WASHINGTON COUNTY ARKANSAS

BIOGRAPHICAL
AND
HISTORICAL MEMOIRS

Goodspeed

Heritage Books
2025

HERITAGE BOOKS

AN IMPRINT OF HERITAGE BOOKS, INC.

Books, CDs, and more—Worldwide

For our listing of thousands of titles see our website
at
www.HeritageBooks.com

A Facsimile Reprint
Published 2025 by
HERITAGE BOOKS, INC.
Publishing Division
5810 Ruatan Street
Berwyn Heights, MD 20740

Previously published:
Mountain Press
Signal Mountain, Tennessee
2005

— Publisher's Notice —
In reprints such as this, it is often not possible to remove
blemishes from the original. We feel the contents of this
book warrant its reissue despite these blemishes and
hope you will agree and read it with pleasure.

International Standard Book Number
Paperbound: 978-0-7884-9879-4

HISTORY OF WASHINGTON COUNTY.

TOPOGRAPHY, GEOLOGY, ETC.

WASHINGTON COUNTY, next to Benton County on the north, is in the northwest corner of Arkansas, lying against the Indian Territory on the west, and bounded on the east and south by Madison and Crawford Counties, respectively. It embraces twenty-seven townships and an area of 569,600 acres, divided almost equally into valleys, plateaux and inclined surfaces or terraces. An idea of the general surface may be gained by considering the county to have once been a rolling plateau with for its southern, eastern and western margins the Boston Mountains and their several branches; then allowing Fayetteville's region to be the highest point, with gentle slopes of the county to the northwest and northeast, you have the White River on the east and the Illinois River on the west, both with a bewildering network of tributaries washing out among the plateaus, the terraces and valleys, giving a somewhat "islanded" appearance. What is known as East Heights at Fayetteville has an altitude of 1,731 feet above sea level, while some valleys are probably not more than 1,000 feet above the sea. The Illinois River, with its main branches, Clear Creek, the Evansville, Ballard and Barren Forks, drain probably the largest part of the county, while the White River, and its Main, Middle and Southwest Forks cover the remainder excepting that part below the Boston Mountain ridge, which is drained chiefly by the tributaries of Frog Bayou and Lee's Creek. The drainage is even, and the streams are fed almost entirely from splendid springs which burst from the mountain ledges, in some cases affording excellent water power at their source.

In geology few regions show the diversity observed in Washington County. Almost every geological period is represented, from the protruding ancient sandstones to the quarternary formation, which is most prevalent. According to David Dale Owen's report the base rock of the county is the cherty barren limestone, although some of the deepest cuts on White River in the northeast exhibit black shale below that. The following lists show the superposition of rocks in various parts of the county, according to Prof. Owen's approximation. In Townships 17 and 18, Range 29 west: (1) White, yellow and brown sandstone, some of cellular structure, 200 feet; (2) ferruginous and dark shales, 40 feet; (3) chert, 40 feet; (4) cherty limestone, 35 feet; (5) black cherty shale, 40 feet. In the ridge southeast of Fayetteville: (1) Sandstones of the mill grit series with peculiar fossils, 100 feet; (2) calcareous bands; (3) sandstone of the millstone grit series, cellular and carbonaceous, 125 feet; (4) shales, including eight inches of coal and fire clay, 40 feet; (5) sandstone, 6 feet; (6) pentrimital limestone, 4 feet; (7) shales, including an inch or two of coal, in the cut below Cato's Spring; (8) Archimedes limestone, 30 feet; (9) shales, calcareous bands with pyrites, gypiferous shale, black shale with carbonate of iron, 40 feet. In Township 15, Range 29 west, on Wood's branch, Middle Fork of White River: (1) Brown sandstone with amygdaloidal cavities; (2) (space concealed with shales); (3) Archimedes cavernous limestone; (4) grey and black shales, with perhaps some interstratified sandstone, and including, near its base, a band of dark fossiliferous, pyritiferous limestone, and segregations of carbonate of iron. Another section on the Middle Fork of White River: (1) Sandstone, probably underlaid with shale, 50 to 100 feet; (2) Archimedes, cavernous and concretionary limestone, 40 to 60 feet; (3) grey shale, pyritiferous limestone shale. In the ridge at the point where the road crosses East Fork of the Illinois River: (1) Soft brown sandstone, a few feet of limestone followed by sandstone, 80 feet; (2) ferruginous, sandy shales, 30 feet; (3) Archimedes limestone, 70 feet. The succession at Cane Hill: (1) Fine grained sandstone, 15 to 20 feet; (2) limestone, a few feet; (3) coarse yellow sandstone, 40 feet; (4) greenish grindstone grit, 45 to 70 feet; (5) Archimedes limestone, 60 feet; (6) marly shales in the bed of the branch. Superposition from Cane College Hill to Barren Fork of the Illinois River: (1) Shistose sandstone of College Hill, Archimedes limestone over Boonesboro Spring, 45 feet; (2) dark shales, 10 to 15 feet; (3) freestone or building stone; (4) shale; (5) chert; (6) fossiliferous limestone; (7) sandstone; (8) chert and cherty limestone of the Barren Fork of Illinois River; (9) black shale. In Vineyard Township the succession is: (1) Fine grained silicious rock, approaching the texture of white stone in its character; (2) limestone; (3) shale; (4) yellow, coarse sandstone; (5) finer grained shistose sandstone of the character of grindstone grit; (6) Archimedes and other limestones; (7) dark shale rocks; (8) brown freestone; (9) shale; (10) fossiliferous chert; (11) fossiliferous limestone with marly and shaly partings; (12) chert; (13) cherty limestone; (14) black shale.

Although near Fayetteville the strata in places dip to a considerable degree, so that elevations occasionally may be due to that cause, the greater number of them are probably due to their composition of less easily eroded rock. The limestones have, through the action of water, become cavernous in many places, and this is no doubt the prevailing source of springs. The great variety of rock formation, from which the soils are formed by erosion and decomposition, gives rise to a marvelous variety of soils, which are so continually renewed that they seem inexhaustible.

The great variety of mineral resources are probably due to the results of the igneous disturbances farther south, which gives to the strata of Washington County its occasional dips. Prof. F. L. Harvey has given a remarkable list of minerals and rocks found in the State, and this county includes a large proportion of them.

It is estimated that 60 per cent of the whole area of the county is timber land, the leading varieties of wood being white oak, hickory, red oak, post oak, walnut, ash, elder, elm, dog-wood and locust. The timber is so important a feature and of so excellent a quality that the St. Paul branch of the " Frisco Railway" was built especially for making the timber accessible to supply several railways. At Fayetteville natural gas has been found in three different places, at the depths of 225, 140 and ninety feet. Its coal has not been developed, although there are evidences of a fair supply. The agricultural products are corn, wheat, grasses and clovers, oats, Irish and sweet potatoes, sorghum and tobacco, particularly; the sorghum cane is peculiarly suited to Washington County surroundings, and is rapidly acquiring importance. But little cotton is grown. The horticultural phase of the county is especially striking; its apples are first premium fruits wherever exhibited; peaches, grapes, pears, plums, cherries, berries and other small fruits follow, in excellence and abundance not far behind the apples. These, heretofore raised for home consumption, have, since the advent of the Frisco Railway, been raised almost exclusively for commercial purposes, and become famous throughout the country. Irish potatoes, onions, cabbage and turnips have increased manyfold in quality and abundance, and are shipped to Little Rock, Fort Smith, Springfield and other places.

The stock embraces hogs, chiefly Berkshire; large horses for city purposes are bred; mules for the Southern market; cattle, sheep and poultry are also raised, and in all branches new breeds are constantly being introduced. "The egg shipment is nearly double in value that of the wheat crop," says Dr. J. F. Simonds, an authority on Washington County produce. The value of live stock in the county (assessed) is $747,784; number of horses, 8,007; mules, 3,703; cattle, 21,242; hogs, 31,655; sheep, 13,021; number of acres of public land in the county, 150,477, 80,000 of this being United States land, and the rest State land; number of acres taxed, 419,123; assessed value of all lands taxed, $2,436,-316.80; assessed value of personal property, $1,662,309.42; total assessed value of real and personal property, $4,098,626.22; total revenue collected in the county for 1887, $78,029.16.

SETTLEMENT AND EARLY SCENES.

The Indian occupation of Northwestern Arkansas presents few points of interest. This territory was first claimed by the Osages, and was frequently visited by them in their hunting tours, but it is not probable that they had any established villages in this region. As early as 1806 some of the Cherokees settled above Point Remove, on the Arkansas River, and by a treaty made July 17, 1817, acquired title to all the country west of a line from the mouth of Point Remove, on the Arkansas, to a point on White River, three miles above Batesville, thence up White River to where Dubuque now is; thence west of south to the mouth of Frog Bayou. To this country a large number of Cherokees were transferred from the country east of the Mississippi. Bands of Shawnees and Delawares also established themselves in this region, and had quite a large village near the present town of Yellville, in Marion County. Hunting parties frequently came into what is now Washington County, where they found an abundance of game. It is said that they usually encamped on the elevation south of Fayetteville, which was then destitute of trees. This isolated hill commands a view of the surrounding country for several miles, and they were there protected from any unexpected attack from their old enemies, the Osages.

By the treaty of 1828 the Cherokees exchanged the territory occupied by them, between White River and the Arkansas, for that west of the present State line, to which they were removed. This country embraced the greater part of Lovely County, which was by force of treaty abolished, and the citizens of the country removed east of the western boundary line of the State. They were indemnified from such loss, by reason of such removal, by a grant of 320 acres of land to the head of each family, to be located within the limits of the State.

The first regular explorer of this portion of the State was Frank Pierce, who, about 1819, came up White River trapping and hunting. On reaching the mouth of West Fork, he ascended that stream to within two miles of Fayetteville, where he discovered a herd of buffalo. In attempting to kill one of them to get some meat for his supper, he saw a band of Indians. He lowered his gun without firing, dropped under the bank and retired for the night under the friendly shelter of a large elm. The next day he struck the waters of the Illinois, and followed that beautiful stream to its mouth, then down the Arkansas to where Lewisburgh now is, thence across to Batesville. About the year 1828 he came back and settled near the place where nine years before he had spent the night in hiding from the Indians.

The following facts concerning the settlement of Washington County are from the pen of the late Rev. John Buchanan:

"In the year 1826, before the treaty was made giving white people the right of settling in what is now Washington County, six families, to wit, John Alexander, two McGarrahs, two Simpsons and one Shannon, moved there. Their settlement being a trespass, a command of soldiers was sent from Fort Gibson to move them off. This was done in August, 1826. The settlers each had a small field of corn, which the soldiers cut down with their swords. After the soldiers returned to the fort the families shocked up their corn, and remained at their homes.

"In 1828 the treaty was made with the Cherokees, giving the right of settlement to the whites, and fixing the line which now divides the country from the Indian Territory. The immigration into and settlement of the country by the white people was rapid. Among the first were the Billingsleys, Pyeatts, Carnahans, Blairs, Simpsons, Marrs, Shannons and others, from Kentucky, and the Buchanans, Beans, Woodys, Parks, Evanses, Weddingtons and others, from Tennessee—the latter from South Carolina, and others from different States too numerous to mention. *   *   *   *

"The first resident ministers of the Gospel were Revs. Fisher, Poston and Holcomb, of the Baptist; Sexton, Covington and Harrell, of the Methodist, and Carnahan, Blair and Buchanan, of the Cumberland Presbyterian. The first Sabbath-school was organized at the house of James Buchanan, on Cane Hill, in October, 1828, by Rev. John Carnahan, with thirteen scholars. This school has been kept up, with slight intermissions, for fifty years. Samuel Carnahan, the son of the founder, was its superintendent for twenty years, during which time he was absent only two Sabbaths. Rev. John Carnahan preached his first sermon at Crystal Hill, near the mouth of Palarm, fifteen miles above Little Rock, in the year 1812, which was perhaps the first Protestant sermon ever preached in Arkansas."

The western, northwestern and central part of Washington County was the first settled. The settlements began at Evansville and Cane Hill, and extended in the same direction to Fayetteville. The Cane Hill country presented the greatest attraction to immigrants, and that section was quite compactly settled before some other parts of the county contained a single habitation. This region was one of the most fertile spots in the State. For a distance of four or five miles hill and dale were covered with a heavy growth of sycamore, walnut and linden, intertwined with grape-vines, and underneath and between the trees was an almost impenetrable cane-brake. So thick was the cane, and so luxuriant the vines, that horses and cattle of the settlers frequently became entangled in them, and perished of hunger and thirst before their owners could find them.

The settlements here began in 1828. As mentioned by Mr. Buchanan, the Pyeatts were among the first to arrive. James and Jacob Pyeatt, as early as 1811, set out from Northern Alabama, in company with James and Samuel Carnahan, sons of Rev. John Carnahan. They embarked in flat-boats, and floated down the Tennessee, Ohio and Mississippi Rivers to the mouth of the Arkansas, then worked their way up the Arkansas to Crystal Hill, fifteen miles above Little Rock, where they were subsequently joined by several relatives and friends. All were natives of Kentucky, but had removed to Alabama to locate upon certain Indian lands, which, upon their arrival there, they found were not yet open for settlement.

As soon as Washington County was formed Crystal Hill community removed to Cane Hill, and they and their descendants have since been among the best people in Northwestern Arkansas.

The Buchanans were from Tennessee, and were among the most influential of the pioneers. There were six brothers of them: John, Andrew, Robert, James, Alexander and Isaac. Andrew and John Buchanan were ministers in the Cumberland Presbyterian Church. The former, familiarly known as "Uncle Buck," located at Prairie Grove, where his step-son, Col. James P. Neal, now lives. He died in 1857. James Buchanan located near the site of the White Church, where he passed the remainder of his life. Rev. John Buchanan was "Uncle John" to every one. For forty years or more he was one of the leaders of his church in Arkansas, and died at a ripe old age, beloved by every one who knew him.

The Billingsleys, together with Charles Adams and Samuel

Williams, came from Tennessee to Arkansas Post in 1814, and in 1816 located on Big Mulberry. Two years later they removed to near Fort Smith, and in 1828 or 1829 came to Washington County.

Mark Bean was a well-to-do and influential pioneer of the Cane Hill country. He was a native of Tennessee, and had come to "Lovely's Purchase" among the first immigrants. He was there engaged in the manufacture of salt. When driven out he went to Crawford County, where in 1829 he was elected to the Territorial Legislature. Soon after he came to Washington County, where he remained until his death. He is said to have been originally a Democrat, but having quarreled with A. H. Sevier, he allied himself with the Whigs, and became one of the leaders of the party in Washington County.

Of the Parks there were three brothers, Robert, Aaron and Joel, who lived on the Fayetteville road not far from the White Church. Robert was a farmer and Aaron and Joel kept a store. Afterward Joel went to Texas, and Aaron located on White River. The first stores on Cane Hill were opened by William Dugan and S. D. Lowell.

In 1830 James Coulter came from East Tennessee and settled on the place where Joseph Moore now lives. The next year James B. Russell, his son-in-law, with other relatives followed. Mr. Russell is still living. After living one year near Rhea's Mills, he removed to near where Boonsboro now is, and has since been identified with that community. In 1832 a school-house was built near Boonsboro, and Maurice Wright, a brother-in-law of Mr. Russell, was the first teacher. The next year Mr. Russell himself taught the school. Here attended the youth for the whole Cane Hill neighborhood, but not long after two schools were established, one at the White Church and the other at Elm Spring or Salem Church.

Among the pioneers of the Cane Hill region, besides those already mentioned, there were Thomas Pogue, who located on the site of Boonsboro; William Woody, at one time a judge of the county court; William Rhode and Hay Crawford, William Maxwell, Henry E. Campbell, William Wright, Isaac Spencer, Levi Richards, James Mitchell, A. Whinnery, Charles McClellan, Joseph and Benjamin Garvin.

The settlements in the vicinity of Evansville were made at a slightly earlier date than those on Cane Hill. Mr. Buchanan's recollection of them has been given. Other pioneers of this part of the county may be mentioned as follows: Samuel and Daniel Vaughn, William Reed, Coleman Cox, George Gibson, Thomas Tennant, Jesse Goddard, Charles J. Sievers, Thomas Ballard, George Morrow, John Morrow, John Ish, John Williams, Lewis Evans, S. F. Gray, Henderson Bates, D. C. Edmiston, John Cole and William Oliver. Coleman Cox came from Warren County, Ky., with his family in 1821, and lived in Sebastian County until 1828, when he removed to Washington County, and located on the head of Barren Fork, four miles south of Boonsboro. He had three sons, Edmiston, Samuel and Burwell, and two daughters, one of whom married Peter Pyeatt. Rev. Thomas Tennant came to Arkansas in 1819, and lived in Pulaski County until 1829, when he took up his residence in Washington County. He died near Evansville in 1885, at the extraordinary age of one hundred and fourteen years. He was a minister in the Methodist Church for ninety years. Thomas Ballard, George Morrow, S. F. Gray and Henderson Bates are still living. D. C. Edmiston, who was a native of Tennessee, came to the State when thirteen years of age. He lived in Clark County until 1835, when he removed to Washington County, and resided four miles south of Cane Hill until his death. In 1831 Lu C. Blakemore, the father of Dr. F. Blakemore, of Greenwood, Ark., came from Sumner County, Tenn., and after living a year or two in Fayetteville located eight miles east of Boonsboro. Other pioneers in the latter vicinity were Claiborne Lewis, Stephen Talkington, Elisha Dyer, John Billingsley and his father, James Billingsley, John Rutherford, William Stirman, Benjamin and William Strickler and James and David McWilliams.

Among the first settlers in the neighborhood of Walnut Grove were John Conner, Josiah Trent, David Reese, Ralph Skelton, Henry Tollett, G. A. Pettigrew, William Bonham, Joseph Lewis, John Pierce, Robert Anderson, Abel Johnson, George Lawrence, Samuel Woolsey, John Hart and Hugh, Abram and William Allen. John Conner was a Georgian by birth, but had been reared in Kentucky and Indiana, and had lived for a time in Illinois. In 1827, in partnership with several other families, he built a keel-boat, and set out for Arkansas. He remained one year in the vicinity of Evansville, where he found John Alexander, James Simpson, Hugh Shannon and John and William McGarroh. He made a permanent location near the present village of Farmington, and his daughter, who married A. W. Arrington, is still living in the neighborhood, an intelligent chronicler of pioneer days.

Josiah Trent was also a Georgian by birth. He first located in the southern part of the State, but in February, 1829, came to Washington County, and pitched his tent on the place where his son now lives. There he remained until his death, in 1877. For many years he was a local preacher in the Methodist Church. He was the son-in-law of Samuel Woolsey, who came to the county at about the same time.

George A. Pettigrew was a North Carolinian by birth, but had lived in Georgia, Kentucky and Missouri. From the latter State he came to Arkansas in 1825, and after a residence of five years in Hempstead County removed to Washington County. He lived one year on Cane Hill, and then made a permanent location seven miles west of Fayetteville. He was a prominent Whig, and in 1840 was elected to the Legislature. He was the father of Col. James R. Pettigrew and Z. M. Pettigrew.

The Allens were brothers, and old bachelors, and lived together for many years. Anderson, Click and Pierce all lived on the Illinois River. Among the first school-teachers in this neighborhood were Pleasant Tackett, Stephen Strickland and Alfred W. Arrington.

Of the first settlers in the Mount Comfort neighborhood may be mentioned Solomon Tuttle, William Cunningham, Isaac Murphy, W. A. and James McCurdy and Hezekiah Appleby. Tuttle and Cunningham were both men of wealth and substance, and had grown-up families. Murphy located here, and taught school before he began the practice of law. This was an intelligent and progressive community, and the first school of more than local reputation was established here. It was called "Far West Seminary," and was presided over by Robert Mecklin, the founder of Ozark Institute. The seminary was opened about 1835, in the brick church erected at this point by the Cumberland Presbyterians.

It has been mentioned that Rev. Andrew Buchanan made a settlement in Prairie Grove Valley in 1829, but a settlement had been made by Isaac Marrs nearly two years earlier, on the creek which bears his name. This was, doubtless, the first settlement in Prairie Grove Valley. The next year, his brother, James Marrs, settled what is now known as the Patton place. Both reared large families, and several of the prominent citizens of the county are numbered among their descendants. They came to Arkansas from Logan County, Ky., as early as 1817. Alexander Marrs, a member of another family, was also a pioneeer of the county.

About 1830 James Crawford came from Tennessee and located near Viney Grove. He reared a large family of sons and daughters. The former numbered five—William, James, John, Mack and Robert, and the latter, four. Among his sons-in-law were John Moore, William Morton and James West.

One of the first settlers of the county was Eli Bloyed, who located on West Fork, several miles south of Fayetteville, and for the first year lived upon the flesh of wild animals alone. Among others of the pioneers in this portion of the county were John and Christy Horness, Samuel Mayes, P. and J. H. Estes, Jacob Coats, Alexander Rutherford and George Reed.

Among the early residents of the White River country, and that part of the county east of Fayetteville, were Dr. James Boone, Robert McCarny, Peter Mankins, Cortez Hitchcock, Rial Williams, Thomas Smith, Robert Marshall, James West, Daniel Ritter and Jacob Sheay. McCarny was from Alabama. He was the first county judge of Washington County; was elected to the Territorial Council in 1831; to the Constitutional Convention in 1836, and to the State Senate in 1836, in 1844 and 1848, retiring from the office in 1852.

Dr. Boone came to the county in 1830, and remained until his death, in 1856. He was a Whig in politics, and was a member of the Constitutional Convention of 1836. He also served one term in the House of Representatives.

Peter Mankins came to the county from Illinois in 1832, and

although then past sixty years of age, he lived an ordinary life-
time after his arrival here. He was born on September 19, 1770,
in Maryland, and died in 1881 at the age of over one hundred
and eleven years.

The settlements in the north part of the county, in the vicini-
ties of Springdale and Elm Springs, are mentioned in connection
with those villages.

To "Uncle An" Fitzgerald, of Springdale, this chapter is
indebted for some of the following notes on early "Arkansaw"
life, so variously pictured by our humorists, and none give them
with greater gusto and humor than "Uncle An" himself. Bear,
deer, elk, buffalo, wolf, panther and wildcat were their next door
neighbors in those days, and in true cannibal fashion these neighbors mutually preyed on each other. Cornmeal hoe-cakes being so
prominent a feature of their eatables, their ingenuity hit upon the
following unique form of perpetual motion: choosing a spring
with a high opening, a forked stick was fastened before it, and
balanced in the fork a pole, on one end of which was placed an
inclined water trough, which, when filled by the flowing spring,
would drop, raising the heavy pestle hung to the other end of the
pole; the water at once being spilled, the trough would resume
its position, and down went the pestle into the wooden mortar
below, pounding whatever the mortar contained into fine powder.
A half bushel or more of corn placed in the mortar at night
would be transformed into palatable meal by sunrise. Home-
made clothes of cotton, flax and wool were common; the husband
and wife seeding enough cotton by the light of a pine knot or
"tallow dip" to keep the busy wife with spinning material for
the next day. Wild honey supplied the place of sugar, and when
the first coffee appeared, "we tried to bite it like ye do beans, ye
know," said "Uncle An." Letters were seldom received, but
the advent of a missive was the signal for the neighborhood to
gather round the 'Squire, whose learning enabled him to read to
them news from the hieroglyphics; and when a like document
was to be written, the 'Squire sharpened his goose-quill and, dipping it into the oak-ball ink, became amanuensis for the neighborhood. Card-playing was an amusement, and the settlers
knew where Troy Gordon's "still" was, but "Uncle An" and

his gray-haired compeers affirm that none of the well-known evils of to-day were attached to them then. "Hoe-downs" and reels— "none o' yer huggin' dances"—were tripped lightly, and with jollity, to the tune of "Roarin' River," etc., which some deft musicians drew from the gourd "fiddle" with its horse-hair strings and bow, and the gourd banjo with its squirrel-skin head and horse-hairs. "We had debatin' sasieties too—bony-fide (*bona fide*) debatin'," said "Uncle An." "Pursuit and Possession," "Art and Nature," and "Which would a man go futher fur —money 'er his best gurl?" were passed upon, and when it came time to walk home with some bright-eyed lass, "we walked a leetle ways off," said "Uncle An," "we didn't clevis arms uz they do now!"

The physical features of Washington County have undergone a very decided change in the last sixty years. When the pioneers first made it their home there were large areas of prairie which are now covered with a more or less dense growth of timber. The site of Fayetteville and several of the surrounding elevations, as well as the intervening valleys, were bare of timber, and were covered with a luxuriant growth of grasses, which afforded excellent pasturage for buffaloes and other herbivorous animals.

For the following account of the wild animals of Prairie Grove Valley this chapter is indebted to Col. James P. Neal. With little modification it applies to the whole county. He says: "My first acquaintance with the valley was in 1829. The buffalo had then receded some fifteen or twenty miles to the northwest. Their paths were still numerous, leading mainly from one lick to another. Their heads were scattered all over the prairies, one perhaps to every three acres of land. These licks were depressions in the earth, filled with water a little brackish in wet weather. In summer, when dry, they were the resorts of buffalo for the salt with which the earth was saturated, and were known as buffalo licks. They afforded salt for stock for many years after the country was settled, and even yet when not enclosed. In an early day hunters often captured and brought in buffalo calves, and tried to domesticate them, but they invariably died in one or two years. In that day buffalo skins were used for carpets, door mats, hearth rugs, mattresses, bed covers, saddle blankets and numerous other things. It is said that Thomas Wagnon, an old timer, while out hunting, wrapped himself, arms, hands and all, from shoe-top to chin, in a green buffalo hide at night. In the morning it was frozen and would not enroll, and when found he was well nigh dead. This same man burned out the first stump in which to pound corn into meal at this place, which was the only evidence of civilization when we first camped here. This we used until mills were built.

"There never were many panthers here. Capt. Mark Bean, who resided in the valley a few years in an early day, often related his panther experiences. He was on the snow looking for deer when he came across panther tracks. He followed the trail for an hour or more, when, passing under a large post-oak tree, he looked up and saw the panther crouched on a limb about twelve feet above his head, intently watching him. It was with an effort that he suppressed a scream. His hair stood straight up on his head. He walked on some steps, adjusted his hunting knife, turned and fired. The panther made a leap, screamed and fell to the ground dead.

"Bear were never numerous in this valley, the smooth open country not suiting them.

"The wolf, the great depredator on small stock, comes next in the scale of importance, and their name was legion, the black and gray. About dark in the evening they began to howl in four or five directions. At first their howls were piteous and doleful, making the most cheery household lonely. One or two at the different points at first, then others would join in until the packs would increase seemingly to forty or fifty, and as they joined in the howl became more earnest, increasing until it became an indescribable medley of whining, yelping, yelling, howling, discordant sounds that would make the hair rise on one's head. Then they would hold up five or ten minutes, after which a repetition of the performance would occur, the whole lasting from one to two hours. At about the hour the wolves opened, each family would begin to blow a horn. Some had two or more. This would put the dogs to howling, and was thought to keep the wolves near their hiding places. The hour of horn-blowing soon became of much interest to the settlers. It was a sort of evening roll-call, and if any family had failed to join messengers would have soon been at their doors inquiring the cause."

Up to the year 1838 the peaceful settlements of Northwestern Arkansas were rarely disturbed by serious crimes or acts of violence. It was almost Arcadian in its virtue and simplicity. Rarely were the courts called upon to investigate anything more serious than some trivial misdeameanor, and frequently the grand jury reported that there was no business before them. In 1838 the Cherokee Indians were brought from Tennessee and Georgia, and located on the territory since known as the Cherokee Nation. This immigration brought with it a cloud of those doubtful characters that have always been found upon the extreme frontiers of our civilized settlements. They were attracted here in unusual numbers by the fact that the Indians had been paid a large sum of money for the improvements upon their old reservation, and all were flush with gold and silver. They came to sell them whisky, to gamble and to trade with them.

" Runaways from every State in the Union were collected along the Cherokee line, and preyed alike upon the whites and the Indians. For the especial benefit of these desperadoes, as it seems, groceries were erected immediately upon the line, one-half the house being in Washington County and the other in the Cherokee Nation, so that when a crime was committed in one part of the grocery, the offender had but to step across a plank in the floor, and, lo ! he was in another jurisdiction, beyond the reach of legal process issued by the court on the side he had left."*

With the advent of these desperadoes peace and quiet were at an end. Murders, robberies and other outrages were of almost monthly occurrence, but what was still worse these crimes went unpunished. Numerous suspected persons were arrested, indicted and tried, but convictions did not follow. The culprit had only to summon a few of his friends, prove an *alibi*, and be discharged. This state of things existed until law-abiding citizens lost confidence in the courts, and declared that they were in

*Arrington

league with the assassin and the robber. The culmination was reached on both sides of the State line in 1839. On the Indian side the rival parties of Ross and Ridge had continued the deadly quarrel begun in their native country. On the night of June 20, 1839, the leaders of the Ridge party, Maj. Ridge, his brother, Elias Boudinot and his son John Ridge were assassinated by members of the Ross party. John Ridge was taken from his bed by a band of men, and in the presence of his family stabbed to death. Maj. Ridge had started for Van Buren, and was waylaid and shot from a bluff near the road, about seven or eight miles from Evansville. Boudinot was killed near his home at Park Hill, within about a mile of John Ross' house. Others of the Ridge party fled to escape a similar fate. These disturbances in the Cherokee Nation enabled the white desperadoes to commit crimes along the borders, and to cast the suspicion upon their savage neighbors, which proved a most convenient cloak to cover their evil deeds. On the night of June 15, 1839, the people living in the vicinity of Boonsboro, on Cane Hill, were aroused by the burning of the house of William Wright, and the cries for help from his terror-stricken wife and children. A neighbor was awakened by Mrs. Wright, who informed him in accents of indescribable terror that the Indians were upon them, that they had killed her husband and children and burned the house, and that they would all be massacred if they did not flee for their lives. In a few minutes the scattered neighbors were aroused, and many of them, taking their families upon horses, in buggies or on foot, set out to seek refuge from the savage hordes that were swooping down upon them. They spread the news of the Indian invasion, and soon the entire country was aroused. Others of the Boonsboro people, more courageous, decided to hold their ground until the danger became more imminent, and finally two young men, that had previously lived with Esquire James B. Russell, who resided a short distance from the Wright family, observing that he had not put in an appearance, resolved to reconnoitre his house and ascertain whether he had been killed. They did so, and found Mr. Russell unharmed and asleep in his bed. He was aroused, and the fear of the Indians having somewhat subsided, a party was made up to visit the scene of the

murder at Wright's.   There a harrowing sight met their eyes.
In the yard and close to the burning house lay the body of
Wright, pierced with a half dozen dagger thrusts and burned to
a crisp; beside it was the body of his second daughter, a girl
fourteen or fifteen years of age, with a bullet hole in the forehead.   At a little distance was an infant, its brains dashed out.
Upon the bed in the burning dwelling could be seen the forms
of two little girls interlocked in each other's arms, as they lay
when the revolvers and the bowie knives of the assassins began
their bloody work.   Upon further search two little boys, aged
about six and ten years, respectively, were found at some distance from the house administering as best they could to their
elder brother, a youth of some eighteen years, whose skull had
been fractured.   Another child, a little toddling thing, was found
uninjured in a cornfield near by.   The eldest daughter had also
made her escape.

A jury was impaneled, and, in the absence of the coroner,
an inquest was held by Esquire Russell, when the following facts
were ascertained: Mr. Wright, who was a hard-working, honest
farmer, and one of the first settlers on Cane Hill, had the previous autumn purchased a large number of hogs, which he converted into bacon, and during this spring had been selling it to the
newly arrived Indians.   From this source he had received a considerable sum of money, a part of which he had deposited with
his brother, a merchant at Boonsboro, and a part he kept in his
house.   On the night of the murder the family retired early, but
about 10 o'clock Mrs. Wright arose to get a drink of water for
one of the children.   While in a back room she heard a noise at
the gate, and, peering out at a crevice between the logs, she saw
three men approaching.   A sudden pang of fear and suspicion
seized her, and she crouched down where she stood.   The next
instant a knock was heard at the door, and her husband arose
and opened it.   Instantly three gleaming bowie knives were
sheathed in his bosom, and he was dragged, dying, out of the
door.   His daughter, awakened by the disturbance, sprang to
his assistance, only to receive a bullet in the forehead from the
revolver of an assassin, who was so near that the powder burned
her face.   Mrs. Wright saw no more, but fled from the back door,

and escaped to a neighbor's. The two older children, aroused by the confusion, attempted to make their escape; the girl was successful, but the boy was stretched upon the floor by a blow from the butt of a pistol, which fractured his skull. The two little girls were shot as they lay in bed, and the butchery was made as atrocious as possible to give color to the suspicions against the Indians. Two little boys were sleeping in a trundle-bed, under the one occupied by the parents, and were not noticed by the assassins. They did not awake until after the departure of the robbers, when the heat from the burning house aroused them. They arose, and with wonderful presence of mind succeeded in rescuing the wounded elder brother from the flames.

By daylight on the morning after the murder people from the surrounding country began to come in, and by noon hundreds, perhaps a thousand, had assembled. That night a council of old citizens was held, and the question of public safety was discussed in all its phases. The powerless condition of the courts was recognized, and after a long debate it was decided to take the matter into their own hands. A committee of thirty-six discreet and reliable citizens was selected to direct investigations and to punish the criminals should they be apprehended. The names of the members of the committee, as given by Col. James P. Neal, are as follows: Mark Bean, Rev. Andrew Buchanan, James Coulter, Levi Richards, Rev. Samuel Harris, Robert Bedford, John R. Pyeatt, Lewis Evans, John D. Moore, Rev. B. H. Pierson, William Oliver, Garvin Dunn, Leander Burnham, James Buchanan, James Hamilton, Aaron Parks, Robert Parks, T. C. Wilson, James Mitchell, William D. Crawford, Samuel Carnahan, James Crawford, Sr., Henry E. Campbell, John Tilly, Sr., Thomas Tiner, Rev. Thomas W. Norwood, William Crawford, Richard Bean, M. W. McClennan, Robert Buchanan, Isaac P. Spencer, William Munkress, Samuel Marrs, John Campbell, Henry E. Campbell and John Latta. Rev. Samuel Harris was chosen president of the committee. One hundred able and energetic men were selected as a company of light horse. They were sent in tens over the county, with instructions to arrest and bring before the committee all suspicious persons, gamblers, idlers and stragglers. Meantime the committee was engaged in trying to get some clue. Suspicion finally rested on James Barnes, William Bailey, Taylor S. Barnes, John Asbury and Alexander Richmond and Ellery Turner, all of whom were taken into custody and brought before the committee. Witnesses both for and against the prisoners were summoned before the committee, and several days were consumed in the trial. One by one they succeeded in establishing plausible *alibis*, and it became evident that all must be discharged. Bailey was a gambler and a stranger in the country, and was looked upon with greater suspicion and dislike than any of the others. The circumstantial evidence was much stronger against him, although he had proven as good an *alibi*. While the guards were conveying him to Boonsboro, where the committee was in session, he threw away a letter, which was recovered. It was written to his father, and stated that he had killed a man, and was about to leave for Texas. Also a shirt, sprinkled with blood, was found in his saddle-bags. For these he had a plausible excuse, and his *alibi* was good, but some of the citizens were not satisfied of his innocence. The night before the men were to be released they took him from the guards, and taking him to a neighboring mountain, endeavored to extort a confession from him by whipping him, but failing in this they turned him loose, and he disappeared from the neighborhood.

All of the suspected men lived near the Cherokee line. John and Alexander Richmond were small farmers, and Turner a farm laborer, who lived with his mother and sister. James Barnes was much superior to the others in education and intelligence. He had come from Howard County, Mo., a few years previous, and had lived in the family of Rev. Andrew Buchanan at Prairie Grove, where he attended school. He came of a highly respectable family, and is said to have been a man of unusually fine appearance. At this time he was married, and was keeping a grocery on the Cherokee line.

After the discharge of these prisoners the people returned to their homes and the excitement abated, but the light horse continued to ride, and the committee came together whenever circumstances rendered it necessary. About ten days or two weeks later Asbury Richmond was at his brother John's, and being intoxicated became angry with his brothers, John and

Alexander. A Mr. Hornage lived some sixty or eighty steps from John Richmond's, and he, his wife and daughter, and a young man who was boarding with him, heard Asbury Richmond accuse his brothers of several acts of stealing, and at last say: "You, you d—d rascal, helped to murder that family on Cane Hill, and I was taken up for it and disgraced in consequence." This was communicated to the committee, who had Asbury Richmond brought before them. He there made a statement in substance as follows: He said that his brother, John Richmond, James Barnes and William Bailey once proposed to him to go into an arrangement to get some money, but that he did not join them; that on Sunday after the murder John Richmond told him that they had done the business on Cane Hill, and that in a few days he would be able to pay the money he owed him. Upon his testimony John Richmond, James Barnes and Ellery Turner were arrested and taken before the committee. William Bailey had fled the country, but a search for him was instituted. As at the former trial witnesses were summoned for both the prosecution and the defense. James Barnes produced several witnesses to prove an *alibi*. Nathan Wofford testified that Barnes was at his grocery until about sunset, and that at dark they ate supper. After supper himself and one McCrackin went to the grocery and slept there, leaving at the house James Barnes and his wife, Taylor S. Barnes and Jacob and Patsy O'Bryant. Jacob O'Bryant, who was an honest and highly respectable young man, testified that he and his sister, having been belated on a journey, had slept for the night at Barnes'; that he had slept in the same room with Barnes; that from this room the only means of egress was by a door, and the night being warm he had placed his pallet immediately in front of the door, so that Barnes could not have left the house except by passing over him. This testimony was corroborated by the others present.

Against Barnes was introduced the testimony of Mrs. Wright, who swore that he had been at their house for bacon two or three times; that on the day before the murder Wright's wagons, loaded with bacon, had passed Barnes' grocery on the way to the Nation, yet during that day Barnes had called at Wright's for bacon, and while waiting for Wright to come from the field had asked many questions concerning the amount of bacon he had sold, the money received, etc.; that Wright had asked Barnes why he did not get his bacon from the wagons, and that he replied, he had not seen the wagons when they passed.

James Shelby, the driver of one of the wagons, was then called, and testified that he had stopped and talked with Barnes at his grocery on the morning referred to. This constituted the case against Barnes, outside of the confession by John Richmond.

In behalf of Turner, William Hunter, his brother-in-law, Mrs. Turner, his mother, and Mrs. Hunter, his niece, all testified that he, accompanied by William Bailey, had come home on the fatal night from a ball play, a short time after dark, and that they were at home at the hour at which the murder was committed. John Raymond, when brought before the committee, denied the charges that had been made by his brother Asbury, and refused to answer the questions of the committee. Finally, watching an opportunity, he broke from his guards, and made a dash for liberty, but being weighed down by chains he was quickly recaptured. After sitting speechless for a time, under pressure from the committee he at last agreed to make a full confession. He stated that the murder and robbery had been planned and committed by himself, Jack Nicholson, a resident of the Cherokee Nation, who was never captured, James Barnes, William Bailey, Ellery Turner and another man whose name has been forgotten. He related all the harrowing details of the horrible butchery, stating that their object had been to do the murder in Indian style.

After this confession Barnes and Turner still denied all knowledge of the affair, and demanded to know if they had not proved good *alibis*. The prisoners were remanded to the guard-house, an old log building formerly used as a school-house. After some deliberation, the committee took a vote upon the question: "Shall these men suffer death?" and it is said that but one vote was cast in the negative. The condemned men were then once more brought before the committee, and were sentenced to be hung on the following Monday, July 29, 1839. On the morning of that day about a 1,000 people assembled at the scene of the execution, just south of the present town of

Boonsboro, near the residence of Thomas Pogue. By 10 o'clock, the hour appointed for the execution, the gallows was surrounded by a surging mass of humanity, white, black and red, all impatient for the exciting event, and fearful lest it be postponed. At last the wagon bearing the victims appeared. Each sat on his coffin, Richmond wearing a shroud, and Turner and Barnes in their accustomed dress. Arrived at the scaffold, they were given a few minutes in which to take leave of their relatives and friends. The confession of Richmond and the evidence produced at the trial was then read from the stand, after which the prisoners were ordered to stand up, facing the people. The chairman of the committee arose and requested all who sustained the action of the committee to raise their hands. About ninety-nine out of every 100 pairs of hands went up. The ropes were then adjusted, the victims standing on the rear of the wagon. A fervent prayer was offered by the Rev. Andrew Buchanan, the order to move on was given to the driver, and the next instant three writhing forms hung swaying to and fro beneath the gallows tree. Thus ended the first chapter in one of the most remarkable incidents in the whole history of lynch law. A second was to follow. William Bailey, whom more than any of the others was thought to have deserved punishment, had escaped, but the committee had been tracing his footsteps. He had gone from Cane Hill to Van Buren; thence to Shreveport, and from there to his father's home on the Hiwassee River, in East Tennessee, where all trace of him was lost. About the middle of December following a message was received on Cane Hill from Rev. Guilford Pylant, who lived a few miles south, that Bailey was at his house in charge of Creed Taylor and "Bill" Mussett, who had captured him in Pulaski County. A guard was sent down to bring him to Cane Hill, and the committee of thirty-six was again convened. The trial began the next morning, and, before the close of the day, the sentence of death was passed upon William Bailey. The execution was fixed for the next day but one, and at the appointed time he was hung in the same way, and at the same place, as his alleged confederates, David Donaldson acting as hangman. It had been thought that at the last moment he would confess the crime, but he died protesting his innocence.

After the excitement attendant upon these executions had somewhat subsided, a reaction naturally set in, and it began to be asserted that the men who had been hung were innocent, and the severest censures were placed upon the committee. In time there grew up two distinct parties in the county, the one upholding the action of the committee and the other condemning it, and to this day a reference to the "Cane Hill" tragedy arouses the gray haired pioneer, and you are soon made aware to which party he belonged. Some seven or eight years after the occurrence of these events A. W. Arrington, the talented preacher and lawyer mentioned in another chapter, wrote a highly imaginative account of the Cane Hill affair, which was published in a pamphlet entitled "The Desperadoes of the Southwest." It very unfairly reviewed the trial, and was filled with abuse of some of the leading members of the committee, and was justly denounced by those persons and their friends as an infamous slander. The members of the committee of thirty-six were men of high character, in fact it embraced some of the ablest Christian men in the county. The work they did they thought to be necessary, and they performed it deliberately and conscientiously. If they erred in their judgment it was an awful thing, but it was an error of the head and not of the heart.

In the year 1840 the committee officiated at another execution. This time a slave-girl, Caroline, was hung for the murder of her mistress, the wife of Andrew A. Crawford. Mr. Crawford lived at what is now known as the Neil place. He was subsequently a judge of the county court, and died at Corinth during the war. After the chores about the house had been done, it was customary for Caroline to assist her master on the farm, which was some half mile from the house. One morning upon reaching the field she informed her master that a tramp had called at the house just before she left, and she feared that he had some evil intentions upon her mistress. Mr. Crawford paid but little attention to this, but when he reached the house at noon he was horrified to find the bleeding and mangled body of his wife lying upon the floor near the fire, with wood piled around it as though the intention had been to burn it. He quickly gave the alarm, and the surrounding country was searched for the tramp who had committed the foul deed, but no such individual could be found. Caroline, however, by peculiar actions, attracted attention, and suspicion was turned upon her. She was examined and blood was found upon her clothes. She was tried by a committee of citizens, and made a full confession of the crime. A gallows was made by putting a pole in the forks of two dogwood trees standing about fifteen feet apart. The girl was placed in the hind end of a wagon, and the rope adjusted. All was in readiness for the fatal movement of the wagon, when the wretched creature appealed for one more drink of water. There was none at hand, and she was somewhat roughly denied this last request. With the cry of "water" upon her lips, she was swung off. When life was pronounced extinct, they cut her body down, and buried it at the foot of the gallows tree.

From this time matters quieted down, and although occasional crimes were committed, society resumed the even tenor of its way. In 1849 the "gold fever" reached the county, and many of the citizens became infected with it. From a letter written in April, 1849, to the Van Buren *Intelligencer*, the following facts concerning the Washington County company which went to California are gleaned.

The company met on April 21, and elected the following officers: Lewis Evans, of Evansville, captain; Thomas Tyner, first lieutenant; P. Mankin, second lieutenant; James S. Vaun, secretary, and Martin Scrimpsher, of the Cherokee Nation, commissary. The company left the rendezvous on April 24, and five days later they had reached Grand Prairie. The company consisted of nearly ninety members from Washington County, thirteen from Madison, nine from Benton and fourteen from the Cherokee Nation. Those from Washington County were as follows: Lewis Evans, Hiram Davis, A. G. Evans, Leonard Shuler, Gus A. Shuler, William Hoge, Enos Slover, Isaac Hale and wife, James Blake, William Wilson, William Goddard, John Van Hoose, George Lewis, Wiley Cosby, Peter Mankins, James Dickinson, Jacob Strickler, Nathan Lewis, John Lewis, Nathan Thorp, John Ingram, John Powers, W. F. Woodruff, John Sanders, James L. Cartwright, J. R. Cline, George C. North, Edward Freyschlag, H. J. McRoy, Samuel McCulloh, James L. McCulloh,

George McKey, James Carter, George McClure, K. Crumley, Thomas Creamer, James Morrow, Hugh Morrow, A. B. Crawford, J. M. Mathews, J. P. Kellum, A. B. T. Pyatt, Squire B. Marrs, James Carnahan, John Carnahan, James Pierce, John Carter, Cane Hill, Thomas and Aaron Tyner, William and Hiram Shores, Thomas Maxwell, John Newman, B. Whitley, Christian Freyschlag, Henry Freyschlag, Joseph Chew, William Mallett, W. R. Cunningham, Fred P. Sime, James Ingram, William Crawford, Holy and James Hand, Misses Barbara and Mira Freyschlag, James Cartwright, Isaac Murphy, E. W. Avaid, James and William Irvin, Jacob Meyers, John M. Wham, James Divin, Mathew A. Divin, J. T. Edmondson, A. E. Edmondson, J. S. Crawford, A. A. Crawford, Robert Epperson, C. H. Holmes, J. J. Bean, Oscar Bean and Benjamin Sanders.

COUNTY ORGANIZATION.

The territory now embraced in the State of Arkansas was included in the purchase made from France in 1803. It belonged to what was denominated Upper Louisiana, which was formally transferred to the United States in March, 1804, and by Congress was placed under the jurisdiction of the Territory of Indiana, of which William Henry Harrison was governor. Soon after the transfer Congress passed an act for the organization of two Territories, Orleans and Louisiana, the boundary between which was the thirty-third parallel of north latitude. The latter Territory was divided into five districts, one of which, New Madrid, included the present State of Arkansas. In 1806 the district of Arkansas was created, but it was abolished the following year, and remained a part of New Madrid until after the organization of Missouri Territory. On December 31, 1813, the Territorial Assembly passed an act creating the county of Arkansas, and the following year Lawrence County was organized. The latter embraced all of the present State north of the mouth of Little Red River. On December 15, 1818, the southwestern part of the county of Arkansas was divided into three separate counties, Pulaski, Clark and Hempstead. By an act of Congress approved March 2, 1819, the Territory of Arkansas was established, and on August 3, of the same year, it was organized. The first session of the Territorial Assembly was held at the post of Arkansas in 1820, and during the session two new counties, Miller and Phillips, were organized. Upon the reassembling of the Legislature in October of the same year, Pulaski County was divided and Crawford County was formed. At the same time Independence County was erected from a portion of Lawrence County. In 1823 Chicot County was organized from a part of Arkansas County, and two years later the counties of Crittenden and Izard were established. During the session which convened in October, 1827, the counties of St. Francois, LaFayette and Lovely were created. The last named county included the western part of what is now Washington County, and also extended into the Cherokee Nation. It was formed by an act approved on October 13, 1827, and was in existence but one year. To understand its organization and abolition it is necessary to refer to some of the Indian treaties. The first treaty was made and concluded on November 10, 1808, between Pierre Choteau, agent for the Osages, and the chiefs and warriors of the Big and Little Osages at Fort Clark, on the Missouri River, in the then Territory of Louisiana. The Osages agreed that the boundary line between them and the United States should begin at Fort Clark, and run thence south to the Arkansas River. They did not claim below the Arkansas, and all the territory north of the Arkansas and east of the above line were by this treaty relinquished to the United States. Later, by treaties in 1818 and 1825, the Osages gave up their title to the greater portion of the land lying west of the line. The treaty of 1825 was made at St. Louis between Gov. William Clark and a deputation of chiefs and warriors of the Great and Little Osages. By it the title to the following territory was relinquished: "Beginning at Arkansas River at where the Osage boundary line strikes it at the mouth of Frog Bayou, thence up the Arkansas and Verdigris to the falls of the Verdigris, thence eastwardly to the said Osage line at a point twenty leagues north from the Arkansas River, and thence to the place of beginning." This tract was known as "Lovely's purchase," and afterward constituted Lovely County.

By a treaty between the United States and the Cherokees, who had been located in Arkansas, made on May 6, 1828, the western boundary of the State was defined as follows: "A line shall be run commencing on Red River at a point where the eastern Choctaw line strikes said river, and runs due north with said line to the river Arkansas, thence in a direct line to the southwest corner of Missouri." This cut off the greater part of Lovely County, and October 17, 1828, the Legislature passed an act extinguishing the county and establishing the county of Washington with the following boundaries: " Beginning at a point where the western boundary line of the territory strikes the northern boundary line of Township 12 north; thence east with the northern boundary line of Township 12 north to the western boundary line of Range 25 west; thence north with said line to the south boundary line of the State of Missouri; thence with said boundary line to the southwest corner of the State of Missouri; thence south with the western boundary line of the Territory of Arkansas to the beginning." By reference to a map it will be seen that Washington County at that time embraced all of its present territory, all of what is now Benton County, a little more than one-half of Madison County, and about one-fourth of the present county of Carroll.

The first court for the county was held in March, 1829. The following is a transcript of the record of the first day's proceedings :

At a circuit court in and for the county of Washington and Territory of Arkansas, on Monday, the 2d day of March, 1829, present: The Hon. James Woodson Bates, circuit judge, Lewis Evans, sheriff, returned into court list of grand jurors to serve as a body for the county at this term of the court, viz.: James Buchanan, foreman; James Billingsley, John Billingsley, John Conner, David Conner, James Simpson, Hugh Shannon, William L. Weddington, John Woody, William B. Woody, Benjamin Garvin, Daniel Vaughn, Alexander Buchanan and R. G. Crisp, who were sworn, received their charge and withdrew to deliberate. Lewis Evans, sheriff, was sworn into office and gave bond and security for faithful performance of his duties as sheriff of Washington County, which is approved by the court.

Ordered, That Larkin Newton, John Billingsley and Nathan Caughin be appointed a committee to view and work a road leading from the county seat to the southern boundary of the county at or near Cove Creek.

Ordered, That all that part of the county south of a line commencing at a point where the western boundary of the county crosses Matthew's Mountain, thence easterly with the boundary of said county until it strikes the Barren Fork, thence up the same to the forks, thence eastwardly through the prairie, so as to leave John Ish to the south of said line 100 yards, thence direct to a point 100 yards north of Coleman Cook's, thence due east to the eastern boundary line of the county, be established as a separate and distinct township, to be known as Vineyard Township.

Ordered, That that part of the county north of Vineyard Township and south of a line commencing where the western boundary of the county crosses Illinois River, thence up said river to the mouth of Marrs' Creek, thence up said creek to the forks near the Widow Edwards', thence up the left hand fork of said creek to its source, thence due south until it strikes Vineyard Township, be established a separate and distinct township, to be known and called by the name of Cane Hill Township.

Ordered, That all that part of the county lying north of Vineyard and Cane Hill Townships, and west of a line commencing where White River leaves the county, thence up said river to the mouth of Friend's Fork, thence with the dividing ridge between Friend's Fork and the middle fork of said river until it strikes Vineyard Township, be established a separate township, to be known and called Prairie Township.

Ordered, That all that part of the county north of Vineyard Township and east of Prairie Township be established a separate and distinct township, to be known and called by the name of Richland Township.

It is ordered by the court that John Woody, James Simpson and James Buchanan be appointed as commissioners to view and blaze out a road leading from the town of Franklin to George McInturff's mill, thence to the south boundary of the county toward Damon's Lick on Lee's Creek.

On motion, ordered that Thomas Wilson be appointed constable of Prairie Township, and that the clerk take bond and security of said Wilson in the sum of $400.

James Simpson is appointed constable of Cane Hill Township with the same bond.

Benjamin Garvin is appointed constable of Cane Hill Township.

Samuel Vaughn is appointed constable of Richland Township, bond and security $400.

John Wilson is appointed county surveyor of Washington County.

Ordered, That court now adjourn until 9 o'clock to-morrow morning.

On the following day the grand jury returned an indictment against Hiram Johnson for larceny, and reported their business completed. They were discharged, and court adjourned until court in course.

At the July term following Judge Benjamin Johnson presided. Thomas Garvin acted as foreman of the grand jury, which body, after one day's investigation, reported no business before it. Up to this time the courts were held in the dwelling house of John McGarrah. McGarrah had built two log cabins, one of which had a floor of puncheons, while the other was without a floor. The courts were held in the former; the latter was used as a dining room. At this term of the court the sum of $49.75 was appropriated for the purpose of building a court-house. The contract was awarded to Samuel Marrs, and was completed before the next term. The building was made of logs, and a fire-place occupied an entire end of the house.

At the July term, 1829, a new township, called Illinois, was formed, with the following boundaries: "Beginning on the western boundary of the county, and running eastwardly with the north boundary of Vine Township to the forks of Barren Fork Creek, a little west of John Ish's; thence up the left hand fork near Pyeatt's mill, so as to leave all the present settlers on said creek east of said line; thence northwardly to the top of the dividing ridge between the Barren Fork and May's Creek; thence on said ridge with its meanders to Marrs' Creek; thence due north to the northern boundary of the county."

At this time, also, judges of election were appointed for the various townships, as follows: Illinois, elections to be held at the house of Joseph St. Clair, Richard Price, Job Ratliff and William Bowers; Richland, elections to be held at the house of Robert McCarny, Rial Williams, Stephen Holmesly and Robert Fletcher; Cane Hill, elections to be held at the house of William B. Woody, John Dodson, James Buchanan and Thomas Kiser; Vineyard, elections to be held at the school-house near Hugh Marrs', Jonathan Allen, Hugh Shannon and John Ish; Prairie, elections to be held at the court-house, Larkin Newton, John Wilson, Jr., and Christopher Harness.

In 1830 a county court was established, and Robert McCarny appointed county judge. No record of this court, prior to 1835, could be found. Meantime several new townships were formed, as is indicated by the following list of judges of election appointed for August, 1836: Prairie Township, Solomon Tuttle, James Byrnside, W. S. Wallace; Osage Township, J. B. Dixon, George Wallace and David Woods; Benton Township, Samuel Tiner, John McPhail and John McLaughlin; Clear Creek Township, Joseph Sinclair, William Clary and Isaac Cate; Illinois Township, Thomas Wagner, John Odle and A. Smith; Vineyard Township, Jacob Chandler, William Hunter and Jesse Goddard; Cane Hill Township, Henry E. Campbell, James Mitchell and H. Crawford; Mountain Township, John Ferguson, Samuel Stevenson and William Stirman; Helburn Township, William

Ake, Ambrose H. Helburn and J. P. Cross; Bowen Township, William Cantwell, John Bowen and Henry McElhany; War Eagle Township, John Long, William Gage and Isaac Crow; Brush Creek Township, Abram Buck, Nathaniel Henderson and John Harp; Richland Township, Ryal Williams, John Slover and Thomas M. Duckworth; Sugar Creek Township, William Reddick, William Ford and Stephen Case.

The first Legislature created the counties of Madison and Benton, and the townships of War Eagle, Bowen, Osage, Sugar Creek, Clear Creek, Benton and Helburn, and parts of Richland and Brush Creek were cut off. In January, 1837, the court re-established Brush Creek and Richland Townships, and at the following April term made an order creating White River Township, which included all the territory south of White River, and the northern boundary of Township 15, and west of the range line between Ranges 29 and 30. In 1839 Mountain Township was divided, and the eastern portion was erected into a new township by the name of West Fork. Three years later Mountain Township was again divided, and the part south of the dividing ridge, between the waters of the Illinois River and Cove Creek and Lee's Creek, was erected into a new township, called Cove Creek. Prior to this time, however, in July, 1841, Clear Creek Township was re-established, and in 1852 it was divided, and Elm Springs Township created. From that time until the close of the war there were no further changes in the municipal townships.

The first county court after the organization of the State government was begun and held on January 9, 1837. There were present the following magistrates: John Cureton, John G. Stout, James Owens, Booker Smith, John T. Edmiston, L. C. Blakemore, Thomas Wilson, John Robinson, Lorenzo D. Pollock, Nathaniel Burdire, Samuel Wilson, John Campbell and John D. Moore. John Cureton was elected judge; B. H. Smithson, clerk, and Lucius C. Pleasants, sheriff.

At about this time a new court-house was completed by the contractor, William M. Kincaid, at a cost of over $5,000. It was a brick structure, and was a very creditable building for a new county. In October, 1839, the county court made an order for the erection of a new jail, and appropriated $5,000 for the purpose. Archibald Yell was appointed to superintend its construction. It was to be built of stone, and was to be 42x22 feet, two stories high. In the lower story were to be the dungeon and the debtors' room, and in the upper story the jailor's residence. The walls of the dungeon were to be forty-two inches thick, constructed of rock in two layers, with upright sawed timber or round locust poles, six inches thick, between them. The contract was let to Mathew Leeper for $4,460, and the building was erected in accordance with the above specifications.

In January, 1852, James P. Neal, William M. Bowers and A. W. Brownlee were appointed to select and purchase a poor farm. At the April term they reported that they had purchased the farm of Elias Muncie in Township 17, Range 29 west, containing eighty acres. It was then ordered that two log buildings be erected for the accommodation of the paupers, and John R. Glazebrook was appointed poor-house commissioner. Here the poor of the county have since been cared for. The present superintendent is John A. Beckett. In June, 1854, James H. Stirman, Alfred M. Wilson and Jonas M. Tibbetts were appointed to let the contract for a new court-house, which was accordingly done. George D. Baker bid $6,900, and received the contract. He completed the building and turned it over to the county in October, 1855. This building was burned during the late war, and in April, 1868, the county court appointed James H. Van Hoose and Thomas J. Pollard, commissioners to superintend the erection of a new court-house. The contract was let to Alexander Hendry for $22,500, and was completed about two years later.

Within the past ten years a large number of new municipal townships have been formed. On July 5, 1878, Goshen Township was erected from portions of Richland and Brush Creek, and in October of that year a part of West Fork Township was constituted Crawford Township, with the voting place at Crawford school-house. In 1880 three new townships were established as follows: Lee's Creek, from parts of Crawford and Cove Creek; Reed, from a part of White River, and Center, from portions of Prairie and Marrs' Hill. In July, 1884, the townships of Durham, Price, Star Hill and Winslow were formed, and since that time three others have been added: Dutch Mills, in January, 1885; Wheeler, in July, 1885, and Weddington, in July, 1886.

COUNTY OFFICERS.

The following is a complete list of the officers of Washington County since its organization:

Judges.—Robert McCarny, 1830–32; John Wilson, 1832–33; J. M. Hoge, 1833–35; W. B. Woody, 1835–36; John Cureton, 1836–38; Thomas Wilson, 1838–44; Jonathan Newman, 1844–60; A. A. Crawford, 1860–62; R. W. Mecklin, 1862–64; C. G. Galbreath, 1864–66; L. Tankersley, 1866–68; C. G. Galbreath, 1868–72; Hiram Davis, 1874–79*; Thomas Mullins, 1879–86; H. P. Green, 1886.

Associate Justices.—William Kiser, W. S. Oldham, R. W. Reynolds, David Williams, April to October, 1837; Thomas Wilson, 1837–38; Booker Smith, 1837–39; William Kiser, 1839–40; John Robinson, 1839–40; James Pittman, 1840–41; Noah Reeder, 1840–41; J. C. Pittman, 1841–43; Jonathan Newman, 1841–45; William S. Hamby, 1843–44; Cyrus G. Galbreath, 1844–45; John Robinson, 1845–47: Asa Combs, 1845–47; C. G. Galbreath, 1847–51; W. O. Spencer, 1847–48; Asa Combs, 1848–51; William O. Spencer, 1851–52; A. W. Brownlee, 1851–56; Ed. S. Dawson, 1852–53; T. D. Wisener, 1853–57; William E. Smith, 1856–57; A. W. Brownlee, 1857–60; Jones Pierson, 1857–58; M. D. Frazer, 1858–59; C. G. Galbreath, 1859–62; M. D. Frazer, 1860–61; Larkin Tankersley, 1861–62; Samuel May, 1864–66; Abraham C. Males, 1864–66; William C. Graham, 1866–67; J. L. Carlisle, 1866–67; John B. Rainwater, 1867–68; Lee C. Blakemore, 1867–68; Elijah Davidson, 1868; John Pearson, 1868–71; Abraham Jack, 1870–71; J. L. Carlisle, 1868–70; E. B. Harrison, 1871–73; William Todd, 1871–72; M. H. Mayes, 1872–73.

Clerks of the County Court.—Larkin Newton, 1828–30; B. H. Smithson, 1830–40; Benjamin H. Pierson, 1840–44; James Pittman, 1844–46; P. R. Smith, 1846–62; S. D. Lowery, 1862–64; G. W. M. Reed, 1864–66; P. R. Smith, 1866–68; G. W. M. Reed, 1868–72; P. R. Smith, 1872–80; H. F. Reagan, 1880–84; J. B. Shannon, 1884–88.

---

*Died March, 1879.

Clerks of the Circuit Court.—Jo. Holcomb, 1866–76; A. S. Gregg, 1876–84; John N. Tillman, 1884–88.

Sheriffs.—Lewis Evans, 1828–36; L. C. Pleasants, 1836–40; P. R. Smith, 1840–44; Elijah O'Brien, 1844–48; B. H. Smithson, 1848–52; Z. M. Pettigrew, 1852–56; John Crawford, 1856–60; George Gibson, 1860–62; A. S. Gregg, 1862–64; J. W. Carney, 1864–66; Jacob Yoes, 1866–68; Benjamin F. Little, 1868–72; Z. M. Pettigrew, 1872–80; C. M. Henry, 1880–84; George F. Dean, 1884–88.

Treasurers.—Isaac Murphy, 1836–38; W. S. Wallace, 1838–40; Mathew Hubbard, 1840–44; William M. Bowers, 1844–52; James B. Simpson, 1852–60; W. A. Watson, 1860–64; Thomas Carlisle, 1864–66; James B. Simpson, 1866–68; Thomas Carlisle, 1868–72; A. B. Lewis, 1872–74; Lafayette Boone, 1874–80; J. B. Rainwater, 1880–84; W. S. Tunstill, 1884–88.

Assessors.—Wilson Shreve, 1868–72; G. H. Pettigrew, 1872–74; William Mitchell, 1874–78; J. W. M. Trent, 1878–86; G. W. Morrow, 1886–88.

Coroners.—John Skelton, 1828–30; James Marrs, 1830–32; James Coulter, 1832–33; James Crawford, 1833–35; W. W. Hester, 1835–36; D. Callaghan, 1836–38; L. W. Wallace, 1838–40; John Brickey, 1840–42; Ewing Rabb, 1842–44; W. Skelton, 1844–46; H. W. Fincher, 1846–48; Peter Van Hoose, 1848–50; H. W. Fincher, 1850–62; J. R. Jackson, 1862–64; M. Gregg, 1864–66; Peter Mankins, 1866–68; William Graham, 1868–72; W. D. Holland, 1872–78; J. J. Mount, 1878–80; George W. Van Hoose, 1880–82; W. R. Phillips, 1882–86; George W. Van Hoose, 1886–88.

Surveyors.—Y. Caruthers, 1830–32; J. T. Edmundson, 1832–33; John McClellan, 1833–40; E. H. Shipley, 1840–44; W. D. Sullivan, 1844–48; H. P. Ross, 1848–54; E. H. Shipley, 1854–56; H. P. Ross, 1856–64; William Mitchell, 1866–68; G. W. Cline, 1868–72; L. A. Buchanan, 1872–74; A. Buchanan, 1874–78; J. A. Buchanan, 1878–82; Hugh Scott, 1882–84; William Mitchell, 1884–88.

Representatives in the Legislature.—Session October 5 to November 25, 1829, John Alexander; session October 3 to November 7, 1831, James Pope and A. Whinnery; session October

7 to November 16, 1833, J. B. Dixon, J. Reagan, John Alexander and James Byrnsides; session October 5 to November 16, 1835, no record of members to be found; first State Legislature, session September 12 to November 8, 1836, A. Whinnery, James Boone, J. C. Blair and J. M. Hoge; session November 6, 1837, to March 5, 1838, A. Whinnery, James Boone, J. C. Blair and W. B. Woody; second Legislature, session November 5 to December 17, 1838, W. S. Oldham, W. L. Wilson, John McGarroh, R. Bedford, G. W. Sanders and Robert Hubbard; third Legislature, session November 2 to December 28, 1840, John McGarroh, W. L. Larremore, L. C. Blakemore, W. D. Reagan and G. A. Pettigrew; fourth Legislature, session November 7, 1842, to February 4, 1843, W. S. Oldham*, A. W. Arrington, Lee C. Blakemore, George Cline and Moses Stout; fifth Legislature, session November 4, 1844, to January 10, 1845, John Billingsley, C. A. Miller, I. Strain, Lee C. Blakemore and Thomas Wilson; sixth Legislature, session November 2 to December 23, 1846, R. Buchanan, John Billingsley, R. A. Sharpe, M. Stout and Isaac Murphy; eighth Legislature, session November 4, 1850, to January 13, 1851, Lee C. Blakemore, G. B. Anderson, George Cline, J. M. Tibbetts and Thomas Wilson; ninth Legislature, session November 1, 1852, to January 12, 1853, George Cline, W. N. Bowers, Thomas Wilson, S. R. Moulden; tenth Legislature, session November 6, 1854, to January 22, 1855, Lafayette Gregg, S. R. Moulden, B. H. Smithson and Thomas Wilson; eleventh Legislature, session November 3, 1856, to January 15, 1857, John Billingsley, Benjamin F. Boone and William T. Neal; twelfth Legislature, session November 1, 1858, to February 21, 1859, William T. Neal, Thomas Wilson and Jeremiah Brewster; thirteenth Legislature, sessions November 5, 1860, to January 21, 1861, November 4 to November 18, 1861, and March 5 to March 22, 1862, John Crawford, B. F. Boone, J. Mitchell and L. M. Bell; fourteenth Legislature, session November 5 to December, 1862, E. H. Phillips, J. M. Tuttle, R. C. Byrd and C. R. Fenton; fifteenth Legislature, sessions April 11 to June 2, 1864, November 7, 1864, to January 2, 1865, and April 3 to April 22, 1865, J. Pierson, W. H. Nott, Y. D. Waddle and William J. Patton; Con-

*Speaker.

federate Legislature, session September 22 to October 2, 1864, E. H. Phillips and R. C. Byrd; sixteenth Legislature, session November 5, 1866, to March 23, 1867, J. R. Pettigrew, J. B. Russell, W. H. Brooks and John Enyart; seventeenth Legislature, sessions April 2 to July 23, 1868, and November 17, 1868, to April 10, 1869, S. Bard and J. Yoes; eighteenth Legislature, session January 2 to March 25, 1871, Thomas Wilson and James M. Pittman; nineteenth Legislature, session January 6 to April 25, 1873, D. Bridenthal and T. W. Thomason; twentieth Legislature, sessions November 10, 1864, to March 5, 1875, and November 1 to December 10, 1875, W. F. Dowell, J. S. Williams and T. J. Patton; twenty-first Legislature, session January 8 to March 8, 1877, T. W. Thomason, W. C. Braley and C. W. Walker; twenty-second Legislature, session January 13 to March 13, 1879, W. C. Braley, B. F. Walker and E. B. Moore; twenty-third Legislature, session January 8 to March 19, 1881, E. B. Moore, T. W. Thomason and S. E. Marrs; twenty-fourth Legislature, session January 8 to March 28, 1883, E. B. Moore, S. E. Marrs and W. C. Braley*; twenty-fifth Legislature, session January 12 to March 28, 1885, B. F. Walker, H. P. Green and R. A. Medearis; twenty-sixth Legislature, session January to March, 1887, Robert J. Wilson, W. M. Davis and H. M. Maguire.

Members of the Upper House of the General Assembly.—Territorial council, James Billingsley, 1829; Robert McCarny, 1831; Mark Bean, 1833; State Senate, W. McK. Ball and Robert Mc-Carny, 1836; O. Evans and A. Whinnery, 1838; O. Evans and David Walker, 1840; David Walker and M. Bean, 1842; Mark Bean and Robert McCarny, 1844; Robert McCarny and J. E. Mayfield, 1846; J. E. Mayfield and R. McCarny, 1848; R. Mc-Carny and J. Billingsley, 1850; John Billingsley, 1852; John Enyart, 1854, also 1856; B. H. Smithson, 1858; R. W. Mecklin, 1860; Hiram Davis, 1862; J. M. Gilstrop, 1864; F. R. Earle, 1866; T. J. Hunt,† 1868; A. Caraloff,† 1870, also 1872; B. F. Walker, 1874; A. M. Wilson, 1876, also 1878; J. S. Williams, 1880; Thomas Wainwright, 1881, also 1882; T. W. Thomason, 1884, also 1886.

Members of Constitutional Conventions.—Convention of 1836,

---

*Speaker.
†From the district composed of Washington and Benton Counties.

David Walker, Mark Bean, A. Whinnery, William McK. Ball, James Boone, Robert McCarny; convention of 1861, David Walker (president), J. H. Stirman, J. P. A. Parks and T. M. Gunter; convention of 1868, Charles W. Walker and James M. Hoge; convention of 1874, Benjamin F. Walker, M. F. Lake and T. W. Thomason.

ELECTIONS.

Washington County has always been strongly Democratic in politics. In its early history the Whig party had some very able leaders, and through their superior ability were frequently able to secure an election to some legislative or judicial office. In 1836, and again in 1838, the Democrats elected solid delegations to the Legislature, but in 1840 David Walker, a Whig leader, was elected to the Senate, and two of the representatives, W. D. Reagan and G. A. Pettigrew, were Whigs. In 1842 the failure of the State Bank still farther strengthened the Whigs, and Mark Bean, another Whig leader, was elected to the Senate, while David Walker held over. At this election there were also two Whigs chosen representatives. Two years later the Democrats regained their lost ground, and held it until the opening of the Civil War.

The first election statistics that could be obtained were for the year 1860. The September election resulted as follows:

Governor, R. H. Johnson, 969; H. M. Rector, 1,305. Representative in Congress, J. N. Cypert, 662; T. C. Hindman, 1,606. Circuit judge, J. M. Wilson, 718; J. J. Greene, 1,440. Representatives in the Legislature, R. West, 1,132; John Crawford, 1,530; W. Hulse, 1,044; L. M. Bell, 1,293; G. W. Tate, 505; B. F. Boone, 1,194; D. C. Smithson, 407; James Mitchell, 1,297; T. J. Kelly, 354; Dr. Cansler, 282. Prosecuting attorney, John R. Cox, 744; Lafayette Gregg, 1,534. Clerk of the courts, Z. M. Pettigrew, 946; P. R. Smith, 1,424. Sheriff, W. P. Taylor, 557; George Gibson, 1,688. County judge, Jonathan Newman, 944; A. A. Crawford, 1,225. Treasurer, Joseph Holcomb, 833; W. A. Watson, 978. Surveyor, H. P. Ross, 1,703. Coroner, A. Beattie, 476; H. Fincher, 829. School commissioner, F. Smiley, 739; P. P. Van Hoose, 1,375.

In 1866 the Union party nominated the following county ticket: Representatives in the Legislature, Thomas J. Hunt, Jacob Yoes, W. H. H. Nott and Wilson Rizley; county judge, W. E. Graham; sheriff, J. W. Carney; circuit court clerk, George W. M. Reed; treasurer, Thomas Carlisle; coroner, J. J. Hutchinson; surveyor, G. M. Cline. This ticket was defeated by the Conservative Democrats, but by what majority could not be ascertained. In 1868, at the election to vote upon the adoption of the new constitution, the majority against adoption was 550, but it was adopted by the State as a whole, and under its provisions the Radical party easily maintained its ascendancy.

The campaign of 1872 marks the beginning of the end of "carpet-bag" rule in Arkansas. The Radical party became divided within itself, and two tickets were placed in the field. One was headed by Elisha Baxter and supported by Gov. Clayton, and the other by Joseph Brooks, a "carpet-bagger" from Ohio, supported by those who opposed the administration, which included the Democratic minority. The result of the election in Washington county was as follows: For governor, Joseph Brooks, 1,178; Elisha Baxter, 738; for lieutenant-governor, Daniel J. Smith, 1,216; V. V. Smith, 710; for secretary of state, Edward A. Fulton, 807; James M. Johnson, 712; for auditor, James R. Berry, 1,232; Stephen Wheeler, 696; for treasurer, Thomas J. Hunt, 1,024; Henry Page, 715; for attorney-general, Benjamin T. DuVal, 1,211; T. D. W. Yonley, 702; for congressman-at-large, William J. Hyne, 1,227; John M. Bradley, 696; for congressman third district, T. M. Gunter, 1,218; W. W. Wilshire, 701; for representatives to the Legislature, David Bridenthal, (Dem.), 1,216; T. W. Thomason (Dem.), 1,183; James H. Berry (Dem.), 805; David Chandler (Dem.), 824; W. E. Gould (Dem.), 254; — McGaugh (Dem.), 273; H. S. Coleman (Rad.), 608; J. F. Johnson (Rad.), 393; — Rutherford (Rad.), 433; for sheriff, Z. M. Pettigrew (Dem.), 1,060; William Mayes (Lib.), 304; W. J. Gilliland (Rad.), 497; for circuit clerk, J. H. Van Hoose (Dem.), 529; Joseph Holcomb (Dem.), 663; J. Q. Benbrook (Rad.), 652; for county clerk, P. R. Smith (Dem.), 1,082; R. Putnam (Lib.), 214; G. W. M. Reed (Rad.), 536; for treasurer, A. B. Lewis (Dem.), 1,061; John A. Pearson (Rad.),

769; for assessor, — Moore (Dem.), 1,127; — Reed (Rad.), 445; for county judge, E. T. Stirman, 665; A. J. Hale, 603; for coroner, W. D. Holland, 998; — Cate, 431; for surveyor, L. A. Buchanan, 1,089; W. L. Alexander, 376.

In 1874, at the first election after the adoption of the present constitution, there was no Republican State ticket, and B. F. Walker was elected to the State Senate without opposition. For circuit judge J. M. Pittman received 1,994 votes, and J. H. Huckleberry, 242. For prosecuting attorney the vote was: Peel, 1,247; Cullom, 482; Dougherty, 192. Two county conventions were held. The first met at Prairie Grove, and nominated what was termed the farmers' and laborers' ticket, which was elected by a large majority. A week or two later a second convention was held at Mt. Comfort, and an " Independent " ticket placed in the field. The result was as follows:

Representatives in the Legislature: J. S. Williams, 1,731; W. F. Dowell, 1,721; T. J. Patton, 1,430; William Alexander, 660; J. B. Russell, 570; John Enyart, 127. Sheriff, Z. M. Pettigrew, 1,376; J. D. Henry, 977. County clerk, P. R. Smith, 1,952; J. P. Pyeatt, 201. Circuit clerk, Joseph Holcomb, 1,517; Dr. Putnam, 855. County judge, Hiram Davis, 1,403; George Gibson, 99; A. J. Hall, 643. Assessor, William Mitchell, 1,699; "Sid" Williams, 455. Treasurer, Lafayette Boone, 1,429; John Mayes, 858. Surveyor, A. Buchanan, 1,706; Mark Cline, 714. Coroner, W. D. Holland, 1,859; — Arnett, 450.

In 1876 the Republicans met in convention and decided to nominate no county ticket, but to give their support to the best men announced as candidates. The result was the distribution of the votes among a large number of candidates. The following was the vote:

Representatives in the Legislature: W. E. Braly, 1,576; T. W. Thompson, 1,342; C. W. Walker, 1,327; W. C. Roberts, 1,250; D. M. Fields, 945; John Billingsley, 577; Thomas Wainwright, 305; John Enyart, 289; S. T. Kennedy, 292. County judge, Hiram Davis, 1,888; W. W. Brownlee, 749. Sheriff, Z. M. Pettigrew, 1,755; J. D. Henry, 1,216. Circuit clerk, A. S. Gregg, 1,409; R. H. Smith, 1,228. County clerk, P. R. Smith, 1,964; C. C. Conner, 1,069. Assessor, William Mitchell, 1,113;

G. W. Van Hoose, 207; John Pearson, 500; A. Tankersly, 124; George Gibson, 437; O. M. Rieff, 50; W. B. Brodie, 294; F. F. Curtis, 47; J. F. Johnson, 262; C. B. Pettigrew, 34. Treasurer, Lafayette Boone, 1,754; A. B. Lewis, 991. Surveyor, A. Buchanan, 1,694; G. M. Cline, 645. Coroner, W. D. Holland, 1,207; H. West, 170.

At the same election the vote for governor was W. B. Miller, 2,320; A. W. Bishop, 751. For prosecuting attorney, E. T. Stirman, 1,682; George J. Crump, 950. For senator, A. M. Wilson, 1,404; W. D. Reagan, 1,060; B. F. Williams, 505. For congressman, T. M. Gunter, 1,936; J. H. Huckleberry, 774. For President, Tilden, 1,888; Hayes, 817; Cooper, 87.

The election of 1878 resulted as follows: Circuit judge, J. H. Berry, 1,872; J. M. Pittman, 1,406. Prosecuting attorney, H. A. Dinsmore, 1,799; E. I. Stirman, 1,562. Representative, W. C. Braly, 2,191; Thomas Mullins, 1,272; E. B. Moore, 2,071; Thomas D. Boles, 1,060; W. T. Walker, 2,128; Trueman Niman, 1,054. Sheriff, Z. M. Pettigrew, 1,761; John Garrett, 943; William Mitchell, 934. County clerk, P. R. Smith, 2,236; John Mayes, 1,202. Circuit clerk, A. S. Gregg, 2,481; Thomas Wainwright, 876. Treasurer, Lafayette Boone, 1,280; John Pearson, 901; T. H. Cartner, 291. County judge, Hiram Davis, 1,980; Harris, 1,150. Assessor, J. W. M. Trent, 2,120; A. B. Lewis, 204; J. R. Beaman, 1,030. Surveyor, — Hale, 1,648; J. A. Buchanan, 1,362. Coroner, J. J. Mount, 1,855; Hanna, 226; — West, 228.

The Republicans nominated no State ticket this year, but at the November election there were three candidates for Congress, and the vote was as follows: T. M. Gunter (D), 1,253; James F. Cunningham (I), 405; Byrd Smith (G), 79.

In 1880 there were two county tickets, the straight Democratic ticket and an Independent ticket, supported by the Republicans and Greenbackers, with the following result:

Representatives: E. B. Moore (D), 1,884; Trueman Niman (I), 1,416; S. E. Marrs (D), 2,107; R. R. Fallen (I), 1,495; T. W. Thomason (D), 2,118. County judge, A. S. Vandeventer (D), 1,381; Thomas Mullins (I), 2,343. Sheriff, G. H. Pettigrew (D), 1,264; C. M. Henry (I), 2,466. Circuit clerk, A. S.

Gregg (D), 1,915; T. W. Cline (I), 1,806. County clerk, P. R. Smith (D), 1,417; H. F. Reagan (I), 2,312. Treasurer, A. B. Lewis (D), 1,695; J. B. Rainwater (I), 1,997. Assessor, J. W. M. Trent (D), 2,093; Pearson (I), 1,533. Surveyor, J. A. Buchanan (D), 1,810; P. R. Bates (I), 1,807. Coroner, A. A. Maguire (D), 1,504; George Van Hoose (I), 1,682.

At the November election the vote for congressman was T. M. Gunter, 1,430; S. W. Peel, 719, and Samuel Murphy, 816. For President, Garfield electors, 788; Hancock electors, 1,936, and Weaver electors, 262.

In 1882, in the county election, the contest was the same as in 1880, and resulted as follows:

Representatives: E. B. Moore (D), 1,908; H. D. Gorham (I), 1,246; S. E. Marrs (D), 1,879; Jesse Jones (I), 1,082; W. C. Braly (D), 1,722; T. L. Harvey (I), 931; R. R. Fallen (I), 235. County judge, Robert J. Wilson (D), 1,704; Thomas Mullins (I), 1,781. Circuit clerk, A. S. Gregg (D), 1,578; Thomas Welch (I), 554; Mack Devin (D), 827; Henry Cartner (I), 487. County clerk, P. R. Smith (D), 974; Hugh F. Reagan (I), 2,434. Sheriff, C. M. Henry (D), 1,469; C. M. Henry (I), 1,538; P. McGuire (D), 467; Z. M. Pettigrew (I), 135. Treasurer, J. B. Rainwater (D), 1,369; J. H. Van Hoose (I), 1,257; A. B. Lewis (I), 793. Assessor, J. W. M. Trent (D), 1,705; J. R. Beaman (I), 1,036; William Mitchell (I), 741. Coroner, W. R. Phillips (D), 1,705; George Van Hoose (I), 1,120. Surveyor, Hugh Scott (D), 2,124; Thomas J. Campbell (I), 986. The vote for governor was, for J. H. Berry, 2,296; for R. K. Garland, 506, and for W. D. Slack, 688.

In 1884 the contest lay between Republicans and Democrats in the State and county elections, with the following result:

For governor, S. P. Hughes, 2,692; Thomas Bates, 1,176. Representatives: B. F. Walker, 2,390; E. Webb, 1,115; H. P. Greene, 2,574; C. L. Howell, 1474; R. A. Medearis, 2,484; D. M. Moore, 1,481. County judge, R. J. Wilson, Thomas Mullins. Circuit clerk, J. N. Tillman, 2,318; T. W. Cline, 1,978. County clerk, J. B. Shannon, 2,342; H. B. Collier, 1,832. Sheriff, George F. Drane, 2,196; Pat. Mouldin, 1,937. Treasurer, W. S. Tunstill, 2,425; J. B. Rainwater, 1,849. Assessor, J. W. M.

Trent, 2,415; J. C. Fletcher, 1,350; G. H. Cartner, 424. Coroner, W. R. Phillips, 2,473; J. R. Harris, 814. Surveyor, William Mitchell, 2,288; P. R. Bates, 1,964.

The vote at the November election was, for Congressman: S. W. Peel, 2,496; W. R. Keener, 1,275. For President: Cleveland electors, 2,455; Blaine electors, 1,387.

In 1886 the vote for governor was 2,730 for S. P. Hughes and for Lafayette Gregg, and 50 for C. E. Cunningham.

For county officers the vote was as follows:

Representatives: W. M. Davis, 2,881; S. D. Gilbreath, 1851; H. M. Maguire, 2,824; James Oates, 1,850; R. J. Wilson, 2,854; O. D. Slaughter, 1,742. County judge, H. P. Greene, 2,767; Elijah Webb, 2,764. Circuit clerk, J. N. Tillman, 2,764; L. W. Gregg, 1,880. County clerk, J. B. Shannon, 2,550; C. R. Gilbreath, 2,003. Sheriff, George F. Drane, 2,679; Thomas Brooks, 1,932. Treasurer, W. S. Tunstill, 2,679; C. M. Greene, 1,772. Assessor; G. W. Morrow, 2,864; John Pearson, 1,819. Surveyor, William Mitchell, 3,034. Coroner, G. W. Van Hoose, 2,886; Davis, 1,774.

WASHINGTON COUNTY FINANCES.

The financial condition of Washington County is excellent. It is true it has a considerable bonded indebtedness, but it is no greater than can be sustained without placing unusual burdens of taxation upon the people. The following is the last report of the clerk of the county court, giving a statement of the financial condition of the county for the year ending July 14, 1888:

Total amount outstanding warrants, including allowances of record July 14, 1888	$4,074 09
By amount cash in treasury July 14, 1888, belonging to general county fund	597 02
Total indebtedness other than bonded indebtedness July 14, 1888	3,477 07

A. I. U. Bonded Indebtedness.—This amount includes 8 per cent bonds issued December 1871, due January, 1903, $100,000. The interest on these bonds has been paid up to July 1, 1888, leaving a balance in the county treasury on account of interest of $688.57.

The above bonds are credited with $16,000 refunded by the State to the county on account of two years' interest erroneously collected on said bonds, which amount is in State 6 per cent bonds, the interest on which is payable semi-annually. Also by $10,708.41 collected and paid into county treasury as an A. I. U. sinking fund, of which amount $5,620 is invested in four bonds of the State drawing 6 per cent interest per annum, dated 1869 and 1870, and due thirty years from date. Balance in county treasury, cash uninvested July 14, 1888, $5,006.47.

Amount and Sources of Revenue collected for the year ending July 14, 1888, to wit:

Total current expenses	$19,728 12
Fines, forfeitures, licenses, etc	3,284 38
Tax for interest on A. I. U. bonds	8,028 07
Interest on $16,000 State bonds	960 00
Tax A. I. U. sinking fund	4,007 22
Common school tax, penalties, etc	5,394 15

Total amount received, other than special school $41,401 94

Total amount expended during the year ending July 14, 1888, which amount includes the county court, and all other incidental expenses, divided as follows, to wit:

Circuit court expenses	$5,776 95
County court expenses	3,822 18
Justice of the peace court expenses	475 65
Jail expenses	1,419 77
Paupers	907 48
Paupers paid in cash, $201.75*	
Inquisition	90 10
Assessment of 1887	825 37

$13,317 50

Total orders on treasury, including *$201.75 for paupers in cash, and treasurer's commission on general county fund	1,634 68
Interest on A. I. U. bonds, including $120 on interest of 1887	8,120 00
Amount A. I. U. sinking fund in State bonds	5,620 00
Treasurer's commission on A. I. U., A. I. U. sinking fund and common school tax, as above	369 02

Total $29,061 20

RAILROADS.

The subject of railroad communication early engaged the attention of the people of Washington County, and it was almost constantly agitated for more than a quarter of a century before any tangible result was secured. One of the first schemes was for the construction of a grand trans-continental line, on or near the thirty-fifth parallel. This engaged the attention of the whole country, and a survey of the land was made, but nothing resulted from it. Other schemes, however, were not wanting. Early in the fifties the Legislature of Missouri chartered a road to be built from St. Louis to Springfield, and work upon it was soon after begun. It was thought that by proper effort an extension into Northwestern Arkansas could be obtained, as witness the following order of the county court of Washington County, made in 1855: "In view of the growing population, and the great success of our agricultural and commercial interests, it becomes imperative on us to use every reasonable exertion for the purpose of securing for ourselves a cheaper and more speedy means of transportation. The State of Missouri, having by an extension of her credit, and her congressional donation of the public domain, put in operation the construction of a railroad to run from St. Louis to Springfield, putting it in our power, by proper exertion being used, to have like facilities, by a continuation of said road to this place, it is ordered by the court that the clerk of the county be, and hereby is, ordered and instructed to prepare two additional columns on the poll books of an election to be held in August next, for a representative to Congress. In these columns he shall place the words 'For Railroad Tax' and 'Against Railroad Tax,' and all persons voting are requested to record their votes in one or the other columns." The result of the vote could not be ascertained, but it was doubtless in favor of the proposition. The road, however, with all the aid extended to it by the State of Missouri, had only reached Rolla when the war put an end to the work.

In 1868 two proposed railroads were presented for the consideration of the people of Northwestern Arkansas. One was for a railway to be built across the State from east to west, and a company known as the Pacific & Great Eastern Railway Company was organized, with James H. Van Hoose as president. No work was done beyond a partial survey of the line. During the same year an act was passed granting the usual State aid of $15,000 per mile, to the Northwestern Border Railroad Company, upon the completion of a road from Van Buren to the Missouri State line, by the way of Fayetteville and Bentonville. From this time forth numerous conventions were held, and many plans for the building of various proposed lines were presented, but the railroads were as far away as before. At last the St. Louis & San Francisco Railroad Company decided to extend their line into Texas, by the way of Fort Smith. Two lines were surveyed, one to pass through Prairie Grove Valley, and the other by the way of Fayetteville. To secure its construction over the latter the business men of Fayetteville purchased the right of way from the Missouri State line to Fayetteville, at a cost of over $8,000, and also donated $2,500 for the building of a depot. The first train over this road reached the town on June 8, 1881, amidst great rejoicing. A celebration was held, and appropriate addresses delivered by Col. T. M. Gunter, E. C. Boudinot, John O'Day and others.

In 1884 the Pacific & Great Eastern Railway Company was revived, or rather a new company was formed with the same objects as the old company of that name. It was incorporated on October 23, 1884, with an authorized capital stock of $8,877,000, by the following citizens of Fayetteville: B. R. Davidson, J. W. Stirman, C. A. Mulholland, J. D. Van Winkle, Maurice Coffey, P. F. Davidson and J. H. Van Hoose. During 1885 eight miles of road were constructed from Fayetteville eastward, but no further work has been attempted. Regular trains are run, however, and negotiations are now pending for the further building of the road. Should the line be completed it will open up a fine mineral and timber region, hitherto undeveloped. The present officers of the company are B. R. Davidson, president; P. F. Davidson, secretary; H. H. Dorsey, treasurer, and George S. Albright, superintendent.

In 1886 H. F. McDanield, a tie contractor, surveyed a line of railroad from Fayetteville to St. Paul, in Madison, and procured the right of way. He then interested the St. Louis & San Francisco Company in the proposed new road, and they undertook its construction. It has been completed to St. Paul, with the intention of continuing it to Little Rock.

SOCIETIES.

The organization of an agricultural and mechanical association early engaged the attention of some of the most progressive citizens of the county. Such a society was organized in 1856, and the first fair was held in that year. The court yard was used as a fair ground, and the agricultural and mechanical productions were exhibited in the court-house. A track was around the outer edge of the yard, and here several races were run. Capt. S. P. Pittman rode the winning horse, which belonged to Maj. W. D. Reagan. This fair was declared a success, and the next Legislature granted a charter to the association. Five acres of land were donated by Judge David Walker, and grounds, several acres in extent, were inclosed and improved. These grounds lay south of town, and there in October, 1857, the second fair was held. The third was held at the same place a year later. At each of these fairs from $150 to $200 were awarded as premiums. The first list of officers that could be found are for 1858. T. B. Van Horne was then president; J. W. Washbourne and John Enyart, vice-presidents; P. P. Van Hoose, secretary, and J. L. Dickson, treasurer. The last fair held by this association was in September, 1859.

In 1869 it was determined to revive the society, or rather to organize a new one. A meeting was held in Fayetteville on May 1, and preliminary arrangements made. After the matter had been thoroughly discussed throughout the county a permanent organization was effected, with Thomas Wilson as president; H. C. Botefuhr and T. J. Patton, vice-presidents; C. R. Buckner, recording secretary; James P. Neal, corresponding secretary, and J. D. Henry, treasurer. Fourteen acres of land lying west of Fayetteville were purchased, and the first fair was given, beginning on November 1, 1869. This was fairly successful, and a second fair was held the following year. The interest in it then failed, and the society was disbanded.

In 1872 the *Prairie Grove Valley Agricultural and Mechanical Association* was organized; held a fair in Prairie Grove Valley on October 17 and 18 of that year. The officers of the association were Samuel P. Pittman, president; Robert J. West and M. F. Lake, vice-presidents; J. J. Baggett, secretary, and B. F. Totten, treasurer. These fairs were continued for three or four years, but it was found that the interest in them was not general enough to justify the stockholders in maintaining.

In 1877 the *Washington County Agricultural and Mechanical Society* was once more revived, and this time existed for four years. Recently attempts have been made to organize a new society, and the prospects of success are much better than ever before.

The Washington County Medical Society was organized July 2, 1872, at the office of that veteran among Arkansas physicians, Dr. T. J. Pollard, of Fayetteville. Those who signed the constitution of the society on that day are as follows: Drs. T. J. Pollard, W. B. Welch, S. F. Paddock, R. J. Carroll, George W. Holcomb, E. F. Brodie, H. D. Wood, F. N. Littlejohn, John M. Lacy and John C. Grace. They elected as president, Dr. T. J. Pollard; vice-president, Dr. W. B. Welch; recording secretary, Dr. R. J. Carroll; correspondent, Dr. J. C. Grace, and treasurer, Dr. G. W. Holcomb. Drs. Littlejohn, Carroll and Holcomb comprised the credential committee, and those on publication were Drs. Paddock, Wood and Brodie. The society has a membership of seventeen at present, and always sends delegates to both State and national associations. Dr. T. W. Blackburn, of Boonsboro, Dr. O. L. Wilson and Dr. A. S. Gregg, respectively, fill the office of president, vice-president, and secretary and treasurer (combined).

The Western Arkansas Fruit Growers' and Shippers' Co-operative Association is composed largely of Washington County men, and has its headquarters at Springdale. It was organized June 30, 1888, at the latter place, with for its first officers the following: President, S. B. Wing; vice-president, G. W. Umbaugh; secretary, John B. Gill; corresponding secretary, W. G. Vincenheller, and treasurer, J. W. Kimmons. The following committees were also appointed: On transportation, J. L. Rea, of Van Buren; on commission merchants, D. D. Ames, of Avoca; on claims, E. Arkebauer, of Van Buren, and on handling fruits, John W. Phillips, of Springdale. The officers and committees show the scope of the association's intentions, and it is thought that it will be a powerful agent in the development of the fruit growing of the whole region. It has seventeen members.

The Northwest Arkansas Horticultural Society, having its present headquarters at Springdale, was organized at that place in December, 1886, with sixteen members, representing Washington, Benton, Carroll and Madison Counties. Its first officers were: President, E. Arkebauer, of Van Buren; vice-president, George F. Kennan, of Rogers; secretary, John B. Gill, and treasurer, C. Petros, both of Springdale. The president and vice-president have since been succeeded by W. J. Todd, of Rogers, and I. D. Raders, of Springdale, respectively. The society is in a prosperous condition, and has a membership of about twenty persons. A successful fair was held by this society at Rogers in 1887, and at Springdale in 1888.

The Washington County Horticultural Society was organized at Fayetteville August 6, 1887. The first officers elected were Hon. W. J. Patton, president, and Dr. J. F. Simonds, secretary, and at the annual election in January, 1888, these gentlemen were retained for the coming year. Meetings for the discussion of subjects pertaining to horticulture are held on the last Saturday of each month.

POPULATION.

In 1830 Washington County, which then embraced an area almost three times as great as at the present time, had a population of 2,007 whites, 5 free colored and 170 slaves. In 1840, with the county reduced to its present limits, its population was 6,246 whites, 19 free colored and 883 slaves. The following table shows the population by townships at the end of each decade, beginning with 1850:

TOWNSHIP.	1850.		1860.		1870.		1880.
	White.	Colored	White.	Colored	White.	Colored	White & Col'd.
Brush Creek...............	583	6	778	9	722	18	790
Cane Hill.................	803	279	1150	342	1503	108	1744
Clear Creek..............	672	5	691	25	1191	8	....
Cove Creek..............	408	3	405	15	505	9	571
Elm Spring..............	...	....	704	9	1063	8	1677
Illinois.................	987	325	1699	461	1146	52	2195
Marrs' Hill.............	526	64	926	26	1272	8	1746
Mountain...............	804	105	927	158	882	54	1068
Prairie.................	1657	223	2307	278	3554	330	5110
Richland...............	382	107	666	96	1139	17	1087
Vineyard...............	647	64	913	77	871	16	1233
West Fork..............	605	....	707	15	1226	17	798
White River............	663	32	1233	29	1516	29	1766
Prairie Grove..........	....	....	....	...	....	....	994
Crawford...............	....	....	....	....	....	....	572
Goshen.................	....	....	....	....	....	....	788
Springdale.............	....	....	....	....	....	....	1265
Lee's Creek............	....	....	....	....	....	....	500
Total.................	8737	1213	13102	1538	16590	674	23844

COURTS AND CRIME.

The organization of the circuit court in 1829 has already been noticed. Washington County then constituted a part of the Second Judicial Circuit, of which Benjamin Johnson was judge. There was much interchanging of circuits, however, and the court at Fayetteville was presided over successively by Thomas P. Eskridge, Edward Cross and S. S. Hall, and from 1833 to 1837 by Archibald Yell. During that time no very notable or curious cases were tried. At the June term of 1833 Samuel Wackard was called upon to answer the charge of stealing a steer, valued at $12, from one John Musick. The jury decided that he was guilty, and that he should pay to the owner of the steer $24, pay a fine of $24, receive five lashes upon his bare back and stand in the pillory fifteen minutes.

At the December term of 1835 Ellis Gregg was tried upon an indictment for murder, and the jury returned the following verdict: "We, the jury, find the defendant guilty of manslaughter, and sess the fine to $1 and one hour's imprisonment."

The first circuit court held after the organization of the State government was begun on April 15, 1837. The county then formed a part of the Fourth Judicial District, of which J. M. Hoge was judge until 1844.

The first conviction for murder occurred at the September

term, in 1838, when Spencer Asbury was tried for the killing of Enoch Chandler, of Illinois Township, on August 1,
1838. A verdict of murder in the first degree was found, and
he was sentenced to be hung on September 28, but before the
day of execution arrived he made his escape and was never recaptured.

At the May term, 1839, Willis S. Wallace was tried upon the
charge of manslaughter, for the killing of a Cherokee named Orr.
The jury, composed of James Campbell, Jefferson Cabe, Wilson
Chapman, Jacob Coats, James R. Wilson, Bailey Marshall,
James C. Gilliland, Ralph Skelton, A. H. Bryant, George A.
Pettigrew, Jesse Pruett and Daniel Rose, returned a ver-
dict of "not guilty." At the time the killing occurred the
Cherokees were on their way from Tennessee and Georgia to the
Indian Territory, and were passing through Fayetteville. It had
been their custom on reaching small towns to imbibe freely of
"fire water," then to take possession of the town and terrorize
the inhabitants. Fayetteville was made no exception to the rule.
The following account of the affair here, by Alfred W. Arrington,
is said to be very correct: "It was a beautiful Sunday in mid-
summer that a band of 1,000 Cherokee emigrants, from their
homes east of the Mississippi, passed through Fayetteville to the
country provided for them by the Government in the distant
west. The scene of their passage through the principal streets
of the village was picturesque in the extreme. Long lines of
wagons rolled slowly forward, creaking with a dull sound under
their heavy loads. Then followed the troops of pedestrians of
all ages and conditions; hunters with their rifles and tomahawks;
barefoot squaws with their babes tied on their shoulders; little
Indian boys leading their lean, wolf-like dogs by long strings
fastened around their necks, and half-naked girls driving herds
of cattle before them. Next came lines of those on horseback
(these belonged to the middle class), and these too were of every
variety of description: sober and sedate members of the church;
half-breed braves in the wild costume of the desperado; white
gamblers, who had married Indian women; and beautiful quad-
roons, with whose dark and fascinating eyes and raven ringlets,
still more bewitching, if possible, floating in the wind around their

fine graceful shoulders. After these followed the families of wealth—the Cherokee aristocracy—in their splendid carriages, many of which were equal to the most brilliant that rattle along Broadway. And next, and last of all, came hundreds of African slaves on foot, and weary and worn down by the heavy burdens they were compelled to carry.

"It was earnestly hoped by the citizens of Fayetteville that no grocery would be opened on that day to afford the many Indian vagabonds and desperadoes an opportunity of becoming intoxicated, which would very likely result in some serious mischief. But the Wallaces could not let pass so excellent a chance of making a few dollars. Accordingly their door was thrown open and dusky-faced crowds flocked in thick as honey bees to their evening hive. The door was literally blocked up with the dense throng of savage bacchanals, and more than 100 were compelled to remain outside, who passed into the liquor shop their money from hand to hand and received in the same manner large quart and gallon measures of old, rich-beaded whisky, which they gulped down eagerly as if it had been nectar newly drawn from Paradise. But this was found to be too slow a method of satisfying their fiery thirst, and, accordingly, they made up a pony purse, as it is called in the backwoods, bought a whole barrel of brandy at a four-fold price, rolled it out before the grocery door, knocked in the head and commenced dipping and drinking with those little tin cups and gourds, one of which every Indian carries about his person. Men, women, and even children, joined in the spree, and in an incredibly short time were sufficiently drunk to commence yelling and shouting as if a whole army of fiends had just arrived in town from the infernal regions. As yet all went on peaceably; all was fun and frolic; music not over musical, and dancing which, from the verticose motion of the dancers, might be literally termed a reel. The main body, comprising the most respectable portion of the emigrants, had gone on through the village without making any halt, and camped about two miles beyond on a little creek, there to spend the night.

"It was growing late in the evening, the sun being about an hour high, when an event took place to change the boisterous mirth that reigned about the grocery into madness.

"A brutal loafer, citizen of Fayetteville, who was busy in the wassail, offered a gross insult to a Cherokee woman. A half-breed desperado, by the name of Nelson Orr, avenged her by knocking down the ruffian on the sill of the grocery door. He did not stop with this, but jumped on his foe, and commenced choking and gouging him at his leisure.

"Riley Wallace, who was standing near, thinking the chastisement sufficient, pulled Orr off his prostrate enemy, though in as gentle a manner as possible to effect the object. Orr immediately turned his wrath against Wallace, drew his bowie knife and made a bold cut at his breast. The latter retreated into his grocery pursued by his foe, furious with rage and bent on slaughter. Willis S. Wallace, seeing the peril of his brother, sprang over the counter, unsheathed his knife, and plunged it up to the hilt in Orr's side, who reeled and fell on the floor. A deafening outcry was raised by the Indians, who sought to lay hands on Wallace, and prevent his egress from the room. Five or six caught him by different parts of his clothing, but he cut them loose with his bloody knife-blade, and made his escape to his own dwelling, where he armed himself more effectually with gun and pistols.

" The rumor of the affray was speedily carried to the Indian encampment for the night, which, as we have said, was two miles west of Fayetteville, and in a short time hundreds of Indians with their guns were seen approaching the town. About a quarter of a mile ahead of the main body rode, at swift gallop, a company of twenty horsemen under the command of William Coody, a quadroon brave. These dashed up the principal street, and into the public square, with the silver handles of their bowie knives and pistols gleaming in the beams of the setting sun.

" As soon as Coody got sufficiently near the whites, who had armed themselves, and gathered in a crowd around Wallace, he addressed them in hurried accents, informing them that he had come to prevent bloodshed, and that for that purpose it was necessary for Wallace to leave town immediately, for several hundred furious Cherokees would be there in a few minutes, and that if they found their enemy a scene of slaughter would certainly ensue, and if resistance were offered they would not hesitate to burn down the village! He had scarcely finished the sentence, when a hideous war-whoop was heard in the distance. Coody and his troop of horse then rode rapidly back, to stay if possible the advance of the furious savages.

"Wallace was at first unwilling to retreat, swearing that it should never be said that he fled before the face of mortal man. His friends, however, conjured him by every consideration of principle and policy, for the safety of the village and of innocent blood. At length, moved by the urgent entreaties of all present, in company with several friends, he rode off and disappeared in the adjacent forest. The utmost exertions of Coody and the more rational leaders of the Cherokees were barely sufficient to persuade the remainder that Wallace had made his escape, and thus induce them to return without committing any serious outrage.

"Orr lingered several days in excruciating torture, and expired as he had lived, a fearless desperado to the last."

This case had scarcely been disposed of when Willis Wallace killed another man. On one Sunday morning L. D. Pollock, Thomas Wagnon and one Curry, his brother-in-law J. Wagnon, all fairly respectable citizens of the county, came to Fayetteville, and became engaged in a game of cards. This was reported to some of the citizens, and Willis Wallace, his brother, Riley and two or three others, resolved to put a stop to the game. They went to where the men were playing, and threatened them with arrest. This very naturally enraged them and a quarrel ensued. Wallace and his party were getting the better of the card players, and Wagnon started to run away. He ran across the public square, and passed out on the other side of town. All the party followed, and Willis Wallace attempted to take Curry's horse from the rack on the square to pursue Wagnon. At this Curry pulled a pistol from his saddle-bags, but Wallace was too quick for him, and without waiting for further demonstrations drew his own revolver and shot Curry dead.

As he fired, Pollock, who was close by, threw a stone, striking Wallace upon the head and knocking him down, whereupon Riley Wallace, in a similar manner, struck down Pollock. He remained unconscious for several seconds. Meantime Willis Wallace regained his feet, and going up to Pollock plunged a bowie knife through his body, pinning him to the ground. It was at first thought that he was killed, but Dr. P. J. Pollard, who had witnessed the fight from his window, had him at once removed to the hotel, dressed his wounds, and by his skill in a few weeks restored him to health. Two or three years later Pollock and Riley Wallace met at a saloon in Fayetteville. Both instantly recognized that it was "kill or be killed." Wallace drew first, but his pistol missed fire. Pollock was either too nervous or too drunk to take advantage of this accident, and before he could fire Wallace drew a bowie knife and plunged it into his heart, killing him instantly. He then fled the country, and was never captured.

Willis Wallace gave himself up to the authorities, but was released upon bail. After the Cane Hill murder occurred the public mind became agitated about Wallace's being at large. This feeling was encouraged by A. W. Arrington, until finally a mob gathered in Fayetteville, and placed itself under his leadership for the arrest of Wallace. The latter had in his possession a cannon or two, and some small arms and ammunition, which had been placed under his care by the State, and with a party of his friends he fortified himself in his store-house on the west side of the public square, where the arms were stored. Arrington and his party occupied the court-house. The excitement became intense, and bloodshed seemed inevitable. Families within range of the guns took refuge in cellars, and all waited in breathless anxiety for the battle to begin. It did not take place, however. The party in the court-house did not venture an attack, and finally dispersed. At the next term of the circuit court Wallace was tried upon an indictment for manslaughter, and was acquitted. He soon after moved to Texas.

In 1846 one of those brutal murders, of which there had been so many, was committed on the Cherokee line. This time the victim was George Harnage, and the motive as usual was robbery. John Work, a desperado living in the west part of the county, was suspected, and anticipating capture he disappeared. The grand jury found an indictment against him, and a warrant was placed in the hands of the sheriff for his arrest, but he could not be found. Some time after Sheriff Elijah O'Brien and a posse were hastily summoned by Jacob Funkhouser, of Cane Hill, to his residence. There it was learned that Work was in hiding in the vicinity, and could be captured. It appeared that before the murder of Harnage, Work had become intimate with a black man belonging to Funkhouser, and had planned to go with him to the free States or to Canada. This made the slave his fast friend, and after the murder he sought the negro, and induced him to supply him with food. He told the negro that he wished to kill his master, Jacob Funkhouser, against whom he had a grudge, and would then flee the country with him. The negro supplied him with food, answered the questions concerning the movements of his master, and did his bidding for some time. But Work could find no opportunity to accomplish the murder, and chafing under his involuntary seclusion became as ferocious as a caged tiger. He became more outrageous in his demands upon his slave friend, and finally began to use threats against him. This frightened the negro, who in reality did not wish to see his master murdered, and at last he decided to make a clean breast of it and make known the hiding place of Work. He related the whole matter to his master, who quietly summoned the sheriff, and instructed the negro to keep up his relations with the murderer as though nothing had occurred. It was decided that the negro should inform Work that the time for him to act had come, that at a certain hour that evening he would find Funkhouser in his field, and that he, the negro, would have a horse ready for him to make his escape. The sheriff and his posse then stationed themselves near the spot where Work and the negro had been in the habit of meeting, and the remainder of the program was carried out as arranged. The negro met the murderer and gave him his instructions, and as the latter started for the spot where he was to meet his victim the officers fired upon him, mortally wounding him. He instantly recognized that he had been betrayed, and drawing a bowie-knife sprang at the negro, but fell dead when just beyond reach of him.

Work was about thirty-five years of age, and a Hercules in size and courage. Ordinarily he was social and pleasant, but belonged to that class denominated " dangerous." Of the posse who accompanied Sheriff O'Brien two are still living. They are Thomas Ballard and W. B. Taylor.

In 1845 occurred the first legal executions in Washington County. In the autumn of that year Crawford Burnett, his wife Lavinia, and his son John, were hung for the murder of Jonathan Selby. Selby was a bachelor living some few miles from Fayetteville, and was murdered for the money he was supposed to keep in his house. Much excitement was aroused, and suspicion fell upon the Burnetts. They were taken into custody, and a daughter, a young girl about fifteen years of age, confessed that her parents had planned the murder, and that her brother, John, had executed it. Before the arrests the latter had gone to Missouri, and only Burnett and his wife were taken into custody. They were tried at a special term in October, 1845. A. B. Greenwood was prosecuting attorney, and the judge assigned Isaac Strain and James P. Neal to defend the prisoners. Isaac Murphy also volunteered his services for the defense. The defendants were tried separately, and a verdict of guilty returned in each case. The trials were short, the principal witness being the daughter that had confessed to the guilt of the parents. They were sentenced to be hung on November 8, 1845, less than thirty days after the trial. At the appointed time a gallows was erected on the hill south of town, not far from the National Cemetery, and there in the presence of almost the entire county Crawford and Lavinia Burnett were landed into eternity. Soon after their execution John Burnett was arrested, and returned to the county. He was indicted, and after a brief trial found guilty, and on December 4, 1845, was sentenced to be hung on the 26th of the same month. His attorneys were Isaac Murphy and A. M. Wilson. They believed their client innocent of the crime, and did all in their power to save him, but, in the face of the two prior convictions and the testimony of the sister, that was but little; he was hanged on the day named, on the same scaffold where his parents had met their deaths less than two months before.

In 1856 Dr. James Boone, an old and prominent citizen living about five miles from Fayetteville, was brutally murdered by three slaves, two of whom belonged to him, and one was the property of a neighbor. The negroes conspired to kill him, and going to his house at night they created sufficient disturbance to bring him to his door, when they felled him to the ground with a blow from a bludgeon, and continued to beat him until he was dead. When accused they confessed to the crime, and a band of men, led by the sons of Dr. Boone, took the two negroes that had belonged to him from jail and hung them. The third one was tried at the next term of the circuit court, and was also hung.

In 1860 an old man named Mullis, living in Mountain Township, was murdered in his house at night by a negro man belonging to him. Mullis, a man beyond middle life, had come from Indiana a few years before, bringing with him a young woman whom he called his wife. It was rumored, however, that he had been a well-to-do farmer in Indiana, and that he had left a wife and several children, and eloped with a servant girl. After coming to Arkansas Mullis purchased a negro man, and between his so-called wife and this negro there grew up a criminal intimacy. It was this that led to the murder. After his arrest the negro confessed to the killing, but plead self-defense. He was lodged in the jail at Fayetteville, but was not allowed to remain there long. A mob, raised in the neighborhood where the crime was committed, came to Fayetteville, and hung him. The woman, his guilty partner, was in the town at the time, and it was only through the intervention of citizens that she was saved from the same fate.

During the war, and immediately after, numerous homicides were committed in Washington County, but these were incident to the demoralized state of society. Under normal conditions there is no more peaceable and quiet community.

In 1868 a deadly feud arose between the Shannons and Fishers and their friends, in which several persons on each side lost their lives. All the parties at the time lived at or near Evansville and were considered desperate characters. The trouble grew out of a gambling transaction. Maj. Fisher won a horse from M. K. Shannon, but the latter's father claimed $30 of the value of the horse, and Fisher paid it. About a week later he met M. K. Shannon in a saloon in Evansville, and asked him to make good the amount he had paid his father. While they were parleying F. M. Shannon, a brother of M. K. Shannon, entered the saloon and shot Fisher through the head, killing him instantly. Shannon was tried before a justice of the peace, and released. Soon after

John Fisher, a brother of the murdered man, and Calvin Carter' returned from southern Arkansas, where they had been attending races, and had Shannon re-arrested, taken to Fayetteville, and again tried, with the same result as before. They returned to Evansville, resolved to kill Shannon, but he remained away. Dr. J. C. McKinney, the father-in-law of Shannon, took an active part in his defense, and attempted to raise a mob to drive Fisher and Carter from the country. One morning in February, 1869, he entered G. W. McClure's store to make some purchases, and was followed by John Fisher, who without many words shot him through the heart. He then went to Mrs. Alberty's, where he re-enforced himself with Calvin Carter and Charles Bush. All mounted horses, and armed with guns and pistols passed several times up and down the streets of Evansville. Some half hour later they rode out of town into the Nation. In a short time F. M. Shannon, with John Finley, W. M. Finley, J. W. Bell, M. K. Shannon and John Brotherton, arrived in Evansville and started in pursuit. After going some eight or ten miles the party separated, and taking a circuitous route returned to Evansville. Bell, Brotherton, W. M. Finley and M. K. Shannon arrived first, and dismounted at the store where McKinney had been killed. Fisher and his party, who in the meantime had returned and were at Gillett's grocery, fired upon them, wounding Sam Alberty, an old citizen, in the hip, and breaking the leg of a horse.

F. M. Shannon and John Finley arrived at this juncture, and a large number of shots were fired by both parties, but no serious damage was done. Matters then quieted down for several weeks, but each party watched the other, hoping to take them at a disadvantage. Meantime the Fisher party was re-enforced by Scott Reed, and one who was thought to have been Frank James. Not long after this party gave a dance in Evansville, and the Shannons, together with the sheriff, Benjamin Little, and a posse, in all about thirty men, attempted to capture John Fisher, for whom Gov. Clayton had offered a reward. They made the attack, and killed Scott Reed at the first fire, but Fisher rallied his men, and drove the Shannons into an old stable near by. He then took refuge in the house where his sisters lived. The two parties maintained their respective positions, firing occasional shots back and forth all day. When night came on Fisher and his men escaped into the Territory, and the sheriff took Fisher's horses and left. The sheriff then took a posse, and went to Texas in search of the outlaws, and upon his return reported that Fisher had been killed. Fisher's sisters brought suit for the horses taken by the sheriff, and gained the suit, but it is said, that the Shannons, as soon as the judgment was rendered, went to the stable and shot one of the horses, a fine race mare. Soon after this occurrence the Fisher sisters removed into the Cherokee Nation, where they joined their brother and his party. On June 2, 1869, John Fisher, Cal Carter, Charles Bush, James Reed and John Coleman entered Evansville, and waylaid and killed two of the Shannon faction, Noah Fitzwaters and Newton C. Stout. They then returned to the Nation, and the Governor offered a reward for their arrest. Capt. Anderson, of Crawford County, with a posse, went in pursuit, and succeeded in killing two of the party, Edmondson and Coleman, in Benton County. By this time the law-abiding citizens had become weary at these continued outrages, and A. G. Lewis, William Littlejohn, Capt. Adair and several others organized themselves into a company, and forced both parties to leave the country.

Two or three years after the above occurrences two young men from Kansas passed through Evansville, with a drove of some twenty-five horses, on their way South. They had been gone but a short time when a printed circular was received at the Evansville post-office, offering half of the horses to any one arresting the men, who, it was stated, had stolen them. John and Jack Richmond, Lafayette Shultz and Bud Morris, residents of the vicinity of Evansville, started in pursuit. A. G. Lewis, deputy sheriff of Washington County, wished to accompany them, but they refused him. They overtook the horsemen below Van Buren, and started back with them, but when they reached Lee's Creek Mountain they took them into a ravine near the road, shot them, and went on to Evansville with the horses. A man by the name of Dodge came from Ellsworth, Kas., rewarded the captors with half of the horses, and returned. Subsequent investigation showed that the circular referred to was the only one sent out, and that the Richmonds called for it as soon as it reached the office. John Richmond was arrested by Deputy Sheriff Lewis, and was tried. The jury failed to agree, and pending another trial he made his escape. The others of his party had fled, as soon as suspicion fell upon them, but about seven years later Bud Morris was arrested and brought back, and while out on bond again made his escape.

The demoralizing effects of the war were slow in dying out. In Washington County, before the war, there lived three brothers, all natives of the county, John, George and James Reed, sons of Richard A. Reed, who was himself born in the county. All were known as industrious young men, and were well respected. John entered the Federal army, and at the close of hostilities returned home, and engaged in farming on White River. He was a resolute but quiet man when sober, but quarrelsome and disposed to play the bully when intoxicated, and his character had not been improved by his war experience. He was a Republican in politics, and while this had nothing to do with his death, it doubtless involved him in difficulties which would not otherwise have arisen. He had more than once defied the authorities of Fayetteville, and had come to be looked upon by them as a "bad man." In February, 1879, Deputy Sheriff John R. Serrell arrested John Rutherford, a friend of the Reeds, for an assault, and, as he failed to furnish the required bond, was proceeding to put him in jail, when John Reed arrived and demanded his release. For some reason he refused to bail his friend, and when the jailer, J. B. Moore, opened the cell door to put the prisoner in, Reed struck him on the head with a bottle filled with brandy, felling him to the floor. Two shots were instantly fired, and Reed fell mortally wounded. Deputy Sheriff Serrell was arrested, charged with the homicide, but upon trial was discharged. George Reed swore revenge, but it was generally believed that he did not have sufficient courage to put his threats into execution. He was apparently afraid of Marshal Stirman, and once begged him not to shoot him if he ever had any trouble with him. The officer would not promise, and soon after the conversation Reed, while mounted, drew a revolver on the marshal, who quickly sprang under the horse's neck and pulled Reed to the ground, punishing him quite severely. Not long after Stirman resigned, and William Patton was appointed to succeed him. George Reed at once told his friends that he was going into town to try the new marshal. This intention he carried into effect. He entered the town and, having got into a quarrel with the officer, was attempting to draw his revolver, when the marshal shot him from his horse, killing him instantly. This occurred on June 4, 1881. Patton was tried and honorably acquitted, but the friends of Reed were not satisfied, and swore to avenge his death, and from that time Patton lived in constant fear of assassination. He took every precaution to save his life, but fate was against him. About 9 o'clock on Saturday night, July 2, 1881, while Patton and Deputy Sheriff and Night Watchman John Mount were conversing on the public square, they were fired upon by unknown parties, and both instantly killed. Patton was shot three times and Mount twice. No clue was ever obtained to the assassins, but they were, without doubt, the friends of Reed.

THE BAR.

The bar of Fayetteville has always been one of eminent ability, and has numbered among its members some of the most brilliant legal lights in the State. One of the first lawyers to locate here was Judge David Walker, who came to Arkansas in 1830, and, after standing an examination by Judges Cross and Johnson, was admitted to the bar, and located in Fayetteville. He was born in what is now Todd County, Ky., in 1806, and had but meager opportunities for securing an education. He, however, had an indomitable will, that enabled him to rise above adverse circumstances, and he soon became a leader in the profession which he chose. In September, 1833, he was elected prosecuting attorney, and at the expiration of his term was re-elected. He was chosen a member of the convention which framed the first State constitution, and took an important part in the deliberations of that body. In 1836 he was a presidential elector for Hugh L. White, and in 1840 was elected to the State Senate. He was a strong supporter of the Whig party, and in 1844 made a canvass for Congress against Archibald Yell, who was doubtless the only man that could have defeated him. In 1848 he was elected by a Democratic Legislature to a seat in the Supreme Court, where he served until 1855, when he resigned. In the campaign of 1860 he supported the Bell and Everett ticket, and in 1861 was elected to the Constitutional Convention, of which body he was chosen president. During the war he served in the military court of Price's army, and in 1866 was elected chief justice of the Supreme Court. He continued in that position until ousted by the reconstruction acts. In 1874 he was again elected to the Supreme Court, from which he resigned in 1878. He died in 1879. He was a man of uncompromising integrity, indomitable energy and strong native ability, and he has had few equals in Arkansas, either as an advocate or as a jurist.

Soon after Judge Walker's arrival in Fayetteville, Archibald Yell located in the suburbs of the town on a place now owned by Col. T. J. Hunt, which he called "Waxhaws." Gov. Yell was born in North Carolina in 1797 of poor parentage, and received a limited education in his youth. In 1812 he volunteered in a Tennessee regiment, having previously removed to that State, and by his gallant service attracted the attention of Gen. Jackson, by whom he was attached to the company that constituted his life-guards. When the war was over Yell returned to Middle Tennessee, and after studying law engaged in the practice of his profession at Fayetteville, in Lincoln County. About 1833 Gen. Jackson, then President, appointed him a judge in the Territory of Arkansas. Upon the admission of Arkansas into the Union, he wished to be the first Governor, but it was discovered that he was ineligible, and he was elected to Congress. He was re-elected in 1838, and in 1840 was elected Governor. He continued in that office until 1844, when, at the request of the Democratic party, he resigned and entered upon a canvass for Congress. He was elected, and in 1846 was re-elected, but soon after resigned his seat, returned to Arkansas, organized a regiment for service in the Mexican War, and was killed at the battle of Buena Vista. His remains were returned to Arkansas, and buried with Masonic and military honors at Fayetteville. In 1872 his remains were removed by Washington Lodge from their first resting place, and deposited in Evergreen Cemetery.

While Gov. Yell was not the equal, perhaps, of some other

Arkansans in either native intellect or education, he possessed, in a remarkable degree, that indefinable quality called personal magnetism, and as a politician, in the best sense of that term, he was without a peer.

Among the other early attorneys in Fayetteville were Stephen G. Sneed, W. McK. Ball, W. S. Oldham, L. D. Evans, R. T. Wheeler, Isaac Murphy, Jonas M. Tibbetts, A. W. Arrington, John B. Costa, Mathew Leeper, W. D. Reagan and A. M. Wilson. Stephen G. Sneed came to Arkansas from Missouri sometime about 1830, and subsequently removed to Austin, Tex., where he died in 1883. In 1831 he was elected prosecuting attorney of his circuit, and was a candidate for re-election, but was defeated. In 1844 he was elected judge of the Fourth Judicial Circuit, and remained upon the bench for four years. He was not highly educated, and had but a limited acquaintance with the text books of his profession, yet he was a very successful advocate, and a powerful adversary before a jury. He was a man of fine physique, was thoroughly versed in human nature, and during his residence here was one of the most conspicuous figures before the bar in Northwest Arkansas.

Williamson S. Oldham was a native of Tennessee, who came to Arkansas in 1835. He had previously been admitted to the bar, and in 1837 was made attorney for the Fayetteville Branch of the State Bank. In 1838 he was elected to the Legislature, and six years later was again elected. In 1845 he was elected to a seat on the bench of the Supreme Court, but the duties of that office were distasteful to him, and he soon resigned. In 1846 he was a candidate for Congress, but was defeated by Robert W. Johnson, and soon after removed to Texas, which State he represented in the Confederate States Senate.

William McK. Ball was one of the most popular lawyer politicians of Washington County during the "thirties." It was a popular saying at that time, referring to politics, "As goes McK. Ball, so goes Washington County, and as goes Washington County, so goes Arkansas." His influence secured for him the position of cashier of the Branch Bank at Fayetteville, and the failure of that institution cost him his prestige. He was accused of having appropriated some of the funds to his own use. He soon after removed to Texas.

L. D. Evans came to Arkansas from Tennessee, and, after several years residence in Fayetteville, removed to Texas, where he became a judge of the supreme court. He was not a good speaker, but was a close student, and was a fairly successful lawyer. Physically he was a large, fine looking man, and possessed a strong intellect.

R. T. Wheeler came to Fayetteville from Kentucky, but did not remain long. He married a sister of Judge David Walker, and removed to Texas, where he was elected a judge of the supreme court. He was a highly educated and polished gentleman, and a lawyer of fine ability.

Jonas M. Tibbetts was a native of New Hampshire. He came to Fayetteville in the "thirties," and remained until the beginning of the Civil War, when he returned to the North. In 1844 he was elected prosecuting attorney, and in 1850 became a member of the Legislature. Subsequently, as attorney for the State Bank, he accumulated a goodly fortune.

Mathew Leeper came to Fayetteville from Tennessee, under an appointment by President Jackson, as receiver of the land office, and was never actively engaged in the practice of his profession. He was an ardent Democrat and a man of some influence in political circles. Soon after his arrival in Fayetteville he was challenged to a duel by Judge Jesse Turner, who considered himself insulted by some remarks of Leeper. The latter accepted the challenge, and chose Judge S. G. Sneed as his second, while B. H. Martin acted as second for Turner. The parties met at some point across the line in the Cherokee Nation, but when all was in readiness for the principals to take their position, Mr. Leeper made an apology and the duel was declared off, much to the disgust of the many Indians that had gathered to witness the affair. Mr. Leeper subsequently removed to Texas, where he is still living.

Judge J. M. Hoge was born in Tennessee in 1806. In early youth he attracted the attention of Felix Grundy, and became a sort of protege of that distinguished gentleman. After graduating in the Nashville University, he studied law with Judge Grundy, and in 1827 was admitted to the bar. Soon after he came to Washington County, and for the first two years lived in a cabin on the farm of Rev. Andrew Buchanan, where he engaged in teaching school. He then removed to Fayetteville, and opened a law office. In 1836 he was elected a judge of the Fourth Judicial Circuit, and in 1840 was re-elected. Near the close of his second term he removed to Bentonville, and just before the opening of the Civil War he went to California, where he acted as, correspondent for various newspapers. He died in Colorado in 1874. He was an able jurist, and wielded a facile pen, but he was not a ready debater.

Isaac Murphy was a Tennesseean who came to Fayetteville about 1840, and subsequently removed to Huntsville, in Madison County. In 1856 he was elected to represent Madison and Benton Counties in the State Senate, and in 1861 was chosen a member of the constitutional convention, which passed the ordinance of secession. He was a Union man and voted against the ordinance and when the Federal Army secured control of the State in 1864, he was made governor, serving in that capacity for four years. He was a quiet, unobtrusive man, somewhat visionary in his ideas, but always throughly honest.

Alfred W. Arrington was one of the most unique characters ever at the bar in Northwestern Arkansas. He came to the State some time in the "thirties" from Missouri, and for a time was a school teacher and Methodist circuit rider. He finally turned his attention to the law, and soon became noted for the brilliancy of his imagination and the success which attended his practice in the courts. He was of a poetic temperament and possessed much dramatic power, and as a reporter of remarkable trials he became even more celebrated. Among his most famous reports is the imaginative account of a trial in Conway County, in which Rev. John Taylor and an Indian maiden were the chief characters. In a collection of similar sketches, which were published in a pamphlet entitled "The Regulators of the South and Southwest," he gave an account of the hanging of the supposed murderers of the Wright family at Cane Hill, which gave great offense to those engaged in the affair, and their friends. In 1842 he was elected to the Legislature on the Whig ticket, and soon after the expiration of his term he went to Texas; subsequently he removed to Chicago, where, after attaining a high reputation as a lawyer and orator, he died early in the "seventies." He was very erratic in his manner of living, and lacked mental balance. He frequently indulged in fits of dissipation, and did many things to destroy the confidence of the public in him.

John B. Costa was an Italian by birth. He studied law under Judge Sneed, and became his son-in-law. He went to Texas with him, and died there a few years later.

Of those pioneer lawyers of Washington County, but two, W. D. Reagan and A. M. Wilson, are now living. The former has now retired from practice, but both for nearly half a century have been among the most able and honored members of the Fayetteville bar. Mr. Wilson came to the county in 1837, and almost before he considered himself a lawyer he was appointed prosecuting attorney of the Fourth Judicial Circuit, then embracing ten counties. He served in that capacity for four years, and subsequently he was appointed attorney to wind up the business of the Branch State Bank of Fayetteville. In 1848 he was elected to the Legislature, and in 1852 was appointed by President Pierce United States District Attorney for the western district of Arkansas. He was re-appointed in 1856, and completed a second term. He espoused the cause of the Southern Confederacy, after the efforts to secure a peaceable settlement of the difficulties had failed, and during the war his property was nearly all swept away. He has since held no official position except that of State Senator, but he has exercised a very considerable influence in the Democratic party of Arkansas, and was an important factor in delivering the State from the rule of the "carpet-baggers."

Wilbur D. Reagan came from Tennessee in 1830, and located in what is now Carroll County. He followed school teaching for two or three years, and then began the study of law under Judge S. G. Sneed. In 1835 he was admitted to the bar, and the next year was elected to the Legislature. In 1838 he removed to Fayetteville, and with the exception of some eight or ten years in Texas, has been a resident of that town. As a practitioner he was industrious and energetic, and highly successful. He was excessively aggressive, and was wont to rely for success upon sarcasm and invective, and his ability to browbeat witnesses and overawe juries, rather than upon a knowledge of the law and a skillful presentation of his case.

Among the lawyers that began practice at Fayetteville, at a little later date than those mentioned above, were Gen. H. F. Thomason, Col. James P. Neal, P. V. Van Hoose, Hiram Davis, Senator J. D. Walker, Lafayette Gregg and J. R. Pettigrew. Out of this number only two, Senator Walker and Judge Gregg, are now members of the Fayetteville bar.

Gen. Thomason came to Washington County with his father in 1829, and in 1846 began the study of law with W. D. Reagan. He was admitted to the bar in 1847, and in 1851 was elected prosecuting attorney, which office he filled for two terms. In 1856 he was a candidate for Congress upon the Know-nothing ticket, and in 1860 was a presidential elector on the Bell and Everett ticket. In 1857 he removed to Van Buren, and has since been identified with the interests of Crawford County.

James P. Neal also came to Washington County in 1829. He was a stepson of Andrew Buchanan, and remained with him until 1840, when he removed to Fayetteville, and entered the clerk's office. A year or two later he entered the office of W. D. Reagan, and began to prepare himself for the practice of law. In 1844 he was admitted to the bar, and remained at Fayetteville until 1854, with the exception of one year spent in fighting the Mexicans. In 1854 he removed to Texas, where he was engaged in the practice of his profession until about 1870. He has since resided upon the farm settled by his stepfather, where he founded the pleasant village of Prairie Grove.

J. R. Pettigrew was a native Arkansan, having been born in Hempstead County in 1829. He was educated at Ozark Institute and Arkansas College, and about 1850 entered upon the study of law with Maj. Reagan. Two years later he was admitted to the bar and soon after formed a partnership with his preceptor, whose son-in-law he became. During the war he served in the Confederate Army, and in 1866 he was elected to the Legislature. In 1879 he was elected journal clerk of the United States Senate, and in 1882 President Arthur appointed him the Democratic member of the Utah commission, which position he held at his death in 1886. Col. Pettigrew possessed a good degree of natural ability, and in manner was modest and retiring, but pleasant and companionable. His connection with journalism is mentioned elsewhere.

Hiram Davis was a native of Missouri. He came to Washington County in 1832 or 1833, and shortly afterward married and removed to Carroll County. Upon the election of B. H. Pierson to the office of clerk of Washington County, he returned and assisted him in the office. At the end of the term he became a law student under Judge David Walker, and subsequently was a partner with him. He was a thorough lawyer and a good counselor, but was not a fluent speaker. In 1874 he was elected county judge, and filled the office from that time until his death in 1879.

P. P. Van Hoose, a brother of Mayor J. H. Van Hoose, was educated at Ozark Institute, in which he subsequently became a professor. He was a thorough scholar, and lawyer of high ability, but was cut off by death in the prime of life.

The present bar of Fayetteville is composed of the following members: A. M. Wilson, J. D. Walker, Lafayette Gregg, T. M. Hunter, B. R. Davidson, J. W. Walker, J. V. Walker, C. W. Walker, William L. Gregg, R. J. Wilson, C. R. Buckner, S. H. West, I. M. Partridge, S. E. Marrs, E. B. Wall, George W. M. Reed, Jr., J. W. L. Stuckey, D. M. West and R. W. Carter.

The present bar of Fayetteville is composed of the following members: A. M. Wilson, Lafayette Gregg, J. D. Walker, T. M. Gunter, B. R. Davidson, J. W. Walker, E. B. Wall, G. W. M. Reed, Jr., C. W. Walker, J. V. Walker, William L. Gregg, R. J. Wilson, J. W. L. Stuckey, S. H. West, C. R. Buckner, S. H. West, D. M. West, S. E. Marrs, I. M. Partridge and R. W. Carter.

WAR RECORD.

One company of mounted volunteers was raised in Washington County for service in the Mexican War. It consisted of 110 men, and was organized in the spring of 1846, with Stephen B. Enyart as captain, James P. Neal, first lieutenant; Mack O'Brien, second lieutenant; J. F. Rieff, ensign, and Mark Cline, orderly sergeant. The company marched to Washington, Hempstead County, but were too late to be received. They returned to their homes, and held themselves in readiness for the next call for troops. This came about the 1st of March, 1847, and the company marched to Fort Smith, the mustering place, near the middle of that month. About the 1st of April they left for Mexico by the way of San Antonio. They marched to Monterey, and were employed in the country between that city and the Rio Grande, in guarding wagon trains and doing scout duty, until the close of the war. They participated in several skirmishes, but took part in no pitched battle. The company was never assigned to any regiment. It was mustered out at Carmorigo in June, 1848, and returned home by way of New Orleans.

The position of Washington County on all the questions which led up to the Civil War was similar to that of the State as a whole. She was reliably Democratic, and at the presidential election of 1860 gave Breckenridge a majority of 149 votes; her interests and sympathies were all with the South, but there was a decided feeling against disunion until the war had actually begun.

On January 24, 1861, the Legislature passed a bill providing for an election to vote upon the calling of the State Convention, and also to select delegates to the convention, provided it were called. A call was at once issued for a mass meeting, to be held at Fayetteville on February 2, and at the appointed time some 400 or 500 persons assembled. B. F. Boone was called to the chair, and the convention was addressed by R. W. Mecklin. Dr. T. J. Pollard then read a series of resolutions, that had been adopted by a convention at Boonsboro on January 26, 1861. The principal clause was as follows: "*Resolved*, That it is the sense of this meeting that if the efforts of the border States, to wit: Virginia, Maryland, Delaware, North Carolina, Tennessee, Kentucky and Missouri, shall fail to adjust the present political troubles of our country, that the interests of Arkansas being common with theirs, she shall take such action as those of the older and more powerful slave States shall indicate for themselves." The resolutions also declared in favor of J. B. Russell, David Walker, C. W. Dean and James H. Stirman for delegates to the convention. After the reading of these resolutions Dr. G. W.

Taylor moved that a committee of fifteen be appointed to draft a report expressive of the sense of the meeting, whereupon Stephen Bedford took the floor, and charged that the chairman had been selected a week before, that the resolutions to be reported by the committee were already prepared, and that the secretaries [J. H. Van Hoose and M. C. Duke] were secessionists. These charges threw the meeting into the greatest confusion, and it adjourned *sine die*. No further attempt was made to formally nominate delegates. The election took place on February 18, and the *Arkansian* announced the result in the following: "The election on Monday passed off, under all circumstances, as quietly as our elections generally do, without bloodshed or angry feeling, and the Union is doing as well as could be expected. The following is the result: Convention, 569; no convention, 1,541; for delegates, J. H. Stirman, 1,924; T. H. Gunter, 1,780; David Walker, 1,777; J. P. A. Parks, 1,713; C. W. Dean, 410; John Billingsley, 364; W. T. Neal, 353; scattering, 42.

"From Benton, Madison, Crawford and Sebastian Counties we learn that the Southern Rights men have been defeated by as heavy majorities, in proportion to the number of votes polled, as in the county."

On the 5th of March a meeting was held in the court-house "to take the sense of the people on the inauguration of A. Lincoln." Judge B. J. H. Gaines was called to the chair. He explained the object of the meeting, and stated that although he had before been a Union man, he was now for secession. The inaugural address was taken up, and read by M. C. Duke, and a committee of five was appointed to report resolutions upon it. C. W. Deane, J. P. Doss, James D. Walker, Robert Buchanan and John Crawford were appointed the committee, but Mr. Walker declined to serve, and Dr. S. R. Bell was substituted. The committee reported the following resolution, which was unanimously adopted:

WHEREAS, The inaugural address of Mr. Lincoln clearly indicates his intention to retake the forts and arsenals of the seceded States, and, also, to collect the revenue in said States, and,

WHEREAS, Virginia, Kentucky and other border States have declared that such an attempt WOULD BE COERCION. Therefore, be it

Resolved, That in our opinion, the inhabitants of Arkansas being inseparably connected with the Southern States, she should immediately take such steps as would guarantee her safety.

This expression of opinion was, of course, taken to influence the convention which had met at Little Rock the day before, but the great mass of the people were even yet loth to give up the Union, and it was not until after the fall of Fort Sumter, and the call for troops by President Lincoln, that the convention decided to pass the ordinance of secession.

The events that led to that ordinance are, briefly, as follows: The convention deliberated from March 4 until the 21st, when it adjourned to meet at the call of Hon. David Walker, its presiding officer. In the meantime union and non-union addresses were issued to the people of the State; one, entitled " Union Address to the People of Arkansas," was signed by the union members of the convention, among the first of whom were David Walker, J. H. Stirman, J. A. P. Parks, and T. M. Gunter, of Washington County. The object of this address was explanation of their action and the urgency of a popular election to vote on the question: " Shall Arkansas co-operate with the border, or unseceded slave States, in efforts to secure a permanent and satisfactory adjustment of sectional controversies disturbing the country, or immediately secede?" Says an extract from the address: " Thus, it will be seen, that while Arkansas is not committed to the doctrine of secession, she condemns coercion by the Federal Government, and recommends the removal of causes that might lead to a collision; and the adoption of constitutional means to restore peace and fraternal relations between the sections, and happiness and prosperity to our once united, but now distracted, country." The remainder of the address was an appeal for union.

Before the May meeting of the convention its chairman, the Hon. David Walker, issued the following address:

To the People of Washington County:

Under existing circumstances, I feel it to be my duty to take your advice upon some important questions which will, in all probability, arise for the consideration and action of the convention, now shortly to be convened. Your delegates were elected under a pledge to co-operate with the border slave States in an effort to settle our difficulties with the Northern States upon honorable and just terms, and under no circumstance to vote for an ordinance of secession, unless the same was referred back to you for your rejection or approval. The majority received by myself and colleague was very large, so great as to leave no doubt but that you heartily approved our position. You will see by reference to the journals of the convention that our grievances were defined, our rights asserted by way of instruction to commissioners to be elected to co-operate with the border slave States in an adjustment of the questions at issue between the North and South. Commissioners were elected to meet at Frankfort, Ky., on the 27th of May, and after full consideration it was left to a majority of the voters of the State to say whether they would co-operate with the border States in such a settlement or would secede.

Thus matters stood, and the friends of the Union and co-operation, and of secession, had taken the field upon this issue, when news reached us that the United States troops had not been withdrawn from Fort Sumter, and that in anticipation that supplies, if not also reinforcements, were to be sent, a fight ensued, which resulted in the destruction and evacuation of the fort, since which time has followed a proclamation of the President, calling for troops to retake the forts in the seceded States, and enforce the laws. Amongst other States, Arkansas was called upon to furnish a regiment for that purpose. The reports as to the ground upon which the fight was commenced are contradictory, as well as to the extent of the preparation for a general war, between the slave and free States, but enough is known to leave but little doubt that there is imminent danger of a protracted and deadly civil war. Against the coercion policy of the Government this, as well as the other border slave States, protested, and by a resolution of our convention we declared that we would resist coercion if attempted. In view of these facts, and after seeking information as well from the border States as to their action, as from citizens of this State, I felt it to be my duty, in obedience to an order for that purpose, to call the convention together, to meet on the 6th of May. The question presented for your consideration is, under existing circumstances, what will you have your delegates do? Shall they adhere to the position taken by them before the election, and which you so unanimously endorsed, or will you expect of them to vote for an unconditional ordinance of secession, which is not to be referred back to you for approval? Do you wish to remain in connection with a government that, if not already at war with a large proportion of the slave States, is threatening and preparing to engage in such a war? Or would you prefer to cut loose from the old confederacy, and free yourselves from all further alliance to it? The effect of this act would be, on the one hand, to release you from all obligations to the old government, and, on the other, to deprive you of its protection and aid, such as its military defense on our borders, its Federal courts, land office, mail service, etc. Of this you will consider.

But again, will you secede and maintain an independent position, and await some general settlement and co-operation of all the slave States, or will you secede and unite at once with the Confederate States? Should you prefer the former, that is, to maintain an independent position until a government may be formed by the border States in common with the seceded States, and act in concert with them, you will necessarily incur the expense of supporting your own government and of defending it; but should you, on the other hand, prefer to unite with the Confederate States, and make common cause with them, you will necessarily assume the responsibility of furnishing men and money to aid them in the support and defense of their government.

I am induced to call your attention particularly to this matter, because I find a strong if not a prevailing opinion here that in no event should troops be drawn from this portion of the State; that our exposed condition in event of secession will demand that the troops in this part of the State should be kept here for our own defense. None should be misled or deceived in this matter. If the State unites with the Southern Confederacy she must necessarily come under obligations to furnish troops to fight at any and all points, at home and abroad, wherever required. And the fact is not to be disguised, that as the northern and western counties have the largest white population, a heavy demand must be made on them. There is but little hope, for a time at least, of a reunion of the States under the old Government, and as the border slave States contain, according to the late census, 2,085,858 more inhabitants'than the Confederate States, we can readily see, that should they act together in the establishment of a government, composed of the fifteen slave States, they will have it in their power, in such organization, as far as may be practicable, to protect our rights and promote our interests in common with theirs.

I have thus hastily and imperfectly presented for your consideration the outlines of our present condition, and of the prominent question likely to be considered by the convention. There never was a time when we should act with more prudence than the present, and, as our interests are one, we should, if possible, act as a united people. I desire to know your will, what would you have me do? I hope you will act at once, and can, in conclusion, only pledge myself to obey your instructions, and reflect your will fearlessly and faithfully. I have intentionally omitted a reference to the original cause of our present difficulties, or to those upon whom rests the fearful responsibility of destroying and breaking up our once glorious and happy, but now prostrate and ruined, government. You all know my sentiments. I have endeavored to avert the calamity that is now upon us, with regard to which my mind has undergone no change. But it would be useless and improper to dwell upon the past.

Our duty to ourselves and our country demands all our thoughts and all our energies. Let us look to the present and the future, and do all that we can to save our people from the calamity of civil war and utter ruin. *For weal or woe, my destiny is yours.* Your obedient servant,

(Signed)   DAVID WALKER.

We have seen how the convention at Fayetteville expressed itself on March 5, and now, in answer to the above call, the voters of West Fork Township assembled on April 27 and passed the following resolutions:

Resolved, First. That we are opposed to any ordinance of secession.

Second. That we utterly oppose any action in the State convention that will sever the State of Arkansas from the Federal government without a full and fair expression of the loyal voters of the State.

Third. That in case of an ordinance of secession we wish to co-operate with the other border State or States.

Fourth. That we are opposed to any act of the convention that would unite us with the Southern Confederacy as it now exists.

Among the names attached to these resolutions were C. G. Gilbreath, chairman; W. R. Dyer, secretary; J. C. Stockburger, D. E. Robinson, A. W. Reed, John A. Rutherford, Thomas McKnight and W. D. Dye, committee on resolutions.

These two conventions represent the various conflicting instructions.

After the act of the convention at Little Rock, martial activity was rife in every quarter. In Washington County, where sentiments were so divided, there was more or less uncertainty. The governor had ordered proclamations for troops, and those of this section were placed under Gen. Pearce. Then Brig.-Gen. Ben. McCulloch, who was in charge of Confederate troops protecting the Indian Territory and Arkansas, issued his proclamation for troops about the 1st of July, 1861. Under the latter several hundred men recruited at Fayetteville, in charge of Col. McRae. This raw material operated about Springfield and at Oak Hill.

No opportunity, so far, had appeared for Federal recruiting; but the halting action of the county was evidence that there was a large latent element of neutrality or Federal sympathy. Indeed the men of Washington County were in a peculiarly trying position. With a large element of educated men, who felt the conviction that union was the only hope of the land, the strong fraternal feeling with the Southern States whose interests were similar, a stronger hope that their homes might not be laid waste by invasion, and that the secessional rupture might still be healed, all this certainly was an explanation, if not an excuse, for a great mass of uncertain and changeable action.

In all these acts, however, the *right* of secession, if not silently assumed, was at least not denied, so that, without positive conviction on that right, all the motives that would appeal to citizens of Arkansas could not but lead to just such procedure as was adopted. And when once the secessional course was chosen it was natural for the authorities to take all measures for identifying the interests of the State with the Confederate States. The State government was in the hands of ultraists, and it is not strange that their radical measures should not be met by universal enthusiasm in Northwestern Arkansas; for, to quote from Col. A. W. Bishop, "Though bordering on the Cherokee line, it has been the intellectual center of the State, with Fayetteville as the point from which its intelligence radiated. Settled principally by Kentuckians and Tennesseeans, whose early teachings under

Henry Clay and Andrew Jackson gave to their politics life, and to their loyalty vigor, attachment to the Federal Union has, from its settlement, been the prevailing sentiment of this section; a result attributable, in no small degree, to the educational institutions of Fayetteville and vicinity."

The time had come, however, when Washington County was supposed to furnish every able-bodied man to fight for State protection against the Federal Government and for the Confederate cause; and the most severe military measures were adopted to enforce this throughout the county, means which, to those not realizing the necessities of war, seemed hideous and barbarous.

Those with neutral inclinations, or those in whom union convictions were supreme, were compelled to flee the country, hide in caves, use any deception to cover their intentions until a favorable opportunity arose, go armed, or, in some cases, suffer death. This state of affairs continued during 1861, and up to March 29, 1862, at which time the Union "Army of the Southwest" was lying at Cross Timbers, Mo., when refugees from all parts of this section applied to the Federal officers for protection and enlistment. The battle at Pea Ridge, in which McCulloch lost his life, was the signal for the exodus of Union sympathizers to the Federal lines, and it gave them more boldness at home in Washington County. The movement also aroused more severity among the State and Confederate authorities in their hopes to prevent it, until the lot of any in Washington County, except active adherents of the Southern cause, was far from pleasant. Neutral citizens of the county often joined one army or the other as seemed necessary to save their lives; Unionists thus became, in varying numbers, members of regiments from probably every State whose troops came within reach of Washington County— those of Kansas, Missouri, Iowa, Illinois, Indiana, and, probably, others.

To illustrate this movement, the following from the over-caustic, though otherwise excellent, pen of Col. A. W. Bishop is inserted: " Prior to that event (Pea Ridge) the loyal (Union) citizens of Arkansas were cowed and powerless. With difficulty they avoided enlistment in the rebel army, and now that the reins of persecution began to slacken they availed themselves of every opportunity to strike for the Federal lines.   The army of the Southwest moved to Batesville, and Cassville, Barry Co., Mo., became the outpost of the frontier, with Lieut.-Col. C. B. Holland, of 'Phelps' Missouri Volunteers,' as commander of the post, and M. La Rue Harrison, then of the Thirty-sixth Illinois Infantry Volunteers, as quartermaster and commissary of subsistence.   Cassville was also at this time the seat of a general hospital, and in other respects a position important to hold.

" On May 10, 1862, there came to its pickets a band of eleven Arkansans, led by Thomas J. Gilstrap and Furiben Elkins, of Crawford County.   Listening to their story of suffering and wrong, and learning that others still were toiling their way northward, the idea occurred to Harrison of applying for authority to raise a regiment of Loyal Arkansans for the cavalry arm of the service.   *   *   *

" On June 16, 1862, a special order of the War Department was issued authorizing the raising of the regiment, and Col. Harrison, with increasing zeal, now bent his energies to the task. Meantime, other fugitives had crossed the Missouri line.   On May 14 there came into Cassville a band of thirty, led by Thomas Wilhite, of Washington County, men of nerve and activity, whose undesirable life on the Boston Mountains had, nevertheless, fitted them admirably for the wild-wood skirmishing in which they were destined to act a conspicuous part.

" On June 20 there arrived another detachment of the yeomanry of Washington County, 115 strong, under the leadership of Thomas J. Hunt."

The return of the remnants of McCulloch's army, after the death of their leader, and the laying waste of supplies on the retreat, left Washington County open for occupation by the new Federal troops under Col. Harrison, who had soon after organized the First Arkansas Cavalry, and afterward came to Fayetteville to establish a post, which was to be the key of Northwestern Arkansas, as it had been under Gen. McCulloch.   In July, 1862, Maj. Hubbard, of the First Missouri Cavalry, and Maj. Miller, of the Second Wisconsin, appeared at Fayetteville on a raid of capture and recruiting.

Meanwhile, all manner of Confederate guards, squads, companies and battalions, were organizing under the following:

GENERAL ORDERS, NO. 17.

HEADQUARTERS, TRANS-MISSISSIPPI DISTRICT,
LITTLE ROCK, ARK., June 17, 1862.

I. For the more effectual annoyance of the enemy upon our rivers and in our mountains and woods all citizens of this district, who are not subject to conscription, are called upon to organize themselves into independent companies of mounted men or infantry, as they prefer, arming and equipping themselves, and to serve in that part of the district to which they belong.

II. Where as many as ten men come together for this purpose they may organize by electing a captain, one sergeant and one corporal, and will at once commence operations against the enemy without waiting for special instructions. Their duty will be to cut off Federal pickets, scouts, foraging parties and trains, and to kill pilots and others on gunboats and transports, attacking them day and night, and using the greatest rigor in their movements. As soon as the company attains the strength required by law, it will proceed to elect the other officers to which it is entitled. All such organizations will be reported to these headquarters as soon as practicable. They will receive pay and allowances for subsistence and forage, for the time actually in the field, as established by the affidavits of their captains.

III. These companies will be governed in all respects by the same regulations as other troops.

Captains will be held responsible for the good conduct and efficiency of their men, and will report to their headquarters from time to time.

By command of MAJOR-GENERAL HINDMAN.

(Signed.)   R. C. NEWTON, *A. A. General.*

During the summer Gen. Hindman's pickets were near the southern boundary of Washington County, and the territory between that and the Missouri line was harried by parties from both armies, engaged in all that is included in bushwhacking, scouting, recruiting, foraging, burning, and all this not unattended by independent bands of robbers and assassins, who were fighting for no cause but plunder.

So the situation continued in Washington County until December 7, following (1862). Meantime, the gallant and indefatigable Col. W. H. Brooks had become commander of that famous Washington County regiment known as the Thirty-fourth Arkansas Confederate Infantry, and on December 7, 1862, they engaged in the hard-fought battle of Prairie Grove, so graphically described by one of its participants elsewhere in this chapter. The Thirty-fourth Arkansas was to the Confederate cause in Washington County what the First Arkansas Cavalry was to the Unionists of this county, and T. M. Gunter, of the former, and T. J. Hunt, of the latter, both of Fayetteville, were their respective lieutenant-colonels, who were Washington County men.

The retreat of Hindman's army after Prairie Grove left the county in charge of the Federals, with headquarters at Fayette-ville, where, January 8, 1863, Lieut.-Col. A. W. Bishop was made provost marshal and Col. M. La Rue Harrison was post commander. The First Arkansas Cavalry, under the immediate command of Maj. Thomas J. Hunt, bore the brunt of the service in scouring the country to relieve it of the independent bush-whackers, who were the result of Hindman's order, No. 17.

In March, however, the following proclamation offered new developments:

To the People of North and West Arkansas:
In obedience to special orders from Headquarters Trans-Mississippi District, I this day assume command of all the troops, of whatever kind, in Northwest Arkansas. In doing so, I hope to be able in a short time to rid that section of the State of the presence of an insolent and unscrupulous abolition invader. To do this I must have the hearty co-operation and sympathy of the citizens, and the united and determined effort of the soldier. I bring with me to the task the life-time experience of a soldier, coupled with the zeal of a citizen. Arkan-sas is the home of my adoption, and that part of it which I am assigned to com-mand is my favorite locality.

The soldiers of Arkansas have, in the present struggle for independence, distinguished themselves on every battle-field. The record they have made on the bloody plains of Virginia, Missouri, Tennessee and Mississippi have shed a halo of glory around their name, and I know that in defending their homes and families they will maintain the character they have made in other States. I therefore ask every man in Northwest Arkansas, capable of bearing arms, to rally to the defense of their homes and their firesides. Every man knows he owes his country service, should come forward at once, and enroll themselves beneath their country's flag, to protect their rights and their liberties. Come at once! In war, moments are precious.

Those who betake themselves to arms are expected to do their whole duty; those who remain at home should do theirs. The soldiers must be fed and clothed. I hope that a spirit of industry will pervade all classes; that farms will be cultivated with care; that the hum of the busy wheel will be heard in every household, and that the women of Arkansas will emulate the mothers and daughters of the Revolution. We are engaged in a war with a bitter, unscrupulous and mercenary enemy—our success alone can terminate it. The motto of our enemy is: "Subjugation and spoliation;" ours is: "Peace—inde-pendence."

We must conquer it. The enemy must be driven from the soil of Arkan-sas, and beyond the borders of Missouri. The war has now assumed such vast proportions, and is being prosecuted with so much vigor, that it can not, in the nature of things, be of long duration. One united and vigorous effort on the part of the soldiers in Arkansas will expel the invader. He will not return.   (Signed)   W. L. CABELL,
Brigadier-General, Commanding Northwest Arkansas.

Events following the issuance of this proclamation are explained in the succeeding official report of Gen. Cabell's attack on Fayetteville the following month:

HEADQUARTERS POST,
FAYETTEVILLE, ARK., April 19, 1863.

MAJ.-GEN. S. E. CURTIS, *Commanding Department of the Missouri:*

General: The following report of the battle of yesterday, at Fayetteville, is respectfully submitted, in addition to the telegraphic dispatches of last evening. On Friday, 17th inst., a scout under command of Lieut. Robb, First Arkansas Cavalry, returned from the direction of Ozark, and reported no apparent preparations of the enemy to move in this direction. Having no fresh horses I ordered Lieut. Robb to take his command to quarters, expecting to be able to send a small scout again on the next day. On Saturday morning, 18th inst., at a few minutes after sunrise, the enemy, having made a forced march from the Boston Mountains during the night, surprised and captured our dismounted picket, on Frog Bayou road, and approached the town with wild and deafening shouts. Their cavalry charged up a ravine on the east of the city, and attacked my headquarters (Col. Tibbett's place). The firing of the picket had alarmed the command, and by the time the enemy had reached town the First Arkansas Infantry had formed on their parade ground under command of Lieut.-Col. E. J. Searle, assisted by Maj. E. D. Ham, and slowly retired by my orders toward the cavalry, then formed, dismounted at their camp. Fearing that, not being uniformed, they might be mistaken for the enemy, and be fired upon by the cavalry, I ordered Lieut.-Col. Searle to post seven companies as a reserve, in a sheltered position in our rear, two of which were afterward ordered to support the left wing. The remaining three companies of the First Infantry, together with four companies of the First Cavalry, formed the center of our line, under my own immediate command. The right wing was composed of the Third Battalion, First Cavalry, under command of Maj. Ezra Fitch; and the left wing, Second Battalion (First Arkansas Cavalry), was commanded by Lieut.-Col. A. W. Bishop, assisted by Maj. T. J. Hunt. Headquarters was made the "bone of contention," and was repeatedly charged by the rebels, who were gallantly repulsed by our men. In less than thirty minutes after the first attack the enemy planted two pieces of artillery, one a twelve-pounder and one a six-pounder, upon the hillside east of town, near Col. Gunter's place, and opened a sharp fire of canister and shell upon the camp of the First Arkansas Cavalry, doing some damage to tents and horses, but killing no men. At 8 A. M. our center had advanced and occupied the house, yard, out-buildings and hedges of my headquarters; the right wing had advanced to the arsenal, and the left occupied the open field northeast of town, while the enemy had possession of the whole hillside east, the Davis place, opposite to, and the grove south of headquarters. This grove was formerly occupied by the buildings of Arkansas College. At about 9 A. M., or a little before, Col. Monroe led a gallant and desperate cavalry charge upon our right wing, which was met by a galling crossfire from our right and center, piling rebel men and horses in heaps in front of our ordnance office, and causing the enemy to retreat in disorder to the woods. During this charge Capts. Parker and Smith, of the First Infantry, while bravely cheering their men, were both wounded in the head, though not dangerously. At about the same time, by my order, two companies of the First

Cavalry, led by the gallant Lieut. Robb, advanced within rifle range of the enemy's artillery, and, guided by the blaze of its discharges, fired several volleys into the midst of the artillerists, which effectually silenced their battery and caused its precipitate withdrawal from the field. The enemy's center, occupying the Davis place, made a desperate resistance for nearly an hour after both wings had partially given away, and skirmishing continued at intervals for some time with pickets, reconnoitering parties and stragglers. At 12 M. their whole force was in full retreat for Ozark. Having only a very few horses, and those already on duty with picketing and reconnoitering parties, I was utterly unable to pursue them. During the whole action the enemy occupied ground covered with timber and brush, while my command were in the streets and open fields.

Since the battle I have ascertained the following particulars: Gen. Cabell and staff, with about 2,000 men and two pieces of artillery, left Ozark on Friday morning with three days' rations and a full supply of ammunition. They halted at the crossing of the mountains a little past noon, and rested until nearly sunset, afterward marching rapidly toward Fayetteville. They were delayed by the darkness of the night and the incumbrance of their artillery, so that they did not commence the attack as early by nearly two hours as they had intended. Col. Monroe recommended a cavalry attack, to be supported by the artillery, but was overruled by Cabell, and a halt was made until the artillery could come up. Their force was made up as follows: Brig.-Gen. W. L. Cabell commanding, accompanied by staff and escort; Carroll's First Arkansas Cavalry Regiment, Col. Scott, of Virginia, commanding, assisted by Lieut.-Col. Thompson; Monroe's Second Arkansas Cavalry, Col. Monroe commanding in person; First Battalion Parson's Texas Cavalry, Lieut.-Col. Noble commanding; one section of artillery, commanding officer not known; four companies of bushwhackers, commanded by Mankins, Palmer, Brown and others. The enemy left all their dead and wounded, which they could not take away on their retreat, in our hands, leaving Surgeon Russell and Assist.-Surgeon Holderness to take charge of them. To-day Capt. Alexander arrived at our picket with a flag of truce, bringing a communication from Gen. Cabell, a copy of which I enclose. The flag was immediately ordered back with my reply, a copy of which is also enclosed. The following is a list of casualties on our side:

First Arkansas Infantry: Killed—S. Cockerill, Company A. Wounded—Capt. Randall Smith, Company A, head, slightly; Capt. William C. Parker, Company H, head, slightly; Corp. John Woods, Company A, slightly; James Shackley, Company A, mortally; Niles Slater, Company A, slightly; Daniel Rupe, Company E, slightly; William Rockdey, Company F, severely; —— Nolin, Company H, slightly.

First Arkansas Cavalry: Killed—Privates H. Morris and J. D. Bell, Company I; R. B. Burrows, Company A. Wounded—Capt. W. S. Johnson, Company M, right arm, dangerously; Sergt. Frederick Kise, Company A, slightly; Sergt. John Asbill, Company D, severely; First Sergt. W. M. Burrows, Company E, severely; Com. Sergt. Benjamin K. Graham, Company L, slightly; Corp. Josiah Fears, Company A, slightly; Corp. Henry C. Lewis, Company D, slightly; Corp. George A. Morris, Company G, slightly; Corp. Doctor B. Morris, Company M, slightly; Farrier William Wooten, Company C, slightly; John Hays, Company A, severely; James Jack, Company A, severely; William J. Qunton, Company D, slightly; Francis M. Temple, Company D, John Grubb, Company E, slightly; Jordan Taylor, Company E, severely; William F. Davis, Company G, slightly; George Davis, Company H, mortally; William J. York,

Company H, severely; Davis Chyle, Company M, slightly. Missing—thirty-five (mostly stampeded toward Cassville during the engagement). Prisoners—one lieutenant and eight men First Arkansas Cavalry, taken while absent without leave at a dance nine miles from town; also one private First Arkansas Infantry, and six privates in other commands, taken in town. Total killed, 4; wounded, 26; prisoners, 16; missing, 35.

The enemy's loss is not accurately known. At and about this post are not less than twenty killed and fifty wounded. Citizens report one colonel and several men as having died on the retreat, also a large number of wounded still moving on with the command. We captured during the engagement Maj. Wilson, Gen. Cabell's commissary, wounded, and Capt. Jefferson, of Carroll's regiment; also four sergeants, three corporals and forty-six privates, a part of them wounded; also not less than fifty horses and one hundred stand of arms, mostly shot-guns. Among their killed are Capt. Hubbard, of Carroll's regiment, and a captain of bushwhackers. The enemy admit the loss of over 200 horses, killed, taken and stampeded. Enclosed please find a rough sketch of the position of forces at 9 A. M., when the battle culminated.

Every field and line officer, and nearly every enlisted man, fought bravely, and I would not wish to be considered as disparaging any one when I can mention only a few of the many heroic men who sustained so nobly the honor of our flag. Lieut.-Col. Searle and Maj. Ham, in command of the reserve, did good service in keeping their men in position, and preventing them from being terrified by the artillery. Lieut.-Col. Bishop and Majs. Fitch and Hunt, of the First Cavalry, led their men coolly up in the face of the enemy's fire, and drove them from their position. Capt. W. S. Johnson, Company M, First Cavalry, had his right arm shattered while leading his men forward under a galling fire. Lieut. Roseman, post-adjutant, and Lieut. Frank Strong, acting adjutant, First Cavalry, deserve much praise.

I remain, General, your most obedient servant,
[Signed]   M. La Rue Harrison,
Colonel First Arkansas Cavalry, Commanding.

P. S.—We had actively engaged during the battle between three and four hundred men only. I should not neglect, also, to mention that S. D. Carpenter, assistant surgeon of volunteers, assisted by Assist.-Surgeons Coffee, Drake and Tefft, were actively engaged during the contest in carrying the wounded from the field and attending to their wants.
[Signed]   M. La Rue Harrison,
Colonel First Arkansas Cavalry, Commanding.

This defeat of Confederate arms, although not gaining to them their object, the capture of Fayetteville, was followed by the evacuation of that city on April 25 (1863), a few days later, under the order of Gen. Curtis, to "fall back by forced marches on Springfield," thus leaving Washington County open to Confederate occupation. During the summer both Confederate and Federal troops were largely drawn off toward Vicksburg, and on the return of Col. M. La Rue Harrison from a raid down on the

Arkansas River, he reoccupied Fayetteville on the 22d of September. The remainder of 1863 and the early half of the following year was occupied by the Fayetteville post in scouring the whole region for bands of bushwhackers, and by the Confederate bushwhackers in threatening and annoying the enemy in all ways possible, and who in October made a concerted attack on the city, but failed. On October 3 (1864), a detachment of Gen. Price's army, under the command of Maj.-Gen. Fagan, which had circled about on its Missouri raid, and was lying at Cane Hill, made an attack on Fayetteville. About 800 of the First Arkansas Cavalry and others, making the number 1,128 men, were stationed in a fort, and behind a line of rifle-pits, and although the attack was kept up all day, and many attempts were made to storm the fortifications, they were repelled. On the morning following Gen. Curtis appeared with his army, in pursuit of Gen. Price, and, joined by the First Arkansas Cavalry, ended the great raid some time later, leaving Washington County comparatively quiet during the winter. During 1865 guerrilla warfare was carried on with varying degrees of intensity, until about the 1st of July, when news of the surrender of Gen. E. Kirby Smith, then commanding the Confederate trans-Mississippi department, reached Fayetteville, and on the 23d of August the sturdy First Arkansas Cavalry was mustered out of service.

The following letter to Lieut.-Col. Bishop, acting adjutant general, Arkansas, gives an idea of a feature of Washington County life during 1865:

FAYETTEVILLE, ARK., December, 23, 1864.

Colonel: * * * * I write this as a simple memorandum to guide you in your entreaties for the suffering women and children of Northwestern Arkansas. There are thousands of old men, women and children left here yet. You know their condition. I have from time to time worked to assist and protect them. Since you left I have established, at their request, post colonies at Rhea's Mill, Engle's Mill, Bentonville, Pea Ridge, Elm Spring and Huntsville, and am about organizing others at Mudtown, Mount Comfort, Oxford Bend, Richland, McGuire's, Middle Fork, West Fork and Hog Eye.

The plan is: 1. Fifty men, capable of bearing arms, unite and ask to be organized into a home guard company, and permission to settle on a large tract of abandoned land, which is all in one body.

2. They are organized, armed and move their families to the place.

3. They build a block house or small fort in the best point on the land (selected by me).

4. They sign articles agreeing to be loyal to the United States authorities; to abide by the laws and orders from the nearest military post; the laws and present constitution of Arkansas; the proclamation of the President, etc., and are all mustered in as home guards.

They also agree to parcel out the land by vote, giving to each one all he wants to cultivate, but to have nothing in common, except common defense and obedience to law. Thus all persons within ten miles of these settlements are expected to enroll their names and belong to them, and none but rebels have, so far, objected.

Six of the settlements have made such progress that each will raise large quantities of corn next season, and the Union Valley settlement has agreed to deliver one thousand tons of hay next season, if needed.

Bentonville and Elm Springs are filling with people who have moved in. Winningham is going to settle Mudtown with fifty Arkansas families returned from Missouri.

All this is no chimera, it is half accomplished now, and the other companies are forming and will be at work in ten days. Some of the forts are nearly done. The refugees have nearly all left this place and gone to the colonies.   *   *   *   *

[The rest pertains to the revocation of Gen. Canby's evacuation order.]

Yours, for Arkansas,

(Signed)   M. LA RUE HARRISON,
Colonel First Arkansas Cavalry.

The most famous Washington County Federal regiment, the one mostly drawn from that county, and most active in it, was the First Arkansas Cavalry Volunteers, who were mustered into service August 7, 1862. Their regimental organization is as follows: Colonel, M. La Rue Harrison; lieutenant-colonel, Albert W. Bishop; lieutenant, Thomas J. Hunt; majors, James J. Johnson, Ezra Fitch, Charles Galloway, John I. Worthington, Richard H. Wimpy, Hugo C. C. Botefuhr, Frank Strong; surgeon, Henry J. Maynard; assistant surgeons, William Hunter, Amos H. Coffee, Jonathan E. Tefft; chaplain, Reuben North; adjutant, Denton D. Stark, Henry M. Kidder; adjutant first battalion, E. B. Harrison; adjutant second battalion, Frank Strong; regimental quartermasters, J. H. Wilson, John M. Bigger; regimental commissaries of subsistence, Thomas J. Rice, John A. Maxwell. Non-commissioned staff—Sergeant-majors, Robert Thompson, Thomas Brooks, Warren W. Munday, Simeon A. Baker, Jonathan Douglass; regimental quartermaster-sergeants, John M. Bigger, James C. Summers; regimental commissary-sergeants, Thomas H. Scott, Jeremiah B. Hale; hospital stewards, Amos H. Coffee, W. E. Maynard, Melancthon Hilbert, Thomas J. McCord, S. W. Chism;

chief trumpeters, John Pool, O. A. Whitcomb, James Lusk. Company A—Captain, M. La Rue Harrison, Steward H. Carlile, Joshua S. Dudley; first lieutenants, James J. Johnson, Thomas J. Gilstrap, William J. Patton, Frederick Kise; second lieutenant, Charles F. Eichacker. Company B—Captains, Thomas J. Hunt, Bracken Lewis, Hugo C. C. Botefuhr; first lieutenants, William Hunter, Denton D. Stark, Thomas Wilhite, Gustavus F. Hottenhauer; second lieutenants, Crittenden C. Wells, Owen A. Whitcomb. Company C—Captains, Ezra Fitch, Charles C. Moss, Elizur B. Harrison; first lieutenants, Samuel W. Chism, James R. Ivie; second lieutenant, Philip McGuire. Company D—Captains, Jesse M. Gilstrap, William L. Messenger, James Allison; first lieutenants, James H. Wilson, George W. M. Reid, William P. Clark; second lieutenant, Jacob H. Keiser. Company E—Captains, Charles Galloway, George R. King; first lieutenants, Philip M. Slaughter, Elam O. Kincaid, George W. Rowe; second lieutenant, George A. Purdy. Company F (Benton County). Company G (Carroll County and Missouri). Company H—Captains, John I. Worthington, Lawson L. Jernegan; first lieutenants, John W. Morris, Hugo C. C. Botefuhr, James G. Robertson, Warren W. Munday; second lieutenant, Melancthon Hilbert. Company I—Captain, DeWitt C. Hopkins; first lieutenants, Jacob J. Reel, Henry W. Gildemeister, John Vaughan; second lieutenant, Willis E. Maynard. Company K (Southeast Arkansas). Company L—Captains, John Bonine, Joseph S. Robb, Frank Strong; first lieutenants, George S. Albright, Thomas Brooks; second lieutenant, Simeon A. Baker. Company M—Captains, Robert E. Travis, William S. Johnson, John B. C. Turman; first lieutenants, James Roseman, Alvin D. Norris; second lieutenant, Thomas J. Rice. Causalties by companies: Company A, killed and died, 41; Company B, killed and died, 25; Company C, died, 33; Company D, killed and died, 21; Company E, killed and died, 41; Company H, killed and died, 36; Company I, killed and died, 24; Company K, killed and died, 21; Company L, killed and died, 15; Company M, killed and died, 22. Total, 279.

The following is the history of the regiment, as given by the report of Adj.-Gen. A. W. Bishop, of Arkansas: "On March

29, 1862, while the 'Army of the Southwest' was lying at Cross Timbers, Mo., M. La Rue Harrison, of the Thirty-sixth Illinois Infantry Volunteers, applied for and received authority from General Curtis to recruit a company for the Sixth Missouri Cavalry Volunteers, and proposed to enlist citizens of the State of Arkansas, many of whom had escaped conscription, and were then entering various regiments of the national army.

"On the 12th of May, 1862, eleven men from Washington County, Ark., made their appearance at the post of Cassville, Mo., and were sworn into the service of the United States; on the 18th of the same month about twenty more were added, and on the 1st of June the organization, numbering forty-five men, moved from Cassville to join a battalion of the Sixth Missouri Cavalry Volunteers, then stationed at Forsyth, Mo. On the march Capt. Harrison learned that many more than were enough to complete one squadron were on their way from Arkansas to join him, and he telegraphed to Hon. John S. Phelps, tendering, through him, to the President, a regiment of loyal Arkansans, for the United States volunteer army. On the following day a reply was received that the President would accept the regiment, provided it was completed within twenty days. [An inserted letter here is omitted.]

" Recruiting parties had already been sent into various parts of Arkansas, and squads of from six to thirty men were constantly arriving at Springfield and enlisting in the regiment. On the 20th of June a raid was made into Fayetteville, Ark., from Cassville, by a detachment of the First Missouri and the Second Wisconsin Cavalry, under command of Maj. Hubbard, at which time 115 recruits were brought out, mostly from Washington County.

"July 1 Capt. Harrison, with about 200 recruits, left Cassville with the Thirty-Seventh Illinois Infantry, and established his rendezvous at Springfield, Mo. July 3, the authority for mustering having been received, four companies were mustered into service, and on the 7th day of August a minimum regiment. On the 11th day of August Col. Harrison was, by order of Brig.-Gen. E. B. Brown, appointed chief engineer for the district of Southwest Missouri. About the 1st of September the first battalion, under Maj. Johnson, was ordered to join the command of Gen. Brown, in the field, west of Mount Vernon, Mo. It was engaged, September 15 and October 13, in the battle near Newtonia, Mo., and during the campaign furnished most of the scouts, guides, and messengers for the army, besides being frequently engaged in skirmishes with the enemy's scouting and reconnoitering parties. On the 2d day of October, 1862, the regimental organization of the twelve companies was completed.

" On the 3d day of October the second battalion, having been mounted and armed, was sent to the southwest to join the ' Army of the Frontier,' under Gen. Schofield, and during that month it, with the first, constituted the advance of that army in its march through Northwestern Arkansas. On the return of Gen. Schofield, about the 20th of October, these battalions were stationed at Elkhorn Tavern and Cassville, as outposts, and there remained until the next forward movement of that army. November 11 three companies of the third battalion, under command of Lieut.-Col. Bishop, left Springfield and joined the regiment at Elkhorn Tavern, on Pea Ridge, which place was held by him as the extreme outpost south of the second and third divisions of the Army of the Frontier, until its second advance, which resulted in the battle of Prairie Grove.

" On the 5th of December, in obedience to orders from Gen. Herron, Col. Harrison, who had been relieved from duty as chief engineer of the district of Southwest Missouri, left Elkhorn with eight companies of the regiment and a train of twenty wagons, and moved forward to join Gen. Blount, then at Cane Hill, Ark. On the night of the 6th the detachment camped at Prairie Grove, ten miles southwest of Fayetteville. During the night orders were received from Gen. Blount for the detachment to move at day-break and join Gen. Solomon near Rhea's Mill. Messengers also brought information from Gen. Blount that the enemy were west of Cane Hill, and would probably attack him in the morning; that the road between himself and Col. Harrison was clear.

" At daylight on the morning of the 7th the detachment moved forward, but at sunrise was met by detachments of Missouri troops retreating, who had been attacked by Hindman's advance at their camp two miles south of Illinois Creek. A determined attack was made by the enemy at this point, and within half an hour a serious panic ensued, which resulted in the capture of the train of the First Cavalry and the temporary demoralization of the regiment. Falling back to the Walnut Grove Church Col. Harrison rallied his men upon the right of Gen. Herron's army, which was met at that point, and advanced with it to Prairie Grove.

" On the following day Col. Harrison made a raid south to the Boston Mountains, pursuing some of the routed detachments of Hindman's army and capturing twenty-nine prisoners.

" 1863—On January 8 a detachment under the command of Lieuts. Thompson and Vaughan participated in the defeat of Marmaduke, at Springfield, Mo., Lieut. Vaughan and Sergt. L. D. Jernigan were severely wounded during the engagement. About January 25 a detachment, commanded by Capt. Galloway, participated in a raid into Van Buren, under command of Lieut.-Col. Stuart, Tenth Illinois Cavalry, at which time a steamer and 315 prisoners were captured. On February 3 a detachment of eighty-three men, under Capt. Galloway, routed 180 rebels near White Oak Creek, in Franklin County, and on the following morning Capt. R. E. Travis was mortally wounded in an attack upon a party of guerrillas, who had fortified themselves in a log house near Thurlkill's ferry, on the Arkansas River.

" On April 18, at sunrise, the post at Fayetteville was attacked. [Elsewhere described.]

" In September Col. Harrison attacked a detachment of rebels under Coffee, in the Seneca Nation, pursuing them down the Indian line to Round Prairie, Ark., and on the 22d of that month the First Cavalry reoccupied Fayetteville. On October 4 a detachment of the regiment, 450 strong, with two sections of Battery A, First Arkansas Light Artillery, and one section of mountain howitzers, under command of Col. Harrison, left Fayetteville in pursuit of the rebel Gen. Shelby, who at that time was moving north from Neosho, Mo., with 2,000 men and two pieces of artillery. Marching through Pineville, Newtonia, Granby, Carthage, Lamar and Greenfield toward Warsaw, countermanding orders turned the column toward Bower's Mill, and thence by way of Mount Vernon and Cassville to Fayetteville, to relieve the garrison at that place, which was being seriously threatened by a superior force under the rebel Col. Brooks. At sunrise, on October 15, a part of the detachment, while in camp at Cross Timbers, and having in charge a train of twenty-five wagons loaded with supplies for Fayetteville, was attacked by Brooks, but through the timely return of Col. Harrison, who, having gone forward toward Fayetteville with a portion of his men, had heard the firing, the attack was repelled. On October 23 a portion of the regiment, with its howitzer battery, under command of Maj. Hunt, joined Gen. McNeil at Huntsville, taking the advance in the pursuit of Gen. Shelby across Arkansas River.

"On November 7 an expedition, 435 strong, under Col. Harrison, left Fayetteville, moving eastward, and on the morning of the 9th routed a force of rebels near King's River; and again, on the following day, at sunrise, at Kingston; at noon, on the Dry Fork of King's River, and in the evening near Mulberry Mountain. On the 11th and 12th Capt. J. I. Worthington drove the same irregular forces across Arkansas River, carrying his howitzers by hand across the Frog Bayou Mountain, and on the 23d and 25th engaged and routed bands of guerrillas near Sugar Loaf Mountain, in Marion County, and on Richland Creek, in Searcy County, the last time with considerable loss. Lieut. L. D. Jernigan was here severely wounded and taken prisoner.

"1864—During the months of January and February a detachment of the regiment, commanded by Capts. Galloway and Boteführ, served in Carroll, Marion and Searcy Counties, under orders from Brig.-Gen. C. B. Holland, from the district of Southwest Missouri. They were engaged repeatedly with the enemy, and received high praises in Gen. Holland's official report.

"During this year detachments of the regiment were very frequently engaged with guerrillas, who were still infesting Northwestern Arkansas, and on October 28 a concerted attack upon Fayetteville was defeated. On October 3 the town was again attacked by a largely superior force, detached from Gen. Price's army, then lying at Cane Hill, the whole under the command of Maj.-Gen. Fagan. [Mentioned elsewhere.]

"All summer long the First Cavalry had been actively employed against the enemy, who increased in strength until in autumn they swarmed through the county, but Price's retreat and the approach of winter secured, for a time, comparative quiet.

"1865—During this year a relentless warfare was carried on against the small bands of guerrillas who infested Northwestern Arkansas, and many were killed. * * * * [The mustering out of the regiment on August 23 is mentioned elsewhere.] From May, 1863, until the disbanding of the regiment a cornet band was maintained at the private expense of the officers, and at the close of the war the instruments were presented to the city of Fayetteville."

The Fourth Arkansas Cavalry Volunteers was commanded by a citizen of Fayetteville, Col. Lafayette Gregg, but, as its further county representation was very small, this mention will suffice.

The First Arkansas Infantry Volunteers was recruited at Fayetteville after the battle of Prairie Grove, by Dr. James M. Johnson, of Huntsville, Madison County, and contained Washington County men in various parts of its organization. The following is a brief account of its history, by F. M. Johnson, major, commanding regiment: " At the time of the muster-in of J. M. Johnson as colonel of this regiment it numbered thirty-six commissioned officers and 810 enlisted men, recruited in the previous sixty days in Madison, Washington, Newton, Benton, Searcy and Crawford Counties. It participated in the battle of Fayetteville, under the immediate command of Lieut.-Col. E. J. Searle and Maj. E. D. Ham, on the 18th of April, 1863, and marched for Springfield on the 25th of that month. On the 6th of July it was ordered to Cassville, Mo., where it shortly afterward arrived, and on the 17th of August joined the Army of the Frontier, under command of Maj.-Gen. Blount, at Fort Gibson, Cherokee Nation, pursued the rebels under Cooper and Stanwatie to Perryville, in the Choctaw Nation, and, returning to Fort Smith, was the first regiment to enter the garrison on the 1st of September, 1863. Shortly afterward, by order of Brig.-Gen. McNeil, the regiment proceeded to Waldron, and remained there until February, 1864, when it was again ordered to report at Fort Smith to take part in the movement southward under Brig.-Gen. Thayer; left Fort Smith with the frontier division on the 24th of March,

1864, forming part of the first brigade under Col. John Edwards; participated in the battle of Moscow, losing three men killed and several wounded; entered Camden on the 16th of April, 1864, and was engaged in a reconnoisance of the enemy after the battle of Poisoned Springs; left Camden on the 26th of April, and, as a part of the right wing of the Union army, was engaged with the enemy at the battle of Saline River, where it repulsed a strong flanking party with considerable loss to the enemy, and losing no men itself. On the 1st of May, 1864, the regiment arrived at Little Rock, and proceeded thence to Fort Smith, where it arrived on the 17th of the same month; since which time it has been engaged in escort and guard duty on the frontier. The greatest aggregate was in November, 1863—979 officers and men; the lowest in March, 1865—774; present aggregate, 788, 31 commissioned officers and 757 enlisted men."

The regimental officers and captains are as follows: Colonel, James M. Johnson; lieutenant-colonel, Elhanon J. Searle; majors, Elijah D. Ham, Francis M. Johnson; surgeon, William B. Waterman; assistant surgeons, Thomas B. Drake, Harvey H. Bolinger, Robert B. Campfield; chaplains, Francis Springer, John M. Leard; adjutants, Francis M. Sams, William Patterson; regimental quartermasters, Crittenden C. Wells, Jonathan H. Hewes; Company A, captains, Randall Smith, Daniel E. Sutcliffe; Company B, captains, Elith Haynes, Thomas H. Scott; Company C, captain, James R. Vanderpool; Company D, captains, Ransom R. Rhodes, William H. Newman; Company E, captains, James M. Hutchings, John W. Spralding; Company F, captains, John McCoy, George W. Raymond; Company G, captain, George W. R. Smith; Company H. captain, William C. Parker; Company I, captains, William J. Heffington, John Whiteford, Samuel Bard; Company K, captain, Abial Stevens. Total casualties, 184.

The Second Cavalry and Second Infantry of the Federal Arkansas troops had but few representatives from Washington County. Col. Edward J. Brooks, of Fayetteville, was given authority to organize a Fourth Arkansas Infantry Volunteer troop at Fayetteville, but his recruits were absorbed into other commands or disbanded.

Battery A, First Arkansas Light Artillery Volunteers, known

as "Stark's Battery," was raised by Denton D. Stark, then adjutant First Arkansas Cavalry. "April 1st the battery was full," so says the adjutant-general's report, "but was not mustered into service until August 31, 1863. Meantime and until the 25th of April, of this year, it was stationed at Fayetteville, Ark., (though officers and men were absent in Missouri procuring horses when the battle of the 18th of April took place), when, by orders from headquarters of the department of the Missouri, Northwestern Arkansas was evacuated. From May 4th to September 21st, 1863, the battery was stationed at Springfield, Mo., receiving, while there, guns and equipments. In September Lieut. Robert V. Thompson, with one section of the battery, participated in an expedition under the command of Col. M. La Rue Harrison, through Southwestern Missouri and Northwestern Arkansas, in pursuit of Col. Coffee's command, then raiding that section of country, and proceeded thence to Fayetteville, Ark. The remaining two sections of the battery, under the command of Capt. Stark, left Springfield, Mo., September 21, 1863, for Fayetteville, marching first, however, as far north as Greenfield, Mo., under Col. Harrison, who was then in pursuit of Gen. Shelby. Moving thence to Fayetteville, one section of the battery took part, about October 20, in a skirmish with the enemy, under Col. Brooks, at Cross Timbers, Mo. The battery remained at Fayetteville until March 19, 1864, when, by order of Brig.-Gen. Thayer, it marched to Fort Smith. On the 23d of March it joined the expedition to Camden, forming a part of Col. Adams' brigade. It was present in the skirmish at Moscow on or about the 13th of April, with four guns in action, and relieved the Second Indiana Battery, under a severe fire from the enemy's artillery. Leaving Camden with the retreating force under Gen. Steele, April 28, it reached Little Rock May 3, 1864, and moved thence with the frontier division of the Army of Arkansas, to Fort Smith. In October one section of the battery, under Lieut. Mayes, was sent with other troops in pursuit of Col. Gano, who had captured a supply train between Fort Scott and Fort Smith, making a forced march to Cabin Creek, north of Fort Gibson, where they came up with the enemy retreating, but he escaped. The battery occupied Fort No. 2, at Fort Smith, until the 30th

of August, 1865, when it was mustered out of service. * * *
* * [The men] were faithful, brave and efficient, and reflected great credit upon the battery and the State."

The officers were Captains, Denton D. Stark and Henry H. Easter; first lieutenant, Robert Thompson; second lieutenants, Edward D. Brogan, William Mayes; first sergeant, Alex Thompson; quartermaster-sergeant, John B. Malidon.

The battery was largely represented by Washington County men. Their casualties were twenty-five, who were killed and died of disease.

Independent companies were organized in the autumn of 1863, under orders of Maj.-Gen. Schofield, and among those organized in Washington County were Capt. Bracken Lewis' company, Capt. Mackey's company, and a West Fork Township company. The first two companies served in the defense of Fayetteville, November 3, 1864.

The total number of Washington County men in the Federal army, according to an estimate of Col. T. J. Hunt, is between 500 and 800.

Col. W. H. Brooks was probably the most active representative of the Southern cause for Washington County. Among the first organizations was Brooks' battalion of cavalry (State troops), which afterward became E. I. Stirman's battalion, and later on was transferred to the Cismississippi Department, where it was known as the Sharpshooters' battalion. A few of these were Washington County men. Capt. Lafayette Boone's company, which served at Elkhorn, was officered as follows: First lieutenant, L. P. Beavert; second lieutenant, Sam. H. Smithson, and third lieutenant, John O. Parks.

The well-known Thirty-fourth Arkansas Infantry then fell to the command of Col. Brooks, and for an account of its formation a portion of the address of Col. J. R. Pettigrew, delivered at the Grand Reunion of ex-Confederates at Prairie Grove, on August 19, 1886, is here inserted: "Mr. Chairman, Ladies and Gentlemen: Twenty-five years ago this beautiful valley was a military camp; red battle had stamped his foot, and the nation had felt the shock. Peaceful pursuits had been abandoned, and all was busy preparation for the inevitable conflict. In September, 1862, at this place, the Thirty-fourth (Brook's) Regiment of Arkansas Infantry was organized; shortly thereafter the regiment went into camp at Mount Comfort, then at Elm Springs, then to Elkhorn, thence to Camp Reagan, then to Spadra, on the Arkansas River, where we received our arms, Enfield rifles; thence we marched to Mazzard Prairie, near Fort Smith, where the regiment became a part of Fagan's Brigade. All the points named were camps of instruction, and the 'tramp, tramp' of the soldier was heard on every hand. The hot blood of youth coursed in our veins then, and the 'pomp and circumstance of glorious war, was hailed with delight. The enemy was approaching; patriotism and desire to defend homes and firesides was at fever heat. The order to march at length came; the Arkansas River was crossed. At Lee's Creek the head of the column was halted, the different commands massed, and the solemn ceremony had of presentation of battle flags to each regiment. No more impressive scene was ever witnessed in all this land than on that calm winter morning, to see thousands of soldiers kneeling with their faces northward, and the solemn invocation commending them and their fortunes to the arbitrament of arms and the God of battles. Thenceforth the red flag of battle waved over each command. The march was resumed, and on the 7th day of December Prairie Grove was reached.

" The stillness of the early morning was broken by the clash of arms. about 200 of the enemy's cavalry were captured near the church. Our infantry coming up, met the prisoners; enthusiasm and eagerness for the fray were aroused to the highest pitch. We moved rapidly to the battle-field, and the long line of infantry and artillery was placed in position, where we awaited the approach and attack of the enemy. About noon the cavalry were withdrawn, pickets driven in, and the enemy charged the whole line of Fagan's Brigade; the battle of Prairie Grove had opened in earnest, and Fagan's Brigade, from that time until shortly before sundown, repelled charge after charge of the enemy under the gallant Herron. About an hour before sunset the enemy withdrew his infantry, and opened a terrific fire upon our lines. The enemy was reinforced by Gen. Blount's command, which at once opened a terrible fire upon our left.

Gen. Parsons and his invincible Missourians met him with great gallantry and success. The battle of Prairie Grove, while of short duration, will compare, perhaps, with any fought during the war, in fierceness and desperate gallantry. The rattle of musketry often rose above the roar of artillery, and the bright sunlight gleamed from bayonets held by hands as steady as Napoleon's veterans at Austerlitz or Waterloo. Officers and soldiers were alike brave, and there were feats of individual prowess that stamped the actors heroes. Thus it was the logic of fate that Brooks' regiment received its first shock of battle, and baptism of blood, almost on the very spot of its origin. * * * * Many a gallant life went out in that fierce conflict; Capt. William Woosley (or Owsley), Lieuts. Ben Boone and James Pollard, as brave and good men as ever breathed the breath of life; Tell Duke, the gifted and intrepid lieutenant, whose spirit rose from the din of battle, the rattle of musketry, and the roar of artillery to the peaceful bosom of its God; William Gray, color-bearer; John Sharp, Henry Morrison, Cy Graham, Clem Kirksly, James Gray, and others whose names I cannot now recall, went down in the shock of battle to fill heroes' graves, and left names with immortality synonymous. Brooks' regiment can well claim to be the child of Prairie Grove. It had its origin here, and aided in making its fields and groves historic. * * * * Night closed the scene at Prairie Grove with the victorious Confederates occupying the field, and the wearied soldier sought whatever of repose he could get on the perilous edge of battle, which he expected to be resumed on the morrow, dreaming, fitfully, perchance, of home and loved ones whom he expected soon to greet; but late at night the order was silently passed along the lines to prepare to march. The soldiers who expected to follow up the victory were not slow in getting ready; such, however, was not the case; it was a retreat, and Gen. Hindman's army were subjected to the trying ordeal of turning their faces from home and loved ones, and a hard-earned victory. Thus we came to Prairie Grove, and thus we left its fields, made forever historic by the valor and blood of patriots."

The regiment served after this at Helena, and were in the retreat from Little Rock. At the action at Jenkins' Ferry they sustained greater losses probably than during all their career; here it was that Capt. Walker was killed and Col. Brooks was wounded.

The most reliable information obtainable gives the following regimental organizations of Col. Brooks' command, with changes, and as complete as possible where companies are from Washington County: Colonel, W. H. Brooks; lieutenant-colonels, T. M. Gunter, J. R. Pettigrew; majors, James Owsley, J. R. Pettigrew, F. R. Earle; adjutants, M. C. Duke, Peter Carnahan; quartermaster, James Trott; commissary sergeant, Capt. Robert Tyus; sergeant-majors, Frank Watson, Henry Keyser; surgeon, Dr. W. B. Welch; assistant surgeon, Dr. J. M. Lacy; hospital steward, G. M. Cox. Company A—Captains, T. M. Gunter, J. W. Walker; acting captain, Lee Taylor; first lieutenant, Pomroy Hart; second lieutenant, J. M. Roark. Company B—Captains, F. R. Earle, James Mitchell, George Gibson; first lieutenants, James Mitchell, Peter Carnahan; second lieutenant, William Buchanan. Company C—Captain, Samuel H. Smithson; first lieutenant, John O. Parks; second lieutenant, Isaac Roark; third lieutenant, James Pollard; orderly sergeant, Robert Anderson. Company D—Captain, William Owsley. Company E—Captain, James E. Wright; second lieutenant, J. M. Pittman. Company F—Captain, C. L. Pickens. Company G—Captain, James Owsley. Company H—Captain, Wallace; first lieutenant, Mayes; second lieutenant, Albert Brodie; third lieutenant, J. L. Duke. Company I—Captain, A. V. Edmondson. Company K—Captains, J. R. Pettigrew, A. Wilson; first lieutenants, M. C. Duke, S. P. Pittman; second lieutenants, B. F. Boone, C. F. Reagan; third lieutenants, A. Wilson, James Beard.

At Camden the following consolidation seems to have been completed in 1863: Companies C, H and A were consolidated into Company A, Company G was merged into Company D and Company I was placed in Company K.

The Sixteenth Arkansas Confederate Infantry was organized under Gen. McCullough's order, at Rogers (then Calahan Springs), about the middle of November, 1861, with the following officers, the list being made most complete when there is Washington County representation:

Colonels, J. F. Hill, W. T. Neal, David Province; lieutenant-colonels, W. T. Neal, B F. Pixley, J. M. Pittman; majors —— Farmer, J. M. Pittman. Company A, captains, L. Swagerty, Jesse Adams. Company B, captains, —— Turner, Jesse Cravens. Company C, captains, John Connelly, J. J. Yearwood. Company D, captains, John Smith, E. G. Mitchell, J. Bailey. Company E, captain, W. S. Poyner. Company F, captains, David Good-night, —— Stephens. Company G, captain, J. P. Carnahan; first lieutenant, W. E. Pittman; second lieutenants, B. F. Pixley, B. Carnahan; third lieutenants, V. A. Ross, John Eggers. Company H, captains, —— Kelley, J. P. Cloud. Company I, captains, Dan Boone; first lieutenant, John Garrett; second lieutenant, Abe Wilson. Company K, captains, John Lawrence, James Waldon.

The last change of officers occurred at the reorganization at Corinth, Miss., where Col. David Province took charge of the regiment. The general course of the regiment was as follows, after its organization at Calahan's Springs: It first went to Elm Springs, thence to Cross Hollows with Gen. Price, then Elkhorn and Van Buren, thence with Gen. Price to Corinth, Tupelo, Iuka and Corinth again, where it was the only Arkansas regiment in the First Missouri Brigade. Their next move was to Port Gibson, where they were captured. The officers were imprisoned and the privates paroled. The greatest casualties occurring to the Sixteenth Regiment was at Corinth, where seven-twelfths were reported "killed, wounded and missing."

The following State troops were in service at Oak Hill: Col. Gratiot's Third Arkansas Infantry, Col. Walker's Fourth Arkansas Infantry, Col. Dockery's Fifth Arkansas Infantry, Col. Churchill's First Arkansas Cavalry and Col. Carroll's Cavalry.

Their Washington County representation was somewhat as follows:

Colonel, Gratiot, Third Arkansas Infantry; lieutenant-colonel, David Province; Company ——, captain, Bell, and Company ——, captain, Pleasant Buchanan; first lieutenant, J. M. Lacy; colonel, J. D. Walker, Fourth Arkansas Infantry; lieutenant-colonel, T. D. Berry; major, S. W. Peel; Company ——, captain, T. M. Gunter; first lieutenant, Wythe Walker; colonel, ——, Dockery, Fifth Arkansas Infantry; captain, W. T. Neal; colonel,

T. J. Churchill, First Arkansas Cavalry; colonel, Carroll; Company ——, captain, Jeff Kelly; first lieutenant, Lafayette Boone; second lieutenant, James A. Ferguson; third lieutenant, Samuel H. Smithson.

Col. Walker's regiment was organized about July 8, 1861, at Camp Walker, in Benton County, and was disbanded about the last of August, of the same year, at Walnut Springs. Among the other captains of the regiment were Denny, Fancher, Johnson, Pittman, Sanders, Bunch and Tinnin. An independent company, under Capt. J. F. Rieff, also did excellent service.

The Fifteenth Arkansas Mounted Infantry of the Northwest, so distinguished from another Fifteenth Arkansas Infantry, did service at Wilson's Creek. In it was organized by Capt. James Richards, probably in November, 1861, a company which took the title Company G, and also one under Capt. Pleasant Buchanan, called Company H. Capt. Richard's company was partly of Washington County men, but Company H was entirely from that county. The company was organized at Cane Hill, with First Lieut. Patton Inks and Second Lieut. A. A. Evans. The captain and first lieutenant were captured at Elkhorn, and A. A. Evans became captain. The regiment then started for Pittsburg Landing, but the battle was over. Iuka and Corinth were their next points of action. At the latter place Capt. W. H. Holcomb, of Springdale, became captain of Company G. Companies G and H were next among the forces that moved to Port Gibson, then Jackson, Miss., and Champion Hill. At Black River, on May 17, 1863, Capt. Holcomb was captured and sent to Johnson's Island, Ohio, and after the siege of Vicksburg Companies G and H were returned to Arkansas and consolidated under Capt. A. A. Evans. The organization of Company G was: Captains, James Richards, W. H. Holcomb; first lieutenants, William Cooper, J. H. Williams; second lieutenants, Marion Mosier, Evan Atwood; third lieutenants, James Cooper, White.

In the Seventeenth Arkansas Infantry, under Col. H. M. Rector and Lieut.-Col. Griffith, there was but one company, that of Capt. T. W. Thomason.

The total Confederate representation from Washington County is estimated at about 2,000 men by Col. T. M. Gunter *et al.*

It is greatly to be regretted that the records of Confederate soldiery in Washington County have all been lost except those uncertain traces left in the treacherous memories of those, now growing old, who passed through the distracting struggles.

In the tombs that dot the cemeteries lying on the hills east and west of Fayetteville are the certain records of the deadliness of the conflict.

The National Military Cemetery, lying about three-quarters of a mile southwest of the court-house, is a natural mound embracing six acres, surrounded by a columned brick wall, and surmounted by a flag-staff, about which in concentric circles lie 1,214 of the victims of Pea Ridge, Prairie Grove and Fayetteville. The place was located by the Government in 1867, and stationed in the brick lodge, with its adjoining stables, is the keeper, who is now in constant charge—Capt. A. Pettit. The grounds originally contained about 1,900 graves, but many have been removed by friends.

The Confederate Military Cemetery lies on the slope of East Heights. It is an octagon, surrounded by a stone wall, with a smaller octagon in the center, intended for a monument, but which now contains the grave of Gen. Slack, who fell at Prairie Grove. The cemetery is divided into eight convergent sections, the four sections of graves alternating with the remaining four, which are devoted to ornamental shrubbery. Here lie about 700 who wore the gray at Pea Ridge, Prairie Grove and Fayetteville, embracing citizens of Texas, Louisiana, Missouri and Arkansas; and it represents a greater mausoleum in the hearts of the wives, mothers, sisters and daughters of those men, or such of them as lived in Washington County, for it is the result of the efforts of the Southern Memorial Association, a society of ladies organized in Fayetteville, and other parts of the county, in June, 1872; it was dedicated by them precisely a year later. For some twelve years the president of the society has been an earnest and intelligent Christian lady—Mrs. Lizzie Pollard—to whose efforts the success of the movement is in no small degree due.

CITIES, TOWNS AND VILLAGES.

FAYETTEVILLE.

The enterprising town of Fayetteville dates its history from the organization of Washington County in 1828. At about that time George McGarroh, the father of James, John and William McGarroh, removed from the neighborhood of Evansville, and located near the spring in what is now known as the Masonic addition to Fayetteville. The next year James Leeper, the father of Mathew W. Leeper, came, and after living for a time in a camp, built a small log house near where the Mountain House now is. Soon after Reuben W. Reynolds and the Sweeneys arrived. One of the Sweeneys built a house, and kept a sort of hotel. In February, 1830, the first store-house was erected. It was built by James Holmsley and two other young men for one John Nye, an Eastern man. They built it of black oak poles, and covered it with boards made from a large oak tree that stood on the branch below the spring west of town. It was without a floor. It stood on the west side of the public square. This building was completed in one day, and the next day the same young men erected a similar structure for two brothers, Seviers, who opened a store near what is known as the Blockmill corner. The Seviers remained but a few months. Nye continued for two or three years.

The above were the first settlers of Fayetteville. The McGarrohs were of the true backwoods type, and not a few of the now well-worn newspaper anecdotes of early Arkansas are said to have originated with them. They were entirely uneducated, not able even to read or write, but John, or Jack, as he was more popularly known, was a man of considerable native ability, and was twice elected to the Legislature. As a member of that body he assumed much dignity, and sedulously sought to conceal his illiteracy. To this end he frequently procured a newspaper, and while sitting in his seat in the House scanned its columns long and earnestly. A member, one day observing that he held his paper upside down, accosted him with: " Uncle Jack, what is the news?" " I see they have had a thundering big storm on the river," replied Jack, "and capsized every durned boat." The paper was filled with advertisements of boats, each accompanied by a picture of a boat, from which, in the inverted position of the paper, he drew the inference, they had been capsized.

William McGarroh was for a long time a grocery keeper in Fayetteville. He never kept any books, and although he did a considerable credit business he is said never to have made but one mistake. On one occasion he charged a customer with a cheese, when he had purchased a grindstone. Upon settlement the customer objected to the item. McGarroh turned to the wall back of him, which was covered with marks and signs, and after studying it for a moment, broke out with: "I'll be durned, if I didn't forget to put an eye in that cheese."

In a letter to Mr. J. H. Van Hoose, in 1879, Rev. John Buchanan has the following to say of the early history of Fayetteville: "The town of Fayetteville was located at the county site of Washington County in 1829. The territory now embraced in Benton and Madison Counties then belonged to Washington County. This is the reason why the location was made so far northeast of the center of what is now Washington County. Two of the commissioners who located the county site were former residents of Lincoln County, Tenn., and Fayetteville was the county site of Lincoln County, hence the name Fayetteville was given to the new town.

" So soon as the location was made Capt. Jack McGarroh moved to the place and camped there until a house was built. The first court was held there in August, 1829. Two log houses were erected at the time of the court. One was floored with hewed puncheons; the court was held in it. The other had only a dirt floor, which was used for a hotel. Forks were driven in the ground, poles laid in them, and boards placed upon the poles for a table.

" I do not remember who presided as judge of the court, but think it was Judge Johnson, father of Hon. R. W. Johnson, now of Little Rock. There were two lawyers present, but their names I do not remember.

" McGarroh's table was well supplied with pound cake, beef, venison and turkeys, as wild game of every description was abundant about there at that time.

"The first store-house ever built in Fayetteville was put up for two brothers by the name of Sevier, nephews of the Hon. Ambrose H. Sevier, one of our first lawyers and statesmen. They brought their goods to Cane Hill, and deposited them there with Col. W. B. Woody until their house was built in Fayetteville. In December, 1829, they hired me to haul their goods to Fayetteville. They remained in business there but a short time."

The commissioners of the seat of justice were Lewis Evans, Larkin Newton, Samuel Vaughn and John Woody. They fixed upon the site of Fayetteville, and when the government survey of land was made, it was found to be upon a sixteenth section, the school section. A special act of Congress was therefore passed transferring the school section of Township 16, Range 30 west, to the twentieth section. The patent for the town site was issued February 27, 1835. It granted to the commissioners the south half of the northeast quarter and the north half of the southeast quarter of Section 16, Township 15, Range 30 west.

The survey of the town was made by Charles McClellan, then deputy county surveyor, assisted by John West, John Smallman, James Parr, William McGarroh and A. Mankins as chain carriers.

Sale of Lots.—The lots were sold chiefly at public sale, A. Whinnery being the auctioneer. The following is a statement of the sales up to 1837, the names of the purchasers and the price paid:

NAMES.	Block.	Lot.	Price.	NAMES.	Block.	Lot.	Price.
A. B. Anthony.....	16	5	$100.00	Matthew Leeper....	15	9	$70.00
A. B. Anthony. ...	16	4	10.50	Matthew Leeper...	15	10	76.00
A. B. Anthony.....	29	1	10.00	Matthew Leeper...	15	11	50.00
A. B. Anthony.....	29	2	10.00	Wm. McK. Ball...	16	6	82.00
A. B. Anthony.....	29	3	10.00	Wm. McK. Ball...	16	3	12.00
A. B. Anthony.....	29	4	15.00	Wm. McK. Ball...	4	....	50.00
A. B. Anthony.....	29	5	15.00	John McGarroh....	16	9	65.00
A. B. Anthony.....	29	12	10.00	John McGarroh....	16	12	12.00
A. B. Anthony.....	29	7	80.00	John McGarroh....	16	13	11.50
A. B. Anthony....	29	8	20.00	John T. Powers....	17	6	65.00
A. B. Anthony.....	29	9	15.00	John T. Powers....	17	12	12.00
A. B. Anthony.....	29	10	10.00	James P. Humes...	32	1	16.50
A. B. Antbony.....	29	11	10.00	James P. Humes...	32	2	17.00
A. B. Anthony.....	29	6	10.00	James P. Humes...	32	3	11.00
A. B. Anthony.....	30	....	30.00	John West.........	7	1	27.00
Matthew Leeper...	16	7	82.00	Alfred Wallace....	26	4	76.00
Matthew Leeper...	15	7	40.00	Alfred Wallace....	14	8	56.00
Matthew Leeper...	15	8	60.00	Alfred Wallace.....	14	1	34.00

NAMES.	Block.	Lot.	Price.	NAMES.	Block.	Lot.	Price.
Dillin Irby	18	4	$12.50	M. H. W. Mahan	31	2	$30.00
Dillin Irby	18	2	10.00	M. H. W. Mahan	31	3	20.00
Dillin Irby	13	8	22.00	M. H. W. Mahan	31	4	14.00
Dillin Irby	13	9	16.50	L. C. Pleasants	28	12	67.00
Martha Tramell	24	2	15.00	C. M. McClellan	30	7	125.00
Martha Tramell	24	1	25.00	C. M. McClellan	30	8	10.00
David Walker	28	6	46.00	C. M. McClellan	30	9	10.00
David Walker	28	4	40.00	William M. Kincaid	30	6	114.00
David Walker	16	11	100.00	William M. Kincaid	25	7	32.00
David Walker	25	3	26.00	John T. Cox	28	11	75.00
David Walker	25	4	26.00	John T. Cox	19	1	25.00
David Walker	25	5	20.00	B. H. Martin	26	12	50.00
David Walker	25	9	18.00	John B. Webster	26	13	32.00
David Walker	13	11	10.25	John B. Webster	31	9	31.00
David Walker	13	4	10.00	John B. Webster	19	2	25.00
David Walker	13	12	10.00	John B. Webster	35	....	10.00
David Walker	13	3	10.00	John B. Webster	36	....	13.00
David Walker	13	1	10.00	John B. Webster	34	....	12.50
David Walker	13	8	10.00	M. H. Clark	26	15	50.00
David Walker	13	2	11.50	M. H. Clark	17	4	28.00
David Walker	25	2	23.50	M. H. Clark	18	3	15.00
David Walker	16	2	21.00	M. H. Clark	18	1	12.50
David Walker	42	5	35.00	M. H. Clark	22	....	15.00
W. T. Larremore	28	10	66.00	M. H. Clark	11	....	21.00
W. T. Larremore	3	....	50.00	W. D. Hart	26	8	21.00
W. T. Larremore	7	2	10.00	W. D. Hart	23	....	20.50
John Tuttle	25	8	25.00	P. V. Rhea	17	8	41.00
W. F. Denton	17	3	25.00	R. W. Reynolds	28	9	55.00
B. H. Smithson	17	1	25.00	R. W. Reynolds	28	8	55.00
B. H. Smithson	17	2	18.00	R. W. Reynolds	28	7	101.00
B. H. Smithson	25	1	31.00	George Freyschleg	30	4	80.00
B. H. Smithson	1	....	127.00	George Freyschleg	31	1	131.00
E. A. Sweeney	17	9	50.00	James Sinclair	30	11	25.00
E. A. Sweeney	18	8	20.00	James Sinclair	30	10	10.00
A. Yell	41	....	15.00	James Sinclair	30	12	18.50
A. Yell	42	1	16.00	Isaac Murphy	12	1	11.00
L. Brodie	17	7	55.00	Isaac Murphy	12	2	10.00
H. M. Hill	8	....	30.00	Isaac Murphy	12	3	14.00
William Dugan	30	1	85.00	Isaac Murphy	12	4	14.00
William Dugan	30	3	70.00	L. Evans	17	5	35.00
William Dugan	25	11	10.00	L. Evans	13	5	10.00
William Dugan	25	12	21.00	J. M. Tuttle	31	10	45.00
William Dugan	25	10	16.00	Wilson Bros	16	3	87.87
J. M. Sweeney	18	7	20.00	John S. Blair	6	....	150.00
Oneismus Evans	16	15	10.00	Matthew Hubbard	42	3	7.00
Oneismus Evans	16	2	50.00	Matthew Hubbard	42	4	17.00
George McGarroh	13	15	30.00	John Lewis	28	5	60.10
William Skelton	15	4	13.00	John Lewis	28	15	16.00
William Skelton	15	3	13.00	John Lewis	16	10	100.00
William Skelton	15	2	16.00	Samuel O. Harris	28	17	10.00
William McGarroh	15	7	100.00	Samuel O. Harris	28	16	14.00
A. S. Walker	5		50.00	Samuel O. Harris	32	7	22.50
James Byrnsides	16	6	52.00	Samuel O. Harris	14	4	20.00
James Byrnsides	16	7	144.00	Samuel O. Harris	14	5	15.00
James Byrnsides	16	10	25.50	Samuel O. Harris	14	2	15.00
James Byrnsides	16	11	40.00	Samuel O. Harris	14	3	15.00
James Byrnsides	31	7	17.00	William Meek	16	8	85.00
James Byrnsides	31	8	23.00	W. Marrs	w¼4	....	12.00
Alfred Dobbs	30	5	82.00	J. M. Hoge	13	7	15.50
M. H. W. Mahan	26	5	60.00	J. M. Hoge	13	10	12.00
M. H. W. Mahan	26	3	50.00	D. R. Mills	28	18	11.50

NAMES.	Block.	Lot.	Price.	NAMES.	Block.	Lot.	Price.
D. R. Mills	28	2	$15.00	John Ransom	28	1	$11.50
J. H. George	28	19	10.00	Samuel Alexander	37	....	17.00
Jackson Bigelow	26	14	39.00	Samuel Alexander	33	....	12.00
Jackson Bigelow	26	1	106.00	Samuel Alexander	32	6	10.50
Solomon Tuttle	15	6	22.00	Samuel L. Marrs	32	5	10.50
Solomon Tuttle	15	5	20.50	Samuel L. Marrs	38	....	10.00
John G. Stout	21	....	15.00	James Boone	31	6	10.00
William Wilson	26	14	26.00	James Boone	14	7	17.00
J. & G. Laplin	26	9	19.00	James Boone	14	6	11.50
J. & G. Laplin	18	6	16.00	James Boone	39	6	14.00
James Irvin	30	2	101.00	James Boone	32	4	11.00
James Irvin	30	13	11.25	James Boone	9	4	20.25
James Irvin	30	14	10.50	James Boone	16	1	12.75
James Irvin	30	15	10.00	James Boone	e¼40	....	12.00
N. Coffman	28	3	22.00				

These sales in the aggregate amounted to $6,339, of which nearly the whole sum was expended in the erection of public buildings.

Early Settlers, etc.—Of above purchasers several were not residents of the town, but all, it is believed, were citizens of Washington County. A. B. Anthony was a merchant, associated in business for several years with L. Brodie. He succeeded in accumulating a large fortune, but subsequently removed to Texas, where he lost it all. Brodie died at his residence near Fayetteville. Mathew Leeper, W. McK. Ball, David Walker and Isaac Murphy were lawyers, and are mentioned elsewhere. W. T. Larremore was a prosperous merchant. He was also a minister of the Cumberland Presbyterian Church, and was in great demand as a camp-meeting preacher. He subsequently became a convert to the teachings of Alexander Campbell, and united with the Christian Church. After several years' residence in Fayetteville, during which time he represented the county in the Legislature one term, he removed to Texas, where he died two or three years later.

In this connection mention of Moses Campbell should not be omitted. He was one of the leading merchants of " the thirties," and built what at that time was considered the finest dwelling in this portion of the State. It was the house now occupied by Mr. Prentice. Mr. Campbell remained but a few years, and when he left sold the property to W. S. Oldham.

The Wallace family consisted of William Wallace, the father, and four sons: Willis S., Alfred, Leonard and Riley. They came to the county about 1831, and located on a farm some four or five miles east of Fayetteville. Soon after Alfred Wallace opened a general store on the west side of the public square, where for several years he carried on a prosperous business. Willis S. Wallace and one of the other brothers were the proprietors of a grocery.

James Byrnsides kept a hotel in a log building standing on the site of the Star livery stable. He was a man of some influence in the community, and in 1833 was elected a member of the Territorial Assembly. H. W. Mahan was a physician, and was killed by W. T. Blakemore, a son-in-law of Byrnsides.

William Skelton was a farmer and hatter, and lived two or three miles from town. W. D. Hart was a cabinet maker, and P. V. Rhea a blacksmith. John Lewis was also a blacksmith, and kept a hotel on what is known as Stone's Corner. M. H. Clark was a physician, and resided where Z. M. Pettigrew now does. Onesimus Evans was president of the Fayetteville branch of the State Bank. This institution was established in 1837, and did business in the two-story brick building standing about where the Van Winkle Hotel now is. William McK. Ball was the cashier. After an existence of four or five years it suspended, and the officers were charged with having stolen a part of the funds. Upon investigation it was found that the books had been carried away. One of them was subsequently found in White River, another in a stable loft in Fayetteville, and a third in an old stove. All had been badly mutilated, and the exact condition of the bank at the time of its failure was never ascertained. The most of those connected with it removed to Texas.

About 1839 Fayetteville received several citizens. Among them were James Sutton, Dr. T. J. Pollard, Stephen K. Stone, Dr. Charles W. Deane, Dr. Throckmorton, father of ex-Governor Throckmorton, of Texas; Dr. John I. Stirman, James H. Stirman and Alfred Stirman. Of these only two, Dr. T. J. Pollard and Stephen K. Stone, are now living. James Sutton was a Kentuckian, but had resided in Missouri prior to his coming to Fayetteville. He was engaged in merchandising until his death some time in "the fifties." His brother, Seneca Sutton, was also a merchant of Fayetteville for a time. Dr. Throckmorton lived in the country near town, and was a partner of Dr. Pollard until he removed to Texas. Dr. Deane came from Tennessee, and for nearly half a century was a leading physician and prominent citizen of Washington County. The Stirmans came from Kentucky. James H. and Alfred Stirman were brothers, and were partners in a general mercantile business. The former was afterward a member of the firm of Stirman & Dickson, and was a member of the constitutional convention of 1861. Dr. John I. Stirman was a brother of James H. Stirman, and from March, 1860, to November, 1862, was Secretary of State. A correspondent of the Van Buren *Intelligencer*, writing in 1849 from Fayetteville, describes the town as follows:

"The population of this place has not increased since 1844, rather diminished—it has followed the business and taken abode at Van Buren. The retail business here is important, and the merchants engaged in it are 'coining money' faster than they could do it in California. Messrs. Stirman and Dickson and James Sutton are indeed doing a fine business; and I must say that dry goods are retailed here as cheap as at Van Buren. This they are enabled to do on account of the small expense of store-keeping, living, etc.

"Fayetteville is the foremost town of Arkansas in the cause of education, and Washington stands second to no county in the State for schools. The Rev. C. Washbourne and Miss Sawyer are sturdy pioneers in the cause, and are entitled to the gratitude of parents and guardians for their perseverance under so many adverse circumstances. It was under Mr. Washbourne's charge of the matter that the Ozark Institute took its rise, under the style of 'Far West Seminary,' which, though it was destroyed by fire, phœnix-like rose from its ashes, and is now spreading its wings of literature and science over a pupilage of sixty scholars. This institution is under the control of Mr. Robert W. Mecklin, who is in every way qualified for the charge. His reputation has reached over the whole of Western Arkansas. He is assisted by Messrs. Lockhart and Van Hoose, both gentlemen of high literary acquirements. I learn that Rev. Robert Graham, a gentleman of high literary attainments and fine reputation as a scholar, h as been engaged, and will, some time next month, commence as assistant to Mr. Mecklin. This school, even in its infancy, far excels any other that I know of in the State. The Ozark Institute is about three miles from Fayetteville, in a beautiful and highly cultivated neighborhood, distinguished for its health.

"Miss James has a fine academy for young ladies, about a mile from the institute. It is a new establishment, but is in a progressive and flourishing condition. Miss J. has the reputation of being a fine teacher, and of an indefatigable spirit. At an early day she will, I doubt not, have a fine academy.

"At this place Miss Sawyer's Female Seminary stands No. 1 in the whole country, and the success of this institution is a gratifying testimonial to laudable perseverance. Miss S. commenced with a small beginning against many odds, which she controlled with an energy that would do honor to any leading spirit. Hers, indeed, is a leading spirit. She first sounded the tocsin of education, and sounded the death-knell of ignorance and vice. By her exertions a degree of intelligence and refinement is spread over this county, unseen and unfelt in other new countries. But I was going to speak of the school. The building is new, copious, convenient and neat, combining all the necessary requirements. About fifty pupils attend, the largest number of whom reside in the neighborhood, yet a considerable number are from abroad, who either board with Miss S. or in the neighborhood among the many clever families that reside here. The school has the benefits of the erudition of a splendid teacher and enlarged scholar in the person of Rev. C. Washbourne.

"Among the many beautiful cottages in sight from this place is the ' Waxhaus,' the homestead of the gallant and lamented Yell. Upon a high hill, about a mile off in the northwest, stands the residence of Judge Oldham, by far the most beautiful seat of all around. The judge has moved off to Texas, as I understand, about a week ago. Col. Leeper has built upon a neighboring hill. His fine improvements present a beautiful prospect, and as fine as is the view of this residence from town, yet much more so is the magnificent scenery around from thence. At one glance a beautiful panorama of nature and art is beheld —hill, valley, forest, prairie and stream.

" The ' yaller' fever rages here to a considerable extent, and for so healthy a country many will be carried off with it. About 100 will go from this county. They intended to go up the Arkansas and cross the mountains on Col. Fremont's last trace. The only reason I can learn for taking an unexplored route is that they believe Fremont has gone to some rich diggings that are not known to the public, and they wish to share the fruits of his discoveries. Among those going are Judge Murphy, Judge Davis, Dr. Cunningham, Dr. McCulloh and Lewis Evans, of this county, Judge Hoge, J. W. Washbourne and Pierce Miller, of Benton."

The following description of Fayetteville as it was in 1852 is condensed from an interesting sketch written by Hon. J. H. Van Hoose in 1882. Thirty years ago Fayetteville was a pretty little village of about 600 inhabitants, all of whom were industrious and happy. Arkansas College, presided over by Rev. Robert Graham, was fast coming into notice, and a large number of boys and young men, sons of wealthy planters of the South, were sent here each year to be educated. There was also a female seminary, founded by Miss Sawyer, who, with such assistants as those accomplished young ladies, Miss Foster and Miss Daniels and Prof. Zilliner, an accomplished musician, added much to make Fayetteville *then* famous for its educational facilities. Many beautiful young ladies from Missouri, the Indian country and South Arkansas attended this school. These school girls and the young men of Arkansas College, together with the young men of the town and our own beautiful girls, made Fayetteville society second to none in the State; in fact, from 1851 to 1861 there were very few towns in the South or West the size of ours where there could be found more prosperous business men, more gallant beaux, more charming and beautiful young ladies, better schools or more intelligent, industrious, happy and contented people than our own loved Fayetteville could produce.

In 1852 we elected a town council, with Col. James P. Neal as chief alderman or mayor, and Jim Ballard as town constable. There were then six dry goods stores in Fayetteville, all doing a profitable business. People from King's River and War Eagle country, from Benton and Crawford Counties and the Indian

Nation, bought all their goods here. James Sutton sold goods on the corner now occupied by Achard & Co. His store-room and warehouse was 30x150 feet, and he sold immense quantities of goods, and bought everything the farmers brought to him. Stirman & Dickson sold goods in a brick store-house located on the lot now occupied by the drug store of Whitlow & Lake. They, too, did a large business. S. K. Stone was selling goods in a small, one-story brick on the same spot where his splendid fireproof brick now stands. L. B. Cunningham did business in a two-story frame house on the corner where Hansard's gallery is now located. W. L. Wilson was selling goods in a frame house where Mulholland's grocery store is. Baker & Bishop, of Van Buren, had a store here in charge of William A. Watson. Merchants then bought goods only once a year, and it required about eight weeks to make the trip to New York and buy the year's goods.

There was no regular drug store in the town until 1854, when a young doctor named James Stevenson came here from Kentucky, and opened a drug store in a building about where the *Democrat* office is located.

There were two groceries or saloons in the town then, one kept by Capt. William McGarroh, on the McGarroh corner, and the other by Bill Throckmorton, on the west side of the square.

There were two hotels. One was on the corner where Kell's livery stable is, and was known as the "Byrnside House." The other stood on the south side of the street on a lot now occupied by the lumber yard, near the Methodist Church. This hotel was kept by John Onstott, and a man could get as good a dinner there for ten cents as any hungry man could wish for.

There were three blacksmith shops, run by John Lewis, John Krim and Jim and Dan Stone, and two wagon shops, one run by W. B. Taylor, now of Prairie Grove, and the other by Asmos Outzen. Joseph Dunlap carried on a saddlery shop, and Nathan Wilcox, a shoe shop. There was one cabinet shop, in which William M. Bowers made tables, bedsteads, coffins, etc., and two tailor shops, run by W. G. Bassore and James B. Simpson, respectively.

On July 4, 1860, Fayetteville was first placed in telegraphic communication with the remainder of the world. On that day Stebbins Telegraph Company completed a line from Jefferson City to Fort Smith, *via* Fayetteville. The first message was sent by Col. J. R. Pettigrew to the mayor of St. Louis, who returned an appropriate answer.

Newspapers.—The first newspaper published in Fayetteville was the Fayetteville *Witness*, in 1840, by C. F. Town. It was short lived, and there was no further attempt at newspaper publication in Washington County until the year 1852. On the 8th of May, 1852, the first number of the *Western Pioneer* was issued by William E. Smith, who had previously published the *Mountaineer*, at Huntsville, Ark. This paper was followed two years later by the *Southwest Independent*, William Quesenbury, editor and publisher. He was a racy and vigorous writer, an accomplished editor, and something of a humorist and poet. He continued the publication until some time in 1856. The town was then again without a newspaper until 1859. In that year J. R. Pettigrew and E. C. Boudinot established the *Arkansian*, a six-column folio, the first number of which appeared on March 5, 1859. The following were some of the objects for which the publishers stated the paper was established: "To advocate the principles of the Democratic party, and to stay the onrushing tide of abolitionism, which threatens to overwhelm the South; to advocate the building of a railroad from the Atlantic to the Pacific, and to secure its location on or near the thirty-fifth parallel, and to promote the cause of education." The paper was conducted with so much ability as to make it one of the most influential papers in the State, outside of Little Rock, and its circulation soon reached two thousand copies weekly. It reputation was supported not only by the well-known ability of its editors, but such writers as Quesenbury and Washbourne were frequent contributors to its columns. It was published until some time in 1861.

In August, 1860, W. W. Moore began the publication of the Fayetteville *Democrat*, but discontinued it during the war, owing to the destruction of the press and materials by the Confederates when evacuating Fayetteville. Moreover, the publisher joined the army and served until the close of hostilities.

In 1867 one Brown established a radical Republican paper,

called the *Radical.* Soon after R. C. Brown began the publication of a Democratic newspaper, called the Fayetteville *Times.* The two Browns became involved in a quarrel, and the latter fought and whipped the editor of the *Radical.* Shortly afterward the name of the *Times* was changed to the Fayetteville *Arkansian,* while the *Radical* was purchased by Bard & Richardson, and became the *Mountain Echo.* Richardson soon sold to Mr. Lindsay, and in 1870 Daniel Webster became the proprietor of the *Echo,* but Col. Bard had a claim upon the office and the material. He obtained possession of it, and established the *News,* which remained under his control until 1874, when it was suspended. Webster obtained new material, and continued the publication of the *Mountain Echo* until about January 1, 1873.

In 1868 E. B. & W. B. Moore purchased the press and material of the *Arkansian,* and re-established the *Democrat,* the first number of which was issued on the 4th of July, 1868. They conducted it until 1884, when it was purchased by S. E. Marrs and J. N. Tillman, the present proprietors. It has since been under the able editorial management of Mr. Marrs.

In the fall of 1879 Revs. Floyd and Shepherd, of the Christian Church, began the publication of a religious weekly, the Fayetteville *Witness,* which they continued about eighteen months.

On September 2, 1875, the first number of the Arkansas *Sentinel* appeared. It was established by the Sentinel Publishing Company, with the late Col. J. R. Pettigrew, one of the founders of the old *Arkansian,* as editor, and it was published under his name until his death. For several years, however, his control of it was only nominal. It is now owned by I. M. Patridge and H. F. Reagan, and is one of the most widely circulated and influential Democratic papers in Northwest Kansas.

Early in 1885 the Fayetteville *Republican* was established at West Fork. Jacob Yoes furnished the capital, and G. S. White became the editor. In the summer of 1886 it was purchased by W. M. Simpson, who removed the office to Fayetteville. He transferred it to Thomas Wainright, but, at the end of one month, resumed charge of it. In December, 1886, he sold out to Thomas Brooks and Damon Clarke. At that time it was a six-column folio, "patent outside," and had a subscription list of about 300. Messrs. Brooks & Clarke made it a seven-column folio, printed it all at home, and within a year had increased the circulation to 1,500 copies weekly. On January 10, 1888, Mr. Clarke purchased the interest of his partner, and has since been the editor and proprietor. The *Republican* is the organ of the Republican party in the Fourth Congressional District, and wields a decided influence in public affairs. For a short time in 1885 a daily paper, named the *Evening Call*, was published at Fayetteville, by T. P. Price, with Frank J. Price and Albert H. Price as editors.

A "Greenback" organ, called the *Blade*, was established in 1880 by John Moore, who, after about two years, sold out to F. M. Wolf, now of Springfield, Missouri. Wolf, changing the name and the politics of the paper, published for about six months the *Times*, a Republican sheet.

Societies.—The society of a town may in general be gauged by the number and character of its churches and societies. Measured by this standard Fayetteville ranks high, having seven churches and eight lodges, besides several other benevolent and social organizations. Washington Lodge No. 1, A. F. & A. M., as its number indicates, is the oldest Masonic lodge in the State. In 1835 a number of Masons in this part of the State petitioned the Grand Lodge of Tennessee for a lodge at Fayetteville, and on November 5, 1835, a charter, signed by Hugh L. White, Grand Master, was issued to Washington Lodge No. 82. Among the charter members were Onesimus Evans, W. M.; James McKissick, S. W.; Mathew W. Leeper, J. W.; Archibald Yell, Samuel Adams, Abram Whinnery, W. L. Wilson and William McK. Ball.

This charter has a history of its own. In 1862, when the Federal troops took possession of the town, it was thrown with other papers into the street, where it was picked up by a member of an Iowa regiment, a Mason, who sent it to Past Grand Secretary A. O. Sullivan, of Missouri. In 1866 it was sent to W. D. Blocher, and was by him transferred to J. H. Van Hoose, who returned it to the lodge. It is now in the possession of the Grand Lodge of Arkansas.

On November 21, 1838, representatives of four lodges met at Little Rock and organized the Grand Lodge of Arkansas. The delegates from Washington Lodge were Onesimus Evans, Washington L. Wilson, Robert Bedford, A. Whinnery, R. C. S. Brown, Samuel Adams and Williamson S. Oldham. Washington Lodge No. 82 now became Washington Lodge No. 1. About 1840 a two-story frame building was erected for a hall. The lot was donated by Governor Yell, who also gave $100 toward the erection of the building. This hall was remodeled in 1875, and is in a good state of preservation. In the winter of 1862, after most of the members of Washington Lodge had gone South, the Federal troops took possession of the hall, and Col. La Rue Harrison, the Post Commander, was here initiated into the order, as were also a number of other officers and privates. To this circumstance was doubtless due the preservation of the hall, when every other public building was destroyed.

The following is as complete a list of the Past Masters as could be obtained: John B. Costa, 1843; J. H. Stirman, 1848; W. R. Quarles, 1850; W. L. Wilson, 1851; J. M. Tibbetts, 1852; Robert Graham, 1855; W. R. Quarles, 1858; J. B. Simpson, 1859; Robert Graham, 1860; P. P. Van Hoose, 1861–65; J. H. Van Hoose, 1865–68; D. B. Jobe, 1868; J. H. Wilson, 1869; J. D. Henry, 1870–73; J. H. Kelton, 1873; W. O. Lattimore, 1874; P. R. Smith, 1874*; O. C. Gray, 1875; R. Putman, 1876; O. C. Gray, 1877; A. S. Gregg, 1878; J. H. Van Hoose, 1879–81; R. Putman, 1881; J. H. Van Hoose, 1882; J. R. Southworth, 1883; W. B. Welch, 1884; O. C. Gray, 1885–87; D. W. C. Davenport, 1887, and James J. Boss, 1888.

In 1841 the General Grand High Priest of the United States issued a dispensation to the Far West Chapter at Fayetteville, in answer to a petition signed by Joel Haden, Samuel Harris, William Shannon, Onesimus Evans, Thomas J. Pollard, Richard P. Pulliam, Alfred A. Stirman, Thomas Bean and Abraham Whinnery. The following year a charter was granted by the Grand Chapter, which, after the organization of the Grand Chapter of Arkansas in 1852, was replaced by another. The first records of the chapter, which are now in existence, are dated

---

* Filled the unexpired term of Lattimore.

April 21, 1854. W. L. Wilson was then High Priest, and J. L. Dickson, Secretary. The members numbered twenty. The High Priests since 1854 have been as follows: J. H. Stirman, 1855; W. R. Quarles, 1856; W. L. Wilson, 1857–60. (From October, 1860, to June, 1865, but one meeting was held.) James H. Van Hoose, 1865; D. B. Jobe, 1866; J. H. Van Hoose, 1867–69; Johnson Reynolds, 1869; J. H. Van Hoose, 1870–73; J. D. Henry, 1873; John Mayes, 1874; J. H. Van Hoose, 1875; O. C. Gray, 1876–79; J. H. Van Hoose, 1879–83; O. C. Gray, 1883; J. S. Hurlburt, 1884; T. J. Pollard, 1885–87; E. B. Wall, 1887; J. H. Van Hoose, 1888.

Baldwin Commandery No. 4, Knights Templar, was established in June, 1871, under a dispensation from W. S. Gardner, Grand Commander of the United States. There were then but two Sir Knights in Fayetteville—W. O. Lattimore and J. H. Van Hoose. The first meeting was held June 20, and several members of —— Commandery were present for several days, who assisted in the organization. The first officers elected and appointed were as follows: W. O. Lattimore, Eminent Commander; J. H. Van Hoose, Generalissimo; Abraham Allen, Captain-General; R. T. Lacey, Prelate; George A. Vaughan, Senior Warden; J. R. Pettigrew, Junior Warden; John Mayes, Treasurer; W. C. Roberts, Secretary; Samuel Bard, Standard Bearer; J. L. Lewis, Sword Bearer; B. F. Little, Warder; Henry Reed, Guard. In September of that year J. H. Van Hoose attended the Grand Encampment at Baltimore, and obtained a charter for Baldwin Commandery. The first regular election under the charter took place in January, 1872, when the officers above named were re-elected with the following exceptions: Dr. C. W. Deane was chosen Prelate; J. A. C. Blackburn, Recorder; B. F. Little, Standard Bearer; A. J. Gilbreath, Sword Bearer, and T. M. Gunter, Warder. Since then the Commanders have been elected as follows: George S. Allbright, 1874; O. C. Gray, 1876; J. H. Van Hoose, 1877; J. R. Pettigrew, 1878; George S. Allbright, 1879; D. W. C. Davenport, 1883; J. S. Hurlburt, 1885; J. R. Southworth, 1886.

Fayetteville Lodge No. 10,388, K. of L., dates its organization from June 17, 1887, when it was organized at Byrnes' Hall at Fayetteville.   The first officers elected were as follows: A. C. Hoag, M. W.; J. Tillman, W. F.; C. H. Putman, W. I.; W. Gakin, Almoner; S. H. Smith, F. S.; H. M. Rieff, Treas.; E. D. Erwin, Statistician; C. T. Carr, R. S.; John French, U. K.; A. Hodges, I. E.; John Zilla, O. E.; H. M. Rieff, Judge; D. Calvin, Judge Advocate. These, with twenty-five others, embrace the charter membership.   The lodge is composed of forty-eight Knights at present.   Their list of officers for the current year is F. E. Martin, M. W.; W. H. Merion, W. F.; D. Calvin, W. I.; John French, U. K.; E. Nix, Treas.; J. Nix, F. S.; W. French, R. S.; I. M. Baber, V. S.; T. F. King, Statistician; A. Hodges, I. E.; H. Broadie, O. E.; J. C. Van Hoose, Judge, and A. J. Boatright, Judge Advocate.

Fayetteville Lodge No. 28, A. O. U. W., began its existence December 29, 1887, when it was organized by J. C. Byers, D. G. M. W. of the Grand Jurisdiction of Texas.   Capt. E. B. Harrison was elected P. M. W., together with the following officers: E. Z. Davies, M. W.; G. E. G. Penn, Foreman; A. C. Hoag, O.; J. R. Southworth, Recorder; T. J. Martin, F.; S. H. Blackmer, Receiver; J. A. Hassel, G.; J. W. Bishop, I. W., and J. B. Nix, O. W.   These officers and twenty-two other members embrace the charter membership.   The only change in officers is the succession of W. A. Watson as Recorder.   The society have thirty-five "United Workmen" on their rolls at present, and the lodge is in good condition.   They meet in the Odd Fellows' Hall.

Frontier Lodge No. 1626, K. of H., at Fayetteville, became an independent society May 24, 1879, with twenty-six charter members.   The Knights of Honor have a large number of officers, and their first election resulted as follows: J. L. Cravens, P. D.; O. C. Gray, D.; E. D. Harrison, V. D.; E. B. Moore, Asst. D.; J. J. Vaulx, Chaplain; D. W. C. Davenport, Reporter; C. J. Sumstag, F. R.; J. L. Duke, Guide; H. S. Gray, Guardian; Albert Byrnes, Sentinel; Dr. C. S. Gray, Med. Examiner; J. S. O'Brian, Treas.; W. F. Stirman, L. D. Jernigan and O. C. Gray, Trustees.   Since their organization the Dictators of the order have been as follows: O. C. Gray, E. B. Harrison, E. D. Moore, H. S. Gray, C. M. Greene, Albert Byrnes, D. W. C. Davenport, Cuth P. Conrad, J. L. Cravens, C. S. Gray, Walter Cook, J. L.

Cravens, J. N. Thurmond, the present occupant of that chair. Their present officers are S. H. West, V. D.; Oscar Richter, Asst. Dictator; C. M. Greene, Reporter; W. C. Cardwell, F. R.; W. R. McIlroy, Treas.; J. J. Vaulx, Chaplain; W. W. Harrison, Guide; S. H. Blackmer, Guardian; J. L. Knesal, Sentinel; A. S. Gregg, Med. Ex.; E. D. Harrison, W. E. Nix and O. C. Gray, Trustees. The society meets in the I. O. O. F. Hall, and have rented from that order since the organization of the K. of H. Lodge.

Mountain Lodge No. 15, I. O. O. F., Fayetteville, Ark., was organized August 12, 1856, by Past Grand England and A. Clark, who installed the members. This veteran lodge elected the following officers: J. F. Rieff, N. G.; H. Marshall, V. G.; C. S. Hauptman, Sec., and A. Outzen, Treas. A. Clark was the only other charter member. During the war the general disruption affected the lodge, and the charter was lost; but on November 14, 1866, the lodge was granted a duplicate of the original charter, and on May 1, 1869, they reorganized permanently on a dispensation from G. M. Peter Brugman. Their lodge, on the memorable Sunday night of April 18, 1880, was destroyed by a cyclone, and after a few years of meeting in various places, they leased their present lodge for a term of five years, December, 1885. Among their present members the following are Past Grands: C. S. Hauptman, E. B. Moore, E. B. Wall, D. W. C. Davenport, J. F. Johnson, J. F. Simonds, J. J. Vaulx, H. F. Reagan, J. N. Tillman, B. H. Stone and C. B. Paddock, and their present officers are C. S. Hauptman, N. G.; W. L. Stukey, V. G.; J. F. Simonds, Sec., and J. N. Tillman, Treas. The lodge has $2,000 in the stock of the Building Loan Association of Fayetteville, and at the expiration of their lease propose to erect a commodious hall. At present they rent their rooms to three other local orders.

Travis Post No. 19, G. A. R., Fayetteville, Ark., was organized August 23, 1884, and the members were mustered in by C. M. Barnes, Adjutant General of the Department of Arkansas. The first officers chosen were the following: E. B. Harrison, P. C.; T. J. Hunt, Sr. V. C.; J. B. Coffey, Jr. V. C.; J. B. Cox, Adj.; J. V. Quick, Surgeon; L. D. Middleton, Chaplain; Lafayette Gregg, Quartermaster; C. M. Greene, Officer of the Day; William Mayes, Officer of the Guard; C. F. Lang, S. M.; P. M. Stephens, Q. M. S., and J. H. Harmon, Guard. These, with the following, constitute the charter membership: G. W. M. Reed, T. J. Taylor, W. O'Brian, J. H. Flood, W. Mayes, J. Clancy, Phillip McGuire, B. F. Rice, I. W. Daniel, J. F. Wilson, W. F. Jones, J. Armstrong, H. K. Stephens, Joseph Duncan, T. Brooks, J. K. Pool, S. S. Mayes, George Carney, D. Devilbiss, W. C. Roberts, J. M. Brinson, S. Cox, W. J. York. T. J. Hunt, H. Harmon, J. Harmon, J. H. Johnson, R. H. Clayton, Elias Andrew and C. W. Wright. The lodge lapsed after a few meetings, and was reorganized April 4, 1887. Their hall is on the second floor of the Byrnes & Blackmer Planing-mill Block, where, among the post relics, is a flag-staff, captured from Gen. Caball by the men under Lieut. Brooks. The present officers are Thomas Brooks, P. C.; W. O'Brian, Sr. V. C.; J. W. Quick, Jr. V. C.; W. J. York, Surgeon; Elias Armstrong, Chaplain; R. S. Curry, Officer of the Day; J. R. Lee, Officer of the Guard; J. C. McClellan, Adj.; S. H. Blackmer, Q. M. S., and W. A Todd, S. M. They have thirty-nine members.

Criterion Lodge No. 36, Knights of Pythias, of Fayetteville, was organized June 16, 1887, at the I. O. O. F. Lodge hall. The order began with the following charter members: J. C. Purdy, E. B. Harrison, Chas. M. Greene, R. C. Choate, C. A. Mulholland, John P. Wood, W. C. Cardwell, John A. Reed, J. S. McDanield, H. F. McDanield, Thomas Shores, Thomas W. White, Joseph T. Morris, H. D. Perky, J. L. Bozarth, John T. Jarrell, E. B. Wall, C. Dale, George Reed, Jr., Lafayette Reed, Damon Clarke, Frank Van Horn, J. B. Shannon, John N. Tillman, W. R. McIlroy and J. H. Williams. Of these, Mr. Harrison, P. C.; Mr. Greene, C. C.; Mr. Reed, V. C.; Mr. Clarke, P.; Mr. McIlroy, M. of E.; Mr. Dale, M. of F.; Mr. Tillman, K. of R., and Mr. Reed, Jr. M. at A., constituted the first list of officers. From the organization until the present the Chancellors Commanding have been as follows: E. B. Harrison, C. M. Greene, John A. Reed and John N. Tillman. The lodge now has a membership of fifty-seven, over whom are the following officers: J. N. Tillman, C. C.; W. C. Cardwell, V. C.; T. A. Hancock, M. at A.; W. R. McIlroy, M. of Ex.; W. L. Benbrook, M. of F., and J. J. Vaulx, the Prelate. The society use the I. O. O. F. Hall.

Municipal.—At the January term of the county court, in 1841, a petition signed by more than two-thirds of the taxable inhabitants praying for the incorporation of Section 16, Township 16 north, Range 30 west, was presented and granted. P. V. Rhea was appointed the first alderman, and John W. Johnson, John B. Costa, Richard P. Pulliam, Hosea G. Cardwell and M. W. Thornby, the first councilmen. This organization was maintained until 1859, when a city charter was obtained from the Legislature. The first election under the new charter was held in April of that year, when the following officers were chosen: J. W. Walker, mayor; J. W. Washbourne, C. E. Butterfield, P. P. Van Hoose, J. B. Simpson, A. Crouch, J. H. Stirman and E. C. Boudinot, councilmen. The next year the officers elected were Stephen Bedford, mayor; L. B. Cunningham, J. R. Pettigrew, J. Holcomb, C. E. Butterfield, J. T. Sutton, J. H. Van Hoose and W. T. Pollard, councilmen, and M. D. Frazer, marshal.

During the war the municipal government was suspended, and was not reinstated until 1867 or 1868, when M. LaRue Harrison was elected mayor. Some of the acts of the new municipal government were distasteful to the citizens of the town, and in 1869 an application was made to the Legislature to revoke the charter, which was done. An organization was then effected under a general statute, and E. I. Stirman was elected mayor. The order of incorporation was made by the county court, August 24, 1870, and he was elected in November upon a Democratic ticket. In November, 1871, T. Murray Campbell, a Republican, was elected mayor, A. J. Norris, recorder, and G. W. M. Reed, Alonzo Flanders, G. W. Taylor, Charles Smith and A. J. Blackwell, councilmen. One of the first acts of the new council was to adopt the following ordinance:

"Be it ordained, that all ordinances and parts of ordinances passed by the former council, except those in relation to the agricultural college, be and hereby are repealed up to date of November 7, 1871."

The municipal government was maintained under this organization until 1885, when Fayetteville became a city of the second class.

The following is a list of the mayors elected since the retirement of T. Murray Campbell: J. R. Pettigrew, 1872–73; George A. Grace, 1873–74; Robert J. Wilson, 1874–76; A. M. Wilson, 1876–77; A. S. Vandeventer, 1877–80; J. H. Van Hoose, 1880–81; W. C. Jackson, 1881–83; C. W. Walker, 1883–84; Samuel E. Marrs, 1884–85; W. C. Jackson, April to December, 1885; R. J. Wilson, January to April, 1886; O. C. Gray, April, 1886, to October, 1887; E. B. Wall, October, 1887, to April, 1888; J. H. Van Hoose, elected for a term of two years, beginning April, 1888.

Business Development.—The Civil War dealt harshly with Fayetteville. Her churches and institutions of learning, all of her public buildings, and many others, were destroyed, while her people were scattered all over the South, financially broken and morally disheartened. But an intelligent and enterprising community, possessing the natural advantages that belong to Fayetteville, cannot be permanently "downed." No sooner had hostilities ceased than the work of restoration began, and the city of to-day is a lasting monument to its extraordinary recuperative powers. The location of the State University here in 1871 marks a long step forward, but the completion of the St. Louis & San Francisco Railroad added an element of still greater importance to the growth of the city. The population is now not far from 4,000, and in 1887 the estimated total business transactions amounted to more than a million and a half dollars. The following is a running account of its business:

McIlroy's bank (private) was opened in 1872 under the name Denton D. Stark & Co., with William McIlroy as a large owner in it. Mr. Stark had the management of the business until 1878, when Mr. McIlroy assumed complete control. On July 1, 1886, the present firm name was adopted, the capital being owned by the McIlroy estate. W. R. McIlroy is cashier, and is assisted by C. M. Greene. Their resources are as follows: Loans and discounts, $88,978.60; overdrafts, $1,538.73; building, furniture, etc., $4,500; due from banks (good on draft), $50,487.71; cash, exchange and other items, $26,343.80; total, $171,878.84. Liabilities: Capital, $25,000; surplus and profits, $9,231.67; due depositors, $137,614.42; due banks, $32.75; total, $171,878.84. Loans made during 1887, $50,923.35; correspondents, Chemical National Bank, New York; Continental Bank, St. Louis, and the First National Bank, Little Rock.

The Washington County Bank was chartered November 6, 1884, under the State banking laws, by W. B. Welch, president; J. A. Ferguson, vice-president; B. R. Davidson, T. F. Jones, directors, and S. P. Pittman and A. L. Williams. The first four directors and two officers mentioned, with Mr. MacDevin as cashier, constituted the first organization. These men represent an estimated worth of $320,000. The officers remain unchanged, excepting S. P. Pittman, as vice-president and director, *vice* J. A Ferguson. The resources of the bank are as follows: Discounts and loans, $55,943.25; bonds and stocks, $25,000; county warrants, cash value, $2,300; real estate, furniture and fixtures, $5,700; due from banks, $21,148.32; cash on hand, $20,267.54; total, $130,359.11. Liabilities, capital stock, $12,000; surplus, $6,400; undivided profits, $4,056.42; due other banks, $641.20; due depositors, $107,261.49; total, $130,359.11. Loans made in 1887, $290,000; exchange in 1887, $480,000; average daily clearance, $20,000; correspondents, National Park Bank, New York; Bank of Commerce, St. Louis; First National Bank, Fort Smith; German National Bank, Little Rock, and Merchants' Loan and Trust, Chicago.

Fayetteville Building and Loan Association, No. 1, permanent, was incorporated and began business March 11, 1886. E. B. Harrison was chosen president; J. W. Stirman, secretary; D. W. C. Davenport, treasurer; B. R. Davidson, attorney; E. B. Harrison, J. C. Williams, Albert Byrnes, G. T. Lake, J. L. Duke, H. K. Wade and C. W. Trott, directors. Their stock is divided into two series of $100,000 each, and each series is divided into 4,000 shares, valued at $25 each. Monthly dues are 12½ cents per share, and premiums are from 15 to 30 per cent. The present officers are President, E. B. Harrison; secretary, C. M. Greene; treasurer, W. R. McIlroy; attorney, E. D. Wall; directors, E. B. Harrison, G. T. Lake, A. Byrnes, J. L. Cravens, J. L.

Duke, C. Dale and J. L. Bozarth. The association has been a powerful agent in the development of Fayetteville.

The Fayetteville Electric Light and Power Company was organized as a stock company in January, 1888, with the following officers: President, E. B. Harrison; directors, A. Byrnes, J. S. McDaniel, Lee Baum, J. L. Cravens, G. T. Lake and J. L. Duke. Their chartered stock was $36,000. Their plant, valued at $8,000, has a capacity of 460 Heisler incandescent lamps of 20-candle power each; however, they have now but about 250 lamps, distributed on streets, in churches, hotels, etc. The H. F. McDaniel Railway Supply Company is one of the largest in the State. The Fayetteville Street Railway Company's president is I. J. Ronan, and W. L. Killebrew is secretary and superintendent.

In general merchandise are Baum & Bro., Reed & Ferguson, Campbell & White, C. C. Conner & Co., Wood & Co., B. H. Stone & Co., R. S. Curry, Boles & Co. and "The Famous" of Jesse Ellis. The grocers and general stores are represented by Mulholland & Lake, Gilbreath & Taylor, Wilson & Dickson, W. W. Harrison, C. M. Bigelow, Blakeley Bros., Lantrip & Miller, Moore & Gallaher, A. B. Lewis, Randall & Oliver and D. A. Coker. In the line of bakery, restaurant, confectionery, etc., are August A. G. Hach, Hodge & Riggs, Ira Turner, C. M. Bigelow, U. G. Pearce, N. L. Dickson & Co., T. Satterfield & Co. and J. F. Johnson. Hardware is headed by E. B. Harrison, E. Z. Davies, W. N. Crenshaw and R. R. Smith. W. F. Russell and John Cox are barbers. Jesse Ellis deals in, and John Feathers manufactures, boots and shoes. J. L. Duke and J. Wadkins have jewelry and time-piece establishments. Z. Thomas is a cigar maker. Mrs. S. J. Young and J. W. Hansard are photographers. Books and stationery are handled by J. D. Van Winkle and W. C. Cardwell. Gregg & Smith, Benbrook & Co., W. H. Whitlow, J. H. Williams & Co. and W. W. Dickey are in the drug and pharmacy trades. John F. Buie, undertaker. Saddlery and harness are in the hands of George Sutton and S. J. Jones. Implements of various kinds are sold by S. L. Kyle, John M. Howe and Cato Bros. Mrs. M. M. Allbright & Co. deal in musical instruments. D. M. Harbison and Carter & Taylor have meat markets. The Van Winkle House, by R. S. Miller, Mountain House, by Thomas Jennings,

Tremont House, by H. L. Glass, and Quarles House, by E. Quarles represent the hotels. The Sweitzer Wagon Co., president, E. B. Harrison, and Ellis Duncan, secretary and superintendent. The Fayetteville Evaporator Company, by Campbell & White. The Bed Spring Manufacturing Co., proprietor, Thomas Jennings. The tailors are Baum Bros. and McFadden. W. L. Call, R. T. Smith and J. W. Quick are blacksmiths. H. F. Buie has a billiard hall. The legal fraternity are L. Gregg, B. R. Davidson, A. M. Wilson, J. V. Walker, J. D. Walker, C. W. Walker, J. W. Walker, T. M. Gunter, W. L. Gregg, R. J. Wilson, J. W. Stuckey, E. B. Wall, S. H. West, G. W. M. Reed, Jr., R. W. Carter, W. J. Patton and C. R. Buckner. Real estate is handled by Davidson & Jones and Dickson & Pettigrew (also abstractors of title), Reed & Carter and E. B. Wall. Mr. Keenan buys wheat. Drs. W. B. Welch, H. D. Wood, T. J. Pollard, Wade Pollard, C. S. Gray, A. S. Gregg, J. B. Massie and O. L. Wilson represent the medical fraternity, while the dental profession has Drs. J. R. Southworth, S. D. Luther and R. B. Horton for their representatives. The newspapers are elsewhere mentioned. Livery, Simmon & Ferguson, J. E. Vaughan and Thomas Jennings. The Fisher Transfer Company. Furniture, J. L. Bozarth, The Fayetteville Manufacturing Company, and McClelland. Produce shippers, Campbell & White, McNabb & Rogers and Oscar Richter. The Waters-Pierce Oil Company, J. P. Marbut, manager. Brick and stone masons, Willard Algine & Company and S. H. Blackmer (brick yards also), Charles Dodt and R. M. Jestice. Fayetteville Bottling Works. City Laundry, A. A. Hollister, proprietor. City Bath Rooms, J. T. Watson. The Fayetteville Steam Dye Works. Millinery, Baum & Bros., B. H. Stone & Co. and Mrs. Abbott. Mills, Byrnes & Blackmer and J. S. McClelland (planing), and the Fayetteville Flouring Mills, J. F. Cravens, lessee. The Fayetteville Foundry and Machine Shops, manager, A. Volner. Lumber trade, C. Dale and Cazort Bros. Contractors and builders, Mix & Co., I. N. Baker, F. P. Milburn and O. H. Marion. Architect and superintendent, C. M. Prentice. Insurance, J. H. Van Hoose and E. B. Wall. Sewing machines, L. Matney.

SPRINGDALE.

This is now a horticultural and commercial place, although its founding was due to religious purposes. As in many other cases the immediate cause of the settlement was the noble spring near a tree across the road west of Haxton & Co.'s woolen mills, but which, during the war, broke out at a period about 400 feet distant from its first opening, and south of the mills. The following entries of land in this part of the county will show what material there was for a settlement: Township 18 north, Range 30 west, Section 36—John Holcomb, September 1, 1845; S. P. Fine, February 29, 1840; W. G. Quinton, March 16, 1840; John Holcomb, September 18, 1856; Joseph Holcomb, December 29. 1852; James Fitzgerald, March 7, 1840; Isaac S. Fitzgerald, December 29, 1849, April 2, 1853, December 26, 1849, and April 9, 1855; W. H. Holcomb, January 11, 1853; Section 35—Freeborn Graham, February 28, 1840; Section 30 —John Ingram, April 24, 1840; Thomas M. McLain, January 2, 1831; Section 31—William Barrington, September 5, 1849; Jacob Pearson, November 29, 1851; Section 32—John Ingram, November 22, 1848; John Hamilton, November 7, 1840. Township 17 north, Range 30 west, Section 1—James Brandon, Octo- 29, 1838; W. D. Quinton, September 19, 1839; Section 2—John Fitzgerald, February 9, 1839; Isaac S. Fitzgerald, October 25, 1838. Township 18 north, Range 29 west, Section 30—John Fitzgerald, June 6, 1840; Joshua Fitzgerald, June 6, 1840; Section 29—S. White, September 12, 1840; W. Graham, June 12, 1840, and J. S. Graham, August 2, 1848. These are some of the earlier entries of the region of Springdale and Elm Springs, covering the plats of both places. The earliest settlers, then, about Springdale's site were the Fitzgeralds, James Brandon, W. D. Quinton, the Grahams, S. P. Fine, the Holcombs and S. White, together with some others at various dates, as Elijah Lee, William Easley and James Mayfield.

Many of these were adherents of the Primitive Baptist faith, and soon after their arrival held meetings at various places, and among the first visiting preachers were Rev. James Mayfield and Rev. John Holcombe (he retained the final *e*). Mr. Joseph Holcomb thinks the first members were Elijah Lee, William

Graham, William Easley, Freeborn Graham and wife, Ira Graham and wife.   The church was organized in 1840, and given the biblical name Shiloh, and on Christmas day, 1841, William D. Quinton deeded a plat at the spring, six rods by twenty rods, to the trustees of the church, William Easley, Elijah Lee and Freeborn Graham, for the site of a church.   They soon erected a log church, and in 1843 found their first regular pastor in the person of Rev. John Holcombe, who bought of W. D. Quinton, and entered all the present plat of Springdale, and more, to the amount of 600 acres.   From this time on to the present the place attracted attention through the well-known and largely attended " May Meetings " of this sect, in which the ceremony of " feet-washing " is performed.   They have been held regularly, with three exceptions during the war.   Rev. Holcombe built him a home, and also established a wagon-shop in which he employed four or five men, but aside from these and his wife and several children, and Shelby Fitzgerald, there were no residents on the site of Springdale for over twenty years.   With dangers of the opening war arising, Rev. Holcombe and the most of his family sought refuge in Texas, and during the first year all their buildings were burned by men claiming to be Federal soldiers.

Following the close of hostilities he and the family returned, at once rebuilt the church, and built his home on the elevation just east of the woolen mills.   This was in 1866.   In July, 1868, he laid out the original town of Shiloh, on the west side of Spring Creek, about the old church plat.   The first store was opened by R. S. Coon, whose stock was purchased the following year by Holcomb & Putman.   In 1870 Joseph Holcomb returned from his travels succeeding his war service, and bought the old homestead, excluding the town plat.   The Missionary Baptist College was about the next addition to the town of Shiloh, although it was short lived.   It was organized in 1872.   (Its growth will be treated of in the chapter on schools.)   Then Mr. Jack Steele opened a general store.   In 1875 the post-office was established, and the name changed to Springdale.   The postmaster appointed was B. E. Putman, and the successors to that position have been W. H. Lovelady, C. C. Phillips, B. W. Gregg, J. B. Gill and W. Y. Winton, the present incumbent.

Its Growth.—The growth of the village was so marked that incorporation began to be agitated, and the most active in this, as in other enterprises for the good of the place, was Joseph Holcomb, "the father of the town," as he is familiarly styled. By an order of the county court on April 1, 1878, "the town of Springdale" was incorporated. June 14, 1879, the following officers were elected, and on July 4 sworn in: Joseph Holcomb, mayor; W. R. Ritter, C. Petross, A. J. Hale, J. B. Baggett and R. M. Huffmaster, aldermen, and S. S. Purcell, recorder. The successors of Mr. Holcomb to the mayoralty have been: R. M. Huffmaster, O. C. Ludwig, Mr. Holcomb a second time, W. G. Prunner, S. L. Staples, for two terms, and Millard Berry, who is now serving his second term. The present aldermen are Joseph Holcomb, J. F. Barr, N. S. Haxton, E. A. Linebarger and Wilson M. Davis; treasurer, C. Petross, and recorder, E. H. Bryant.

During about a decade, in the earlier half of which was the date of incorporation, some of the following firms opened their respective places: W. H. Lovelady, the successor of Holcomb & Putnam; Slaughter & Seacy, A. M. Phillips and Joseph Holcomb with general stores; in the hardware line, J. A. Coffelt, Gill & Harris (afterward Deaver & Harris, and Deaver & Co.); wagon-shop, Drum & Phillips; flouring-mill, Petross & Son; evaporator, D. Wing & Bro.; nursery, J. B. Gill; Springdale Canning Co., president, J. R. Harris; lumber yard, A. J. Armstrong, and a newspaper, mentioned elsewhere.

The construction of the "Frisco Railway" during 1881 gave an impetus to the growth of Springdale, greater, probably, than any other place in the county, and it has been so marked as to be denominated a "boom." Putman's Addition to the town was laid out on the west, and afterward Joseph Holcomb laid out Railroad Addition on the south and east. Business spread itself along the street leading to the depot. The railway outlet for produce and fruit made those two industries the most prominent, and gave Springdale a leadership in the general fruit-growing interests of this part of the State, equal to any.

The general merchandise trade is represented by B. F. Deaver & Co., Dodson & Co., Lane, Linebarger & Co., Searcy & Sons, D. A. White and Martin & Livingston, while the grocers are G. M. Gabbert, C. W. Wright and Theo. Parker. W. T. Farrar and J. R. Harris & Bro. deal in hardware, and the drug trade is handled by H. A. Daily, W. Y. Winton and A. Starkweather. The Springdale Canning Co., a stock company, has a large factory. The Springdale Nurseries, owned by Gill & Vincenheller, another owned by A. M. Kennan & Son, and Zimmerman & Bryan represent the fruit interests. The W. B. Haxton & Co. Woolen Mills and the Springdale Milling Co. (roller mill) represent the mills. Phillips & Phillips and J. R. Harris & Bro. have lumber yards. Real estate is handled by Berry & Harris, while Millard Berry and A. J. Hale are lawyers.

The Springdale House, Thomas Gladden, proprietor, is the only hotel, while the bakeries, restaurants, confectioneries, etc., are represented by R. E. Renner, J. W. Kensil, Mr. Yocum and Mr. Davis. Drs. John Young, D. Christian, J. M. Kennedy and W. J. Wilkerson are the medical representatives, while Dr. J. B. Dare cares for the dental needs of the community. A. M. Kennan and Roach & Vinson are shoemakers; Charles A. Minney, barber; Sevier & Lewis, J. B. Baggett and G. W. Bowman care for wagon and blacksmith interests; Bobert Orr and W. H. Russell have tin shops; Stokes & Bro. are liverymen; W. T. Farrar, harness-maker; E. T. Caudle and J. W. Carter have brick yards; a dairy is owned by W. Hewitt; milliners, Miss Mary Hodges and Miss Fannie Kensil; furniture is handled by B. H. Welch and B. F. Pollock; meat market, J. B. Henson; jeweler and photographer, George F. Kennan; plasterers, Van Dyke & Bartholomew; and among the sixteen or seventeen contractors and builders are C. W. Phillips, Stork & Gaut, D. M. Linebarger and C. A. Jones.

The Springdale *News* is the only newspaper. Its existence began in 1882 under the title of the Springdale *Enterprise*, O. C. Ludwig, editor, and a year or so later H. C. Warner purchased it and gave it the name Springdale *Yellow Jacket*. Price & Bro. then ran it for a brief interval under the cognomen Springdale *Journal*. Damon Clarke gave it its present title when he assumed control in 1886, but he sold out to H. M. & J. Van Butler, whose editorial charge, under the appellation *The Arkansaw Locomotive*, with which they headed the paper, closed May 1, 1887. The present editor, John P. Stafford, has since had charge of it, and has resumed the title *News*. Its political policy is Democratic.

The schools and churches of Springdale appear in the chapter on those subjects. Three societies, a farmers' club, the Masonic and G. A. R., are in a prosperous condition; two, the I. O. O. F. order and the W. C. T. U., once organized, are abandoned.

The Springdale Farmers' Club was organized in January, 1886, with W. M. Davis, president, and John B. Gill as secretary. The club has been one of the powerful instruments in the development of Springdale. They have introduced fine stock, particularly a Holstein bull and Berkshire hogs, the latter being the property of the organization. New varieties of fruit have been introduced and experimented with, amongst which is the noted early red peach, "The Gov. Garland," named and discovered by J. B. Gill. The shipping interests have been worked up by them. A successful live-stock show was held at Springdale in the fall of 1887 by the society, and they now have the finest collection of grains and grasses in the State for exhibition in the fall of 1888. The society has fifteen wide-awake members. I. D. Rader and John B. Gill have filled the office of president since the first incumbent. J. D. Beck is secretary.

Societies.—Springdale Lodge No. 316, F. & A. M., was chartered in 1873, and organized by James D. Henry, D. D. G. M. The first officers chosen were J. B. Steele, W. M.; W. H. Lovelady, S. W.; D. C. Smithson, J. W.; A. G. Smith, Treas.; J. R. Harris, Secy.; C. Petross, S. D.; Peter Graham, J. D.; and W. B. Smith, Tyler. They began with seventeen members, and have increased to fifty, with lodge property valued at $500. The present officers are D. Christian, W. M.; B. S. Williams, S. W.; W. N. Pierce, J. W.; C. Petross, Treas.; Evans Atwood, Secy.; L. D. Petross, S. D.; W. F. Daily, J. D., and E. Adams, Tyler. A list of Masters is as follows: B. Putman, N. D.; J. B. Steele (chartered), H. G. Hartley, W. H. Lovelady, W. M. Harris, J. A. Armstrong, B. F. Deaver, J. S. Patterson and the present incumbent. Messrs. Putman, Hartley, Harris, Lovelady and Deaver have served more than one term.

U. S. Grant Post No. 34, G. A. R., at Springdale, was chartered October 30, 1886, and the members were mustered in by S. P. Gilbreath, of West Fork. They had nineteen members, and elected the following officers: B. R. Butcher, C.; J. Smith, Sr. V. C.; C. W. Wright, Jr. V. C.; B. C. Cox, Adj.; A. W. Baker, Q.; R. E. Renner, Chaplain; J. T. Sullivan, Surgeon; John Vernon, O. of D.; J. W. Langford, O. of G.; S. Mayes, Q. S. They have a hall in the Searcy Block, and number sixty-five members. Present officers: J. Smith, C.; W. Mayes, Sr. V. C.; A. W. Baker, Jr. V. C.; C. W. Wright, Q.; R. E. Renner, Chaplain; E. P. Hall, Adj.; J. Vernon, O. of D.; E. A. Ellis, O. of G.; J. Pollett, S. M.; J. Conger, Q. S.; J. T. Sullivan, Surgeon.

OTHER TOWNS AND VILLAGES.

Elm Springs.—This name is derived from probably the largest of Washington County springs, and is a settlement six miles west of Springdale, located among great springs of such power that, not far from their openings, John Ingram, in 1844, found them strong enough to run a water-mill. This was the earliest mill in this part of the county, and was the nucleus of the village.

From the entries given in connection with the Springdale land entries, it is seen that Mr. Ingram made the first entry on the site of Elm Springs, in 1840, and that in that region Thomas M. McLain entered land as early as January 2, 1831. William Barrington, Jacob Pearson and John P. Hamilton made entries in 1849, 1851 and 1840, respectively. A Mr. Rose was a very early settler there, but no record of his having entered land exists. After the location of the mill Mr. Ingram was joined by William Barrington, who also opened a store, and gave the name Elm Springs to the new settlement. His miller was W. F. Deaver. Mr. Barrington bought out Mr. Ingram, and some time afterward sold a half interest in the mill to B. J. Deaver—the firm then bearing the name Deaver & Barrington. After 1852 a blacksmith shop was added, and soon the schools under Rev. and Mrs. Jesse McAllister were opened. At this period the population of the place had probably reached its highest. A few years later an epidemic broke up the school. One of the first stores opened was owned by Barrington, Shelton & McAllister, and a pioneer named "Hosey" Moses had a small establishment. Early church buildings will be mentioned in the pages devoted to those subjects. Among the business men since the war have been Dr. Christian, F. F. Webster, James Pollock, Trotter & Wasson, B. J. Davis, Farrar & Reed. Elm Springs post-office was established in 1848, W. Barrington, postmaster. In 1852 W. S. Deaver was postmaster, and was followed by John Reavis, who held the office until the discontinuance of mails, in 1861. The postmasters since 1865 have been Miss M. W. Pearson (now Mrs. Wasson), J. R. Pollock, James Grimsly, James Trotter, T. F. Webster, R. L. Ritter, W. T. Farrar, R. L. Ritter, B. J. Beaver and W. V. Steele, the present incumbent.

The war almost depopulated Elm Springs, and its business has not since risen above its present condition. The mills, which once made the place a center of trade, have long since disappeared, and what remains is general business, represented by the following firms: In general merchandise—M. D. Steele, R. L. Ritter, G. A. Wilkerson and W. V. Steele deal in drugs, notions, etc.; Garrison & Pearson manage the marble trade; Smith & Robinson are blacksmiths; E. M. Hilsabeck holds the shoe trade; Drs. T. G. Welch, D. C. Summers and G. A. Wilkerson are the physicians; J. M. Robinson, J. P., and B. J. Deaver, N. P., are the sources of legal light. One lodge is also in operation, the F. & A. M.

West Fork.—This place and its vicinity had settlers who entered land as early as April 25, 1836. The following entries were made in that region: William Bloyd, October 24, 1840; James Wynn, July 16, 1840; Eli Bloyd, August 19, 1840; Peter Bloyd, November 10, 1840; John Graham, May 7, 1836; George Putmer, April 10, 1837; Robert McPhail, April 25, 1836; Moses Graham, July 9, 1838; Evan Harrer, July 10, 1838; J. F. Tamison, December 12, 1838, and Benjamin Hardin, April 25, 1836. The general settlement went under the name of West Fork, but its village life did not begin until about 1875 or 1876, when the old water-mill plant at the head of the creek was moved there, and the steam mills built. This was carried out by H. H. Davis, D. Robinson and W. H. Brock. Following this was a carding-machine, introduced by M. M. Morrow, and John Hughes became the first merchant. A spoke-factory was established by J. M. Langston, soon followed by a Mr. Bentley. H. H. Davis and J. M. Langston soon became proprietors of the mill, and added a black-smith shop; and a Mr. Bell soon added another place where the anvil's ring could be heard. Hughes, the merchant, soon disposed of his stock to Jacob Yoes and a Mr. Simco, but on the completion of the "Frisco" railway he reopened another establishment.

The construction of the St. Louis & San Francisco Railway was as great a boon to West Fork as to other places along the line. An outlet for its fruits, produce and timber led to rapid development in the village, until its business is now represented by the following establishments: Jacob Yoes and Gilbreath & Langston lead in merchandise; F. J. Males has a fine drug store; J. P. Cox deals in groceries; hardware and implements are handled by Jacob Yoes; a meat market is owned by Thomas Everett; C. Stapleton deals in furniture; J. W. Bell, and D. H. and D. K. Barron are blacksmiths. The West Fork Hotel is owned and managed by Dr. A. S. Fleming. The proprietors of the West Fork Flouring Mills are Yoes & Crider. The West Fork Canning and Evaporating Company is a local stock company, with a capital of $25,000, and $8,500 already invested in equipment. The president is S. P. Sample; secretary, G. S. White, and superintendent, C. K. Winslow. Mr. Sample, H. H. York, G. A. Yoes, J. W. Robertson, Thomas Walker, J. F. Collyer and J. C. Oldham are directors. The company also own a can factory. Lozier's Nursery is owned by Fred. Lozier. J. M. Phillips is a contractor and builder. Drs. J. S. Cannon, S. P. Sample and A. S. Fleming represent the medical fraternity. Thomas McKnight, J. P., J. C. Oldham, N. P., and G. S. White, N. P., attend to legal business.

The post-office was moved from the present site of Pitkin, which then bore the name West Fork. The first incumbent of that office was H. H. Davis; he was followed by J. W. Hughes, W. Simco, himself and J. P. Cox, who is now in charge. A well-known deputy postmaster was J. M. Langston.

Four fraternities are represented, the G. A. R., F. & A. M., I. O. O. F. and Knights of the Horse.

West Fork was incorporated in May, 1885, and the following officers chosen: Mayor, J. M. Phillips; recorder, J. A. Smith; marshal, Joshua Carmen; aldermen, H. H. Davis, H. H. York, S. P. Sample, W. E. Shanks and N. Northern. Messrs. Simpson and Emerson have served as mayors, also. The officers for 1888 are as follows: Mayor, J. M. Phillips; recorder, J. B. Lansdell; treasurer, S. P. Sample; marshal, N. Northern; aldermen, J. C. Carmen, J. F. Collyer, J. D. Sample, Thomas McKnight and James Emerson.

Prairie Grove.—This is the third town in Washington County in population and importance. It is situated in the midst of one of the most beautiful valleys in Northwestern Arkansas, and within a short distance of the geographical center of the county. Its site was first settled by Rev. Andrew Buchanan in 1829, and by his influence a school and a church were established soon after. He died in 1857, leaving his real estate by will to his widow during her life-time. At her death, with the exception of eighty acres, it was to go to Cane Hill College, and in event of the failure of that institution it was to become the property of the Cumberland Presbyterian Book Concern, at Nashville, Tenn. The eighty acres were to go to two servants. This bequest naturally produced serious complications in the title. In 1871 Col. James P. Neal, a step-son of Mr. Buchanan, obtained deeds from the various parties interested in the property, and took up his residence on the old homestead. He then conceived the idea of founding a town, and soon after secured the establishment of a post-office, of which he was made postmaster. In 1872 a blacksmith and wagon-shop was opened by Rogers & Baggett, and in 1875 a store-house was erected, and a stock of goods put into it. The following year McPhetridge, Baggett & Rogers erected a large steam flouring-mill, and in 1877 the town was regularly laid out. The first sale of lots took place on March 24 of that year. Since that time the town has steadily improved, and now has a population of about 500.

In 1885 a weekly newspaper called the Prairie Grove *News* was established by Joseph Garrison, and published for about one year. In April, 1887, H. Milton Butler began the publication of the Prairie Grove *Banner*, which he has since continued. The

Rising Sun was published for a short time in 1887, but was soon bought out by the *Banner*.

The two most important manufacturing enterprises of the town are the Prairie Grove Mills, now owned and operated by H. C. & G. W. Crowell, and the Prairie Grove Canning and Evaporating Factory, operated by a joint-stock company. The latter enterprise was recently established. The officers of the company are E. G. McCormick, president; D. F. McMillan, vice-president; W. I. Cook, secretary; W. T. McCormick, treasurer; D. K. Hulbert, superintendent. The directors are E. G. McCormick, C. G. Marrs, J. O. Parks, W. P. Dyer, D. F. McMillan, S. B. Hardy and J. H. Flood. The authorized capital stock is $25,000, of which $8,000 has been paid in. The factory is supplied with all the latest improved machinery for canning and evaporating fruit. It has a capacity of 10,000 cans per day by the canning process, and 250 bushels per day when evaporating fruit or vegetables.

The mercantile interests of Prairie Grove are represented by the following individuals and firms: General stores, H. C. & G. W. Crowell, B. A. Carl, W. N. Butler & Co., Hardy & Marrs, W. P. Dyer and D. F. McMillan; furniture, H. H. Collier; harness and saddlery, A. Dixon & Co.; druggists, McCormick & Co. and H. C. Crowell; jewelry, musical instruments, etc., Simmons & Henderson; marble works, Leach & Dorman; hardware, Baggett & Sanders; lumber, J. V. Rich.

Occidental Lodge No. 436, A. F. & A. M., of Prairie Grove, was organized March 20, 1886, with the following officers: J. E. Mock, W. M.; E. G. McCormick, S .W.; J. J. Baggett, J. W.; G. E. James, S. D.; J. O. Parks, J. D.; W. R. Wallace, Treas.; R. S. Staples, Sec., and W. D. Rogers, Tyler. The membership at present numbers twenty-eight. The meetings are held in the institute building. E. G. McCormick is now W. M.; W. W. Mahan, S. W.; A. Sanders, J. W.; W. N. Butler, Sec., and J. J. Baggett, Treas.

Boonsboro.—Eight miles southwest of Prairie Grove is this flourishing community of two or three hundred souls. It is in one of the oldest settled sections of the county, and dates its existence as a village from the "thirties." The first store was opened by Morris Wright in 1834 or 1835, in a little log cabin, just north of the present village. In 1840 he removed a little further south, and continued in business until the war. At about the same time Levi Richards and White McClellan opened a second store, and John F. Truesdale erected a steam mill just below the town, where some ten years before a small water mill had been built by Thomas Garvin.

The establishment of Cane Hill College in 1852 somewhat increased the importance of the village, but in 1860 it could boast of only two stores. These were kept by McClure & Mc-Clellan and Wright & Lewis. At the close of the war E. W. McClellan & Son, Lewis & Ayres and Warren Stewart were among the first merchants to resume business.

The great distance of the town from the railroad has somewhat obstructed its growth, yet it has made steady improvement. The following is a directory of its present business interests: Edmiston & Co., J. Edmiston, S. T. Cole, McBride & Haygood and Cowley & Welch, general stores; J. W. Cope, druggist; Ross & Blackburn and Mrs. M. L. Mann, millinery; W. F. Easterley, wagon-maker; Russell & Wood and A. E. Andrews, blacksmiths; Moore & Pyeott, roller flouring-mill; J. M. Russell & Co. and R. H. Bean, grist-mills; canning factory, operated by a stock company. The canning factory is similar to the one at Prairie Grove, and was recently put into operation. The president of the company is J. S. Edmiston, and the secretary, H. W. Moore. The raising of nursery stock is an extensive business in the vicinity of the town. The leading nurseries are owned by J. B. Russell & Co., Haygood & Co. and D. M. Moore & Son.

When Cane Hill Lodge No. 57, A. F. & A. M., was organized is not now known, as the charter and records were destroyed during the war. The first meeting of which any record could be found was held on August 3, 1865, when J. A. L. McCulloch was W. M.; George W. Scott, S. W.; L. W. Yates, J. W.; F. R. Earle, S. D.; R. H. Bean, J. D.; E. W. McClellan, Secretary; A. Mitchell, Treasurer, and W. B. Brodie, Tyler. The next year a building committee, composed of J. W. Staggs, J. A. L. McCulloch and L. W. Yates, was appointed, and a second story was built over E. W. McClellan's store for a lodge room. It was occupied until December, 1886, when the building was destroyed by fire.

Meetings have since been held over the Methodist Church. The following is a list of the Worshipful Masters since 1865: W. B. Welch, 1866; J. M. Lacy, 1867; F. R. Earle, 1868; R. D. Hays, 1869; James Mitchell, 1870; J. P. Carnahan, 1871; H. M. Welch, 1872; C. McCulloch, 1873; H. M. Welch, 1874-76; J. A. L. McCulloch, 1876; J. A. Buchanan and J. P. Carnahan, 1877-79; T. S. Tennant, 1879; J. P. Carnahan, 1880; W. B. Welch, 1881; R. H. Bean, 1882; H. L. Routh, 1883-85; T. W. Blackburn, 1885-87; J. P. Carnahan, 1887. The members of the lodge now number about thirty.

Evansville.—This village was named in honor of Capt. Lewis Evans, who opened a store there about 1830. He was succeeded by Charles McClellan, and about 1838 a flood of merchants came in, bringing large stocks of goods to sell to the immigrant Cherokees, to whom large sums of money were due from the Government. As payment was delayed for fifteen years, many of these merchants failed, and the business interests of the town were seriously impaired. Soon after the town was laid off Leonard Schuler established a tan-yard, the most extensive ever in the county. A horse-mill was built by Evans soon after he opened his store, and for a short time it supplied nearly the whole county with meal. There are now in the town two steam saw and grist mills, with cotton gins attached. The first was erected by C. E. Rose, in 1870, and the other by Littlejohn & McCormick, about five years ago.

The first schools in Evansville were taught by Allen M. Scott, who was succeeded by Mrs. Dr. Bartlett. For four years, from about 1874 to 1878, a graded school was maintained, but it has since been abandoned.

The business interests of the town are now represented by the following firms: J. A. Bacon, Basham & Goodrich, J. M. Chandler, J. R. Flinn, F. N. & N. B. Littlejohn and G. W. McClure, general stores; L. W. Rosser, cabinet maker; W. L. Childress, cabinet and wagon maker, and J. C. Ferguson, wagon maker. About one mile north of Evansville is a little village known as Greersburg, containing a store, a blacksmith shop, carpenter shop, a Masonic lodge and a school-house.

Cincinnati.—This is one of the best inland towns in the

county. It is situated in Section 29, Township 16 north, Range 33 west, and is the center of a rich grain and live stock region. It is within one and a half miles of "the Nation," and has a good trade from that country. The amount of business transacted in 1887 is estimated as follows: Aggregate, $224,935; merchandise, wagons and agricultural implements, $82,865; grain and grain products, $43,500; cattle, hogs, sheep and mules, $91,750; miscellaneous, $5,000. There are in the town five general merchants, two milliners, one druggist, one wagon factory, one agricultural implement factory, two blacksmiths, two tanneries, two harness shops, one undertaker, two shoe-shops, one merchant and custom mill, two physicians, one dentist, one hotel, one livery stable, an academy and two churches. One of the most important enterprises is the wagon factory of James Oates, who located in Cincinnati in 1868. His sales in 1887 amounted to $15,000. The oldest mercantile establishment is that of R. J. Rhea, who in 1884 succeeded W. H. Rhea, who began business in 1849. Among the others are Rhea & Watts, Spivey & Marquess Bros., Moore Bros., H. Shields and C. M. Cox. Moore Bros. are also proprietors of the Eureka Mills.

Farmington.—A little village six miles west of Fayetteville is called Farmington. It was laid out about 1870, by W. H. Ingles, and for a number of years grew quite rapidly, but of late it has somewhat deteriorated. The principal business is carried on by C. C. Conner & Co., who have a general store, and also operate a flouring-mill. Reed & Son and Rieff & Macy are the other merchants. A wagon-shop is conducted by J. H. Cato.

HAMLETS.

Dutch Mills, on Section 28, Township 14, Range 33; Greensburg, on Section 16, Township 13, Range 33; Viney Grove, on Section 1, Township 15, Range 32; Sulphur City, on Section 15, Township 15, Range 29; Brentwood, on Section 29, Township 14, Range 30; McGuire's Store, on Section 25, Township 16, Range 29; Winslow, on Section 13, Township 13, Range 30, and Salem Springs, on Section 8, Township 14, Range 33, are smaller places, some of which promise growth.

EDUCATION.

Lands and Funds.—Washington County, if she could have controlled Arkansas, would, no doubt, have dotted the State with schools and colleges; as it was she was among the first counties to encourage the proper use of the great United States land grants for public institutions of learning. It was not because there were not large grants made to the commonwealth that the public-school movement languished until 1868, for with the "16th section" grant, " the 72 sections seminary land grant," the 640,-000 acres, and "the swamp lands grant" of September 28, 1850, there were from nine to eleven millions of acres of school lands at the disposal of the commonwealth for the education of its children; and some of this, too, as early as "the forties."

Every State has its periods of fraudulent administration, but in no part of the history of Arkansas has fraud and plunder been more rife than in the early administration of the most precious of its funds and resources, the school funds and lands. The lands were sacrificed at 50 and 75 cents an acre, and even then the funds were misappropriated and misloaned, until the statutes teemed with acts to suppress the evil. The office of county school commissioners was established in the hope that evils of caring for the fund might be lessened, and so the situation continued until 1868.

Earliest Schools.—Washington County suffered with the rest of the State, as far as the fund was concerned, but her settlers and pioneers, like their forefathers from the "old world," brought their schools and churches along with them, and welcomed others, who were pioneer planters of such institutions. Many parents taught their own children, and then sent them to other States. Some lady or gentleman would take a few boys and girls of the neighborhood to his or her own home and hold a " subscription school." But the poorer people and the colored race had not even these advantages. There is no certain information as to the first teacher in the county. A Mrs. Hoge held one of the earliest private schools, in her home near Evergreen Cemetery, at Fayetteville. (Governor) Isaac Murphy was also a teacher at the county seat in the latter part of "the thirties."

His was a mixed school. A Dr. Sanders was one of the earliest pedagogues there also. Mr. and Mrs. Dickson were among the number about the year 1840. In the region of Springdale probably "Uncle Joe" Holcomb taught the first schools, as early as 1844; he was followed in 1845 by "Tom" Cannon; Harvey Adams covered the time to 1850, when Miss Jennie Mills took up the birch for the two years following; D. A. White in 1853, George Hancock in 1854, and Charles Wildes covered the most of the period before the war. "Abe" Whaley and a Mr. Allbright were among those after the war.

The Far West Seminary.—This institution was intended to be the first college in Arkansas, and some place its earliest beginnings, before 1835, in a brick church at Mount Comfort. In 1843 its board of visitors included Rev. C. Washbourne, G. W. Paschal, A. W. Arrington, Robert W. Mecklin and Isaac Strain, who published in the *Arkansas Intelligencer* a three-column article on the purposes of the institution. Rev. Washbourne was sent east to solicit aid for it, and great exertions were made to get it firmly on foot. It was incorporated in 1844—then the only college in Arkansas, and Ozark Institute was to become a preparatory school. Good buildings were started, but on February 27, 1845, the still unfinished structures were burned, causing a loss of from $12,000 to $13,000. This seemed to be the death-blow to the enterprise. Rev. Robert W. Mecklin was among its principals, and Col. J. P. Neal, of Prairie Grove, was one of the many young men who attended it. It was suspected of being a political move, for some reason, and that, no doubt, had much to do with the lack of encouragement extended to it.

Cane Hill Schools.—Cane Hill was settled in the main by educated Christian people, and it early became distinguished for its churches and schools. Both were established as soon as the first settlers had located their land, and secured shelter for themselves and families. At first one school supplied the youth for several miles around with instruction, but as the settlements became more numerous better educational facilities were demanded. On October 28, 1834, a meeting of the Cumberland Presbyterians, of Washington County, was held in the Cane Hill meeting-house for the purpose of taking the necessary steps to establish a school. Rev. Samuel King was called to the chair, and presided over the deliberations. A board of trust was chosen, and the Rev. B. H. Pierson, D. D., was elected president and Ezra Wilson clerk. This school was opened in April, 1835, and was probably kept up in some form until the founding of Cane Hill College.*

Cane Hill College.—This latter institution was chartered in 1852, and went into operation in a brick building erected for the purpose at Boonsboro'. Rev. Robert M. King, of Missouri, was president, and Prof. S. Doak Lowry, assistant. After laboring for about six years Mr. King resigned, and his place was filled by the promotion of Prof. Lowry. James H. Crawford and P. W. Buchanan were at the same time made assistants. An effort was made to raise an endowment by scholarships, and Rev. W. G. L. Quaite was appointed endowing agent. He received in donations and scholarships about $1,000, but owing to the loss occasioned by the war very little was realized from this effort.

In March, 1859, Rev. F. R. Earle, of Greenville, Ky., accepted the presidency, and was formally inaugurated the following June. At the close of the collegiate year, in June, 1859, two young men, S. H. Buchanan and J. T. Buchanan, were regularly graduated, receiving the first diplomas given by the institution. At that time, also, the first catalogue was issued. S. H. Buchanan was employed as tutor for the next session, and at the close of the school year, in 1860, Prof. Lowry resigned. In 1861 work was necessarily suspended, and in November, 1864, the college building with all its contents was destroyed by fire. A building previously used as a boarding-house escaped the flames, and after the close of hostilities the president began preaching and teaching there. In 1868 a new frame building, valued at $5,000, was completed, and in September the president, assisted by Prof. James Mitchell, opened the college. The next year J. P. Carnahan was added to the teaching force. In 1874 Prof. Mitchell resigned, and his place was filled by Prof. Harold Bourland. In 1875 the trustees resolved to admit pupils of both sexes, and Rev. H. M. Welch was placed in charge of the young ladies' department. He retired in 1879. In the four years following Mrs. Earle, Miss Welch, Miss Moore and Mrs. Whittenburg were

*History of Cumberland Presbyterianism.

employed as teachers whenever the patronage demanded it. In 1883 Prof. Carnahan retired, after eighteen years' service. The president then had entire charge of the work until 1885, when he too resigned, and Rev. J. P. Russell was placed in charge. Mr. Russell taught for two and one-half sessions. In the second session of his administration the college building was burned. In this emergency the Methodists offered their house, and this, with a small dwelling, furnished accommodations for the school. Upon the resignation of Mr. Russell, Dr. Earle again undertook the management of the institution, and in 1886 there was completed a new brick building, better than either of the former ones, at a cost of about $8,000. In 1887 the president, assisted by two good teachers, began work in the new building, and a fairly successful year ensued. Dr. Earle is an able educator and a faithful worker, and Cane Hill College is doing much for the cause it represents, but it is now under the shadow of the State University, and is so far removed from railroad communication that it can scarcely hope to regain its old-time prosperity.

At about the time Cane Hill College was established Esquire James B. Russell, who had previously done much for the promotion of education in the community, erected a large frame building about one mile south of Boonsboro, furnished it with a library and apparatus, and installed Thomas G. McCulloch as teacher. McCulloch, who was an excellent instructor, although a somewhat severe disciplinarian, remained in charge of the school for four or five years, and under his administration the attendance became so great that an addition to the building was made. After Prof. McCulloch's retirement the school was successively under the direction of Miss Coleman and Miss Lloyd.

Upon the establishment of Cane Hill College Mr. Russell proposed to donate the property to the church, provided $500 was raised for the college in his name. This was done, and Cane Hill Seminary became as famous an institution for the education of young ladies as Cane Hill College was for the education of young men. During the three or four years before the war this institution was under the care of Prof. Newton Gibens and three assistants.

Prairie Grove Institute is the name of a high-school conducted under the auspices of Fayetteville District Methodist Episcopal Church, South. It was opened in 1883, under the care of N. J. Foster, in a two-story brick building, erected for the purpose in a beautiful grove near the town of Prairie Grove.

The Fayetteville Female Seminary.—In 1839 this institution was founded by Miss Sophia Sawyer. This lady had left her New England home to become a missionary to the Cherokee Indians in Tennessee, and on their removal to the Indian Territory she followed them, in company with the Ridge family. Indian troubles led to her locating at Fayetteville, whither she brought fourteen young Cherokee girls, daughters of prominent Cherokee families. Among these maidens were four who bore the names Susan Drew, Amanda Drew, Maggie Harper and Julia Rogers. She opened her school near the present residence of Stephen K. Stone, and in time had an assistant, a Miss James (afterward Mrs. Marshall), and later on Miss Lucretia Foster and Miss Mary T. Daniels. Rev. C. Washbourne at one time was instructor in literature. Two Misses Freyschlag also assisted at one time. In about 1854 Miss Lucretia Foster became principal, and in 1859 the institution was incorporated. A neat catalogue, issued for 1859–60, gives the following faculty: Mrs. Lucretia Foster Smith, principal; Miss Mary T. Daniels, associate; Miss Annis C. Feemster, teacher in primary department; Madame Marie Janssen, teacher in French and embroidery; Mr. F. F. Zellner, professor of music. The whole number in all departments was 103; number in music, twenty-four; number in embroidery, thirty. The students were largely from Fayetteville, but some were from such distant points as Salem, Tenn. The first year of the war, however, closed this institution, but not before the first class received its diplomas. Elizabeth F. Massie, of Fayetteville, and Cener Boone, of Bedford County, Tenn., constituted the class.

Ozark Institute.—On May 19, 1845, Rev. Robert W. Mecklin, having withdrawn from The Far West Seminary, opened a well-attended male seminary about three miles northwest of Fayetteville, and gave it the title "Ozark Institute." Its reputation spread throughout the region, and its attendance often numbered over a hundred students. To it were attracted as teachers such brainy young men as Rev. Robert Graham, who became the partner of Rev. Mecklin. Under them were assistants A. S. Lockert and Z. Van Hoose. The institution continued until February 17, 1857, and remained inoperative until after the war, when for a time it was revived by Prof. C. H. Leverett.

Rev. Robert Graham was a Christian gentleman of remarkable abilities, and of excellent scholarship; he was a man who left his impress upon any society in which he moved, and with these abilities was coupled the earnestness and zeal of a convert of Alexander Campbell. He was not only a pastor, but an educator, and not only formed but was able to execute plans for the higher education of the youth of Washington County and the Southwest. He had made a strong impression on the students of Ozark Institute, and on his withdrawal from that school in 1850, to found a college in Fayetteville, he was followed by about twenty pupils. In October of that year he founded Arkansas College, and began the school on the lot now occupied by the residence of Mr. Prentiss. The enterprise was a private one, entirely under Mr. Graham's control, and in 1851 his situation was such that he felt warranted in building a new structure in McGarroh's grove, on the site of the present Fayetteville Christian Church. Mr. Graham's first assistant was Prof. John M. Pettigrew, afterward a senator. Among his students were the following well-known names, some of them of national reputation: James R. Pettigrew, afterward editor of the *Sentinel*, and one of the Utah Commission, Robert Rutherford (now Judge), Granville Wilcox, a distinguished lawyer, and editor of the Van Buren *Argus*. Arkansas and John Wilson, T. W. and W. T. Pollard, J. T. Sutton, Maj. Johnson and Mark L. Evans, who became useful men, were also among the number. The school had attained a first-class reputation under the influence of Robert Graham, and its attendance was probably never below 100 pupils after the new building was occupied. In 1859, another Christian minister, Rev. William Baxter, assumed control on the withdrawal of Mr. Graham, and was its president until, like all the other institutions of peace, it gave way to the march of war in 1861. There are conflicting rumors in regard to the destruction of the building;

it is said to have been destroyed by the order of McCulloch, in event of the defeat of his army at Pea Ridge, and according to others it was burned by Federal soldiers as a war signal to Springfield officers toward the North. Certain it is, however, it was reduced to ashes.

The loss of Miss Sawyer's school to Washington County's facilities for female education might have been replaced by the Fayetteville Female Institute, organized in 1858, if the war had allowed it to continue; but it had the misfortune to be used by Gen. McCulloch as an arsenal, and, after fatal Pea Ridge, the bombs and powder it contained were made to do self-destruction to the building and its magazine. Rev. T. B. Van Horn, of Ohio, the founder, in looking about for a site, chose the northwest corner of Dixon and College Avenues, the site of the parsonage of Rev. Dr. Maynard at present; here he built a three-story frame edifice, surmounted by a spire.

As Rev. Van Horn was a strong Unionist, he left Arkansas in 1861, and his institution was converted into a Confederate arsenal, meeting with the fate above mentioned. The attendance had averaged probably fifty pupils.

In 1849 Rev. Jesse and Mrs. S. A. E. McAllister organized two large academies at Elm Springs, Rev. McAllister teaching the male school, and the female school being in charge of his wife. The attendance reached sixty or more in the male school, and probably forty in the girls' school, many attendants of the latter coming from the Indian Nation. The school was under Methodist Episcopal influences, if not entirely controlled by that body. It was not destined to an unbroken existence, for an epidemic a few years after its organization resulted in its abandonment; not, however, before a Mr. Lockhart had served as Rev. McAllister's successor, and a Mrs. E. Saunders, who had been professor of music, had taken the place of Mrs. McAllister at the head of the female school. The deed for the lot for the building site was given May 8, 1852, by W. Barrington, to the trustees of Elm Springs Male and Female Academy, Thomas Stanford, Russell M. Morgan, Thomas McClain, W. N. Carlile, L. H. Blake and Lee C. Blakemore.

A Baptist College.—In 1872 there was organized at Springdale a Missionary Baptist College by the Rev. Barnes, and in the following year it was incorporated. It was under the control of three teachers, and held in a fine two-story brick edifice that rivals the public school building of the town. For some reason the school did not prosper, and in April, 1885, it was bought by the Lutheran Church, and converted into a parochial high-school for a colony of that faith in and to the west of Springdale, and now goes under the name "Lutheran College." Two instructors, Rev. A. S. Bartholomew and Rev. I. E. Rader, have been in charge ever since the new organization, and their enrollment often reaches eighty in number.

Elm Springs Academy.—In January, 1887, Rev. W. W. Lundy, a graduate of Hiwassee College, East Tennessee, leased the school property at Elm Springs, and established "Elm Springs Academy for Males and Females." The first year sixty-five students were enrolled, and in 1888 the enrollment reached 103 pupils. The school offers scientific, commercial, normal and classical instruction, under the able direction of Rev. Lundy and his assistant, Miss Jessie Gotcher.

The period from 1861 to 1867 may be considered practically a blank in the educational history of Washington County. During active hostilities the preservation of life was about all that the harassed mothers, left to care for their families as best they might, could do; and when reconstruction began, the broken up families, who looked round on devastated fields, burned homes, villages and towns, the ruins of everything that had been the fruits of years of labor and care, with scarcely anything to turn to except their orchards and the bare fields, found their situation almost as though they had come as penniless pioneers to a new country, and it needed some time for them to recuperate their exhausted energies and finances. Then, too, the situation had changed; the slaves were free; they were to be a part of the population; free schools were being agitated; the finances of the people and the State were in a lamentable condition; and for many reasons the free school idea did not become suddenly popular; there was still the tendency to cling to the private schools; the school funds from the public lands, so far as sold, were all gone; the State began taking means to secure what could be recovered; and soon a plan of free common schools was presented to the Legislature.

Common Schools.—On July 23, 1868, was approved an act of the State Legislature, entitled "An Act to establish and maintain a system of Free Common Schools for the State of Arkansas." The act begins :

Be it enacted by the General Assembly of the State of Arkansas:

SECTION 1.   That the proceeds of all lands that have been or "hereafter may be granted by the United States to this State, and not otherwise appropriated by the United States or this State; also all (moneys) stocks, bonds, lands, and other property, now belonging to any fund for purposes of education; also the net proceeds of all sales of lands and other property and effects that may accrue to this State by escheat, or from sale of estrays, or from unclaimed dividends or distributive shares of the estates of deceased persons, or from fines, penalties, or forfeitures; also any sales of the public lands which may have been or may be hereafter paid over to the State (Congress consenting); also all the grants, gifts, or devises that have been or may be hereafter made to this State, and not otherwise appropriated by the tenure of the grant, gift, or devise, shall be securely invested and sacredly preserved as a public-school fund, that shall be designated as the "Common-School Fund" of the State, and which shall be the common property of the State.

SECTION 2.   That the annual income from the said fund, together with one dollar per capita, to be annually assessed on every male inhabitant over the age of twenty-one (21) years, and so much of the ordinary annual revenues of the State as may hereafter be set apart by law for such purposes, shall be faithfully appropriated for maintaining a system of "Free Common Schools" for this State, and shall be applied to no other purposes whatsoever, than to the payment of teachers' wages and the salaries of the circuit superintendents of public instruction.

The act provided that the governor, secretary of State and its created head, the superintendent of public instruction, should be the commissioners of the fund; that every county should be divided into school districts, with a trustee as the district officer; that each judicial district should constitute a school circuit, over which a " Circuit Superintendent of Public Instruction " should have supervision, these officers being appointed by the governor; and that among other duties these superintendents should license teachers, hold county teachers' institutes, visit schools, arrange district apportionment of funds, etc.   The salary of these officers was to be $3,000 and office expenses; thus is seen the importance attached to the office.   As an interesting feature of reconstruction days, the act provides for the following " Teacher's Oath: "

" I do solemnly swear (or affirm), that I will honestly and faithfully support the Constitution and laws of the United States, and the Constitution and laws of the State of Arkansas, and that I will encourage all other persons so to do. That I will never countenance or aid in the secession of this State from the United States; that I will endeavor to inculcate in the minds of youth sentiments of patriotism and loyalty, and will fully, faithfully and impartially perform the duties of the office of teacher according to the best of my ability; so help me God."

This act was amended April 12, 1869, to provide for certain district contingencies, and the sale and transfer of lands. On February 4 of the same year it was also amended to adapt the system to the peculiar needs of cities and towns, making them a special school district.

Dr. Thomas Smith was the first State superintendent of public instruction, and under him was W. B. Henderson, the circuit superintendent of public instruction over the districts of which Washington County is a part. Under Supt. Smith about 2,500 schools were organized throughout the State, and Washington County had her share.

Industrial University.—The next most important event in the educational history of Washington County, and of the State also, was an act of the Legislature, approved March 27, 1871, entitled " An Act for the Location, Organization and Maintenance of the Arkansas Industrial University, with a Normal Department therein." It begins thus:

Be it enacted by the General Assembly of the State of Arkansas:

SECTION 1. That the treasurer of said State be a financial agent and trustee of said State, immediately after the passage of this act, to apply for and receive of the United States Government all the land scrip to which this State may be entitled by reason of her acceptance of the provisions of the act of Congress entitled " An act donating public lands to the several States and Territories which may provide colleges for the benefit of agriculture and the mechanic arts," approved July 2, 1862, and acts amendatory thereof.

The act further provides for converting this scrip into funds; for a trustee from each judicial district, who, together with the State superintendent of public instruction, were to constitute the board of trustees; for receiving bids from counties, cities and incorporated towns for the location of the institution; for proceedings for its erection; for the organization and maintenance of it; for the appropriation of $50,000 for these purposes, the 150,000 acres of land scrip being only for endowment; to provide also for the purchase of from 160 to 640 acres of land for the university and its farm, etc.

In 1872 the board, consisting of Hon. Thomas Smith, and Trustees Bennett, Cohn, Prather, Boteführ, Bishop, Searle, Young, Clayton, Sarber and Millen, sent a committee to visit the universities of Illinois and Michigan. Among the bids received by them was one from Hon. Liberty Bartlett, of Pulaski County, offering ninety-two acres; one from Batesville, subscribing $50,-000; one from Washington County, voting $100,000, with the city of Fayetteville voting $30,000 in addition, and one from A. P. Robinson, of Conway, offering a quarter section of land. Washington County was chosen, and the homestead of Mr. William McIlroy, embracing 160 acres, was bought by the committee on buildings and grounds, A. S. Prather, J. E. Bennett and M. A. Cohn, who paid the sum of $12,000, $1,000 of which was at once raised by citizens of Fayetteville. Large donations of land were offered by Hons. Lafayette Gregg and David Walker. Mr. Van Odell, of Chicago, was the architect chosen, and the contract let to Meyers & Oliver for $130,000. Work began September, 1873, and the following is a description of the results as completed August 10, 1875, and as reported by the board of visitors for 1875 to the governor:

We spent half a day in examining the new building, and were impressed with its grandeur. Its foundation is deep, broad, durable and abundantly able to support the heavy and well proportioned superstructure erected thereon. It is replete with beauty, solid in its construction, and well adapted to the purposes and objects for which it was built.

It is 214 feet long by 122 feet wide, covering an area of 26,108 square feet. It is five stories high, with French or Mansard roof, covered with slate and tin. The height of the building is 134 feet.

The basement story is built of stone; the foundation is bedded on solid rock. The three next stories are built of brick, and the attic of wood. The basement story is in height thirteen feet in the clear, first and second stories sixteen feet each, third and fourth fifteen feet, the clock and bell tower extending two stories above the attic.

There was used in the construction of [the] building 2,600,000 brick, 2,300 perch of rock, 719,805 feet of lumber, 260,000 pounds of iron, 250 kegs of nails, 85 doors, 282 windows, and 12,008 square yards of plastering in first and second stories. The building is to be heated with hot air furnaces and lighted with gas.

There are ten rooms 77x61 feet, ten rooms 22x29 feet, ten rooms 22x28 feet, ten rooms 22x25 feet, ten rooms 22x22 feet, ten rooms 22x19 feet, five rooms 15x 28 feet, four rooms 22x20 feet, and one room 77x50 feet, making a total of seventy rooms. In addition there are four corridors 15x28 feet, and four corridors 14x206 feet.

There are four entrances to the building, and three flights of stairs from first to third floor, the principal stairway leading from the main entrance to the attic story. The principal entrance to the first floor is on the east, by circular steps surmounted by a beautiful portico of stone.

The fact that the stone, lumber and brick used in this building were obtained in Arkansas, and that the workmen who wrought so faithfully in "cutting, hewing and carving" are chiefly residents of this State, is, or ought to be, a source of congratulation to the entire commonwealth.

Says Prof. F. L. Harvey: "The brick for that beautiful structure, the Arkansas Industrial University, was made from clay found inside the campus, while the brown sandstone for the basement was quarried a few hundred yards away, and the ornamental grey limestone, used in the façade, procured in Washington and Madison Counties."

The entire value of the university property, as given in its first catalogue (1873–74), was $355,000; and the main building was to be finished by September, 1875.

In a memorial of the board to the United States Senate, praying for aid, they say: "* * in the month of January, 1872, (it) was opened for the reception of pupils;" and that 200 students had become connected therewith. The first faculty was Gen. Albert W. Bishop, A. M., president and professor of mental and moral philosophy; C. H. Leverett, A. M., professor of ancient languages and literature; T. L. Thompson, B. S., professor of theoretical and applied chemistry; Gen. N. B. Pearce, professor of mathematics and engineering; Lieut. E. S. Curtis, Second Artillery, United States Army, professor of military science and tactics; Richard Thruston, M. D., professor of practical and theoretical agriculture and horticulture; N. P. Gates, principal of normal department; Mary R. Gorton, preceptress in normal department; Lu J. Stanard, instructress of training school, and W. D. C. Botefuhr, professor of music. The freshman class opened with 16, the normal class with 13, and the preparatory department with 201.

It proposes as its object in the first catalogue:

First.   To impart a knowledge of science and its application to the arts of life.

Second.   To afford to students, such as may desire it, the benefits of daily manual labor.   This labor is to some degree remunerative.   But its remunerative character is not so much intended to lessen the expenses of students as for educational uses, as it is planned and varied for the illustration of the principles of science.   The preservation of health, and of a taste for the pursuits of agriculture and mechanic arts, are two other important objects.

Third.   To prosecute experiments for the promotion of agriculture and horticulture.

Fourth.   To provide the means of instruction in military science; and to this end skilled instructors and suitable military implements will be secured and obtained as soon as practicable.

Fifth.   To afford the means of a general and thorough education, not inferior to those afforded to all classes in the best colleges.

The experimental farming was to be done entirely by the pupils, under the faculty direction; the number of beneficiaries for Washington County, who were to receive four years' tuition free, was eight; the uniform prescribed for the male students was the West Point cadet suit; the courses arranged were the classical, agricultural, engineering, normal, and preparatory and musical courses; the discipline was to be self-government; one literary society, the " Claiosophic," was established; a mineral and geological cabinet and library was established; likewise a horticultural collection; a four-acre orchard; and the year closed commencement exercises during the first three days of July, 1873.

At the first commencement held June 27, 1872, President Gen. A. W. Bishop delivered an excellent address on the educational history of the county and of the A. I. University movement in particular.

The report of 1874 shows an aggregate attendance of 321, and a commercial course added.   A military band of fourteen pieces was added also, and the cadets placed under military government; a professorship of history and English literature was established.   The report of 1875, with the announcement, shows N. P. Gates as acting president, and Mrs. V. L. Gray as teacher of painting and drawing; a total attendance of 344; the " Mathetian," a literary, and two musical societies, the Euterpean and Philharmonic, were organized; $500 received from the Peabody fund; a branch normal college, for colored students, was opened at Pine Bluff, September, 1875.   The report for 1876, and announcement for the following year, shows the attendance 270; the first graduates, six in number. The report for 1877, and announcement for 1877–78, shows Gen. D. H. Hill, president; total attendance, 287; four prizes are offered. For 1878 the report and announcement show an attendance of 256; morning and evening religious exercises in the chapel; two more prizes added. For 1879, with announcement for 1879–80, the report shows the faculty increased to sixteen; a medical department at Little Rock with a faculty of sixteen; aggregate enrollment, 420 (exclusive of medical department); one prize added; two more literary societies, Philomathean and Phamakopton; general increase in collection and library. The report for 1880, and catalogue of 1880–81, show the attendance 450; cadet battalion of three companies; uniform for ladies; large contributions to collections, library and reading room; number Washington County scholarships increased to twenty-one. For June, 1881, faculty numbers seventeen; attendance (exclusive of medical department and branch normal), 441; Y. M. C. A. organized; seven degrees obtainable; an oratorical contest established; fourth annual meeting of Alumni Association reported; seven literary societies reported; large contributions to cabinets, library, etc.; twenty-two scholarships for Washington County. For June, 1882, attendance 363. In 1888 a new three-story brick dormitory was opened; it contains forty rooms, and is lighted by electric light. The officers (at Fayetteville) are as follows: E. H. Murfee, A. M., LL. D., acting president, professor of mathematics, logic and astronomy; J. M. Whitham, A. M. (late assistant engineer United States Navy), superintendent of mechanic arts, and professor of engineering; H. Edwards, A.M., professor of history, English, French and German; F. W. Simonds, M. S., Ph. D., professor of biology and geology; E. L. Fletcher (first lieutenant Thirteenth Infantry, United States Army), professor of military science and tactics; A. E. Menke, F. C. S., superintendent of agriculture, and professor of chemistry and mineralogy; J. F. Howell, A. M., instructor in pedagogics and senior assistant; W. E. Anderson (graduate Miller Manual Labor School), assistant professor of mechanic arts, and instructor in mechanical drawing; S. S. Twombley, B. S., assistant professor of chemistry and agriculture; C. H. Leverett, A. M., assistant professor of ancient languages; G. W. Drake, A. M., assistant in preparatory department; A. M. Waggoner, assistant in preparatory department; J.C. Massie, Jr., A. B., assistant in preparatory department; N. J. Williams, assistant in preparatory department; K. V. King, instructor in music; C. B. Lyon, B. P., instructor in free-hand drawing and industrial art; J. W. Mayes (graduate Miller Manual Labor School, Va.), instructor in iron work; L. C. Gardner (graduate Chicago Manual Training School), instructor in foundry and forging; W. F. Bates, foreman of the farm; L. Treadwell, instructor in field engineering; P. H. Babb, instructor in wood work; W. N. Crozier, instructor in English; I. Pace, English instructor; M. Danaher, instructor in Greek; G. A. Warren, English instructor; A. Polson, English instructor; J. H. Hobbs, English instructor; Prof. Edwards, librarian; Prof. Howell, secretary of faculty; Miss Taff, assistant librarian; Prof. Drake, superintendent of dormitory; Mrs. F. W. Washington, matron; W. French, engineer, and W. W. McCant, janitor. The State Agricultural Experiment Station, located here, have a board of control, station council, and eleven station officers.

The students are as follows: In the agricultural course, 48; mechanical engineering, 26; civil engineering, 68; scientific, 46; classical, 55; normal, 54; irregular, 6; literary, 2; in lowest preparatory, 112; total matriculates at Fayetteville, 417; music, 27; medical department at Little Rock, 67; branch normal at Pine Bluff, 181; total, 665. Eight courses are offered, and among the degrees gained at Fayetteville are B. S. A., B. M. L., B. C. E., B. S., B. A. and L. I. Three post-graduate degrees are conferred, M. A., M. S. and Ph. D. Nineteen agricultural journals are taken for that department. Six shop-rooms accommodate fifty pupils at one time. Thirty-three engineering journals and about sixty volumes of proceedings of various societies in Europe and America are used in that department. Over 160 machines or models are in the museum of that department. The Gordon Engineers' Club, organized in 1887, have had six prominent lecturers during the year. A battalion of three companies is thus officered: E. L. Fletcher, first lieutenant Thirteenth United States Infantry, colonel; G. C. Shoff, first lieutenant and adjutant; W. N.

Crosier, first lieutenant and quartermaster; W. E. Dickson, first lieutenant and ordnance officer; G. A. Humphreys, sergeant-major; Company A, Capt. G. A. Warren; Company B, Capt. J. H. Hobbs; Company C, Capt. Press Boles. The property is valued at $300,000. There are three literary societies. Library, apparatus, museums, cabinets, etc., are good. The long vacation is now had in winter. The classes have been as follows: 1875 numbered 8; 1876 numbered 9; 1877, same; 1878, 5; 1879, 8; 1880, 10; 1881, 6; 1882, 15; 1883, 7; 1884, 10; 1885, 6, and 1886, 5.

Other Educational Matters.—From time to time the public school laws have been changed and amended, but the greatest change was made about 1875, after the change of administration in State affairs. An effort was made to abolish the supervision system, including the offices of State and circuit superintendents, and replacing the latter by throwing their duties on the county judge and county examiners, and substituting a district board of three directors for the trustee. J. L. Denton, then State superintendent, and *ex-officio* receiver of the George Peabody fund, on the prospect of the success of the anti-supervision element, telegraphed the manager, J. P. Curry, who at once went to Little Rock, and urged upon the Legislature the retention at least of the office of State superintendent. The great indebtedness of the State made this seem necessary, but it was a vital blow against the public-school system. Whatever the cause, however, the retrenching process cut out all supervision except the office of State superintendent. Aside from the poll-tax and other funds, a State tax of 2 mills is a source of revenue, and an optional district tax of 5 mills for districts who will vote it.

To trace out the statistical growth of the common-school system in Washington County is impossible, on account of the lack of records, and the absence of reports where records have been kept. The State superintendent's reports to the governor, excellent as they otherwise are, are thus rendered practically worthless as far as this feature is concerned. Both the State superintendent and county examiner lament the fact, and point to that as an argument for supervision of county work.

The report of June 30, 1881, shows the enrollment in Washington County to be: White, 8,292; colored, 342; increase, 216. Those pursuing studies to be: Reading, 1,222; orthography, 1,706; penmanship, 309; mental arithmetic, 410; written arithmetic, 610; English grammar, 337; geography, 259; history, 100; higher branches, 37; whole number taught, 2,354; whole number last year, 3,396.

The report of 1882, when there were 121 districts, but thirty-five districts reported, showing the number enrolled to be: White, 2,330 (the enumeration being 9,158); colored, 84 (the enumeration being 325 and the increase 849). Those pursuing studies to be: Reading, 1,274; orthography, 1,444; mental arithmetic, 356; written arithmetic, 549; English grammar, 156; geography, 152; history, 141; higher branches, 35.

For June 30, 1881, the number of teachers are given as: Male, 39; female, 7; with first grade certificate, 32; with second grade certificate, 13; with third grade certificate, 1. The average wages of first grade males, $33.66; first grade females, $48.33; second grade males, $20.71; total paid out, $7,781.39.

For June 30, 1882, the number of teachers given are: White males, 33; colored males, 2; white females, 7; average monthly salaries for males of first grade, $33.11; first grade females, $23.24; second grade males, $25.09; third grade males, $20.62.

June 30, 1881, number of buildings erected during the year, two of wood, costing $611.30; number erected previously, eighty of wood, costing $20,650; total valuation, $21,261.30; number of districts reporting, two.

June 30, 1882, eleven districts only reported.

The receipts and expenditures of the public-school fund in Washington County, as given June 30, 1881, is as follows: Received from all sources, $17,171.34; expended for all purposes, $7,781.39; amount unexpended, $9,389.95. As given June 30, 1882: Received from all sources, $14,615.55; expended for all purposes, $10,990.81; amount unexpended, $3,624.74.

In 1883 the enumeration was: White, 9,732; colored, 382; increase, 631; number of districts, 130; number reporting, 53; enrollment, white, 3,328; colored, 104; total, 3,432; pursuing, orthography, 2,254; reading, 2,050; mental arithmetic, 607; written arithmetic, 980; English grammar, 373; geography, 510; history, 163; higher branches, 15; penmanship, 926.

In 1884 the county examiner reports: Enumeration, 10,785; enrollment, 2,926; number of districts, 135; number of districts reporting enrollment, 53; number of teachers employed, 56; the county treasurer reports amount on hand July 1, 1883, $5,424.26; from common-school fund, $6,097.57; district tax, $1,702.17; poll tax, $3,954.24; other sources, $652.05; total, $17,830.29; amount expended, $12,254.72; balance on hand June 30, 1884, $5,775.57.

(In 1884) number of districts, 135; number reporting, 43; enrollment, white, 2,957; colored, 5; total, 2,962; pursuing orthography, 2,266; reading, 1,870; mental arithmetic, 835; written arithmetic, 901; English grammar, 436; geography, 408; penmanship, 548; history, 219; higher arithmetic, 11.

In 1883 the number of teachers reported are: Male, 47; female, 9; total, 56; average monthly salaries of first grade males, $32.55; first grade females, $26.66; second grade males, $28.75; third grade females, $20.00.

In 1884 the number of teachers reported are: Males, 35; females, 21; total, 56; average monthly salary first grade males, $33.00; females, $27.20; second grade males, $29.41; females, $22.50; third grade males, $22.50.

In 1883 Washington County reports twelve wooden school-houses, erected at a cost of $22.58; whole number, 123, valued at $24,600; and in 1884 reports three wooden buildings, constructed at a cost of $379; and the whole number reported are but eleven buildings, valued at $1,297.

In 1883 the school fund received was: Amount on hand June 30, 1882, $3,642.61; from common-school fund, $4,757.33; from district tax, $3,162.11; from poll tax, $3,583.79; from other sources, $101; total, $15,246.75; and in 1884, amount on hand June 30, 1883, $5,424.26; common-school fund, $6,097.57; district fund, $1,702.17; poll tax, $3,954.24; from sixteenth section sales or leases, $328.20; other sources, $323.85; total, $17,830.29.

Expenditures for 1883, teachers' salaries, $9,390.42; treasurer's commissions, $232.07; total, $9,822.49; amount unexpended, common-school fund, $4,214.46; district fund, $1,209.80; total, $5,424.26; and for 1884, teachers' salaries, $11,834.10; building repairing, $216.64; treasurer's commissions, $203.98; total, $12,-

254.72; amount unexpended, common school fund, $828.14; district fund, $3,125.03; funds from all other sources, $1,622.40; total, $5,575.57.

Of the $2,800 received by the State from the Peabody Educational Fund in 1883, all but $150 was expended, and the only direct aid received by Washington County was her share of $1,300 applied to the district normal institutes, one of which, in 1884, was held within her borders, at Springdale. In the latter year, of $2,000 received, all but $667.10 was expended for these institutes, as directed by the general agent of the fund. In addition to the above Washington County students have the privilege of competing for the eight Peabody scholarships in the State Normal College at Nashville, Tenn., each scholarship allowing $200 per annum for the expenses of its holder in the above college.

In his report for 1883 and 1884 the State superintendent showed the great need for revision of the school law in almost every department, but especially in regard to county supervision and school districting, and to provide free text books. He also states the condition of the permanent school fund, whose interest only is used as follows: Loughborough bonds, 6 per cent., $170,-000; auditor's certificates of 1883, $270.91; reclamation certificates, $76.00; total, $170,346.91.

The fact is also mentioned of the loss of funds by fire in 1874 and 1879 to aggregate (with interest) over $300,000, and the replacement of this is urged.

In the report for 1885 and 1886 the State superintendent, Hon. W. E. Thompson, again urges county supervision in a masterly manner, and no doubt the public sentiment will soon demand it as the greatest need of her public-school system. His report shows a general advance in the schools of the State, and in public sentiment in regard thereto, which has no doubt been largely fostered by the district normal institutes, which are supported by the Peabody Fund. This fund is reported as follows: To balance on hand November 1, 1884, $667.10; to normal institutes in 1885, $1,500; total amount for 1885, $2,167.10; by amount expended for institutes in 1885, $1,087.90; to balance on hand January, 1886, $1,079.20; to amount received for public schools in 1886, $1,800; to amount for institutes in 1886, $1,500;

total amount, $4,370.20; by amount expended for institute work, $1,678.75; balance on hand December, 1886, $2,700.45.

Two more scholarships in the Nashville State Normal College were given to the State.

September 30, 1886, the permanent school fund was as follows: Currency, $174,554.33; State scrip, $652.02; reclamation certificates, $76; refunding certificates, $100; total, $175,382.35.

The report for Washington County June 30, 1885, is: Amount received from common-school fund, State, $14,690.05; district tax, $11,262.12; poll tax, $4,307; other sources, $361; total, $30,-620.17.   Amount expended for teachers' salaries, $7,670.32; building and repairs, $1,493.32; treasurer's commissions, $222.79; total, 9,386.43.   Balance unexpended of common-school fund, $7,640.73; district fund, $10,641.12; other sources, $2,951.89; total, $21,233.74.   Enumeration, white, 9,947; colored, 227; total, 10,913; enrollment, white, 3,016; number of districts, 134; number reporting enrollment, 40; number districts voting tax, 4; number teachers employed, 50; number school-houses, 11; value of school-houses, $3,305; number of institutes held, 3.

The county's report for June 30, 1886, is as follows: Balance on hand June 30, 1885, $21,233.74; common-school fund, State, $8,056.40; district tax, $7,483.10; poll tax, $4,685.60; other sources, $500; total, $41,958.84.   Amount expended for teachers' salaries, $15,301.57; building and repairs, $10,157.94; treasurer's commission, $414.48; other purposes, $279.76; total, $26,153.75.   Balance unexpended common-school fund, $4,143.-04; balance unexpended district fund, $6,580.16; balance of fund from other sources, $5,081.89; total, $15,805.09.   The enumeration, white, 11,286; colored, 438; total, 11,724; enrollment, white, 2,946; number of districts, 150; number reporting enrollment, 104; number voting tax, 38; number of teachers employed, 114; number of school-houses, 80; value of school-houses, $26,177.29; number of institutes held, 4.

The county examiner's report for 1888 gives total white enumeration, 12,800; total colored, 430; grand total, 13,230; total white enrollment, 6,965; colored, 201; grand total, 7,166; average male daily attendance, 1,871; female, 2,443; total, 4,314; whole number of teachers, 124; amount paid teachers, $16,043.-

42; number of schools taught, 116; number of days schools were taught, 8,474; visits of directors, 345; amount of taxes levied for schools, $12,514.04; number of school-houses erected during the year, 10; cost of same, $2,200; whole number of school-houses in county, 84; total value of same, $35,782; value of all other property belonging to districts, $2,213; receipts for the year, $23,742.95; expenditures for the year, $18,516.60; balance, $5,237.57; number of districts voting tax, 75; total number of districts in county, 164; number of institutes held during year, 2; teachers attending same, 60; number of children deaf, blind, insane, etc., 7.

The public-school system has kept pace with the rapid growth of the county since the advent of the " Frisco Railway," and has made greater progress in the last semi-decade than in any twenty years previously. The growth in the attendance of three institutes held in the county since 1886, is significant; the first, at West Fork, had only seventeen in attendance, the second numbered eighty, and the last, at Fayetteville, had an attendance of 125. In September, 1887, a Directors' Annual Meeting was organized, which is expected to be an influential agent in the improvement of district management.

Among a large number who might be mentioned as active in the promotion of public-school interests in various parts of the county are Prof. E. H. Howell, Judge L. Gregg and Col. Thomas Hunt, of Fayetteville; William Mitchell, of Prairie Grove; County Examiner C. H. Inman, of Springdale; H. P. Sloan, of Pitkin; William Mayes, of Johnson; Dr. B. F. Williams, of McGuire's Station, *et al.*

It is but natural that Fayetteville, which had long had such excellent private seminaries and colleges, should be loth to exchange them for the undeveloped public schools, which, for some time, were considered not unlike schools for paupers. It was organized under Circuit Supt. E. E. Henderson as District No. 1, with J. Q. Benbrook as trustee, and schools with not to exceed three teachers, including those for colored schools. Among the various buildings rented from year to year were the Masonic Hall, the old Female Seminary, the Methodist, Baptist and Christian Churches. Under the corporation school law

Fayetteville was made a special district, and March 20, 1871, the following school board met: J. C. Massie, J. Q. Benbrook, H. C. C. Boteführ, Thomas D. Boles, D. D. Stark and Charles L. McClung. Mrs. Smith then had charge of the white schools, and Miss Dora Ford and a Miss Mannels taught the colored students, under the care of the American Missionary Society.

No school building was erected by the city until their present edifice was built, in 1885, under the direction of the following board: L. Gregg, president; B. H. Stone, O. C. Gray, E. B. Harrison, J. T. Reynolds and another. The board made the following report September 1, 1885:

"We report that for the last school year the district voted a five-mill tax for building purposes, and for this year a five-mill tax for all teaching purposes."

The directors drew from the county treasury for building purposes during the year $2,468.63 from the State; from the common-school fund, $1,120; the amount received from other sources was an accumulation from previous years in the treasury.

We report one school-house built during the year. Its foundation is stone; its walls, brick; its roof, iron; contains two large halls and six good class rooms; materials and finish, good; location, on an eminence in a seven-acre lot; cost of building and grounds about $9,131.55, and the grounds unenclosed; amount in the treasury, in State scrip, $557.03.

One school building was erected for colored children in the city several years ago, of stone foundation, brick walls, and wooden roof, by the American Missionary Association and by individual contribution; it will accommodate about eighty or 100 pupils; the grounds (donated) and the house are worth about $2,500 to $3,000. The school board paid $150 to a colored teacher for the colored schools this year.

The following enumeration was reported: White, 602; colored, 139; total, 741.

The school building was rented to private teachers on its completion, on account of lack of funds; but the following year the public schools opened in full force, and have made rapid advancement.

In 1886–87 the first public school was held in the new building, under the following corps of teachers: Superintendent, Col. O. C. Gray; assistants, Miss Ella Carnall, Mrs. F. L. Sutton, Miss Anna Putman, Miss Jessie Cravens, Mrs. Alice Adams and Mrs. M. W. Alex.

The school graduated its first class of three pupils in 1888, and starts out for the coming year with the following corps of teachers: Superintendent, A. S. Stultz, a graduate of the Cook County Normal School, under the famous educator, Col. Parker; assistants, Miss Anna Putman, Miss Jessie Cravens, Mrs. Annie Stapp, Miss Mollie Dickson, Miss Mattie Ralston, Miss Mary Leverett and Miss Lena Rhodes, most of whom are graduates of the Arkansas Industrial University. Their curriculum is of a high-school grade, enabling its graduates to enter the A. I. U. The principal of the colored school is A. L. Richardson, and his assistant is W. J. Kidd.

The financial report of the school board for June 1, 1888, is: Total receipts, $6,394.41; total expenditures, $4,205.11; amount on hand, $2,188.20.

Among the earliest teachers at West Fork were Prof. Thomason and H. Lafferson. A log building was long used as an ordinary district school. In 1886 the growth of the town led to the erection of a special building of two stories. It is a neat frame, 36x40 feet, situated in the west part of town. G. S. White and the present incumbent have been the teachers in the new building.

In 1885 the Springdale district erected a fine two-story brick edifice, containing four rooms. Before this date, and even until 1888, private schools seemed to have a strong hold on the people. The first private school was in the old Baptist Church, a three-months' school "after corn was laid by," in which "Readin', Ritin', Rithmetic and Spellin'" were conned over. The date of the first is uncertain, but the old church answered this pedagogic purpose until the "fall of Sumter." The first public-school building was a frame, built about 1868–69. That built in 1885 is 40x70 feet, and is an ornament to the town. Three teachers, Principal J. W. Coltrane, assisted by M. W. Davis and H. M. Grenade, have charge of about 150 pupils. Principal Coltrane has been in charge since the erection of the building, which, like the house at West Fork, is a special district building.   Other places in the county are ordinary members of the public-school system.

RELIGION.

Cumberland Presbyterians.—One of the first religious organizations to enter Washington County was the Cumberland Presbyterian.   The first Cumberland Presbyterians to locate in Arkansas were the Pyeatts and Carnahans, who, in 1812, emigrated from Northern Alabama, and located at Crystal Hill, fifteen miles above Little Rock.   The party consisted of James and Jacob Pyeatt and James and Samuel Carnahan.   The next year the father of the Carnahans, Rev. John Carnahan, removed to Arkansas, and, in the house of Jacob Pyeatt, preached the first sermon delivered in what is now Arkansas by a Cumberland Presbyterian.   He formed a circuit, and was placed on the roll of Elk Presbytery.   In 1814 he was licensed, and in October, 1816, was ordained.

The intermediate meeting for the organization of the Presbytery of Arkansas was held at the house of John Craig, on White River, in 1823.   R. D. King, Reuben Burrow, John Carnahan and W. C. Long were present, and James H. Black and J. M. Blair were received as candidates.   The presbytery was constituted at the same place in May, 1824, by Revs. John Carnahan, W. C. Long and William Henry.   At the next meeting, in the fall of the same year, a quorum was not present, but Rev. Andrew Buchanan presented himself as a candidate, and in the spring of 1826, with three others, was licensed.   Soon after the Carnahans, Blairs, Buchanans, Pyeatts and Crawfords removed to Cane Hill, in Washington County, and there, on August 30, 1828, Revs. William T. Larremore and J. M. Blair organized Cane Hill Cumberland Presbyterian Church, with James Billingsley, James Buchanan, William Reed and Robert Buchanan as elders.   Meetings were held for four or five years in a log school-house, standing where the grave-yard near Boonsboro now is.   One session of the presbytery was also held there.   About 1832 or 1833 a large log house, 35x50 feet, was erected, and was occupied until 1858, when the building known as the White Church was completed. It is a frame structure, 40x50 feet, and cost about $1,500. Among the pastors who have served this congregation are John Carnahan, J. M. Blair, Samuel Harris, George Morrow, B. H. Pierson, John Buchanan, J. T. Buchanan, F. R. Earle, R. F. Adair and J. T. Molloy. Soon after the organization of the church a Sabbath-school was established, and, with the exception of a short time during the war, it has since been maintained.

During the pastorate of Rev. Samuel Harris the congregation was divided, and Salem Church organized. A portion of the members became dissatisfied with Mr. Harris, and elected another pastor. His adherents then organized a new congregation, with James B. Russell, James Haygood and Lewis Haygood as elders. This occurred in 1844. The successors of Mr. Harris have been Rev. Mr. Braly, B. H. Pierson and Dr. F. R. Earle. A school building located near Boonsboro was used as a place of worship until the erection of Cane Hill College. The congregation now numbers about 110 members. The officers are as follows: W. C. Braly, G. M. Haygood, J. R. Pyeatt, H. C. Pyeatt, A. E. Andrews and Z. B. Edmiston, elders, and W. F. Moore and J. S. Edmiston, deacons. Recently about eighteen members have withdrawn, and organized a new congregation about one and one-half miles south of Boonsboro.

Billingsley congregation of Cumberland Presbyterians was organized some time about 1850, and for many years was known as Mount Zion Church. Among the first members were G. B. Nolen and wife, Merritt Baker and wife, Nancy Stevenson, John Billingsley and Miriam Dodson. The elders were John Billingsley, G. B. Nolen and Merritt Baker. Until the Civil War the congregation was under the care of Rev. Ambrose Williams, and since that time it has been chiefly supplied by B. F. Totten, J. T. Molloy and F. R. Earle.

Previous to May, 1888, services were held in school-houses, but at that date a neat frame building was completed, at a cost of $540. In 1887 seventeen members of this congregation withdrew and organized Pleasant Grove congregation, with L. Tankersly, S. Dell and L. C. Blakemore.

The Fayetteville Cumberland Presbyterian Church is a part

of the Arkansas Presbytery. Its early records were destroyed during the war, so that reliable information of the pre-war period is very meager. A Rev. Feemster is given as one of its earliest preachers. On June 3, 1867, the following members reorganized themselves into a church: Samuel H. Buchanan, E. H. Buck, M. G. Bonham, L. F. Graham, J. D. Henry, Dr. James Stephenson, Sarah Sellars, M. S. Bonham, Esther Crockett, L. M. and A. E. Routh, Adeline Graham, M. J. Reif, Margaret Calfee, Sarah Hodges, Martha Stephenson and L. A. Henry. Since 1867 the pastors have been as follows: Revs. Samuel H. Buchanan (now Dr.), John Buchanan, F. R. Earle (now D. D. and president of Cane Hill College), S. S. Patterson, J. L. Dickens, Rev. E. E. Morris, G. A. Henderson and J. T. Molloy, the present pastor. Dr. Earle was recalled three different times after his first pastorate. The largest accessions to the church have been made under Rev. A. M. Buchanan, R. G. Pearson, an evangelist, and Rev. Molloy, the total membership now being 114. Their first building was of brick, erected at a cost of $2,500. Their present church edifice is a frame structure, built during the centennial year. Two ladies' societies, the Aid and Foreign Missionary, are in a flourishing condition.

West Fork Cumberland Presbyterian Church was organized in the summer of 1853, in a school-house one mile and a half from the town of West Fork. Two years later a log building was erected. The original members numbered about twenty-five, of whom four are now living. They are J. C. Stockburger and wife Martha A., Maria Brown and William Hutcheson. The first elders were J. C. Stockburger and E. Baker. There is now a membership of over fifty, and in 1881 a new frame church house was completed.

Barker Cumberland Presbyterian Church was organized in 1881 by Rev. Samuel Cox, with the following officers and members: N. Rose, E. P. Haynes, S. A. Cox, elders; J. L. Barker, deacon; M. Hodges, treasurer; Margaret Cox, L. Landon, E. Haynes, A. D. Haynes, Tennie Haynes, Clara Cox, Jessie Loften, Margaret Loften, Mrs. Rose Huston Landon. During the same year a house of worship was erected. It was a frame building, and stands on the "old Barker farm." The pastors have been Rev. Samuel Cox, J. H. Pigman and S. L. Robinson.

Middle Fork Cumberland Presbyterian Church was organized in August, 1887, with L. J. A. Prather as pastor. G. W. Van Hoose and Pleasant King, elders; George King, deacon, and G. W. Van Hoose, clerk. The congregation was composed of members from White River congregation at Maguire's Store. The petitioners were, besides the above officers, John C. and M. L. Moore, F. L. Davidson, J. Maguire, Matilda Maguire, members. E. A. Hammontree was chosen clerk, and John Wells ordained deacon. The pastors have been M. Smith, Mathias Spires, M. D. Cox and J. C. Peters. The congregation, now numbering thirty-two members; worship in a school-house.

Little Elm Baptist Church was organized by Elder T. H. Day, with the following members: M. W. Marrs, deacon; D. K. Clevenger, C. T. Clayton, James Jackson, Annie Day, Mary J. Clayton, Sallie Beaver, Lucy Slaughter, Belle Gibson and Mary Shelly. The church was organized in a school-house, but in 1883 a union meeting-house was erected. It is situated nine miles west of Fayetteville. T. H. Day served the congregation as pastor for six years, and was then succeeded by H. B. Borders, the present pastor.

Spring Valley is the name of a flourishing church at Spring Valley, organized by Elders A. J. Vaughn and C. S. Fritts. It now belongs to Spring Valley Association, which was organized in October, 1877.

Beersheba Cumberland Presbyterian Church is situated on the Middle Fork of White River. It is a member of Arkansas Presbytery, and was organized about 1878 by the Rev. Samuel Black. Among its original members and officers were Elders A. Hight, W. C. Douglass, J. S. Guinn and George W. Arnett, and Deacon Nathan Reed. The first building, erected in 1878, was built at a cost of about $200. The pastors have been Revs. Prather, Black, Goin and Pigman, under whose charge the membership has reached to the number of about twenty persons.

The Barker Cumberland Presbyterian Church, a member of Arkansas Presbytery, was organized in 1881, by Rev. Samuel Cox. Elders N. Rose, E. P. Haynes, S. A. Cox, Deacon I. L. Barker, Margaret Cox, E. Haynes, A. D. Haynes, Tennie Haynes, M. Hodges, Clara Cox, Jessie Loften, Margaret Loften, Mrs.

Rose, Huston Landon, L. Landon and W. Cornstep were the original members. Rev. Samuel Cox was followed in the pastorate by Rev. Benj. Pigman and Rev. Benj. L. Robinson. The society has twenty-three members, and a house of worship valued at $1,051. It is a frame structure, located on the old "Barker farm," and erected in 1881.

The Cumberland Presbyterian Church, located five miles east of Prairie Grove, was organized in 1887, by Rev. T. Molloy, of Fayetteville. Their membership has increased from twenty-four, the original number, to thirty-four, the present membership. They occupy a union church with the Church of Christ at that point.

Methodist Episcopal Church, South.—The Fayetteville Methodist Episcopal Church, South, was organized about 1834 or 1835 at the home of Lodowick Brodie. Among its first members were Mr. Brodie and wife, Martin Frazier, Dr. Adam Clark and wife, David Reise and wife, a Mr. Avard and wife, a Mrs. Anthony, Mr. and Mrs. John Skelton, and a Mr. Cardwell and wife. They held services in Mr. Brodie's house, and after the completion of the first court-house used that as a place of worship. Their first church, which was afterward burned during the early years of the war, was built in the spring of 1840, and it was about 1868 that their present brick structure was erected. David Reise was the first class-leader, and among their earliest ministers and circuit riders were Rev. John Havel, Rev. Bump, Rev. Avery, Dr. Adam Clark, Rev. Custer, Dr. John Hunter, Dr. Sanders, Rev. William Cobb, Richard Cardwell and Rev. Carlyle. After 1840, among those who preached here were Revs. Young, Ewing, Lively, Thomas Stanford, Benona Harris, and Rev. Danley.

The Elm Springs Methodist Episcopal Church, South, is a very old society, organized probably in the earliest thirties, by Rev. H. G. Joplin, its pastor. The earliest members received into the church, of which information could be obtained, was Margaret S. Webster in 1834, John B. Webster in 1839, Kilby Saunders in 1851, Sarah E. Deavers the same year, Rev. Jacob Pearson the same year, M. W. Wasson in 1852, Zachariah Ennis the same year, Marion D. Steele in 1857, Mary E. Steele in 1854, Catherine M.

Glover in 1855, Sultana D. Pearson in 1858, Thomas F. Webster in the same year, and Elizabeth A. Webster in 1860. The society erected a neat frame structure in 1850, and on their reorganization in 1866 their present building was put up. It is a frame, valued at $400. Rev. Joplin's successors are W. A. Cobb, G. Boyd, J. Banks, T. Stanford, M. D. Steele, H. M. Granack, E. J. Downe, S. D. Gaines, D. Sturdy, W. H. Corley, T. J. Smith, J. F. Hall, James A. Walden, C. R. Taylor, P. B. Summers, B. Williams, B. C. Matthews and J. M. Clayton. The church was reorganized in 1866, by Rev. M. D. Steele, and the officers were J. P. Simpson, W. S. Deavers and J. P. Birch. The present membership numbers fifty-four persons.

Sulphur Springs Methodist Episcopal Church, South, belongs to the Prairie Grove Circuit, and was organized about 1850. Larkin Tanksley, class-leader; Green Harrison, steward; Mrs. Tanksley, Mrs. Green, R. J. West and wife, John Mock and wife, Robert Houck and wife, Mr. Larabee and wife and a few others were the original members. They erected their first church soon after organization, about five miles south of Prairie Grove. It is of hewn logs, and cost probably $300. It still serves as their house of worship. The pastors of the society have been Revs. David Carethers, L. P. Linely, Thomas Stanford, John Mathis, W. W. Mathis, Dr. Andrew Hunter, J. W. Shook, —— Woods, T. J. Smith and all others who preached at Prairie Grove. Their membership is fifty-one.

The Illinois Chapel Class of the Prairie Grove Circuit was probably organized as early as 1842, and among its first members are Mr. Ross and wife and James Young and wife. Rev. Young Ewing traveled the circuit in 1852. The church is three miles east of Prairie Grove.

The Stonewall Class of the Prairie Grove Circuit was organized by Rev. P. B. Hopkins, August 6, 1887. For its first members and officers there were J. N. Wheeler, steward; H. Davenport, class-leader; Jesse Wheeler, J. P. Bennett, Sarah Bennett, S. E. Davenport, J. H. Davenport, A. Allen, Ada Bennett, M. J. Sanders, F. E. Mahery, J. Mahery, Mittie Parker, S. J. Bates, Mary Wheeler, M. A. Taylor, Tenna Bates, Virgin Mahery, F. A. Taylor and M. E. Allen. The society hold services in a school-house three miles west of Prairie Grove.

Viney Grove Methodist Episcopal Church, South, another member of the Prairie Grove Circuit, began its existence in 1853, under the guidance of Rev. David Carethers. P. B. and Lucinda H. Tucker, James Branenburg and Thomas West (two officers of the church), Adeline Howel, Armind West, James West and Jetta West constituted the first membership. The first church, a log house situated on the prairie west of the present Viney Grove, was built in 1854, but suffered destruction during the late war. The next church, erected in 1869 at Viney Grove, was built at a cost of $1,200. It was dedicated by Bishop G. F. Pearce in 1869, but was burned in October, 1844. The present house, a good frame structure, was built in 1885, at a cost of $1,500, and has not yet been dedicated. The society numbers seventy-six persons. The pastors, beginning with Rev. David Carethers, have been Revs. Young Ewing, Jordan Banks, Walter Thornburg, J. W. Shook, W. W. Mathis, —— Gering, Thomas Stanford, L. P. Linely, G. A. Danly and others mentioned among the Prairie Grove pastors.

Zion Methodist Episcopal Church, South, is a member of the Elm Springs Circuit, and was organized in 1857 by Rev. John S. McCarven, with the following members: Richard W. Cardwell, class leader; Mary L. Cardwell, William H. Cardwell, D. Cardwell, Jane C. Ford, Amilla Ford, W. H. Eidson, Susan Eidson, Wilson Cage, Mary B. Cage, David Willeford, Martha Willeford and Mary J. Ruth. The first building was erected in 1857; it is a frame house, valued at $500, and is located six miles northeast of Fayetteville. Their pastors since Rev. McCarven have been Revs. Josiah A. Williams (P. C.), Thomas Stanford (P. E.), J. Banks (P. C.), J. W. Shook (P. E.), M. Granade (P. C.), William Mathis (P. E.), E. J. Dawn (P. C.), J. M. Clayton (P. E.), T. Wainwright (P. C.), James A. Walden (P. E.), T. J. Smith (P. C.), J. J. Roberts (P. E.), J. F. Hall (P. E.), David Sturdy (P. C.), James A. Anderson (P. E.) and William Mathews (P. C.). They have fifty members.

The Prairie Grove Methodist Episcopal Church, South, is the center of a considerable circuit bearing its name. The society was organized in 1869 by Rev. David Sturdy, with the following as a partial list of members: W. D. Rogers, steward; L. T. Sanders, class leader; John Mock, S. E. Rogers, Martha Rogers, Julie Rogers, Margaret Mock, M. J. Sanders, Martha J. Mock and Mary A. Mock. They erected a good frame church in 1880, at a cost of $1,500, and dedicated it the following year, Rev. R. S. Hunter officiating. The pastors of the society have been Revs. David Sturdy, J. Atchley, Jerome Haralson, W. H. Carley, R. M. Tydings, S. J. Stone, J. F. Hall, P. B. Summers, C. R. Taylor, J. P. Calloway, S. N. Burns, B. H. Greathouse, T. J. Reynolds, Young Ewing, J. A. Walden and P. B. Hopkins, the present incumbent of the pastoral office. The congregation numbers 107 members. It was for several years an appointment on the Cane Hill Circuit before its organization, and services were held in the Cumberland Presbyterian Church.

Mount Carmel Methodist Episcopal Church, South, is on the Cincinnati Circuit, and was made a separate society in 1877 by Rev. T. F. Bremer. Samuel Gilbreath, Luretta Gilbreath, J. J. Clayton, Lewis Collins, Sallie Collins, N. J. Christian, Elizabeth A. Christian, E. M. Tullis, Mary Holt, H. Fosselman, E. Fosselman, Carol Moore, Isabell Washington and about ten others constituted the original membership. They have a small pine church building, valued at about $175, located about three miles east of Cincinnati. It was built in 1866. Revs. T. F. Bremer, Robert Johnson, J. W. Stone, —— Dikes, P. B. Hopkins, W. M. Baldwin and J. H. Meyers, the present incumbent, have filled the pastoral office. The membership is now twenty-four persons.

The following list of appointments for the Methodist Episcopal Church, South, in Washington County was obtainable:

1874—J. A. Walden, P. E.; J. J. Roberts, Fayetteville Station; W. H. Corley, Fayetteville Circuit; J. Harolson, Boonsboro Circuit; R. M. Tidings, Viney Grove Circuit; J. E. Martin, White River Circuit.

1875—J. A. Walden, P. E.; S. A. Mason, Fayetteville Station; D. J. Smith, Fayetteville Circuit; R. M. Tidings, Boonsboro Circuit; W. H. Carley, Viney Grove Circuit.

1876—J. A. Walden, P. E.; R. S. Hunter, Fayetteville Station; J. A. Hall, Fayetteville Circuit; T. F. Brewer, Boonsboro Circuit; A. Summers, Viney Grove Circuit; J. Shook, White River Circuit.

1877—J. A. Walden, P. E.; R. S. Hunter, Fayetteville Station; J. F. Hall, Fayetteville Circuit; W. J. Stone, Viney Grove Circuit; T. F. Brewer, Boonsboro Circuit; J. N. Pace, White River Circuit; D. C. Ross, Illinois Circuit.

1879—J. F. Hall, P. E.; F. A. Jeffett, Fayetteville Station; J. A. Walden, Fayetteville Circuit; W. J. Stone, Boonsboro Circuit; C. R. Taylor, Viney Grove Circuit; D. C. Ross, Illinois Circuit.

1880—J. F. Hall, P. E.; George W. Hall, Fayetteville Station; P. B. Summers, Fayetteville Circuit; J. W. Shook, Illinois Circuit; J. P. Calloway, Viney Grove Circuit; W. J. Stone, Boonsboro Circuit; J. H. Bradford, White River Circuit.

1882—S. H. Babcock, P. E.; T. J. Reynolds, Fayetteville Station; W. H. Corley, Springdale Circuit; D. C. Ross, Weddington Circuit; Frank Naylor, Goshen Circuit; W. A. Derrick, White River Circuit; S. F. Dykes, Boonsboro Circuit; S. N. Burns, Viney Grove Circuit

1883—S. H. Babcock, P. E.; W. Penn, Fayetteville Station; W. H. Corley, Springdale Circuit; T. J. Reynolds, Viney Grove Circuit; S. S. Key, Boonsboro Circuit; L. W. Harrison, White River Circuit; A. M. Elam, Brentwood Circuit; R. R. Moore, Goshen Circuit; W. A. Derrick, Weddington Circuit.

1884—J. A. Anderson, P. E.; M. E. Butt, Fayetteville Station; B. C. Mathews, Springdale Circuit; W. T. Keith, Cincinnati Circuit; L. W. Harrison, Illinois Circuit; J. A. Walden, Prairie Grove Circuit; P. B. Hopkins, Boonsboro Circuit; J. R. Maxwell, White River Circuit; D. C. Ross, Goshen Circuit.

1885—J. A. Anderson, P. E.; M. E. Butt, Fayetteville Station; B. C. Mathews, Springdale Circuit; L. W. Harrison, Illinois Circuit; J. A. Walden, Prairie Grove Circuit; P. B. Hopkins, Boonsboro Circuit; W. T. Keith, Cincinnati Circuit; J. R. Maxwell, White River Mission; D. C. Ross, Goshen Circuit.

1886—J. A. Peebles, P. E.; G. W. Evans, Fayetteville Circuit; B. C. Mathews, Springdale Circuit; H. A. Armstrong, Illinois Circuit; P. B. Hopkins, Prairie Grove Circuit, J. A. Walden, Boonsboro Circuit; J. H. Meyers, Cincinnati Circuit; D. C. Ross, Goshen Circuit.

1887—J. A. Peebles, P. E.; B. H. Greathouse, Fayetteville Station; J. M. Clayton, Elm Springs Circuit; H. A. Armstrong, Illinois Circuit; P. B. Hopkins, Prairie Grove Circuit; J. A. Walden, Boonsboro Circuit; J. H. Meyers, Cincinnati Circuit; J. R. Maxwell, White River Mission; J. H. Sturdy, Goshen Circuit.

Christian Church.—The West Fork Christian Church is probably the oldest organization of the followers of the teachings of Alexander Campbell in Washington County. It was organized in 1837, with the following officers and members: Elders, William Robinson, Stephen Strickland and Alfred Arrington; deacons, Levi Combs and Shelby Conner, and members, Mrs. S. Strickland, Mrs. A. Arrington, Mrs. Shelby Conner, Thomas Wilson and wife, Mrs. W. Robinson, Benjamin Miller and wife, Samuel Alexandel and wife, Daniel Conner, Eli Bloyd and wife, John Wilson, Joseph Lewis, Betsy Conner, Christopher Harness and wife, Joseph Miller, Sr., and wife. They were first organized under an elm tree, and held services there until soon after the ruling elders built a church of hewed logs. Elder Stephen Strickland seems to have been the first pastor, and among others who held services there afterward were Rev. John Robinson, the well-known Rev. Robert Graham, Rev. Elijah Northam and Rev. Eli Baker. The present membership numbers about thirty persons.

The Fayetteville Christian Church is not only one of the oldest and largest churches in Washington County, but is probably the largest Christian Church in Arkansas. This is largely due to the character of its founder, Rev. John T. Johnson, its pioneer educator, Robert Graham, and its present pastor, Rev. N. M. Ragland. Rev. Johnson, a brother of Vice-President Richard M. Johnson, became a convert to the teachings of Alexander Campbell, and giving up his seat in Congress, took the water route to Little Rock, Van Buren and other points in the Southwest, to spread the new teachings, whose followers here became known in popular terms as "The Campbellites," "Stoneites" and "New Lights," as well as "Christians" and "Disciples." The following extract from a letter explains itself:

VAN BUREN, March 7, 1848. }
Tuesday morning.   }

Beloved Brother Campbell: I am here, in good health, about 1,500 miles from home, laboring in the cause of the reformation, for which you have sacrificed so much, and nobly struggled for a quarter of a century. The success has been far beyond the expectation of the most sanguine. Thank the Lord that your writings ever fell in my way ! I shall ever feel the debt of gratitude that you taught me how to read the bible—the book of the Lord. It imparts to me a happiness that no language can tell. [Here he speaks of visiting Little Rock and Van Buren.]

3. I visited Fayetteville, fifty-two miles north, and labored twelve days with great success. We had about thirty-five additions, and organized a church fifty strong, with elders and deacons. We have four able lawyers, an able physician, and a distinguished preacher of the Cumberland Presbyterians in the congregation. I left rejoicing! [He then speaks of other matters, and closes with the following]:

This is a great country. The success of this precious cause is the only motive that could induce me to make such immense sacrifices of domestic happiness.   (Signed),   J. T. JOHNSON.

From the date of the above letter we see that the church was organized about February, 1848, and we also see that there was a settlement of probably fifteen adherents of this faith already there, among whom were Dr. and Mrs. Pollard, and a Mrs. Onstott, probably the first three members of the congregation. Among the ministers who preached before Johnson's organization was a Rev. Stirman. After the organization Rev. Robert Graham, a man of great natural and scholarly ability, was their next pastor, and he it was who founded Arkansas College, which, although a private school, was a powerful agent in the growth and character of the church. He was both president of the college and pastor of the church during a considerable period, until he was succeeded, in both positions, by another able and scholarly man, Rev. William Baxter, whose period of service covered the remaining time before the war. With three so able men as these in succession, the rapid growth of the new church is not surprising.

Among those that followed Rev. Baxter were Revs. A. B. Murphy during the war, Kirk Baxter, S. K. Hallam, a Mr. Rice, J. M. Shepherd and a Mr. Floyd, who were editors of *The Faithful Witness*, a religious journal, Gay Waters, James Elliot and the present pastor, Rev. N. M. Ragland. The increase in membership and the extension of church work has been greater under Rev. Ragland, probably, than under the guidance of any of his predecessors. The membership is about 300. A mission at Farmington, a frame building costing about $1,500, was dedicated May 27, 1888, and now has a flourishing Sunday-school. A mission chapel in the southeastern part of Fayetteville has lately been built, and is used for Sabbath-school purposes, chiefly. It is a frame structure, valued at $1,000. Another flourishing mission is held in a school-house about two miles north of Fayetteville. The following annual financial report for the year ending November 15, 1887, will illustrate the extent of their work:

To amount paid out by church for incidental expenses and improvements, $353.63; to amount paid out for various missions, $130.11; to amount paid by C. P. S. Club, $73.95; to amount paid by Dorcas Society, $97.35; to amount paid by Sunday-school, $84.09; to amount paid by mission school, $12.60; to amount paid on minister's salary, $900; total, $1,651.73. By regular and special collection, $417.64; by collection on subscription, $900; by collection from Dorcas Society, $138; by collection from C. P. S. Club, $73.94; by collection from C. W. B. M., $27.75; by collection from Young People's Mission, $12.45; by collection from Sunday-school, $173.56; by collection from mission school, $12.62; total, $1,755.97. To amount on hand, $104.24. T. J. Conner, church treasurer.

They have also a Ladies' Missionary Society, which meets once a month.

The first church building of the denomination was built on the site of the Tremont House, but that was, with many other buildings, burned during the war. The old Masonic Hall was their next church house, until the present brick structure on College Avenue was completed, about 1871.

The Christian Church, unlike many others, was not broken up or disturbed by political issues during the great conflict.

The Christian Church, on the middle fork of White River, was organized in 1840 by Rev. S. Strickland, with Elders Samuel Hanna and Bracken Lewis, Matilda Lewis, Francis Hanna, Owen Ramey and wife, William Chandler and wife, Eleazer Lancaster and wife, F. Lancaster and William Hunt as members. After the war Rev. John S. Robertson, an evangelist, reorganized the church, with Elders Owen Ramey, E. Hanna and S. Hanna, Deacons W. Kelley and W. Chandler, and Clerk W. H. Campbell as officers, and over 100 members. It then took the name Union Church, and at one time reached a membership of 300. A frame church building was erected in 1854, at a cost of about $1,000, but it was destroyed by fire in 1882. A new frame was begun in 1884, which, when finished, will equal the first in value. On account of branch churches forming from this congregation the present membership is but eighty-three. These branches are Black Oak Grove, the elders of which are Andrew Hobbs, James Mahon and James Dockery, and Clifton Church, two miles west of the old church, whose pastor is Rev. F. A. Hobbs. The pastors have been as follows: Revs. Stephen Strickland, John S. Robertson, A. B. Murphy, E. Baker, Isaac Tellis, S. R. Beaman, William McDonnell and C. H. O'Bryan, the present incumbent.

Pleasant View Christian Church was organized in the spring of 1867, by Rev. Elder James W. Garrett, Elder John Read, William Russell, N. McIlroy, William Cranby, Caroline Read, O. A. Russell, Malissa Garrett, Malinda English, J. English and S. English, the original members.

The society has a membership of sixty, and before branch churches were organized from it at Antioch and at Cherryvale in the Indian Territory they numbered about 100. Their neat frame building, erected in 1883 at a cost of $500, is situated in Vineyard Township. Rev. Elder J. W. Garrett has been in charge from the first, but occasionally services have been held by the following ministers: Revs. Gage, Baker, Beaman, McDonnell, Williams, Allison, Ferguson, Elliot, Moore, Ragland, Geddens and others.

Evening Shade Christian Church is a young society, organized the first month in 1888 by Rev. John Williams. The officers chosen were Elders James Privett, R. R. Falin, W. J. Malone, S. W. Passick, and Deacons A. C. Males, W. Pearson and John Phelan. The other members were Lidie Males, R. E. Malone, S. C. Brown, Mary Hall, Mollie Webb, John and Sarah Malone and Z. Rutherford. The society have met in the school house of District No. 137. Their pastors have been Revs. John

Williams and H. C. Crowell. Thirty persons constitute their membership, most of whom are from Greenland and West Fork congregations.

Black Oak Church of Christ began its separate existence in 1880, with the following officers: Elders, J. J. Dockery, J. S. Mahone and L. A. Hobbs; deacons, E. T. Dockery and Robert Skelton, and thirty-six members. They built a hewn log house in 1878, as a community, for a school-house which is now used as a church, but the society contemplates the early erection of a larger structure, 34x46 feet. They have a membership of 105 persons. Rev. Daniel Chich, the pastor who organized the society, was succeeded in his pastoral duties by Revs. J. S. Mahon, C. H. O'Bryan and the present minister, Rev. L. A. Hobbs.

The Christian Church, situated five miles east of Prairie Grove, was organized in 1884 by Rev. C. Sperry. They have thirty members at present. They have a weather-boarded ceiled building, 24x36 feet, erected in 1884 at a cost of $400.

The Church of Christ at Mountain View dates its organization from 1886, when it was effected by Revs. M. N. West and B. M. Curtis. The elders were Eli Winn and J. H. McDonald, and J. W. Fitts, Sr. and Jr., were deacons. The church began with ten members, and have now increased their number to thirty-seven, who meet in the school-house of District No. 92. Revs. H. C. Crowell and B. M. Curtis have been the pastors.

The Christian Church of Prairie Grove was organized some time in July, 1885, by Dr. William Judd. It began with between forty and fifty members, and the following year was able to build a neat frame church, valued at about $700. Rev. H. C. Crowell has been its pastor from the beginning, and now counts their membership at about fifty persons.

The Church of Christ at Springdale was reorganized in 1887, by Elder Evan Thompson, with the few members scattered about that place. At the present writing the foundation of a tasteful frame structure, about 30x40 feet, is in progress. The society numbers twenty-five members.

Presbyterians.—The Presbyterian Churches in Washington County are members of the Presbytery of Washbourne, named in honor of the Rev. Cephas Washbourne (or Washburn), who was an early missionary to the Indian nations, and who was probably the first Presbyterian preacher to hold services in Washington County. The presbytery was first ordered by the Synod of Arkansas, convened at Pine Bluff, Ark., in 1883, and met on October 24, 1884, in the Presbyterian Church at Fayetteville. Rev. S. W. Davies, D. D., opened the meeting with a sermon from Numbers XI, 10-17. Those present were Rev. S. W. Davies, W. A. Sample, J. L. D. Houston and S. B. Ervin, and Ruling Elders O. C. Gray, of Fayetteville; M. G. Hearn, of Mount Zion; T. P. Allison, of Big Springs; J. D. Reinhardt, of Alma; J. C. Clift, of New Hope; J. F. Nolen, of Prosperity; S. W. Dinsmore, of Bentonville; J. A. Dibrell, of Van Buren, and John Smith, of Fort Smith. Revs. W. M. Crozier and D. C. Boggs were also among the number. Rev. W. A. Sample was chosen moderator.

The second meeting was held at Alma Church, April 16, 1885, and one was held with Bethel Church in October following.

Presbyterian influences gained an early foothold in Washington County, not only through Rev. Washbourne's great labors, but they radiated also from the faculty of Miss Sawyer's school at Fayetteville, although not so directly in ministerial work.

The Fayetteville Presbyterian Church dates its present organization from November 9, 1872, when a Presbyterial committee, composed of Rev. W. A. Sample, of Fort Smith, Ruling Elder A. W. Dinsmore, of Bentonville, assisted by Rev. D. C. Boggs, of the latter place, effected it. There had been services held here before the war, by Rev. Washbourne, in whose honor the presbytery is named, and among the members of this faith here at that time were Miss Lucretia Foster and Miss Mary T. Daniels, instructors in Miss Sophie Sawyer's school; but the present church is the only complete organization, probably. The original members were Prior N. Lea, ruling elder; Mrs. Elizabeth Lea, Misses M. Lizzie, Laura J. and Emma Lea, Denton D. Stark, Mrs. M. C. Stark, H. M. Lyon, Mrs. Fannie Springer, Mrs. M. A. Harris, John Barnett, Mrs. Susan H. Barnett, Mrs. Mary T. Smith, Mrs. Lizzie Lattemore, Mrs. E. M. Cox and B. F. Cherry. In January, 1876, they completed and paid for a good frame church, costing $1,750, which is located on the corner of College Avenue and Spring Street. It was dedicated the following year, on February 18, by Rev. Dinsmore offering the dedicatory prayer and Rev. S. W. Davies, D. D., the pastor, reading a sketch of the organization. Rev. Davies has been their only regular pastor, and under his management the church has risen to a membership of eighty-three on the rolls, with the various societies connected with it in active operation.

The Springdale Presbyterian Church was organized May 1, 1882, at Springdale, by Rev. S. W. Davies, D.D., and Rev. J. L. D. Houston. Its first members under the organization were Elder and Mrs. A. G. Hill, Deacon and Mrs. J. G. Bratten, Deacon R. M. Huffmaster, Thomas M. Hill, Miss A. E. Hill, E. M. Bratten, Miss Belle Bratten, Miss M. F. Huffmaster, Mrs. A. A. Overton, James J. Fleming, Mrs. E. C. Fleming, Mrs. Cynthia Morgan, Mrs. Lavinia W. Phillips, Mrs. Emily Lichliter, Mr. and Mrs. G. W. Armstrong and Miss Mattie Armstrong. Their pastors have been the Presbyterial evangelists, Rev. J. L. D. Houston and Rev. A. W. Milster, the present pastor, under whose ministry their membership has reached twenty-three. They have a neat brick house of worship, which was built about 1883 at an estimated cost of $1,000.

The Big Spring Presbyterian Church was organized in October, 1880, at Big Spring, by the Revs. S. W. Davies, D. D., and D. C. Boggs and Ruling Elder O. C. Gray. The congregation began with the following sixteen members: Mr. and Mrs. T. P. Allison, Mr. and Mrs. R. O. Hannah, Mr. and Mrs. T. A. Hannah, Mr. and Mrs. A. V. Hannah, John Hannah, Miss Elizabeth Hannah, Mr. and Mrs. W. A. Skelton. The ruling elders were T. P. Allison and R. O. Hannah. Their church building is a neat frame structure, erected in 1881 at a cost of $500; and was dedicated during the following year by Rev. Dr. S. W. Davies, of Fayetteville. This is one of the congregations under the charge of the Presbyterial evangelist, Rev. A. W. Milster, who assumed his duties in 1888; his predecessor was Rev. J. L. D. Houston, whose ministry in the same office dated from 1880. The membership of the church numbers twenty-three.

Prairie Grove, Boonsboro, Cincinnati and Viney Grove all have small congregations, but have never had any organization, if Cincinnati be excepted, which had a church there before the war, but which was among the large number of societies broken up during those chaotic days. These places are under the charge of the Presbyterial evangelist, Rev. A. W. Milster, of Fayetteville, who holds services at each place at regular intervals.

Baptists. — The Baptist Churches in Washington County belonged to Bentonville Association until 1871, when the Fayetteville Baptist Association was organized. The Bentonville Association is now in its forty-eighth year.

The Missionary Baptists did not begin the organizing of churches so early as some of the other denominations by several years. The oldest congregation of which any record could be found is styled Friendship Baptist Church. It was organized about three miles southeast of Springdale, in May, 1847, by R. C. Hill and J. F. Mitchell. Among the first members were Joseph Baker, James Meek, James White, Isaac Horton, Rhoda Baker, Elizabeth Meek and Nancy Fitzgerald. James Meek was the first deacon, and James White, clerk. The next year a small frame building with a chimney at each end was erected. It was used as a house of worship until 1861, when the present building was put up. Among the pastors who have served this church have been the following: J. F. Mitchell, Joseph Baker, Louis Heath, B. D. Gray, T. B. Van Horn, Asa Brown, Z. M. Vaughn, G. Bryant, A. D. Slaughter, E. Newton, J. C. Renfro, C. P. Tupper, J. T. Boyd, R. Hall, Mac. Slaughter, G. P. Hanks and J. B. Stark.

Mount Vernon Baptist Church was organized in 1848, by R. C. Hill and Joseph Baker. Among the pioneer members of this church were Isaac B. and Samuel H. Vernon, Brinson Sears, Sarah A. Meyers, Nancy Vernon, Emeline Phillips, Christiana Henson, Ann Pinkman and Elias Moncy. The last named was the clerk. The first house of worship was destroyed during the war, and a school-house was the meeting place from 1866 until 1877, when a frame building, 20x40 feet, was erected upon land donated by Dr. O. D. Slaughter. Among the preachers who have administered to this congregation may be mentioned Rev. Joseph Baker, O. D. Slaughter, R. Allen, T. Boyd, A. Huckaby, W. F. Green, C. P. Tupper, M. Slaughter and H. C. Calvert. The present membership of this church is seventy-five.

Valley Grove Baptist Church was organized in 1855, with the following constituent members: T. B. Van Horn, James Shults, Sarah Shults, Jackson Dyer, James F. and Sarah Hood, and Benjamin F. and Susan Boone. T. B. Van Horn was chosen moderator, and B. F. Boone, clerk. The congregation worship in a union meeting-house, which was erected in 1870, on the northeast quarter of Section 1, Township 15, Range 29 west. A former building was destroyed during the Civil War. Among the pastors of this church have been T. B. Van Horn, William Blakely, James Campbell, W. G. Slinker, J. Mayes, J. M. Haycraft, A. Huckaby and J. Crawford.

About June, 1866, a Baptist Church, formerly known as New Prospect, but now called Sulphur City, was organized by Elders John Mayes and James Isacks. The former became the first pastor. His successors have been J. C. Renfro, W. G. Slinker, J. Crawford, A. Huckaby, J. A. Smith and J. H. Calvert. The first house of worship was a log building, erected by the Baptists, Methodists and Presbyterians. The meetings are now held in a house erected by the school district.

Weddington Gap Baptist Church was organized on March 20, 1871, by Elders E. Baker and Elijah Burkett. The deacons elected were John England and George Dickison, the first of whom is still occupying that position. Among the other members were H. M. Davis, John T. Davis, Melvina F. Davis, Edward England and J. A. Cooper, who was the first and is the present clerk. Among the pastors have been C. Williams, H. J. Scruggs, J. B. Harralson, J. Robertson, T. H. Day, L. H. Palmer and H. C. Winstead. The congregation up to this time have worshiped in a school-house and Methodist Church, but is now completing a building.

Oak Grove Baptist Church is situated on Fall Creek. The congregation was organized on July 25, 1875, by Thomas Smith, with twelve members. G. M. Farmer and J. Swinford were chosen deacons, and J. Rogers, clerk. Since its organization the church has baptized thirteen members, licensed two ministers and ordained two deacons and one minister. The present officers are G. M. and C. O. Farmer, deacons; J. M. Carter, treasurer, and C. O. Farmer, clerk.

Mt. Gilead Baptist Church situated at Dripping Springs, eighteen miles south of Fayetteville, was organized on September 2, 1877, by Elder M. Smith, with nine members.

The Fayetteville Missionary Baptist Church was organized in 1857, at a private house about two miles south of Fayetteville, by John, Sarah, Martha and W. Z. Mayes, J. W. Buie, Sister Watson, Amanda (afterward) Peer, and a few others. The pastor was the Rev. Elder John Mayes, and their services were held at the various homes of the members until they were interrupted by the war, in 1863. The membership was then scattered and the records all destroyed, but in 1866, under their indomitable leader, the Rev. Mayes, nine of the old members resumed worship at a church in Fayetteville, and during the first month admitted thirty members. Their meetings were held in the Masonic Hall and other places until about 1879(?), when through the untiring zeal of Rev. Mayes, acting as pastor and carpenter, their present neat frame structure on College Avenue was completed, at a cost of, probably, $1,500. It was dedicated by Rev. J. P. Eagle, of Lonoke, Ark. Compelled by the weight of years to resign his pastoral duties, Rev. John Mayes was succeeded in his work by the following pastors: Revs. T. P. Boone, B. W. N. Simms, C. W. Callahan, M. L. Ball and Dr. B. G. Maynard, the present incumbent, who was formerly president of Tazewell and Mossy Creek Colleges, Tenn. The church has now a membership of about 118. It also has its various subordinate organizations, Sabbath-schools, etc.

The Springdale Missionary Baptist Church was organized about 1870, as Liberty Church, by Elders Bryant and Putman, and formed part of the Fayetteville Missionary Baptist Association. The moderator was Elder B. Putman, and W. A. Hunter was church clerk. The other members were John and Louisa Hychloter, Margaret and Elizabeth Fitzgerald, Margaret Baggett, Lucinda Baker, Fanny A. Putman, Isaac and Phœbe Lynch, William M. Blakely and James Meek. The society built their first church in the north part of Springdale in 1872; it is a frame structure, valued at about $1,500, and was dedicated by Elder Putman the following year. The Masonic order and the Primitive Baptist society have a financial interest in the building.   Under the charge of the following pastors, the membership has reached seventy-five: Revs. B. Putman, H. R. Barnes, T. P. Boone, O. D. Slaughter, W. F. Green, I. C. Robison, C. P. Tupper, Elder Huckleberry, John Mayes, B. W. Neal and A. M. Kennan, clerk.

The Valley Grove Missionary Baptist Church was organized in 1855 by Rev. T. B. Van Horn, with the following members: James Shultz, Sarah Shultz, J. Dyer, James F. and Sarah Hood, Benj. F. Boone and Susan Boone.   Rev. Van Horn was chosen moderator, and B. F. Boone became clerk.   The first building erected by the society was some time previous to the war, but during that conflict it was burned, and no house of worship was had until the erection of the present one in 1870.   It is a frame structure, situated in Section 1, Township 15, Range 29.   It is a union building, also occupied by the Cumberland Presbyterians and a Methodist society.   Rev. Van Horn's successors have been Revs. William Blakely, James Campbell, W. G. Slinker (?), J. Mayes, J. M. Haycraft, A. Huckaby and J. Crawford.   The society has thirty-seven members.

Vineyard Missionary Baptist Church is another member of the Fayetteville Association, organized December 14, 1867, but there seems to have been an organization before the Civil War, which erected a good frame church in 1859.   At the reorganization in 1867 there were but seven members: Elders G. Bryant and Asa Brown, Thomas Kimbrough, Sarah Kimbrough, J. S. Butler and M. E. Greer.   Some of their pastors have been as follows: Rev. T. B. Van Horn, Elders G. Bryant, F. R. Ferguson, J. W. McCurly, A. J. Estes, T. P. Boom, G. A. Latinn (?), C. P. Tupper and T. H. Day.   The society has eighty-four members.

The Valley View Missionary Baptist Church has a membership of twenty-nine persons.   Its records have been destroyed. It was organized June 24, 1877, by Elders J. C. Peters and J. C. Swainford, with the following officers: deacons, A. E. and W. R. Bridges, and clerk, W. D. Bridges.   Their church building, a neat frame, is located on Lee's Creek, about two miles north of the Crawford County line.   The following ministers have filled their pulpit: Revs. J. C. Peters, Aaron Peters and W. C. Eads.

Bethlehem Missionary Baptist Church, of the Fayetteville Association, became a separate society on May 11, 1879, by the agreement of the following members: Elder Joab and Sarah Caviness, Elder Mathias and M. A. Spyres, Joseph and Polly York, Peleg Rigsbee and daughter, Winifred, and Mahlon and Rhoda A. E. Spyres. The society previous to 1881 held their worship under a brush arbor in summer, and in private houses in winter. During the latter year, however, they erected a hewn log house, 20x24 feet, located on Lee's Creek, four and one-half miles southwest of Woosley. They have plans afoot at present for the erection of a frame church, 26x35 feet. Under the administration of the following pastors the membership has reached sixty persons: Rev. Elder Joab Caviness, Elder M. Spyres, Elder Keggel, Elder J. D. Woolsey and Elder M. H. Spyres. Their present officers are Deacons, A. T. Hopkins and Mahlon Spyres, and clerk, Henry Spyres.

Little Elm Missionary Baptist Church is a large society of seventy members, who have a small frame church about nine miles west of Fayetteville. The church building is valued at about $200, and was built in 1883, as a union church, before which date meetings were held in a school-house. The society was organized in 1881, by Rev. Elder T. H. Day and Deacon M. W. Marrs. D. K. Clevenger, C. T. Clayton, James Jackson, Anice Day, Mary J. Clayton, Sallie Beaver, Lucy Slaughter, Bella Gibson and Mary Shelley constituted the membership. Rev. Day served as pastor for six years, and the present minister in charge is Rev. H. B. Borders.

Rock Spring Missionary Baptist Church, meeting about two and one-half miles northwest of Rhea's Mills, at a school-house, is a comparatively young organization, whose existence began in 1882, on the third day of September, by the agreement of twelve members. The first pastor was Rev. T. H. Day, and Deacon S. W. Gleason and Clerk J. P. Jordan were the first officers. Rev H. C. Winstead, pastor, and R. Diment, the church clerk, constitute the present officers. Thirty-three members form the present society.

Fairmount Missionary Baptist Church, another young society of twenty-nine members, was formed in March, 1886, by Elder

M. Spyres and Deacon A. S. Hopkins. Besides these G. Spyres, John Jackson and Richard Daniels were the first members. The society was formed at a school-house two miles northwest of Winslow, and have so far been unable to provide a separate building for church purposes.   Rev. M. H. Spyres is the pastor in charge, and B. F. Johnston the church clerk.

The Garret Creek Missionary Baptist Church is a flourishing society of twenty-eight members, under the pastoral charge of W. C. Eads. J. W. Tapp is the present clerk. When the society began its separate existence, in September, 1886, as a member of the Fayetteville Association, the following members and officers were enrolled: Deacons, A. F. Sooter and G. W. Walton; clerk, Thomas Baker; E. V. McBroom, J. T. Smith, Annie Rickets, Elizabeth Fleming, Louisa Smith, N. M. Walton and Nancy Sooter.

Evening Shade Missionary Baptist Church, whose pastor is Elder J. C. Williams, has a membership of twenty-five persons. Its elders are Joseph Malone, Robert Fallen and Mr. Parish.

Methodist Episcopal.—The Methodist Episcopal Church of Springdale was organized at Liberty, a defunct village two miles from Springdale, and the property there was sold and the congregation established at the latter place in 1870.   The time of its organization at Liberty is approximated as 1852.   The original congregation included Joseph Holcomb and wife, Mr. and Mrs. W. B. Smith, Mr. J. B. Banks and wife, and Mrs. Wagoner. After the removal they united with Shiloh Baptist Church to build a union church.   In 1884 their present church, a frame building 32x50 feet, was built.   Their membership has increased to about 100.   Among the pastors in charge have been Revs. J. M. Clayton, Thomas Smith, J. R. Tydings, J. A. Walden, Hall, W. H. Corley, Summers, Williams and B. C. Matthews.

Fayetteville Methodist Episcopal Church, North, was organized in 1866, by Rev. W. L. Molloy.   There were few members, who were under the successive pastoral charges of Rev. Molloy, Revs. H. G. Hopkins, C. L. Howell, A. W. Fields and W. H. Gillam.   Under the aid of the Church Extension Society a church was built by Rev. Fields, but about 1874 the Rev. Gillam was compelled to see the church sold as the only means to extricate the body from a lamentable financial situation, and the congregation was disbanded.

Primitive Baptists.—Shiloh Church of Primitive Baptists at Springdale, Ark., belongs to the Washington Association. It was organized August 22, 1840, with the following members: William Graham, Levi Graham, Nancy Graham (the only one alive at the present writing), Moses Lee, Lucinda Graham, James Owens, Ellen Owens, Margaret Wolf and Sarah Graham. Elders Samuel Wheat, of War Eagle Church; William Poston, of Union Church; John Holcombe, of West Fork Church, and Deacons John Wood and Berry D. Graham, of West Fork Church, were the presbytery who established it. Elder James Mayfield was the first pastor, followed by Elder John Holcombe, until his death in 1876; then Elders A. G. Smith and Norman F. Goodrich were elected jointly, but since the death of Elder Smith his colleague has served. The records of the first four years are lost, but the church, it is known, was established three miles east of its present location; on its removal, however, to Springdale a log house was erected within a few rods of the site of the present building, which is a neat frame structure, erected in 1871, at a cost of about $1,000. The present membership of the church numbers about 100. This denomination figured largely in the growth of Springdale.

The Catholics.—St. Joseph's Catholic Church, of Fayetteville, was first organized by Father Curry, of Little Rock, about forty years ago. This generous priest bought a section of land near the site of Fayetteville, and sold it at a merely nominal rate to a company of Rhode Island Catholics, among whom were William Flynn, Patrick Hennessy, Philip McCoy, Charles Healy, Albert Byrnes, Maurice Coffey and Peter Smith, the original members of the congregation. The next visiting priest was Father Lawrence Smythe. The congregation soon felt able to build and support a church, and through the active work of Patrick Hennessy and others, the present neat frame building on the corner of Willow Street and La Fayette Avenue was completed by a Fort Smith carpenter named "Bill" Sullivan. The edifice cost about $2,500, and in June, 1878, was dedicated by Bishop Fitzgerald. The priests located here have been Fathers Thomas

O'Rielly and Joseph Phillip Maurel, the latter being the present incumbent. They have a membership of 120, and is the only congregation of that denomination in the county.

Protestant Episcopal.—St. Paul's Protestant Episcopal Church is one of the oldest churches in Washington County, and the only one of this denomination. It was organized May 23, 1848, by Rev. W. C. Stout, and the following officers were chosen: C. W. Deane, M. D., as S. W.; J. W. Chewas, J. W.; John Campbell, William McIlroy and Charles W. Washington, as vestrymen. On February 3, 1854, the corner stone of their first church was laid, and on October 29, following, the neat frame structure was consecrated by the Rt. Rev. Bishop Freeman. Their present edifice is of brick, and the date of erection is 1872, the corner-stone being laid on October 26. The dedication was not made until April 8, 1888, when the Rt. Rev. H. N. Pierce, D. D., LL. D., bishop of Arkansas, performed the ceremony. Under the charge of the following rectors the church has increased the number of its communicants to 112: Revs. William Scull, W. C. Stout, C. C. Townsend, Otis Hackett, J. Sandels, C. M. Hoge, T. M. Thorpe, and J. J. Vaulx, the present incumbent.

Evangelical Lutheran.—The Salem Evangelical Lutheran Church is a part of the English Conference of Missouri, and was organized in 1879 by Rev. I. E. Rader. The original members were I. D. Rader and wife, D. M. Linebarger and wife, W. F. Renner and wife, C. S. Hawn and wife, J. H. Bird, Mrs. Jacob Mason and Mrs. I. E. Rader. Mr. Linebarger and I. D. Rader were the elders, and Mr. Renner and the first mentioned elder were trustees. In 1880 they built their first church in Springdale, but have since replaced the frame structure by a brick edifice costing $4,800. Their parochial school has an enrollment of eighty-eight scholars, in charge of two instructors; and their Sunday-school, managed by a superintendent and three teachers, is attended by seventy-five persons. Of the 140 in connection with the church fifty-six are communicants. Since Rev. I. E. Rader's pastorate Rev. A. Sloan Bartholomew has been in charge.

Adventists.—The Seventh Day Adventists are represented in but one portion of Washington County, namely, at Springdale. One feature of their faith, however, the observance of Saturday as Sabbath, has created no small degree of interest in political circles, and this gives them a prominence that their comparatively small numbers would hardly justify otherwise.

The Springdale Seventh Day Adventists Church began with the following officers: Elder, J. A. Armstrong; deacons, Z. Sweringen and William Martin; trustees, William Martin and P. M. Ownbey. In 1886 they built a good frame church at a cost of, probably, $800, situated not far from the "Frisco" depot. The new house of the society was dedicated by J. G. Wood, and since then the work has been in the charge of the following pastors: Revs. J. G. Wood and J. P. Henderson. The pastor who, in company with D. A. Wellinsin, organized the church was Rev. J. W. Scoles. The society belongs to the Arkansas Conference. Their members at present number 106.

Congregationalists.—The Congregational Church of Fayetteville (colored) was organized in 1883, under the auspices of the American Congregational Missionary Association of New York City. The church now used was a school-house on College Street, and was bought by the society that year. Their membership is seventeen, and they have been under the charge of the following pastors: B. F. Foster, J. M. Shippen, W. R. Polk and L. B. Moore.

Bible Society.—The Washington County Bible Society was a pioneer institution. Its first meeting was held in March, 1831, when the following officers were elected: Rev. A. Buchanan, president; John Truesdale and Robert McCarny, vice-presidents; Maurice Wright, recording secretary; Lewis Evans, corresponding secretary; James Coulter, treasurer; C. M. McClellan, depositary; John Carnahan, Thomas Garvin, John Alexander, Joseph Reed and Jesse M. Blair, directors. The entire amount collected for the first year was only $63.47½. The society appears to have gone down about 1839, and was not revived until about 1850, when James Orr was elected president; Rev. John Buchanan and Robert W. Mecklin, vice-presidents; Rev. Cephas Washbourne, secretary; Maurice Wright, treasurer; Rev. Andrew Buchanan, James Crawford, Pressly R. Smith, Samuel Carnahan and Rev. Guilford Pylant, managers. This society continued in existence until the war, the last record being the report of Rev. John Buchanan, secretary, on June 14, 1860.

Y. M. C. A.—The Fayetteville Young Men's Christian Association was organized March 22, 1887, through the exertions of Mr. Ellis Duncan and Mark Dean. The original members were S. W. Barnett, R. S. Curry, W. N. and A. W. Crozier, Mark Dean, Messrs. Ellis, N. L., Garnett, Robert W. and Thomas G. Duncan, W. M. Flynn, W. McBride and Morton Milburn. The society is now in a prosperous condition, with parlor, reading room and hall in the post-office block. They have lately secured a general secretary, Mr. H. W. Hutchins, who devotes his entire time to the work, and is rapidly establishing all the various departments of Y. M. C. A. work. The following is a list of presidents since organization: W. McBride, Lee Treadwell and C. A. Davies, the present incumbent.

POST-OFFICES.

The number of post-offices established in Washington County from 1829 to 1888 was ninety-five, with names of postmasters and dates of appointments, as follows:

Ada: Archibald Borden, July, 1857; Hugh Rogers, July, 1858; discontinued February, 1867.

Albia: Jacob Yoos, April, 1871; discontinued July, 1873.

Aquilla: Owen D. Slaughter, May, 1884; Jeptha Johnson, May, 1885; John S. Johnson, November, 1885; Robert I. Fink, May, 1886; discontinued November, 1887.

Arnett: Luke Arnett, April, 1883.

Billingsly: Hiram H. Barrow, March, 1854; Lemuel G. Bassord, February, 1858; discontinued June, 1866; re-established July, 1866, Henry A. Sawyers; William K. Dye, April, 1867; Hiram H. Barrow, November, 1868; John C. Hanna, June, 1871; Horton M. Parks, April, 1872; Robert O. Ellis, July, 1872; Mathew M. Morrow, July, 1873; Houston M. Parks, February, 1877; Hiram H. Barrow, September, 1878; J. M. Burrow, April, 1883; Hiram H. Barron, June, 1883; discontinued August, 1883; re-established April, 1884, Thomas H. Cartner; Charles Marrs, April, 1885; John S. Darring, October, 1886; Ben. Elder, November, 1886; discontinued August, 1887.

Blackburn: Z. C. Winn, July, 1880; Hiram Mannon, February, 1882; John H. Mannon, March, 1882; discontinued, August, 1887; re-established August, 1888, Alice F. Nicholds.

Boone's Grove: Benjamin F. Reagor, June, 1851; discontinued June, 1851; re-established with B. F. Boone, September, 1858; M. P. Pool, April, 1866; G. W. Lewis, June, 1867; Susan Boone (Mrs.), July, 1868; discontinued January, 1869.

Boonsborough (late Steam Mill): Samuel Newton, August, 1843; Ewing W. McClure, July, 1845; John P. Truesdale, February, 1866; John S. Wilson, May, 1866; discontinued August, 1866; re-established with E. H. Blome, February, 1868; Nancy E. Brooks (Mrs.) January, 1869; W. D. McBride, January, 1870.

Boston: John Wilson, December, 1858; A. M. Kennon, June, 1860; discontinued June, 1866; re-established, O. Adkins, May, 1867; discontinued June, 1868·

Bostonville: Tandy K. Kid, July, 1844; discontinued May, 1848.

Brentwood (late Gunter): Dock W. Fuller, November, 1881; James J. Crawford, May, 1882; Henry C. Skelton, October, 1882; Frank H. Rizer, April, 1886; Thomas J. Bell, March, 1887.

Brush Creek: Robert Garrett, April, 1840; discontinued February, 1841.

Cane Hill: William B. Woody, June, 1830; Philemon H. Trout, December, 1833; Benjamin G. Estill, August, 1835; Lewis Henderson, February, 1837; Shepherd F. Atherton, May, 1840; James Hamilton, April, 1842; discontinued August, 1843; re-established with William W. Watson, February, 1867; Joseph H. Delap, November, 1867; discontinued February, 1868.

Carter's Store: John C. Carter, July, 1875.

Cherokee Agency (late in Crawford County): Hercules T. Martin, January, 1840; discontinued December, 1841; re-established with P. M. Butler, July, 1845; Frederick A. Kerr, October, 1845; discontinued May, 1849.

Cincinnati: William S. Walker, February, 1857; John A. Dienst, March, 1866; Henry S. Martin, October, 1867; Hagermon Shields, November, 1871; James Oates, October, 1876; James T. Walker, December, 1878; William S. Walker, December, 1878; H. Shields, January, 1879; Walter Bates, May, 1881; W. S. Baker, August, 1882; James Oates, October, 1882; James H. Barton, December, 1885.

Cleveland: Jesse C. Williams, June, 1879; discontinued December, 1880.

Clyde: William C. Russell, February, 1887.

College Grove: Thomas Wainwright, December, 1874; James D. Winning, January, 1876; Moses Dutton, January, 1876; changed to Goshen June, 1876.

Cove Creek: John Morrow, July, 1844; David Lichlyter, January, 1847; discontinued July, 1848.

Cross Roads: Wiley D. Deen, November, 1875; discontinued October 1876; re-established September, 1878, Louisa M. Piper; discontinued March, 1880; re-established with John F. Mason, March, 1883; discontinued February, 1884.

Devore: Elijah Devore, June, 1884.

Dump: William Guinn, February, 1885; discontinued July, 1886; re-established, January, 1887, William Guinn.

Durham: Charles C. Warner, August, 1873; John M. Smith, October, 1875; William A. McKinzie, July, 1885; John I. Vanhoose, February, 1887.

Dutch Mills: Frank H. Warren, October, 1871; George Heron, March, 1876; Ephraim M. Evans, August, 1877; Olney S. English, April, 1883; Valentine S. English, June, 1883; John V. Edmiston, October, 1887; Joseph R. Kimbrough, January, 1888.

Elm Springs: William Barrington, April, 1848; discontinued July, 1848; re-established with William S. Deaver, July, 1853; Thomas J. Sherman, July, 1858; Thomas F. Webster, May, 1860; Jonathan H. Reavin, March, 1861; Marinda W. Pearson, February, 1866; James R. Pollock, December, 1872; discontinued October, 1874; re-established November, 1874, James R. Pollock; James Trotter, August, 1875; Thomas F. Webster, February, 1876; R. L. Ritter, September, 1879; William T. Farrar, October, 1881; Ransom L. Ritter, January, 1888; Benjamin J. Deaver, August, 1883; William V. Steele, January, 1886.

Eutaw: Samuel Wilson, April, 1838; discontinued July, 1838.

Evansville (late Vineyard): Lewis Evans, December, 1838; Jacob Chandler,

December, 1846; Granville B. Shannon, November, 1847; Daniel W. Dennenberg, September, 1851; John H. Barney, February, 1852; George McClure, January, 1854; Elias H. Gilbert, May, 1834; Daniel W. Dennenberg, July, 1854; John H. Barney, April, 1856; Harrison J. Paden, May, 1857; Thomas B. Greer, April, 1861; Charles B. Withrow, May, 1866; Preston Chandler, December, 1866; John Adams, April, 1867; Orville Gillettzen, November, 1868; William N. Martin, November, 1869; Thomas N. Evans, May, 1872; James M. Chandler, May, 1875; J. W. Waters, March, 1878; James M. Chandler, April, 1878; John R. Flinn, October, 1878.

Evergreen: Maston S. Gregg, July, 1866; Benson W. Gregg, September, 1868; discontinued December, 1872; re-established September, 1874, Benson W. Gregg; discontinued November, 1878; re-established March, 1884, Wilson M. Davis; Henry Bell, September, 1884; discontinued October, 1884.

Farmington: William F. Martindale, June, 1868; William H. Engels, October, 1868; John W. Reed, September, 1881.

Fayetteville: Larkin Newton, August, 1829; Bryan H. Smithson, October, 1833; Onesimus Evans, July, 1839; John I. Stirman, December, 1841; Isaac Strain, February, 1844; John B. Costa, October, 1847; Henry Reiff, September, 1848; John W. Chew, February, 1850; William F. Blakemore, September. 1853; John W. Chew, March, 1854; William Adams, January, 1856; Dudley W. Fillingim, August, 1856; James B. Simpson, April, 1857; Elias B. Moore, January, 1860; William A. Watson, March, 1861; Hugo C. C. Botefuhr, February, 1866; Mary Lowe (Mrs.), December, 1866; John Richardson, January, 1868; Martin G. Bonham, February, 1868; James T. Harn, March, 1869; E. E. Henderson, March, 1871; Daniel Webster, April, 1871; Roderick A. Caldwell, December, 1874; Jesse L. Cravens, December, 1877; Elizur B. Harrison, June, 1884; Jesse L. Cravens, June, 1886, reappointed August, 1888.

Felix (late Swaggerty): William H. Ladd, November, 1886; Jasper N. Clark, April, 1887; Dominicus Gray, November, 1887.

Georgetown: Joseph L. Carter, July, 1884; changed to Lincoln January, 1885.

Goshen (late College Grove): Moses Dutton, June, 1876; Edmon B. Shipley, January, 1877; Jesse B. Kelley, October, 1877; Sterling H. Slaughter, October, 1882; Johnson A. Bryant, September, 1888.

Greenville: Hiram H. Barrow, March, 1854; Jeremiah Brewster, March, 1855; Levi Howell, September, 1857; Leroy Roberts, March, 1858; Benjamin Strickler, January, 1860; discontinued February, 1867; re-established July, 1867, Marshall N. Dale; William S. Crawley, October, 1868; John R. Hobrick, May, 1871; Adam W. Dobbins, October, 1871; discontinued October, 1872; re-established October, 1873, Robert E. Elmore; discontinued February, 1874.

Gunter: Thomas Custer, January, 1880; discontinued, January, 1881; Dock W. Fuller, June, 1881.

Harris: John Sword, April, 1888.

Hazel Valley: James R. Dean, July, 1875; discontinued July, 1878; re-established August, 1878, Paschal P. Bogan.

Helth (now in Madison County): John S. Brannon, February, 1884.

Hermansburgh: James S. Hukill, September, 1853; John H. Hermann, April, 1856; Frederick C. Hermann, October 1859; discontinued February, 1867.

Hilochee: Daniel B. Neal, September, 1850; discontinued July, 1866; re-established September, 1867, Samuel Cook; discontinued October, 1868.

Holm: P. A. Johnson, July, 1881; discontinued October, 1881.

Hood: Robert A. Rutherford, February, 1885; Moses D. Lewis, May, 1887.

Howe: John Craig, October, 1884; David Mallory, February, 1886; Lizzie M. Key, June, 1887.

Hubard: Francis M. Dyer, February, 1888.

Johnson: Joseph Ellis, March, 1887; Charles W. Spencer, May, 1888.

Liberty Grove: Jasper Farmer, June, 1875; discontinued July 1878.

Lincoln (late Georgetown): Joseph L. Carter, January, 1885; Noble Carter, July, 1886; John W. Smyth, May, 1887.

Little Spring: Anderson Sanders, March, 1876, changed to Spring Valley May, 1876.

Lone Star: Marshall N. Dale, July, 1883; discontinued April, 1884.

Lynch's Prairie: Albert G. Gregg, January, 1859; discontinued September, 1866.

Maguire's Store: Benjamin F. Williams, August, 1867; George W. Maguire, December, 1886; Benjamin F. Williams, May, 1887; discontinued October, 1888.

Malta: Hezekiah H. Alexander, June, 1887; Alexander Charley, September, 1887; discontinued April, 1888.

Mankins: Clark L. Burchett, September, 1882; Joseph H. Laymon, January, 1887; changed to Sulphur City April, 1887.

Mares Hill: James Mares, June, 1840; discontinued July, 1841.

Moffit: J. B. Mangrum, May, 1888.

Morrow: William M. Dyer, June, 1883; G. W. Morrow, July, 1883; discontinued December, 1883; re-established April, 1886, John G. Barnes.

Mountain: John Billingsly, December, 1883; discontinued January, 1839.

Mount Hayes: Emily Beaty, July, 1877; discontinued March, 1879.

Ocoee: Thomas A. Hannah, December, 1883; discontinued December, 1885.

Pitkin: Charles Fierce, May, 1884; James M. Karnes, September, 1884.

Prairie Grove: Abraham Price, July, 1867; Eliza E. Remheart, February, 1868; discontinued October, 1871; Tilghman H. Addison, November, 1871; James P. Neal, May, 1873; Joel P. Neal, March, 1887.

Rhea's Mills: Hugo C. C. Boteführ, July, 1867; William H. Rhea, December, 1874; Samuel V. Rhea, March, 1884; William C. Stone, March, 1886.

Richland Creek: Thomas Smith, December, 1832; Wilson R. Smith, June, 1831; Robert Buchanan, January, 1843; B. J. Helmesly, February, 1849; changed to Titsworth, Madison County.

Rugby: Andrew J. Vanlandingham, August, 1882; discontinued July, 1883; William J. York, December, 1885; David S. Miller, May, 1886; changed to Staunton December, 1886.

St. Patricks: George Lewis, June, 1840; James C. Dickerson, ——; discontinued January, 1843.

Sexton: William M. Goddard, June, 1882; William H. Sexton, March, 1884; John Gaylord, October, 1885; Ephraim M. Evins, December, 1885; Norman Gaylord, April, 1887; Robert C. Ridley, November, 1887; Watie Cagle, March, 1888.

Springdale: Bennett Putnam, May, 1872; William H. Lovelady, April, 1876; Christ C. Philips, May, 1877; Bemon W. Gregg, April, 1881; John B. Gill, December, 1884; Walter Y. Winton, July, 1885.

Spring Mill: Seneca Sutton, July, 1858; James T. Sutton, August, 1858; George W. Late, April, 1860; discontinued July, 1866.

Spring Valley (late Little Spring): Anderson Sanders, May, 1876.

Staunton (late Rugby): David S. Miller, December, 1886.

****

Steam Mill (changed to Boonsboro): Samuel Newton, April, 1839.

Strain: Joseph J. Morgan, January, 1884; Osborne L. Wilson, October, 1884; Joseph J. Morgan, November, 1885; James O. Johnson, April, 1887; discontinued December, 1887.

Strickler: Marshall N. Dale, April, 1878; John H. Worley, January, 1883; Mirander Brewster, August, 1883.

Sulphur City (late Mankins): James H. Laymon, April, 1887.

Summers: Benjamin N. Wortham, June, 1882; Henderson Elens, October, 1882; discontinued April, 1883; re-established April, 1884, John F. Summers.

Summit Home: William J. Reed, December, 1876; discontinued October. 1879; Elijah J. Woodburn, December, 1879; changed to Winslow August, 1881.

Sunset: Jerry M. Osburn, October, 1888.

Swaggerty: Gen. W. Stone, September, 1885; changed to Felix November, 1886.

Sweet Home: James C. Pittman, September, 1840; discontinued November, 1844; re-established with James C. Pittman, January, 1845; William D. Shorse November, 1845; discontinued April, 1846.

Sylva: John Cole, May, 1838; Charles I. Severs, November, 1843; Martin W. Thornberry, June, 1848; Joel P. Blair, May, 1849; Joseph M. Dickson, November, 1850; William Jones, March, 1851; Martin W. Thornberry, December, 1851; changed to Cincinnati February, 1857.

Taney: D. E. Jackson, March, 1879.

Tansy: William D. Shores, April, 1848; John Crawford, November 1852; discontinued June, 1857; Rufus K. McCollum, April, 1857.

Tolu: Thomas B. Greer, July, 1887.

Tranquilla: Joseph Arnett, May, 1870; discontinued October, 1871.

Vineyard (changed to Evansville): Lewis Evans, February, 1829; John Latta, December, 1833.

Viney Grove: William E. Zellner, August, 1870; James B. Gillis, July 1874.

War Eagle (changed to Sevierville, Marion County): Isaac Crow, December, 1832; John Buckhanon, December, 1835.

Wedington: Joseph D. Powell, March, 1879; Robert F. Flatt, August, 1882; Dan Thomason, May, 1884; Robert M. Delozier, October, 1886; Andrew J. Webb, December, 1886.

Wesley (now in Madison County): Calloway C. Baker, September 1867; discontinued August, 1870; re-established July, 1872, Joseph B. Shannon; James McMahon, May, 1873; Keble C. Cumings, February, 1874.

West Fork: James C. Hearer, May, 1848; John W. Harer, February, 1850; James Winn, October, 1850; John W. Harer, March, 1851; discontinued March, 1852; re-established with O. L. Karnes, May, 1854; W. H. H. Nott, February, 1866; W. T. Woolsey, June 1871; H. H. Davis, July, 1878; J. W. Hughes, December, 1879; William Simco, March, 1880; S. C. Robinson, August, 1880; Harris H. Davis, September, 1880; Jefferson P. Cox, January, 1886.

Wheeler: Thomas F. Weldon, March, 1873; Seth T. Kennedy, June, 1874; John Nickols, December, 1874; Eli H. Langston, February, 1876; David C. Guthrie, August, 1876; James Hogg, December, 1876; Henry Barker, August, 1878; Lue F. Barker, September, 1878; Charles F. Overman, September, 1878; Washington Pinder, November, 1878; William I. Hogg, November, 1880.

Winslow (late Summit): Elijah J. Woolum, August, 1881; James R. Yoes, January, 1883; John B. Kelton, August, 1883; Jobe A. Williams, November, 1885.

Wyman: William L. Lively, March, 1886; Francis M. Boyd, December, 1886; discontinued September, 1887; re-established May, 1888, Francis M Boyd; William T. Harmon, September, 1888.

The number of post-offices in Washington County now (October, 1888,) existing is forty-two, as follows: Arnett, Boonsborough, Brentwood, Carter's Store, Cincinnati, Clyde, Devore, Dump, Durham, Dutch Mills, Elm Springs, Evansville, Farmington, Fayetteville, Felix, Goshen, Harris, Hazel Valley, Hood, Howe, Hubard, Johnson, Lincoln, Maguire's Store, Morrow, Pitkin, Prairie Grove, Rhea's Mills, Sexton, Springdale, Spring Valley, Staunton, Strickler, Sulphur City, Summers, Tolu, Viney Grove, Wedington, West Fork, Wheeler, Winslow, Wyman.

WASHINGTON COUNTY.

William Agee.   The mercantile interests of Hood, Washington Co., Ark., are ably represented by the firm of Agee & Reagan, who carry a $2,000 stock, and do an annual business of $7,000.   Mr. Agee, the senior member of the firm, was born in Todd County, Ky., March 16, 1818, and is a son of John M. and Martha (Christian) Agee, who were born in Virginia, in 1792 and North Carolina in 1794, respectively,   They were married in the mother's native State, and moved to Kentucky, thence to Pettis County, Mo., in 1836, where they both died, the former when about eighty-five years of age, and the latter at the age of fifty-seven. The father was a farmer and Democrat, and was twice married, his second wife being Nancy Palmer, a native of Kentucky.   She died in Missouri, previous to the death of her husband.   Eight children were born to the first marriage, six of whom are living: Mary J., wife of James Combs; Caroline A., wife of M. J. P. Drake; John C., Miles A., James M. and William.   The latter began clerking in 1837, and followed that occupation for twelve years at Georgetown, Mo., after which he went into the mercantile business, but at the end of two years discontinued the business at this point.   He entered 280 acres of land west of Sedalia, and laid out the town of Dresden.   He sold a portion of his land for town lots, and did business there until several years after the war.   He then purchased his father's old home and farmed for six years, and then traded this farm for a stock of goods in Lamonte, Mo.   At the end of three years he moved his stock of goods to Washington County, Ark., and two years later went to Fayetteville, where he resided four years.   He afterward located in the place where he now resides, forming a partnership in March, 1887, with Hugh F. Reagan.   He served in the Federal army about seven months during the late war.   In October, 1842, he wedded Susan M. Courtney, who was born in Shelby County, Ky., in 1825, and died in Jackson County, Mo., in 1845. Two years later Mr. Agee led to the altar Miss Bohannon, a daughter of Charles Bohannon.   She was born in Woodford County, Ky., in 1828, and died the same year of her marriage.   Oswald Kidd's daughter, Jemimah A., became his third wife.   Her birth occurred in Pettis County, Mo., about 1830, and she died in 1851, leaving one daughter, Kate, the wife of W. H. Longan.   In 1852, Mr. Agee married his present wife, Elizabeth Christian, a daughter of Harris Christian.   She is a native of Todd County, Ky., born in 1825, and four of her five children are living: William H., Mary B., (wife of Hugh F. Reagan,) Thomas J. and George F. Mr. Agee and wife are members of the Christian Church, and he is a Democrat and Mason.

John T. Appleby, farmer and stock raiser, is the son of Hezekiah and Margaret (Herron) Appleby, natives of Georgia and Kentucky, respectively, the father born in 1797 and the mother in 1793. They were married in 1819, and afterward settled in Bedford County, where they remained until 1830, and then came to Arkansas, locating in Washington County. During the war the father went to Texas, on account of trouble at home, leaving his wife, and in 1864 her house was burned, and she mounted a horse and rode to Texas only to find that her husband was dead. The following year she, too, passed away. He was a Democrat in politics, and both were members of the Old School Presbyterian Church. He was an extensive farmer and stock raiser. Of their eight children, four sons and two daughters, all the sons served in the Confederate army. The third child, John T., was born August 17, 1826, in Bedford County, Tenn.; was reared on a farm, receiving a fair English education, and ran his father's farm until twenty-nine years of age. In 1855 he married Miss Almyra Standfield, who was born on the farm where the subject now lives, April 23, 1836. In 1863 he enlisted in Capt. Brown's company, Brooks' regiment Arkansas Cavalry, Confederate States Army, and in October, 1863, he was taken prisoner and was confined at Springfield, Mo., until the close of the war. He then returned to farming, and is now the owner of 200 acres of land, 125 of which are under cultivation. All this he has made since the war, having lost all his property during that eventful struggle. He and wife are members of the Cumberland Presbyterian Church, he being an elder of the same for the last twenty-one years. Mr. and Mrs. Appleby are the parents of five children: Annice L., Charles W., Ida M., George and Bertha A.

John J. Arnold, one of the prominent farmers of Goshen Township, was born in North Carolina about 1833, and is the son of John and Sallie (Murray) Arnold, both natives of Virginia. They moved to North Carolina after marrying, and from that State to Cass County, Ga., making their home there, six years. Later they went to Alabama, where the father died, in Benton County, of that State, in the spring of 1849. The mother afterward moved to Pulaski County, Ark., and still later to Washington County, where she died August 26, 1874. Mr. Arnold was a farmer, and had followed this occupation all his life. Their son, John J. Arnold, went to Phillips County, Ark., where he remained nine months, and from there went to Conway County, of the same State, but after a residence there of about eight or nine years he moved to Pulaski County, and in 1871 moved to Washington County, where he purchased his present farm, which consists of 170 acres, nearly eighty under cultivation. Mr. Arnold is a blacksmith, wagon-maker, carpenter and mill-wright by trade, but his principal occupation during life has been farming. He was married July 12, 1859, to Misa Ann Davenport, a native of New York. To them were born five children: George E., deceased; Christopher C., deceased; Josephine, wife of A. L. Nelson; Ella, wife of James Tunstill, and John N., at home. During the late unpleasantness between the North and South, Mr. Arnold served a short time in the Confederate army. He is a conservative Democrat in his political views, has been a successful farmer, and is an honorable, straightforward citizen. Mrs. Arnold is a member of the Methodist Episcopal Church South.

Dr. Evans Atwood, a practicing physician of Springdale, Ark., was born in Vermilion County, Ill., in 1836, and is a son of Simeon and Eliza (McGary) Atwood, and grandson of James Atwood, who was a Virginian and one of the pioneer settlers of Kentucky. He immigrated to Kentucky, and afterward moved to Ohio, thence to Vermilion County, Ill., where he died in 1853 or 1854. He was one of the pioneers of early times, the most of his life having been spent on the extreme borders of civilization. His son Simeon was born in Adair County, Ky., in 1807, and July 31, 1835, was married to Miss Eliza McGary, born in Posey County, Ind., in 1820, by whom he became the father of eight children, Dr. Evans Atwood being their eldest child. They immigrated to Texas in 1840, where they resided ten years, and then came to Washington County, Ark. Here they spent the remainder of their days, the father dying June 10, 1888, and the mother May 18, 1883. Dr. Atwood was taken to Arkansas at the age of thirteen years, and has made that State his home up to the present time. He studied medicine under a preceptor for about two years, and during the winters of 1873 and 1874 took a course of lectures in the Louis-ville (Ky.) Medical College, after which he returned home and began practicing, meeting with good and well-deserved success. He is one of the oldest practi-tioners in this portion of the county and is well to the front in his profession. November 6, 1859, he was married to Miss Lucy Jane Roberts, who was born in East Tennessee June 29, 1841, and by her became the father of two children: Martha J. and James C. They were divorced in 1867, and the Doctor married Miss Susan Wilson February 17, 1867, who was born in Washington County, Ark., on the 31st of July, 1839. The following children were born to them: Robert L., John W., Lettie E., William A., Herman E., Rettie M., Rilla B., Simeon D., Hugh and Thomas J. Dr. Atwood is a member of Springdale Lodge No. 316, A. F. & A. M., belongs to the Primitive Baptist Church, and votes the Democratic ticket. During the late war he served as lieutenant in the North West Fifteenth Arkansas Infantry, Confederate States Army, and in his four years' service was wounded but once, slightly; was taken prisoner at the battle of Bayou Pierre, near Port Gibson, Miss., May 1, 1863, and was held a prisoner at Alton, Ill., Johnson's Island, Ohio, Point Lookout, Md., and Fort Delaware, Del., until the war closed. His maternal grandfather, Hugh McGary, served in the Indian Wars of Florida and the "Black Hawk" War as an officer.

Philip Hudson Babb, teacher in the mechanical department and wood-shops of the A. I. U., was born in Greeneville, East Tenn., June 14, 1844, the son of Philip and Artaminca (Hale) Babb, and grandson of Philip Babb, a native of North Carolina, and a mill-wright by occupation. He built the first mill in East Tennessee. The Babbs now living in America date their ancestry in this country back to the landing of two brothers at Plymouth Rock in early colonial times. They were from England, and both took part in the war for independence. Afterward one settled in Massachusetts, the other in North Carolina, and from the latter descended the present Babbs of North Carolina, Tennessee and Arkansas. The father of the subject of this sketch was a native of Tennessee, and a farmer by occupation. He assisted in moving the Indians from the Georgia Reservation to their present quarters in the Indian Territory, and afterward moved to Tennessee, where he died at the age of fifty-three years. His son Philip was reared in Tennessee, learned his trade at Knoxville, of that State, and spent three years in bridge building in connection with the East Tennessee & Virginia Railroad Company. He afterward went to Northern Missouri, and spent about two years in that State, then made his way to Arkansas, March 14, 1872, and has since been actively engaged in the building interests of Western Arkansas. Among the many buildings erected by him may be mentioned the Benton County Court-house at Bentonville, and he had the con-tract for building all the stairs for the Cherokee schools at Tahlequah, I. T., the Orphan Asylum at Grand Saline, I. T., and the Indigent school, five miles from Tahlequah. Mr. Babb was married in Tennessee to Miss Mary Correll, a native of Rockingham County, Va., and the daughter of Rev. Andrew Correll, who was of the Dunkard faith. To Mr. and Mrs. Babb were born two sons and a daughter: Effie, Roten and Delmer. Mr. Babb was reared in the Methodist faith; he is a member of the Masonic order, being insured in that society.

Jeremiah Barnes, among the old and enterprising farmers of Illinois Town-ship, was born in Lancaster County, Penn., May 10, 1815. The Barnes family were originally from Ireland, and after reaching this country they settled in Maryland, where Gilbert Barnes, father of Jeremiah, was born. He grew to manhood in that State, but afterward went to Pennsylvania, where he married Miss Catherine Ford, a native of the last named State. Her father was from England, and deserted the British army to join the colonists in the Revolu-tionary War. The parents of our subject were married in Pennsylvania, and there lived until about 1842, when they moved to Springfield, Ill. The father was a farmer, also a cooper, and could turn his hand to almost any kind of work. He was a member of the Presbyterian Church, and died at the age of eighty-five. The mother was a member of the Lutheran Church, and died at the age of eighty-four. Their family consisted of ten children, five sons and five daughters. Jeremiah, the youngest but two of this family, received a very lim-ited education, and at the age of sixteen began learning the carpenter's trade, and this he has followed all his life. Having found his way west as far as Law-rence County, Ind., he met Miss Eunice Beasley, a native of Orange County, Ind., born November 12, 1823, and the daughter of Silas and Cynthia Beasley, who were born in Tennessee and Kentucky, respectively. Richard Beasley, the father of Silas Beasley, was born in Ireland. Silas Beasley was an excellent farmer and trader in produce, shipping it to New Orleans by the old flat-boat method, and died at the age of seventy-four. Of his ten children, Eunice was the third. In 1840 she and Mr. Barnes were married, and after living in Lawrence County, Ind., until 1854, they moved to Washington County, Ark., and here they have since lived. They became the parents of four children: Emily A., Clark, George and Lewis. Emily is the only one now living, and is the wife of Thomas Phelan. Mr. Barnes was the first justice of the peace of Illinois Township after the war, and like his father before him is a Democrat in politics. Mr. Barnes has 300 acres in the home place, and his wife has 283 acres of her own. She looks after all the business, and is accounted as competent for that kind of work as anyone. Both Mr. and Mrs. Barnes are members of the Christian Church, and are excellent citizens.

John F. Barr. Among the worthy tillers of the soil of Washington County, Ark., who have become extensive land holders and acquired a handsome competency, may be mentioned Mr. Barr, who is a native of Lawrence County, Ala., and was born on December 27, 1829. His parents, Isaac and Sarah (Holt) Barr, were married in Tennessee, and soon after that event moved to Alabama, where the father died. She was a Georgian by birth, he a Virginian, but reared in Tennessee, and throughout life was a farmer. He died in Alabama, and his widow and seven children moved to Washington County, Ark., where she met and married John C. Neill, and died about 1845. John F. Barr attended the common schools of Arkansas. At the age of seventeen he crossed the plains to New Mexico, and returned the following year. At the age of twenty years he was married to Miss Mary A. Boyd, a native of Washington County, Ark., and by her became the father of seven children: Ardilla, Mell and Belle (twins), Dora and Ida, five girls, four of whom are married; two boys, Humphrey and Frankie. Humphrey graduated from the Commercial College of Lexington, Ky., in 1883, also from the literary department of the Rogers Academy, with class honors, June 1, 1887. John F. Barr has farmed in Washington County, Ark., ever since marriage, with the exception of four years, from 1852 to 1856, which he spent in Oregon and California, having crossed the plains in a "prairie schooner" drawn by four yoke of oxen, making the trip to Oregon City in seven months and two days. After remaining in the West four years he returned home by sea, crossing the Isthmus of Panama, via New Orleans. He has ever since assiduously followed his avocation of farming until, recently, he has sold his farms of 450 acres, and has moved to Springdale, where he has some valuable property, to pass the remainder of his days. He is a strong supporter of Democratic principles.

George Wesley Barringer, carpenter and builder, and son of Peter and Maria (Caldwell) Barringer, was born in Union County, Ill., near Jonesboro, July 3, 1841. The parents were natives of North Carolina, and Peter Barringer was a wagon manufacturer by trade. About 1815 he went with his father, Peter Barringer, to Illinois, and there settled on a farm, where he followed agricultural pursuits for many years. George W. Barringer attained his growth on his father's farm, and later learned the carpenter and builder's trade of Jacob Lant, a leading builder of Jonesboro. In 1862 Mr. Barringer abandoned all his business prospects for a time and enlisted in the Union army, Company A, Ninety-seventh Illinois Volunteer Infantry, and was in active service for three years. After the war he returned to his home and followed his trade here until 1876, when he moved to Washington County, Ark., and located in Fayetteville. Here he has followed his business ever since, and has erected some of the finest residences and best business buildings in the city, viz.: Bole's store, William Barry's residence (by Babb & Barringer), Mr. Mock's residence, Prof. Leverett's residence and numerous others that might be mentioned. He was married in Illinois to Miss Kate Stuernagle, of Indiana, whose parents were natives of Germany. Seven children were the result of this union, three sons and four daughters: Lewis, Annie, John, Frank, Mollie, Evaline and Kate. Mr. Barringer has been a member of the Odd Fellows fraternity, and he and family worship at the Christian Church.

Richard H. Bean, farmer, miller and native of Washington County, Ark., was born on the 16th of December, 1837, and is a son of Hon. Mark Bean, who was born at Bean Station, Tenn., and came with his parents to Arkansas about

1820. He was married in Batesville, Ark., to Miss Hettie Stuart, and soon after settled on a farm in Franklin County, which county he afterward represented in the State Senate, being a member of that body several terms. In 1834 he took up his abode in Washington County, settling near what is now known as Rhea Mills, but afterward moved to Cane Hill, where he resided until his death, which occurred in February, 1862. His wife died while they were living in Franklin County, and he afterward married Nancy J. Parks, a native of Tennessee, and a daughter of Robert W. Parks. Richard H. Bean was educated in the Cane Hill College, and grew to manhood in Washington County. When the war broke out he enlisted in the Arkansas State troops, but at the end of three months they were disbanded. In 1863 he joined Col. Jackman's Missouri regiment, Shelby's brigade, and served, mostly on detached duty, until the close of the war. He then returned home and erected a large steam saw and grist mill near Cane Hill, which he managed up to 1879, when he sold out and retired to his farm and engaged in stock farming, at which he has been entirely successful. He has been breeding and dealing in fine cattle, hogs and sheep for several years, and has as good blooded stock as there is in the county. He was one of the prime movers in establishing the Cane Hill Canning and Evaporating Factory, and has about $700 invested in that enterprise. He is one of the enterprising business men of Washington County. In May, 1866, he was married to Mary L. Lacy, a native of Alabama, and daughter of T. H. Lacy, by whom he is the father of seven children : Bettie, Ola S., William H., John L., Mary L., Nancy and Ruth. Mr. and Mrs. Bean are members of the Cumberland Presbyterian Church, and he is a Royal Arch Mason.

John M. Bell was born in the Indian Territory, near Evansville, Ark., on the 9th of July, 1829, and is a son of James C. and Matilda (Woolsey) Bell, and grandson of John Bell, who was born in the "Emerald Isle," and in 1780 immigrated to the United States, locating in North Carolina. He was a farmer by occupation, and followed that occupation in Tennessee, Arkansas and Texas. He died in the latter State in 1850. James C. Bell was born in North Carolina in 1796, and in 1823 came to Arkansas, locating first in Hempstead County, thence to the Lovelace Purchase, where he took a claim, which he afterward lost when the Indian Territory was laid off, and in 1831 came to Washington County. He entered the farm now owned by his son, John M., and at his death, in 1848, left his family in comfortable circumstances. He was an active member of the Whig party. He was married to Miss Woolsey in 1825, by whom he became the father of eight children, six of whom lived to maturity. After the father's death Mrs. Bell married (in 1853) Judge Jonathan Newman, of Washington County, and died in November, 1862. John M. Bell was born on the farm where he now resides, and was reared in the house where he is now living, which was built by his father in 1834. He attended the common schools in his youth, and in 1857 entered the mercantile business at Bentonville, but in 1861 married Miss Elizabeth C. Hale, of Davidson County, Tenn., and located on his farm in Washington County. In 1862 he enlisted in Company K, Thirty-fourth Arkansas Infantry, in the Trans-Mississippi Department, and was a faithful soldier until the close of the war, when he was mustered out as orderly-sergeant. His farm was in a very bad condition, but he immediately set to work, and by industry and good management soon accomplished wonders in the way of improvements, and now has ninety of his 160 acres under cultivation. His wife, who was born December 16, 1840, is a daughter of J. T. B. Hale, who came to Benton County in 1855; she is the mother of four children: William F., Minnie L. (wife of J. N. Woodruff), Samuel E., and Thomas (deceased). Mr. Bell is a member of the A. F. & A. M., and a Democrat politically. In 1880 he took the census for two townships in his county.

Alvin J. Bellamy, farmer of Vineyard Township, is the son of William and Sallie (Martin) Bellamy. The father was born in Virginia, and moved with his parents to Franklin County, Ga., where he married a Miss Westbrooks, who bore him two children, one son and one daughter. After her death he married Miss Martin, and nine children were the result of this union. He was a wheelwright by trade, although he made farming his chief occupation. He died at the age of eighty-four, and was a member of the Missionary Baptist Church, as were also his two wives. The paternal and maternal grandfathers of our subject were both Revolutionary soldiers. Alvin J. Bellamy was born in Franklin County, Ga., January 6, 1844, on a farm; received a limited education, and in

September, 1861, he enlisted in Company B, Twenty-ninth Georgia Infantry, (Confederate States Army), and served until the close of the war. He participated in the battles of Jackson, Chickamauga, Lookout Mountain, Missionary Ridge, Dalton, Resaca, Altoona, New Hope Church, Atlanta, Jonesboro, Columbus. After the battle of Jonesboro he was promoted to the rank of second lieutenant of Company A, Col. Bryant's cavalry. Returning to Georgia, he married Miss L. Ballenger in 1866. She was born in Franklin County, Ga., April 19, 1845, and by her marriage became the mother of six children, four sons and two daughters. The same year of his marriage Mr. Bellamy moved to Red River County, Texas, but the following year moved to Washington County, Ark., locating where he now lives on a fine farm of 190 acres, 150 under cultivation. He is one of the best farmers in his community, and one of the most successful. He is a Democrat in politics; is a Master Mason, and both he and Mrs. Bellamy are members of the Methodist Church.

John Quincy Benbrook, merchant druggist, was born in St. Charles County, Mo., July 17, 1833, and moved with his parents, Nathan and Sarah (Maguire) Benbrook, to Arkansas a few years later. He received a good practical education in the schools of his locality, and later engaged in school-teaching, but abandoned this and engaged as clerk in the dry goods store of Boone & Reagor, at Boone's Grove, where he remained two years. He then left the store and completed his education. In 1856 Miss Mary J. Campbell, daughter of J. M. Campbell (deceased), became his wife. After his marriage Mr. Benbrook engaged in agricultural pursuits, but in 1858 removed to Texas, and spent a year in that State, where he still followed farming. He then returned to Arkansas, where he engaged in merchandising in 1863, and has continued this occupation ever since. To this marriage were born three sons and three daughters: E. L., a tinsmith by occupation, and a resident of Phœnix, Arizona; Alice C., wife of T. J. Conner, a resident of Fayetteville; Minerva, Catherine; W. L., a druggist with his father; J. C., a student at the A. I. U., and Agnes May. August 25, 1882, Mrs. Benbrook passed away in full communion with the faith of the Methodist Episcopal Church, in which she had been an active worker. Mr. Benbrook has served on the school board of Fayetteville at different times, and was clerk of the circuit court at this place from 1870 to 1872. He is a member of the Masonic fraternity, is an Odd Fellow, a Knight of Honor, and belongs to the Baptist Church. His parents were natives of Simpson County, Ky., and his paternal grandfather rendered active and honorable services in the War of Independence. Owen Maguire, his maternal grandfather, was a farmer and carried on this occupation all his life.

Allen H. Bennett, another successful agriculturist of Goshen Township, was born in North Carolina October 6, 1834, the son of Richard and Rachel (Watson) Bennett. The father was born in Virginia, and went to North Carolina with his parents when but a year old. There he was reared to manhood, married and there passed his last days. The mother was a native of Tennessee, and moved to North Carolina, where she received her final summons. Their son, Allen H., remained under the parental roof until twenty-two years of age, when he began farming for himself, and when the war-cloud threatened the nation he enlisted in the Confederate service, and was in active duty from 1861 to 1865. He was in the Virginia army, and was through all the important battles of the East, and was wounded, at Seven Pines, in the small of the back, and was also wounded in the shoulder at Bull Run. He is still troubled with the latter. After the war he returned home, and at the end of twelve months came to Carroll County, Mo., where he married (1867) Miss Miranda A. Watson, of Carroll County, Mo., and they became the parents of three children: Laura A., Rachel E. and Maud A. After his marriage Mr. Bennett moved to Washington County, Ark., and located on the farm where he now lives. It consists of 120 acres, eighty under cultivation and six in fruit, and is situated two and a half miles from Goshen. He is a Democrat in his politics, and he and wife and two daughters are members of the Missionary Baptist Church.

Millard Berry, real estate agent and mayor of Springdale, Ark., was born in Daviess County, Ind.; and is a son and only child of Walter E. and Angeline (Cross) Berry, who were born, respectively, in Kentucky and Indiana in 1832 and 1836. The father was a farmer, and was reared, educated and married in Indiana. In 1879 he immigrated to Texas, and at the end of four years came to Springdale, Ark., where he is now living a comparatively retired life, and, so far as it is possible for one of his energy and habits of industry to do, is enjoying a well deserved rest. His son, Millard, was reared in Daviess County, Ind., and was educated in the common schools of Washington, the county seat. He studied law for four years after leaving school, and then formed a law partnership with James W. Ogdon, the firm being known as Ogdon & Berry. Two years later Mr. Berry dissolved the partnership with Mr. Ogdon, preparatory to going west, and immediately went to Dallas County, Tex., coming to Springdale, Ark., four years later. During the greater portion of his residence in the "Lone Star State" he served as justice of the peace, which in his precinct was quite a lucrative position. After coming to Springdale, Ark., in November, 1883, he was engaged for a year and a half in selling machinery and farming implements, and during the next two years he traveled through Arkansas and Texas as general agent for the Kansas Manufacturing Company, of Leavenworth, Kas., but being of a domestic nature he abandoned the road to remain more at home with his family, and is now engaged in the real estate business, and also practices law to some extent in addition to his duties as mayor. While a resident of Indiana he was married to Miss Mary I. McHolland, and by her is the father of three children: Thaddeus, Ethelyn and Walter. Mayor Berry is a stanch Democrat in his political views, and whether he has given his constituents a Democratic administration or not, it is conceded that the town of which he has been mayor for two consecutive terms is in excellent condition, there being no indebtedness, but, what is better, a gradually increasing fund in the treasury, while all public improvements have been carefully looked after and kept up. Mr. Berry is also interested in, and personally connected with, the business of the Springdale Canning Company, which is one of the most important manufacturing concerns in the county, and does a very extensive business.

Sheppard Hubbard Blackmer, builder, and member of the firm of Byrnes & Blackmer, was born in Washington County, Ark., and is the son of Sheppard and Charity (Looper) Blackmer, the former a native of Massachusetts, and the latter of Bedford County, Tenn. She was the daughter of Allen and Polley Ann Looper. To Sheppard and Charity (Looper) Blackmer were born four children, three sons and one daughter: Sheppard Hubbard was born September 2, 1844; Mary Ann was born April 20, 1846; Hiram Vaughan was born January 20, 1848; Henry Allen was born April 14, 1850. Sheppard Blackmer, Sr., left home in Washington County, Ark., April 22, 1850, and went to California; was there two years, and died in California. Charity Blackmer died in November, 1858, leaving the children all small. Sheppard H. was left at the age of fourteen years to work for himself. He began learning the trade of brick-making and plastering, but at this juncture the war broke out, and he enlisted in the Union army, and was a corporal in Company A, First Arkansas Infantry Volunteers, serving from February 14, 1863, to August 10, 1865. He then returned, and completed the trade of plastering at Springfield, Mo., where he actively engaged in this business until 1870. He then moved to Fayetteville, and has been since actively engaged in mason work and the building industry. He was married in Springfield, Mo., August 25, 1869, to Miss Docia Virginia Fallin, a native of Washington County, Ark., and the daughter of Robert R. and Nancey D. (Cabe) Fallin, who were natives of Maury County, Tenn. To Mr. and Mrs. Fallin were born five children, two sons and three daughters: Mary Emily, Holmes Lafayette, Docia Virginia, Joseph Anthony, Elizabeth Delitha and Martha, and to Mr. and Mrs. Blackmer were born four children, two sons and two daughters: Alonzo Clinton was born August 21, 1871; Mary Stella was born February 22, 1873; Lillie Lois was born September 23, 1878; Albert Hiram was born July 14, 1883. Mr. and Mrs. Blackmer are members of the Christian Church, of which he has been deacon for some time. He is a member of Washington Lodge No. 1, A. F. & A. M., and Frontier Lodge No. 1626, Knights of Honor, and Fayetteville Lodge No. 28, A. O. U. W., and Travis Post No. 19, Grand Army of the Republic, and is a stockholder and an original charter member of the Electric Light Company. Mr. Blackmer has put up most of the brick work on the south side of the square in Fayetteville, the White & Campbell store, the Welch & VanWinkle Block, and the company have built the dormitory and laboratory of the A. I. U. and many other important buildings of Fayetteville.

Jesse Lee Blakemore. Prominent among the early settlers and farmers of Washington County, Ark., are the Blakemores, who first became represented in this county, in 1831, by Hon. L. C. Blakemore, who was a Tennesseean, born in 1800. He was married to Charlotte Johnson, a native of North Carolina, and on coming to Arkansas first located in Fayetteville, where he was engaged in the hotel business for about two years, and then engaged in farming; was in the Legislature, and was afterward appointed register of lands. He returned to Fayetteville, where he filled the duties of that office for four years. He was afterward chosen to represent Washington County in the State Legislature, and after serving three or four terms retired to his farm in the country, where he spent the remainder of his days, dying in August, 1882, at the age of eighty-two years. He had lived a long, active and useful life, and his death was lamented by a large circle of friends and acquaintances. Jesse L. Blakemore was born in Sumner County, Tenn., March 29, 1827, and was reared on a farm, making his home with his father until he attained his twentieth year, when he began fighting the battle of life for himself. He enlisted in an independent company, under Col. S. B. Everett, and served in the Mexican war for about thirteen months, but although he saw some hard service he was in no battles. In July, 1848, he returned home, and, after making his home with his father for nearly two years, was married in 1849 to Eliza Jane Wheeler, and began farming on rented land. In 1852 he bought a farm on White River, which he sold at the end of two years and bought his present home. His farm consists of 216 acres, 150 acres of which are under fence and cultivation, and he has a fine young orchard of 400 apple and peach trees, just beginning to bear. His wife is a daughter of John A. Wheeler, who first settled in Yell County, Ark., in 1841. She was born in Campbell County, Tenn., and is the mother of thirteen children, ten living: Mary (wife of J. J. Pearson), Sally (wife of W. B. Harrison), Charlotte (wife of W. West), Belle (wife of George Lisenby), Lee D., William W., Jesse J., James A., Benjamin I. and Burk F.; those deceased are John T., Anna E. and Lulie A. Mr. and Mrs. Blakemore are members of the Methodist Episcopal Church South, and he is a member of the A. F. & A. M. and the Masonic fraternities.

Hon. Benjamin F. Boone (deceased), attorney, merchant and farmer, of Washington County, Ark., was born in Tennessee December 29, 1828. His father, James Boone, was born in North Carolina, December 12, 1788, and was a soldier of the War of 1812; died June 11, 1856. His wife, Sophia Boone, reared a family of five children: Daniel T. Beya, F. E. Bernoulli, Cornelia, Veleria and Lafayette. The parents of the above-named children came to Arkansas in the spring of 1830, and settled in Washington County, where they spent the remainder of their days. He, James Boone, was chosen and served as a delegate from said county in the territorial convention that framed the first constitution of the State of Arkansas, he being a second blood cousin of the noted Indian fighter of Kentucky fame, Daniel Boone. Benjamin F. Boone was brought to Arkansas by his parents and grew to maturity in Washington County, where he studied law, and after being admitted to the bar practiced his profession a few years. Later he located at what is known as Boone's Grove, where he engaged in merchandising and held the position of postmaster until the breaking out of the war, when he enlisted in Brooks' Confederate regiment, being promoted to the rank of second lieutenant. December 7 he received a gunshot wound, from which he died March 1, 1863. He was one of the leading men of the county and held several important offices, having represented Washington County in the State Legislature two regular and one called session, being elected on the Democratic ticket. He was a leading member of the I. O. O. F., and his death was universally lamented by all who knew him. November 25, 1852, his marriage with Miss Susan A. Robertson was celebrated. She was born in Tennessee July 10, 1833, and was the daughter of John and Priscilla (Howry) Robertson, natives of Tennessee, and immigrated to Arkansas in 1845. Here the father died in 1884, followed by the wife seven months later. They were the parents of twelve children, of whom are now living Eliza Sharp, Margaret Danields, Thomas H. and R. J. Robertson and Mrs. Susan A. Boone. There were four children born to Mr. and Mrs. Boone: DeWitt T., living in Texas; Bernoulli, and Ines, wife of Ruford D. Robbins, a well-to-do farmer, and Edwin G., who is residing on the home place with his mother. He was born on the 16th of December, 1859; was born and reared on the farm where he now resides, being a young man of energy, ability, sturdy and prosperous habits, a Democrat in politics, and is a stanch supporter of the principles of that party.

Francis M. Boyd. Among the representative farmers of Washington County, Ark., may be mentioned Mr. F. M. Boyd, who was born near where he now lives on the 14th of June, 1840, and is a son of William D. and Elizabeth (Oxford) Boyd, the former of whom was born in North Carolina in 1806, and the latter in East Tennessee in 1811. They were married in Tennessee, and in 1829 moved to Arkansas, where they gave their attention to farming. The mother's death occurred on the 31st of July, 1879. She and husband were members of the Methodist Episcopal Church for many years; he is a Democrat. Out of a family of ten children born to them the following are those living: Mary A., wife of John F. Barr; Lavina, widow of V. B. Johnson; Francis M.; Albert W.; Rebecca, wife of Sylvanus Walker, and William A. Those deceased are Nancy, Malinda, Clementine and Benjamin F. Francis M. Boyd remained at home until the breaking out of the war, when he enlisted in the Confederate State service, Company K, and served until the army was disbanded at Marshall, Tex. He was in many battles and skirmishes, but was never wounded nor taken prisoner. He returned home and resided with his parents until his marriage, in February, 1866, to Arminta Walker, a daughter of Tandy W. Walker. She was born in Marion County, Mo., March 12, 1836, and died at her residence November 12, 1885, and was buried at Sun's Chapel November 14. (As one of God's chosen, she rests in peace.) She was a member of the Methodist Episcopal Church, South. Mr. Boyd is a Democrat, and gives his aid to all laudable enterprises. He is the present postmaster at Wyman, and has been engaged in business in that place for three years. He is a member of the Methodist Episcopal Church, South.

J. L. Bozarth, furniture dealer and one of the first-class citizens of the county, was born in Dade County, Mo., October 16, 1863. His parents, William M. and Eleanor D. Bozarth, were natives of Kentucky and Missouri, respectively. The father was born in Christian County May 28, 1812, and followed agricultural pursuits until 1833, when he learned the blacksmith trade in the little village of Belleview. In 1839 he went to Henry County, Mo., and here carried on his trade for several years, but in 1866 moved to Washington County, Ark., where he has since been identified with the mercantile interests of the county. He is the son of Abner and Fannie (Means) Bozarth, natives of Virginia. The Bozarths were frugal, industrious people, and were strong Baptists, holding closely to the faith of that church. Of the Means very little is known farther than that they made early settlements in Kentucky. Mr. Bozarth was married twice, his first marriage resulting in the birth of two children: Elizabeth F., widow of James Conner, and Franklin S., both of Henry County, Mo.; and his second resulting in the birth of Lillie, wife of T. J. Rogers, and J. L. Mr. Bozarth is a member of the Masonic fraternity, and for five years filled the position of sheriff of Henry County, Mo. He deviated somewhat from the religious faith of his forefathers, and is a member of the Methodist Episcopal Church South. J. L. Bozarth moved with his parents to Washington County, Ark., in 1866, and there grew to manhood. He learned the furniture business in Fayetteville, and in 1882 engaged in the same for himself. In this county he married Miss Sue S. Schoolfield, of Fulton. Ark., daughter of Mrs. Mary A. Schoolfield. Mr. Bozarth is an organizer and member of the Fayetteville Gun Club, and an official in the same. He is a member of the K. of P., in which he is master of arms. He also adopted his father's religious belief, and joined the Methodist Episcopal Church, South, in April, 1882.

Hon. David Bridenthal, whose name is closely associated with the farming interests of Washington County, Ark., is the son of John A. and Elizabeth (Hoevel) Bridenthal. The father was born in Germany, and when about eight years of age he and a younger brother were playing on an emigrant ship when it set sail. They were found on board, but as they were only two little Dutch boys, it was thought best not to turn back. On reaching Baltimore, Md., they were sold to a restaurant keeper, but a few years later John A., coming to the conclusion that he did not want to open oyster shells any longer, ran away to Pennsylvania, and was afterward joined by his brother, who became a wealthy iron manufacturer. John A. Bridenthal, as he grew up, evinced a strong liking for his books, and became an intelligent man. He was a weaver by trade. After reaching manhood he married Miss Hoevel, a native of Pennsylvania, and when their son, David, was an infant, they moved to Ohio. In their old age they resided with a married daughter in Moniteau County, Mo., where they died, she at the age of fifty-six and he at the age of eighty-eight. Both were members of the Missionary Baptist Church, and he was a Democrat in politics until the slavery question was brought up, when he became an Abolitionist. In their family were six children, three sons and three daughters. The youngest of these children, David, was born July 7, 1824, near Woodbury, Penn., and was educated first in the common schools, and afterward attended select school in Wooster, Ohio. At the age of about seventeen he entered Granville College, where he attended through the sophomore year. Afterward he taught for several years, and in 1847 was elected professor of Latin and Greek in Union University, at Murfreesboro, Tenn., where he continued for about three years. In 1850 he established the Mountain Home Female Academy, in the mountains of Northern Alabama, and conducted the same for several years, after which he moved to Texas, where he entered the legal profession, being admitted to the bar about 1856. In 1862 he enlisted in the Confederate army, and was in service for about two years. While in Murfreesboro, in 1848, he married Miss Catherine L. Ashford, a native of North Alabama, and to them were born five children: Ada, Thomas J., Lizzie H., David A. and Maud. Ada is deceased and the rest are all married. Mrs. Bridenthal died in 1876. She was a member of the Baptist Church. They came to this county in 1866, and here Mr. Bridenthal has been very successful, being the owner of 700 acres of land, which he has divided among his children. He is a Democrat in his political opinions, and represented Washington County in the Arkansas Legislature during the session of 1873 and 1874.

Thomas Brooks. This gentleman is one of the most prominent farmers of Washington County, Ark. He was born in Hawkins County, Tenn., April 6, 1832, and is the son of William D. and Susan (Price) Brooks, and the grandson of Thomas Brooks, who was one of two of the first settlers of Hawkins County, Tenn. William D. Brooks was born in Hawkins County, Tenn., was of English descent and a farmer by occupation. He reared seven sons and seven daughters to be men and women, five sons and three daughters now living. The mother was born in Hawkins County, Tenn., also, and died in that county, on the old homestead where she spent her life. The father died in 1854, and the mother in 1859; both lived to be more than three score years. Thomas Brooks (subject) was reared on a farm in his native county, and remained with his parents until twenty-two years of age, or until April 6, 1854, when he married Miss Lucinda Maddox, a native of Hawkins County, Tenn., born in December, 1834. Her parents were among the earliest settlers of that county, and both died in Overton County, of that State. To Mr. and Mrs. Brooks were born eleven children: Mary E. (wife of Willis Rider), Laura M. (deceased), Eliza K. (deceased), John W. (deceased), Francis M., James S., Marquis D. L., Susan K., Maggie E., Nora B. and Effie E. After marriage Mr. Brooks moved to Newton County, Mo., but after a residence there of three years he moved to Washington County, Ark., near where Brentwood is now located, and lived there until the breaking out of the war, when he enlisted in Company B, First Arkansas Cavalry, United States Volunteers. After nine months he was promoted to sergeant-major, and February 28, 1864, he was promoted to the rank of second lieutenant of Company L, First Arkansas Cavalry, etc. January 11, 1865, he was promoted to first lieutenant, and was a brave and gallant officer. He served his country with credit for more than three years. After the war he purchased his farm two and a half miles southeast of Fayetteville, where he owns 250 acres, 165 under cultivation. His wife, three sons and four daughters are members of the Baptist Church; he is a Master Mason, a G. A. R., and is now commander of Travis Post No. 19. Politically he is a firm Republican, having been a Whig before the Republican party existed. He takes an active interest in politics and all public affairs, and was a Republican when it "tried men's souls."

Javan Bryant, M. D., of Evansville, was born in Spartanburgh, S. C., November 5, 1839, the son of Reuben and Sarah (Kirby) Bryant, both natives of South Carolina, and the mother of Scotch descent. The Bryant family were of the original Brittons, and came to America about four generations back. Reuben and Sarah (Kirby) Bryant were married in their native State, and both were professing Christians, he a member of the Baptist and she a member of the Methodist Church. He was a well-to-do farmer, and died in his native State at the age of sixty-eight. The mother died at the age of forty-eight. In their family were two children, a son and a daughter. The father had previously

married a Miss Dillard, who bore him five children. His second marriage was
to Miss Kirby, and after her death he married a Miss Harvey, who bore him
one child. The eldest of the second set received his education in the high-
school at Glenn Springs, S. C., and at the age of eighteen began the study of
medicine, which he continued until twenty-one years of age, when he graduated
at the Medical College of the State of South Carolina, and afterward located
in Spartanburgh County. In 1861 he married Miss Susannah N. Littlejohn, also
a native of South Carolina, who bore him five children—three sons and two
daughters. Dr. Bryant practiced his profession in Spartanburgh County until
May, 1862, when he enlisted in Company I, Thirteenth South Carolina Infantry,
Confederate States Army, serving as a private several weeks, when he received
a commission as assistant surgeon, which position he held until the surrender
of Johnston. His chief service was hospital duty at Richmond, Va., Raleigh,
Wilmington and Kittrell's Springs, N. C. He surrendered at Thomasville,
N. C., and afterward returned to Spartanburgh County, where he continued his
practice. In 1879 he and family moved to Hot Springs, Ark., where his wife,
who was an invalid, hoped for recovery. The same year they located at
Evansville, Washington County, and here his wife died in July, 1883. She was
a member of the Missionary Baptist Church, as is also Dr. Bryant. Dr. Bryant
represented Spartanburgh County in the State Legislature of South Carolina during the sessions of 1868–70. He has been a very close student all his life, and his
special diversion is language, being able to speak and read, more or less fluently,
seven different languages, and he is deeply interested in the improvement and
propagation of Volapük. In 1878 he took an *ad eundem* degree at the Atlanta,
Ga., Medical College. Dr. Bryant is a member of the Washington County
Medical Association, has practiced medicine twenty-seven years, and is accounted
a skillful physician, receiving a liberal share of the patronage. He is a contributor to periodical literature, both medical and literary.

Charles Ratcliffe Buckner, a successful legal practitioner at Fayetteville,
Ark., was born in Hopkinsville, Ky., May 8, 1844, the son of George and Jane
Critcher (Ratcliffe) Buckner (the former a lawyer by profession), and grandson
of George and Annie (Madison) Buckner. George Buckner, Sr., was a native
of Virginia, and of old Virginia stock. He served in the Revolutionary War,
and his wife was a niece of James Madison, President of the United States.
George Buckner, Jr., was a man of undoubted integrity and loyalty, and as
a representative for his district, opposed the secession of his State. Jane
Critcher Ratcliffe was the daughter of Charles Ratcliffe, a physician by profession, and son of an important aid-de-camp to Washington in his struggle for
independence. Charles Ratcliffe Buckner grew to manhood in Hopkinsville,
Ky., and March 22, 1862, he enlisted in Woodward's squadron, Confederate
Kentucky Cavalry, which was organized at that time in Tennessee, and afterward became known as Company A, First Kentucky Cavalry, and after its reorganization was known as Company A, Second Kentucky Cavalry. Mr. Buckner rendered honorable and active service until the close of the war. The first
year he was in the quartermaster's department of the regiment, but abandoned
this for more active service during the latter years of the war. He was detailed
as scout, and served in various capacities, taking great risks. After the war he
attended school, and in the fall of 1865 he went south and made his home in
New Orleans, engaged in clerical work, until January 1, 1868, when he came to
Little Rock. In February of the same year he moved to Washington County,
Ark. He read law while in New Orleans, under the preceptorship of Maj.
Levey, a nephew of Judah P. Benjamin, and after coming to this county was
admitted to the bar, and has practiced ever since. He was married in this county
to Miss Nannie, the youngest daughter of Hon. David Walker. [See sketch
elsewhere]. To Mr. and Mrs. Buckner were born three sons and a daughter:
Jennie, George, Charles and Walker. Mr. Buckner would never accept any
public positions, and has never been a member of any secret societies. Mrs.
Buckner is a worthy member of the Baptist Church.

H. Milton Butler, editor and proprietor of the Prairie Grove *Banner*, was
born in Fairmount, Gordon Co., Ga., February 12, 1859, and is a son of James
F. and Flora Ann S. (Watts) Butler, who were born in South Carolina, November 2, 1821, and Georgia, March 19, 1826, respectively. They were reared and
married in the latter State, and at the breaking out of the late Civil War the
father enlisted in the Confederate army, and served as corporal with Gen. Joe

Johnston until the close of the war. He then returned to his home in Georgia, and in the winter of 1868 moved to Arkansas, and settled near Springtown, Benton County, where he still resides. H. Milton Butler came to Arkansas with his parents, and received the advantages of a good common-school education, which he has since improved very much by self-application at leisure moments. At an early age he manifested a desire for reading, and the ablest newspapers of the day were eagerly devoured by him. After his marriage, which occurred September 14, 1879, he was engaged in agricultural pursuits for about seven years, and then he and a brother began editing a paper at Springdale, Ark., but after a very short time he removed to Prairie Grove and established the *Banner*, which has a large and increasing circulation. The *Banner* is a neat, newsy little paper, and is published in the interests of the Democratic party, and for the development and upbuilding of the beautiful and productive Prairie Grove Valley. Mr. Butler is not a member of any church, but is a firm believer in the teachings of the Bible, and is ever ready to assist the cause of Christianity. He is an active worker in the Sabbath-school, and was recently (May, 1888) elected secretary of the Washington County Sunday-school Convention. September 30, 1888, he was elected city recorder of the incorporated town of Prairie Grove. His wife, Susan A., is a daughter of James and Nancy (Sparks) Deatherage, of Benton County, and was born in Boone County, Ark., September 5, 1861, and is now the mother of seven children: Orlando E., Sylvester J., Ethel P., Talitha A., W. H. Milton, Bertha A. (deceased) and James G.

Albert M. Byrnes, carpenter, builder and proprietor of the planing-mill at Fayetteville, was born in Dublin, Ireland, August 2, 1849. His parents, Michael and Charlotta (Hatton) Byrnes, were natives of Ireland, and came to America in 1850. The father was a wagon-maker by occupation, and died in California three years after reaching the United States. Their son, Albert M., was reared to manhood in his native country, and at the age of seventeen crossed the ocean and with his parents made a home in America. After spending a year in New York City, he spent four years in Springfield and Southwest Missouri, after which he came to Fayetteville, Ark., and has since been closely associated with the business interests of that city. He was married in Washington County to Miss Mary McCoy, a native of Providence, R. I., and the daughter of Philip McCoy, of Prairie Township. One son and six daughters were the result of this union: Dora and Mary, are students of St. Joseph's Convent; Nellie, Bessie, Emma, Annie and Albert Harrison. Mr. Byrnes would never accept any official positions, and as a consequence has never been an office-holder. He is a member of the K. of H., the K. of P., and he and family worship at St. Joseph's Roman Catholic Church. He is a stockholder and organizer of the Electric Light Company; is director of the Building and Loan Association, and is a stockholder and an active organizer of the Sweetzer Wagon Company. Many marks of his handicraft are to be seen in the fine residences and business blocks of Fayetteville and vicinity.

A. J. Campbell, whose birth occurred in Wooster, Wayne Co., Ohio, August 23, 1845, is the son of Jared and Mary A. (Breidenthal) Campbell, the former a native of Ohio, and a blacksmith by trade. A. J. Campbell remained in his native State until sixteen years of age, and then went to Missouri with his parents, who settled in Moniteau County, where A. J. read medicine for some time. After completing his medical course he practiced for four years, and then attended the St. Louis Medical College, from which institution he graduated some time later. He was married in Moniteau County, Mo., to Miss Laura E. Houston, daughter of Dr. C. C. Houston, who was born in Tennessee, and who was a lineal descendant of the family of Gen. Samuel Houston. To this marriage were born four sons and a daughter: Edgar, J. Herbert, Judson, Oscar and Elfie. In 1884 Mr. Campbell left his lucrative practice in Morgan County, Mo., made a location at Lowell, Ark., and here engaged in merchandising until the spring of 1888, when he moved to Washington County, Ark. Mr. Campbell is a member of the Masonic fraternity, and he and wife are members of the Christian Church.

James B. Campbell is one of the well-to-do agriculturists of Washington County, Ark., and is a native of Middle Tennessee, born in Bedford County May 15, 1835. His father, Berry Campbell, was born in Kentucky, but was married in Tennessee to Mary E. Butler, who was also born in Kentucky.

His death occurred previous to the birth of his son, James B. His widow continued to reside in Tennessee until 1848, when she came to Arkansas, locating
first in Pike County and afterward in Washington County, where she died in
1878. James B. Campbell made his home with his mother until her death. In
1861 he enlisted in the Confederate army, in the Sixteenth Arkansas Infantry,
and served until the close of the war, being a participant in the battles of Pea
Ridge, Corinth, Iuka, Port Hudson, Mark's Mill and Saline River. In the
winter of 1859 Mr. Campbell was married to Miss Hannah Buchanan, a daughter
of Leander Buchanan, one of the early settlers of Washington County, and
their union has resulted in the birth of six children: James E., William R.,
Wiley B., Mary E., John and Claude. In 1874 Mr. Campbell located on his
present farm of 207½ acres, and is considered one of the prosperous farmers of
the county. He has a pleasant and comfortable home, and has a nice orchard of
two acres of select and grafted fruits.

Thomas J. Campbell, assistant assessor of Washington County, Ark., was
born in Somerville, Morgan Co., Ala., April 18, 1833, the son of Judge William
H. Campbell and Olivia (McLellan) Campbell, and grandson of William Campbell,
who was a native of Dumfries, Va. Judge William H. Campbell is now eighty-
two years of age, and has held important membership with the Somerville bar
since his twenty-first year. He held the judgeship there for twenty-five years,
and served in the State Legislature of Alabama for 1852 and 1853. He filled the
position of bank attorney for the Decatur Bank, of Alabama, and many other
official positions. He has held more commissions from the State government of
Alabama than any other man in that State, and he served with honor and credit
in both Federal and Confederate capacities. Olivia (McLellan) was the daughter
of Col. John McLellan, of Indian War fame, serving from Tennessee, although
a native of Virginia. Thomas J. Campbell was reared in Somerville, and at the
age of eighteen entered the probate judge's office, where he served as clerk for
about eighteen years. He served throughout the entire war; the first year was
in the Army of Virginia, Twelfth Alabama Regiment, and for three years was
with Forrest's cavalry. In 1871 he left his position in the probate office and
moved to Arkansas, locating at Cane Hill, and filled the position of justice of
the peace at this place for two years; also served as assistant assessor, deputy
sheriff and in other capacities. He was married, in Alabama, to Miss Sarah P.
Welsh, sister of Dr. W. B. Welsh [see sketch], and to them have been born two
sons: Clinton C., clerking in Fayetteville, and William Booth. Mr. Campbell
and wife are worthy members and attendants at the Methodist Episcopal
Church.

William H. Campbell, a progressive and enterprising farmer of Washington County, Ark., and native of the same, was born in 1846, and is a son of
William H. and Julia (Rutherford) Campbell, who were natives respectively of
Virginia and Tennessee. After residing in his native State until grown, the
father moved (about 1838), locating first in Fort Gibson, I. T., and later in Washington County, Ark. At the beginning of the late Civil War he was quartermaster under Gen. McCullough, but was taken sick and died December 18,
1861, leaving a widow and ten children, of whom our subject, a lad of fifteen
years, was the third. The mother was but four years old when she was brought
to this county, and here she was reared, married and spent the remainder of
her days, her death occurring on the 30th of December, 1884. The following
are her children: John E. (who died in February, 1888), James B., William H.,
Joseph W., Elizabeth (wife of Dr. George Carter), Julia (wife of Zachariah Van
Hoose), Thomas H., Mary H., Noel G. and Richard. William H. Campbell had
the advantages of the common schools during his father's life-time, and acquired a sufficient knowledge of the English branches for ordinary purposes.
His finances were very limited when he began life for himself, but by prudence
and good management he has acquired considerable property, and has a sufficient competency for his wants. His farm consists of 260 acres of good land,
with ninety acres in a fine state of cultivation. He also deals quite extensively
in stock, and is considered one of the representative citizens and farmers in the
community in which he resides. During the latter part of the Rebellion he
served his country under B. F. Johnson, and did effective service. He is a Republican in his political views, and has always given material assistance to all
laudable enterprises. February 15, 1846, his wife, whose maiden name was
Mary Hanna, was born. She is a daughter of J. C. Hanna, and is the mother of

three children : Nora (deceased), Mollie (living) and Maggie (deceased). Mrs. Campbell is a consistent and prominent member of the Christian Church.

Barton A. Carl may be mentioned as one of the prosperous merchants of Prairie Grove, Ark., and was born in Coffee County, Tenn., September 12, 1832, being a son of Thomas and Nancy (Shed) Carl, who were natives respectively of New York and Tennessee, and were married in the latter State. After residing in Tennessee for several years they removed to Arkansas (about 1839) and located, first in Franklin County, then in Benton County, and in 1850 came to Washington County, locating on a farm about two miles south of Prairie Grove, where they made their home until their family was reared. The father is now residing in Benton County and is eighty-six years of age. The mother died in Franklin County about 1841, having reared a family of six sons and one daughter to maturity, all of whom are living, with the exception of one son, at this writing. Barton A. Carl grew to manhood in Benton and Washington Counties, and made his home with his father until he attained his majority, when he determined to seek his fortune in the West, and after a journey of five months over the plains, at last reached California. Here he spent three years engaged in mining, and then returned home via Nicaraugua and New Orleans, and as his stay in the gold fields had been successful he purchased a farm in Washington County and settled down to tilling the soil. In 1883 he came to Prairie Grove, leaving two of his sons to till the farm, and has since been engaged in merchandising, carrying a large and select stock of goods. He is a charter member of the canning association, and is also one of the trustees of the Prairie Grove College. He has taken a deep interest in all enterprises calculated to benefit the town and county, and is a citizen worthy the esteem of all. He was married January 20, 1857, to Miss Sarah S. Parks, a native of Tennessee, and daughter of John P. A. Parks, and by her is the father of the following family: Elbridge D., Atlantic (deceased), John F., Charles (deceased), E. Clint, Frank H., Walter W. and Van W. The family worship in the Methodist Episcopal Church, South, and Mr. Carl is a member of the Masonic fraternity.

Obed C. Cate, farmer, stock raiser, and trader, was born in Jefferson County, Tenn., September 15, 1831, and is the son of Charles and Rachel (Thornburg) Cate. The father was born in Jefferson County, Tenn., September 9, 1805, and the mother in the same county January 21, 1808. They lived in their native State until 1847, when they moved to Washington County, Ark., and purchased the property where their son, Obed C., is now living. Here they passed their last days, the father dying December 3, 1869, and the mother February 14, 1863. The father was a thrifty farmer, was a Whig before the war, and during that eventful period he was a Union man. Both were members of the Missionary Baptist Church. Their family consisted of seven children, three sons and four daughters. Obed C. Cate and his sister Jane were twins. He was educated to a limited extent in the old subscription schools, and after working for his father until twenty-one years of age, he began as an independent farmer. October 9, 1853, he married Miss Mary Miller, who was born in Washington County, and who bore him ten children, Sidney M., Lafayette, William A., Annie J., Charles E., Laura A., John O., Aimy, Carrie and Mary A. In 1862 Mr. Cate was conscripted in the Confederate army, but succeeded in getting out after four months' service. After marriage he settled upon the farm where he now lives, and which consists of 300 acres. Mr. Cate is a Republican in his political views, and is a member of the I. O. O. F. He has lived in this county for forty-one years, and is accounted one of the most successful farmers in his community.

Alexander Caton is one of the prominent fruit growers of Washington County, Ark., and in 1883 located on the farm on which he now lives. His orchard consists of 1,500 apple trees, 200 peach trees, and he raises all kinds of small fruit and garden vegetables, being exceptionally successful in that line of business. He was born near Wheeling, West Va., January 22, 1835, and is a son of Alfred and Sarah (Sheddock) Caton, who are Virginians, and are residing in Montgomery County, Mo. He is eighty-nine years of age, and she is about seventy-five. They were married in their native State, and lived there and in West Virginia until 1840, when they moved to Ohio, and at the end of fifteen years took up their abode in Missouri. They have been farmers all their lives, and have been members of the Missionary Baptist Church for many years. Two sons and five daughters are living of their family of eleven children. Alexander was their fourth child. He left home at the early age of fifteen years and began working for wages at anything he could get to do.   He resided in the following States, in the order in which they are named: Indiana, Louisiana, Mississippi and Tennessee.   While in the latter State the war broke out, and in May, 1861, he joined Henderson's Scouts and served until the close of the war.   He was in many skirmishes and did considerable scouting.   He was taken prisoner near Holly Springs, Miss., and retained at Cairo, Ill., for about one month, when he was exchanged.   He was again captured at Walnut Hill, and was kept a prisoner at Rock Island until the close of the war.   He then located in St. Louis County, Mo., where he farmed until 1874, when he went to Texas and spent about seven years in freighting from Fort Worth south.   He then came to Washington County, Ark., where he has since resided.   In 1873 he was united in marriage to Elizabeth Allison, who was born in Missouri and died in Texas.   She was the mother of two children, both of whom died in infancy.   In 1881 Mr. Caton married his present wife, Elizabeth Crawley, who was born in Arkansas in 1865 and is the mother of three children: Jennie F. (deceased), William A. and Ada A.   Mr. and Mrs. Caton are members of the Christian Church, and he is a Democrat.   The Richhill fruit farm, owned and cultivated by Mr. Caton, is located on the Wyre road, twenty-two miles south of Fayetteville.   This, the southern portion of Washington County, is the best belt for fruit growing, and finer land for berries and vegetables is not to be found in any of the Middle or Western States.

James M. Chandler, merchant at Evansville, Ark., is the son of Jacob and Elizabeth (Reeder) Chandler.   The father was born in Kentucky in 1793, and when a child moved with his parents to Tennessee, where he married Miss Reeder.   About 1825 he and his family moved west of the Mississippi River, locating in the territory now occupied by the Choctaws, but two years later they moved in the vicinity of Evansville, where the father died in 1876.   He was a farmer all his life, a Democrat in politics, and for many years was justice of the peace.   The mother died when quite young (1836), and was but thirty-six years of age.   Both were members of the Methodist Episcopal Church, South.   Their family consisted of eight children, six now living.   The youngest son, and the subject of this sketch, was reared a farmer boy, and received his education in the subscription school, also at Cane Hill College.   At the age of eighteen he began teaching in the Cherokee Nation at $33⅓ per month, but thinking that he could not rise in the profession he hired as clerk in a store for $12 per month.   After working for his employer until almost as much was due him as the stock was worth, he and a partner, N. B. Dunhurg, took the stock in 1853 and began merchandising at Dutch Mills.   Soon after he moved to Wilsonville, one and a half miles north of Evansville, and here carried on farming in connection with merchandising.   In 1856 he married Miss Margaret L. Morrow, daughter of Rev. George Morrow, and to them was born one son, William M.   Mrs. Chandler died in 1861, and four years later Mr. Chandler married Miss Helen M., daughter of Rev. Young Ewing.   This union resulted in the birth of five children: Charles H., Addie D., Lulu E., Lillie and James E.   In 1862 Mr. Chandler enlisted in the Confederate army, and served in the commissary department most of the time until the close of the war.   In 1867 he opened a store in Evansville, and has operated the same ever since.   He was also postmaster at Evansville for five years, is a Democrat in politics, and he and wife are members of the Methodist Episcopal Church, South.   He owns 100 acres of land, a good store, and has made it all by his own industry.

Joel L. Cherry, a prosperous farmer and stock breeder of Washington County, Ark., is a son of John Cherry, who was born, reared and married in Tennessee, and afterward became a farmer of Howard County, Mo.   He was a soldier in the War of 1812 under Gen. Jackson, and was at the battle of New Orleans, and died in 1858.   His wife, Elizabeth Boyer, was born in Tennessee, and became the mother of ten sons, four of whom served in the Confederate army and one in the Union army.   She died in 1868 at the old home in Linn County, Mo.   Joel L. Cherry was born in Howard County, Mo., September 19, 1823, and was reared in Linn County, marrying there, in 1842, Miss Mary A. Hines, a native of Howard County.   She became the mother of nine children, six of whom are living: Isaac, Lewis, John T., Elizabeth (wife of Walter Asher), Susan (wife of John Cohea) and Mary (wife of Murray Cowan).   Mr. Cherry resided on a farm in Linn County until the fall of 1860, when he came to Washington County, locating on the farm of 200 acres where he now lives.   He has

150 acres under cultivation, and is in a prosperous condition financially. In 1861, as his sympathies were with the South, he joined the Confederate army, and was a faithful soldier until the close of the war. After his return home he and his sons began to improve the farm, which had sadly deteriorated during his absence, and their efforts were attended with good results. The family are members of the Primitive Baptist Church.

Dr. D. Christian, physician and surgeon of Springdale, Ark., was born in Warren County, Tenn., in 1851, and is a son of W. T. and Lucy (Dodson) Christian, who were born, reared and married in Tennessee and who became the parents of four children. W. T. Christian's birth occurred in 1831, and throughout life he was one of the honest tillers of the soil. He died in Little Rock, Ark., in 1863, but his widow, who still survives him, resides in Benton County, Ark., and has attained the age of fifty-five years. Dr. D. Christian was taken by his parents to Northwestern Arkansas when a child, and was there reared to manhood and educated. Before commencing the study of medicine, he was engaged in farming and pedagoguing, which occupations he followed with good results; and he first became a disciple of Æsculapius under the instruction of Dr. Hubbard. In 1880 he was graduated as an M. D. from the St. Louis Medical College, and soon after returned to Springdale, where he was successfully engaged in practicing his profession until the fall of 1877, when he went to New York City and began attending the Bellevue Hospital Medical College, from which institution he was afterward graduated. He then took a course in the New York Post Graduate Medical School. He graduated in 1880, and then settled at Elm Springs, a few miles west of Springdale. There he practiced medicine three years, and then, in 1883, he removed to Springdale, and has since been successfully engaged in practicing. Dr. Christian has arisen to prominence in his profession, and has an extensive and increasing practice, which his success as a physician fully justifies. He began his medical career with small means, but by indomitable energy and perseverance has acquired an enviable knowledge of his profession. In 1872 Miss Emily J. Cowen, who was born in Benton County, Ark., in 1853, became his wife and she is now the mother of one child, J. Otto. Dr. Christian votes the Democratic ticket, and is a member of the A. F. & A. M. and the I. O. O. F.

Ambrose H. Clark, who is one of the old settlers of Arkansas, and was first identified with the interests of Washington County in 1841, was born in Ross County, Ohio, April 28, 1818. His parents, John and Nancy (Humes) Clark, were born in the "Green Mountain" State, the former's birth occurring in 1783 or 1784. He died in Dade County, Mo., in 1849 or 1850, his wife's death occurring in Indiana in 1841. They first emigrated from their native State to Ohio, and thence to Indiana, and then to Illinois, and afterward to Missouri. They were members of the Christian Church, and became the parents of eight sons and one daughter, only two of the family now living. Ambrose H. Clark only remained at home until fourteen years of age, and then began working on a farm in Ohio, but afterward went to Indiana, where he lived four years, and then came with a family, by ox team, to Arkansas. He has ever since made his home in Washington County, where he has a good farm of 300 acres, a portion of which is under cultivation. He started out in life with no means, but being of an ambitious and energetic disposition, and having a true helpmate in his wife, he has surmounted many obstacles, and can now enjoy the fruits of his labor. His wife, who was a Miss Selina Hash, is a daughter of Alvin Hash, one of the old settlers of Washington County, and was born on the 20th of October, 1823. Her father and mother died in Illinois in 1844 and 1878, respectively. Mr. and Mrs. Clark became the parents of eleven children: Mary, Frances, Martha E., Esther, William, John, Mestlina, Josephine, Ida, Lydia and Augustine, all of whom reside in Washington County. One child died in infancy. Mrs. Clark and four of her children are active members of the Christian Church. Mr. Clark is a Republican, and takes an active interest in all enterprises for the public weal. During the late war, although he was not a regular soldier, he was in Price's raid and participated in the battle of Richland.

B. F. Clark. Prominent among the successful and enterprising farmers of Goshen Township stands the name of B. F. Clark, who was born in Conway County, Ark., April 1, 1834, and is the son of Morris and Lucinda (Jones) Clark. The father was born in Tennessee, and grew to manhood within thirty miles of

Nashville. He was a farmer all his life, and lived in Tennessee until a young man, when he went to Conway County, Ark., and here married Miss Jones. He remained in this county until 1844, when he moved to within a mile of Goshen, Ark., and there received his final summons. His death occurred about 1870. The mother was born in Kentucky, and died on the old homestead near Goshen about 1874. They were the parents of nine children, six now living: B. F., Susan (wife of Levi Phillips), John J., Elizabeth (widow of Charles Phillips), Richard M. and Ellery W. B. F. Clark was the oldest of this family. He remained at home until twenty-one years of age, and then engaged in farming near Goshen. He has always lived in this vicinity, and on the present farm for twenty-one years. This farm consists of 140 acres, eighty under cultivation. He was married March 22, 1855, to Miss Martha A. Counts, who was born in Madison County, Ark., October 13, 1838. They had twelve children, ten of whom lived to be nearly grown and nine now living : John H., George H. (deceased), William H., Benjamin F., Jr., Henry M., Ashley, Lawson, Eliza J., Mary, Sarah and two infants who died unnamed. Mr. and Mrs. Clark are members of the Primitive Baptist Church, and Mr. Clark has always been a firm Democrat in politics. During the late war he was in the Confederate service for four years; was wounded in the right leg, and carried the ball six months. This wound was received at Fayetteville and will cripple him all his life.

Ellery W. Clark. This prominent and widely known farmer was born in Washington County, Ark., on the farm where he now lives, August 22, 1852, the son of Norris and Lucinda (Jones) Clark. The father was born in Tennessee in 1809, was reared in that State, and when a young man came to Conway County, Ark., where he followed agricultural pursuits until coming to the farm one mile south of Goshen. Here he continued farming, and here he died December 29, 1869. The mother was born in Kentucky in 1811, and died in Washington County, Ark., December 9, 1873. They were members of the Regular Baptist Church, and were the parents of nine children, six now living, viz.: Benjamin F.; Susan H., wife of Levi Phillips; Polly, deceased; Nimrod, deceased; John J.; Elizabeth M., widow of Charles Phillips; Richard M., Norris, deceased, and Ellery W. The last named was reared on the farm, and assisted his father in tilling the soil, until after the death of both parents, when he continued to improve and farm the old home place. He has 180 acres, 120 under cultivation, and a fine two-story residence, one of the best in the neighborhood. April 3, 1873, he married Miss Ann Garrett, daughter of James B. and Charity Garrett. She became the mother of ten children: Walter K., James, Joseph H., Edgar, Pearl, Jewell, Garrett, Norris, Ruby and Grace. Mr. Clark is a Democrat in politics; has never aspired to official positions, but is one of the prominent and successful farmers of the county.

Damon Clarke, proprietor and editor of the Fayetteville *Republican*, was born at Macomb, McDonough Co., Ill., May 20, 1861. He received a fair common-school education during his youth, and in 1879 went to Topeka, Kas., where he remained one year, being employed as a clerk. He then became connected with C. C. Chapman & Co., publishers, of Chicago, and remained with them until the fall of 1881, when he joined the historical corps of J. H. Beers & Co. (subsequently Warner, Beers & Co.), for whom he worked until the fall of 1883. The following winter he was employed as secretary of the Union Publishing Company, of Springfield, Ill., after which he traveled a year as general agent for a Grand Army of the Republic history. In November, 1884, he came to Bentonville, Ark., where his parents, C. C. and Martha (Lea) Clarke, still reside. In February, 1886, he purchased the Springdale *News*, selling it in December of the same year to enter into a copartnership with Thomas Brooks in the purchase of the Fayetteville *Republican*, of which Mr. Clarke became manager and editor. In January, 1888, he assumed the sole proprietorship of that organ. Mr. Clarke is a member of the Arkansas Press Association, and belongs to the Young Men's Republican Club, of Fayetteville. He was also a charter member and the first prelate of Criterion Lodge of the K. of P., of Fayetteville. He is now secretary of the Washington County Republican Central Committee, and has been secretary of the Congressional Committee of his party. In 1888 he was an alternate delegate from the Fifth Arkansas Congressional District to the National Republican Convention.

Charles T. Clayton, farmer and brick-maker of Center Township, Washington Co., Ark., was born in Cooper County, Mo., October 21, 1831, and is a son of

John and Sarah (Leath) Clayton. John Clayton was born and reared in Eastern Maryland, and in his youth learned the harness maker's trade. He obtained a good education and began the study of medicine, but before completing his course enlisted in the War of 1812, nearly losing his eyesight during one of the battles of that war by the explosion of a piece of artillery, and was never afterward able to resume his studies. After the war he immigrated to Cooper County, Mo., in 1828, and the remainder of his days were spent in agricultural pursuits and working at his trade. He and his wife were married in 1817 and became the parents of seven children, three of whom are living: Charles T., Martha (wife of John Killbrith) and William. The father died in 1859, and the mother in 1832. Charles T. Clayton was educated in the common schools of Cooper County, Mo., and in 1856 was married to Talitha Hammond, who was born and reared in Cooper County. They soon after located on a farm in Denton County, Tex., but in 1861 Mr. Clayton enlisted in the Confederate army, and was wounded and taken prisoner at the battle of Chickamauga and taken to Camp Douglas, Chicago, Ill., where he was retained until peace was declared. He then returned to his home in Texas, where he remained engaged in farming and stock dealing until 1867, when he located in Washington County, Ark., on the farm of 220 acres where he now lives. In 1856 he engaged in the manufacture of brick, and now manufactures about 50,000 brick annually. In 1871 his wife died, and the following year he was married to Mary Hawkins, of Cooper County, Mo., by whom he is the father of one child, Thomas. His first union was blessed in the birth of six children: Lucy, wife of William Tucker; Sarah, wife of John Gibson; Mary, wife of Charles Norwood; Lizzie, wife of Joseph Lasater; Talitha and John. He takes an active interest in the cause of Christianity, and organized the first Sunday-school in Center Township, beginning with his own family. Owing to the rapid growth of the school he was compelled to move to the school-house, and has always been an active worker for the Baptist Church. He is a Democrat in politics, and is a member of the Agricultural Wheel.

Samuel T. Cole. The mercantile and farming interests of Washington County, Ark., are well represented by the gentleman whose name heads this sketch. His birth occurred in Jones County, Ga., October 19, 1831, but he was reared to manhood in Kemper County, Miss. He remained with his father until he attained his majority, and then came to Arkansas in 1858, locating in Yell County, where he was married September 25, 1860, to Mary E. Woods. She was born September 20, 1839, in Tennessee and reared in Mississippi, and was the daughter of John Woods (deceased). Up to 1874 they resided in Yell County, but since that time have been residents of Cane Hill Township. He purchased a farm of thirty-six acres, on which is a neat one-story residence and a fine orchard of fifteen acres of well-selected fruits. Since 1887 he has been engaged in merchandising in the town of Boonsboro, carrying a good and fairly large stock. He is one of the directors and treasurer and the largest stockholder in the Cane Hill Canning and Evaporating Factory, and is one of the enterprising citizens of the county. He is the father of the following family: Amanda B., wife of S. J. Harris, of Dardanelle; Dr. John W., of Boonsboro; O. H., who is in the store with his father; Lula L., Mattie I., Mary L. and Carl G. Samuel Walter died in 1884, at the age of fifteen years. Mr. Cole's parents, Reuben and Celia (Wadsworth) Cole, were born in Richmond County, N. C., and Jones County, Ga., respectively. They were married in the latter State, and there made their home until 1841, when they moved to Kemper County, Miss., the father dying in Kemper County April 25, 1857, the mother in Washington County January 26, 1877. He was a soldier in the Creek War, and was major in the State militia of Georgia.

Prof. J. W. Coltrane, of the Northwestern Normal, situated at Springdale, Ark., was born in Randolph County, N. C., June 27, 1852. The Coltrane family are of Scotch-Irish descent, and first came to America in 1665, locating in North Carolina. Here Branson Coltrane, the father of Prof. J. W., was born June 7, 1823, and is still living. His wife, whose maiden name was Martha L. Pool, was born in 1827, and died in 1879, after becoming the mother of nine children. Prof. Coltrane was reared on the old homestead in North Carolina, and after attaining a suitable age entered Trinity College, from which institution he was graduated in June, 1876, with the degree of A. B. Previous to his entering college he had been engaged in teaching, and after graduating he determined to seek his fortune in the West, and accordingly came to Boone County, Ark., where he taught some time in Bellefonte, afterward locating in Valley Springs, where he followed the same occupation for over two years. He next located in Salem, Iowa, where he had charge of the Whittier College for three years, and then came to Bentonville, Ark., where he was engaged in teaching for about three years more. Since December, 1886, he has been a resident of Springdale, and has had charge of the Northwestern Normal, which is one of the first institutions of the kind in the State. Prof. Coltrane has arisen to prominence in his profession, and his efforts as an educator have been attended with universal success. In November, 1878, he was married to Miss Sallie Griggs, and by her is the father of three little daughters: May, Tot and Katie. He is a member of the Quaker Church, and in his political views is a Democrat.

I. G. Combs was born in Prairie Township, Washington Co., Ark., June 3, 1855, and was reared to manhood on his father's farm. After obtaining a good common-school education he took a three years' course in the A. I. U., and after completing his studies in that institution, turned his attention to pedagoguing, continuing that occupation for about four years, teaching in all about eight terms of school. During the summer months his attention was given to agricultural pursuits, and in his farming and other enterprises he has been quite successful, having acquired a comfortable competency. He has always taken an active interest in politics, and is the present sheriff of Washington County. He was married to Miss Martha Cowen, a daughter of Anthony and Georgiana (Hurt) Cowen, who were natives of Middle Tennessee. She is a member of the Methodist Episcopal Church South. The father of the subject of this sketch, Mr. Nathan Combs, was born in Breathitt County, Ky., September 19, 1830, and is a son of Matthew and Frankie (Brown) Combs, both of whom were born and married in Buncombe County, N. C. They removed to Kentucky shortly after their marriage, where they spent the remainder of their days, dying in 1866 and 1868, respectively. They became the parents of nine children, all but three of whom are dead. Their son Nathan was reared on a farm in the "Blue Grass" State, and at the age of twenty-three years came to Washington County, Ark., where he married, and in 1861 settled on his farm of 757 acres, three miles southeast of Fayetteville. His farm consists mostly of bottom land, with 450 acres under cultivation, and he has a fine orchard of 1,500 fruit trees. He has a substantial and commodious two-story brick residence, and for many years has devoted his time exclusively to farming, and has achieved a decided success in that calling. He began life for himself with only $13, and is now ranked among the wealthy and prosperous farmers of the county. June 7, 1854, he was married to Elizabeth Cline, a native of Tennessee, by whom he became the father of one son, Isaac G. He and wife are members of the Methodist Episcopal Church, South, and in politics he has always been a Democrat, and has taken a deep interest in the political affairs of the country. His wife's parents were Virginians, and her father, George Cline, was a captain in the War of 1812, and served two terms in the Legislature of Arkansas, having moved to the State about 1838.

C. C. Conner, president of the Conner-Boles Mercantile Company, whose birth occurred three miles southeast of Fayetteville, April 11, 1842, is the son of Isaac Shelby and Elizabeth (Ingram) Conner, and grandson of Daniel Conner, who was a native of Tennessee, and who made a settlement in Arkansas, among the very first pioneers of Southeast Arkansas. He was a native of Virginia or South Carolina, and some of the members of his family were soldiers in the War of 1812. Shadrick Ingram, the maternal grandfather of Caleb C. Conner, was a native of North Carolina, and made a settlement in Southeast Arkansas, possibly a few years later than the Conner family. He was a soldier in the War of 1812. Caleb Chapman Conner, after reaching manhood, enlisted in the Confederate service, and was in Brooks' regiment all through the war, participating in every battle of his regiment. After the war he returned home, and after farming a year or two he engaged in teaching school, and followed this for a year and a half. He then engaged in merchandising, and has been identified with the mercantile interests of Washington County ever since. He was married in his native county to Miss Sarah Trent, daughter of Josiah Trent, of the Methodist Episcopal Church, South, and Elizabeth (Woolsey) Trent, very early settlers of Washington County. To Mr. and Mrs. Conner have been born five children, a son and four daughters: William Clinton, who is associated with his

****

father in the mercantile business; Maggie, Lillie Bell, Birdie and Katie. Mr. Conner is a member of the school board; is a Mason, and is a man who takes an active interest in all public enterprises. He is an active member of the county fair. He has a steam mill at Farmington, and also a branch store there, and is one of the wide-awake men of the county. He and family are members of the Christian Church.

John M. Cox, merchant, and son of Lloyd A. and Sarah (English) Cox, was born June 12, 1831, in Greene County, Tenn. The father was born in Sullivan County, Tenn., though the Cox family originally came from Maryland. The mother was born in the same State, and was of English descent. After their marriage, which occurred in Sullivan County, Tenn., they moved to Rheatown, Greene County, in the same State, and here passed their last days. He died at the age of fifty-five, and she at the age of sixty-two. The father was a merchant by occupation, and held the office of sheriff of Greene County, Tenn., one term. Both were members of the Methodist Church, and he was a Democrat in his political principles. Their family consisted of seven children, all sons. The eldest of this family, John M. Cox, grew to manhood and received a good education in the academy at Strawberry Plains. He assisted his father in the store until 1852, when he married Miss Mary E. Powell, daughter of Dr. Samuel Powell, and a native of Washington County, Tenn., born in 1831. After marriage they moved to Florida, and four years later came to Cincinnati, this county. He then engaged in merchandising with William H. Rhea, with whom he continued until 1862. During the fall of 1863 he received the appointment of purchasing agent for the transportation department of the Confederacy. After returning he again engaged in merchandising, which occupation he has since continued. In 1862 he opened a tan-yard in Cincinnati, which lay idle until 1867, when he and a partner put it into operation again, but since then Mr. Cox has disposed of his interest in the same, and made merchandising his main business, though he is the owner of 220 acres of land. He has but one child, Charles M., who has grown up in the store, and now has charge of the business. Mrs. Cox died in February, 1882. She was a member of the Methodist Episcopal Church, South. Mr. Cox is a Democrat in politics, and is a Master Mason. A month before he was twenty-one years of age he applied to the lodge to be admitted as a member, but the master proposed to reject it on the grounds of his age. Andrew Johnson, afterward President of the United States, made a speech in his favor, and as a result Mr. Cox was admitted as a member. He is liberal toward schools, churches and other worthy enterprises, and is a good citizen. He has made the most of his property by his own industry.

Samuel Cox was born in Ohio in the year 1827, and is the son of Nathan and Ruth (Bruer) Cox, both natives of North Carolina. The father was a farmer and blacksmith by occupation, and at the breaking out of the War of 1812 he enlisted in the army of his country and went to the front, serving under William Henry Harrison until the close of the war. He moved to Washington County, Ark., in 1842, and here died in 1859. Samuel Cox was educated in this county, and remained with his parents until he reached manhood, working in the shop and learning the trade of his father. In 1853 he married Miss Pamelia A. Ingram, of Washington County, Ark., and eight children were the result of this union: Elizabeth R., Jeanette, Samuel, William N., Adaline, Lucinda, Jacob and Nathan. In 1863 Mr. Cox enlisted in Company A, First Arkansas Independent Light Artillery, United States Army, commanded by Benton D. Starks, and served for two years or until the close of the war. During the war he had the misfortune to lose his hearing by the heavy firing of cannons. He fought in fifteen engagements when artillery was used, and did his share of the fighting. When peace was declared he returned home to Washington County, and engaged in blacksmithing. He has succeeded in accumulating considerable of this world's goods; has a fine farm of 120 acres, all well cultivated and well improved. He is a Mason and Odd Fellow, and he and wife are members of the Baptist Church.

Samuel A. Craig, general merchant, who carries a stock of goods valued at $2,000, and whose annual sales equal $6,000, has been in business at Wedington, Ark., for the past six years, and has met with flattering success. He was born in Greene County, Tenn., February 14, 1826, and is the son of James and Jane (Hall) Craig, both natives of Greene County, Tenn. The father died in Hamblin County, of that State, in 1884, and was eighty-four years of age at that time.

The mother died in 1836, and when comparatively a young woman. They were married in Greene County, Tenn., and lived in that and Hamblin County all their lives. The father was a member of the Presbyterian Church, and after the death of his wife married Mrs. Barton, a widow, who died in 1878. Mr. Craig had followed farming all his life, and in this occupation was very successful. By his first marriage were born four children, two now living: Samuel A. and John; the latter, living in Carroll County, Ark., is a prominent citizen and a leading farmer. At the age of twenty-one Samuel A. left home, and learned the tanner's trade in Parisville, Cocke Co., Tenn., and worked at his trade in that and Greene County, Tenn., for several years, but gave that up and engaged in trading, selling goods for himself and other people. A few years before the war he left Tennessee and located in Johnson County, Mo., but soon after moved to Cincinnati, Ark., where he sold goods for W. H. Rhea for sixteen years. He then came to this county. He was in the Confederate army during the war, and was in Capt. Eubanks' company. In 1860 he married Miss Sarah Rhea, a sister of W. H. Rhea, and a native of Benton County, Ark., born in 1833. This union was blessed by the birth of one child, a son, P. V., who is now in his uncle's store at Cincinnati. Mr. Craig is a Democrat in his political views, and is a good citizen.

Hon. Johnson Crawford. A history of the prominent families of Washington County, Ark., would be incomplete without mentioning the Crawfords, who have long been residents of the State and county. The family was first represented in the State by John Crawford, who moved from Virginia to the far West with his wife and five small children, locating in Lawrence County, where he is supposed to have met a violent death, either by drowning or being devoured by some wild animal, as he went out hunting one spring day and never returned. His son Arthur, who was born in Augusta County, Va., in 1806, was only a small boy when his father disappeared. He remained with his mother, he being the only son, until he was twenty-two years of age, and then began doing for himself, coming to Washington County about 1832, and locating on the farm where his son, Hon. Johnson Crawford, is now living. He moved from West Fork to Sulphur Springs in 1876. He is yet living, and was married, in 1842, to Miss Sarah Wood, who was born in Tennessee in 1814, and died in February, 1885. Her seven children were as follows: Rebecca, wife of W. P. Loudon; Jesse, who was killed in West Fork Township in 1864, a soldier in the Confederate army; Mary, wife of James Brown; Johnson; Adaline, wife of John West; James, deceased, and John, who died in Washington County in July, 1886. Johnson Crawford was born in Washington County, Ark., July 9, 1843, and resided under the paternal roof until the breaking out of the war, when he enlisted in Company K, and was with Gen. Price on his raid through Kansas and Missouri. At the battle of Prairie Grove he had his hat-band shot in two twice, and he also participated in the battle of Helena. When peace was declared he came home to his parents, with whom he remained until 1867, at which time he was united in matrimony to Miss Clementine Gilland, and engaged in farming on the west fork of White River, where he remained eight years. Since that time he has resided on the farm of 200 acres where he now lives. In 1876 he established a general merchandise store, and the place took the name of Sulphur Springs from the large number of springs in the vicinity, but is now called Sulphur City. He continued in this business until 1878, when he sold his store and stock of goods, and since that time has been engaged in farming. Mr. Crawford and wife are members of the Baptist Church, and he is a minister of that denomination, being ordained in 1876, and is now the pastor of two churches. He is a Democrat in his political views, and has always taken an active interest in politics, being the present representative of his county in the State Legislature. The following are his children: Effie (wife of H. Layman), James A., John P., Jesse D., Jordan O., Pearl, Eli D., Maude M., Ina and an infant.

Leonidas E. Crawford deserves honorable mention as a successful farmer and stock raiser of Washington County, Ark. He was born on the farm on which he now resides, November 11, 1850, being one of six children born to R. D. Crawford, who was born in Tennessee in 1818, and left that State at the age of twelve years, locating in Washington County, Ark. Here he was married to Eliza Henderson, and afterward bought the place known as the Henderson farm, which consists of 500 acres, and as he is unable to care for all his land, his boys left their cattle ranch in Texas, and are now cultivating the farm and raising stock. His orchard consists of 800 bearing trees of fine varieties of apples, peaches and pears, and his residence is commodious and comfortable. Mr. Crawford was captain of a company of militia five years in early times. He and wife are worthy and consistent members of the Cumberland Presbyterian Church. Leonidas E. Crawford grew to mature years on his father's farm, and in 1879 went to Texas, where he and his brothers were ranching cattle; spent one year in the management of the cattle, the herd consisting of 1,000 head, branded thus: E. W. T. November 15, 1880, while in Western Texas, he was united in marriage to Miss Sallie E. Woodruff, who was born in Washington County, Ark., and a daughter of F. M. Woodruff, a native of Tennessee, and an early settler of Washington County, and their union has been blessed in the birth of three sons: Francis R., Clifford P. and Clyde. In 1880 Mr. Crawford left Texas and returned to Arkansas, but for several years retained his interest in the cattle ranch in the Lone Star State. Since his return he has resided on and managed a part of the old farm. He and his brothers are extensively engaged in stock dealing (1888).

Rev. Henry C. Crowell, pastor of the Church of Christ, Prairie Grove, Ark., and a member of the mercantile firm of H. C. & G. W. Crowell, of the same place, was born in Benton County, Ark., December 18, 1851, and is a son of Charles Crowell, who was of German descent, and was born, reared and married in Tennessee. His wife, whose maiden name was Lavina Foster, was born in Bedford County, Tenn., and became the mother of fourteen children, all of whom except four lived to be grown, and seven sons and three daughters are now living. Soon after their marriage the parents moved to Arkansas, being among the early settlers and farmers of Benton County, but since 1877, or 1878, they have been residents of Prairie Grove. Their son, H. C. Crowell, was reared to manhood in Benton County, and at the age of sixteen years began working at the jeweler's trade, serving a two years' apprenticeship. He then began working for himself at Ozark, Ark., but at the end of one year went to Crawford County, where his parents had located, and engaged in the general merchandise business, but with a very small capital. About 1878 he became a resident of Prairie Grove, and was the second merchant in the town, and has helped materially in making the place what it is. He and his brother have built twenty-one residences and five business houses, and are also extensively engaged in milling. He and his brother have a large and select stock of general merchandise, and are doing well financially. They also own and operate a drug store in the town. In August, 1873, Mr. Crowell was married to Miss Emma Foster (no relation of his mother), a daughter of Josiah Foster, and by her is the father of six children, four of whom are now living: Minnie Lee, Arthur, Neta and an infant daughter named Sudie. Mr. Crowell was ordained a minister of the Christian Church in 1884, and is now the local preacher of that church at Prairie Grove. He is the author of a work entitled "Exposition and Bonding of Satan."

James C. Cunningham. Among the honest and prosperous tillers of the soil of Prairie Grove, Washington Co., Ark., worthy of mention is Mr. Cunningham, who was born in Bedford County, Tenn., November 29, 1841. His parents, M. T. and Nancy G. (McGill) Cunningham, were born, reared and married in Tennessee, and there spent their days. The father was a blacksmith, wagon-maker and miller by trade, and followed those occupations throughout life. James C. received a good education in the Flat Creek Academy, acquiring a thorough knowledge of the common and higher English branches and the higher mathematics. He remained with his father until eighteen years of age, and in the fall of 1859 came West to seek his fortune, locating in Washington County, Ark., where he has since made his home, with the exception of a few years. He raised a crop in 1860, and part of one in 1861, but the breaking out of the war interfered with his labors, and he enlisted in the Confederate army, in McCrea's regiment, for three months, at the end of which time he returned home. In October, 1861, he enlisted in Hart's battery of Arkansas troops for twelve months, but when it was reorganized, about three months later, he joined the Third Texas Cavalry, with which he remained until April, 1862. He was then detailed on detached duty for a short time, and afterward joined the Nineteenth Texas Infantry, serving with the same until the close of the war. In June, 1865, they were disbanded at Hempstead, Tex., and he remained in that

State until 1866, engaged in teaching school. After returning to Arkansas he was engaged in teaching the young idea for about one year, and then turned his attention to farming and stock raising, which occupation has received the most of his attention up to the present time. He rented land for some time, and in 1880 purchased his present valuable bottom land farm of 280 acres, 175 acres of which are under cultivation. He also owns 120 acres of land at Viney Grove, eighty acres of which are under cultivation. He was married in Washington County, January 24, 1867, to Miss Jennie Rollins, a native of the county, and daughter of Moses Rollins, deceased, and by her became the father of three daughters: Nancy N., Mary and Susie. The wife died in October, 1871, and in January, 1877, Mr. Cunningham married his second wife, Miss Fannie Shofner, a native of Bedford County, Tenn., and daughter of Newton K. Shofner. Four children have blessed this union: Newton, William, Tennie and Earl. Mrs. Cunningham is a member of the Cumberland Presbyterian Church.

Hiram Abiff Daily is a prominent young druggist of Springdale. Ark., and was born in the "Blue Grass" State in 1855. He was reared and educated in Texas, and before entering the drug business was engaged in mercantile pursuits. Since 1880 he has been engaged in selling drugs at Springdale, and is the popular druggist of the town. He began his present business with a $200 stock, and now his goods are valued at $5,000, and he has a pleasant and comfortable home worth at least $1,000. Owing to his excellent business qualifications he promises to become one of the wealthy citizens of the county, as he is now one of the popular young business men. He votes the Democratic ticket, and is a strong supporter of the principles of that party. His marriage with Miss M. T. Ellis was celebrated in 1882. She was born in Illinois, and she and Mr. Daily are the parents of three children: Floy, Nina and Gus D. H. Daily, M. D., father of Hiram Abiff, was born in Smith County, Va., in 1797, and was reared in Tennessee. He commenced the practice of medicine in 1822, and has been a resident of and followed his profession in the following States: Tennessee. Virginia, Kentucky, Texas and Arkansas, and is now residing at Springdale, but is retired from active business life. He was twice married, his first wife becoming the mother of nine children. His present wife, who was a Miss Sarah Pruner, was born in Virginia in 1825, and is the mother of ten children, H. A. Daily being one of her sons.

Charles Dale, lumberman of Fayetteville, Ark., was born in Port Huron, Mich., April 17, 1846, and is a son of Perry H. Dale, a contractor and builder of that city, a native of Rochester, Genesee Co., N. Y., being a son of an English gentleman who came to America and made a settlement in York State. Perry H. Dale was married to Miss E. A. Spalding, a daughter of Jedediah Spalding, of New Hampshire. Charles Dale grew to maturity at Port Huron, and at the age of eighteen years left his father's sash and door factory, in which he worked, and went to Cleveland, Ohio, where he enlisted in the Tenth United States Infantry April 16, 1864, and was soon sent to the front. The first important battle in which he participated was the battle of the Wilderness, and he afterward took an important part in the following battles: Spottsylvania Court House, North Anna River, Cold Harbor, Siege of Vicksburg, and Weldon Railroad. He was severely wounded in the right foot at the latter engagement, which incapacitated him for further service. After recovering from his wound he was appointed to special duty as clerk at the general headquarters at New York City, afterward filling the same position for Gens. Hooker, Sherman, Cook and Terry, and was mustered out of service at Fort Snelling, Minn., in 1867. After spending a few months at home he went West, visiting Kansas City and Sherman, Tex., and on his way home visited Fayetteville. Ark., and Springfield, Mo., spending some months in the latter place. In 1869 he went to Kansas, where he was engaged in the lumber business for one year, and after his return to Michigan he accepted the agency for the Port Huron & Lake Michigan Railway, spending two years in the employ of that corporation. He resigned his position March 4, 1873, and after a short time went to Cincinnati, Ohio, thence to Chicago, where he was engaged in the patent right business for a number of years. In 1879 he went to Kansas with S. A. Brown & Co., and was engaged in the lumber business in that State until 1883, when he came to Fayetteville, Ark., and purchased the lumber interests of S. A. Brown & Co., which business he has conducted with good success up to the present time. He was married at Vicksburg, Mich., to Miss Prudence Williams, a daughter of Myron Williams, a leading mill owner, lumberman, merchant and vessel owner of that place, and their union has been blessed in the birth of one child, Nina. Mr. Dale and wife attend the Episcopal Church, and he is a member of the K. of P., of which society he is a charter member, and is also a charter member of the Fayetteville Gun Club, the Fayetteville Electric Light Company and the Building and Loan Association.

James E. Davis, whose name takes the lead in the list of prominent land-holders of Washington County, was born in Blount County, Tenn., August 10, 1831, and is the son of James and Charity (Philips) Davis. The father was born in Blount County, Tenn., was a successful farmer, was a member of the Missionary Baptist Church, and was a Union man and a Republican in politics. The mother was a native of North Carolina, and was married to Mr. Davis in Blount County, Tenn., where they both passed the greater part of their lives. He died at the age of seventy-three, and she at the age of sixty-five. She was also a member of the Baptist Church. In their family were twelve children, seven now living. James E. Davis, when twenty-one years of age, went to Cass County, Ga., but one year later returned to Tennessee and located in Blount County. In the year 1854 he moved to Washington County, Ark., where he has since resided. Although commencing without means he is now the owner of 2,000 acres of some of the best land in the county, with 600 acres under cultivation. October 12, 1857, he married Miss Elizabeth Woolsey, who was born in Washington County, Ark., February 12, 1838, and who is the daughter of Samuel Woolsey. To Mr. and Mrs. Davis were born eleven children, five sons and six daughters, nine of whom are now living, viz.: James W., Nina E., John S., George W., Mollie T., Nolie L., Cora B., Ella E., Ida M., Edgar C., Caleb L. Those deceased are Nolie L. and Edgar C. Mr. Davis served four years in the Confederate army, in Col. Carroll's regiment, and was in many skirmishes. He was taken prisoner, was taken to Fayetteville, and there confined for two months. Another time he was a prisoner a short time, doing the duty of a scout. During this eventful period he lost all his property but his land, he being the owner at that time of about 300 acres. Mr. Davis, in his political views, has been a Democrat, but now votes for the best man. He is the largest land-owner in Washington County, and has some property in Benton County. He is one of the enterprising citizens of the county, and at all times supports the cause of education.

Hon. Wilson M. Davis, who is at present ably representing Washington County, Ark., in the State Legislature, was born in Missouri in 1852, and made his native State his home until six years of age, at which time he was taken by his parents, Green and Tirzah (Banks) Davis, to the "Lone Star State." Here he resided until fourteen or fifteen years of age, when, being of an independent and enterprising disposition, he determined to make his own way in the world, and, accordingly, came to Washington County, Ark., and engaged in farming, and, after receiving sufficient education in the common schools, engaged in teaching school. He has resided in Springdale for about seventeen years, and is well known throughout the county as a man of integrity and ability. In 1885 he was elected, on the Democratic ticket, to the State Legislature, and is now filling the duties of that position to the entire satisfaction of his constituents, having introduced several important bills, among which was the railroad bill for prohibiting discrimination in freight rates and one for reducing car fare to 3 cents per mile. Both bills were passed. In 1875 he was united in marriage to Miss Ardilla Barr, who was born in 1858, and their union has resulted in the birth of four children. The family worship in the Methodist Episcopal Church South.

George Freeman Deane, sheriff of Washington County, and a prominent citizen, is a son of Charles W. and Eliza Ruth (McKissick) Deane, and grandson of Job Deane, who was a native of Virginia, and a planter and merchant by occupation. He settled in North Carolina at a very early date. The parents of the subject of this sketch were natives of South Carolina and Tennessee, respectively, and the father was a physician by profession, making his home in Washington County, Ark., at an early date. He died in this county March 4, 1886, full in the faith of the Episcopal Church. The Deanes were originally from Virginia, and were long-lived people. Mrs. Deane was the daughter of Col. James McKissick, a native of South Carolina, who made a settlement here in early times. George Freeman Deane attained his majority in Fayetteville, and followed agricultural pursuits for some time.   His early inclinations were for stock raising, and after the war, in which he served about thirteen months in the Southern army, he began dealing and trading in stock.   He was married in Fayetteville to Miss Mary Elizabeth, daughter of Judge Hiram and Elizabeth (Anderson) Davis.   Three children were born to Mr. and Mrs. Deane, two sons and one daughter: Sidney E., Ruth Elizabeth and Charles Volx.   Mr. Deane has 160 acres in the home place and 160 acres in another tract.   He is using his influence in the introduction of Holstein cattle and Spanish jacks in the county, with a fair prospect of success before him.   He has always taken an active interest in the agricultural society in the county, and has served as an official in the same.   He was also interested in the Grange movement.   He is just closing his second term as sheriff of the county, which position he filled with credit to himself and his constituents.   He and Mrs. Deane are worthy members of the Methodist Episcopal Church.

William S. Deaver was born in Maryland on the 14th of April, 1813, and September 21, 1842, was married, in Virginia, to Sarah M. Martin, who was born on the 8th of June, 1823.   In 1850 they started out to seek their fortunes in the far West, and located in Arkansas, where they resided until their respective deaths, May 9, 1876, and January 9, 1853.   They were the parents of five children: John Richard, Mary Elizabeth, George William, Benjamin Franklin and David Wilson, out of which only three are living, the two oldest boys, J. R. and G. W., having lost their lives in the Southern army.   After his wife's death William S. Deaver was married to Sarah E., a daughter of Jacob Pearson, of Elm Springs, their union taking place August 11, 1853.   This wife died on the 29th of May, 1887, leaving one son, J. P. Deaver.   Benjamin Franklin Deaver, a son born to the first marriage, was born in the "Old Dominion" December 27, 1849, and came to Arkansas with his parents.   He resided in Elm Springs until eight years of age, and then was taken to a farm about two miles east of that place, where he resided until 1880.   October 11, 1874, he was married to Miss Ellen, daughter of William H. and Rebecca Holcomb, and by her became the father of three children, only one of whom is living, Bertha S., who was born May 14, 1879.   Mrs. Deaver died on the 19th of June, 1882.   In 1881 Mr. Deaver moved to Springdale, Ark., and engaged in merchandising, being the senior member of the general dry goods firm of B. F. Deaver & Co.   He has sole charge of the store, and is the first dry goods merchant of the town.   He has been a member of the Methodist Episcopal Church since 1878; was made a Mason at Elm Spring Lodge No. 154 in 1875; has been a member of Springdale Lodge No. 316 since 1881; since that time has served as W. M. four years.   In his political views he supports the principles of the Democratic party.   On the 4th of June, 1884, Mr. Deaver married his second wife, Mary B. Putman, a daughter of Dr. R. and Elizabeth Putman, of Fayetteville, Ark.   She was born four miles south of Fayetteville August 27, 1859.   She lived and was principally educated at the State University of Fayetteville, and graduated at Woodland College, Independence, Mo., June 7, 1881.   She became the mother of one child, that was born and died September 10, 1885.

Wiley D. Deen, farmer of White River Township, Washington Co., Ark., was born in Hamilton County, Ill., in January, 1841, and is a son of William and Barsheba (Durham) Deen, who were born respectively in Tennessee and North Carolina, in 1799.   The father was nearly grown when he left home and went to Illinois, and he was a farmer of Hamilton County until he was nearly seventy-nine years of age, dying in 1878.   His wife resided in her native State until about fourteen years of age, when she was taken to Tennessee by her parents, and there resided for about twenty years, then moving to Illinois, where she met and married Mr. Deen.   She died in Washington County, Ark., June 13, 1888, being the mother of two children: Martha, who died when three days old, and Wiley D.   The father was previously married to a Miss Jane Coffee, of Illinois, by whom he became the father of eight children, three of whom are living: Jacob (who lives within 300 yards of where he was born, and is about sixty-five years of age), Susan (the wife of Henry Davis, residing in Illinois) and Frances (the wife of James Johnson).   Wiley D. Deen came to Phelps County, Mo., with his parents, when he was in his eighteenth year, and located on a farm heavily covered with timber, which they began to improve.   About 1864 he came to Benton County, Ark., where he resided two years, and then came to his present location.   During the war he was a Confederate soldier in a Missouri cavalry regiment, serving as third lieutenant, but the company was soon after disbanded, and after visiting in Illinois for some time he returned to Missouri the following year (1866). He participated in the battles of Oak Hill and Springfield, and was in numerous skirmishes. He was married in June, 1862, to Margaret J. Brown, of Phelps County, Mo., born in 1841, and died November 23, 1883, having borne a family of twelve children: Andrew J. (deceased), Melvina (wife of G. W. King), Barsheba (wife of J. N. Jarvis), Ashal, Albert, Martha, Wiley, Alfred and Allen (twins), William, Leta and Amos. Mr. Deen was again married, March 1, 1888, to Mrs. Mary E. (Parker) Woodruff, who was born in Arkansas in 1853, and was first married to James Adair, and became the mother of two children: Emma and George. Their father died in 1881, and she afterward married J. Woodruff, who died four years later. To them was born one child, Viola. Mrs. Deen is a member of the Missionary Baptist Church, and Mr. Deen is a member of the Methodist Episcopal Church, South, of which he is a steward, and he takes an active interest in church work. He is a Democrat, and is the present justice of the peace of his township. Our subject has a good farm of over seventy-seven acres, with forty acres under cultivation, and a fine bearing orchard of over 600 trees.

Mac Devin, one of the enterprising and respected young men of this city, was born in Marr's Hill Township, now Rhea's Mill Township, December 3, 1856, and is a son of James Crawford and Elizabeth Jane (Edmiston) Devin. The father is a substantial farmer of Washington County, and was born in Tennessee, his father being Irben Devin, who settled in Prairie Grove Township in 1833. The mother of our subject was born near Ft. Smith, on the Poteau River, in what is now Indian Territory. Her father, John T. Edmiston, was a native of Georgia, who settled in Arkansas before it became a State. Mrs. Devin died in 1885, a member of the Cumberland Presbyterian Church, and is buried in Prairie Grove Cemetery. Mr. Devin still resides upon his farm in Marr's Hill Township. Young Mac passed his youth upon the farm, and received a common-school education, which was supplemented by a course at the Viney Grove High-school. In 1878 he was appointed deputy county clerk, which office he filled with satisfaction for two years. He then spent two years in the sheriff's and collector's office, leaving that position to accept the position of cashier of the Washington County Bank. Upon the organization of the Bank of Fayetteville he was offered the same position in that corporation, and in November, 1888, he began to fulfill the duties of that office. Mr. Devin is a business man of sterling integrity, and is a stockholder in the Switzer Wagon Company and the building and loan association. He married Miss Nancy Louisa, the third daughter of the Hon. Hosea Maguire [see sketch], who has borne him one son and two daughters: Earl, Paul and Josephine. Mrs. Devin is a member of the Cumberland Presbyterian Church, in which her hussand is a deacon. Mr. Devin is a Royal Arch Mason and a Knight of Pythias.

David Divelbiss, a prominent citizen of Richland Township, Washington Co., Ark., was born in Morrow County, Ohio, on the 25th of October, 1834, and is a son of Frederick and Elizabeth (Henline) Divelbiss, whose ancestors were Germans, and came to the United States prior to the Revolutionary War. The Divelbiss family first located in Maryland, and afterward in Pennsylvania, where Frederick Divelbiss was born in August, 1809. He is now residing in Huntington County, Ind. His wife was born in Huntingdon County, Penn., in June, 1809, and died in Huntington County, Ind., November 11, 1881. They were married in Ohio, and there resided until 1849, at which time they moved to Indiana. The father has been a life-long farmer, and is a Republican in his political views. David Divelbiss was the third of nine children, seven of whom are living: David; Samuel; Maria, the wife of John Christman; Jonas; Sophia, wife of Elias Patterson; Marian, the wife of George Seese, and William C. At the early age of seventeen years David began to earn his own living, by hiring out by the month. In 1860 he purchased land in Huntington County, Ind., and began his career as a farmer, but October 21, 1862, left the plow and enlisted in the United States army, in Company C, Thirty-fourth Indiana Infantry, and served until October 20, 1865, when he was discharged at Brownsville, Tex. He was in many hotly contested battles, and after the war returned home and again turned his attention to farming. In the spring of 1876 he came to Washington County, Ark., and bought the farm of 320 acres on which he now lives. He is also engaged in the stock and dairy business, and in 1887 sold $700 worth of butter. His cattle are full-blooded Jerseys. Mr. Divelbiss is a stanch Republican, and is a member of the G. A. R. and I. O. O. F. June 5, 1859, he was married to Mary, a daughter of Albert Draper. She was born in Huntington County, Ind., March 14, 1842, and she and Mr. Divelbiss are the parents of the following family: Rachel, wife of B. F. Johnson; Mary C., Francis E., Sarah T., Frederick W., Albert D., Solomon B. and Samuel C. Those deceased are Nora A. and Anna M. Mr. and Mrs. Divelbiss are worthy members of the Missionary Baptist Church, and are well known and respected in the county in which they reside.

Dryden Dold, M. D., retired physician and farmer, of Washington County, Ark., was born in Augusta County, of the "Old Dominion," May 17, 1812, and was reared and educated in his native county. At an early day he began the study of medicine, and took two courses of lectures in the medical department of the University of Virginia, and one course of lectures in Philadelphia, Penn., in the winter of 1834-35. In the spring of the latter year he began practicing his profession in Middlebrook, Va., and at the end of twelve months came west, and located first in St. Louis, and then in Natchez, Miss., remaining in the latter place six months. He then returned to Virginia, and shortly after located near Knoxville, Tenn., where he made his home, and practiced his profession for about fifteen years. The following four years were spent in Georgia, and after a short residence in New Orleans he came up the Mississippi River as far as Cane Hill, Ark. (in 1848), where he located and practiced medicine for about thirteen years, his practice extending within a radius of from twenty to thirty miles. He became a resident of Benton County, Ark., in 1861, and owned considerable land where Siloam Springs is now located, but in 1874 he returned to Washington County, where he has since made his home, and where he has had an extensive and increasing practice. He was married while residing in East Tennessee, but about 1858 his wife died, and he married his second wife, Nancy Reed, in Washington County, Ark. She is a native of the county, and a daughter of John R. Reed, one of the early settlers of Arkansas. Dr. and Mrs Dold are the parents of the following family: William A., John Philip, Mary M., Sarah E., wife of Robert Simpson, and Laura Virginia. The family are members of the Cumberland Presbyterian Church.

James Dodson, senior member of the mercantile firm of Dodson & Co., of Springdale, Ark., was born in Tennessee in 1836, and at the age of fifteen years came to Arkansas with his parents. He farmed for a short period, and for about five years was one of the popular local educators of Northwest Arkansas. In the fall of 1866 he entered mercantile life in Randolph County, where he resided until 1883, when he took up his abode in Imboden, and followed the same occupation until February, 1887. Since that time he has resided in Springdale, and is doing a thriving business. He has some valuable town property, besides his spacious store building, and is considered one of the progressive and prosperous citizens of the county. Miss Julia D. Henderson became his wife and the mother of his three children: Fannie S., wife of J. L. Davis; John S. and Nettie M. Mr. Dodson and family worship in the Primitive Baptist Church, and he is a Democrat in his political views. In 1861 he enlisted in the Confederate army, and served four years. He was in eighteen different battles, but was never wounded. His parents, Sampson and Celia (Rogers) Dodson, who were born in Tennessee in 1809 and 1814, respectively, were reared and married in their native State, and in 1851 immigrated to Arkansas. They were the parents of four children, James being the second in the family, and their deaths occurred in 1877 and 1874, father and mother, respectively.

Rev. William A. Douthit, merchant at Salem Springs, Washington Co., Ark., and a successful farmer, is the son of Thomas and Sarah Douthit, both natives of North Carolina. When young they moved with their parents to this county, were married April 10, A. D. 1842, and here in this county they have resided ever since. The father is a tiller of the soil, and he and wife are members of the Methodist Episcopal Church, South. He is sixty-nine years of age, and is of Irish and English descent. His grandparents came from Ireland. The mother's maiden name was Alburty; she is sixty-five years of age, and is of German descent. Her grandparents came to America with the first settlers of New York. William A. Douthit was born November 5, 1848, and was one of eight children born to his parents, six sons and two daughters. He was reared to farm life, and had very poor educational advantages in early life, the Civil War depriving him of such educational advantages. After reaching manhood he educated himself in an academy at Evansville, and afterward taught for about six months. He then turned his attention to farming, which occupation he still carries on, and is now the owner of eighty acres of good land. In 1872 he married Miss Belle Bowden, a native of Pope County, Ark. She was the daughter of John and Elizabeth Bowden, who came from Maury County, Tenn., in an early day. John S. Bowden was elected to the Legislature in the year 1856, was re-elected in 1858 and 1860, and was in the State Legislature when the State seceded, and was re-elected when the north part was admitted to the Union. He was killed by the rebel guerrillas in April, 1865. The mother still survives, and lives on the old homestead. To William A. and Belle Douthit were born six children, three sons and three daughters. Both he and wife are members of the Methodist Episcopal Church. October, 1887, Mr. Douthit built a store-house in Salem Springs, and soon after engaged in merchandising at that place. With the exception of about ten years Mr. Douthit has made this county his home all his life. He is a Republican in politics, and was elected justice of the peace in the fall of 1884, which he faithfully filled. In 1881 he was licensed to preach in the Methodist Episcopal Church, and preached the second sermon at Salem Springs in a brush arbor in July of that same year.

Julius Linn Duke, jeweler at Fayetteville, Ark., was born in Pike County, Mo., August 5, 1843, and is a son of Courtney M. and Catherine (Jackson) Duke, natives of Virginia and Missouri, respectively. The father was a merchant by occupation, and a descendant of a long line of ancestors of the Old Dominion. In 1854 he immigrated to Fayetteville, Washington Co., Ark., and here died in 1876, after a long and useful life. He was buried with the honors of the Odd Fellows society. His wife, Catherine (Jackson) Duke, was the daughter of Cornelius Jackson, a native of Pennsylvania, who made a settlement in Missouri at a very early date, and was a farmer and trader by occupation. Julius L. Duke attained his growth in Washington County, Ark., and here learned the jeweler's trade. He entered the ranks of the Confederate army, Third Arkansas Volunteer Infantry, State Militia, and was at the battle of Wilson's Creek. Upon the organization of the Confederate regular service, he enlisted in Company H, Thirty-fourth Arkansas Volunteer Infantry, and participated in the battles of Prairie Grove, Helena, Jenkins' Ferry, and numerous other minor engagements. He remained in the service until the close of the war, and then returned home and engaged in the jewelry business, and has been prominently identified with it ever since. He was married in Fayetteville, in 1868, to Miss Helen M. Gaines, daughter of Judge B. J. H. Gaines, of Sebastian County, Ark. They have one daughter, Annie G. Mr. Duke has served in the courts of the city, also the school board, is a member of the Masonic fraternity, the K. of P., the K. of H., and he and wife and daughter are members of the Christian Church.

Zebulon B. Edmiston, retired merchant, of Boonsboro, Ark., is a native of Clark County, Ark., born April 17, 1830. His father, David Edmiston, was born in Tennessee, and came to Arkansas when a lad of thirteen, with his father (who also bore the name of David), and located in what is now Clark County. Here David C. Edmiston grew to manhood, and was afterward married to Rebecca Thornton, a native of Illinois, moving to Washington County, Ark., in 1835, where he was engaged in farming until his death, in April, 1884. His wife died in August, 1882. Zebulon B. spent his youthful days on his father's farm, and received a fair common-school education. On December 16, 1852, he was married to Miss Eunice Jane Gray, a daughter of Sanford F. Gray, who bore him three sons: James P., David N. and John S. Mr. Edmiston farmed until 1872, when he moved to Boonsboro to give his children the advantages of the schools of that place, and four years later engaged in merchandising, which occupation he successfully carried on until 1884, when he retired from active business life and left his store to the management of his sons. When the Boonsboro Canning and Evaporating Factory was organized, in 1888, Mr. Edmiston became one of the stockholders and did all in his power to further the enterprise. John S. Edmiston, son of Zebulon B. Edmiston, was educated in the Cane Hill College, and graduated from that institution in the summer of 1876, and in the fall of the same year began teaching in the primary department of the same institution. He then taught in Sebastian County, Ark., for some time, and afterward went to Texas, where he followed the same calling, returning to Arkansas in December, 1878. In February, of the following year, he engaged in merchandising in Boonsboro, and has been actively engaged in that business ever since. He became a director and president of the Cane Hill Canning and Evaporating Company, of which B. J. Wade was made vice-president; S. T. Cole, treasurer; Dr. W. H. Moore, secretary, and the following are the other directors: F. R. Earl, W. S. Moore, J. H. Marler and William M. Lewis. May 6, 1886, Mr. Edmiston was married to Miss Alice L. Lacy, who was born in Alabama and was reared and educated in Arkansas. They have three children: Erin, Lacy and Clem Gray. The family are members of the Cumberland Presbyterian Church.

Howard Edwards, A. M., Professor of History, English and Modern Languages in the A. I. U., was born in Fauquier County, Va., November 7, 1854, and received his education under his father, who was a noted educator. By the time he was twelve years of age he had read many of the classics with his father, and when seventeen years of age he entered Randolph Macon College, near Richmond; graduated in 1876 with the degree of A. M., being first honorary man in mathematics and also in Latin. The last year of his course he was elected assistant professor of Latin. Having taught a year in private schools, he studied in the universities of Leipsic and Paris, making language his chief study. Returning, he was instructor in English, German and History in Bethel (Va.) Academy, for two years, and was also two years at the Bingham (N. C.) School. He was then acting principal of Bethel (Va.) Academy, for two years, then principal of Tuscumbia (Ala.) Academy, and in 1885 he was elected to his present position. March, 1888, he was elected librarian of A. I. U. In 1881 he married Miss Elizabeth Smith, a native of Fauquier County, Va., and by this union were born two children, Norman and Bland. Both Prof. and Mrs. Edwards are members of the Methodist Episcopal Church South. Rev. Francis M. and Frances (Bland) Edwards, parents of Prof. Edwards, were born in Virginia and North Carolina, respectively. The father was a native of King George County, was left an orphan when quite young, and was reared in Baltimore by a brother, Rev. William B. Edwards, D. D., where he received a fine classical education. He taught in private schools until the close of the war, and since then has been engaged in the ministry. The mother was a direct descendant of Theodrick Bland, of Colonial fame. In their family were three living children, two sons and one daughter. Clarence is a prominent educator of New York, and in his politics affiliates with the Democratic party.

S. L. Eidson, proprietor of Eidson's Distillery, of Washington County, Ark., was born in the county in 1852, and is a son of W. H. and Susan Eidson. He was reared on a farm and followed that occupation until a few years ago, when he commenced distilling apples and peaches and manufacturing whisky. He has on hand at the present time 3,500 gallons of whisky, of the finest quality, on which he has a good trade, and which he ships principally south and west. Besides his distillery, he owns 220 acres of fertile and well-improved land, from which he derives a comfortable competency. He votes the Democratic ticket. About 1876 he was married to Miss Amanda Harper, but has since been married to Miss Sallie Payne. His first union was blessed in the birth of four interesting children.

William Harrison Eidson, another citizen whose name is synonymous with the farming interests of the county, is a son of William and Martha (Wilson) Eidson. The father was born in North Carolina about 1782, and the mother in Hawkins County, Tenn., being about eight years younger than her husband. When a young man the father immigrated to Tennessee, where he met and married Miss Wilson. They spent their lives on a farm in Hawkins County, Tenn., and both lived to be about seventy years of age. He was an old-time Democrat, and she was a member of the Missionary Baptist Church. They were the parents of eleven children, six sons and five daughters. The sixth child, William H. Eidson, was born in Hawkins County, Tenn., April 19, 1823, was reared on the farm and educated to a limited extent in the old subscription schools. At the age of nineteen he married Miss Susan Begley, a native of Hawkins County, Tenn., born November, 1822. Having farmed in that county until 1851 he moved to Washington County, Ark., located in the woods on the place where he now lives, and here first entered forty acres of land. Since then he has added thereto, and now has about 1,200 acres. To Mr. and Mrs. Eidson were born ten children: McCoy, John D., Henry, Mary J., Samuel L., William S., Martha E., Ellen C., George P. and Orlena B. The eldest two were killed

****

at the battle of Vicksburg, while in service on the Confederate side. As a business man Mr. Eidson has been eminently successful, and is one of the largest land owners in the township. He has been a resident of this county for thirty-seven years, and has lived on his present property all that time. He is Democratic in his political views, was justice of the peace four years, and both he and wife are members of the Methodist Episcopal Church, South.

William H. Engels, farmer, was born in Independence County, Ark., August 27, 1830. His father, Henry A. Engels, was born and reared in Washington, Ky., and at the age of nineteen years left his home to seek his fortune in the West, locating in Independence County, Ark., where he engaged in farming, and became one of the leading citizens of the county. He was the first sheriff of the county after the State was admitted, and held the office six years. He died December 9, 1843, and his wife, whose maiden name was Eliza Allen, and whom he married in 1829, died in 1835. She was born in Alabama, a daughter of Andrew Allen, one of the prominent men of Independence County, and became the mother of three children: Abraham A., Sarah J. (wife of W. F. Woodruff) and William H. The latter was but five years old when his mother died, and he was reared by his uncles, William and Abraham Allen, of Washington County, Ark. He returned to his father in a few years, but at the latter's death returned to his uncles, with whom he remained until grown, In 1852 he went to Fort Smith and entered the employment of Sutton, Griffith & Co., wholesale merchants, with whom he remained four years. In 1854 he went overland to California with a drove of stock, returning the following year, and in 1856 returned to Washington County, where, in December of that year, he was married and settled on the farm where he now lives. During the war, being exempt from service, he remained at home and had charge of the Allen Grist-mills, and in 1865 removed the mills to Farmington, built the Farmington Grist-mills, and also operated a saw-mill. He laid out the town of Farmington, and owned the land on which the town was built. In 1876 he retired from the milling business and devoted his attention to farming, and for about ten years operated a steam thresher. His wife, Isabella (Kinnibrugh) Engels, was born in Washington County in 1834, and to her union with Mr. Engels four children were born: Mary (wife of John Smith), Alice, William A. and Bertha. Mr. Engels owns a good farm of 140 acres, with eighty under cultivation, and he and wife are devoted members of the Methodist Episcopal Church. Mr. Engels supplies the following data of interest: The first thresher was brought to Washington County in 1844; the first reaper in 1857; in 1858 he (Mr. Engels) went to St. Louis in a two-horse wagon for a reaper, a distance of 350 miles, taking twenty-nine days to make the trip. The first steam flouring mill in the county was erected in 1854, at Fayetteville, by Stirman & Dickson, merchants of that place. There are now (close of 1888) sixteen in the county.

J. T. Evins, farmer and merchant at Dutch Mills, was born in Washington County, Ark., November 17, 1856, and is the eighth of ten children, four sons and six daughters, born to Ephraim M. and Mary A. (Crozier) Evins. The father was born in South Carolina, although his parents came from Wales, and the name was originally Evans. Grandfather Evins and his brother came over from Wales and took different sides in the Revolutionary War. So hostile were the feelings of Grandfather Evins toward his brother for fighting against the colonies that he changed the spelling of his name. Ephraim M. Evins went to East Tennessee, and was here married to Miss Hannah D. Crozier, who bore him four children. After her death he married Miss Mary A. Crozier, and with her moved to Washington County, Ark., in 1854. She died about 1864, and since that time Mr. Evins has remained single. While in Tennessee he engaged in merchandising, also ran a mill, and since coming here he has followed farming. He is still living, is seventy-eight years old, is a Democrat in politics, and is a member of the Methodist Episcopal Church. His son, J. T. Evins, was educated in the common schools and also at Cane Hill College. Having farmed a short time he began merchandising at Dutch Mills in 1881, and has continued there ever since. The following year J. C. White joined him, and the firm became as it now stands, Evins & White. They have an unusually large and select stock of goods, and are doing well at this business. In September, 1882, he married Miss Alice, daughter of James S. White, and a native of Washington County, Ark., born February, 1860. Three children were the fruits of this union: Theodore F., Ava P. and Thaddeus W. Mr. Evins has made all his property by industry and saving, never having spent his money foolishly. He is a Democrat politically, and he and wife are members of the Cumberland Presbyterian Church.

Jasper Farmer is a well-to-do citizen of Washington County, Ark., and was born near where he now resides in February, 1840, being a son of William and Eliza (Putnam) Farmer, who were of English descent. The father was a Tennesseean, born in 1816, and grew to maturity in Indiana, but was married in Fulton County, Ill., in 1836, and soon after removed to Arkansas, dying in Franklin County in 1865. His wife was a daughter of R. Putnam, who served in the Black Hawk War, and who located in Indiana when a boy, and in 1836 came to Arkansas, after a short residence in Illinois. He died in Washington County. Mrs. Farmer became the mother of one daughter and four sons: Jasper, Stacy, Isaac N., J. M. and William R. She is yet living, and resides on the old home farm with her daughter Stacy. Jasper Farmer's early days were divided between attending the common schools and assisting his father on the farm, and he remained under the parental roof until the breaking out of the late war, when he (in 1862) enlisted in the Confederate service, but at the end of four months returned home, where he was married in 1878 to Martha Woolsey, a daughter of W. T. Woolsey, and located on the farm where he now resides. He is a thrifty and progressive tiller of the soil, and his dealings with his fellow men are above reproach.

James Felton may be mentioned among the prosperous farmers and stock raisers of Washington County, Ark. His birth occurred on the 5th of December, 1826, in Smith County, Tenn., his parents, Thomas and Polly (Glover) Felton, being natives of the same State. About 1841 the family moved to Missouri, and in Greene County the father improved a farm and reared his family. His death occurred in 1862. James Felton made his home with his father until he attained his majority, and September 1, 1853, was married, in what is now Christian County, to Miss Cordelia P. Tillman, a native of Tennessee. After his marriage he farmed in Christian County until the breaking out of the war, and in 1861 enlisted in the Confederate service, First Missouri Infantry, serving until the surrender of Vicksburg, and participating in the battles of Elk Horn, Grand Gulf, Corinth, Iuka, and the siege and surrender of Vicksburg. He was taken prisoner in the last engagement, and was kept at Camp Morton until the close of the war. Four of Mr. Felton's brothers were in the same regiment as himself; one was killed and the other three were wounded, but he escaped unhurt. After receiving his discharge he returned to his family in Missouri, and shortly after removed to Texas, where he raised one crop. In February, 1867, he came to Arkansas, locating in Washington County, where he purchased his present farm of 200 acres, three miles east of Boonsboro. He has 100 acres under cultivation and a good frame residence and good barns. He has a family of six children: Buena Vista (wife of J. A. Nugent), L. J., E. W., Veta (wife of William Huffaker), Lenora and Zulah. The family attend the Missionary Baptist Church, of which Mr. and Mrs. Felton are members.

James Andrew Ferguson, merchant, banker and dealer in real estate, was born in Mountain Township, Washington Co., Ark., January 28, 1840, and is the son of John C. and Elizabeth (English) Ferguson, the father a native of Virginia, and the mother of Tennessee. John C. Ferguson was of Scotch descent, was married in Tennessee, came to Arkansas about 1833, and settled in Washington County, where he passed his last days. He died in 1862 or 1863. The mother was of English descent, and the daughter of Mathew English, who was captured and reared by the Indians. She died in 1844. James Andrew Ferguson was the fifth of a family of seven children, three sons and four daughters. He grew to manhood in his native State, and enlisted in the war as second lieutenant of Carroll's regiment, Confederate army, and was subsequently promoted to the rank of first lieutenant, holding this position with honor and credit until the fall of 1863, when he had the misfortune to have his leg broken by a fall from his horse. He then resigned, spent a year in California, and after the war returned to Fayetteville, where he has since been identified with the interests of the county. He was married, in Washington County, to Miss Nannie E. Tuttle, daughter of J. M. and Evaline (Smith) Tuttle, and a native of Tennessee. Five sons and one daughter are the result of this union: George (who is actively engaged in the stock business), James Wallace, Arthur Lee, Augusta, Harry and John Middleton, who was the fifth child, and who is now deceased.

Upon the organization of the Washington County Bank, Mr. Ferguson took an active interest in its establishment, rendered important aid and has held connection with it since. He is a member of the Masonic fraternity, is a K. of H., and he and family worship at the Episcopal Church.

T. R. Ferguson, whose post-office is Spring Valley, is a native of Indiana, born in 1820, and the son of William and Nancy (Ross) Ferguson. The father was a farmer, was a soldier in the War of 1812 under Gen. Jackson, and was at the battle of New Orleans. He moved from Virginia to Indiana in his early youth, and there died. His son, T. R. Ferguson, was educated in the State University at Bloomfield, and studied medicine at Springfield, Ill., under Dr. Darlin, graduating from McDowell College a year or so later. He then began to practice his profession, and has continued at this ever since. In 1840 he espoused religion, joined the Christian Church, and soon after was ordained. He follows his ministerial duties as a local preacher when possible to do so. He entered the Southern army in 1861, under Gen. Price, and served with him until the close of the war. He was taken prisoner several times, but was exchanged. Previous to this, in 1841, he married Miss Liza J. May, of Macon County, Ill., and they are now the parents of six children: Mrs. Nancy Purdy, Mrs. Catherine Muse, Mrs. Annie Denningbery; Walter, who married Miss Alice Sanders; George, and James, who married Miss Ellen Hice. The same year of his marriage Mr. Ferguson left Indiana and moved to Springfield, Ill., but soon left there and moved to Buchanan County, where he remained until the close of the war. After that eventful period Mr. Ferguson moved to Washington County, Ark., where he has remained ever since, practicing his profession and engaged in his ministerial duties. He is a member of the Masonic fraternity, an Odd Fellow, is a member of the Agricultural Wheel, and his family are all members of the Christian Church. In 1883 Mr. Ferguson was the candidate of the Union Labor party for State senator.

John R. Flinn, merchant and miller of Evansville, is the son of Hugh and Martha A. (Cottrell) Flinn. The father was born in Ireland in 1803, and the mother in Alabama in 1806. The father immigrated to America in 1835; had previously served a seven years' apprenticeship at the stone-cutter's trade, and was an excellent workman. He cut the columns for the Missouri State capitol, and did the carving on the seminary at the capital of the Indian Territory. Having found his way to Arkansas, he made this State his home until his death, which occurred in 1880. The mother grew to womanhood in her native State, and here married a man by the name of Thurston. She bore him two children, and after his death she moved to Arkansas, where she married Mr. Flinn, and bore him two sons. She is still living. The youngest son, John R., was born December 15, 1847, in Crawford County, Ark., where he was reared and educated. In 1865 he married Miss Julia A. Snodgrass, a native of Franklin County, Ark., and to them were born nine children, six now living. After farming until 1875 Mr. Flinn left Crawford County, and moved to Washington County, locating in Evansville, where he bought the Evansville Grist and Saw-mill. This mill he has owned ever since, and has just added a cotton-gin, in which Mr. J. M. Chandler is partner. Mr. Flinn is a member of the Masonic fraternity, is Democratic in his politics, and has been postmaster at Evansville for eight years. His wife, his mother and his eldest daughter are members of the Presbyterian Church.

Jonathan Foust, one of the wide-awake, thorough-going farmers of Goshen Township, was born July 28, 1838, in Highland County, Ohio, and is one of nine children born to his parents, Jonathan and Anna (Shaffer) Foust. The father was born in Westmoreland County, Penn., October 15, 1802, moved to Ohio in 1817, and in 1838 moved to Huntington County, Ind., where he and wife are residing at the present time. Both are eighty-six years of age. Their son, Jonathan Foust, was but one year old when his parents moved to Indiana, and here he attained his growth and received his education. During the late war he served three years with the Federal army, and rendered effective and valuable service. February 12, 1867, he chose Miss Matilda E. McElhaney as his companion through life, and the following children were the result of this union: Florence F., Minerva E., David M., William H., Rosa B., Charles F., Nellie M., Alvin E., Elmer F., Grover C. and M. T. One daughter, Ida Rebecca, died in infancy. Mrs. Foust was born January 19, 1848, and is the daughter of David McElhaney, who was born in West Virginia June 18, 1810, and moved to Preble

County, Ohio, in 1844. In that county he married Miss Sarah Scott, and in 1850 they moved to Huntington County, Ind. He has been a farmer all his life, and he and wife are now living. In 1886 Mr. Foust and family moved to their present farm in Washington County. This farm of ninety-five acres is located eight miles east of Fayetteville, and is in White River Valley. Mr. Foust has succeeded admirably in farming and stock raising, and makes a specialty of thoroughbred Poland-China hogs. He is a Democrat in politics, takes an active interest in public enterprises, and he and wife are members of the Christian Church.

Stephen D. Gilbreath, merchant of West Fork, Ark., is a native of Washington County, Ark., born May 28, 1845, and is a son of Cyrus D. and Sarah (Craig) Gilbreath. The father was born in North Carolina in 1808, and as his educational advantages were quite limited in his boyhood days, he attended school with his own children in order to obtain the coveted education. In 1833 he located on a farm in Independence County, Ark., and two years later came to Washington County, and became one of the leading farmers and stock raisers of the county, owning a good farm of 200 acres. He always took an active interest in politics, and held the office of justice of the peace a number of years, and was also judge of the county court several terms. His death occurred in October, 1880. His wife, who became the mother of nine children (five living), died in 1847, and in 1851 he married Mrs. Cynthia Bloyd, and their union was blessed with two children. Stephen D. Gilbreath received a fair English education, and was reared to manhood on his father's farm. In 1862 he was compelled to hide in the woods to save his life, and in 1863 he enlisted in Company D, First Arkansas Cavalry, United States Army, and did honorable and active service until the close of the war. After his return home he located on a farm, and in February, 1865, was married to Susan Billingsley, a native of Washington County, and by her became the father of five children: James M., Sarah R., John, Dayton W. and Amy E. In 1882 Mr. Gilbreath gave up farm life and engaged in merchandising at West Fork, in partnership with John Lane. At the end of three months he purchased his partner's interest, and after carrying on the business in his own name for some time, formed a partnership with J. M. Lagster, with whom he has since been connected. Mr. Gilbreath is a Republican in politics, and is a member of the G. A. R., Post No. 14, at West Fork, and he and family attend the Christian Church.

Thomas Gladden, the accommodating proprietor of the Gladden Hotel at Springdale, Ark., was born in Tennessee in 1815, and is a son of William and Violet (Wilson) Gladden, the former of whom was born in North Carolina, and the latter in Tennessee, in 1772 and 1779, respectively. They became the parents of fourteen children. William Gladden moved to Missouri in 1815, and there died in 1882, lacking only three months of being one hundred and ten years old. His wife died in 1883, aged one hundred and four years. Thomas Gladden was three months old when he was taken to Missouri, and in that State he was reared and educated and resided for fifty-two years, being engaged in farming and stock trading. He was also married while in that State to Miss Sarah G. Huff, by whom he became the father of eight children: Alexander; Dr. R. B., of Purdy, Mo.; Lucy, Elizabeth, Mary, Atinina, Sarah E. and J. I. Mr. Gladden became a resident of Benton County, Ark., in 1867, and from there went to Boonsborough, where he lived five years. He has now been residing in Springdale for thirteen years, and during that time has been engaged in keeping hotel, purchasing his present large house in 1887, which is largely patronized by the traveling public. He supports the principles of the Democratic party, and his first presidential vote was cast for Martin Van Buren.

Dr. H. D. Gorham. The Gorham family was first represented in America by the great-grandfather of Dr. Gorham, who came from England at an early day and settled in Connecticut. While serving in the Continental army, during the Revolutionary War, he was killed at the battle of Bunker Hill. His son, Seth Gorham, was born in Connecticut, served throughout the Revolutionary War and lived to a ripe old age, dying in 1854. His son, Deming Gorham, father of the Doctor, was born in Rutland, Vt., in 1798, and was a farmer by occupation and also followed the cooper's trade. He became one of the wealthy land owners of Rutland County, Vt., and died in his native State and county in 1861. He was married to Sabra Gates, who was also born in Rutland, Vt., and a daughter of N. Gates. She was the first cousin of Gen. Ethan Allen, of Revolutionary fame, and became the mother of three children: Dr. H. D.; Sarah J., wife of J. M. Goodno, and Elizabeth J. (deceased). She died in 1869. Dr. Gorham grew to manhood on a farm in Vermont, and was married in 1831 to Electa D., daughter of Josiah Duten. She was born and reared in New Hampshire, and was the mother of two children: Ellen, wife of Rollin Mead, and George W. His second wife was Jane Duten, who bore him two children: James K. and Mary, wife of G. W. Smith; she died in 1853. He married his third wife, Esther M. Cook, who was reared in Morgan County, Ohio, and by her became the father of five children: Wallace D.; Harriet M., wife of W. P. Williams; Mariette H.; Austrilla, wife of H. B. Minnie. and Larilla, wife of J. L. Burns. In 1838 the Doctor moved to Ohio, where he was engaged in farming until 1843, when he moved to Van Buren County, Iowa, and opened the first coal mines on the Des Moines River. In 1850 he made an overland trip to California, and was engaged in mining for one year. He then returned home, and in 1856 went back to his old home in Vermont, and took charge of the old home farm until his father's death. While residing in Iowa his eyesight failed him, and he was blind for eighteen months, but doctored with some of the best physicians of the West and East, all to no purpose, until he engaged the services of a man by the name of Campbell, residing in Iowa, who eventually restored his sight. He obtained the prescription from Dr. Campbell's son, and after locating in Michigan, in 1863, began making the treatment of the eye his especial business, practicing at Grand Rapids, Mich., and Fort Wayne, Ind., and is now known in many portions of the United States. Since 1870 he has resided in Washington County, Ark., where he has a good farm of sixty acres. He is a member of the A. F. & A. M., Viney Grove Lodge, and he and family worship in the Cumberland Presbyterian Church.

James S. Graham, farmer of Washington County, Ark., and native of the "Blue Grass State," was born in 1820, and while an infant was brought by his parents, William and Lear (Boyd) Graham, to Arkansas. William Graham was born in the "Old North State" in 1777, and in 1782 was taken by his parents to Kentucky, where he resided until 1820, and then came to Arkansas and spent the remainder of his days. He was married in Kentucky, and became the father of eleven children, four of whom are living. His principal occupation throughout life was farming. His wife died in 1836. Their son, James S. Graham, was reared in Northwestern Arkansas, and is one of the thrifty farmers of that locality. Rebecca Jane Patton, who was born in Tennessee in 1826, became his wife and the mother of nine children: Vachiel C., Peter, Rachel, Dorothea T., Amanda A. (widow of Robert Graham), Benjamin P., Orlena J., J. Willy and Cynthia. After suffering many of the privations and hardships of pioneer life Mr. Graham, by hard work and good management, is now the owner of 327 acres of land. He is one of the oldest residents of the county, and is highly respected and esteemed by a large circle of acquaintances and friends. He and his two eldest sons served in the Confederate army from 1863 until the close of the war, his eldest son volunteering in the first company ever organized in Arkansas. Peter, the other son, was a member of the third company that was organized. Mr. Graham is a member of the Primitive Baptist Church, the A. F. & A. M., and in his political views is a stanch Democrat.

Riley Graham, one of the leading farmers of Wedington Township, was born in Casey County, Ky., September 23, 1827, and is the son of Littleton F. and Catherine (Carson) Graham, both natives of Kentucky, the father born in Casey County April 12, 1799, and is still living near Fayetteville. The mother was born about 1800, and died near Fayetteville, Ark., in 1857. They were married in Casey County, and there lived until 1836, when they moved to Lincoln County, Tenn., and there lived until 1852. He is a member of the Cumberland Presbyterian Church, as was also his wife, and has been a life-long Democrat. He was a successful farmer, and since the death of his wife has lived with his children, seven now living of a family of ten: Ewing, John C., Riley, Minerva, Cyrena, Clarinda and Melvina Adaline. Those deceased were named Cyrus M., Catherine and America. Cyrus M. was in the Confederate service during the late war, and was killed by the bursting of a shell at the battle of Prairie Grove. Riley Graham remained at home until twenty years of age, and has always followed the occupation of a farmer. In 1853 his father gave him a small tract of land, and in 1857 he sold this and bought land near Fayetteville. He is now the owner of a well-located and well-improved farm, the result of his own and his wife's hard labor. October 13, 1853, he married Miss Elizabeth Jane Wilson, daughter of Hon. Thomas Wilson, who was born in Kentucky in 1812, and who died at the age of seventy-three. He was one of the first settlers of Washington County, and a prominent citizen, at different times county judge, and also represented Washington County in the Arkansas Legislature several times; was also a farmer. Mrs. Graham was born near Fayetteville, Ark., June 1, 1836, and by her marriage became the mother of ten children, nine now living: James C., died when an infant; Bell D., Thomas G., William R., Len F., Cora Alice, Emma C., Virginia W., Cyrus E. and Kate May. July, 1862, Mr. Graham enlisted in Company A, of Brooks' infantry, Confederate army, and after serving a short time was captured at Fayetteville, and paroled. He re-enlisted in the fall of 1864, and served until the close of the war. Mr. Graham, his wife and all the children but the youngest and fifth are members of the Methodist Episcopal Church, South. He is a Democrat in politics, and a member of the I. O. O. F.

Clifton Sidney Gray, M. D., and one of the prominent practitioners of Fayetteville and vicinity, is a native of Missouri, born near Sedalia January 2, 1850, being the son of Hon. Hampton P. Gray, and grandson of John Gray, who was a native Virginian, and who made a settlement in the then Territory of Missouri, and was a planter by occupation. He was an active and useful citizen in the gradual development of his locality, and amassed considerable wealth. Hon. Hampton P. Gray was an attorney by profession and a native of Missouri, born in that State while it was yet a Territory. He was married to Miss Amanda Snell, daughter of John Snell, a planter and farmer near Sedalia, and a native of England, who made a settlement there in early times. Dr. Clifton S. Gray was reared in Columbia, Mo., whither his father had removed, supplementing his public school training with a thorough literary and classical course at the University of Missouri, at Columbia. At the end of four years and when in his seventeenth year he graduated from this institution. After graduating he began the study of his profession under the preceptorship of Dr. Norwood, of the chair of chemistry and physics in the University of Missouri, but afterward spent two academic years in the University of Louisville, Ky., and one year at the St. Louis Medical College, graduating from that institution in the class of 1871 and 1872. He did not enter into any regular practice on account of ill health, and came to Washington County, Ark., in 1876, to try a change of climate. He was greatly benefited by the change, and soon engaged in the active practice of his profession, which was only disturbed by trips through Utah and Colorado for his health, and one year spent in Bellevue Hospital Medical College in New York. He was married in Little Rock, Ark., to Miss Fannie A. Ashley, a graduate of Mrs. Cuthburt's Female School, of St. Louis, and daughter of William Ashley, who is a son of Senator Chester Ashley, of the United States Senate. Dr. Gray is a member of the American Medical Association and of the Arkansas State Medical Society, serving as the honored vice-president of the latter society. He has made some few contributions to literary journals of his profession, and is considered one of the intelligent and prominent citizens of his county. He is a member of the I. O. O. F. and K. P. societies, and he and Mrs. Gray worship at the Presbyterian Church. Mrs. Gray is a member of the Ladies' Aid Society of that church, and is active in general church work.

Prof. Oliver Crosby Gray, A. M., LL.D., was born in Lincoln County, Me., December 30, 1832, the son of Dr. Peter T. Gray and grandson of Rev. Thomas Gray, who was a clergyman of the Unitarian Church, and who spent a long, useful life in his ministerial work in Maine and Massachusetts. Dr. Peter T. Gray was a native of Massachusetts, a graduate of the medical department of Cambridge University, and an eminent physician of Jefferson, Me. His wife, Elizabeth (Kennedy) Gray, was a lady of unusual attainments, and the daughter of Nathaniel Kennedy, a worthy citizen of Waldoborough, Me., who dated his ancestry back to early Scotch-Irish settlers in that State. Prof. Oliver C. Gray was the eldest of a family of three sons: Thomas K. is a druggist at Minneapolis, Minn., and a man of wealth, and John D. is a druggist of Stockton, Cal. The boyhood days of Prof. Gray were spent in his native State, and in 1849 he entered Waterville (Me.) Classical Institute, where he spent two years in a preparatory course. In August, 1851, he entered Colby University, graduating with the class of 1855 in a thorough literary and classical course, taking his A. B. After graduating he went to Minneapolis, where he had charge of the public schools, and was the first superintendent of those schools. He remained here two years, and then spent two years as principal of the Monticello Academy, of Wright County, Minn. After this he was located for one year at Princeton, and took charge of the female academy in Dallas County, Ark., but the breaking out of the war caused him to leave his charge at that place and accept a responsible position in the Confederate army. After the war he resumed his labors at Princeton, and there remained two years, after which he accepted the position of professor of mathematics in St. John's College, Little Rock, Ark. Here he remained seven years, and was president of the college the last three years of his stay, resigning his position to accept the position of professor of mathematics in the A. I. U., which position he held until 1885. During the seven years in St. John's and eight and a half years in the A. I. U., he served as commandant of cadets, and this, including four years in the war, makes a total of nineteen and one-half years in military service. In 1886 Prof. Gray was placed in charge of the public schools of Fayetteville, and held the superintendency until May, 1888. During his incumbency of St. John's College, in 1869, he was made M. A. by his Alma Mater, and in 1884 he had the degree of Doctor of Laws conferred upon him by that university. He was elected to the office of mayor of Fayetteville, and filled the position from 1886 to 1888. He was married in Cushing, Me., to Miss Virginia L. Davis, a lady of education and refinement, who died in full communion with the faith of the Presbyterian Church. She had been a teacher of art in the A. I. U. for several years, and died in 1886, leaving a son and daughter: Carl R., a young man of unusually good business qualities, who is now holding the responsible position of commercial agent of the 'Frisco Railroad, with headquarters at Wichita, Kas., and Ethel, a student of the Lewis Academy at Witchita, Kas. Prof. Gray is a charter member of Frontier Lodge 1626, K. of H., and was representative to the Grand Lodge this year. He is a Mason, knighted in Hugh De Payne Commandery, Little Rock, Ark., made in Princeton Lodge No. 16, Princeton, Ark., and to the thirtieth degree of the Ancient Scottish Rite at Little Rock in 1872. In July, 1888, he was re-elected to his old chair of mathematics in the A. I. U., which position he now holds.

A. J. Greathouse may be mentioned as one of the prosperous farmers of Elm Spring Township, Washington Co., Ark., and was born in the county in which he now resides in 1852. His boyhood days were spent in assisting his father on the farm and in attending the common schools, where he received a good practical education; afterward attended the State University at Fayetteville, Ark. After finishing his education he engaged in pedagoguing, becoming one of the successful educators of Northwestern Arkansas, but discontinued this occupation to engage in agricultural pursuits, which have received his attention up to the present time. He owns a good farm of 120 acres, from which he is deriving a comfortable competency; is a member of the Methodist Episcopal Church, South, and in his political views is a Democrat. He is one of eleven children born to the marriage of Robert and Margaret (Blunt) Greathouse, who were born in 1826 and 1831, respectively.

Hon. Henderson Parmer Greene, county and probate judge of Washington County, Ark., was born in White County, Tenn., on the 4th of June, 1828. His parents, Wesley and Catherine (Gentry) Greene, were natives of the "Old North State," the former a millwright by occupation, and a direct descendant of Gen. Nathaniel Greene, of Revolutionary fame. This branch of the Greene family have all the characteristics of their ancestors, and are a square-built, hardy, long-lived and courageous people, inheriting Scotch-Irish blood from their paternal ancestors. Catherine (Gentry) Greene is a descendant of a prominent old North Carolina family, and she and her husband, Mr. Greene, died in Montgomery County, Tenn., when their son, Henderson, was a small lad of seven years. He became a bound boy in the family of Alfred Davidson, and with them removed to Greene County, Mo., in 1839, where he grew to manhood, and acquired sufficient knowledge in the common schools to enable him to engage in teaching as a profession. He followed this occupation in Greene and Christian Counties from 1849 until the breaking out of the War of the Rebellion. In 1860 he was elected to represent Christian County in the State Legislature, and served two terms, the latter term including a call session. In 1861 he organized Company F, Fourth Regiment Missouri Volunteers, Confederate States Army, of which company he became commander upon its entering the field, and after serving about two years was taken captive while doing recruiting service as quartermaster, and was kept a prisoner until near the close of the war. After the cessation of hostilities he went to Texas, where he remained about two years, and then came to Cane Hill, Ark., and engaged in farming and teaching school. In 1884 he was elected to the Lower House of the State Legislature, and two years later was elected county and probate judge of Washington County, and has filled the duties of that office with ability and to the entire satisfaction of his constituents. While residing in Christian County, Mo., he was married to Miss Elmina Elizabeth Tillman, who was a daughter of Reuben Tillman, a native of Tennessee. She was an honored and worthy member of the Missionary Baptist Church, and her untimely death was mourned by her husband and five children. The latter's names are as follows: William F., a physician and druggist at Lowell, Ark.; James A., who is studying medicine with his brother, Thomas O., who is a teacher by profession; Minnie, who is yet single, and Mattie, wife of Andrew Hanna. Judge Greene was married in Washington County, Ark., January 9, 1874, to Miss M. J. McLothlin, a native of Arkansas, and two daughters have been born to this marriage: Emma Otelia and Caddie A. Judge Greene has been a member of the Missionary Baptist Church since 1854, and was a charter member and active worker in the Grange movement at Cane Hill, being master of that organization for several years.

Andrew Smith Gregg was born in Lawrence County, Ala., December 7, 1827, and is the son of Samuel and Mary (Smith) Gregg, both natives of Tennessee. The parents were frugal, industrious people, and settled in Oxford's Bend of White River, Washington County, Ark., in 1835. Here the mother died in 1847, and the father followed her in 1867. Andrew S. Gregg was reared to manhood in Arkansas, and has since been closely identified with the stock dealing interests of Washington County. He also followed, for six years, the teacher's profession in Washington County, Ark. In 1861 he was elected to the office of sheriff of Washington County, served one year, and was re-elected to the same position in 1862. In 1876 he was elected circuit court clerk, and held the position eight years, being re-elected to succeed himself three times. He was married, in Washington County, to Miss Sarah L. Muncy, daughter of Nathaniel Muncy, a native of Virginia, and became the father of a son and three daughters: Fannie E. (wife of Thomas G. Walker), Mary Elizabeth (wife of Thomas Gray), Dora I., Washington Alexander. During war times Mr. Gregg clerked in the State treasurer's office, and during the latter part of the war had charge of the archives of the State. He is a Mason, knighted in Baldwin's Commandery No. 4, is a member of the I. O. O. F., and a member of Springdale Horticultural Society. Mr. Gregg, his wife and daughter are members of the Methodist Episcopal Church, South, of which he has been steward for the past twelve years.

H. P. Gregg is one of the worthy tillers of the soil of Washington County, Ark., and is a son of A. G. and S. J. (Barr) Gregg, who were the parents of six children. (The father had four other children by a second wife.) A. G. Gregg came from Alabama to Arkansas with his father, Henry C. Gregg, when about eighteen years of age, and made his home in Washington County. His son, H. P. Gregg, was born in Washington County, Ark., September 22, 1842, about one and a half miles south of his present farm, which consists of 100 acres, and has always made his native county his home. He was first married to Miss D. A. Nichilson, who was born in Georgia, and by her became the father of six children: A. L., J. E., M. E., S. E., Laura and M. A. Mrs. Gregg died on the 3d of August, 1881, and Mr. Gregg afterward married his present wife, Mrs. Ownbey, by whom he has one child, W. F. Mrs. Gregg owns 100 acres of land, and their farms bring them in a comfortable competency. She was previously married to J. W. Ownbey, by whom she had three children. Mr. Gregg is a Democrat, and during the late Civil War served in the Confederate army for three years and six months.

Thomas B. Greer, a prominent merchant of Greersburg, Ark., was born in Lafayette County, Mo., December 4, 1839, and is one of ten children born to James W. and Michel E. (Brown) Greer. The father was a native of Davidson County, Tenn., and the mother of Williamson County, of the same State, where they were married. They moved to Lafayette County, Mo., in 1821, and here the father engaged quite extensively in farming. In 1854 they moved to Washington County, and engaged in merchandising in connection with farming, which he continued until 1863, when he was killed by the Pin Indians.

He was fifty-eight years of age at the time of his death; was a Democrat in politics, and he and wife were members of the Missionary Baptist Church. The mother died at the age of seventy-seven years. Of their large family of children, seven sons lived to be grown, but the only one now living is Thomas B. Greer. He was educated in the common schools, also attended one term at Cane Hill, and assisted his father on the farm until sixteen years of age, when he began clerking for his father. Four years later he became possessor of half of the stock, but lost it all during the war. Previous to this, in 1859, he married Miss Mahala E. Denton, a native of Bradley County, Tenn., and six children were the result of this union. In the spring of 1862 Mr. Greer enlisted in Company I, Second Cherokee Regiment, Confederate Army, served throughout the war, was taken prisoner at Boston Mountain in November, 1862, and remained as such for five weeks, when he was exchanged. After the war he farmed until 1870, when he laid off Greersburg, built a store, and the following year began merchandising, which he has since continued, and has a large stock. Besides this he is interested in farming, and is the owner of 180 acres of land. He is a Democrat in politics, has been notary public for fifteen years, and was appointed postmaster of Tolu in 1887. He has been a Master Mason since 1869, and he and wife are members of the Missionary Baptist Church. Mr. Greer contributes liberally to all worthy enterprises, and has been successful as a business man. He was nominated by the Democratic party on the 18th of August as one of the three to be elected to represent his county in the Lower House of the General Assembly, and was elected on the 3d of September, 1888, to that position for two years, running ahead of the ticket.

Major James M. Grimes, farmer and miller, is the son of William and Elizabeth (Harris) Grimes. The father was a native Virginian, was of Welsh descent, and was a soldier in the Creek War. Grandfather Grimes was a captain in the Revolutionary War, and Grandmother Grimes lived to be one hundred and ten years of age. At the age of one hundred she could walk a mile as quickly as when a girl. The mother of the subject of this sketch was born in North Carolina, was of English descent and a member of the Methodist Episcopal Church. After marriage Mr. and Mrs. Grimes immigrated to Tennessee, settling in Rutherford County, and there passed the remainder of their days. Of the six children born to their union, two sons and four daughters, Maj. James M. Grimes was the youngest but one. He was born May 1, 1826, in Rutherford County, Tenn., was reared on a farm and there educated to a limited extent. After reaching manhood he began for himself, and for five years was overseer on a plantation, after which he married and began farming on his own account. Miss Balsora Patterson became his wife in 1852, and to them were born twelve children, four sons and eight daughters, of whom eight are now living. In the days of militia Mr. Grimes held the office of major, and in November, 1861, he enlisted in Company D, Forty-fifth Tennessee Infantry Volunteers, Confederate States Army. He went out with the rank of orderly sergeant, and a year later was elected second lieutenant, which position he held until the close of the war, serving four years. He was in the battles of Shiloh, Murfreesboro, Chickamauga and Jonesboro, and at the first-named battle had one of the bones in the left forearm broken by a ball. After the war Maj. Grimes followed farming in Rutherford County until 1868, when he moved to Washington County, Ark., and located in Prairie Township. In 1879 he lost his wife, and the following year he married Miss Brunetta J. Rieff, a native of Wilson County, Tenn., who bore him one child, a daughter. He and Mrs. Grimes are members of the Christian Church, as was also his first wife. He is a Democrat in politics, casting his first presidential vote for Lewis Cass, of Michigan. Maj. Grimes is the owner of 280 acres of land, 160 of which are under cultivation and well improved. In 1886 he built a saw-mill on White River, and is now adding a flour mill. All his property is the result of his own industry and good management. He is a liberal supporter of schools, churches and all other worthy enterprises. In September, 1888, he was chosen justice of the peace of Prairie Township.

Hon. Thomas Montague Gunter, one of Washington County's representative men, and one who has been closely identified with her interests, was born on a farm in Warren County, Tenn., September 18, 1826, the son of John and Lavina (Thomason) Gunter, natives of North Carolina and Tennessee, respectively, and grandson of Augustus Gunter, of North Carolina, who settled in Tennessee at an early date. The Gunters were people of fine physical development, and were strong in their convictions. They were believers in the Presbyterian doctrine. The Thomasons were of similar characteristics, and Mrs. Lavina (Thomason) was the daughter of William Thomason, of Tennessee. Thomas M. Gunter was reared to manhood on the farm, and secured a fair education in the common schools, supplementing it with a collegiate course at Irvin College, near McMinnville, Warren Co., Tenn., from which institution he graduated in 1849, as valedictorian of his class. He had, in early manhood, formed strong inclinations for the study of law, and after graduating he taught school for twelve months in Alabama, and with the means thus obtained was enabled to further prosecute that study. In 1852 he moved to Arkansas, and on the 2d of January, 1853, he moved to Fayetteville, where he entered the office of Gen. H. F. Thomason (a cousin), completing a thorough course of study under him, and was admitted to the bar in 1854, by Hon. Felix I. Batson, circuit judge of this district. He served in the Forty-third, Forty-fourth, Forty-fifth, Forty-sixth and Forty-seventh General United States Congress. He also served as prosecuting attorney for the ten counties of Northwest Arkansas, served under the Murphy Government, and was reconstructed out of that office upon the reconstruction of the State. He was married in Louisiana, Mo., December 4, 1854, to Miss Marcella Jackson, whom he buried, in 1856, at Mount Comfort Cemetery in full communion with the Christian Church; she was a noble woman, and left a son, Julius C., attorney at Trinidad, Colo., and a graduate of the University of Virginia. He settled there at first on account of his health, and afterward permanently located there. Mr. Gunter took for his second wife Miss Jennie Bragg, of Charleston, Va., who is a relative of Gen. Bragg, of the Confederate States army. They have a son and daughter: Walker T., reading law with his brother, and Gertrude. When the war broke out Mr. Gunter enlisted in the Confederate army, in the Arkansas State Militia, and participated in the Wilson Creek battle, commanding Company A, Walker's regiment, under Gen. Pierce, and, upon the formation of the regular service, entered it as captain. He was subsequently promoted to the rank of lieutenant-colonel upon the organization of the Thirty-fourth Arkansas Infantry, known as Brooks' regiment, and rendered active and honorable service until the winter of 1864, when he was elected lieutenant-colonel of a battalion of cavalry upon the reorganization of the troops, and held command of this battalion (Gunter's battalion of cavalry) until cessation of hostilities. He went with Gen. Price to Missouri, and, after Gen. Cabell's capture, commanded the brigade at Newtonia. He participated in the battles of Oak Hill, Elk Horn or Pea Ridge, Prairie Grove, Poison Spring, Jenkins' Ferry, and after the last named battle made the raid to Missouri. As before mentioned, he commanded the brigade after Cabell's capture, fought at Neosho. While a member of Congress Mr. Gunter was chairman of the committee on private land claims, and served in that capacity for eight years. He was also a member of the committee on Indian affairs, etc. He retired on his own account, after serving his tenth year. He was a delegate to the seceding convention of Arkansas, and felt opposed to the principles, holding that the matter should be settled without difficulty. He is considerably interested in agricultural pursuits, and is a successful breeder of Jersey cattle and Southdown sheep. In 1880 he built large flouring mills at Siloam Springs, which he has lately remodeled by the roller process. Mrs. Gunter is a member of the Episcopal Church, and an ardent worker in the Ladies' Aid Society of that church. Mr. Gunter has held affiliation with the Masonic body since his early manhood. He has passed all the chairs of that body, and is a worthy Sir Knight of Baldwin Commandery No. 4.

James S. Gwinn, a wealthy agriculturist and stock farmer of Washington County, Ark., was born in Lee County of the "Old Dominion," October 19, 1831. His grandfather, James Gwinn, was born near Richmond, Va., and afterward moved to North Carolina, where his son William, the father of James S. Gwinn, was born in 1800. He afterward moved back to his native State, where he died while in the prime of life. He was the father of three sons and three daughters, all of whom lived to rear families. His son William was the eldest of the family, and while still a resident of his native State was married and became the father of seven children. In 1837 he moved to the "Blue Grass State," where he became the owner of a large tract of land, and was engaged in horse training and racing. He was a Democrat, and died in 1861. His wife was born, reared and married in Virginia, and reared to maturity a family of six children, all of whom are living save one son, who was a soldier in the Confederate army, and was killed about the close of the late Civil War. Their names are as follows: John; Sally, widow of Isaac Deaton; Drury F. (deceased); Elizabeth, widow of D. C. Richardson; James S., and Charlotte, wife of W. T. Mahon. The mother of these children, who was born in 1804, is still living, and makes her home with her daughter Elizabeth. She has been a professor of religion since thirteen years of age, and is a warm-hearted and benevolent Christian lady, and is now a member of the Baptist Church, although formerly a member of the Methodist Episcopal Church. James S. Gwinn was but six years of age when his parents came to Kentucky, and he was reared to manhood on his father's farm, being also engaged in horse-racing for about ten years. He began doing for himself after attaining his majority, and when the war broke out he was the owner of about 1,000 acres of land, with 150 acres under cultivation. He enlisted in Company I, Tenth Kentucky Volunteer Infantry, serving first as first lieutenant and afterward as captain of his company. He was captured in April, 1864, and taken to Johnson's Island, Ohio, where he was kept a prisoner until the close of the war in 1865. He returned to his farm in Kentucky, but soon became dissatisfied and removed to Arkansas in 1866, leaving his farm in charge of his brother-in-law, Samuel Grigsby. He sold out shortly after and located permanently in Washington County, where he purchased a good farm of 300 acres, and has been largely engaged in farming and stock raising, and although he has only resided in Washington County for a short time he is already identified with its best farming interests, and takes a deep interest in all worthy public enterprises, and holds the mail contract between Hood, Sulphur City, Carter's Store and Hazel Valley. He has always affiliated with the Democratic party. In 1858 he was united in marriage to Martha Napier, by whom he is the father of seven children: Rosanna, wife of H. C. Osborn; Henry; Lewis; Melissa, wife of C. M. Rogan; Mahala; Nancy Ann and Emma.

A. J. Hale. Success in life is mainly dependent on determined and persistent effort, and these qualities are the characteristics of Mr. Hale; consequently his career in life as an attorney at law and farmer has been a reasonably successful one. He was born in the "Old North State" in 1823, and is one of five children born to the marriage of John H. Hale , of English and Scotch descent, and Margaret Hunt, who were also natives of North Carolina. The father was a hatter by trade, but the latter portion of his life was devoted to agricultural pursuits, which occupation he was following at the time of his death in North Carolina in 1865. His widow, with her youngest son, Edward E., immigrated to Arkansas in 1868, and here her days were ended. A. J. Hale received his academic education in Normal College (now Trinity College) North Carolina, and afterward pursued his law studies under the direction of Jonathan Worth, of Randolph County, N. C., who afterward became governor. Mr. Hale was admitted to the bar before the supreme court of North Carolina in 1859, and soon after immigrated to Missouri, and was a resident of Marshfield until 1866, at which time he came to Fayetteville, and has since been a resident of Washington County. He has been engaged in practicing his profession and farming, and is also engaged in the real estate business, being the owner of some valuable property in Springdale. He was married first to Miss Elizabeth Goss in 1845, who died in 1860, having borne eight children, six of whom are now living: Martha L., Margaret E., Mary E., William B., Joseph G. and Flora M., who are all married and have families. He married his present wife, Miss Leona Stark, in 1883. Mr. Hale is a member of the A. F. & A. M., and belongs to the Methodist Episcopal Church, South. He was twice elected to the office of clerk of the superior court of Randolph County, N. C., and served in that office for eight years.

Rev. G. P. Hanks, pastor of the New Hope Church, of Elm Springs Township, and the Pleasant Valley Church, of Cane Hill Township, was born in Washington County, Ark., in 1836, and is one of eight children born to the marriage of Nathan D. Hanks, who was born in North Carolina in 1811, and Martha B. Baker, who was born in Tennessee in 1816. After their marriage they came to Arkansas, and were among the first settlers of the State, and are at present residing in Cane Hill Township. G. P. Hanks was reared to manhood in Northwest Arkansas, and received his education in the Cane Hill College, in which institution he remained four years. In the fall of 1857 he went to Illinois, and was engaged in pedagoguing until the breaking out of the Rebellion, when he enlisted in Company A, Sixty-first Illinois Infantry, serving until the close of the war. He served as captain one year, and after peace had been proclaimed he began the study of theology, being ordained a minister of the Gospel in 1869. He preached in Illinois for about seventeen years, and in 1885 came to Arkansas, and has been a resident of Washington County ever since. While residing in Illinois (in 1858) he was married to Miss Cynthia C. Carager, who was born in Illinois, and died about one year after her marriage, leaving one child, Thomas W. He married his second wife, Miss Nancy Braden, in 1861, and by her became the father of four children, three of whom are living: Wilbur, Melvin and Virgil. The mother of these children died in 1875, and in 1888 Mrs. Fannie M. Fears became his wife. She was born in Bedford County, Tenn., but was reared in Arkansas. The two first wives were born in Illinois. Mr. Hanks is a stanch Republican in politics.

Samuel A. Hanna is a prominent and successful stock farmer of Reed Township, Washington Co., Ark., and was born in the county in which he resides April 20, 1838, being one of six surviving members of a family of eight children born to the marriage of Jeremiah C. Hanna and Mary A. Watson. The former was born in Kentucky in 1817, and in 1828 removed with his parents to Vermilion County, Ill., where he remained until 1832, then coming to Benton County, Ark., and to Washington County a year later, where they entered a tract of land and began making a farm, on which Jeremiah C. resides at the present time. He has been an active farmer all his life, and has been a member of the Christian Church for many years. His wife was born in Southern Arkansas in 1821, of Scotch descent, her father having been born in Glasgow, Scotland. He came to America with British troops during the War of 1812, and while at New Orleans deserted the British army and joined Gen. Jackson's army, and was commissioned major. He died in Texas August 10, 1861. He was very finely educated, was a school teacher by occupation, and was twice married, Mrs. Hanna being a child born to his first marriage. She died May 4, 1884, having borne the following children: Susannah (Mrs. Hughes), James W., Mary (wife of W. H. Campbell), George W., Maggie (wife of A. E. Hutchens) and Samuel A. The latter is the eldest of the family, and has always resided in his native county, where he has been engaged in farming and the practice of medicine. In 1862 he began the study of medicine under his uncle, E. Hanna, and for about eight years gave his entire attention to the practice of his profession. Since that time he has been engaged in farming and stock raising, at which he has been quite successful, having a fertile farm of 200 acres, with ninety acres under cultivation. He was married in 1858 to Femmon E. Barron, who was born in Tennessee, and died May 12, 1874, having borne a family of four children: James H., Antonia (wife of E. W. Hutchens), Filenia (wife of P. A. Hutchens) and George M. Mr. Hanna's second wife was born in Lawrence County, Mo., March 2, 1852. Her maiden name was Martha E. Hughes, and she is the mother of four children: Samuel B., Denton E., Eli B. and Maude B. Mr. and Mrs. Hanna are members of the Christian Church, of which he has been deacon for fifteen years and clerk twelve years. He is a stanch Republican in politics, and has held the office of justice of the peace since September, 1888. His paternal grandfather, Samuel Hanna, was of Irish descent, and was born in Pennsylvania, and died in Washington County, Ark., in 1837. He was a Baptist minister for many years, being one of the pioneer ministers of Washington County. He and wife were the parents of three daughters and five sons, all but two being deceased: J. C. Hanna and Margaret (widow of Jonathan Stout).

Robert O. Hannah was born on the 1st of November, 1844, in Polk County, Tenn. His parents, Capt. John F. and Gracie (Telford) Hannah, were born in East Tennessee, February 18, 1797, and June 4, 1810, and died in Arkansas and Kentucky, October 13, 1868, and November 16, 1867, respectively. They were married in their native State, and in 1867 removed to Washington County, Ark. The father was a surveyor and farmer, and became an extensive land-holder, and owned some slaves. He was a heavy loser during the late war, and during that time organized the first company in Polk County, Tenn., and joined the Third Tennessee Confederate Infantry, and after serving twelve months retired from the service, owing to his age and disability. He was county trustee for years, and filled some office during his entire residence in Polk County. He also represented the county in the State Legislature. He was a life-long Democrat, and was always opposed to secret societies and monopolies. His wife was for many years a member of the Old School Presbyterian Church. They were the parents of six sons and two daughters, three sons and two daughters now living: Vance, Elizabeth, wife of E. H. Stephens; Jane M., wife of William A. Skelton; George W. and Robert O. Those deceased are Thomas A., William and John H., who was captain of the third company that was organized in Polk County, and served in the Confederate army throughout the war, and afterward became major of the regiment. Robert O. Hannah remained at home until November, 1862, and then enlisted in Company F, Nineteenth Tennessee, Confederate States Army, and served until the close of the war. He was in the battles of Chickamauga and Missionary Ridge, and was taken prisoner at Mill Creek, Ga., and was kept at Rock Island, Ill., for fifteen months. After the war he returned home and remained with his father until his death, at which time he began farm for himself, and is now the owner of 415 acres of land. He held the office of justice of the peace for four years, and for the past four years has been deputy sheriff. August 29, 1867, he was united in marriage to Mary E., daughter of Absalom Armstrong. She was born in Polk County, Tenn., November 2, 1845, and died in Washington County, Ark., October 22, 1871, leaving one daughter, Mattie, who is now living with her grandmother, in Polk County, Tenn. On the 15th of October, 1872, Mr. Hannah married Susan A. Pierson, who was born in Madison County, Ky., February 3, 1850, and is a daughter of Eli Pierson. They have three sons and four daughters: Mary, Emma J., Gracie E., Norah Lou and James B. William B. and Owen W. are dead. Mr. and Mrs. Hannah are members of the Presbyterian Church, and he is a Mason, a K. of H. and a Democrat, and he is ruling elder in the church, the highest office of his life.

Isham Harrell, who is also successfully engaged in agricultural pursuits in Price Township, is a native of Fort Gibson, I. T., born February 25, 1832, and is the second of four children born to his parents, Joel and Elizabeth (Carter) Harrell. The father was born in North Carolina in 1801, and the mother in Virginia in 1805. They were married at Fort Tousen, I. T., and from there moved to Fort Gibson, I.T., where they remained some time. In 1839 they moved to Washington County, Ark., where they passed the remainder of their lives. He was murdered in 1864 by a band of robbers, and she died in 1880. He was a farmer by occupation, although he furnished horses and provisions for the Government while in the Territory, and he and wife were members of the Cumberland Presbyterian Church. He was a Whig until the demise of that party, and then affiliated with the Democratic party. Isham Harrell moved with his parents to Washington County in 1839, and received a very meager education, owing to the fact that the nearest school was a distance of over three miles from his home. He remained with his parents until grown, after which he engaged in farming and stock raising for himself, and this continued until the fall of 1864, when he enlisted in Capt. A. C. Baty's company of the Second Cherokee Regiment, serving until the surrender. He then returned to farming and stock raising, which he has continued ever since. Previous to the war, in 1856, he married Miss Mary L. Thomason, a native of Washington County, Ark., born November 11, 1836, and a daughter of Col. Daniel Thomason. To this union were born six children, four now living: Jennie E., T. H., Nolie and Mary J. After marriage Mr. Harrell settled upon his present farm, which consists of 380 acres, 125 being under cultivation. He has made this county his home for forty-nine years, and is a successful farmer and a good man. He is a member of the Masonic fraternity, and Democratic in his political views. Mrs. Harrell is a member of the Christian Church.

J. R. Harris. Prominent in the business circles of Springdale, Ark., as a man of push, enterprise and intelligence, is J. R. Harris, who is a dealer in hardware and lumber, and is president of the Springdale Canning and Packing Company. He was born in Missouri in 1847, and is a son of James R. and Annie (Cunningham) Harris, who were born in South Carolina and Tennessee, February 17, 1814, and December 11, 1820, respectively. They grew to maturity and were married in Tennessee, emigrating to Missouri in 1836, and after a thirty years' residence in that State emigrated to Arkansas. Here the father died in 1880. His widow is still living, and resides with her son in Springdale. J. R. Harris was nineteen years old when he came to Arkansas. He received good educational advantages, and spent two consecutive years in the "Shiloh Baptist High-school," receiving in that institution sufficient mental training to fit him for the business affairs of life. After leaving school the first three years were spent in pedagoguing, in which time he became well known as one of the successful educators of Northwestern Arkansas. At this period, as he had always wished to see something of the world, he began traveling. He left home, westward bound, and after reaching Oregon engaged in teaching school, which occupation he followed in that State for eight months. After a sojourn of one year in Oregon and California he returned to Benton County, Ark., and the following year was engaged in trading and speculating in stock. The next three years he officiated as chief assistant in the sheriff's office in Benton County, but his career in that direction was terminated owing to the death of his father, as he immediately left there and came to Springdale. Here he was successfully engaged in the milling business for five years, and at the end of that period sold his interest and engaged in the hardware and lumber business, which he has as successfully managed. He is one of those men who always endeavor to promote the welfare and growth of the town, and was among the first to suggest a canning and packing company, and the first to take stock in the same, of which he is now president. Mr. Harris is unmarried, the family consisting of himself and mother. He is a member of the Missionary Baptist Church, a Democrat in his political views, and is a Master Mason.

William A. M. Harris, ex-merchant, but now a prosperous farmer of Richland Township, Washington Co., Ark., was born in McMinn County, Tenn., May 5, 1836, and is a son of William and Basheba (Fagan) Harris, who were born in South Carolina and Virginia, and died in 1876 and 1860, respectively. They were early residents of Tennessee, and in 1854 came to Arkansas, where they afterward made their home. They were farmers, and members of the Methodist Episcopal Church, and became the parents of thirteen children, four of whom are living: Minnie J. (widow of J. C. Carigin), Nancy (wife of A. Brown), William A. M. and Wilbur F. William A. M. Harris began life for himself at the age of eighteen years with no capital except a liberal supply of pluck and energy. He engaged in stock trading and farming, and by good management eventually became the owner of 500 acres of land, with over 200 acres under cultivation. December 14, 1854, he was married to Sarah H. Carigin, who was born in McMinn County, Tenn., December 13, 1836, and by her became the father of twelve children, the following four being the only ones now living: Basheba (wife of G. W. Hannah), Mary A. (wife of J. McGuire), Laura C. and Jettie I. Mr. Harris and wife are members of the Methodist Episcopal Church, and he is a stanch Republican. In 1861 he enlisted in Company B, First Arkansas Cavalry, and served with credit until the close of the war. He was taken prisoner in Washington County, Ark., and taken to Little Rock, but succeeded in making his escape one month later. He was ten days in making his journey home, traveling nights and sleeping in the brush during the daytime. He was in several prominent engagements and numerous skirmishes.

Fielding Hash, one of the very prominent farmers of the township, was born in Sangamon County, Ill., December 29, 1828, and is the fourth of twelve chidren, ten now living, born to Alvin and Esther (Drake) Hash. The father was born in North Carolina, and partly attained his growth in that State. Later he moved to Tennessee, was married here, and after remaining in this State until 1836, moved to Arkansas, and settled in what is now Washington County. He was a farmer, and was one of the pioneer settlers of the county; was justice of the peace several years, and was a prominent and highly respected gentleman. He died about 1842. The mother was born in Tennessee, and died in Washington County, Ark., in 1878. Their son, Fielding, was but eight years old when his parents moved to Washington County. He remained under the parental roof and assisted his mother on the farm until twenty-three years of age, or until his marriage to Miss Nancy C. Counts, daughter of George Counts, who was one of the early settlers of Madison County, Ark. Mrs. Hash was born June 20, 1833, and by her marriage became the mother of nine children: Lindsey L. (wife of A. A. Laugham), Martha A. (wife of Thomas Mays), Ezra J. W., John D., Edna P. (wife of Willis Boyd), Susan B., Conrad A., Mary E. and George H. Mr. and Mrs. Hash are members of the Christian Church; he is a Republican in his political views, and is an honorable, straightforward citizen. During the late unpleasantness between the North and South Mr. Hash served in the Kansas Militia, and was in the fight at Westport.

W. B. Haxton. Among the prominent industries that have materially benefited Washington County, Ark., and are worthy of mention, are the woolen mills owned by W. B. Haxton.   He was born in the "Buckeye State" in 1824, and is a son of James and Catherine (Cary) Haxton, who were born in Rhode Island and Pennsylvania, in 1799 and 1806, respectively.   The father was a tanner and currier by trade, and died in Indiana in 1848.   His wife died in 1886. W. B. Haxton is the eldest of their ten children, and was reared in Indiana. He entered the woolen mills when about fifteen years of age, and served a three years' apprenticeship with Lowrey & McCuen, of Rockville, Indiana.   He located in Illinois in 1836, and operated the first woolen mills ever run at Danville, and ten years later moved to Iroquois, where he was engaged in farming for some time.   He then went to Williamsport, and in 1863 or 1864 engaged in the woolen business again.   This enterprise was a complete failure owing to war troubles.   The following three years he was engaged in peddling, and in this way secured enough money to come West.   He located in Arkansas in 1871, and in 1877 erected the Springdale Woolen Mills, and is doing a thriving business.   He furnishes all the woolen fabric for the public institutions of the Cherokee Nation, and besides this does a large wholesale local business.   Four years ago there were four woolen mills in Arkansas, but at this date Mr. Haxton's is the only one that has survived and prospered.   At the North-western Agricultural Fair, held at Fort Smith, Mr. Haxton took the premium on the following fabrics: Jeans, blankets, stocking yarn, and a diploma on flannels.   He was married April 30, 1846, to Margaret Foote, who was born in Indiana in 1826.   Ten of their twelve children are living: Elizabeth C., S. N., Thomas J., Sarah F., Lillie D., Rose, Melissa, Nettie, William L. and James E.   Three of this large family, S. N., Lillie and Rose, were married on the same day.   The family are Universalists, and Mr. Haxton is a Republican in politics.

Harvey F. Head, a member of the mercantile firm of Laymon & Head, of Sulphur City, Ark., was born in Murray County, Ga., December 26, 1844, being a son of John C. and Elizabeth (Stanton) Head, who were born in Georgia June 25, 1819, and South Carolina in 1820, respectively.   The mother was taken to Georgia when a small girl, where she attained her majority and was married to Mr. Head in 1839.   They shortly after removed to Kansas, and in 1858 came to Arkansas, where the father was engaged in tilling the soil until his death, which occurred in 1862, followed by his wife a year later.   He and wife were consistent members of the Methodist Episcopal Church, South, and he was a Democrat in politics, although he had formerly been a Whig.   His father, John Head, was of English descent, a native of North Carolina, and died in Georgia.   The maternal grandfather, John Stanton, was of Scotch lineage, a native of the "Palmetto State," and at an early day immigrated to Tennessee, thence to Georgia, where he died.   To Mr. and Mrs. Head were born five children: Sarah J., wife of John D. Woods; Harvey F.; Minerva P., wife of Thomas Cavin; Joseph E., and Anna S., wife of Thomas J. Harp.   Harvey F. Head resided with his parents until their respective deaths, when he and an elder sister took care of the younger members of the family until the spring of 1864, when he enlisted in Company D, First Arkansas Cavalry, United States Army, and served until August, 1865, when he returned to his home and again began caring for his younger brothers and sisters, and during the winter months taught school, and farmed during the summer.   In March, 1888, he formed a partnership with Mr. Laymon in the general mercantile business at Sulphur City, which he has since continued with increasing popularity as a business man and citizen.   All his transactions are conducted with the most scrupulous honesty, and that this quality is appreciated by the public is shown by the large trade which he is gaining.   February 25, 1866, Miss Sarah, daughter of Moses Long, became his wife.   She was born in Hawkins County, Tenn., in 1841, and died October 8, 1881, having borne two children, John W. and Mary L., both residing with their father, who was married the second time, May 10, 1885, to Belle Van Zandt, born near Marshfield, Mo., May 25, 1857, and a daughter of Jehu and Sarah Van Zandt.   They became the parents of one son, Robert H., who died when five weeks old.   Mr. Head is an honored and consistent member of the Baptist Church, and is now officiating as its clerk.   He is a member of the G. A. R., I. O. O. F., K. of H., and in his political views is a stanch Republican.   His wife is a member of the Methodist Episcopal Church.   J. H. Laymon, junior member of the mercantile firm of Laymon & Head, was born in Clark County, Ind., June 4, 1854, and is a son of J. M. and M. B. (Hall) Laymon, born in Ohio and Indiana in 1832 and 1833, respectively.   They were married in Jackson

County, Ind., and resided in that State until 1872, when they moved to Kansas and lived in the following counties of that State, in the order in which they are named: Lyon, Montgomery, Chautauqua and Elk, coming to Washington County, Ark., about 1880, where they are now residing. The father has been a farmer throughout life, and in his political views is a stanch Democrat. He and wife are members of the Baptist Church. The Laymons first came from Ireland to America about 1600, and finally located in Ohio. The Halls came originally from England. To Mr. and Mrs. Laymon six children have been born, two of whom are living: J. H. and H. H. J. H. Laymon, when a small boy, began learning the blacksmith's and gunsmith's trades, under Joshua Cotton, and followed these occupations in Sulphur City from 1880 until March, 1888, when the above partnership was formed. In January, 1886, he was commissioned postmaster at Sulphur City, which position he is now holding. In 1882 he joined the Baptist Church, and in 1887 was ordained a minister of that denomination. He is an earnest adherent of the Democratic party, and as a citizen is highly respected and esteemed, being a kind and considerate neighbor and friend. October 18, 1876, he was married to Miss Mary E., a daughter of Joshua Cotton. She was born July 28, 1854, in Pennsylvania. Four children have been born to them: Ida May, Clarence M., Cora B., and Laurance L., who died at the age of nineteen months.

Armstrong Hendricks, farmer, stock raiser and mechanic, of Prairie Grove Township, Washington Co., Ark., was born in Pulaski County, Ky., November 22, 1836, being a son of Green and Rutha (Hall) Hendricks, who were born, reared and married in their native State. They came to Arkansas about 1838, locating on the farm on which Armstrong Hendricks now resides, and owns, and here the father's death occurred in 1840, and the mother's in 1850. They were the parents of two sons: Armstrong and Gibson H. The former was reared in Washington County, and at the breaking out of the war enlisted in Col. Brooks' regiment, serving with him two years, and the following two years served on detached duty. He was in a number of engagements, but escaped unhurt, and after the cessation of hostilities returned home and began working at the blacksmith's trade, which he had learned previous to the war, continuing the same about three years, after which he began improving his home farm, which consists of 153 acres, with about seventy-five acres under good cultivation, on which is a good two-story residence. Besides this he has another good farm of 100 acres. He is doing well, and his farms yield him a comfortable competency. May 13, 1875, his marriage with Miss Nancy B. Rainwaters was celebrated. She was born in Washington County, and is a daughter of Matthew Rainwaters, who was formerly from Tennessee. Mr. and Mrs. Hendricks are the parents of three sons: James Pressley, Edgar Austin and William Perry.

Alexander Hendry, carpenter and builder, was born in the parish of St. Fergus, Aberdeenshire, Scotland, October 18, 1820, and is a son of James and Margaret (Reid) Hendry. Alexander learned his trade in Aberdeenshire, and for a number of years worked in Glasgow. In 1853 he came to America, and spent twelve years in Tecumseh, Mich., where he was engaged in contracting and building. In 1866 he came to Fayetteville, Ark., where he has since been identified with the building and milling interests of the place. Among the many structures he has erected may be mentioned Judge Gregg's residence, the Washington County court-house and mills, the university, the public school buildings, the opera house and many others. He is now in the foundry and machine-shop business. Mr. Hendry was married in Scotland to Miss Mary Duncan, who died January, 1887, having borne one son and one daughter: John, a miller at Walla Walla, and Mary, wife of John Clancy. Mr. Hendry is a member of the Masonic fraternity, Baldwin Commandery No. 4.

Patrick Hennessey, who is accounted one of the best farmers of his vicinity, was born in County Cork, Ireland, March 17, 1818, and is the son of James and Fannie (Cantley) Hennessey, both natives of the same county as their son. The father was a farmer by occupation, and the Hennessey family from time immemorial have been Catholics. The mother died in Ireland, but the father died in Providence, R. I. They were the parents of six sons, all of whom came to this country. The second child, Patrick, was left an orphan at the age of six years, or nearly the same as an orphan, for his mother died, and his father was banished from home for threshing his landlord, with whom he had gotten into trouble. The children were thus thrown upon the world to look out for themselves, and Patrick never saw the inside of a school-house as a pupil, though his parents were well educated. In 1839 he left his native land for America, and located at Providence, R. I., where, several years later, his father and all his brothers joined him. The same day he left Ireland he married Miss Mary Welch, a native of Cork County, and by her became the father of thirteen children, five sons and eight daughters. After living in Rhode Island until 1859, he moved to Washington County, Ark., and has made this his home ever since. When he first came to America he had very little means, and for fourteen years he worked for a wholesale merchant of Providence. He saved his money, and after coming to this county he purchased a good farm, but the war gave him quite a back-set. He now owns 296 acres of land, 210 being under cultivation. He is a Democrat in politics, and he and family belong to the Catholic Church.

Daniel Harvey Hill, lieutenant-general in the Confederate States army, and president of the Arkansas Industrial University, was born July 12, 1821, at Hill's Iron Works, in York District, S. C. His father was Solomon Hill, a slave-holder, planter and Presbyterian elder; his mother was, before her marriage, Nancy Cabeen, the daughter of Sumpter's scout, Thomas Cabeen, whom Sumpter declared to be "the bravest man in my command." The Cabeens were from Scotland, and were strict Presbyterians and men of wealth and influence. Col. William Hill, the grandfather of General Hill, was an Irishman; he rose to the rank of colonel in the Revolutionary army, was badly wounded at Hanging Rock, and was at home recovering from it when the battle of King's Mountain was fought. The battle-field was only a short distance from his iron works, which was the only furnace in that section of the country, and he made it so useful in manufacturing guns and other munitions of war that it was the daily prayer of his devout compatriots, "O Lord, protect us from the enemy and save Billy Hill's Iron Works." Although without his command, he volunteered for the battle and planned the attack on King's Mountain, and served as a private in that great battle where the British met their first repulse in their southern campaign. Col. Hill was prominent in politics after the War of the Revolution closed, and represented his district in the State Senate for many years. He was an intimate friend of Patrick Calhoun, the father of John C. Calhoun. Two uncles of Gen. Hill, Robert and William Hill, distinguished themselves as soldiers, William Hill as an Indian fighter under Andrew Jackson, and Robert Hill as a major in the War of 1812. Gen. Hill's mother was left a widow when the General, her youngest child, was only four years of age, and her husband having been careless in business matters, and having stood as surety for many friends, found that his estate was badly involved; she sold her negroes and put her sons at work until every claim against her husband, both just and unjust, was fully satisfied. She was a woman of remarkable intellect and learning, and as a girl was one of the beauties and belles of the State. She was noted for her piety and good works, was a Presbyterian, and reared her family in that faith and thoroughly indoctrinated them with the tenets of that church, and made them become thorough Bible students. She died at the residence of her eldest son, Col. W. R. Hill, at Canton, Miss., at the age of seventy-two. Gen. Hill received an appointment to West Point, and in 1838 entered the National Military Academy there. He was graduated in 1842, standing twenty-eighth in a class of about sixty. His class has been considered the ablest and strongest that ever graduated at West Point; among other distinguished and brilliant men who were members of it were Rosecrans, Pope, Sykes, Doubleday, Laidley, Longstreet, Stewart (A. P.), Van Dorn, G. W. Smith and R. H. Anderson. Grant, Stonewall Jackson and George B. McClellan were at the Point while he was there, but in different classes. After graduation he was appointed second lieutenant of artillery, and his first service was on the Canadian frontier, where trouble was anticipated over the boundary. He entered the Mexican War, and was successively brevetted for gallant and meritorious conduct from second lieutenant to major, which rank he held at the close of the war; he acted and served as a captain almost continuously throughout the two years spent in Mexico. After the close of the Mexican War the State of South Carolina presented him an elegant gold sword for the honor which his gallant conduct had brought upon his native State. After his service in Mexico he resigned from the army and was elected professor of mathematics in Washington College (now Washington and Lee University). Before going to Lexington to enter upon his college duties, he was married, at Cottage Home, Lincoln Co., N.

C., to Miss Isabella, the eldest daughter of Rev. Dr. R. H. Morrison, the first president of Davidson College, and a distinguished Presbyterian divine. Mrs. Hill's mother was, before her marriage to Dr. Morrison, Mary Graham, the daughter of Maj.-Gen. Joseph Graham, who was distinguished in the wars of the Revolution and of 1812. Mrs. Hill made her *debut* in society at the executive mansion of North Carolina, when her uncle, William A. Graham, was governor. He was afterward United States Senator, Secretary of the Navy, candidate for Vice-President on the Whig ticket with Gen. Scott, and Confederate States Senator. Another uncle, James Graham, was a member of Congress from North Carolina for many years. Gen. Hill filled the chair of mathematics at Washington College until 1855, when he accepted the same chair in Davidson College, North Carolina, and filled that until 1859, when he was called to the superintendency of the North Carolina Military Institute, at Charlotte, which position he was occupying when the Civil War broke out. In the meantime he had published several works, besides contributing largely to the magazines and newspapers, generally writing on mathematical or theological subjects. His "Elements of Algebra" was fast obtaining a hold in the leading colleges as a text-book when the war broke out. The preface to this work was written by his friend and brother-in-law, Thomas J. (Stonewall) Jackson. He also published "The Sermon on the Mount" and "Crucifixion of Christ," works that were well received by the religious world. At the outbreak of the war Gen. Hill immediately tendered his services to his State. He organized the first camp of instruction at Raleigh, N. C., and when the First North Carolina Regiment was organized he was elected its colonel and immediately went to the front. He fought the first real battle of the war (Sumter being but a bombardment), the battle of Bethel, in which he defeated Gen. Benjamin F. Butler and a Massachusetts brigade. Immediately after Bethel he was promoted to the rank of brigadier-general, which was soon followed by that of major-general, and as such commanded a division under Lee, which rank he held until a short time before the battle of Chickamauga. He participated in the battles of South Mountain, Antietam, Fredericksburg, Seven-days battle, Seven Pines, Petersburg, Cold Harbor, Chickamauga, Bentonville and many others. Just before Chickamauga, President Davis promoted him to the rank of lieutenant-general and sent him with a corps to re-enforce Bragg. In the great battle of Chickamauga he bore the brunt of the fighting. After this battle he was assigned to duty in eastern North Carolina, and did very effective service until the surrender. He was surrendered with Gen. Joseph E. Johnston. It would be impossible to give a history of his services to the Confederacy without giving a history of the operations of the Confederate armies. Probably his greatest service was at the battle of South Mountain, called "The Thermopylæ of America" (Boonsboro), where, with little more than 3,000 men, he kept McClellan's whole army at bay for over a day, saving Lee's supply trains from capture and his army from being cut in two. Suffice it to say that the military record that he made has caused him to be ranked as one of the "great captains" of the Confederate armies. He served the "Lost Cause" without fear and without reproach. After the war he returned to Charlotte, and soon began the publication of a magazine, *The Land We Love*. It had the largest circulation ever obtained by any Southern magazine. He sold it in 1872, and from that date until 1877 edited the *Southern Home*, a weekly newspaper devoted to the agricultural and literary interests of North Carolina. In 1877 he was, without his knowledge or consent, elected president of the Arkansas Industrial University, the State University of Arkansas, located at Fayetteville. He accepted, and when he took charge of it the attendance was but little over 200, largely made up of school children in the primary and preparatory departments from Fayetteville and surrounding country; within a few years he had increased the attendance to about 500 from all portions of the State, and raised the standard of the university until it became the first in the Southwest. He resigned in 1883, but was prevailed upon to withdraw it. He staid until 1884, much to the detriment of his health, when he finally severed his connection with the institution that he had done so much to build up. He carried away with him the loving regard of hundreds of his students, and the good will of the people of the State. He spent a year in Georgia in search of health, and being much improved in health he accepted the presidency of the Middle Georgia A. & M. College, at Milledgeville, a position which he still holds. This college has an attendance under his administration of over 500 students. Gen. Hill has always been a

Democrat, as were his father and grandfather before him. While never a politician he has been a devoted and enthusiastic member of the great party which has produced Jefferson, Jackson, Calhoun and Cleveland. He never held civil office, always declining to be a candidate or accept one tendered by the appointing power. He has been an elder in the Presbyterian Church ever since he was twenty-five years old, and throughout his long and eventful life has been a pure-minded Christian gentleman. He has been a profound student of theology, mental and moral science and all scientific subjects bearing on Christianity, and is a constant contributor to religious periodicals. Gen. Hill has written several articles for the *Century* for its series of war papers. In 1885 he was the orator at the reunion of the Army of Northern Virginia, at Richmond, and delivered an address on the "Confederate Private;" in 1887 he was invited to address the Maryland division of the Army of Northern Virginia, and at Baltimore delivered an address on "The Old South;" in 1888 he delivered the university address at Austin, Tex., to the Texas University. Gen. Hill has always been received, when he appeared on the public platform, by large and enthusiastic audiences. In the three instances mentioned, his reception by the people amounted to ovations, such as would honor a conquering general returning from his conquests; how much greater is the honor, that they have been tendered to an aged veteran of a "Lost Cause!" Gen. Hill is very simple and domestic in his way of life; he is without ostentation or pride, and full of charity and help for the needy and the afflicted. Gen. and Mrs. Hill have had nine children, four of whom died before reaching the ages of maturity. Their eldest, Eugenia, is married to Thomas Jackson Arnold (a nephew of Stonewall Jackson), formerly of West Virginia, now of San Diego, Cal. Mr. Arnold is a lawyer of excellent standing; he is now collector of the port of San Diego; they have three children. Dr. Randolph William Hill has recently been compelled, on account of poor health, to give up a lucrative practice in New York City, and is now living and practicing his profession at San Pedro, Cal. Miss Nannie Hill resides with her father; she is an artist of considerable talent. Daniel Harvey Hill, Jr., is professor of English literature in the college of which his father is the president; he was elected to this position soon after his graduation (in 1880) at Davidson College, North Carolina, and has acceptably filled it ever since. Joseph Morrison Hill is an attorney, and lives and practices his profession at Fort Smith, Ark. In personal appearance Gen. Hill was always of pleasing, but not handsome, address. He is about five feet ten inches in height, has large deep-blue eyes; his hair was light as a youth, but turned very black in manhood, as was his beard. Now both hair and beard are snowy white; he is erect in his bearing, and shows his military training even in his old age. This article could not be better concluded than was another of like character concerning Gen. Hill:

"This sketch is so true, just and unpretending that nothing more need be said to chronicle the career and noble character of this great soldier, spotless gentleman, and invaluable educator of the youth of the country. No man in the Confederate or any other army was regarded as more coolly brave—brave in every sense, in war and in peace—physically and morally courageous."

Albert J. Hodges, one of the independent and enterprising farmers of Dutch Mills Township, is the son of William C. and Nancy (Davis) Hodges, both of whom were natives of Tennessee, the father born in Lincoln County, and the mother in Wilson County. In early life they moved with their parents to McNairy County, Tenn., and later in life were married in this county, where they located. The mother died in 1846, and afterward the father married Miss Julia A. King. In 1854 they moved to Denton County, Tex., where the father died in 1860. He was a farmer and stock dealer, and during the Mexican War he raised a company, of which he was elected captain, and during the days of militia he was elected major of a regiment. Mr. Hodges was the father of nine children by his first marriage and three by the second marriage. Albert J. Hodges was the eldest of these children. He was born September 15, 1833, in McNairy County, Tenn., was reared to farm life, and educated in the primitive log school-house of pioneer times. At the age of eighteen he began business for himself on a farm, where he remained for a short time, and then engaged in the carpenter's trade for about two years, after which he returned to farming. In 1858 he married Miss Mary M. Thornton, a native of Hardin County, Tenn., and by her became the father of nine children, five sons and four daughters, eight of whom are living, the youngest having died a few weeks ago. Previous to his marriage, in 1853, Mr. Hodges moved to Grayson County, Tex., and soon after to Denton County. In 1861 he enlisted in Capt. O. G. Welch's company of Texas volunteer cavalry, and served until the close of the war. He participated in the battles of Pea Ridge and Cabin Creek, and at the latter place was captured and held a prisoner at Camp Morton, Ind., for about eighteen months, being paroled at Richmond, Va. He then returned to his family in Texas, and in 1867 moved to Washington County, where he has followed farming and trading ever since. He, like his father, is a Democrat in politics; he is also a Master Mason, and both he and wife are members of the Missionary Baptist Church. He is the owner of 230 acres of land, besides property in Salem.

Jo Holcomb, retired merchant, now living at Springdale, Ark., was born in the State of Illinois in 1825, and is a son of John and Dorothea (Willbanks) Holcomb, who were born in North Carolina December 10, 1797, and January 15, 1808, and died December 10, 1876, and February 17, 1874, respectively. They were married in Indiana, and soon after took up their residence in Illinois. After residing in the latter State seven or eight years they returned to Indiana, and four years later came to Washington County, Ark. They were the parents of fourteen children, and the father was a minister in the Primitive Baptist Church. Jo Holcomb, whose name heads this sketch, remained on the farm until nineteen years of age, and then began attending the schools of Fayetteville, and supported himself by working in the circuit court clerk's office. He then spent some time in clerking in a mercantile establishment, and after accumulating enough money purchased a one-half interest in the store, continuing in this occupation until the breaking out of the war, at which time he joined the Confederate army and served until after Lee's surrender. He then located in Hempstead County, Ark., where he was engaged in mercantile pursuits for about four years, and was also proprietor of a steam saw-mill. He was married to Miss Cener Boone, who died while they were residing in Hempstead County. She was a descendant of Daniel Boone, and was the mother of one child, Hubert. Mr. Holcomb returned to Washington County, Ark., in 1869, and purchased and has since resided on the old homestead. In 1872 he was elected circuit court clerk of Washington County, and was re-elected two years later. He then returned to his farm. He is a stanch Democrat in his political views, and belongs to the Masonic fraternity. In 1869 he was united in marriage to Miss Belle Smith, and their union has resulted in the birth of four children: Cener, Bruce, Jo Belle and George R.

William H. Holcomb is one of the honest and prosperous tillers of the soil of Washington County, Ark., and was born in Gibson County, Ind., on the 28th of October, 1827, being a son of John and Dorothea (Willbanks) Holcomb. The father was born in North Carolina in 1797. William was twelve years of age when he was brought by his parents to Arkansas, locating in the southern part of Washington County. Here they resided until the fall of 1843, when they moved to the northern part of Washington County, and located on the present site of Springdale. He was educated in the common schools, and was reared on a farm, and in July, 1847, was united in the bonds of matrimony to Miss Rebecca Baker, a Tennesseean, born in 1829, and their union resulted in the birth of eight children, three of whom are living: Calvin, William H. and T. J. Ellen, the fourth child, died after she was married and had become the mother of three children. Mr. Holcomb engaged in wagon making in 1851, and also farmed until 1860. At the breaking out of the war he enlisted in the Confederate service, serving in Company G, Fifteenth Arkansas Infantry. He was wounded at the battle of Elk Horn, and at the battle of Corinth was wounded in the arm. While at Black River, Miss., May 17, 1863, he was captured by Gen. Grant's army, and was sent to Johnson's Island, where he was retained until near the close of the war. He then came home, and engaged in farming near Springdale, and also sold goods. In 1872 he moved to his present farm of 207 acres, where he expects to pass the remainder of his days. He is a member of the Primitive Baptist Church, and is a Democrat in his political views. His son, William H. Holcomb, Jr., was born in 1861, and was educated in the common schools and the State University of Arkansas. He was married in 1883 to Miss Gussie Givens, a native of Kentucky, and by her is the father of one child, William H. Mr. Holcomb is now engaged in farming, and is a Democrat and a member of the A. F. & A. M. His brother, Calvin Holcomb, is also a Democrat, and was born in 1857. He was educated in the common schools and the Springdale High-school, and to his union with Miss Maggie Huffmaster four children have been born: James R., Ethel, Sarah E. and Henry Leroy. T. J. Holcomb, another brother, was born in 1867, and is a graduate of the Missouri Medical College.

William D. Holland is a prosperous farmer of Washington County, Ark., and was born in Jackson County, Ala., December 3, 1827, and was educated in the common schools. He was married in 1851 to Miss Polly Thomas, of Lincoln County, Tenn., and their union resulted in the birth of three children: Thomas N., John A. and William D. Three years after their marriage they came to Washington County, Ark., locating on a farm which now consists of 176 acres of fertile and well-improved land. He is also quite extensively engaged in breeding fine stock, and his annual sales amount to a nice sum. He served in the Confederate army during the late war, and was on active duty for three years. He was wounded at the battle of Prairie Grove. His parents, John and Rhoda (Davis) Holland, were natives respectively of Tennessee and Virginia. At an early day the father moved to Middle Tennessee, thence across the Cumberland Mountains to Alabama, he being the first man to cross with a wagon. He was a planter by occupation, and owned a number of slaves. He served under Jackson in the War of 1812, and was a participant in the battles of New Orleans and Pensacola. William Davis, father of Mrs. Holland, served in the Revolutionary War under Washington, and was one of the very early settlers of Tennessee, afterward moving to Alabama. Mr. and Mrs. Holland died in Jackson County, Ala., in 1858 and 1878, respectively, and four of their nine children are now living.

B. F. Holway, farmer, breeder and dealer in standard trotters, was born in Syracuse, N. Y., October 22, 1849, and is the son of F. N. and Jane E. (Brown) Holway, natives of Maine and Rhode Island, respectively. The father was born in 1810, was a book-keeper and merchant, and is now living with his son, B. F. Holway. The mother died in Iowa in 1870. B. F. Holway remained with his parents until grown, and then engaged in farming in Iowa, where he also ran a livery barn. In 1870 he married Miss Sophia M. Parsons, of Iowa, and they are the parents of seven children. Mr. Holway remained in Iowa until 1886, when he came to his present property, which consists of 240 acres of land. He has spent all his life in farming and in the horse business, and makes a specialty of standard bred trotters. He has some of the finest horses in the United States: Osmon, No. 1403, by Strader's Clay, 22, his dam being the great producing Mag Ferguson, by Membrino Chief, 11. She is the dam of Piedmont, time 2:17¼, and of Almont Eagle, time 2:27. Osmond is now in the hands of Bostick, of Tennessee, being developed. Mr. Holway has mares as follows: Betula, by Romulus; Lorella, by Almont Rattler; Betsy Babbet, by Richmont; Metella, by Wonder; Roselle, by Star of the West, and a great many others—altogether in this line about forty head, the best lot of this class of stock in the State.

James F. Hood, blacksmith and farmer at Hood Post-office, was born in Greene County, Tenn., July 11, 1833, and is the son of Benjamin and Mary (Draine) Hood, both natives of Greene County, Tenn. They were married in that county, and in 1834 they moved to Alabama, where they remained until their son, James F., was ten years old. They then moved to Dade County, Mo. After remaining here a few years they moved to Madison County, Ark., and located on Loller's Creek, where they lived five years, then returned to Cedar County, Mo. They then moved on White River, Washington County, Ark., and afterward made several trips to Missouri. He was a great rambler, and died at Washburn, Barry Co., Mo., in 1875, at the age of sixty-five. He was an industrious man, an excellent farmer, but was not satisfied to remain long in one place. His father's name was John Hood. The mother of James F. is now living and makes her home with him. She is about seventy-five years of age. She is a member of the Missionary Baptist Church, of which her husband was a member and deacon for many years. James F. was the eldest of eight children, four now living, born to his parents. They are named as follows: James F., Jahue, Henry B. and G. W. James F. remained with his parents until twenty-two years of age, when he began for himself as a farmer and has followed this occupation ever since. Before grown he worked at the blacksmith trade in connection with farming, and this he has also followed all his life. In 1866 he came to Washington County, Ark., set up his shop and is now the owner of 280 acres of land, all the result of his own exertion. August 2, 1855, he married Miss Sarah Shults, daughter of James Shults. She was born in Missouri and died in Washington County, Ark., August 10, 1856, without issue. April 4, 1861, he married Miss Rebecca Springston, a native of Indiana, born December 3, 1838, and the daughter of William Springston. Seven children were born to this union: David L., John F., Thomas C., Millie, Elizabeth Ina and William Benjamin, who died when two years of age. Mr. Hood is a Republican in politics, is a member of the Masonic fraternity, is a member of the K. of H., and he and wife are members of the Missionary Baptist Church, of which he is clerk.

David F. Hope, one of West Fork Township's most prominent farmers and stock raisers, was born in Campbell County, Tenn., in 1829. His grandfather Hope came from England with his wife, who was born there, to America at an early day and located in Tennessee, on the Tennessee River, where he followed the occupation of ship carpenter. He reared his family in Knoxville, Tenn., and was one of the prominent men of that section of the country, dying at the age of seventy years, having lived an honorable, active and useful life. His wife died at the advanced age of one hundred years. Their son, Thomas Hope, was born and reared to manhood in Knoxville, Tenn., and learned the ship carpenter's trade of his father, after which he located in Campbell County, Tenn., where he entered a large tract of land and became an extensive slave owner. He was married in Campbell County to Miss Nancy Smith, and by her became the father of ten children. His death occurred at the age of forty-five years, but his widow, who is a member of an old North Carolina family, was born in Tennessee, and is still living and resides with her son Jordan on the old plantation in Campbell County. David F. Hope is their third son, and was educated in the schools of Knoxville. He came to Arkansas in 1851, where he learned the blacksmith's trade, and was married, in 1853, to Louisa Johnson, daughter of James Johnson, by whom he is the father of the following children: Martha J., wife of J. R. Stockbuger; James T.; Mary E., wife of James Basset; Sarah A., wife of Mark Little; Hugh R., John F., Louisa T. C. (deceased); Nancy C., wife of William Yorks, Alice, Benjamin F., George D., an infant deceased, and Elizabeth. After his marriage Mr. Hope located on the West Fork of White River, in Washington County, where he made his home until 1866, and then purchased his present farm of 240 acres. He has eighty acres of improved land, on which is a neat and commodious two-story frame dwelling house, and after years of well-spent labor is now living at his ease, surrounded by the comforts which he has richly earned.

Julius Franklin Howell, A. M., instructor in pedagogics, Arkansas Industrial University, was born in Nansemond County, Va., January 17, 1846. His early life was spent on a farm and in private schools; later he attended the Reynolds Collegiate Institute, where he took a full classical and mathematical course. In 1862 he enlisted in the Confederate army, detached service, and in 1864 he became a member of Company K, Twenty-fourth Virginia Cavalry, being in active duty until the close of the war. During one of the minor engagements about Richmond, Va., he was slightly wounded in the right leg. After the war Mr. Howell spent another year in school, after which he began teaching, following this profession for two years in Virginia and three years in North Carolina. In 1870 he married Miss Ida C. Hinton, who is a native of North Carolina, born January 12, 1851, and who is a graduate of Murfreesboro Female College, North Carolina. In 1873 Mr. and Mrs. Howell moved to Austin, Ark., where Mr. Howell taught school for five years. He then taught four years at Lonoke, a year at Arkadelphia, two years at Morrilton, and in 1885 he became connected with the A. I. U. When quite a young teacher he felt the need of improved methods in education, and having purchased Page's Theory and Practice of Teaching, Wickersham's School Economy, and several other such works, he applied himself to the study of pedagogics, then comparatively a new science in the Southern States. In later years he spent a short time at the Illinois Normal University, where he caught the inspiration which afterward enabled him to secure his present position. He acknowledges his indebtedness, also, to the Cook County (Ill.) Normal School, where he spent a short but very profitable term. He is Democratic in his political views, is a member of the K. of H., and he and Mrs. Howell are members of the Missionary Baptist Church. They are the parents of seven children: Finley, Hinton, Willey, Carrie, Edward, Elmo and Barnes. Edward Howell, father of Prof. Howell, was born in Virginia; was a Baptist minister and a farmer. In 1818 he was married in his native State to Miss Sallie Barnes, who was also a native of Virginia. They were the parents of sixteen children, seven sons and nine daughters, their son Julius being the only professional man among them. Edward Howell was a Democrat in politics, and died in his native State, where he had passed his life, at the age of eighty-three. The mother died at the age of forty-five. Grandfather Howell was a native of England, and immigrated to Norfolk, Va., about 1730.

Rodham C. Horner, farmer, of Washington County, Ark., is one of four surviving members of a family of five children born to the marriage of Hampton and Sarah E. (King) Horner, both of whom were born in Hawkins County, Tenn., and were there reared, married, and spent the remainder of their days. The father was a farmer and stock trader until the breaking out of the late Civil War, and died in 1864 at the age of about fifty-four years. The mother is still living, and resides on the old home place with one of her daughters. The following are her children: Rodham C., Robert S., James (deceased), Hilah A. (wife of Chauncy McBride, of Tennessee) and John H. Rodham C. Horner made his parents' house his home until he was nineteen years of age, when he went to Little Rock, Ark., and from there to Dardanelle, Ark., thence to the Indian Territory two years later. After residing there one year he returned to Northwestern Arkansas, and at the end of two years took up his abode in Kansas. Since 1884 he has been engaged in farming and stock raising in Washington County, but previous to that time was a bridge-builder and carpenter. He has a fine farm of 228 acres, with about 110 acres under cultivation. August 19, 1885, he was married to Elizabeth Scott, who was born near Little Rock, Ark., and is a daughter of Allen and Eliza Scott, natives of Tennessee. The father died June 11, 1886, but the mother is still living, and makes her home with Mrs. Horner. She is now sixty years of age, and two of her four children are living: Robert R. and Elizabeth. Mr. and Mrs. Horner have two children: Robert H. and Hilah May. The family belong to the Methodist Episcopal Church, South, and in politics Mr. Horner is a Democrat.

Samuel C. Howell, farmer, brick and stone-mason, of Washington County, Ark., was born in Hawkins County, Tenn., in 1833, being a son of Madison and Eliza (Dunavan) Howell, who were born in Tennessee and Virginia, respectively. The father was a boot and shoe-maker by trade, and resided in his native State until 1844, when he came to Washington County, Ark., purchased a farm, and engaged in tilling the soil and working at his trade. He met with the best of success in both occupations, and was in comfortable circumstances at the time of his death, in 1853. Mrs. Howell was taken by her parents to Tennessee at an early day, and was there married in 1831 to Mr. Howell, by whom she became the mother of ten children, seven of whom are living. Her death occurred in 1886. Samuel C. Howell received the rearing of the average farmer's boy, and was educated in the common schools of Washington County. He learned the brick and stone-mason's trade in his youth, and worked at that occupation in Fayetteville. By energy and perseverance he has overcome many obstacles, and is now a well-to-do farmer of the county. He owns 235 acres of good farming land in two different sections, and has an orchard of twelve acres, consisting of the finest varieties of fruits. In 1855 he was married to Miss Mary J. Gibson, who was born and reared in Tennessee, and a daughter of William Gibson, of that State, and their union has been blessed with three children: Francis, Josephus and Angeline, wife of Harvey Keene, of Oregon. Mr. Howell joined the Southern army at the beginning of the war, but was never in active service, being on detailed duty the most of the time, and engaged in the blacksmith and shoe shops. He was an eye witness of the battle of Prairie Grove. He is a firm Democrat in politics, and he and family worship in the Methodist Episcopal Church, South.

Col. Thomas J. Hunt. This gentleman, so well known to the citizens of Washington County, and so well respected, was born in this county April 28, 1839, and is the son of William and Rhoda (Wilson) Hunt, both natives of Russell County, Va., where they were married. They afterward moved to Illinois, and from there to Washington County, Ark., about 1839. The father was of English extraction, was a farmer and stock dealer, and during the late war was veterinary surgeon in the First Arkansas Cavalry, being in service nearly the entire war. He was a man who attended strictly to his business affairs, and was not in public life. He died in 1885, and his wife in 1862. They were the parents of four sons and four daughters, Col. Thomas J. being the youngest of this family. He attained his growth on a farm, and secured a high-school education. He remained with his parents and engaged in school-teaching until the outbreaking of the war, when he enlisted in Company B, First Arkansas Cavalry, United States Army; was made captain, and through regular promotion was made lieutenant-colonel of the regiment. He served until the close of the war, and afterward engaged in farming until 1868, when he was elected to the State Senate and served two sessions. He was then appointed brigadier-general of the militia of his district by Gov. Clayton, and held the position until the militia disbanded. He carried on farming and stock dealing in the meantime, which he has continued to the present. He was appointed assessor of internal revenue under Gen. Grant, and filled that position four years. Col. Hunt has about 1,000 acres of land, 400 under cultivation, and has two farms, the home farm being situated one-half mile south of Fayetteville. He was married May 29, 1863, to Miss Matilda E. Campbell, who was born January 22, 1845. and died October 10, 1868. She was the mother of two children: Nora M., born February 27, 1864, now the wife of William P. Moulden, and Virginia J., born August 18, 1865. May 16, 1870, Col. Hunt married Miss Margaret A. Simpson, a native of Washington County, Ark., born August 14, 1849. This union has resulted in the birth of four children: Gertrude, Marshall L., Nellie and William H. Mrs. Hunt is a member of the Methodist Episcopal Church. Col. Hunt is a member of the G. A. R., and politically takes an active interest in the success of the Republican party, and is depended upon largely for judgment in conduct of that party. He was chairman of the Republican Central Committee for many years, and a member of the State Central Committee. He served in the State Senate for the Seventh Senatorial District in 1868, being elected by the elective franchise of Washington and Benton Counties. He is an active and honored member of the Masonic body, both in the Chapter and Blue Lodge. The attractive residence of Col. T. J. Hunt is located within one-half mile of the public square of Fayetteville, and is on one of the handsomest spots in this portion of the State. It was during the early history of this locality selected as the residence site of Gov. Archibald Yell, and was held by that honored gentleman until his sad death at the battle of Buena Vista, Mexico, while he was serving with honor in the United States army. After some few changes of ownership it became the property of Col. Hunt, a wealthy farmer of Washington County, who has taken the pains to have its portrait placed in this history. The knoll or elevation occupies about ten acres of ground, which slopes gently on all sides to the distance of about 200 yards, and from the residence can be had a fine view of the surrounding country. For many years the remains of Gov. Yell and many of his family were buried in a cemetery selected by him here, but lately the Masonic fraternity, of which he had been a prominent member, had them removed to the Masonic plat in the city's cemetery, through the influence of Col. Hunt, who saw that decay was fast destroying the shafts and tablets which marked their resting places.

John W. Hutchens, a wealthy farmer of Crawford Township. Washington County, Ark., was born in Morgan County, Ill., July 14, 1834, and is a son of Ellis and Mary (Shores) Hutchens, who were born in Surry County, N. C., in 1805 and 1812, respectively. They were married in their native State, and in 1829 immigrated with a colony to Illinois, being among the pioneer settlers of Morgan County. After residing there seven years they sold the land which they had entered and located in Naples, Ill., and three years later came to Arkansas, in 1839, and located on a farm near Brentwood. Here the father resided until his death, May 5, 1869. He served in the Black Hawk War while a resident of Illinois, and throughout life followed the occupations of farming and merchandising. His father, John Hutchins, was married twice, and was the father of twenty children who lived to maturity and reared families of their own, and his father came from Wales and raised four sons, he (John) being one of the four. The family settled in Virginia, from which State some of them served in the Revolutionary War. He, John Hutchens, and his brothers became Quakers, and were extensive planters and slave owners. Ellis Hutchens and wife became the parents of eleven children, seven of whom are living: John W., Alfred, Ellis W., Caroline, Adaline, Telitha and Eliza. John W. Hutchens was five years old when he was brought to Arkansas, and Washing-ten County has since been his home, with the exception of one year spent in Texas in 1864. In 1862 he enlisted in Brook's regiment, and served until June, 1865, when he surrendered at Fayetteville. He was with Price when he made his raid through Northwestern Arkansas, and was taken prisoner by the First Arkansas Regiment, but after being retained one month was exchanged. In 1862 he made his first purchase of land, which consisted of eighty acres, and has since increased his acreage until he now owns 363. His farm is valuable for its position and is rich in soil and production. He is a Democrat in politics, and has held the offices of constable, and deputy sheriff, being the present incumbent of the latter office. February 8, 1857, he was united in the bonds of matrimony, to Miss Mary J. Shumate, who was born in Crawford County, Mo., in 1836, and is a daughter of Nimrod Shumate, a native of Kentucky. She grew to naturity in her native State, and came to Arkansas in 1854. She and Mr. Hutchens became the parents of ten children: Mary, (wife of Alfred Ingram), Balas A., Sterling C., Shelby, Ellis, Jeanette, (wife of William Phillips), John C., Masey, Clementine, and one deceased. Mrs. Hutchens is a member of the Christian Church, and is a lady of exceptionally good mind and amiability of character.

James M. Jackson. Among the many enterprising and successful farmers of Washington County, Ark., none is more worthy of mention than James M. Jackson, who was born in Preble County, Ohio, in the year 1821, and is the son of Hon. Andrew and Amelia (Blancher) Jackson. The father was born in Kentucky in 1801, and at a very early date moved to Ohio, where he engaged in farming. In 1828 he moved from Ohio to Indiana, where he followed agricultural pursuits for some time. In 1831 he served as associate judge of the court, and in 1833 moved to Anderson, and was elected sheriff of Madison County; which position he held for four years, and was extensivly engaged in the milling business. In 1837 he was elected clerk and auditor of Madison County, which double office he held for seven years; but before that office had expired he was elected to the State Senate from Madison and Hancock Counties, in 1844, which position he held for four years. In 1853 he was re-elected to the same office and served two terms, making eight years that he served his county in the Senate, after which he retired to private life, and engaged in agriculture and raising fine stock. He died April 21, 1878, leaving eight children: David, Enoch, Matilda, Mary, Caroline, Eliza, Mattie and James M. The subject of this sketch was reared and educated in Indiana, and remained with his parents until he grew to manhood. In 1844 he married Miss Malinda S. McAllister, daughter of John and Hester (McGrady) McAllister, of Madison County, Ind. Mr. McAllister was a wealthy farmer, and commissioner of Madison County for a great many years, and was a very prominent man. To Mr. and Mrs. Jackson were born these children: Charles C., who married Miss Mattie Passwater, is the father of seven children, and is now living in Indiana; Hester C., married to George W. Spann, has three children, and is living in Indiana; Mary J., wife of J. W. Foland, and mother of two children, who also lives in Indiana; John M., who married Miss Mary Alfred, has three children, and is now living at Springdale, Washington Co., Ark.; Bessie A., wife of J. N. Lee, and the mother of one child (Carrie Lee), married to her second husband, K. Terry, lives in Washington County, Ark.; William W., who married Miss Annie Busey, and the father of one child, also living near Elm Springs, Washington Co., Ark., and engaged in farming. Mr. Jackson first commenced life by being deputy clerk of the county court, under his father, but afterward engaged in the milling business in connection with farming, which he continued until 1863, when he embarked in the dry goods and grocery business at Perkinsville and Anderson, where he continued until 1870, after which he sold out and followed farming alone until 1873, when he moved to Anderson, Ind. Here he was elected city clerk, which position he held for two years, and was then elected justice of the peace, holding the last named office until he moved to Washington County, Ark., near Elm Springs, in 1882. He is a member of the Methodist Episcopal Church, South, and is a Democrat in politics.

Hairl P. Jenkins, a prominent farmer and successful stock raiser of Prairie Township, was born in Sevier Township, Tenn., September 1, 1837, the third of a family of eight children, four sons and four daughters, born to James and Hettie (Smith) Jenkins. The family can be traced back to North Carolina, and ultimately to Wales. The grandfather was a soldier in the Revolutionary War. The ancestors of the Smith family were originally from Virginia. The parents of the subject were married and lived in Sevier County until the death of the father in about 1849, when the mother and part of the children moved to Dunklin County, Mo., and here she married Thomas Brumley. During the war they moved to White County, Ark., where the mother died in 1883. The father was a farmer, was a Whig in politics, and the mother was a member of the Baptist Church. Their son, Hairl P. Jenkins, assisted his father on the farm, and received a limited education in the old subscription schools. At the age of eighteen he learned the carpenter's trade, at which he worked for about fifteen years. In 1858 he came to this county, and has made it his home ever since, with the exception of a few years. June, 1861, he enlisted in Capt. Gunter's company, Confederate State troops, and remained in service three months. In the spring of 1862 he joined Company A, Thirty-fourth Arkansas Infantry, Confederate States Army, and served until the close of the war. He was in the battles of Pea Ridge, Wilson Creek, Prairie Grove, Helena and Jenkins' Ferry, and was never wounded or taken prisoner. After the war he worked three years in Little Rock, then moved to White County, and in 1872 came to Washington County, Ark., where the same year he married Miss Nannie S. Rainwater, who was born January 16, 1848, in Washington County, and daughter of John B. Rainwater. To this marriage were born five children: John T., James P., Ethel, Harvey M. and Jefferson P. Mr. Jenkins filled the office of deputy sheriff for a year and a half, is a Democrat in politics, and is a member of the Presbyterian Church. Mrs. Jenkins is a member of the Cumberland Presbyterian Church. Mr. Jenkins is the owner of over 248 acres of land, of which 175 are under cultivation. He has made every dollar of his money since the war.

Thomas Jennings, proprietor of the Mountain House, Fayetteville, Ark., was born in Fayette County, Ga., April 4, 1830, on the farm of his parents, Allen and Cynthia (Varner) Jennings, both of whom were natives of Oglethorpe County, Ga. The Jennings family traces its ancestry to the early days of Virginia. The family is of English and Welsh extraction, and the ancestors were planters and farmers by occupation. Vobert Jennings, the grandfather of our subject, left his home in Virginia to settle in Georgia. The maternal ancestors were also early settlers of Virginia, and Cynthia Varner was a daughter of Frederick Varner, who also left Virginia to settle in Georgia. Both grandfathers were soldiers in the war for independence. Thomas Jennings grew to manhood in Georgia, and there married Louisa E. Black, daughter of Cyrus and Elizabeth (Harkey) Black, natives of North Carolina and early settlers of Georgia. In 1859 Mr. Jennings removed to Texas with his family, and, locating in Upshire County, made that his home until the Civil War. He then served about a year in the Texas Militia, and then joined the regular Confederate army under Gen. MacGruder, in D. S. Terry's regiment, cavalry corps. After the war he spent a year in Texas, and in 1866 located in Fayetteville, Ark., where he has since been engaged in the livery and hotel business. Mr. and Mrs. Jennings have reared a family of three sons and three daughters: Edgar, Fannie T. (now Mrs. C. G. Waite, of Barton County, Mo.), Thomas A., Lillie, Willie and Lizzie. All of his children are well educated, Edgar being a graduate of the Arkansas Industrial University, and Lillie a graduate of the Daughter's College of Harrodsburgh, Ky. Mrs. Jennings and her daughters are members of the Christian Church. Mr. Jennings is one of the foremost men in all enterprises for the development of the county, and was of great assistance in securing the right of way for the San Francisco road, and the location of its depot at Fayetteville. He is also a liberal contributor to all worthy objects.

Dr. P. A. Johnson, a successful practicing physician of Goshen Township, was born in Guilford County, N. C., April 5, 1829, the son of John and Mary (Delay) Johnson. The father was a native of North Carolina, and was reared in Rockingham County; when married he settled in Guilford County, where he passed his entire life. He was a farmer, and died March 20, 1869. The mother was also a native of North Carolina, and died in that State March 3, 1843. Their son, Dr. P. A. Johnson, attained his growth on the farm, and secured a common-school education. When grown he sought the opportunity of higher schooling in Missouri, where he attended Chapel Hill College, in Lafayette County, three years. He remained there for some time engaged in teaching school, reading medicine, and also practiced medicine there until 1865. He then went to Jacksouport, Ark., and after remaining there for three years moved to his present location. He has continued the practice ever since, and in connection also carries on farming and fruit growing. He has 690 acres, 300 under cultivation and forty acres in fruit. All his business transactions have been successful, and he is a good citizen for any community. September 22, 1858, Miss Elizabeth R. Stark, a native of Illinois, became his wife. To them were born these children: John S., William W., Silas E., Howell, Hurlburt, Grace O. and Grover Cleveland. They also have three children deceased: Mary P., Martha and Ernest. The Doctor has always been a Democrat in his political views, takes an active interest in public affairs, and is regarded as a leading man in his community. He and wife are members of the Christian Church.

Jacob Q. Johnson, one of the wealthy and successful citizens of Washington County, Ark., and the son of James and Mary (Queener) Johnson, was born in East Tennessee in 1828. The father was a native of North Carolina, and was of Dutch descent. He took an active part in the Black Hawk War, and served with great credit to his country. He was a farmer and miller by occupation, and moved from Tennessee to Arkansas in 1851, where he followed farming for some time. He located nine miles south of Fayetteville, and here he died in 1883, from injuries received from falling down stairs. His son, Jacob Q., was educated in his native State, and remained with his father until the war broke out, but previous to to this, in 1852, he married Miss R. J., daughter of C. H. Boatright, of Madison County, and to them were born thirteen children, nine now living: Mary Jane, Tennessee, J. Q., Harriet Eliza, Edna K., Catherine, Susan J., Benjamin F. and Dora H. In 1862 Mr. Johnson enlisted in the Federal army, Company B, First Regiment Arkansas Cavalry, commanded by Col. Harrison, and served three years, three months and seven days. He was in the battle of Prairie Grove, was also in several skirmishes, but was never wounded or taken prisoner. After the war Mr. Johnson purchased his present home, which is one of the finest in the Northwest, and upon this farm he has erected a fine two-story brick residence, valued at $4,000, also a large sawmill, with grist-mill and flouring-mill attached, which is run by a thirty-six foot water-wheel. The water is brought a distance of 500 yards to run the wheel. Mr. Johnson has also steam power attached to run the mill when the water is low or the mill is frozen up. This mill is valued at $20,000. Besides this Mr. Johnson is the owner of 800 acres of valuable land, and has over 200 acres under the plow. He is a member of the G. A. R., is a member of the Baptist Church, and is one of the most respected and enterprising citizens of the county.

Benjamin F. Johnson. Among the most successful farmers and stock dealers and prominent citizens of Washington County, Ark., may be mentioned B. F. Johnson, who was born in Campbell County, Tenn., on the 12th of March, 1835. He is a son of James and Mary (Queener) Johnson, natives of Virginia and Tennessee, respectively. The father was born January 4, 1799. Mary (Queener) Johnson was born September 29, 1803, and died May 22, 1876. The father was a farmer by occupation, and was a soldier in the War of 1812. While a resident of Tennessee he held the office of justice of the peace for several terms, and was county sheriff one term. He was an old-line Whig in politics, and was married in Campbell County, Tenn., coming to Washington County, Ark., in 1850, where he spent the remainder of his days, dying May 6, 1882. He and wife became the parents of ten children, seven of whom are living: O. P., a farmer and miller, residing in Missouri; Lucinda, wife of J. R. Hope; Lovisa, wife of D. Hope; Mary, wife of W. Alexander; J. Q., Benjamin F. and Eliza. Benjamin F. remained under the paternal roof until he attained his majority, when he engaged in farming on his own responsibility, and by close application to the duties of farm life he established those habits of industry and frugality which insured his success in after life. He has been actively engaged as a dealer in stock for many years, and in all his business dealings he is fair and just, commanding the respect and confidence of all who know him; he commenced life with no capital but his two hands and a vast amount of energy and pluck, but is now the owner of 932 acres of land, and has one of the finest residences in the county. He is a notable example of those sound and correct business principles which win success and those genial traits of character which secure and retain public confidence and esteem. He took an active part in the late war, and served for over three years as sergeant of Company D, First Arkansas Regiment, operating the most of the time in Missouri and Arkansas. He participated in more than 100 battles and skirmishes, and was quite severely wounded in the left arm in a skirmish on White Oak. His marriage to Miss Nancy K. Boatwright took place October 1, 1856. She was born February 27, 1839, in Anderson County, Tenn., and died May 26, 1864, in Washington County, Ark., having been the mother of four children, two living: J. O. and Mary L., wife of Joseph Arnett. Mr. Johnson's second marriage was to Miss Lydia Lewis, by whom he became the father of fourteen children, seven of whom are still living: George W., Lydia K., Hugh L., Shirley J., Lettie, Burtos B. and Inez. Mr. Johnson is a strong supporter of the principles of the Republican party, and is a member of the G. A. R. He has always been a strong advocate of public improvements, and has given several hundred dollars to aid in the construction of railroads in his county, and throughout life has taken a deep interest in all enterprises tending to benefit the county and the cause of education.

Preston Johnson, a retired merchant of Fayetteville, Ark., was born in Lawrence County, Ark., April 26, 1824, and is a son of William and Elizabeth Ann (Conway) Johnson, who were born in Tennessee and North Carolina, respectively. The former was born and reared near Nashville, and was a son of John Johnson, who was a farmer by occupation, a native of Ireland, and of Scotch-Irish birth. In 1824 William Johnson removed with his wife and five children to Lawrence County, Ark. (now called Sharp County), and two years later came to Washington County, where he and his wife spent the remainder of their days. Preston Johnson engaged in farming and stock raising in his early manhood, which occupation he pursued until 1870, when he came to Fayetteville and engaged in general merchandising. He abandoned this business in 1879, and retired from active business life, and is now enjoying the fruits of a well-spent life. He is a Democrat in politics, and has always been noted for his liberality, and by his many excellent traits of character has secured the confidence and respect of all. In 1879 he lost his wife, whose maiden name was Miss B. C. Reddick, a daughter of Shadrock Reddick. She left one son and four daughters to mourn her loss: Mary Jane (wife of J. S. Thurman), Sarah C. (wife of Z. A. Thomas), Eliza Catherine (the deceased wife of J. L. Keener), Elizabeth Donaldson, a widow, and William (a stock dealer, of Kansas City).

Samuel P. Jones, farmer and an enterprising citizen of Goshen Township, was born in Lee County, Va., November 2, 1836, and is the fifth of ten children born to his parents, James and Lorinda (Warren) Jones. The father was born in the State of Kentucky, and when nearly grown his parents moved to Tennessee. Here he was married, and a few years later moved to Lee County, Va., where he passed his last days. He had followed the occupation of a farmer and blacksmith all his life. The mother was a native of Virginia, and died in that State. Their son, Samuel P., was reared on the farm, and, like the average country boy, received his education in the country schools. He remained under the parental roof until September 11, 1856, when he married Miss Lyrena E. Baker, a native of Tennessee, born June 16, 1839, and four children were the result of this union, viz.: Mary (wife of L. C. Clark), C. T., F. C. and Pamelia (wife of G. W. Sowel). Mrs. Jones died April 11, 1863, and November 1, 1866, Mr. Jones chose for his second wife Miss Hannah S. Muncy, of Virginia, born April 10, 1836. To this marriage were born six children: Pandora A. (wife of Amos James), Virginia A., Wiley H., Dudley B., Flora P. and Florence L. After his first marriage Mr. Jones moved back to Virginia, where he remained two years, and then moved to where he now lives, three miles southeast of Goshen, on a farm of 200 acres, fifty acres under cultivation. During the war Mr. Jones was in the Army of Virginia, Confederate service, and was in a great many of the principal battles; was wounded at Bean Station fight, and as a result was off duty for eight or nine weeks. He has been exclusively engaged in farming since then, and has made a success of this occupation. He is a good citizen, and he and family have the respect of all acquainted with them. He is a Democrat politically, and he and wife are members of the Missionary Baptist Church.

William A. D. Jones, farmer and stock raiser, is the third of five children, two sons and three daughters, born to Edward and Lucy G. (Lee) Jones, and the grandson on both sides of early settlers of Tennessee. The father was born in North Carolina in 1800, was of Welsh descent, and when a boy moved with his parents to Wilson County, Tenn. The mother was also born in North Carolina, about three years after the birth of her future husband, and moved with her parents to Wilson County, Tenn., when a small girl. She was of the Robert

E. Lee stock. The father was a model farmer, a Democrat in politics, and died in 1870. The mother was a member of the Cumberland Presbyterian Church, and her death occurred in 1861. Their son, William A. D. Jones, was born in Wilson County, Tenn., July 2, 1830, attained his growth on the farm, and received a very limited education. In 1850 he married Miss Emiline Holloway, a native of Wilson County, Tenn., and to them were born seven children, five now living: Lucy J., Margaret A., Alwilda S. F., Henrietta J. and Medorah E. October, 1861, he enlisted in Company I, Thirty-eighth Tennessee Confederate Volunteer Infantry, and served two years; going out as orderly he was soon promoted to the rank of first lieutenant. He participated in the battle of Shiloh, where he led 100 men. In 1863 he was discharged on account of disability, and has followed farming and stock raising ever since. He lost his wife in 1866, and the following year he married Miss Nancy J. Graves, a native of Wilson County, Tenn., who bore him eight children: Robert E., Geneva D., John E., Lorenzo R., Eugene, Wilson R., Wiley and Thomas R. In 1867 Mr. Jones moved to Collins County, Tex., where he remained fifteen years; was then in Grayson County for four years, but he, as well as all his family, being sick, he loaded them in a wagon and started for Eureka Springs, Ark. Upon reaching Siloam Springs, Ark., they stopped there, and here the health of the family was soon restored. The same year (1884) he purchased the place where he now lives, which consists of 238 acres of fine land. While in Tennessee Mr. Jones held the offices of constable and deputy sheriff. He is a Democrat in politics, and he and wife are members of the Christian Church.

Luke L. Kantz, one of the most enterprising, wide-awake farmers of the county, was born January 22, 1845, in McMinn County, Tenn., and is one of five children, three sons and two daughters, born to Frederick A. and Amanda E. (Dill) Kantz. The father was born in Carlisle, Penn., in 1812, was a manufacturer of buggies by occupation, and was also a trader in live stock. He was a Whig at one time, but afterward became a Democrat. He assisted in moving the Indians westward, and was a prominent and successful man. He was a member of the Methodist Episcopal Church, and died in 1867, in McMinn County, Tenn., where he had moved the year after his marriage. His father was a native of France, and came to America when a young man. He married Miss Margaret A. Dunbar, a Scotch lady, and they were the parents of two children, Frederick A. being the only son. Mrs. Amanda E. (Dill) Kantz, mother of Luke L., was a native of Gettysburg, born June 24, 1818. Three years after the death of her husband Mrs. Kantz moved to Washington County, Ark., where she still lives, and is a worthy member of the Methodist Episcopal Church. Her son, Luke L., received his literary education in Hiawassee College, and in 1863 he enlisted in Company G, Forty-third Tennessee Infantry (Confederate States Army), and served throughout the entire war. He was in the battles of Baker's Creek and Big Black River, and was among those captured at Vicksburg. After returning from the war he began the study of law, and was admitted to the bar at Athens, Tenn., in 1866. He practiced a short time at Kingston, and in 1867 moved to Washington County, Ark., where, the practice being scarce, he taught school for some time, but later engaged in farming, which he has since continued. In 1870 he married Miss Martha J. Skillern, a native of East Tennessee, born August 5, 1846, and five children were the result of this union: Mary, Martha V., Frederick S., Willie D. and Nellie W. Mrs. Kantz died May 23, 1886. Mr. Kantz is a Democrat in politics, is a member of the Masonic fraternity, and also a member of the Methodist Episcopal Church, South, as was also his wife. He is the owner of 200 acres of land, 125 being under cultivation.

Daniel H. Karnes, a prominent farmer of West Fork Township, Washington Co., Ark., was born in Hawkins County, Tenn., Oct. 13, 1827, and is a son of Andrew and Eliza (Howry) Karnes, being the eldest of their living children. His early days were spent in Hawkins County, Tenn., and in 1853 his union with Miss Rachel Strickland took place. She was a daughter of Jacob Strickland, and is the mother of five children: James, Ellen (wife of John Clark), William, Laura and Andrew. Mrs. Karnes died in 1877, and Mr. Karnes was afterward married to Mrs. Eliza Winn, by whom he became the father of one child, Samuel C. Mr. Karnes first settled on his father's old farm, where he lived until 1866, and then came to his present location, where he has a very valuable valley farm of 375 acres, which is the result of his own exertions.

With its substantial and convenient dwelling, and its spacious out-buildings, it is regarded as one of the most desirable farms in the county. Mr. Karnes is fair and just in all his dealings with men, and as a consequence commands the respect and confidence of all who know him. He is a Democrat in politics, and is ever ready to support the principles of his party. His Grandfather Karnes came from Germany to America when thirteen years of age, and located in Tennessee, where he became an extensive planter. Andrew Karnes was born and reared in Hawkins County, Tenn., and farmed in that county until 1851, when he came to Arkansas, and located on White River, where he still lives at the age of ninety-two years. His wife died in 1885.

John Karnes, one of the successful agriculturists of Washington County, Ark., is a native of Hawkins County, Tenn., born December 14, 1841. He came to Arkansas with his parents in 1851, and in July, 1861, was united in the bonds of matrimony to Miss Rachel Winn, a daughter of James Winn. She was born in Washington County, Ark., December 6, 1843, and became the mother of four children: James A., born November 30, 1862; Henry L., born August 30, 1865; William C., born December 6, 1868, and Nancy, born August 18, 1877, and died in childhood. Mr. Karnes has some exceptionally fine land in West Fork Township, his acreage amounting to 337, with 150 under cultivation, making the largest and one of the best farms in the township, all of which is the result of his good management and industry. He is a member of the following secret organizations: I. O. O. F., A. F. & A. M., I. O. K. of H., and has always taken a decided interest in the cause of education, all public enterprises and politics, being a member of the Republican party. [For further particulars of his family see sketch of D. H. Karnes.] His wife is an honored and worthy member of the Christian Church, and he is in sympathy with all evangelical churches, and contributes liberally to their support.

William Karnes, a prominent farmer of Washington County, Ark., and native of Hawkins County, Tenn., was born December 21, 1831, and came to Arkansas with his parents in 1851. He made his home with and assisted his parents on the farm, until 1859, and was then married to Lucinda Bloyed, and began doing for himself. He purchased a farm of 300 acres which was heavily timbered, and on which he located in 1860, and now has seventy acres cleared and in a fine state of cultivation. Mrs. Karnes was born July 7, 1840, in Washington County, Ark., and is a daughter of William Bloyed. Mr. and Mrs. Karnes are the parents of two children: A. E., the elder, was born in 1860, married James D. Dearing May 22, 1883, and died May 29, 1887, leaving three children; and Laddie, the younger, a son, was born October 18, 1876. Mr. and Mrs. Karnes have also taken charge of W. L. Byrd, a nephew, left an orphan when one year and ten months old, and who was born December 12, 1869. Mr. Karnes is a strong supporter of Republican principles, is a Master Mason, and he and wife are members of the Christian Church. He is a son of Andrew and Eliza Karnes, whose sketches appear in this work.

Dr. Jesse R. Kelly, one of the enterprising and prominent citizens of Goshen Township, and son of Hiram and Elizabeth (McGee) Kelly, was born in Habersham County, Ga., November 29, 1833. The father was a native of North Carolina, born in 1787, and was reared in his native State. After his marriage he moved to Georgia, and reared his family in Habersham and Cherokee Counties of that State. In 1858 he moved to Madison County, Ark., where he died July 13, 1862, and is buried in that county. He was a blacksmith by occupation, and owned a farm, which he operated in connection with his trade. He was a member of the Methodist Church, was a zealous leader in the same, and was an exhorter, a class-leader and steward nearly all his life. The mother was a native of North Carolina, and died when our subject was fifteen years of age. She was also a devout member of the Methodist Episcopal Church, her faith being none less than her husband's. Their family consisted of nine children, eight now living, four sons and four daughters. Dr. Jesse R. Kelly was next to the youngest child in point of birth. He attained his growth on the farm, and remained with his father until twenty-one years of age, when, in 1855, he married Miss Elizabeth A. Richards, of South Carolina, who was born in 1835. The fruit of this union were nine children: John T. (deceased); Mary A., wife of A. J. Parker; Alexander (deceased); Sarah R. H., wife of James Condiff; Marcus L., Lydia J., Julia L., Hettie and Eddie L. Dr. Kelly attended lectures at the Atlanta Medical College, having studied medicine for some time previous to this, and graduated from this institution in 1859. He then entered upon his practice at Hindsville, Madison County, and continued here for four years with a very successful practice. He then endeavored to retire from practice, and in 1878 moved to Goshen, and lived there until 1884, when he moved to his farm, three miles east of Goshen, where he has a beautiful mountain farm of 360 acres, 175 under cultivation and twenty-five acres in orchard. During the war, from 1862 to 1867, Dr. Kelly resided in Texas, where he was engaged in the practice of his profession. He was detailed by the Confederate government to practice for the people left at home, etc. He engaged in merchandising at Goshen from 1878 to 1883, and continued his practice at the same time. He was licensed to preach in the Methodist Church, South, in 1868, was ordained deacon in 1848, and has been zealously engaged in that work ever since. His wife and all the family, with the exception of the two youngest, are members of the same church. The Doctor has been a Master Mason since 1868, and has always been Democratic in his political views. He was postmaster at Goshen for five years, and is an excellent citizen.

Thomas J. Kelly, one of the old and much respected citizens of Prairie Township, was born in Ray County, Tenn., May 5, 1816, and is the son of Thomas and Nancy (Peters) Kelly. The father was born in Virginia, and when young went to Grainger County, Tenn., where he married Miss Peters, a native of Virginia. In a canoe they floated down the Tennessee River to a place near Washington, Ray Co., Tenn., where he established Kelly's ferry, across the Tennessee, and ran this until his death, The mother then came west with her children, and died in Texas. The father was a Democrat in politics, and for about twenty-seven years represented Ray County in the State Legislature. The mother was a member of the Methodist Church. Thomas J. Kelly was the youngest of six children, three sons and three daughters, born to his parents. He grew up to farm life and received a limited education in the common schools. Having served twelve months in the Florida War, he was appointed subsisting agent at Gunter's Landing, where the Indians were being collected preparatory to their removal westward. With them he came to Benton County, Ark., where he bought a large tract of land. In 1844 he married Miss Margaret D. Dixon, a native of Middle Tennessee. To them were born two children: William T. and Margaret. During the Mexican War Mr. Kelly served as wagon-master for Col. Yell's regiment, and during his absence from home his wife died and he was reported dead. So firm was the belief of his death that when he put in appearance all his property had been divided. In 1848 he married Miss Elizabeth Rieff, who was born in Wilson County, Tenn., and who, by her marriage, became the mother of three children: Josephine (deceased), Madline and John H., who has served eight years as minister in the Cumberland Presbyterian Church. Six years of that time were spent in teaching and in his ministerial duties in the Cherokee Nation. In 1848 Mr. Kelly came to this county and settled where he now lives. He served as sergeant-at-arms of the House of Representatives two terms, 1874 and 1875. He is a Democrat politically, and he and his wife are members of the Cumberland Presbyterian Church, as was also Mr. Kelly's first wife.

Thomas H. Kerby, farmer, fruit grower and native of Washington County, Ark., was born on the 16th of April, 1848, and his early days were spent in following the plow and attending the common schools, where he received a good practical English education. In the fall of 1863 he enlisted in Col. Brook's regiment of cavalry, and served until the close of the war, participating in a number of skirmishes. After his return home he engaged in farming, and has made that his chief occupation through life. He has farmed successively in Washington, Jackson, Bates, Washington, Crawford and Washington Counties, locating on his present farm, about two miles from Boonsboro, in March, 1884. He has a good farm of 113 acres, with seventy-five acres under cultivation, and twelve acres in orchard, and from the products of his farm and orchard derives a comfortable income. While residing in Jackson County he was married January 2, 1870, to Miss Rebecca Ashley, who was born in Fayette County, Mo., and reared and educated there. Their union has been blessed in the birth of six children: William F., Annie Laurie, Alice May, Jessie C., Henry Lee and Charles Thomas. Mr. and Mrs. Kerby and their four eldest children are members of the Cumberland Presbyterian Church. Mr. Kerby's parents, Henry Franklin and Rebecca (Coulter) Kerby, were born in Tennessee, and were married in Arkansas. The father was a farmer, and served as sheriff of Washington County at a very early day. He died on the 8th of January, 1867, having been a resident of the county thirty-six years.

F. G. Kimbrough, merchant at Dutch Mills, was born in Jefferson County, Tenn., November 5, 1842, and grew to manhood on the farm. November, 1861, he enlisted in Company H, First Tennessee Cavalry, Confederate Army, and served three and a half years. He participated in the battle of Bean Station, and was twelve months around Petersburg and Richmond. At the former place 100 of his regiment attempted to take their lost picket line against a brigade. Mr. Kimbrough surrendered at Appomattox, and passed through the war without being wounded or taken prisoner. He then returned to Tennessee, farmed until 1867, and then removed to Washington County, Ark., where he made money, and educated himself at Cane Hill College. In 1874 he married Miss M. E. Whitaker, who bore him one child, Elizabeth A. The following year his wife died, and in 1876 he married Miss Henrietta Baxter, who bore him five children: Daisy, Wilson W., James R. G., Thomas D. and Baxter. Mr. Kimbrough and wife are members of the Missionary Baptist Church, as was also the first wife. In 1878 Mr. Kimbrough began merchandising with V. S. English, and another who withdrew in 1884; this he still continues, and in connection is engaged in farming, being the owner of about 230 acres of land. His father, Thomas Kimbrough, was born in Jefferson County, Tenn., as was also his mother, Elizabeth (Austell) Kimbrough. The father was a Democrat in politics; was a farmer all his life, and died in 1886 at the age of eighty-one years. The mother died in 1874 at the age of sixty-four, and both parents were members of the Missionary Baptist Church. In 1869 F. G. Kimbrough started out in life $150 in debt, which, by industry and economy, he soon paid off, and to-day is in very comfortable circumstances.

William Clay Kuykendall, retired farmer of Washington County, Ark., and a native of Union County, Ky., was born on the 18th of May, 1833, and is a son of William F. and Lucy (Wallace) Kuykendall, and grandson of Simeon T. Kuykendall, who was of German descent, and was born in the "Palmetto State." He removed to Kentucky when it was a Territory, and became an extensive farmer and breeder of blooded horses, owning at one time one of the finest race-horses of his day. His son, William F., was born and reared in Union County, Ky., and after his marriage, which occurred in 1831, began tilling the soil on his own responsibility. He was also an extensive stock raiser and dealt largely in horses and mules. At the breaking out of the war he was strongly opposed to secession, but when he found that opposition was of no avail he and four sons joined the Southern army, and he was on active duty until the close of the war. He died in 1881, lamented by a large circle of friends and acquaintances. His wife was a daughter of James Wallace, who was one of the first settlers of Union County, Ky., and an extensive farmer and stock dealer, noted for his hospitality. Mr. Kuykendall and wife became the parents of four sons and four daughters. The mother died in 1878. William Clay Kuykendall was educated in the common schools of Union County, and in 1850 went to Mississippi and took charge of his uncle's, Jacob Kuykendall's, plantation and negroes for two years. He was then overseer of different plantations in Louisiana until the breaking out of the war, when he immediately enlisted in a Louisiana regiment, and was afterward transferred to the First Kentucky Cavalry. In 1862 he went to Southern Kentucky, raised a company, and was appointed its captain. He afterward returned and organized another company, 156 strong, and again went to the front. While in Gen. Lyon's brigade he was promoted to the command of the regiment, but resigned in 1864 and returned to the command of his company. He was in the battle of Shiloh, and during his entire service was almost constantly engaged as a scout. After the war he returned home and took charge of his father's farm, also going in debt $5,000 for a farm of his own. This he paid off by his own industry and good management. In 1871 he was married to Mrs. Nannie Brooks, widow of John A. Brooks, a leading attorney of Webster County, Ky., and daughter of James Rice, a prominent farmer of Hopkins County. Mrs. Kuykendall became the mother of two children by her first marriage: Sidney J., deputy clerk of Dallas County, Tex., and a young man of marked ability, and Jennie, who resides with her mother. Mr. and Mrs. Kuykendall are the parents of one child, Rice, who is sixteen years of age. In 1875 Mr.

Kuykendall went to the Hot Springs for the health of his family, and while there was engaged in running a hack between that place and Malvern. He next went to Brown County, Tex., where he was engaged in the stock business, and in 1880 came to Washington County, Ark., where he has since been engaged in farming. He owns 2,800 acres of land in Texas, and is a man of excellent business qualifications. The family attend the Cumberland Presbyterian Church, and he is a member of Viney Grove Lodge No. 265, A. F. & A. M., and Columbus Lodge No. 200, I. O. O. F., at Clay, Ky.

Milton F. Lake was born in Davidson County, Tenn., September 4, 1819, and is of German descent. He is a son of Elijah and grandson of John Lake, who was a soldier in the Revolutionary War, and an early settler of South Carolina. Elijah was born in the "Palmetto State" in 1796, but was reared in Davidson County, Tenn., where his father had located about 1800. He was married to Deborah Miller, of Davidson County, her father, William Miller, being born in Virginia, and of Scotch extraction. In 1830 Mr. and Mrs. Lake removed with their family to Ray County, Mo., but six years later returned to Tennessee, where the mother died in 1845. In 1850 Mr. Lake married Mrs. Elizabeth Wilson, and died in 1861, having been the owner of a large plantation and many slaves. Milton F. Lake was reared on his father's plantation in Western Tennessee, and was educated in the common schools. In 1843 he was married to Margaret L. Braden, who was born in Wilson County, Tenn., and by her became the father of ten children, six of whom are now living: James E., William L., George T., Milton F., Jefferson T. and Ella. His wife died July 4, 1869. He was conscripted in the Confederate army, but was captured at the end of three months and was taken to Alton, Ill., where he was held a prisoner for eight months. He then returned to his home and resumed farming, coming to Washington County, Ark., in 1869, where he has since made his home. He has a fine farm of 500 acres. In 1875 he married Mrs. Jennie Phillips, of Washington County. He was a member of the Constitutional Convention for the State of Arkansas in 1874, and in his political views is a stanch Democrat.

George T. Lake, president of the school board of Fayetteville, belongs to that pushing and energetic class of men who are doing so much to increase the industrial interests of this city. He was born in Louderdale County, Tenn., September 6, 1849, and is a son of Milton F. and Margaret (Braden) Lake, natives of Davidson and Maury Counties, Tenn., respectively. In 1860 Mr. Milton Lake, with his family, left Tennessee and located upon a farm near Prairie Grove, of this county, where he at present resides. Our subject was reared upon the farm, and during his youth attended the public schools of that locality. Possessing a desire to embark in mercantile life, when of age he started in life for himself, and passed four years clerking in a store in this city. In 1875 he established himself in business, and being ever ready to meet the wishes of his customers he has steadily increased his business and patronage until he has taken his rank among the prominent business men of this place. His success is mainly attributed to strict attention to business, untiring energy and a high standard of integrity. He was united in marriage at Fort Smith, Ark., to Miss Mary H. Stratton, an estimable lady, daughter of the late D. H. P. Stratton and Louisa (Kransser) Stratton. Mr. Stratton is a descendant from the Strattons of New Jersey, which was his native State. Early in life he sought a home in the West, and settling in Fort Smith, Ark., became one of its honored and respected citizens. Mrs. Stratton was a native of Germany, who carefully reared her children and lived to see them well established in life. Mr. and Mrs. Lake have a family of two children: Horton and Louise. They are well-to-do citizens, and regular communicants of the Presbyterian Church. Mr. Lake has served both in the town councils and on the school board. He is a Royal Arch Mason, an I. O. O. F. and a K. of H.

Thomas Latham, a well-to-do farmer of West Fork Township, Washington Co., Ark., and an ex-Union soldier, was born in Jackson County, Ala., on the 23d of August, 1827, being a son of Jonathan and Elizabeth (Ball) Latham, and grandson of Cornelius Latham, who was a native of the "Old North State," and was an extensive stock dealer and farmer. Jonathan Latham was born in Randolph County, N. C., in 1800, and died in the State of Alabama, December 27, 1887, to which State he had moved in 1821. He was a prominent politician of his State, and during the war was a stanch Union man, and was representing his county in the State Legislature when the war broke out. He was an extensive land-holder, and at the time of his death was the owner of about 1,000 acres of land, nearly all of which was under good cultivation. To his union with Miss Elizabeth Ball, whom he married shortly after coming to Alabama, was born a family of twelve children, all of whom grew to maturity, and ten of whom are living at the present time. The mother died in 1882. Thomas Latham resided in his native State until August 28, 1863, when he enlisted in Company A, First Alabama Volunteers, and did honorable service for his country until 1864, when he was disabled for life, being thrown from his horse while carrying a message from Gen. Morgan Smith to Gen. John A. Logan. He returned home, and in 1867 removed to Tennessee, where he was married to Elizabeth Freeman, and lived until 1869, when he returned to Alabama, and in 1871 came to Benton County, Ark., and two years later to West Fork, where he has since been engaged in farming. He is a member of the A. F. & A. M,, the G. A. R., Lodge No. 14, and in his political views is a stanch Republican. To his marriage with Miss Freeman, who is a daughter of John W. Freeman, an ex-soldier of the Mexican War, seven children have been born: John T., Barbara (wife of John Hope), Julia, Fannie, George, Ada G. and Nettie. Mr. and Mrs. Latham are members of the Methodist Episcopal Church.

A. A. Langham, a successful farmer of Goshen Township, was born in Georgia, and is the son of Simeon and Clarrissa Ann (Nichols) Langham. The father was born in North Carolina in 1804, and the mother was born in Georgia in 1828. They were married in the last named State, and there principally reared their family, which consisted of twelve children. The father has followed agricultural pursuits all his life, and is now living with his son, A. A. The mother is also living. They came to this State in 1869, and are members of the Methodist Episcopal Church, South. Their son, A. A. Langham, remained at home and assisted his father on the farm until nineteen years of age. In 1872 he chose for his companion in life Miss Lenza L. Hash, daughter of F. Hash, and they became the parents of seven children: Allatia A., William C., John F , Maud, Cener, Mabel P. and Harrison G. After marriage Mr. Langham settled on a farm near Goshen, and here he now has 201 acres, ninety under cultivation. He has tilled the soil all his life and has been quite successful. He and wife are members of the Christian Church. He is a Republican in politics, and a highly respected citizen.

Preston J. Lea, one of the old and much respected citizens of the county, was born in Jefferson County, Tenn., November 20, 1814, the son of Maj. and Rhoda (Jarnagin) Lea. The progenitors of the Leas made their first settlement in America, from England, in North Carolina. Maj. Lea, the grandfather of P. J. Lea, immigrated with Daniel Boone to Tennessee, and made a settlement near Cumberland Gap, where he died, a hale man, at one hundred and eight years. He had a son, Maj. Lea, who married Rhoda Jarnagin, whose father came from Virginia to East Tennessee in 1775. By agreement they assumed three spellings of name in order to distinguish the families, Lea, Lee and Leigh. Robert E. Lee and Gen. Leigh are of this stock. The father of our subject was born close to the Virginia and North Carolina line, and when young moved with his parents to East Tennessee, where he married Miss Jarnagin, and where both spent the remainder of their days. The father was killed by lightning, when our subject was but a lad. In their family were nine children, seven sons and two daughters. Both parents were members of the Missionary Baptist Church, and the father was a farmer by occupation. Their youngest child but one, Preston J., attained his growth on the farm and received a very limited education. On reaching manhood he took to river life, and for many years ran flatboats on the Mississippi River and its eastern tributaries. He piloted the first steamboat that ever went up the Holston River. In 1834 he was married in Grainger County, Tenn., to Miss Mary H. Peck, daughter of Benjamin Peck. She was born September 20, 1818. Having lived in Tennessee until the close of the war, they then moved to Ringgold, Ga., and in 1881 came to this county. His chief occupation has been farming, although he ran a flour and saw-mill for many years. Both he and wife are members of the Old School Presbyterian Church. He was a Whig before the war and a Democrat since. Mr. and Mrs. Lea are the parents of sixteen children, six sons and ten daughters. The eldest son, Benjamin H., was lieutenant of a company of United States troops during the late- war. Mr. Lea has never aspired to any office, but has always been a plain, practical business man.

Rev. Thomas Leach was born in Jackson County, Ala., July 14, 1820, and is a son of Thomas and Ruth (Renshaw) Leach, both of whom were natives of the "Old North State." They first moved to Tennessee, and spent five years in Rutherford County, after which they moved to Alabama, and at the end of ten years came to Washington County, Ark., locating on a tract of unimproved land, but a few years later moved to Benton County, Ark., and there the father died in 1880, in his ninetieth year. He served under Gen. Jackson in the War of 1812, and was a faithful and trustworthy soldier. Rev. Thomas Leach grew to manhood in Washington County, and was educated at Bethesda Academy, remaining with his father for several years after attaining his majority. In 1847 he went to North Carolina on business, and while there was married to Catherine Turner, a daughter of Samuel Turner, of that State, and soon after returned to Arkansas, settling on the farm on which he now lives in October, 1848. His first purchase was 120 acres, but he has since added to that until he now owns 225 acres, with ninety acres under cultivation, and fourteen acres in orchard. His wife died in October, 1865, having borne seven children, all of whom are living and the heads of families, with the exception of one, and in August, 1869, Mr. Leach was married to Mrs. Louisa Woods, a native of Virginia, and a daughter of Robert Crockett. She was the mother of four children by her first marriage. In 1850 Mr. Leach was ordained a minister of the Protestant Methodist Church, and has acted as a local minister of that church since his ordination. He is a Royal Arch Mason, and as a true gentleman and honest citizen has the respect and esteem of all his fellow men.

Prof. Charles Hendee Leverett, of the chair of ancient languages, A. I. U., was born in Boston, Mass., November 30, 1833, being the son of F. P. and Matilda (Gorham) Leverett, the father the author of "Leverett's Latin Lexicon," and the mother a descendant of the first families of Massachusetts. They died when their son, Prof. Charles H. Leverett, was but two years old, and he was taken and reared in the family of the Rev. C. E. Leverett, of Beaufort, S. C. After receiving a good literary training he entered South Carolina College in his sixteenth year, and completed a thorough classical and literary course at that college in 1852. His early inclinations were for languages, and after graduating he taught in the academies of South Carolina. He first accepted a position as teacher in the high-school near Charleston, and made a study of the languages during his teaching, thus adding largely to his stock of information. At the breaking out of hostilities between the North and South he entered the ranks of the Confederate army in Colcock's brigade, and served on the coast defenses for about two and a half years. He was also in Hampton's Legion, but returned home in 1864 on account of ill-health. After recuperating he returned to his command and was in active service for some time. In September, 1868, he came to Arkansas, and spent ten months in Searcy, White Co., Ark., in charge of the high-schools at that place. In September of the same year he came to Washington County, took charge of Ozark Institute, and conducted the same for about three years. He then retired from this position to accept the position of professor of ancient languages in the Arkansas Industrial University, in 1871. He continued to fill this position for thirteen years. He was married in Chesterfield District, in 1861, to Miss Julia Blanche Jenkins, daughter of Maj. R. H. Jenkins, of Charleston, S. C. She was a student of the female college at Charleston and at Orangeburgh. To Prof. and Mrs. Leverett were born five sons and six daughters: Julia B., F. P., Mary, Storer, Ammee, Charles, Abbie, Rosa Catherine Elizabeth, Edward, Nina and Whitham. Prof. Leverett is a member of the K. of H., and he and wife worship at the Episcopal Church.

Augustus Buckner Lewis. Closely connected with the mercantile interests of Washington County, Ark., is the name of Augustus B. Lewis, who was born in Hempstead County, Ark., April 28, 1835, the son of Joseph and Mary Bartlett (Brown) Lewis, grandson of John Lewis, and great-grandson of John or Hugh Lewis, who came over from Ireland at an early date, and settled in North Carolina, but afterward moved to Kentucky, where he remained until 1804, when he moved to Washington County, Mo. Joseph Lewis was born in Livingston County, Ky., in 1802, and in 1822 he went on horseback and alone to Lawrence County, Ark., thence to Independence County, thence to Pulaski, and later to Hempstead County, but finally, in 1831, he and a younger brother, Hugh, made a settlement in Washington County, Ark., where he settled with his wife and two sons, Rowland and A. B., in 1836. He died in 1884, and lacked but a few days of being eighty-two years of age. He had been a worthy and consistent member of the Christian Church for over forty years, and died in full communion with the faith of the same. Mrs. Lewis passed away in 1875, and was a little over sixty-six years of age. She was also a devout member of the Christian Church. They reared five sons and one daughter: Rowland M., Henry T. (who now resides in the Indian Nation), A. B., J. C., Mrs. N. J. Rogers and William P., who lost his life at the fall of Atlanta, July 28, 1864, and is now buried in the cemetery there. The five brothers were all in the Confederate army, and rendered active and honorable service. The father of these children went south during the war, and after the storm clouds had passed away he returned to find that he had not only lost $20,000 above all indebtedness, but become heavily involved. He went to work, and with hard work and good managment soon surmounted all his difficulties. Cornelius Brown, father of Mrs. Joseph (Brown) Lewis, was a native of Virginia, and left the home in that State and made a settlement in Miller County, Ark., at what is now known as the Choctaw Nation, adjacent to Dokesville, the capital of that Nation. He died there at a ripe old age. His widow and family then returned to Hempstead County, Ark. Augustus B. Lewis was merchandising on his own account when the war broke out, but had previously received a good education in Arkansas College. He enlisted in the Confederate army, was in service during the entire war, and was a faithful and honorable soldier. After returning home he farmed for four years, and then moved to Fayetteville, Washington Co., Ark., where he clerked from July 20, 1869, until January, 1882. He then engaged in business for himself. December 26, 1869, he wedded Miss Rebecca Sophia Hewitt, daughter of Nelson and Cynthia (Crimm) Hewitt, natives of Tennessee, and pioneers of Washington County. To Mr. and Mrs. Lewis were born these children: Lucius Lucretius, Lena Leota and Linneaus Lamar. Mr. Lewis was elected treasurer of Washington County for four years, but only served two years on account of the change of the State constitution. Mr. Lewis and family worship at the Christian Church—the church of his fathers.

Brackin Lewis, retired farmer and one of the oldest residents of Reed Township, Washington Co., Ark., was born in the Old North State in 1801, and is the only living descendant of Zachariah and Rachel (Brackin) Lewis. The father died in North Carolina, and the mother was afterward married to Peter Mankins [see sketch]. Mr. Lewis, whose name heads this sketch, came with his parents to Arkansas in 1835, but had lived from the time he was eight years old until he was thirty-four in the State of Kentucky, near the Virginia line, with the exception of one year spent in the State of Illinois. After coming to Arkansas he located near the head-waters of the White River, where he has since been engaged in farming, milling and cabinet work. He has lived a very active life, and is one of the prominent and highly esteemed old citizens of the county. He came to Washington when it was in a very primitive state; and has lived to see it grow into a well populated and highly fertile agricultural region. Matilda Preston, who was born in Kentucky, became his wife, and the mother of sixteen children, seven now living: George W., Rachel (wife of H. Wilson), Moses D., Emeline (wife of T. H. Robinson), Zachariah, John and Eliphas. Those deceased are Henry, Elizabeth, Edie, Nathan P., Lydia, Peter, Julia, Ann and Sarah. Mr. Lewis was formerly a Whig in politics, but is now a Republican, and for about fifty years has been a worthy and consistent member of the Christian Church. He has surmounted many difficulties and discouragements throughout life, and now, after a long and well-spent career, can enjoy the fruits of his labor. His son John was born on the 29th of August, 1845, on the old homestead in Reed Township; has always been engaged in farming on the home place, and during the late war served in the Home Guards under B. F. Johnson. He was married to Miss Almeda Ramey, a native of the county, who died in 1880, having borne four children: William H. (deceased), Lydia, Thomas and Peter. Sarah Parker became his second wife. She was born in Kentucky in 1854, and in 1867 came with her parents, Dosier and Melvina Parker, to Arkansas. The parents are yet residing on the West Fork of White River, in Washington County. To Mr. and Mrs. Lewis were born four children: Dosier, Matilda, Burleigh and Anna. Mr. Lewis is a deacon in the Christian Church, and has always taken a deep interest in church, school and public enterprises.

George W. Lewis. The milling and farming interests of Washington County, Ark., are well represented by Mr. Lewis, who was born in Floyd (now Johnson) County, Ky., May 30, 1822, being a son of Brackin and Matilda (Preston) Lewis. The father is a North Carolinian, born about 1801, and is still living, being a resident of Washington County, Ark., to which State he had come in 1835. He was married in Kentucky, and became the father of sixteen children, seven of whom are living: Moses D., Zacharius, John, Eliphas, George W., Rachel (Mrs. Wilson) and Emeline (wife of T. H. Robinson). Those deceased are Edie, Henry, Elizabeth, Peter, Nathan, Lydia, Sarah, Julia Ann and Millie. The mother of these children died in 1883. George W. Lewis was about eleven years old when he came to Arkansas, and remained with his parents until twenty-four years of age, when he married and began doing for himself, and has since been engaged in farming and the grist-milling business. He was also engaged in saw-milling for about three years during the war, and in 1865 was compelled to give up the business and go to Fayetteville for safety. He was married in 1845 to Miss Lettie Mills, a native of Indiana, and the following are their children: Sallie, Lydia (wife of B. F. Johnson), Lavinia (wife of Benjamin Ramey) and Matilda (wife of W. N. Jones). Mr. and Mrs. Lewis are members of the Christian Church, and he is a Republican in politics, a leading citizen of the county, and a member of the A. F. & A. M.

William M. Lewis, a retired merchant of Boonsboro, Ark., was born in the county in which he now resides, September 23, 1833, and is one of four children born to the marriage of John Lewis and Marian Coulter, both of whom were natives of Tennessee. John Lewis came to Arkansas when a young man, about 1829 or 1830, and began blacksmithing at Fayetteville, his shop being in all probability the first one on the place. He worked at his trade for a number of years, and died in 1860, lamented by a large circle of friends and acquaintances. William M. Lewis was reared and educated in Fayetteville and Cane Hill. In 1848 he began clerking in Cane Hill, and two years later began merchandising in that place, continuing until the breaking out of the war, and in 1862 enlisted as a private in Col. Brook's regiment, Confederate States army. He participated in the Prairie Grove battle, and was paroled at Fort Smith, Ark. After his return he clerked in Fayetteville for a year or two, and in February, 1868, was united in marriage to Mary E., daughter of Col. G. W. M. Reed, who is one of the prominent men of Fayetteville, and whose sketch appears in this work. Mrs. Lewis was born in Washington County, and is the mother of three daughters and one son: Josephine, Maggie C., John R. and Lizzie. After his marriage Mr. Lewis re-engaged in merchandising in Cane Hill, and until 1884 was one of the successful business men of the place. Since that time he has been retired from active business life. He is a member of the Masonic Lodge of Cane Hill, and his wife belongs to the Baptist Church. They have a pleasant and comfortable home, and a fine orchard of twenty-five acres.

Benjamin F. Little, ex-sheriff and prominent farmer, was born in Bedford County, Tenn., September 13, 1839, and is the son of John and Margaret (Johnson) Little. The father was born in Rowan County, N. C., was reared there, and came to Tennessee when a young man. He was married in Lincoln County of the last named State, but only lived there a short time, when he removed to Bedford County, of the same State, and remained there a number of years. In 1850 he moved to Washington County, Ark., and settled at West Forks, where he died October 20, 1874. He was a farmer all his life, and also took a great interest in all public affairs. The mother was reared in Lincoln County, Tenn., and died in Washington County, Ark., March 20, 1884. Benjamin F. Little was reared on a farm, and remained with his parents until he was grown, after which he went to Fayetteville, and here, in 1871, was married to Miss Caroline Woolsey, a native of Washington County, Ark., and six children were the result of this union: Mary C. (deceased), John W., infant (deceased), Emily, Lillie D. and Mamie. In 1872 Mr. Little moved to Goshen Township, where he now has a farm of over 222 acres, seventy-five acres bottom land and 120 acres under cultivation. He has devoted his time exclusively to farming, except four years while he served as sheriff of the county, from 1862 to 1872. Mr. Little is a Royal Arch Mason; is a Republican in politics, and is a straightforward, enterprising citizen. During the late war he served as sergeant of Company D, First Arkansas Cavalry, United States Volunteers, three years, and was a competent and gallant officer.

Lane, Linebarger & Co. This is one of the chief mercantile establishments of Springdale, Ark., and is well and favorably known throughout the county. I. T. Lane, the senior member of the firm, was born in Madison County, Ark., May 6, 1849, and is a son of Samuel and Nancy Lane, who were early settlers of Arkansas, and are now residing in Hindsville. I. T. Lane was reared on a farm in Northwestern Arkansas, and after reaching manhood erected the Hindsville Mills, which he conducted for some time, and then entered the mercantile business in the same town. Two years later he came to Springdale, Ark. (August 23, 1887), and has since been a member of the mercantile firm of Lane, Linebarger & Co. Besides his interest in this establishment, he owns a good farm near Hindsville, and some valuable property in Springdale. He was married to Miss Joe M. Seitz, and by her became the father of one child, Samuel. Mr. Lane is a member of the Free-Will Baptist Church, and is a Democrat in his political views. E. A. Linebarger, of the above named firm, was born in North Carolina in 1853, and is a son of M. H. and Elizabeth Linebarger, who were also born in North Carolina. The father was a mill-wright by trade, and came to Arkansas in 1871, locating first in Madison County and then in Springdale. E. A. Linebarger was born in North Carolina, and came to Arkansas with his parents, and began merchandising in Hindsville, and afterward came to Springdale and became a member of the present firm. He was married in 1877 to Margaret Moser, who was born in Tennessee in 1857, and by her is the father of three children: Arthur, Garland and Homer. The family are members of the Lutheran Church. A. E. Smyer, of the firm of Lane, Linebarger & Co., was born in North Carolina in 1853, being a son of Logan and Emeline E. Smyer, who were born and are now residing in North Carolina. At the age of eighteen years A. E. Smyer went to Kansas, but after remaining there a short time removed to Texas, thence to Northwestern Arkansas. He has been a member of the above named firm for one year. His wife, who was formerly a Miss Martha A. Cline, has borne him four children: Dora F., Charles L., Birtie and Sallie. He and wife attend the Lutheran Church, and he affiliates with the Democratic party.

Prof. William W. Lundy, A. B., the successful principal and proprietor of the Elm Springs Academy, was born in Grayson County, Va., in 1853, and is a son of Elias and Jane F. (Ross) Lundy, who were also born in Virginia. Prof. Lundy attended the common schools of Virginia, and at the age of sixteen years entered the Elk Creek Academy, which institution he attended about five years, teaching school about two sessions during this time, to assist in paying his way. He then went to North Carolina, and afterward to East Tennessee, where he entered the Hiawassee College, graduating from the same in 1868. The following two and a half years he acted as principal of the Lansing High-school, and from there went to Texas, where he taught two years in the public schools, and two years was principal of the Gordonville Academy. His health became poor, and he came to Arkansas, locating in Bloomfield, where he spent about five months as assistant of the Bloomfield Academy. He then took charge of the Osage Valley High-school for one year, going to Golden City, Mo., at the end of that time, and teaching four months, as principal of the schools of that place. Since that time he has had charge of the Elm Springs Academy, which institution is in a prosperous condition under his able management. In 1867 he was married, in North Carolina, to Mrs. Barbara A. Goodman, daughter of Daniel and Nancy C. Burkett, and their union has resulted in the birth of five children: Roy B., Elmer J., Virgie A., Brunner E. and Harley S. Prof. Lundy is a local minister in the Methodist Episcopal Church, South, and a stanch Prohibitionist.

Dr. S. D. Luther. Prominent in his professional work, as well as good citizenship, stands the name and record of the gentleman whose name heads this sketch. He is a native of the State of Tennessee, and comes of a long line of ancestry, whose lineage is directly traceable to the great reformer, Martin Luther. Dr. S. D. Luther was born in Dickson County, Tenn., May 15, 1850, the son of Travis Luther, a native of North Carolina, and grandson of George Luther, who made a settlement in that State after coming over from Germany in the latter part of the eighteenth century. Randolph County, N. C., was the early home of the Luthers in America, and from that locality descended to American genealogical history their posterity, who to-day occupy positions of importance in different parts of the United States. They were, in their earlier history, given to mechanical pursuits, and were inventors of considerable note, while in after years they were strong in their professional work and diversified interests.   The mother of Dr. S. D. Luther was Mrs. Lucy (Myatt) Luther, a lady of estimable worth, daughter of Kendrick Myatt, who moved from North Carolina and made for himself and family a home in Tennessee, and whose sterling worth and clever business abilities placed him in the front rank of the bread winners of his locality, and ensured to him great wealth.   To this family union of Travis and Lucy (Myatt) Luther were born five sons and two daughters, all now living and occupying leading and prominent positions in their respective localities.   Dr. S. D. Luther completed a good education in the schools of his district.   His early inclinations were for the study of dentistry, and to the end of completing a thorough knowledge of this business he bent all his energies. While a mere lad he not only read text books upon his profession, but also carried into practice, in his boyish form, the art of his profession, a fact which must be taken into consideration when it becomes known that he is to-day practically a master in his profession.   He completed a thorough course of study, and entered the practice at Fort Graham, Tex., where he was well and favorably known as a skillful operator in dental surgery.   Seeking a more northern climate he reluctantly abandoned Fort Graham, and located at Eureka Springs, Ark., but subsequently located at Tahlequah, I. T., where he carried his professional work to a high state of perfection, and gained a strong friendship in the hearts of the people of that sunny city.   But the longing for travel had impregnated his nature, and he soon left Tahlequah, and settled at Siloam Springs, Ark., which, after a successful practice, he left, and in the spring of 1888 located in Fayetteville, more for the reason of better school advantages than for any other reason.   However, after coming here the Doctor maintained his supremacy as elsewhere, and is to-day probably the busiest professional man in the county, standing at the head of his profession.   He was married in his native State to Miss Fannie Wright, daughter of Isaac Wright, of Hickman County, Tenn., and this union has been blessed by the birth of a son and daughter: Lulu and Clarence, who are proficients in the art of music.   Dr. Luther enjoys a lucrative practice, and is on the high road to prosperity.   He makes a specialty of gold crowns and contour work, and in this takes the lead.   He is a member of the K. of H., holding official position in that order; is a very polite and affable gentleman, a kind and indulgent husband and father, and is held in high esteem by all who know him.

James S. McClatchy, farmer and stock raiser of Vineyard Township, was born in McMinn County, Tenn., October 13, 1828, the son of Adolphus P. and Jane R. (Workman) McClatchy, natives of North Carolina and Kentucky, respectively, and both born in the year 1805.   Grandfather McClatchy emigrated from Scotland to America and settled in North Carolina, but moved from that State to Tennessee when Adolphus P. was sixteen years old.   Grandfather Workman was also a native of Scotland, and after coming to America first settled in Virginia, but later moved to Kentucky.   Miss Jane R. Workman went on a visit to Tennessee, and here met and married Mr. McClatchy, who became an extensive farmer and stock raiser.   He volunteered to go to the Florida War, was colonel of a regiment, and rendered effective service.   During the late war he lost his health, and died in 1863.   He was a Democrat in his political opinions; both he and wife are members of the Methodist Episcopal Church, South. The mother died in 1870.   Of their family of ten children nine are now living, and five of the sons were in the Confederate army.   The eldest child, James S., attained his growth on the farm, and received a good English education.   On reaching manhood he went as rod carrier in East Tennessee and Georgia, and being appointed to learn the use of the instrument, was soon promoted as a sub-engineer.   He superintended the construction of a section of the road, and then the laying of the track.   Having worked for about five years on this road he obtained the position as superintendent of the track-laying on the East Tennessee & Virginia Railroad.   In 1857 he married Miss Ellen Gilbreath, a native of Knox County, Tenn., born May 21, 1837.   She is a member of the Cumberland Presbyterian Church.   In 1858 they moved to Dallas County, Tex., and two years later moved to this county, locating where they now live.   In August, 1862, Mr. McClatchy enlisted in Company A, of Bryant's battalion, and later became second lieutenant of a Cherokee regiment, and served as such until the close of the war.   He was in a number of minor engagements, but was neither wounded nor taken prisoner. Since the war he has followed farming, and is now the owner of 390 acres of land. He is a Master Mason, and a Democrat in politics.

George W. McClure, another successful merchant at Evansville, is the son of John and Margaret (Kennedy) McClure. The father was probably born in Tennessee, although his parents came from Ireland, and the mother was also born in Tennessee. After marriage they remained in their native State until 1834, when they started for Arkansas, but the father died of cholera at Louisburg. The mother and children came on to this county, but soon after she moved to Barry County, Mo., where her death occurred in 1855. The father was a farmer by occupation, and a Democrat in politics, and the mother was a member of the Old School Presbyterian Church. Nine children of their family lived to be grown, and the youngest but one, George W., was born in Ray County, Mo., December 22, 1828. He was reared on a farm, and received a limited education, owing to the deficiency of schools. After remaining with his mother until sixteen years of age he returned to Arkansas, and here worked for a brother, but in 1849 went to California, where he mined for two years. In 1851 he opened a store in Evansville, where he remained until the breaking out of the war. In 1856 he married Miss Sarah Ward, who was born in the Cherokee Nation, and of Indian descent. Two children, Ruth and Alice, were born to this union. In 1862 Mr. McClure enlisted in Waite's Cherokee brigade (Confederate States army), and served until the close of the war. After returning from the war he found his finances very low, and after farming a year hired out as a clerk in a store, and there continued until 1874. Previous to this, in 1866, he had the misfortune to lose his wife, and has remained single ever since. From 1874 to 1877 Mr. McClure was in Flinn's mill, and from the latter date until 1886 he clerked in the store of Flinn. He then opened his present store, and has had a successful trade ever since. He began life a poor boy, but by industry and close attention to business has made all his property. He is a Democrat in politics.

William Allen McCord, M. D., was born in Bedford County, Tenn., November 6, 1858, the son of Thomas N. and Tabitha (Hight) McCord. The father was born in Tennessee December 20, 1836, and was of English descent. He was reared in his native State, and there he has always lived. He engaged in merchandising in early life, sold goods at Rover, Tenn., before the war, and at Unionville after that event. He also followed farming. He was in the Confederate service during the war, and had the misfortune to lose a leg. He is now trustee of Bedford County, Tenn. The mother was a native of Tennessee, born in 1839, and died in 1862. William Allen McCord was the elder of two children born to his parents. He was reared and educated in Bedford County, Tenn., and later read medicine under Dr. W. F. Clary. He entered the Vanderbilt University, medical department, in 1881, and graduated from the same in March, 1883. He then located at Goshen, Ark., in June, of the same year, where he has built up a large and lucrative practice, and has been eminently successful in whatever he has undertaken. He has one-third interest in the store of Slaughter & Co., and owns property, etc., in Goshen. He was married February 28, 1884, to Miss Tennie Shofner, of Wesley, Madison Co., Ark., and who died June 9, 1885. Dr. McCord then married Miss Fannie Hastings, of Chapel Hill, Marshall Co., Tenn., and this union resulted in the birth of one daughter, Alice Hastings. Dr. McCord has been a member of the county medical association since 1885, was vice-president one term, and a delegate to the State association, but did not attend. From his meager start, and from being thrown upon his own resources at an early period, Dr. McCord has made an unusually good beginning, and a bright and prosperous future is before him. He is a Democrat in politics, is a Master Mason, and both he and Mrs. McCord are members of the Cumberland Presbyterian Church.

McCormick Bros. The drug interests of Prairie Grove, Ark., are ably represented by the above named firm, which consists of William T. and Dr. E. G. McCormick, who are the sons of James W. and Mary J. (Zink) McCormick. The father belonged to one of the F. F. V.'s, and was reared and married in his native State, being engaged in the milling business, which occupation he carried on until his death. He moved to Arkansas in 1875, becoming a resident of Washington County in 1877, and in 1884 located at Prairie Grove, where he died the same year. His wife survives him. Their son, Dr. E. G. McCormick, was born in the "Old Dominion," February 10, 1855, and continued to reside in his native State until he attained his twentieth year, when he came to Arkansas with his parents. He received an excellent early education, and after coming to Arkansas began the study of medicine at Carlisle, being several years engaged in studying that science, and in teaching school, following the latter occupation in Arkansas and Iowa. He took his first course of lectures in the winters of 1878–79, at the Missouri Medical College, of St. Louis, and in the spring of the latter year located in Crawford County, and engaged in practicing his profession until 1880, when he returned to college, and was graduated as an M. D. from that institution in the spring of 1881. He then resumed his practice in Crawford County, but in July, 1884, went to Florida, where he spent three months in looking over the State, then returned to Washington County, Ark., where he has since been a successful practitioner. He and his brother have been engaged in the drug business since 1884, and, in connection with their medicines, carry a large line of paints and oils. The Doctor is president of the Canning Association of Prairie Grove. He was married in Crawford County, February 10, 1884, to Miss Mamie Gilliam, a daughter of Dr. C. D. Gilliam, by whom he is the father of two children: William Grover and Myrtle. Dr. McCormick and wife are members of the Presbyterian Church, and he is a Master Mason. William T. McCormick, a member of the firm of McCormick Bros., of Prairie Grove, Ark., was born in Augusta County, Va., October 21, 1858, and came to Arkansas in 1875, and to Washington County in 1877. Like his brother he received good educational advantages, and after coming to Arkansas assisted his father in the mill until 1881, when he located in Prairie Grove, where he clerked for some time in a drug store. They engaged in their present business in 1884, and have built up a large and paying trade. He is one of the stockholders in the Canning Association, and is also its treasurer, being one of the men to establish that enterprise. He is a consistent member of the Methodist Episcopal Church, South, and has the confidence and esteem of all who know him.

Hugh F., J. S. and J. O. McDanield were born in Muskingum County, Ohio, the parents being B. F. and Sarah (Terrell) McDanield. The father was born in Frederick, Md., and when a young man immigrated to Ohio, where he married and reared his large family of eleven children. He and his wife are now enjoying their old age in Wyandotte County, Kas. Hugh F., the elder of our three subjects, was born in 1843, and died June 29, 1888. His boyhood was spent upon a farm, and upon the outbreak of the war, although scarcely of age, he enlisted in the Seventy-sixth Regiment of Ohio Volunteers, serving in battle and on picket line for three years. Re-enlisting at the end of that time in the veteran corps, he served till the close of the war. He then returned home, but being of an enterprising nature soon went to Kansas City, and until 1873 engaged in mercantile enterprises at that place. He then took a contract to build the Kansas Midland Railway from Kansas City to Topeka, and after its completion operated a ranch in the western portion of Texas some time. He then went to Houston and contracted to build the Texas Western Railway, which he completed in 1877. Returning then to Missouri he engaged in the railroad tie and lumber business. In 1881, having learned that the San Francisco Railway would build this way, he came to Fayetteville for the purpose of furnishing ties for the new division. He located permanently at this place, which is in a finely timbered country, and soon began the shipment of railroad ties to western markets, increasing their business year after year until he accumulated a large fortune. They furnished the Santa Fe Railway nearly all its ties, and in 1887 shipped 15,000 car loads, aggregating a business of $2,000,000. In 1886 Mr. McDanield began the building of the Fayetteville & Little Rock Railway, and in 1887 sold it to the 'Frisco Road, which now operates it. He was the founder of the town of St. Paul, which is destined to become a famous summer resort of Northwest Arkansas, being beautifully situated among the mountains. September 9, 1884, Mr. McDanield married Mrs. Emma Coons, of Kirksville, Mo. His death was largely and sincerely mourned, the community thereby losing one of its most honored men, and the State one of its most enterprising and influential citizens. J. O. McDanield was also engaged in farming during his boyhood, and for some years farmed in Benton County, Mo. He joined his brothers in the railroad business in the West, and possesses the same business qualities which contributed to their success. October 16, 1879, he married Miss Frances Haberthier, a native of Warren County, Mo., who is the mother of two children: John and Sarah C. He is a Knight Templar and a Republican.

William McIlroy (deceased), whose early life was one of hardship and pri-

vation, and whose subsequent career shows what can be accomplished by industry, economy and perseverance, was born in Rockingham County, N. C., July
24, 1812, the son of James and Mary (Small) McIlroy, and grandson of William Mc-
Ilroy, a farmer, whose father was a native of Scotland, and whose mother was
born in Ireland. · The parents of the subject of this sketch were natives of Rockingham County, N. C., and the father was a shoemaker by trade.   The mother
died in that county when William McIlroy was but five or six years old, and of
the four children left at her death, none are living.   William received a limited
education, and worked on the farm from early boyhood.   In 1835 he abandoned
farm life and began clerking in the store of Col. John P. Long, at Chattanooga,
Tenn., where he remained two years.   Previous to this, in 1832, he married Miss
Missouri Vandyke, a native of South Carolina, and the daughter of John Vandyke, a farmer and slave-holder.   Two children blessed this union: Andrew
Jackson, who was born in Habersham County, Ga., in 1834, and died in Little
Rock, Ark., in 1863, while serving in the Southern army; and Melinda H. Vanhoose, who was born in Washington County, Ark., and who died in 1864.   Mr.
McIlroy was next married to Mrs. Eliza Jane Russell, in Kentucky, in 1838.   She
was a native of Virginia, and died in Washington County, Ark., in 1864, at the
age of sixty years.   In June, 1838 Mr. McIlroy settled with his family on a
small farm at head-waters of the White River, Madison County, Ark., and here,
in connection with farming, carried on merchandising on a small scale for about
eleven years.   He commenced selling goods in Fayetteville in 1855, on a capital
of $7,500, and in 1872 he commenced banking on a capital of $25,000, and
followed this business up to the time of his death, which occurred in
1886.   By a partnership, with which he started the bank, he lost $40,000 in the
year 1875, and after that Mr. McIlroy ran the business without a partner.
The bank has now a cash capital of many thousand dollars, and besides this
Mr. McIlroy left real estate valued at about $20,000.   The amount of bank de-
posits equals $120,000, and a general banking business is done, with correspond-
ents in St. Louis, New York and Little Rock.   Mr. McIlroy was never engaged
in any public enterprises, has no military record, and never held an office, except
that of road overseer in the Boston Mountains; he never inherited a cent in his
life, and when first starting out for himself worked for $7.50 a month. His habits
were always good; he never gambled, was not dissipated, but amused himself by
going to the country dances, being very fond of that pastime.   He never belonged to any secret organization; was a Whig up to the late war, when he cast
his vote with the Democrats, and after that time affiliated with that party.
Mr. McIlroy's third wife, whom he married in 1865, and whose maiden name
was Martha Brooks, was born in Tennessee, and was left an orphan when quite
young, after which she was partly reared by the family of Mr. McIlroy.   By his
third marriage Mr. McIlroy became the father of five children, all born in Fayetteville: William R., James H., Charles W., Anna May and Kate. Mr McIlroy
died in full communion with the faith of the Episcopal Church, having joined
that church in 1846, and of which he had been vestryman for thirty years.   A
fellow townsman in speaking of him says: "No one surpassed him for industry,
sobriety and precision in all business transactions. He was discreet in all things,
and dealt accurately even to a cent.   He was a quiet, peaceable man, and his
reputation is without a stain.   He leaned too much on certainties not to be a
success."

W. R. McIlroy, banker, is one of the highly respected and representative
young business men of the county.   He was born at Fayetteville October 13,
1866, and is the son of William McIlroy [see sketch].   After receiving a good
public-school education in this city, he entered the Arkansas Industrial University, which he left while in the sophomore year to enter his father's bank, the
health of the latter becoming impaired and his assistance being required.   He
had early in life displayed rare business qualities, and after working some time
in the bank his services became so valuable that he became a member of the
firm, after his father's death, which occurred September 13, 1886.   Mr. McIlroy
and his mother are by the father's will made sole executors of the estate.   In
July the name of the bank was changed from "William McIlroy & Co." to
"The Banking House of McIlroy & Co."   Mr. McIlroy has inherited his father's
characteristics of business integrity and worth, and is deserving of the honor
and respect with which the community regard him.   He is interested in the
growth of the city, and greatly aided in the organization of the Fayetteville

Electric Light Company, in which he is a stockholder.   He is the present city treasurer, and is treasurer in the K. of H. and K. of P. lodges in this place. He is an active member of the Episcopal Church, and is a liberal donator to all laudable charitable enterprises.

William A. McKinzie, retired merchant and farmer, and ex-postmaster of Durham, Ark., was born in Sevier County, Tenn., in 1826. His parents, Charles and Sarah (Ellis) McKinzie, were born, reared and married in South Carolina, and about 1818 located in Tennessee, where they resided until 1847, then going to Georgia; and after living in Murray County eleven years they moved to Comanche County, Tex., where the father was killed by the Indians in 1863. The mother's death occurred in Georgia, leaving a family of five children: John (residing in Texas), Nancy (deceased), James, William A. and Kenneth (who was killed in a battle with the Indians in Comanche County, Tex., in 1858 or 1859). After the mother's death the father married Stacy Murray, who bore him one child that died in infancy. William A. McKinzie was reared in Tennessee, but moved with his parents to Georgia, where he learned the wagon and blacksmith's trade, and also attended school. He was married at the age of twenty-six, and located on a part of the home place, where he lived until about 1856, when he came to Arkansas. After residing near Fayetteville for about a year, he came to Washington County, where he worked at his trade and farmed until 1878, and then engaged in the mercantile business at Durham, being appointed postmaster of the town the same year, and held the position until 1888. He was first married, to Mary Shields, who died October 22, 1873, having borne four children: John H. (deceased), Sarah L., Charles S. (deceased) and William J. (deceased). October 29, 1874, Mr. McKinzie married Mary F. Masters, who died May 19, 1879, and May 29, 1884, he married his present wife. They are members of the church, and he is a Democrat in politics and a Master Mason. He helped organize the township in which he resides, and during the late war served two years in Gen. Cabel's brigade. He has a good farm of 195 acres, with sixty-five or seventy acres under cultivation.

Thomas McKnight, farmer and stock raiser, was born in Lawrence County, Ark., March 23, 1823, and is a son of John and Elizabeth (Dillingham) McKnight, and grandson of William McKnight, who was from North Carolina, and was a soldier in the Revolutionary War. He afterward came to Kentucky, in the early history of that State, and in 1818 came to Arkansas.   John McKnight, the father, was born in North Carolina, and came to Arkansas with his father, and became a representative farmer of Lawrence County. He died in 1858, and his wife in 1832. They were the parents of eight children, two of whom are living. After the mother's death the father married a Mrs. Underwood, by whom he had four children. Thomas McKnight made his father's house his home until fifteen years of age, and then began working on a farm in Washington County.   In 1846 he enlisted in the Mexican War, serving until its close, when he returned home and resumed farming. In 1848 he married Miss Elizabeth Bloyd, who was born on the farm where they now reside, and to their union eleven children were born, seven now living: William G., Elizabeth (wife of William H. Brown), Mary (wife of James Carter), James W., Henry T., Martha (wife of James Gilbreath), and Ollie (wife of Thomas Carter). In 1883 Mr. McKnight laid out the town of West Fork, and has been one of the active men in building up the place. In 1862 he enlisted in Company A, First Arkansas Cavalry, and after serving one year was discharged on account of disability, and after returning home, although sick and unable to work, was continually annoyed by the bushwhackers. He is a member of the Rutherford Post No. 11, G. A. R., and is a member of the Knights of the Horse. He and wife belong to the Christian Church.

Wiley Paul McNair, agent at Fayetteville, Ark., of the 'Frisco Railway, was born in Charleston, Tallahatchee Co., Miss., June 21, 1849, and is a son of Daniel and Elizabeth (Scallion) McNair. The father was born near Edinburgh, Scotland, and at an early day came to America with his parents, who made a settlement in North Carolina near Wilmington. In 1854 Daniel McNair removed with his family to Gibson County, Tenn., where he spent the remainder of his days. His wife was a daughter of Jesse Scallion, a native of Ireland. Wiley Paul McNair was reared in Tennessee, and after acquiring a good education in the common schools began teaching school in order to obtain means to complete his education. He entered Bryant & Stratton's Commercial College at

Nashville, Tenn., from which institution he graduated in 1868.   He had gained a fair knowledge of telegraphy in the meantime, and upon leaving college applied himself to this work, and after spending five years as clerk in a retail house, in 1873 entered the employ of the Atlantic & Pacific (now the 'Frisco) Railroad, at the Ozark Iron Works, Missouri, now Newburg, Phelps Co., Mo., and in 1883 came to Fayetteville, where he remained two years, and then went to Peirce City, Mo., but the following year came back to Fayetteville, where he has since made his home.   He is a Mason and is a worthy Sir Knight of Baldwin Commandery No. 4, and is also a member of the K. of P. and S. K.   He is a stockholder in the Building and Loan Association of Fayetteville.   While a resident of Tennessee he was married to Miss Nancy A. Flippin, a daughter of James A. Flippin, of Gibson County, Tenn., and their union has resulted in the birth of two sons and two daughters: William Daniel, a telegraph operator at Fayetteville and a student in the A. I. U.; Maud and May, who are also attending that institution, and Wiley Paul, Jr.   The mother is a member of the Cumberland Presbyterian Church, which house of worship the family attend.

Hon. Hosea M. Maguire (deceased) was born about 1813 in Simpson County, Ky., near Bowling Green.   His parents were natives of North Carolina, and were of Scotch-Irish extraction, their parents being early pioneer settlers of the Carolinas.   The parents of our subject came to Washington County, Ark., in an early day, where they made a home and lived the remainder of their active and useful lives.   They were faithful and consistent members of the Cumberland Presbyterian Church.   Hosea M. Maguire was reared in this county, and in early manhood adopted merchandising and trading as an occupation.   In these he met with success, but upon the outbreak of the Civil War, being a strong Southern sympathizer, he gave liberally to the cause of secession, and upon the close of that memorable conflict, like a large number of his contemporaries, he found himself without home or fortune.   Being of a sanguine disposition, however, he at once began to retrieve his broken fortunes, and to that end engaged in the manufacture of tobacco.   This industry yielded him a comfortable income, and he later resumed mercantile pursuits with such success that upon his death he left quite a fortune.   In 1850 he was united in marriage to Miss Sarah Louisa Trammel, who bore him a family of two sons (now deceased) and seven daughters.   After the death of his first wife Mr. Maguire married Mary Smith, widow of Andrew Smith and a sister of his first wife.   Three of the daughters borne by his first wife are now living: Mrs. A. L. Williams [see sketch of husband], Mrs. Mac Devin [see sketch] and Miss Addie Maguire.   One daughter (now deceased) became the wife of W. D. Moore [see sketch].   At the time of his death, July 23, 1888, Mr. Maguire was representing Washington County in the Legislature. He was a faithful and consistent member of the Cumberland Presbyterian Church, and a prominent member of the Masonic fraternity, which buried him with full honors.   He was a quiet and unostentatious man, who journeyed through life upon the principle that "whatever is worth doing at all is worth doing well."   His prosperity only enhanced the natural charity with which he was endowed.   The poor and needy were ever sure of receiving words of comfort and material assistance from him, and his death was mourned by a large circle of friends and associates.   He reared and educated his family well, and was rewarded by seeing them become honorable citizens.   His daughters who married became the helpmeets of men of esteem and acknowledged ability.

A. C. Males was born in Knox County, Ind., on the 14th of May, 1820.   His parents, Solomon and Susan (Spain) Males, were born in Knox County, Ind., and Virginia, respectively.   The father's birth occurred in 1790, and he was reared to manhood in his native State, his marriage occurring in 1817.   He located on a farm, where he was engaged in farming and working at the shoemaker's trade, but after a number of years took up his abode in Gibson County, where he died in 1860.   He was a soldier in the War of 1812, and was a participant in the battle of Tippecanoe.   Four of his ten children are living: Thorton, William, Martha (wife of S. F. Tyner) and A. C.   The mother is still living, and resides in Illinois with her daughter Martha.   A. C. Males was reared in Gibson County, Ind., and throughout life has followed the occupation of farming.   He came to Arkansas in 1839, and the following year was married to Martha J. Skelton, who was born in Indiana in 1822, and died in 1863, leaving a family of seven children, five of whom are now living: William N. and John F. (deceased), and James A., John F., Archibald, Francis J. and Prudence J. (wife of John Brown), living.   Mr. Males' second marriage was with Elizabeth Evans, who was born in Kentucky, and died in 1872, having borne one child, Calvin. Lydia A. Keton, of Kentucky, became his third wife in 1873, and their union has been blessed in the birth of three children: George W., Posey and Hamilton.   Mr. and Mrs. Males are members of the Christian Church, in which he has been a deacon for about a year, and they are the owners of ninety-five acres of land, with fifty acres under cultivation.   In 1862 Mr. Males enlisted in Company B, First Arkansas Cavalry, and served until receiving his discharge August 23, 1865.   He is now a member of the G. A. R.

Francis J. Males, druggist at West Fork, Ark., was born in Washington County, Ark., on the 22d of February, 1852, being a son of A. C. and Martha J. (Skelton) Males.   The father was born in Posey County, Ind., and at an early day came to Arkansas, settling on a farm on White River, in Washington County, but in 1855 located on his present farm.   During the late war he served three years in the Federal army, being a member of the First Arkansas Cavalry. Francis J. Males' boyhood days were spent in following the plow and attending the common schools of Washington County.   After his marriage to Miss Mary Reed, which occurred May 15, 1879, he located on a farm near West Fork, Ark., and there his wife died October 20, 1880, leaving an infant daughter, Ora L.   November 29, 1885, Miss Anna Perry became his wife, and has borne him one child, Lillie B.   Mrs. Males is a daughter of Robert Perry, of Washington County.   Mr. Males purchased a distillery in 1881, and after operating it four years sold out, and engaged in the drug business at West Fork, his being the only establishment of the kind in the town.   He is doing a good business, and owns the store building and a good lot and residence in the town.   He is a member of Valley Grove Lodge No. 336, A. F. & A. M., and is J. D. of the lodge, and also belongs to West Fork Lodge No. 90, I. O. O. F.

Peter Mankins is one of the oldest settlers and farmers now residing in White River Valley, Washington County, Ark., and was born in the "Blue Grass State" (Floyd County) August 1, 1813.   His father, who also bore the name of Peter Mankins, was born in Maryland September 19, 1770, and when he was about eighteen years of age went to North Carolina, where he was married to Mrs. Rachel (Bracken) Lewis, and soon after moved to Kentucky.   He resided on the Big Sandy River, in Floyd County, until 1827, when he went to Vermilion County, Ill., but a year later returned to Kentucky.   From 1832 to 1833 they were again residents of Illinois, and in the latter year came to Arkansas, landing near the head-waters of the White River, and shortly after located on the farm now owned by Mr. Mankins, whose name heads this sketch.   Here the father resided until his death, having attained the extreme old age of one hundred and eleven years and five months.   His death occurred very suddenly and without pain, while apparently as well as usual.   He had been extremely healthy all his life, and his mind was clear and active until the last.   He followed the occupation of farming throughout life, and while in Kentucky operated a whisky distillery, and in his political views was a Democrat.   He was married three times, and by his first wife became the father of eleven children, four of whom are now living: Millie, Rachel, Sarah and Peter.   The mother of these children was first married to a Mr. Lewis, to whom she bore three children: George (deceased), Bracken, who resides in Washington County and is eighty-seven years of age, and Lydia (deceased).   Peter Mankins grew to manhood in Floyd County, Ky., and in 1833 came to Arkansas with a man by the name of George Lewis, and was followed by his parents soon afterward.   In 1849 he made a trip to California in search of gold, and his efforts were attended with the best of success, finding one piece that was worth $416.   He returned home in February, 1851, via the Isthmus of Panama and New Orleans, with $3,750, which was one-seventh of what he and his comrades found.   He has dealt quite extensively in stock, and has driven large droves of cattle from Colorado, near the Texas line, to Chicago, and hogs from his home in Washington County to within 150 miles of New Orleans.   During the trouble in Salt Lake, Utah, in 1857, he sold $34,000 worth of cattle to the United States agent, and up to the breaking out of the late Civil War was engaged in stock dealing.   In 1861 he organized a company of eighty-four men as State troops (Brooks' regiment), purchasing clothing for sixty-four of them at a cost of $550, but afterward turned the camp outfit over to George Van Hoose.   In 1863 he swam the Arkansas River with 300 soldiers shooting at him all the time.   Since the war he has been engaged in farming, and owns 120 acres of land in the home place, and has seven claims of mining lands in Polk County, Ark. He was at one time the wealthiest man in the White River Valley, and was very liberal with his wealth, but lost the greater portion of it during the war. He was married to Narcissa Mills, who was born in 1816 and died in 1863, and by her became the father of ten children, nine of whom are living: Rachel, wife of William Ballard; Henry; Nancy J., now the wife of Mr. Causby; Mary, Mrs. Cate; Walter; Priscilla, Mrs. Strain; Elizabeth, Mrs. Simpson; Millie, deceased; Peter, and Sarah, Mrs. Ballard. Mr. Mankins took for his second wife Mrs. Easter (Hanna) Gilliland, who was born in Kentucky in 1824, and their union was blessed in the birth of one child, Easter J., wife of L. A. Gilliland. Mrs. Mankins was first married to J. Gilliland, and by him became the mother of one daughter, Clementine, wife of J. Crawford. Mr. Mankins has given each of his children a start in life, and is one of the old and highly honored citizens of the county. He has always been deeply interested in all matters pertaining to the welfare of the county, and has given substantial aid to educational and religious institutions.

Walter Mankins is one of the prominent farmers and citizens of Reed Township, Washington Co., Ark., and was born on the farm where he now lives, February 2, 1842, and is a son of Walter and Polly (Lowe) Mankins, he being the seventh of their nine children. His father died when he was about nine years of age, and he then made his home with his uncle, Peter Mankins [see sketch], with whom he remained until he reached manhood. At the breaking out of the late Civil War he was seized with the war spirit, and enlisted in the company which was afterward commanded by Capt. Van Hoose, and was a brave and faithful soldier for three years. He was in a number of severe skirmishes, and after being mustered out at the close of the war he returned home, and engaged in the peaceful pursuit of farming. He was married in 1866 to Miss Luvinia Osborne, who was born in Washington County, and is the mother of three children: Martha Ann, Parthenia and Lydia, who are all living with their parents. The family are members of the Protestant Methodist Church, and Mr. Mankins is a steward in the same. He has always taken a deep interest in church and educational work, and is a strong supporter of the principles of the Democratic party. He has a good farm of 280 acres, with ninety under cultivation, and ranks among the prominent agriculturists of the county.

William H. F. Marion, carpenter and builder, and a man prominently connected with that industry in Washington County, is a native of Sullivan County, Tenn., born September 11, 1835, the son of John and Lydia Louisa (Hicks) Marion, both descendants of old families of that State, and grandson of John Marion, Sr., who was a native of South Carolina, and a relative of Gen. Francis Marion, of Revolutionary fame. Lydia L. Hicks' father, James Hicks, was a native of North Carolina, and a farmer by occupation. William H. F. Marion was educated in his native State, and served an apprenticeship at the mill-wright trade with a Mr. Odell. He obtained a thorough knowledge of the business, and in September, 1858, left Rogersville, Tenn., where he spent three years in professional work, came to Fayetteville, Ark., and remained engaged in his trade until July 5, 1861, when he entered the ranks of the Confederate army, serving under Gens. Eagan and Hawthorne, Churchill's division and King's regiment. He served at Oak Hill, Elkhorn, Prairie Grove and many minor engagements; was in active and honorable service until the close of the war, and his regiment was the last to surrender at Fort Smith. When peace once more smiled upon the nation Mr. Marion went to Missouri and Montana, where he was engaged principally in his professional work for thirteen years. He then returned to Fayetteville (1881), and has since been engaged in the building business. He was married in this city to Miss Elizabeth Van Hoose, sister of J. H. Van Hoose [see sketch]. They have an interesting family of children: Lena Annette, Henry Monroe Willie, Frances and Annie. One child, Mabel, died at the age of three years in Montana, and was buried in the beautiful valley of Gallatin, near Fort Ellis. Another, Lula, died at the age of fourteen, after his return to Fayetteville. She was a natural musician, as are the other children. Mr. Marion is a member of the K. of L., and is an attendant at the Cumberland Presbyterian Church, of which his wife and children are members.

Squire B. Marrs. The Marrs family was first represented in Arkansas in 1817 by James and Elizabeth (Robison) Marrs, who were born in the "Old Dominion," and who immigrated first to Kentucky and then to Arkansas.

After residing in Lawrence County, of the latter State, for about five years, they moved to near Fort Smith, and about 1827 took up their abode on Loveless' Purchase. A year later they came to Washington County and entered a tract of land in what is now Marrs Hill Township, and here Mr. Marrs became the first postmaster of the township. The mother died a short time after they located in Arkansas, and the father's death occurred in 1881, at the advanced age of ninety-three years, having lived sixty-four years in Arkansas. Squire B. Marrs is one of their seven children, and was born in Logan County, Ky., in 1811, receiving his education in the common schools of Arkansas. He was reared on a farm, and after his marriage in 1836 to Miss Rachel Kinchelow entered the farm of 350 acres where he now lives. In 1849 he went overland to California, where he was engaged in mining and trading for about three years, and in 1852 returned to his home. His wife was born in Tennessee, and with her parents immigrated to Washington County in 1835. She became the mother of six children, the following of whom are living: William O.; Elizabeth M., wife of Caleb Marshall; Isabel A., wife of Pleasant Marshall, and James R. The mother died in 1848, and Mr. Marrs, in 1852, after his return from California, married Matilda Ervin, a native of Tennessee, who bore him three children: Samuel E., Squire B., Jr., and Susanna C., wife of Hugh Rogers. In 1862 the family located in Belle County, Tex., where they remained until 1866, and then returned to the farm in Washington County, Ark., which had grown up to weeds and brush and was destitute of fences. Mr. Marrs now has his farm well improved and 100 acres under cultivation, and after his long life of well-spent labor can spend the remainder of his days in ease and quietness. He has been identified with Washington County for many years, the interests of which he has ever had deeply at heart. He has served the people in various public positions, and has always been one of the leading citizens of the county.

Charles G. Marrs, a member of the prosperous mercantile firm of Hardy & Marrs, of Prairie Grove, Ark., and a native of Washington County, was born on the 15th of February, 1855. His father, Andy Marrs, was also born in this county, whither his father, Isaac Marrs, had moved, at a very early day, from the State of Tennessee. Andy Marrs was married, in Washington County, to Winnie Carter, who was born in Tennessee, and throughout life followed the occupation of farming. He served in the late war, and while visiting at home was taken ill and died. Charles G. Marrs' boyhood days were spent on the farm and in attending the common schools, and after attaining manhood he began farming on his own responsibility, continuing this occupation for several years, being also engaged in buying and shipping stock. He first began merchandising in Prairie Grove in 1885, and has successfully continued up to the present time. He is a charter member and director of the Canning Association at Prairie Grove, and, in connection with his business, owns and operates a farm near the town. November 27, 1873, his marriage to Miss Effie McKeever was celebrated. She was born, reared and educated in Washington County, and became the mother of seven children: James Andrews, Ellen, Ollie D., Griffin, Mack, Edward and an infant daughter. Mr. and Mrs. Marrs are members of the Methodist Episcopal Church South, and he is a member of the Prairie Grove Masonic lodge.

Hon. Samuel Ervin Marrs. Among the prominent and highly respected citizens of Washington County stands the name of Samuel E. Marrs, who is a native of Arkansas, born on a farm in Marrs Hill Township, Washington County, April 15, 1853, and the son of 'Squire Brooks and Matilda (Ervin) Marrs. His grandfather, James Marrs, left his Kentucky home at an early date, and settled in Lawrence County, Ark., about 1822. Subsequently, about 1827, he moved to Washington County, of the same State, when his son, 'Squire Brooks Marrs, was about sixteen years of age. Samuel E. Marrs grew to manhood on the farm, and after obtaining a good common-school education in public schools supplemented it with a literary and scientific course at the State University. He taught school for some time after graduation, and while engaged in this occupation at Viney Grove was elected to the Twenty-third General Assembly of the Arkansas Legislature in 1880, and re-elected the following term. In the meantime he applied himself to the study of law, and was admitted to the Arkansas bar in 1884. He was then elected mayor of Fayetteville, and filled this position one term. In December, 1884, he made the purchase of the Fayetteville *Democrat*, in company with J. N. Tillman, and since that time Mr. Marrs has been proprietor and editor of this paper.

Daniel B. Mason, one of the oldest and most respected citizens of Cincinnati, Ark., was born in Marion County, Ala., September 23, 1820, and his father is the fifth of seven children born to Elijah and Temple Mason. His father was a gunsmith by trade and a splendid workman. He spent most of his time in Franklin County, Tenn., where he died at the age of ninety-five. The mother died in Alabama in 1826, when her son, Daniel B., was but six years old. After her death Daniel B. was bound out to a man by the name of John Woods, a drinking, worthless fellow, with whom he remained until seventeen years of age. He then ran away to Murfreesboro, Tenn., and here learned the blacksmith trade. In 1840 he moved to Washington County, Ark., having worked in Benton County, Ark., and Indian Territory until 1849; he put up a shop in Cincinnati, Ark., and with the exception of about four years carried on that business until 1882. In 1844 he wedded Miss Elizabeth A., daughter of P. V. Rhea, and a native of Lincoln County, Tenn., born January 8, 1824. She came to this county with her parents when quite young. To the union of Mr. and Mrs. Mason were born ten children, eight now living, five sons and three daughters. Three of the sons are blacksmiths. Mr. Mason has always been an active business man, and is now running the Travelers' Home, the Cincinnati and Fayetteville hack line, and is the owner of 100 acres of land. He is, politically, a Democrat; is a Royal Arch Mason, having held all the offices in the Chapter and Blue Lodge, and has for many years been justice of the peace, still holding that office. He has always been liberal in supporting schools, churches and all other worthy enterprises; he and wife are members of the Cumberland Presbyterian Church.

Zacharias C. Mason, who was born and reared in White River Township, Washington Co., Ark., was born November 27, 1858, and is a son of David C. and Frances J. (Goodrich) Mason, who were born in Arkansas and Missouri, respectively. At the age of sixteen years the father went to Texas, and after residing in that State for three years returned home, and after residing on the old home place for about five years took the California gold fever, and went West to seek his fortune, his mining operations in that State being attended with the best of results. At the end of two years he returned home, via the Isthmus of Panama and New Orleans, and purchased the farm on which he now resides. He was married in 1856, and the following are his children who are living: Zacharias C., John F., James H. (who lives with his father on the home place), Mary A., Joseph P. and Eliza Belle. The mother of these children was born in Missouri, and as her parents died when she was quite young she was reared by her uncle, George Goodrich. Mr. Mason has been a minister of the Protestant Methodist Church for about twenty years and has been president of the Fort Smith District Conference since 1887. He is a Democrat in politics, and is a member of the Masonic fraternity, and the I. O. of K. of the H. His son, Zacharias C. Mason, was reared in Washington County, and attended both the common and graded schools, and in 1878 united his fortunes with those of Miss Jennie Arnett, who was born in Tennessee in 1863. She was brought to Arkansas by her parents, George and Lorinda (Rodgers) Arnett, when she was six years of age and was reared to womanhood in Washington County. To her parents were born six children: John D., Luke, Martha (widow of William Douglas), Joseph C., Addie (wife of R. Sharp), Jennie (wife of Mr. Mason) and Emma. Both parents reside in Washington County, and are members of the Cumberland Presbyterian Church. Mr. Mason and wife became the parents of four children: Walter Lee, George E. (deceased), Roy Ernest and an infant son. Mr. Mason has a good farm of 175 acres, with 120 under cultivation, and in his political views is a Democrat. He belongs to the Protestant Methodist Church and the Masonic fraternity, and his wife is a member of the Cumberland Presbyterian Church.

John Masters, stock farmer, of Durham Township, Washington Co., Ark., and one of its oldest settlers, was born in the " Palmetto State " September 30, 1820, and is a son of Michael and Elizabeth (Homesley) Masters. and grandson of John Masters, who was of German descent, and a soldier in the Revolutionary War, serving as orderly-sergeant under Gen. Morgan. He was the father of a large family who grew to maturity, and he and wife died in Missouri, at an advanced age. Michael Masters located in Wayne County, Mo., in the spring of 1821, but six years later sold out, and came to Washington County, Ark., being the first man to enter land on Cane Hill. He afterward moved to the

White River Valley, where he reared his family, and died about 1831, aged forty years. His wife was born in Virginia, and became the mother of seven children: John, David J. (deceased), Nancy (Mrs. Guthrie), Margaret (Mrs. Hash, deceased), Elizabeth (Mrs. Heiser, deceased), Mary Adaline (deceased) and David, who was a soldier in the Confederate army, and was killed in battle in 1862. The mother of these children, after the death of Mr. Masters, was married to Jesse Hawk, of Tennessee, by whom she had a family of five children, all of whom lived to be grown, and all now dead except George W. and Lucinda E., wife of Andrew Davis. The mother died near Fayetteville, in 1867, at the age of sixty-three years, and Mr. Hawk died in Washington County in 1885, whither he had come in 1834 or 1835. John Masters came with his parents to Arkansas in 1827, and here grew to manhood, was educated, and has since made his home. His first investment in real estate was in 1852, and comprised eighty acres of land, on which he now lives. He has continued to add to this until he now has 420 acres of land in all, and has 140 acres under cultivation. In 1846 he was married to Miss Ann Ball, who was born in Kentucky, and came to Arkansas in 1837, and their union has resulted in the birth of ten children: David J., John L. (deceased), William P. George R., Mary F. (deceased), Martha J. (Frits), Nancy A. (Mrs. Drain), Sarah A. (Mrs. Robbins), Narcissa J. (Mrs. Robbins) and Arizona (Mrs. Largen). Mrs. Masters has been a member of the Baptist Church for fifty years. During the war Mr. Masters served as cavalryman in the Confederate army for over three years, and did all in his power to aid the Southern cause. He is a member of the I. O. O. F., K. of H., is a Master Mason, and is a strong supporter of the Democratic party.

David J. Masters, farmer, of Durham Township, Washington Co., Ark., and son of John Masters, whose sketch appears elsewhere, was born in Madison County, Ark., August 22, 1846, and made his parents' house his home until he attained his twenty-fourth year, with the exception of the time spent in the army. March 10, 1862, he enlisted in Company K, First Arkansas Volunteer Cavalry, and served until receiving his discharge in 1865, when he returned home and continued to reside with his parents until 1870, at which time he began farming for himself on rented land. This he continued for seven years, and then purchased his present farm of 140 acres, partly under cultivation. He has devoted the most of his time to railroad contracting, furnishing timber for railroad bridges, etc., and since the completion of the St. Paul branch of the 'Frisco line, in 1886, he has been dealing in tie timber. He has also done a great deal of freighting for Sedalia, Peirce City, Joplin, Fayetteville, Fort Smith, Ozark and the adjoining counties. Mr. Masters was first married in 1868 to Miss Sarah Ann Thompson, who was born in Benton County, February 5, 1850, and by her became the father of one child, Willie Alice, who is now the wife of W. P. Bruce, of Crawford County, Ark., and the mother of one child, Maud Lee. Mrs. Masters died November 7, 1868, and Mr. Masters afterward married Mrs. Sarah E. (Jones) Morton, a native of Washington County, born February 4, 1846. She grew to womanhood in Texas, and was first married to W. A. Morton, who died about one year after their marriage. Six children have been born to Mr. and Mrs. Masters: Robert Lee, Georgia Ann, John H., Mary V., Katie E. (deceased) and Effie. Mr. Masters is a Democrat, a Master Mason and a member of the Knights of the Horse. His wife belongs to the Christian Church.

John Mayes, an old and prominent citizen of Washington County, Ark., was born in Guernsey County, East Tenn., June 23, 1810. His parents, William and Elizabeth (Moody) Mayes, were natives of Virginia, the father being a soldier in the War of 1812, and a farmer and mechanic by occupation. John Mayes was married in his native State to Miss Sarah McGhee, who bore him four sons and seven daughters; two daughters died in infancy, but the rest grew to manhood and womanhood. In 1848 John Mayes and family left East Tennessee and came to Washington County, Ark., where he has been identified with building interests ever since. He has been a consistent member of the Missionary Baptist Church since 1843, and since 1856 has been a secularized minister of that denomination. He belongs to the Masonic fraternity, is an exemplary citizen, and a kind neighbor and considerate friend. His eldest son, William Zera Mayes, was born in Grainger County, Tenn., May 28, 1835, and was reared in Arkansas, where he adopted his father's calling, that of a house carpenter and builder, and followed that occupation in Colorado from 1859 to 1860. From that date until 1875 he continued his trade in Arkansas, when he removed to his farm and there resided until his death, which occurred August 7, 1888. He was universally respected and esteemed, and his death was lamented by all who knew him. He was a skillful carpenter, and erected some of the finest residences and business blocks in Fayetteville, among which are McIlroy's Bank, the, Mountain House, S. K. Stone's store, and the State University. May 1, 1860, he was united in marriage to Miss Sarah E. Campbell, a daughter of James and Minerva (Simpson) Campbell, natives respectively of Tennessee and Kentucky, the former being born in 1809 and the latter in 1814. They were very early settlers of Arkansas, and were married at Evansville in 1833. Mr. Mayes and wife became the parents of three children: Nora, wife of W. M. Simmons; Ida, and John F., the eldest of the family and the only son. The latter was born in Washington County on the 16th of March, 1862, and, after receiving an exceptionally good common-school education, he entered the A. I. U., taking a scientific and classical course, and graduated from that institution as an A. B. in 1883, ranking third in a class of fifteen. After leaving college he was engaged in stock dealing for about a year, but gave up this position and became superintendent in charge of the lumber department of J. S. McDaniel, of Fayetteville. May 29, 1888, he was married to Miss Sarah Mulholland, a young lady of culture and refinement, and a graduate of the A. I. U., in the class of 1885–86. Mr. Mayes is a member of the Masonic fraternity, is chief of the fire department of Fayetteville, and is a young man who has already taken a representative position among the citizens of the town and county, and by the judicious management of his business enterprises has acquired a comfortable competency.

Robert J. Mayes, a prominent farmer residing one and a half miles west of Goshen, and the son of William H. and Louisa (Joyce) Mayes, was born in East Tennessee April 29, 1856. The father was born in the same State in January, 1832, was reared there, and there married Miss Joyce, who is a native of Tennessee, born in 1833. They remained in that State until 1858, when they moved to Brush Creek, Washington Co., Ark., near their present residence, and here the father has carried on farming, and is one of the prominent citizens of Brush Creek Township. The mother is also living. Robert J. cultivated the soil on his father's farm until the age of twenty-two, or until December 22, 1879, when he married Mrs. Patie L. (Weatherred) McNeely, a native of Middle Tennessee. They have two children, Robert E. and Waller M. After marriage Mr. Mayes engaged in farming and stock raising on the farm where he now resides, and has been very successful. His wife owns an interest in the farm they now live on of 240 acres of valley land, 150 of which are under cultivation, and also an interest in another farm in Little Rock, this State, and one in West Tennessee, near Memphis. He has another farm of 120 acres, seventy being under cultivation. Mr. Mayes is a Republican in his political views, and has always voted that ticket. He is an excellent citizen, and is a member of the Missionary Baptist Church, while Mrs. Mayes is a member of the Methodist Episcopal Church, South.

William Mayes, the son of Edward and Mahala J. (Jones) Mayes, was born in East Tennessee in 1832. His parents were both natives of Tennessee, and the father followed agricultural pursuits for many years, but toward the latter part of his life followed merchandising in Tennessee. He died in 1863. William Mayes was educated in his native State, and assisted his father on the farm until twenty-one years of age. In 1852 he married Miss Louisa Joyce, a native of Tennessee, and to this union were born twelve children, ten now living: Samuel (who married Miss Cynthia Johnson), Robert J. (who married Miss P. M. Needley), Albert W. (who married Miss Mary Stowball), J. L. (who married Miss Mattie Allen), Thomas (who married Miss A. M. Hash), Louisa (wife of Alex. Neal), Allie (wife of Obadiah Harden), Louie and John. Mr. Mayes enlisted in Company A, First Arkansas United States Infantry, under Capt. Rundal, in 1862, and served until the close of the war. He was in several skirmishes, and was at the battle of Prairie Grove, but was fortunate enough to escape unhurt. After the termination of hostilities Mr. Mayes returned to his home in Washington County, Ark., where he had moved in 1858, and here purchased a farm. He now has about 165 acres, well improved and about seventy-five acres under cultivation. He was appointed justice of the peace of Brush Creek Township by the governor of Arkansas before the reconstruction, and has filled this office ever since.   He is a member of the G. A. R. and Odd Fellow's lodges, and he and wife and children are members of the Missionary Baptist Church.

William Mayes, farmer, stock raiser, and native of Washington County, Ark., was born April 19, 1841, and is a son of Samuel and Lucinda (Miller) Mayes, who were born in Illinois, and came to Arkansa in 1832, where they spent the remainder of their days.   The father was a farmer, and after coming to Arkansas served as justice of the peace for a number of years.   William Mayes is the fourth of their seven children, and received his education in the common schools and the Arkansas College, engaging in agricultural pursuits after leaving the latter institution.   Two years later the war broke out, and he was forced to join the Confederate army, but succeeded in making his escape about three months later, at the battle of Prairie Grove, and joined the Union army, and for faithful service was promoted to the post of orderly-sergeant of the First Arkansas Battery.   At a later period he was promoted to second lieutenant, serving in this capacity until the close of the war, when he was mustered out at Ft. Smith, Ark., and returned home.   During eight months just before the close of the war he commanded the First Arkansas Battery, though only lieutenant commanding.   He was appointed and commissioned captain of Company A, Washington County State Guards, by Gov. Powell Clayton, 1866–67.   He and a Mr. Johnson erected a large grist-mill at Johnson, Ark.   He served in this capacity for seventeen years, and then sold his share to Mr. Johnson, and retired to his farm, which now consists of 300 acres of good land.   He is a stanch Republican in his political views, and is commander of the G. A. R., Post 34, Springdale, Ark.   He also belongs to the A. F. & A. M.   In 1869 he was married to Miss Amanda E. Pierson, who was born in Washington County, Ark., in 1841, and by her became the father of three sons: Charles S. (a student in the State University of Arkansas), Robert C. and Etter M. (deceased when an infant.)

William Green Mhoon.   The Mhoon family are of German descent, and were first represented in Washington County, Ark., by Stark and Mathenia (Mullen) Mhoon, who were born in North Carolina, married in East Tennessee, and in 1836 located in Washington County, Ark.   They were the first family who lived on Round Mountain, the country being in a very wild state at that time, and here they followed the occupation of farming.   They moved to Jefferson County, Ill., in 1853, but a year later returned to Arkansas, and lived in the following places in the order in which they are named: Delaware Nation, Kansas, Jackson County, Mo., Newton County, Mo., Washington County, Ark., Newton County, Mo., Washington County, Ark., and lastly to Newton County, Mo., where the father died May 11, 1888.   He was born in 1811.   His wife died in Washington County, Ark., in 1848, when only thirty-seven or thirty-eight years of age.   She was a daughter of Thomas Mullen, who was among the early settlers of Washington County.   After the mother's death Mr. Mhoon married Sarah Mullen, a sister of his first wife.   She died in Washington County, Ark., in 1881 or 1882, aged about sixty years.   The first union resulted in the birth of eight children, six of whom are living: James E.; Elizabeth, wife of James Bledsoe; John Thomas, William Green, Wilson R., and Mary, wife of James Keele.   Those deceased are Margaret J. and Martha T.   Four children were born to the last marriage, and all are living: Marquis Lafayette, John, Roena, wife of John Jenkins, and Robert G.   William Green Mhoon remained with his parents until he was eighteen years of age, and then engaged in teaming.   He was born March 16, 1840, and on the day he was nineteen years of age he was married to Martha, a daughter of William Melaer.   She was born in Washington County, Ark., December 3, 1839, and her union with Mr. Mhoon was blessed in the birth of eleven children, nine now living: Sarah E., wife of William Heaton; Mary A., wife of W. C. Cosbey; William R., James M., Andrew A., Dora F., Albert, George A. and Josie.   Those dead are John Thomas, who died at the age of twenty years of small-pox, and Minnie Belle.   Mr. Mhoon is a prosperous farmer, and owns 208 acres of land, which is in a good state of cultivation.   He enlisted in the Union army in the fall of 1863, and served until the close of the war.   He was then $200 in debt and had only $40 in money.   He hired out the first year and the next year farmed on rented land.   His first purchase was eighty acres of land, and since then he has been buying and selling until he now owns his present farm, which is one of the best on Round Mountain. He and wife are members of the Christian Church, and he supports the principles of the Republican party.

Dr. D. S. Miller. This gentleman is one of the prominent and enterprising citizens of the county. He was born in Rockingham County, Va., March 20, 1839, and is the son of William and Ruth Miller, natives of Pennsylvania and Virginia, respectively. The father, who was of German descent, was a farmer all his life and died in Virginia, in 1857. The mother died in 1860. Their family consisted of five children, Dr. D. S. Miller being the youngest. He was educated in his native State, and about one year before the breaking out of the Civil War he was elected lieutenant of a company of Virginia volunteers, and was called into the Confederate service, but his sentiments were so strong for the Union that he left the South in 1863, and removed to Ohio, and from there came to Stephenville, Erath Co., Tex. He commenced the study of medicine in Preble County, Ohio, where he resided some fourteen years, and has also followed the occupation of painting and other vocations. While there he invented a patent and operated that for two years; also farmed for one year there, and owned and ran a flour-mill and saw-mill for two years. He then removed to Stephenville, Tex., as above related, and here he followed painting, and also studied medicine, which he practiced there for some time, or until he moved to Washington County, Ark., in 1878. He then located five miles south of Boonsboro, where he followed agricultural pursuits for four years, and then sold out and engaged in merchandising at West Fork one year. Three years ago he located at Greenland Station, where he is postmaster, and where he has followed merchandising ever since. During the war, in 1862, he married Miss Delilah J. Blackwell, a native of Virginia, and to them were born eight children: Preston H., Howard K. (deceased), Virginia V., Elmer E., Charles M., Calvin S. (deceased), Oda S. and Osa F. Dr. Miller is a Republican in politics, and takes an active interest in political affairs. He is a Master Mason, and is now candidate for representative in the State Legislature.

George D. Miller. Among the successful farmers, and one deserving special mention, is George D. Miller, who was born one-half mile from where he now lives, January 19, 1840, and is the son of William and Martha (Landers) Miller, and grandson of Joseph Miller, who was one of the earliest settlers of this valley, owning a large farm in the same, which was called Miller's Valley. William followed in the footsteps of his father, and engaged in farming, but in connection also carried on a tan-yard at Fayetteville about six years. He died in 1872. The mother was born in Southern Arkansas, and was reared in the neighborhood of Fayetteville. She was born June 6, 1822, and is now sixty-six years of age. George D. Miller grew to manhood on the farm, but six years of his early life were spent in Fayetteville, with his father in the tan-yard, but this he has not followed since. During the war he drove a government team thirty-three months in Union, Ark. At the age of twenty-seven, or in 1866, he married Miss Nancy Stinebaugh, a native of Missouri, who bore him ten children: Amanda (wife of J. M. Brooks), Annie, Mary F., Martha, Elizabeth J., Dora B., Bertha A., Laura, Julia R. and Sirena. After marriage Mr. Miller settled on his present farm, which consists of 160 acres, eighty under cultivation. He has another farm of 161 acres, eighty acres under cultivation. This farm is situated twelve miles west of Fayetteville. Mr. Miller has been a successful farmer, and is regarded as a good citizen. He is a member of the Knights of the Horse, and is conservative in politics, not adhering to any political party. Mrs. Miller is a member of the Christian Church.

William Mitchell, county surveyor, was born at Cane Hill, Washington County, Ark., May 10, 1834, and is a son of James and Mary A. (Webber) Mitchell, who were born in Indiana and Florida, respectively. The father was a tanner by trade, and located at Cane Hill about 1830, removing from Tennessee. He was married in the latter State, and became the father of six sons and three daughters, and died in Arkansas in 1859, followed by his wife in 1882. Both were worthy and consistent members of the Cumberland Presbyterian Church. William Mitchell is their fifth child, and grew to manhood in his native county. He served in the Confederate army throughout the late war, serving a portion of the time in Company B, Brooks' regiment. He was at the battles of Oak Hill, Prairie Grove, Jenkins' Ferry, also participating in many important skirmishes. After his return home he engaged in farming and surveying, and has served as surveyor of Washington County three different terms, and as assessor two terms. He was married in Fayetteville to Miss Josephine Lewis, a daughter of John Lewis, Esq,, and three sons and four daughters have blessed their union: Jennie; James L., a student in the A. I. U.; William Z., Mary Kate, John M., Nannie and Lizzie. The family attend the Christian Churches, and Mr. Mitchell is a member of the Occidental Lodge of the A. F. & A. M. He was also a charter member of the Prairie Grove Grange, during the flourishing portion of its existence, and is a member of the State Society of Engineers, Architects and Surveyors. Mr. Mitchell has always taken a deep interest in the welfare of the town and county in which he resides, and has assisted materially in furthering all enterprises tending to benefit them, and is regarded as one of the useful and progressive citizens of the county. His grandfather, James Mitchell, was a cooper by trade, and a native of Virginia.

John Mock, farmer and stock raiser of Prairie Grove Township, Washington Co., Ark., was born in Sevier County, Tenn., October 23, 1821, and was reared and educated in his native State. After reaching manhood he came west and located in Washington County, Ark., but after remaining a very short time went to Texas, returning the following spring to Tennessee. He next went to Northern Georgia, where he was married about 1849 to Miss Margaret E. Rogers, a native of South Carolina, reared in Georgia, and daughter of Hugh Rogers, who now resides in Washington County. Mr. Mock purchased a farm in Georgia, which he farmed for four years, then sold out, and in 1851 moved to Arkansas, where he has since made his home. He became a very wealthy landholder, owning at one time nearly 1,000 acres in one body, but has given considerable land to his children, and also sold some, and is now the owner of 668 acres, with about 400 acres, in one body, under cultivation. The land is all very valuable, but the valleys are especially fertile and well adapted for raising corn, wheat and vegetables. Besides attending to his farm he spent a number of years in buying and selling horses and mules, shipping them south, but discontinued this occupation in 1883. In 1861 he enlisted in the Sixteenth Arkansas Infantry, participating in the battles of Oak Hill and Pea Ridge, but was discharged after the battle of Corinth on account of his age; returning home he resumed farming. He is the father of eight children, all of whom are married but two. Their names are as follows: James, Martha Jane (wife of J. J. Baggett), Mary Ann (wife of Frank Lake), Callie (wife of Thomas Cazart), Maggie (wife of Sam Neal), Josephine, John and Willie. Two of the sons are Masons. The family attend the Methodist Episcopal Church, South, and Mr. Mock is a Master Mason, joining that brotherhood in Georgia. His parents, Philip and Jane (Wilson) Mock, were born in North Carolina and Tennessee, respectively, and were married in the latter State. The mother died about 1840.

Moses Mock, a retired farmer of Jefferson County, Ark., was born in Davidson County, N. C., on the 18th of September, 1826, and is a son of Moses and Jane (Williams) Mock, and grandson of Philip Mock, who was of Scotch-German descent, and who, during the Revolutionary War, assisted the colonists in their struggle for liberty. He subsequently made a settlement in North Carolina, at what is now known as Mocksville, where he spent the remainder of his days. The male members of the Mock family are of medium size, dark complexioned and black-eyed, and are noted for their courageous spirit, energy, honesty and intelligence. The maternal grandfather, Francis Williams, was also a soldier in the Revolutionary War, and was of English descent, his people being members of the Presbyterian Church. Moses Mock was reared in his native State, his educational advantages being limited to a three months' attendance at the common schools during the winter seasons, working at farm labor the remainder of the year. He also learned the mill-wright's trade, and followed that occupation for a number of years, accumulating a handsome competency thereby. At the breaking out of the late Rebellion he enlisted in Churchill's Arkansas regiment (having come here in 1849), and served until the close of the war. After the cessation of hostilities he returned to Arkansas, locating on a plantation in Jefferson County, where he began life anew, and eventually became the owner of 1,000 acres of fine farming land, 500 of which are in a fine state of cultivation, and well stocked. His farm is valuable for its position and for the richness of the soil, also for its residence, barns and out-buildings. In 1878 he came to Fayetteville on a visit, and, being pleased with the town, purchased property, and the following year he and family, which consists of a wife and one daughter, located permanently here. His wife, who was a Miss N. S. Dougherty, is a member of the Christian Church, and his daughter, S. Belle, was a student in the A. I. U. Mr. Mock has served in the city council four years, has been the architect of his own fortune, and is in every sense of the word a self-made man.

James E. Mock, farmer and stock raiser of Washington County, Ark., was born in Walker County, Ga., March 23, 1849, and was taken by his parents to Arkansas at the age of two years. Here he grew to manhood, receiving a good education in the common schools, the Cane Hill College and the Viney Grove Seminary, and September 27, 1873, was united in marriage to Miss Eunice Amanda Patton, a native of Missouri, and a daughter of Col. T. J. Patton, of Siloam Springs, Ark. Their union was blessed in the birth of five children: Edward Lee, Lucy Birdie, Ethel M., Robert L. and an infant son. Soon after their marriage they located on a farm three miles south of Prairie Grove, but in 1882 located on their present farm of 200 acres. Forty acres are in a good state of cultivation and sixty acres are under fence. Besides this land Mr. Mock owns the old home place, which consists of 180 acres, 150 of which are under cultivation. His residence is a good frame building, and the barns and out-buildings are all in good condition. He has been master of the Prairie Grove Masonic Lodge for over two years, and his wife is a member of the Methodist Episcopal Church, South. He is a son of John Mock, whose sketch appears in this work.

Albert A. Moore, one of the representative farmers and stock raisers of Prairie Township, Township 16, Range 29, is the son of Thomas and Eliza (Wilson) Moore, both natives of Kentucky, born in 1791 and 1810 respectively. The father was of Irish descent, and was engaged for many years in running a flat-boat down the Green, Ohio and Mississippi Rivers to New Orleans. His health being affected by the river life, he abandoned this business, and moved to the mountains of Arkansas, locating in Prairie Township, Township 16, Range 29, in 1829, and here built the third log cabin, near the three forks of White River. The mother was a member of the Christian Church, and the father was a strong Whig in his political views. He died in 1853, and she in 1866. In their family were thirteen children, eight sons and five daughters, six now living. Albert A. was the seventh child born to his parents, his birth occurring in Prairie Township, Township 16, Range 29, Washington Co., Ark., March 17, 1838. Like the average country boy he assisted his father on the farm, and received a rather limited education in the common schools, though this he has improved to a great extent by general reading. September 23, 1855, when not yet quite eighteen years of age, he married Miss Martha L. Martin, who was born in Kentucky September 22, 1835, but who was reared in Missouri. Nine children were the result of this union: Americus R., David W., Thomas G., Mary A., Peter L., Jesse F., Mark W. and Amanda E. The eldest child died in infancy, and un-named. Mr. Moore is giving his children good educational advantages, and one of his sons, David W., is a minister in the Christian Church. He and wife are members of the same church, as are all the children, with the exception of one. During the war Mr. Moore served about four months in the Confederate army. He is a Republican in politics, and has been solicited several times to run for office, even for representative, but he, so far, has attended strictly to his farming interests. He is a Mason, and is the owner of 249 acres of land.

George P. Moore, who is also connected with the farming interests of Prairie Township, is the son of Joseph P. and Matilda C. (Abbott) Moore, both natives of Tennessee, the father born in Sumner County in 1806, and the mother in Rutherford County in 1813. They were married in 1832, and after living in Rutherford County until 1837 they moved to Washington County, Ark., and settled near Fayetteville. While living in Tennessee the father made spinning machines, though after coming here he followed farming. He was a Democrat until President Jackson vetoed the banks, and was afterward a Whig. He died in 1850. The mother is still living, and is a member of the Presbyterian Church. Their family consisted of seven children, all boys, and only three now living. The eldest of this family, George P., was born in Washington County, Ark., May 6, 1843, was reared on a farm, and educated in the Ozark Seminary. April, 1861, he enlisted in Capt. Bell's company of Third Arkansas Infantry, Confederate Army, and served three months. In the spring of 1862 he joined Company C, of the Third Arkansas Cavalry, and served until the close of the war. He was in the battles of Oak Hill, Fayetteville, and was in many cavalry skirmishes. He went with Gen. Price in his raid through Missouri, and was one of Gen. Cabell's body-guards for nearly two years. Since then he has followed farming. In 1865 he married Miss Alice Nolen, who was born in Washington County, Ark., November 14, 1845, and who became the mother of nine children: May B., Joseph N., Edward C., George C., James M., Samuel T., Nannie J., John S. and Clarence B. Mr. Moore is the owner of 339 acres of land, 160 being under cultivation. He takes great pride in educating his children, and is giving them the best advantages. He is a Democrat in politics, and both he and wife are members of the Cumberland Presbyterian Church, he being an elder in the same.

Wilburn Denton Moore, farmer and stock dealer, was born at Cane Hill, Washington Co., Ark., October 30, 1854, and is a son of David Milton and Pauline Jane (Reagan) Moore. The grandparents, John D. and his wife, who was formerly a Miss Patrick, moved from Kentucky shortly after the birth of our subject's father, and settled in Tennessee. In 1830 they removed to Cane Hill, Ark., where they now reside. They reared eight children to maturity and buried four children in early youth. One son, Thomas David, died while on duty in the Confederate service. David Milton Moore was for many years associated with his father in the mercantile business at Cane Hill, their store being one of the first in that place. After the death of his father he, for many years, was extensively engaged in farming and stock dealing. His son, Napoleon C., is a merchant at Siloam Springs; Edward is a merchant at Witcherville; John R. is now a partner of his father in agricultural pursuits and the nursery business; James O. is a prominent farmer near Cincinnati, Ark., and Robert Lee is engaged in farming at Prairie Grove. He has two daughters, Cynthia Alice and Mary Pauline, the latter of whom is the wife of Dr. Edward Davenport, of Witcherville [see sketch]. Pauline Jane (Reagan) Moore was a daughter of John Reagan, a native of Tennessee, who located at Cane Hill in 1829 [see sketch]. Wilburn Denton Moore grew to manhood in this county, and is now a substantial farmer and stock dealer. He married Mary J., eldest daughter of the Hon. Hosea M. Maguire [see sketch]. Mr. Moore has two sons living: Hosea David Clyde and Horace Duke. Two children died when young, Mallory and Hugh Oscar. Mrs. Moore died December 4, 1885, and is buried beside her two children in Valley Grove Cemetery, Richland. She was a faithful member of the Cumberland Presbyterian Church, and her loss was greatly mourned by her friends and acquaintances.

John B. Morris, whose post-office address is Spring Valley, Ark., was born in Indiana in 1843, and is the son of Isaac and Margaret (Booth) Morris. The father was a native of Virginia, and has followed agricultural pursuits all his life. In 1870 he and family moved from Indiana to Illinois, and four years later he concluded to move to Arkansas, and did so, but only remained in that State until 1877 or 1878, when he moved to Bates County, Mo. Not being satisfied here he returned to Arkansas, and has been living in this State ever since. In 1861 his son, John B. Morris, enlisted in Company B, Thirty-first Indiana Regiment, and served four years and three months. He participated in all the principal battles fought by the Army of the Cumberland, was slightly wounded three times, and served faithfully until the close of the war. In 1862, while in Kentucky, he was taken prisoner, and was exchanged as a prisoner of war the following year. He had a sunstroke at Atlanta, Ga., from the effects of which he has never fully recovered. After the war he returned to his home, and in 1866 Miss Mary E. Davis became his wife. They became the parents of seven children, five now living: Clara J., Mary E., George E., Thomas H. and Robert F. Mr. Morris is a member of the G. A. R. and Odd Fellows' lodges, is also a member of the Agricultural Wheel, and he and wife are members of the Christian Church. It is hardly necessary to add that Mr. Morris is a Republican in his political views.

George Wilson Morrow, assessor of Washington County, Ark., and an enterprising citizen of the same, was born in what is now Dutch Mills Township, Washington Co., Ark., May 2, 1842, and is the son of Rev. George and Elizabeth (Buchanan) Morrow. The former was born in South Carolina, and reared in Kentucky, and the latter was born and reared in Kentucky. They were married at Fort Smith, Ark., and were the parents of six sons and four daughters. George Wilson Morrow, the youngest of the family, attained his growth in his native county, receiving a good practical education, and at the breaking out of the late war he shouldered his musket and enlisted in the Confederate army, Company B, Brooks' Regiment of Arkansas Infantry, and was in active service all through the stirring events of the war. He then returned to his home in Washington County and engaged in agricultural pursuits. He chose for his companion in life Miss Samantha Russell, daughter of James Bryant and Ann (Coulter) Russell, and by this union became the father of two sons and four daughters: Ann Elizabeth, who is a graduate of Cane Hill College; William R., who runs his father's store; Maggie May, Stella J., Hugh Oscar and Ena R. Mr. Morrow has held the office of justice of the peace for several years, and he and family worship at the Cumberland Presbyterian Church. He is the present assessor, and is a candidate for re-election.

William H. Morton, farmer and stock breeder of Center Township, Washington Co., Ark., was born in Washington County July 28, 1861, and is a son of James A. and Harriet (Tollett) Morton, and grandson of William Morton. The latter was born in Lincoln County, Tenn., and in 1830 immigrated to Arkansas, locating near Prairie Grove, where he became a wealthy farmer. He was a member of the Presbyterian Church, and was very strongly opposed to slavery. James A. Morton was the eldest son of a family of five children, and grew to manhood in Washington County. He was educated in the common schools, and in 1860 was married to Miss Tollett, and located on a farm. In 1861 he was strongly opposed to secession, but when the war began he joined the Confederate army and served until the close of the conflict. He was captured about 1862, and was kept a prisoner at St. Louis, Alton, Rock Island and New Orleans until the close of the war. He then returned home to find that his property had all been destroyed, but he immediately set to work, and became one of the wealthy land owners of the county. He died in 1884. His wife, who was the daughter of Henry Tollett, became the mother of three children: William H., Roland M. and James E., and is now making her home with her son, William H., who was reared on a farm in Washington County. He received a good education in the State University, located at Fayetteville, and in 1884 was married to Miss Bettie Smith, who was born near Farmington in 1863. They have three children: Herbert, Julia and an infant. Mr. Morton's farm consists of 220 acres, and is well improved. He is one of the leading stock breeders and fruit raisers of the county, and has charge of a fine Clydesdale stallion and a jack of the mammoth stock. He and wife are members of the Cumberland Presbyterian Church, and he is a young man of good habits, and is an active Democrat. He was elected a justice of the peace in Center Township at the September election in 1888.

Edward Hunter Murfee, president of the A. I. U., is a native of Southampton County, Va., the son of James W. Murfee, and grandson of Rev. Simon Murfee. At the age of sixteen Edward Hunter Murfee was sent to the University of Alabama, in order that he might be in charge of his brother, James T. Murfee, who was a professor in the university, and from the above mentioned institution he received the degree of Master of Arts. Soon after the war he taught select schools in Marion, Ala., and Demopolis, of the same State. In 1871 he was elected professor of military engineering in the Alabama University, and subsequently was elected professor of mathematics in Union University, Tennessee. Resigning from the latter institution, he obtained a charter for the Mississippi Military Institute, and was superintendent of the same until elected to the position of professor of mathematics in the Arkansas Industrial University in 1885. During the fifteen months ending August 29, he was acting president of the A. I. U., and at the latter date he was elected president without solicitation. In 1886 he was honored by two colleges, Bethel College, Kentucky, and Wake Forest College, North Carolina, with the degree of LL.D.

Col. James P. Neal, one of the old residents of Washington County, Ark., who is now retired from active business life, was born in Butler County, Ky., March 24, 1820, and is a son of William Neal, and a grandson of Thomas Neal. The latter was a Virginian, whose ancestors were Irish, and one of the early settlers of Kentucky, in which State William Neal was born, reared and married. His wife's maiden name was Sinai Harreld, whose parents were also Virginians, of English ancestry. After Mr. Neal's death, which occurred when James P. was a child, she married again, and in 1829 moved to Arkansas with her husband, Rev. Andrew Buchanan, a minister of the Cumberland Presbyterian Church, locating on the land on which the Colonel now resides. Here Col. Neal was reared on the farm, and in 1847 volunteered in the Mexican War, marching through Texas into Mexico. He arose to the rank of first lieutenant, and served in this capacity until the close of the war, being mustered out at Comargo in 1848. Previous to his entering the army he had read law, been admitted to the bar, and had practiced his profession in Fayetteville, and after returning home he resumed his profession, which he continued until 1851, when he was elected mayor of Fayetteville, and held the office until 1854. In 1849 he was married to Miss Adaline Bean, daughter of Capt. Mark Bean, and cousin of the late Col. Tom Bean, the Bonham, Tex., millionaire. In 1854 he moved to Austin, Tex., owing to his wife's failing health, where she died in 1863. During the war Mr. Neal was actively engaged in furnishing the Confederate army with supplies. He was a presidential elector, and voted for Jeff. Davis for his second term. In 1868 he returned to Prairie Grove, Ark., then made historic by the battle of December 7, 1862, between the Federal and Confederate forces, commanded respectively by Gens. Blunt and Hindman. In 1869 he was married to the widow of his brother, Col. William T. Neal, who was killed by the Federals in a skirmish near Clarksville, Ark., in 1864. In 1871 he established the town of Prairie Grove, built the first store and engaged in merchandising, being also appointed postmaster of the town. He held this position until 1887, when he was obliged to resign on account of failing health, and is now living at his beautiful suburban residence, free from the cares of business life, surrounded by the lovely groves and grand old trees made memorable by the incidents of the battle, where that famous old spring comes bubbling forth with its crystal water, where both Federals and Confederates slaked their thirst and bathed their bleeding wounds. Col. Neal has held many positions of trust, and has done much to build up the town. His donations of real estate to public and charitable buildings have been munificent. He is a member of the Masonic fraternity, and is a worthy and consistent member of the Methodist Episcopal Church, South. His first union resulted in the birth of six children, only two of whom (Nora and Sam Bell) grew to mature years. To his present union three children have been born: James Preston, Sinai Belle and Jay Dudley. Mr. Neal has written and published many interesting sketches of the early times in Arkansas.

John A. Neill. Among the many successful and enterprising citizens of Washington County stands the name of John A. Neill, who was born in Morgan County, Ill., September 14, 1827, and is the son of Alexander and Martha (Wilson) Neill, both of whom were natives of Logan County, Ky., born in 1802 and August 9, 1807, respectively. The father attained his growth in his native State, was married there, and about 1825 moved to Morgan County, Ill., where he resided until 1832, after which he moved to Northwest Arkansas, and in the spring of the following year moved to a place one mile north of Goshen. Here he remained until October, 1886, when he moved to the home of his son, John A. Neill, and remained with him until August 14, 1888, when he received his final summons. He had tilled the soil all his life, had been a member of the Methodist Episcopal Church since about 1843, and was one of the most highly respected citizens of this part of the county. The mother died at the residence of her son, John A. Neill, September 13, 1884. She was also a consistent member of the Methodist Episcopal Church. They had a family of six sons and four daughters, one son and four daughters now living. The six sons served in the Confederate army, and but one, our subject, returned alive. The latter was reared in the country, and, like the majority of farmer boys, passed his time in cultivating the soil. At the age of twenty-three he left home, and March 28, 1852, married Miss Nancy Sherrod, a native of Tennessee, born January 29, 1830, and a daughter of William Sherrod, who was a Methodist preacher and an early settler of Washington County. Mr. and Mrs. Neill became the parents of eight children, seven now living: Electa P., born March 17, 1854; George M., born January 19, 1856; William A., born March 11, 1858; Thomas J., born June 23, 1860; John F., born February 11, 1863, and died February 22, 1863; Martha L. and Stonewall J. (twins), born May 29, 1867, and Charlotte J., born April 21, 1870. After marriage Mr. Neill followed farming, two and a half miles east of where he now resides, until the fall of 1856, when he went to Texas, and followed the same occupation in that State, together with the carpenter trade, but was routed by the Indians in 1866. He then moved to Arkansas, and settled on his present property, where he has since lived, and where he still continues farming. He has 179 acres, seventy-five under cultivation and well improved.

Mr. Neill, his wife and all but one of the family are members of the Methodist Episcopal Church, South. Mr. Neill is a F. & A. M., W. M. of Goshen Lodge No. 413, H. P. of Hinesville Chapter No. 81, and a member of Hinesville Council U. D. In politics he has always been a Democrat. He is a moral, upright citizen, and bears the highest regards of his fellow men.

Julian Bailey Nix, another successful carpenter, builder and prominent citizen of the county, was born in Newton County, Ga., at Covington, October 11, 1847, and grew to manhood in that county. He there learned his trade, and followed the same until 1882, when he moved to Washington County. He worked as an apprentice under John C. Nichols, a master in the profession, and one who has left the greatest number of monuments of his business than any man of his place. Joseph M. Nix, father of Julian B. Nix, was also a carpenter by profession, and spent the latter part of his life in the employ of Mr. Nichols. He was killed in 1862 by the bursting of an emery wheel, and was buried with Masonic honors. Since coming to Arkansas J. B. Nix has aided in building some of the finest residences in Fayetteville, and some very fine business blocks, viz.: Auction store, inside work; addition to Bozarth's furniture store, residence of H. K. Wade, residence of John Wood, residences of Tom Bonds and J. S. Worsham, and numerous other buildings. He was married in Georgia to Miss Fannie M. Yarbray, daughter of William and Nancy Yarbray, and became the father of six sons and two daughters: Myrtle, Maud, Robert Edward, Julian Hendrick, Erie Ottawa, Emory Linwood, James Stirman and Willard Huber. Mrs. Nix is a member of the Baptist Church. Mr. Nix is a Mason, and a member of the A. O. U. W., in which he has held official position. His grandfather, William Edward Nix, was a farmer by occupation, and moved to Georgia at a very early date.

R. J. Norman, another successful tiller of the soil, was born in Bedford County, Tenn, in 1845, and is the son of Reuben and Cynthia (McFarland) Norman. The father was born in Virginia; was a farmer by occupation, but was also engaged in teaching school some time. He moved to Tennessee in 1828, and was married in 1832, leaving Tennessee in 1850 to try his fortune out West. He located in Washington County, Ark., near Elm Spring, where he passed his last days, being killed by Federal scouts in February, 1865. His son, R. J. Norman, received rather a limited education, remaining on the farm with his father, and assisting him until August 22, 1863, when he enlisted in Brown's company of Confederate Rangers, Confederate States Army; was captured at Huntsville, Ark., October 22, 1863, by the Second Wisconsin Cavalry, and part of the Sixth and Eighth Missouri Cavalry; was taken to Rock Island, Ill., by way of Springfield, St. Louis and Alton, Ill.; was released from prison in January, 1865; was exchanged March 25, 1865; re-entered Confederate service in Company G, Fifteenth Arkansas, at Shreveport. La., and served with it until the close of the war, being discharged at Little Rock. Returning home he remained one year, then went to Texas, remaining there three years, and coming back to Arkansas again was married to Miss Mary A. Truett in 1871. One child, James R., was born to them. Mr. Norman lost his wife in 1874. In 1876 he was married to a Miss Cynthia J. Aaron, and to this union one child, Nora, was also born, in 1877. He is a member of the Masonic fraternity, is a Prohibitionist in political views, and he, his wife and son are worthy members of the Methodist Episcopal Church, South.

James Oates, proprietor of the Oates' Wagon Factory, was born in Halifax, Yorkshire, England, January 5, 1836, the son of John and Rachel (Armatage) Oates, both also natives of Halifax, Yorkshire, England, where nine generations are buried in one grave-yard. The father was a blacksmith and edge-tool maker. He was the first mechanic in his father's family, though three of his four sons were tradesmen. Both parents died in England. Their family consisted of fourteen children, seven sons and seven daughters. James Oates received very little education, owing to the fact that at the age of about eleven he left England, was on the sea for three or four years. and reached this country in 1852. For one year he followed his trade at Key West, Fla., being in the Government's employ, and he here mounted the first guns in that fort. In 1860 he went to Honduras, Central America, with Gen. William Walker, and was with him until the close of his campaign. He assisted in storming Truxillo, and was in every engagement during that campaign, and was captured when Gen. Walker surrendered, and held a prisoner for several weeks. When Louisiana seceded he was offered

****

a commission in the Confederate service, but refused, and because of his Union sentiments was obliged to leave. In April, 1861, he enlisted in Company G, Seventh Illinois Volunteer Infantry, and served three months, and then enlisted in Company K, Ninth Illinois Infantry, for three years. In December, 1861, he was commissioned second lieutenant, and in June, 1862, he was promoted to the rank of first lieutenant. He participated in the battles of Shiloh, Corinth, Resaca, Peach Tree Creek, Fort Donelson, Nashville and others. During his service he was in sixty-seven engagements, and at Fort Donelson was wounded by four balls, three taking effect in his left shoulder and breast. He was discharged at Springfield, Ill., in 1864, and afterward went to Nashville, Tenn., entered the railroad service of the Government, and although a civilian took part in the battle of Nashville. He receives a pension as a partial compensation. In his wanderings he learned the blacksmith and wagon-maker's trade, and opened a shop at Sedalia, Mo., working about thirty hands. In 1866 he married Miss Ellen Severs, a native of Washington County, Ark., and the daughter of an old settler, Charles J. Severs. One child was the result of this union, Ruth. In 1868 Mr. Oates moved to Cincinnati, Ark., where he built a large factory, with a capacity of about 400 wagons yearly, and besides this he deals in agricultural implements. The year previous to this his wife died, and five years later Mr. Oates married Mrs. Martha J. Maurice, *nee* Spence, a native of Rochester, N. Y. The first Mrs. Oates was reared by Methodist parents, but was not a member of the Methodist Episcopal Church, and the present wife is a member of the Catholic Church. In 1886 Mr. Oates was the Republican nominee for representative of Washington County to the State Legislature, and in 1888 he was chairman of the Republican Mass Convention. He is a member of the G. A. R., and although a Democrat before the war, since that time he has been a Republican. He has one of the largest wagon factories in this section of the State.

Dr. Anderson Ott, one of the prominent physicians of Wedington, was born September 10, 1837, in Washington County, Ind., and is the son of Mallichiah and Mary (Ware) Ott, natives of Kentucky and Pennsylvania, respectively. The father was born in 1814, is still living, and is now a resident of Taswell, Ind. He was a blacksmith by trade, but gave that up to engage in merchandising, and is now following the same in Taswell. He is a Republican in politics, is a member of the Methodist Episcopal Church, and is an honest, respected citizen. The mother was born in 1813, and died in 1875. They were married in Indiana, where the mother died and where the father is still living. They were the parents of eight children, six now living: Greenberry S., a mechanic at Leavenworth, Ind.; George W., a farmer in Crawford County, Ind.; Wesley, a merchant at Taswell, and a partner of his father, and William H., a merchant at Eckerdy, Ind. The children deceased were named as follows: Andrew and Mahala. Anderson Ott, at the age of twenty-one, left home and worked at his trade of painter in Southern Indiana for four years, after which he began selling goods, running a notion wagon over the country for several years, or until 1870. Quite a number of years previous to this, in 1857, he married Miss Sarah Roberts, who died three years later, leaving two children: Mary, now the wife of Wesley Wade, a farmer in Newton County, Ark., and William S., who died when sixteen years of age. Mrs. Ott was a member of the Methodist Episcopal Church. In November, 1862, Dr. Ott enlisted in Company K, Twenty-third Indiana Infantry Volunteers, and after serving a short time was discharged on account of disability. In 1865 the Doctor married Miss Elizabeth Roberts, a cousin of his first wife, and she lived but ten months. She was a member of the Methodist Episcopal Church. January 4, 1866, he married Miss Mary Jacobs, a native of Dubois County, Ind., born January 6, 1845, and the daughter of Elisha Jacobs. To this union were born four children, three now living: John W., Willard E. and Leora Elvira. Luella C. died when two years of age. Previous to 1870 the Doctor had studied medicine a great deal, and in the last named year he began practicing, first at Mifflin, Ind. In 1878 he moved to Arkansas, located at Cave Creek, Newton County, and in 1881 he moved to Benton County, where he remained until 1885, when he moved to Washington County and settled on his present location. He studied medicine under Joel Vandever at Mount Prospect, Ind., and has been a student at the Medical College at Louisville. He now has a very large practice, in fact as much or more than one person can attend to, and has been very successful, as his many patients, now living, can testify. Dr. Ott, in his politics, votes for the best man, and is a gentleman respected by all who know him.

John W. Oxford. Among the names of successful and wide-awake farmers of Goshen Township is the name of John W. Oxford, who was born September 3, 1842, and is the son of Jacob and Rebecca (Culwell) Oxford. The father was born in Middle Tennessee in 1801; was reared there, and after marriage (1839) moved from that State to where J. J. McGaroch now lives, in this county and township. Here he passed the remainder of his life, with the exception of three years in Texas during the war. He was a farmer, and died in 1872. The mother was born in Arkansas in 1822, and is now living with her son, John W. She was the second wife of Mr. Oxford. By his first marriage he became the father of seven children, and by his last became the father of nine children, all now living. He was among the prominent pioneer settlers of Washington County, and Oxford's Bend takes its name from him. John W. was reared on a farm in sight of where he now lives, and remained on the farm with his father until the latter's death. He, like his father, has been a farmer all his life. In 1859 he was united in marriage to Miss Livonia C. Gregg, a native of Washington County, and the fruit of this union were five children: Mary, wife of N. B. Clark; John A., Dora M., Fayner N. and Russell A. Mr. Oxford moved to his present farm, which consists of 115 acres, ninety under cultivation, in 1873. He and wife are members of the Methodist Episcopal Church, South, and he is a member of the Masonic fraternity. He was in Company K, King's regiment, Confederate army, and was in service four years; was wounded three times, once at Helena, once at a skirmish in this county, and again at a skirmish in Texas. All the wounds were in the right arm, and within six inches of each other. Mr. Oxford is constable of his township; is a Democrat in politics, and is one of the township's best citizens.

Alexander Parker, whose birth occurred on Middle Fork, White River, Washington Co., Ark., November 22, 1858, is the son of Pleasant and Sarah (Jones) Parker. The father was born in West Virginia, but was reared in Tennessee. He moved to Arkansas in 1851, settling where he is now living, and has farmed all his life. The mother is also living. Alexander Parker was reared on the farm, and spent his youth in assisting his father on the same, and attending the common country schools. In 1885 he chose for his companion in life Mrs. Lucinda (Gilliland) Peerson, widow of John A. Peerson, and to them were born four children, two pairs of twins, Clarence and Clara, Homer and Virgil. Mrs. Peerson was the mother of five children by her former marriage: Paris, Powell, George, Robert and Laura. After his marriage Mr. Parker taught school for a short time, and then settled to farming on his present property, where he has continued ever since. He has made a success of farming and dealing in horses and other live stock. He owns the fine thoroughbred Steel Dust, Bertram, running stallion, named "Burton, Jr.," dapple bay, three years old. Mr. Peerson also owns an interest in the Peerson farm of 300 acres. Mr. Parker is a Republican in politics, but has never aspired to any official position, and is a respected young man.

Col. Isaac Mitchell Patridge, son of Isaac C. and Elizabeth Patridge, was born at Chapel Hill, Orange Co., N. C., November 12, 1833. His father was publishing a paper there at the time, and was also postmaster of the place. His parents were both born and reared in New Berne, on the seaboard of the State, and were representatives of some of the oldest families in that region, whose ancestors were among the first settlers of Eastern North Carolina, and I. M. Patridge is related to the Hawkers, Mitchells, Willises, Pearces and other prominent families of the "Old North State," who have made their mark in political, legal, mercantile and mechanical life. I. M. Patridge received a fair education in the schools of New Berne, where his mother had removed after the death of his father in 1839. His youth was uneventful until he was about prepared for college, when circumstances induced his mother to put him in a newspaper office to learn the printing business. Accordingly he was sent to Norfolk, Va., where he entered the *Beacon* office, a daily paper published by Cunningham & Gatewood, in the spring of 1850. He remained with this paper for several years, and early exhibited a capacity for higher things than the mechanical drudgery; he passed through the position of reporter, until in January, 1855, he was announced as one of the editors of the paper. During the summer of that year a fearful epidemic of yellow fever passed over Norfolk, claiming among its victims both of the proprietors of the *Beacon*, and the paper was suspended and never revived. In the spring of the following year Mr. Patridge moved "out west," and having an uncle at Friar's Point, Miss., George H. Mitchell, an attorney at law, he entered his office to prepare himself for the bar. During that summer, however, in the heat of the presidential contest, he was induced to re-enter the field of journalism. He therefore moved to Memphis, and accepted the editorship of the Memphis *Whig*. The paper, through financial mismanagement, however, survived but a short time, when, upon invitation, he went to Holly Springs, Miss., and conducted the *Times* of that place during the remainder of the canvass of 1856. Returning to Memphis after the election of that year, he did work upon the *Eagle and Enquirer* until the following summer, when, in connection with several other gentlemen, he purchased the Memphis *Evening News*, and remained with it until the fall of 1857, when he accepted a call to remove to Vicksburg, Miss., and take charge of the Vicksburg *Whig*, then published by the venerable Marmaduke Shannon (who still, 1888, survives at the ripe age of nearly ninety years). His connection with this paper continued until the breaking out of the war. Vicksburg has long been noted for its journalistic fights and duels, and Mr. Patridge was not exempt from his share of the troubles. He fought a duel with Maj. William H. McCardle in July, 1858, but several other calls to the field were happily adjusted by mutual friends of the parties. In 1858 he was elected colonel of the Mississippi militia, and in 1860 major-general, but has always borne his first title of colonel. In 1860 he was chosen by the State convention of the "Constitution Union" party of Mississippi a delegate to the National Convention, at Baltimore, which nominated Bell and Everett for the presidency and vice-presidency. He was an uncompromising Union man until his State declared in favor of secession, in January, 1861, when "he went with his State," enlisting for the war in the Vicksburg Southrons. He was subsequently appointed commissary of the Twenty-first Mississippi Regiment, and the following year promoted to the rank of major in the same department, and was assigned to duty with the Mississippi Brigade, commanded by Gen. W. S. Featherston, who was succeeded by Gen. Carnot Posey, and then by Gen. N. H. Harris. At the close of the war he returned to Vicksburg, and finding a paper there called the *Herald*, which had been established after its capture by the Federal troops by an ex-Federal officer, named Ira A. Batterton, he was induced to take charge of its columns. Mr. Batterton a short time after was accidentally killed in a shooting gallery, and the paper passed into the hands of Mr. James M. Swords, Mr. Patridge continuing as its editor until the summer of 1868. His health demanding his removal from the malarial region, Mr. Patridge went north in the following year, traveling for nearly two years, when he finally made his home at Fayetteville, Ark. He was the first manager of the *Sentinel*, a Democratic paper, established by Col. J. R. Pettigrew in 1875. He remained with it until the spring of 1881, when he removed to Meridian, Miss., engaging in newspaper work until December, 1885, when he was induced to return to Fayetteville, forming a partnership with Col. Pettigrew, who had in the meantime been appointed a member of the Utah Commission. Col. Pettigrew died in October, 1886, and Mr. Hugh F. Reagan is his successor in the *Sentinel*, and the paper, since April, 1887, has been under the management of Messrs. Patridge and Reagan, who by their energy and ability have made it one of the leading journals of the State. Mr. Patridge studied law, and was granted a license by Judge J. S. Yerger, of the Vicksburg Circuit Court, in December, 1865, but has never applied himself to legal practice. He has never been a hunter after official positions. Since living in Arkansas he has served twice in the city council of Fayetteville, each time having been chosen to fill vacancies. Col. Patridge, though a gentleman in the highest sense of the term, of genial disposition, a cultivated mind and manners, of generous heart and refined feelings, appreciating and placing the highest estimate upon the fair sex, has never married, and his most intimate friends know of no romance in his life, nor have they ever had a single intimation that he has ever longed for connubial bliss.

Judge William Jesse Patton was born in Washington County, Ark., June 7, 1840, and is a son of Isaac C. and Elizabeth (Jones) Patton, who were born in Tennessee and Alabama, respectively. The father was born in Knoxville, and in his youthful days learned the hatter's trade, at which he worked in after life. His father, Jesse Patton, was a hatter, and was born in Pattonsburg, N. C., which town was named after his father, Robert Wyatt Patton, a native of Philadelphia, whose progenitors were residents of Oxford, England. Elizabeth (Jones) Patton was a daughter of John Jones, who belonged to one of the old Virginia families, and was of Welsh ancestry. Judge W. J. Patton grew to manhood in Washington County, Ark., obtaining his first schooling at Ozark Institute, which was under the management of Prof. Robert Macklin, and after leaving this institution entered the schools of Fayetteville, but at the breaking out of the War of the Rebellion he left his school days behind him to fight for the Union. He enlisted at Fort Scott, Kas., on the 5th of July, 1861, and was detailed for scouting duty, because of his knowledge of the country, and served in this capacity until June 17, 1862, when he was severely wounded in the head, losing the sight of his left eye. After partially recovering from this wound he acted as quartermaster at Springfield for a detachment of the First Arkansas Cavalry for some time, and then joined Company A, First Arkansas Volunteer Cavalry, and participated in the battle of Newtonia, carrying away with him as a trophy of this battle a handsome sabre. He served all through the war, receiving nine gunshot wounds and two contusions. In 1864 he was elected to, in part, represent Washington County in the State Legislature, serving a part of the first and all of the second sessions as speaker of the House. He was a delegate to the National Republican Convention at Baltimore, June, 1864. July 7, 1865, he was appointed collector of internal revenue for the district of Arkansas, and in 1866 was appointed collector of the Second District, which position he held until June 8, 1873. He was presidential elector for the State at large on the Republican ticket in 1880, and in joint discussion with the Democratic electors made a thorough canvass of the State. He was elected county and probate judge for Pulaski County, the county in which the State Capitol is situated, and by his bold and able management of the public finances of the county soon brought order out of chaos and wrought a revolution in the financial affairs of the county, showing himself to be the best financier that county ever had. A bold, outspoken, fearless man throughout his public career, his measures have met with general approval by his constituents. He has a farm of about 250 acres in Washington County, well improved and well stocked. On it he has one of the best selected young apple orchards of some 5,000 trees in Northwest Arkansas. He was married in Youngstown, Ohio, in 1865, to Margaretta Battenfield, daughter of Jacob Battenfield, who was of German noble ancestry. They have two children: Floy, a graduate of St. Mary's Academy, of Little Rock, Ark., and William Jesse, Jr., a student of civil engineering in the State University. Judge Patton belongs to the Masonic fraternity, is a member of Columbia Commandery No. 2, District of Columbia, the G. A. R., and his family attend the Christian Church.

Petross Brothers & Co. (James Blackburn). Among the industries of Washington County, Ark., worthy of special mention are the flouring mills of Springdale, which are managed by the Petross Bros., who are also proprietors of the same. L. D. Petross, one of the brothers, was born in Benton County, Ark., in 1859, and is a son of C. and A. C. Petross. The father was born in Tennessee in 1828, and was a miller by occupation. He came to Arkansas at an early day, and for several years was engaged in saw-milling, and in 1880 erected the Springdale Flouring Mills, which he managed until 1886, and then turned it over to his sons. L. D. Petross was reared and educated in Northwestern Arkansas, and was a popular hardware merchant of Springdale for several years. He and his brothers are noted for their energy and enterprise, and have built up a large flouring trade. They have changed the old buhr process to the roller process, and are skillful workmen and thoroughly understand their business. L. S. Petross, the younger brother, was born in Washington County, Ark., in 1861, and was married to Miss Nettie Haxton, and by her became the father of one child, Earle. B. C. Petross, the third brother, was born in Northwestern Arkansas in 1855, and was married to Miss Mattie Pruner, by whom he is the father of one child, Eula.

James H. Phillips may be mentioned as one of the prosperous farmers and stock raisers of Washington County, Ark. He was born on the 25th of July, 1830, his parents, McCager and Elizabeth (Willie) Phillips, being natives of the "Old Dominion." They were reared in North Carolina, and the father died on the farm where he was reared, in 1856. He and wife were very earnest and worthy members of the Baptist Church, and became the parents of eight children, all of whom lived to maturity. The mother died in 1841. James H. Phillips was born, reared and married in Wilkes County, N. C., and farmed in his native State until 1859, when he came west, and located on a farm in Benton County, Ark. He was married in 1852 to Miss Sarah Lewis, of Surrey County, N.C., who died in Arkansas in 1861, leaving two children, William N. and Mary F. September 19, 1861, Mr. Phillips married Miss Phoebe D. Brown, of Benton County, and their union has been blessed in the birth of six children: John M., Sarah F., Joseph M., Elijah L., M. C. and Daisy D. In 1862 Mr. Phillips enlisted in the Confederate army, in Capt. Tenon's company, Bryant's battalion, and served until the close of the war, surrendering at Fayetteville, Ark., in June, 1865, just three years from the day he entered service. After residing in Texas about ten months he, in 1867, came to Washington County, Ark., and located on a farm in Elm Spring Township, but in 1884 came to his present farm of 220 acres. He has 120 acres under cultivation, and has a good brick residence and a commodious and handsome barn. He and wife are members of the Christian Church.

William M. Phillips, one of the prominent farmers of Goshen Township, was born in Madison County, Ark,, near Wesley, March 1, 1838, and is the son of David and Kittie (Sanders) Phillips. [For further particulars of parents see sketch of W. G. Phillips, Madison County.] William M. Phillips was reared on a farm on Richland Creek, and remained with his parents until twenty-one years of age. October 21, 1858, he married Miss Martha Ann Denton, who was born October 5, 1844, and who is the daughter of Jacob Denton, an early settler of this county. Ten children were born to this union, nine now living: Lockey M., Edwin L. (deceased), Lydia E., Bent B., Cener L., Willie B., Maud A., Ella M., Minnie E. and Charles R. After marriage Mr. Phillips began farming on the Lake farm, five miles northeast of Huntsville, where he remained until the breaking out of the late war, when he volunteered under Capt. Reagan, and was in service four years. He was wounded in the leg at Helena. He was first lieutenant of his company, and commanded the company nearly all the time after the Helena fight. He surrendered at Fort Smith, and returned to Washington County. While living in Madison County Mr. Phillips was engaged in merchandising at Hindsville, and afterward settled in Pawnee County, Kas.; was one of the first settlers, and lived there two years, dealing in stock. After living in Washington County, Richland Township, on the Riley Williams farm, until 1882, he sold out and moved to his present location, where he has 200 acres of fine valley land, with about 100 under cultivation. He has made farming a success, and is one of the enterprising agriculturists of the county. He has always been a Democrat in his political views, and takes a very great interest in political affairs. He was one of the charter members of the late Trammel Lodge of Free Masons at Goshen, and he and wife are members of the Methodist Episcopal Church, South, and are much esteemed citizens.

Capt. Samuel Pinckney Pittman, deputy sheriff, and one of the prominent men of Washington County, Ark., was born ten miles southwest of Fayetteville, in what is now Prairie Grove Township, June 27, 1836, and is the son of James C. and Mary (Tuttle) Pittman, and grandson of Samuel Pittman. The parents were natives of North Carolina and Tennessee, respectively, and were frugal, industrious people. They were married in Arkansas in 1835, at the home of Solomon Tuttle. Their son, Samuel P. Pittman, grew to manhood in Prairie Grove Township, and adopted his father's business, that of farmer and stock raiser. In 1858 he married Miss Sarah Boone, daughter of William Boone (deceased), and niece of Col. Noah Boone, of Rocky Comfort, Mo. They became the parents of two children: William, who died in his eighteenth year of typhoid fever (June 17, 1878), and Mary, a young lady of education and refinement. Mrs. Pittman is a member of the Cumberland Presbyterian Church, and an active worker in the same. In June, 1862, Mr. Pittman entered the Confederate service, and after serving as orderly-sergeant one year was elected lieutenant of Company K, Thirty-fourth Arkansas Volunteer Infantry, Col. Brook's regiment, and rendered active and honorable service for three years. He surrendered his company, Company K, at Fort Smith, June 12, 1865. He was taken prisoner twice, but escaped each time. After the war he returned to his farming and stock raising, which he continued until 1882, when he retired. He took an active part in the organization of the Washington County Bank, became a member of its directory, in 1886 its vice-president, and is its present honored president, by election in 1888. Mr. Pittman served as trustee of the State University for several years, served as captain of the militia for several years after the war, and still holds that position. Upon the organization of the Grange movement in Washington County, Capt. Pittman rendered important aid, and became a charter member of Prairie Grove Grange. He was county master of the Grange for several years, and served as delegate to the State Grange and lecturer of this district. He owned a half interest in one of the first reapers and mowers brought into Northwestern Arkansas, was the first one to bring a wheat drill into the county, and he brought the first herd of Cotswold sheep and thoroughbred Short horn cattle into the county. Upon the organization of the county fair of Washington County, Ark., Mr. Pittman gave important support, and has held official connection with that institution since. He is one of the county's best citizens, and is universally respected.

Judge James Middleton Pittman, one of the distinguished jurists of the Fourth Judicial Circuit of Arkansas, was born near Prairie Grove May 1, 1838, and is the son of James C. and Mary A. (Tuttle) Pittman. Judge Pittman left home at the age of thirteen, clerked in a dry goods store and attended Ozark Institute. At the age of sixteen he became teacher of mathematics in Ozark Institute, and the following year he began reading law in the office of Hon. W. D. Reagan, of Fayetteville, being admitted to the bar from this office in his twenty-first year, before Judge Felix I. Batson. He immediately began practicing at Carrollton, Carroll Co., and continued at this until the war, when he enlisted his services in the State troops, and rendered effective and active service at Oak Hill, or Wilson's Creek, as captain of Company K, Walker's regiment. After the discharge of the State troops he entered the Confederate service as private of Company E, Sixteenth Arkansas Infantry, Hill's regiment, and participated in the battles of Pea Ridge, Corinth and siege of Port Hudson, La. Upon the reorganization, in 1862, he was elected from the ranks as major of his regiment, and was afterward promoted to the rank of lieutenant-colonel, taking command of the Sixteenth Arkansas. He was captured July 8, 1863, at Port Hudson, La., and was confined in the Federal prisons until released July 24, 1865, by special proclamation. After the war Judge Pittman spent a year in Carrollton, and in 1867 moved to Washington County, Ark. He represented that county and Benton County in the State Legislature of 1871. In 1874 he was elected circuit judge, holding the position until 1878. In 1882 he was re-elected, and has been elected to that incumbency ever since. He was married, in Carroll County, to Miss Margaret Peel, daughter of John W. Peel [see sketch elsewhere], and became the father of two sons and one daughter: Hubert N., a law student of promise; Jennie M. and Bob T. Judge Pittman is a member of the I. O. O. F., and Mrs. Pittman is a member of the Episcopal Church, and is an active worker in the same.

Thomas J. Pollard, one of the old and eminently respected citizens of Washington County, Ark., was born near Lexington, Ky., October 27, 1805, and is the son of William Pollard, a native of Fredericksburg, Va., where he grew up and married Miss Frances Hampton, the mother of our subject. After marriage they went to Kentucky, where the father followed farming and stock raising, and was a man of influence. Mr. Pollard was a friend of Daniel Boone, and was a soldier in the Revolutionary War, serving at Yorktown, and was present when Cornwallis surrendered. He was an intimate friend and supporter of Henry Clay, and was a member of the Baptist Church. Of the eight children born to his marriage only two are now living: Dr. Wade Hampton Pollard and Thomas J. Pollard, both of Fayetteville. The mother of these children was born at Winchester, Va., and is the daughter of Charles Hampton, a cousin to the elder Wade Hampton, father of the present United States Senator, Gen. Wade Hampton, of South Carolina. Dr. Thomas Pollard commenced attending school when a lad, first at the common schools, and finished his literary education in Transylvania University, at Lexington, Ky. He was a student all through his early manhood, and has so continued through his life. Of late years he sleeps only five hours per night, passing a goodly share of each night in "reading his journals." He read medicine for three years under Drs. Pindell and Satterwhite, and finished his private course under Prof. B. W. Dudley, at Lexington, Ky. He then attended three courses of lectures at Transylvania, from which institution he graduated as an M. D. in 1828. Dr. Pollard joined the Baptist Church near Lexington, Ky., in 1825, but in 1827 went with his church into the reformation known as the Christian Church. In March, 1828, he entered upon the practice of his profession at Nicholasville, Ky., where he remained about one year, and then went to Versailles in 1829. On April 14 of the same year he married Miss Mary Willis Stirman, who was born in Mercer County, Ky., and reared and educated at Nicholasville. Her father, Rev. William Stirman, was of a Virginia family, and a minister of the Christian Church. Her mother, Mrs. (Willis) Stirman, was of a Kentucky family, and her brothers, Edwin Winfield and Valentine Irwin, are in Texas, and are ministers in the Christian Church. Winfield Stirman served several terms in the Texas Legislature. From April, 1831, to March, 1839, Dr. Pollard practiced his profession in Palmyra, Mo., and in the last named year he settled at Fayetteville, Ark., and has practiced here ever since. He has been practicing for sixty years, and although now in his eighty-fourth year he can do about as much professional work as he ever could. He was the first president of the Washington County Medical Association, and assisted in organizing it. He is president of the District Medical Society of Northwest Arkansas, embracing seven or eight counties, and has been vice-president of the Arkansas State Medical Society. He has given special study to surgery, and has performed successfully most of the capital operations, and has never once failed in them. For a time, during the war, he was post surgeon at Fayetteville, and served as a surgeon in the Confederate army. He was in the battles of Oak Hills, Elk Horn, Fayetteville and Poison Springs. His service was irregular; when needed he would assist all he could. He has followed no business except his profession, has never engaged in any speculation nor held office of any kind. He became a Master and Royal Arch Mason at Palmyra, Mo., and was chairman of the committees that built two Masonic halls at Fayetteville. Dr. Pollard has always been ready to minister to the wants of his fellow man, and has been instrumental in raising the morals of the town to a high standard. On April 14, 1879, Dr. and Mrs. Pollard celebrated their golden wedding at their residence in Fayetteville, on which occasion about 400 of their friends and relatives from several States were present. By his marriage Dr. Pollard became the father of four children; Sarah Frances, who was born in Versailles, Ky., March 6, 1831, and who is a graduate of Johnson's Female Institute, at Georgetown, Ky., now the wife of Dr. Davis Polson, of Fayetteville. Mrs. Polson's daughter, Emma, by her first marriage with William R. Quarles, is now the wife of Richard M. Darnall, a lawyer and planter in Lake County, Tenn., and is the mother of three children: Jefferson Pollard, Mattie and Richard M. Darnall. Thomas William Pollard was born in Palmyra, Mo., March 3, 1853, and was educated in Arkansas College under President Robert Graham. He married Miss Elizabeth Cooper at Glasgow, Mo., and by her has three children: Joel H., an editor by profession; Stirman, in railway work, and Mary Rebecca, who is attending studies at the A. I. U. John Lilbourn, the third child born to Dr. Pollard, is a native of Palmyra, Mo., born in July, 1835, and educated at the Arkansas College (now deceased). Anna Eliza, the fourth living child of Dr. Pollard, was born in Fayetteville, was educated at Springfield, Mo., and is now the wife of John Vaughn, a hardware merchant at Fort Smith. She has three children: Mary Edith, Fannie Lucy and Millie Haley. Dr. Pollard is a persistent worker, is somewhat excitable, and comes to rapid conclusions, but is orderly and methodical in business, although too generous in going security to be called a successful financier. The Doctor was reared by a father whose morality could never be questioned, and Dr. Pollard has followed in his footsteps. He has never drank whisky, never chewed tobacco, never gambled, and has never let a man pay a dime for him in his life. He has been generous, and has lost financially by his generosity. As a reward for his temperate life the Doctor is well preserved, has good health, is cheerful, and most of all he has the unbounded respect of his fellow citizens. Mrs. Pollard, like her husband, was a member of the Christian Church, and passed away an honored life here, full in the faith of that society, and carrying with her a very cordial respect; she was esteemed by all who knew her for her grand wifely and material worth, and her very excellent Christian spirit, which she at all times maintained. She was well educated, and a woman of decision, but never formed opinions without evidence, and when her opinion was once formed was very seldom changed. She was of good conversational powers, had energy of character, was charitable to the poor, and her door was always open to the needy, notably so during the war. The occasion of their golden wedding was a grand tribute to their worth from all classes and creeds of good people, something of which this venerable couple, their children and grandchildren may well be proud.

John K. Pool may be mentioned as one of the progressive farmers of Washington County, Ark., and is also engaged in merchandising at Thompson's Post-office. He was born in Franklin County, Ark., in 1843, and is a son of M. P. and Lucinda (Gailey) Pool, who were born respectively in North Carolina and Georgia. After attaining man's estate the father went to South Carolina, thence to Georgia, where he was married and resided about ten years, and then came to Arkansas, residing successively in Franklin, Madison and Washington Counties. He located in the latter county in 1854, and was engaged in farming until his death in 1869 or 1870. He was justice of the peace of Washington County for about eight years, and was a soldier in the Mexican War. He was twice married, and by his first wife became the father of one son, Joseph, who was killed during the late war. His marriage to Miss Gailey resulted in the birth of ten children, five of whom are living: Augustus C., George W., Franklin M., Nancy (married) and John K. Those who are dead are Claiborne, Andrew, William, Sarah and Louis C. The mother of these children died in 1868. John K. Pool was reared in Washington County, and remained under the paternal roof until 1861, when in the fall of that year he went to Missouri and enlisted in Company B, First Arkansas Cavalry, and served under Gen. Harrison for three years, receiving his discharge in July, 1865, at Fayetteville. After returning home he resided on the old homestead until 1880, when he located on the farm of 235 acres where he now resides, and where he is engaged in stock dealing. He has eighty acres of land under cultivation, and in 1887 engaged in merchandising at Thompson's Post-office, where he has a fairly remunerative trade. He was first married to Miss Elizabeth Hash, and the following are the children born to their union: Claiborne (deceased), Mary (wife of David Moloy), Benjamin, John N., Calaway (deceased), Nettie and Hattie. Mr. Pool took for his second wife Mrs. Sarah Warner, who was born in Scotland, and came to the United States in 1854. To her first marriage was born one child, May. Her union with Mr. Pool has resulted in the birth of one child, Walter. Mr. Pool is a member of the Knights of the Horse, and politically he is a Republican.

George W. Pool, blacksmith, and one of the prominent farmers of the county, was born in Maryland October 23, 1837. His educational advantages were very limited, and at the age of eighteen he began learning the blacksmith's trade, and afterward followed this until 1861. In July of that year he enlisted in Company B, First Maryland Potomac Brigade, United States Army, and served over three years. He participated in the battles of Gettysburg, Winchester and many minor engagements. He was captured at Harper's Ferry, paroled, and exchanged about six months later. At the close of the war he continued blacksmithing, and worked at his trade in Ohio, Indiana, Illinois and Missouri. He afterward worked at Sedalia for his present employer, Mr. Oates, with whom he has been twenty years. In 1870 he came to this county, and in 1875 he chose for his companion in life Miss Louisa McLain, a native of Steuben County, Ind., who bore him five children, four sons and one daughter. Mr. Pool has 150 acres of land, situated two miles from town, and upon this his family are now living, while he works at his trade in Cincinnati. He has made all his property by his own efforts, and is a good, honest citizen. He is a Master Mason, is a Republican in politics, and his wife is a member of the Cumberland Presbyterian Church.

Augustin Clayton Poole is a successful farmer and fruit grower of Washington County, Ark., and was born in Hall County, Ga., August 29, 1828. The farm of 154 acres, on which he located in 1871, is one of the best in the county, and he also has twenty acres of bottom land on the White River. He was named after Judge Augustin Clayton, of Georgia, who was an old and highly esteemed friend of his father. He was reared and educated in Franklin County, Ark., and was there married, in 1849, to Elizabeth Dunn, soon after locating on a farm near Charleston, but in 1858 came to Washington County, Ark., locating on a farm on the White River. In 1863 he enlisted in Company I, First Arkansas Regiment, United States Army, and served his country faithfully until the close of the war. He then returned to his farm, and found it destitute of fencing and stock, and had to begin the battle of life anew. His wife died in March, 1865, having borne a family of five children, and his daughter Jane kept house for him until 1866, when he married Mrs. Elizabeth Lewis, widow of Henry Lewis, and by her became the father of two children. His second wife died in 1877, and in December, 1879, he was married to his third and present wife, Mrs.

Clarissa Lyons, widow of John Lyons, of Illinois. He is a stanch Republican in politics, and is a son of Mastin P. and Lucinda (Gailey) Poole, who were born in Greenville, S. C., and Hall County, Ga., respectively. The father was reared on a tobacco plantation, and in 1818 was married to Miss Gailey, and became a planter of Georgia. In 1830 he located in Hardeman County, Tenn., and four years later came to Arkansas, and improved a farm near where Charleston now is. In 1853 he went to Madison County, and in 1857 located in Washington County. He was a strong Union man during the war, and after suffering many persecutions and indignities at the hands of the Southern sympathizers, he was compelled to locate in Fayetteville for protection. He died in 1868, and his wife in 1867. They were the parents of twelve children, ten of whom lived to manhood and womanhood.

David C. Price, an enterprising farmer of Price Township, is the third of eleven children born to William and Delphia (Stanphill) Price. William Price was born in Kentucky, but his parents were natives of Ireland, who, after coming to America, settled in Maryland, where they remained a short time, and then moved to Kentucky, and from there to Tennessee, where William grew to manhood. Delphia (Stanphill) Price was born in Tennessee, and she, too, was of Irish parentage. Her father came to America when young, and served two years in the command of Gen. George Washington. Mr. and Mrs. Price were married in Warren County, Tenn., and after living there several years moved to McMinn County, of the same State. In 1832 they moved to Alabama, and five years later to Greene County, Mo., where the father died in 1838. The mother died in Crawford County, Ark., in 1873. Both were members of the Methodist Church. He was a Democrat in politics, and while a resident of Alabama held the office of county judge. Their son, David C. Price, was born November 5, 1814, in Warren County, Tenn., attained his growth on the farm, and received a limited education, never attending school more than twelve months altogether. He moved to Missouri with his parents, and was here married to Miss Frances Dillard, who died about five months later. In 1840 he came to Van Buren, Ark., and ran a ferry across the Arkansas River. At this time he was $750 in debt, and had only a miserable pony, which he turned loose after reaching Arkansas. At the end of six months Mr. Price had paid one-half of his debt, and at the close of the year paid the remainder. In 1842 he married Miss Catherine A. Shannon, who bore him six children, two sons and four daughters. At this time he turned his attention to farming, and has since continued this occupation. In 1851 he moved to Washington County, Ark., and located where he now lives. His second wife died in 1870, and the following year he married Miss Sarah Snyder, of Crawford County, and she died a year later. Mr. Price served about three months in the Florida War, and in 1848 he represented Crawford County in the State Legislature. After coming to Washington County he held the office of justice of the peace for about twenty years. He says he never but once had a desire to merchandise, and that was in 1852, when he sold goods for about two years in Dallas, Polk County, at a loss of about $10,000. He was a Whig previous to the war, and since then he has been a Democrat. When the township was laid off the court honored Mr. Price by giving it his name. Although seventy-four years of age he never uses a cane, and walks with the elastic step of youth. He is the owner of 213 acres of land, and has made all his property by his own efforts.

J. R. Pyeatt. The biographical department of this work would be incomplete without mentioning the Pyeatts, who were among the pioneer settlers of Arkansas, and were first represented in this State by James and Kate (Finley) Pyeatt, natives of North Carolina, who, in 1812, removed from Kentucky to about thirteen miles above Little Rock. Here they spent the remainder of their days. J. R. Pyeatt was born in Kentucky in 1805, and came to Arkansas with his parents, and was here reared to manhood. In August, 1827, he came to Washington County, and erected the first frame house ever built in the county, which is in good preservation, and in which he still resides. Having a natural taste for mechanics, he opened a wagon and blacksmith shop shortly after his arrival here, and followed that occupation for a number of years. He and his brother purchased some raw land, which they improved, but in 1861 Mr. Pyeatt engaged in the milling business, in partnership with his son-in-law, William S. Moore, and has since given that business the most of his attention. In 1831 he was married to Miss Elizabeth Buchanan, who was born and reared in West Tennessee. Her death occurred in 1868. William S. Moore, miller and farmer, was born in Greene County, Tenn., February 20, 1835, the son of Capt. Anthony, and grandson of David Moore, the latter being a soldier in the Revolutionary War. Anthony Moore was a farmer by occupation, and died in Greene County, Tenn., in the spring of 1880. His wife, whose maiden name was Nancy Holt, was also born in Tennessee. William S. Moore spent his youthful days on a farm in Tennessee, and made his home with his father until twenty-one years of age. He then learned the wagon-maker's trade, and in the fall of 1858 came to Arkansas, locating in Cane Hill, where he worked at his trade until the summer of 1862, when he joined the Thirty-fourth Arkansas Infantry, Confederate States Army, and served until the close of the war. He participated in the battle of Prairie Grove, and was paroled in the summer of 1865. He then returned home, and formed a partnership with Mr. Pyeatt in the milling business, and erected the Cane Hill Mills, which was in running order by the spring of 1866. The mill has been remodeled and improved since it was erected, and is now one of the finest mills in Washington County. It has a combined roller and buhr process, and has a capacity of about forty barrels per day. They also manufacture some lumber, and in 1869 added a carding machine, which has proved very profitable. In 1861 Mr. Moore married Miss Kate Pyeatt, a daughter of his partner, J. R. Pyeatt, and their union was blessed in the birth of four children: Henry (who is a physician of the county), Charles R., Bettie and Lucy. Mrs. Moore died in 1877, and he afterward married his present wife, Miss Josephine Moore, a daughter of James Moore. She was born in East Tennessee, and was reared in Texas and Missouri. They are members of the Cumberland Presbyterian Church, and are worthy citizens of the county. Mr. Moore has a good farm, which he manages in connection with his mill, and a fine orchard of forty-five acres.

Benjamin F. Ramey, a prominent farmer and citizen of White River Township, Washington Co., Ark., was born near where he now lives, December 16, 1839, and is a son of Owen and Elizabeth (Strickler) Ramey, and grandson of Owen Ramey, who was born in Virginia, and there married and reared a family of three children, his son, Owen, being born in that State in 1814. He was reared to maturity in Kentucky, however, and in 1836 came to Arkansas, after a short residence in Illinois. He located in Washington County, where he took up land, began improving a farm, and resided there until his death in 1878. He was an active worker and elder in the Christian Church, and was a Republican in politics. His wife was born in Hawkins County, Tenn., in 1818, and when about ten years old was brought to Arkansas, where she afterward met and married Mr. Ramey. She died three months after her husband, in 1878, having borne the following family of children: James M.; Benjamin F.; Mary J., wife of R. G. Daniel; Barbara E., who is the deceased wife of W. J. York; Ephraim; William; Sarah, wife of Henry Mills; Albert; Nancy A.; Margaret, wife of Jacob Wright; Henry G.; Mary J. and Sarah. Benjamin F. Ramey was reared under the home roof, in Washington County, where he continued until the opening of the War of the Rebellion, and in June, 1862, enlisted in Company B, First Arkansas Cavalry, and served until the cessation of hostilities. After his release from army life he returned home, and, after farming on the home place for four years, was married, and rented land near his old home, and began farming on his own responsibility. About five years later he moved to a farm about seven miles from where he now lives, but in 1884 came to his present location, where he has a valley farm of 230 acres, partly under cultivation. He has always taken an active interest in all public enterprises, and is especially interested in the cause of education. Mr. Ramey is a true type of the self-made men of Arkansas, and is indebted to self-effort for his success in life. He has acted with the Republican party since attaining his majority, but has never aspired to any political office. He was married to Miss Louvinia Lewis, a daughter of G. W. Lewis, and a native of Washington County, and by her is the father of five children: Matilda C., Lettie E., Lydia E., Daisy M. B. and Hattie G. Mrs. Ramey is a worthy and consistent member of the Christian Church.

Alexander W. Reed, a prominent farmer of Richland Township, was born in Sevier County, Tenn., May 13, 1825, the son of Robert and Elizabeth (Fagala) Reed, natives of Pennsylvania. The father was born August 6, 1788, and died in Washington County, Ark., September 16, 1861. The mother was born May 9, 1806, and is still living in this county. They were married in Sevier County, Tenn., in

1824, and in 1836 moved from there to McMinn County, of the same State, where they lived for seven years. From there they moved to Whitefield County, Ga., where they remained until 1852, and then moved to Northwestern Arkansas, and here the father died. He enlisted in the War of 1812, but was not mustered in. He was a blacksmith by trade, having served an apprenticeship of seven years. His father, Alexander Reed, died in Rockbridge County, Va., at the age of sixty-four, and the maternal grandfather of our subject served in the Revolutionary War. Mrs. Elizabeth (Fagala) Reed became a member of the Presbyterian Church when young; has been a faithful member since, and is a kind and loving mother. Her husband was an old-line Whig, but later a stanch Republican. Their family consisted of thirteen children, eight now living, and all but one in Washington County, Ark. They are named as follows: Adam, Catherine, (Still), Martha (Stockberger), Elizabeth (Putnam), Maria (Brown), Eliza (Webb), Robert A., and Alexander, who was named for his grandfather Reed. Alexander remained with his father until thirty-five years of age, and worked in the blacksmith shop for nine years, but not with the intention of following it in after life. He took charge of his father's business from the time he was fifteen years old, and at the death of his father it was all willed to him. He was married January 15, 1861, to Miss Elizabeth McGarrah, daughter of William McGarrah, a prominent business man of Fayetteville, and very wealthy. She was born in Fayetteville March 9, 1843, and by her marriage became the mother of ten children, seven now living: Mary, Robert W., John A., William M., Emma, Augustine and Jorden C. Three infants, Eliza J., Julia and James, died in infancy. Mr. Reed and wife are members of the Christian Church, and Mr. Reed is a Republican in politics. He has 147 acres of good valley land, with ninety under cultivation, and is an excellent citizen.

Andrew B. Reed, a progressive farmer of Washington County, Ark., and native of the same, was born on the 14th of June, 1830, and is a son of William and Margaret (Robinson) Reed. They were married in Ohio, the mother's native State, and about 1829 moved to Arkansas, and a year later to Washington County. Here the father died about 1845. He was an elder in the Cumberland Presbyterian Church, and became the father of eight sons and two daughters; six of his sons are living, and reside in Washington County. Andrew B. Reed was reared on a farm in Cane Hill Township, and well remembers the very crude implements that were used in tilling the soil and in reaping the grain in his boyhood days. He remained with his mother until he attained his twentieth year, and then began farming for himself, and after his marriage, which occurred in September, 1851, he purchased some land in Cane Hill Township, but at the end of three years sold it and began improving other places. In 1884 he purchased his present home property, which consists of 249 acres, with about 100 acres under cultivation, and besides this has another tract of land consisting of seventy acres, with thirty in cultivation. He has a fine orchard of about twenty acres, with 1,000 trees all in good bearing condition on this farm, and an orchard of six acres on the home place. His wife, Melissa Jane Scott, was a native of Washington County, and a daughter of Nimrod Scott. She died about 1874, leaving four daughters and one son: Margaret, wife of John Nelson, of California; Lizzie, wife of Edward Shirley; Joseph F., Sallie and Anna. Mr. Reed was married in 1876 to Mrs. Elizabeth A. (Pesterfield) Smith, a native of Tennessee. They are rearing an orphan boy by the name of Samuel Clay Reed, whom they took in his infancy.

George W. M. Reed, son of Anthony Alvis and Martha (Martin) Reed, was born in the Arkansas Territory, April 1, 1830, in what is now Franklin County, near Roseville. Anthony A. Reed was born near Pendleton Court House, S. C., and his father, George W. Reed, immigrated to Kentucky at a very early day, and made a home near Elizabethtown, Hardin County. The history of this branch of the Reed family in America dates back to the settlement of four brothers, natives of Wales, and their families, in the Shenandoah Valley, Va., in very early times. Maj. John Reed, one of the brothers, was he who commanded the American forces in the War for Independence, and fought the immortal Ferguson at King's Mountain. George W. Reed, one of the other brothers, made a settlement at a place known as Reed's Post-office and Reed's Creek in 1811. Three of his sons served in the War of 1812, from Bradley County, Tenn., and one of the sons, Alvis Reed, made a settlement on the Lovelace Purchase, Indian Territory, and afterward he settled seven miles southwest of Fay-

etteville in 1830.   He died upon the Elkhorn battle-field December 5, 1862.
John Reed died at Paint Rock, Ala., and George W. died at Lafayette, Ga. Mrs.
Martha (Martin) Reed, mother of subject, was the daughter of Capt. Joseph
Martin, who commanded a company at the battle of New Orleans, in the War
of 1812–14, from Wilson County, Tenn., and who died in Scott County, Ark.
George W. M. Reed spent his boyhood days in Arkansas, and at the age of thirty-two years began merchandising, which industry he has continued for over
twenty years, retiring and leaving it in the hands of Ferguson & Reed, brother-
in-law and son. He has four sons and four daughters living: Mary Elizabeth
(wife of William M. Lewis, merchant of Cane Hill, Ark.), Noah (deceased),
Sophia (deceased), John A. (of the firm of Reed & Ferguson, merchants of Fayetteville, his successors), Maggie (wife of Pressley A. Crawford), Lina, George
W. M. (an attorney by profession, at Fayetteville, associated with his father),
James Lafayette, William L. and Maud. Mr. Reed served as clerk of the circuit
court for six years, and in the late war he was captain of Company D, First Arkansas Cavalry, United States Army, and remained with the same until cessation of hostilities. He was postmaster at Fayetteville for some time, and has
been land agent and pension agent for a number of years. He is a member of
the Masonic fraternity, and a G. A. R.—member of Travis Post.

William D. Reed (deceased), an uncle of George W. M., and an elder brother
of Alvis Reed, made a settlement here in 1829, his farm adjoining A. A. Reed's.
He married Sarah Alexander, daughter of John Alexander, a native of Kentucky, who made a settlement here in 1829.   William D. Reed, by his marriage,
had twelve children, eleven of whom grew to manhood and womanhood, of
whom Ester (who married Jonas Peerson), John H., Richard, William J., George
W. C., Samuel M., Abigail (who married Enos Yoes), Martha (who married
Charles Pence), Sarah (who married Jacob Yoes, Sr.), Mary Ann (who married
Jacob Yoes, Jr.), James W. (who died as bugler of Capt. Reed's company, Company D, First Arkansas Cavalry, Federal service). The following war song,
composed by Col. W. M. Reed, is taken from a file of the Arkansas *Sentinel*, of
October 22, 1885. "It was often sung here by his father, Anthony A. Reed, in
long years ago," says the *Sentinel*, and its publication has been requested. Col.
George Reed sings it well, and says it reminds him of the days when his father
used to sing it around the old hearth-stone in his childhood days:

> When thundering war's loud cannons roar,
>   We left our families and our homes,
> Marched to the field of destiny
>   To die, or gain sweet liberty.
>
> Near Nashville town we did encamp,
>   On Cumberland's bank we pitched our tents—
> Staid there some eight days or more,
>   Boats and provisions to secure.
>
> Some did weep while others rejoice,
>   Their wives and sweethearts for to leave,
> To leave them all so far behind,
>   Awaiting for their long return.
>
> The Mississippi deep and wide,
>   As we sailed down its troubled tide,
> And many dangers we did screen,
>   In sailing down to New Orleans.
>
> But when these dangers were past and gone,
>   We soon did meet a thousand men,
> And in the field of battle go
>   To meet a bloody tyrant foe.
>
> December the 23d, at night,
>   The first attempt was made to fight;
> The volunteers from Tennessee
>   Were, killed and captured, ninety-three.

We kept the ground in battle array,
  Till December the twenty-eighth day,
They marched in order to our lines
  Till we frustrated their designs.

We kept the ground in battle array,
  Artillery on both sides did play;
Their fiery darts they at us threw,
  Were cannon balls and rockets too.

On New Year's morning as the sun did rise
  A heavy fog darkened the skies;
A British cannon did us alarm,
  Which made us fly to our arms.

We kept the ground in battle array,
  Till January the eighth day,
The British charged on us again,
  Which proved to them a day of pain.

Three thousand of their men did yield
  And lay as victims on the field;
The loss to us but did sustain
  In killed and wounded just thirteen.

And now we have gained a victory,
  And caused our enemy for to flee;
We long to hear General Jackson say,
  He will march us home to Tennessee.

And on our journey we will pursue.
  And bid Orleans a long adieu;
To Tennessee our course we'll steer
  To meet our wives and sweethearts dear.

John Reese is a native of Washington County, Ark., and was born in Cove Creek Township February 13, 1841. He remained with his parents until he attained his majority, and in October, 1862, enlisted in Col. Harrison's First Arkansas Cavalry, United States Army, and served until he was discharged in August, 1865. He was captured at the battle of Prairie Grove, and after being kept a prisoner for about a month was released, and rejoined his regiment in March, 1863. After the war he returned to his parents, who were residing in Missouri, and with them shortly after returned to Arkansas. June 4, 1868, he was married, in Cove Creek Township, to Miss Mary Jane Hodges, a daughter of W. H. Hodges, and their union has resulted in the birth of five children: Fannie J., James M., Thomas B., Ollie B. and Orpha J. In 1876 he located upon his present farm, and has 165 acres under cultivation, mostly bottom land, seven acres in orchard, eighty-eight acres in two tracts, besides other unimproved land. Since locating on his farm he has made valuable improvements, and has a good and comfortable home, and substantial barns and out-buildings. His parents, William W. and Frances J. (Halbert) Reese, were born on Duck River, Maury County, Middle Tenn., and Madison County, Ala., respectively, and were married and made their home in the former State until 1839, at which time they immigrated to Arkansas, locating on a tract of land in Cove Creek Township, Washington County, and still make Washington County their home.

Pleasant V. Rhea (deceased), one of the early settlers of this county, was born in Lincoln County, Tenn., grew to manhood there, and there married Miss Fannie B. White. They moved to Washington County, Ark., in 1830, and here Mr. Rhea followed the occupation of a blacksmith, and also taught school, taking his pay in corn, pumpkins, etc. His family consisted of seven children, three sons and four daughters. He was a member of the Baptist Church, and died at the age of sixty-one years. The mother is also a member of the same church, and is now living at the advanced age of eighty-eight years. Their eldest son, William H., was born in Lincoln County, Tenn., in 1825, and came with his parents to Washington County, Ark., where he learned the blacksmith trade.

At the age of twenty-four he opened a little grocery in Maysville, Benton Co., Ark., and after running that a short time he came to Cincinnati, and bought a stock of goods. Being a shrewd business man he gradually arose until at the time of his death he owned three stores, a mill and several farms, amounting in all to about $75,000. He was a public-spirited man, and was ever ready to contribute to worthy enterprises. He was a Democrat in his political views, and a member of the Masonic fraternity. He married Miss Elizabeth C. Powell, daughter of Dr. Samuel Powell, and a native of East Tennessee. This union resulted in the birth of eight children, four sons and four daughters. He died in 1884, but she is still living. Their fifth child, Robert J., is one of the most extensive merchants of Cincinnati. He was born at Rhea's Mills October 15, 1862, and was reared chiefly in the store. He had good educational advantages, and at the age of fourteen he commenced clerking in his father's store, and has handled goods ever since that time. After the death of his father he purchased his present store, and has the largest stock of goods in the county outside of Fayetteville. In 1886 he married Miss Myrtie, daughter of Charles McClellan, and a native of Washington County, Ark., born November 5, 1868. To this union one son, William H., has been born. Mr. Rhea is devoted to his business, and is accounted a wide-awake business man. He is a Democrat in politics, is a member of the I. O. O. F., and his wife is a member of the Cumberland Presbyterian Church.

Oren M. Rieff, a prominent farmer of Washington County, Ark., was born in Wilson County, Tenn., February 27, 1810, and is a son of John and Hannah (Ross) Rieff, and grandson of Christopher and Mary (Wilschannah) Rieff. The grandfather was of German descent, and was born in Pennsylvania, in which State he was living during the Revolutionary War. He settled in Wilson County, Tenn., about 1800, and reared to maturity a family of twelve children. He was a very active and energetic man until about middle age, then he had a stroke of paralysis, which left him helpless the remainder of his days. He died in 1824 at the age or seventy years. His wife was born in Lancaster County, Penn., and died in Tennessee in 1830, in her eightieth year. Their son, John Rieff, was their ninth child, and was born in Winchester, Va., June 9, 1787, and came to Tennessee in 1800. He remained with his parents but a short time after locating in Tennessee, but took up his abode with his elder brother, and began learning the carpenter's trade, and after attaining his majority was married and settled on a farm in Wilson County, Tenn., where he lived until 1838, and then sold out and came to Arkansas, with his wife and two children, taking up his abode near Fayetteville. During the Creek Indian War he, two brothers, Joseph and Jacob Rieff, and three of his brothers-in-law, Allen, James and George Ross, volunteered to serve in that conflict under Gen. Jackson, and Joseph Rieff also served in the Mexican War. Hannah (Ross) Rieff was born in North Carolina December 12, 1784, and was of Irish descent, her father, Henry Ross, having come from Ireland to the United States (in 1750) when a lad six years old, and locating in North Carolina, near Guilford Court House, where he grew to maturity and married Miss Mitchell, who bore him four children: Allen, James, George and Hannah. Mr. Ross was a soldier in the Revolutionary War, and was guarding prisoners when the battle of Guilford Court House was fought. His death occurred in Wilson County, Tenn., about 1825. Mrs. Hannah Rieff died in Washington County, Ark., April 17, 1853, and two of her eight children died in infancy. Those who lived to maturity are Oren M., Washington G. (deceased), Mary (deceased), Martin C. (deceased), Henry (deceased), and Elizabeth, wife of Capt. Kelley. Oren M., the eldest of their children, was reared in Wilson County, Tenn., and received a somewhat limited education in the subscription schools, but the most of his time was spent on the farm until nearly grown. He then began learning the carpenter's trade, which occupation he followed in after life to some extent. He was twenty-eight years of age when he came to Washington County, Ark., and the first two or three years of his residence here he was engaged in teaching school. In 1838 he located on a farm on the west fork of White River, where he lived for about nineteen years, and then settled on a farm of 340 acres where he now lives. He has always taken an active interest in educational matters, and is the oldest pedagogue of the county. He is a stanch supporter of Democratic principles, and has held a number of offices of trust. May 19, 1834, he was married to Matilda A. Fambro, who was born October 13, 1813, in Davidson County, Tenn., and by her became the father of ten children, five of whom are living: Mary J., wife of James Evans; Eliza C., Henry, Margaret D., and Laura, wife of Thomas Fine. Those dead are John W., Robert S., Susan E., Matilda A. and Oren M. John and Robert were soldiers in the Confederate army. May 19, 1884, Mr. Rieff celebrated his golden wedding, his children and all his grandchildren being present, save one. His son, Henry M., resided with him until 1885, when he went to Fayetteville and began keeping a family grocery, which occupation he followed until the spring of 1888. Since that time he has resided with his parents.

R. L. Ritter, dealer in general merchandise at Elm Springs, Ark., and native of the town in which he now resides, was born in 1852, and is a son of James and Julia Ann (Harroll) Ritter. The father was born in 1817 in Tennessee, and was there married to Miss Harroll, by whom he became the father of ten children, R. L. Ritter being the seventh child. The mother died some time in the fifties, and the father was afterward married to Miss Sarah Akin, and resides in Elm Springs. Here R. L. Ritter was reared to manhood and educated. When about twenty-one years of age Miss Margaret A. Painter became his wife. Their union resulted in the birth of six children: Lucy E., Edward N., Georgia May, Allie, Katie, and Robert L. Until 1878 Mr. Ritter was successfully engaged in tilling the soil, but at that date he abandoned that calling, and spent a year each in Texas and Missouri, then returned to Arkansas, and engaged in general merchandising at Elm Springs, where he has a large and lucrative trade, which is constantly on the increase. He began life with a small capital, but has steadily gained ground until he now ranks among the first business men of the town. He is a Democrat, a member of the Missionary Baptist Church, and belongs to the A. F. & A. M.

Thomas Roberts, a successful tiller of the soil, is the son of Wiley and Anna (Tharp) Roberts, both natives of Hawkins County, Tenn., where they grew up and were married. The grandparents on both sides were soldiers in the Black Hawk War. Mr. and Mrs. Roberts remained in Hawkins County until 1853, when they built a boat, started from Rogersville, Tenn., and floated down to the mouth of the Arkansas River. They reached this county in 1854, and here they spent the remainder of their days. He died in 1863, at the age of forty-six, and she died in 1879, at the age of sixty-one. He was a Whig in politics, and had followed the occupation of a farmer all his life. The mother was a member of the Missionary Baptist Church. In their family were eleven children, eight sons and three daughters. The second child, Thomas, was born in Hawkins County, Tenn., May 31, 1840, was reared on the farm and secured a limited education. He remained on the farm and worked for his father until twenty-one years of age, when he engaged in business for himself. September, 1862, he enlisted in the Confederate army, but only remained a short time, when he went north and joined Company M, Eighth Missouri Cavalry Volunteers, United States Army, and served three years. He was in the battles of Little Rock, Jenkins' Ferry, Pumpkin Bend, and many minor engagements. After the war he returned and remained with his mother until 1868, when he married Miss Mary F. Moore, who was born in this county February 19, 1846. They became the parents of four children: Wiley, James, Louis E. and Carrie. Wiley and James both died the same day, August 22, 1877. Mr. Roberts is the owner of 183 acres of land, ninety acres being under cultivation, and this has nearly all been made by his own exertions. He is a Republican in his political views. He and Mrs. Roberts are members of the Missionary Baptist Church, and he is an honest, upright citizen.

Rev. J. C. Robertson, pastor of the Baptist Church at Elm Springs, Ark., was born in Greene County, Tenn., in 1846, and is a son of Jesse and Margaret (Collier) Robertson, who were farmers by occupation, and the parents of nine children, J. C. Robertson being the only one now living. His grandfather was Col. John Collier, of the Revolutionary War. At about the age of twenty-one years he left home and went to Illinois, and became a student in Shurtleff College, which institution he attended four years. Our subject began to preach in the Presbyterian Church in Greene County, Tenn., and one year after, just before entering Shurtleff College, he changed his views and became a Baptist. After attaining his twentieth year he had been engaged in preaching the gospel, and after leaving college he again resumed preaching, his first location being at Beauregard, Miss., where he remained one year. He next removed to Auburn, Kas., remaining three years, and was also pastor of the Dover (Kan.) Church for two years.   He was next pastor of the Cedar Creek (Mo.) Church for three years, and at the end of that period came to Arkansas, and has been pastor of the Wager Mill Baptist Church ever since.   He has organized a church at Elm Springs, to which he is devoting his time and attention.   He is peculiarly fitted for discussing theological questions, having gained considerable notoriety by discussing such questions with able men representing other faiths.   He has the largest library of theological and historical works in the county, and is a constant reader and close student.   He has been clerk and treasurer of the Baptist Association, of Benton County, Ark., for ten years, and is well posted in the history and doctrine of the church which he represents.   He votes the Democratic ticket, and is a member of the A. F. & A. M.   While residing in Mississippi he was united in marriage to Miss Sazine Vitzalon Tillman, who was born in that State in 1852, and their union has been blessed in the birth of five children, two of whom are living, Theodosia and Effie.

David E. Robinson, retired farmer and a prominent old resident of West Fork Township, Washington Co., Ark., was born in Dickson County, Tenn., in 1818, and is a son of William and Sarah (Stafford) Robinson.   The father was born in Kentucky, and after the death of his parents was reared by an elder brother.   He served in the War of 1812 under Gen. Jackson, and was a participant in the battle of Horse-shoe Bend.   After the close of that war he located in Louisiana, and afterward came to Tennessee, where he was married in 1814.   After residing in that State and Illinois until 1834 he came to Arkansas, and in the spring of 1835 located on a farm of 120 acres on the West Fork of White River. While in Tennessee he held the office of justice of the peace, and was a soldier in the Seminole and Indian War.   He died on his farm in Washington County June 8, 1840.   His wife was a native of Tennessee, and became the mother of the following named children (five of whom are living at the present time): Aaron; Lovisa, wife of E. S. Jackson; Susan, wife of C. Harper; Catherine, wife of Mr. Wheeler; David E., Jacon, Sherod, Anson and William.   The mother died in 1877.   David E. Robinson's early days were spent in Tennessee, Illinois and Arkansas, the greater part of his education being received in the two latter States.   He served one year in the Seminole War, and then returned home, and was married in March, 1841, to Mary Harrer, daughter of Enos Harrer, who was a prominent man and early settler of Washington County.   He died of cholera while on a trip to Oregon in 1852.   Mrs. Robinson died February 16, 1882, having borne a family of nine children: Alex., John W., William H. (deceased), Sarah J.; Elizabeth, wife of E. S. Webb; Frank; Dora, wife of J. Emerson; Mary L. (deceased).   Mr. Robinson purchased 320 acres of land in 1850, but has divided it among his children.   He was a strong Union man during the late war, and throughout life has been a Whig and Republican in politics.   He has been a member of the Christian Church for thirty years, and has lived an active and useful life.   His son, John W., was born in Washington County March 10, 1844, and was reared to manhood in his native county.   During the late war he was employed as teamster in the quartermaster's department, being a participant in the battles of Prairie Grove, Ark. and Iron Mountain.   He resided in Illinois for some time after the war, and then returned to Fayetteville, where he was married in 1870 to Miss Mary M. Forrester, and until 1886 resided on a farm on the West Fork of the White River.   Since that time he has resided on the old home farm, where he owns a fine tract of land consisting of 220 acres, with over 100 acres under cultivation.   Mr. and Mrs. Robinson are the parents of four children: Nora, George W., Rosa M. and John Roy.   He is a member of the A. F. & A. M., and Christian Church, and in his political views is a Republican.   Mrs. Robinson is a native of South Carolina, and is also a member of the Christian Church.   Her father, William Forrester, is still living, and resides in Texas.

John M. Robinson, a skillful blacksmith, of Elm Springs, Ark., was born in Alabama in 1838, and is a son of Archibald Robinson, who was also born in Alabama, and was overseer on a plantation.   He was married to Sarah French, and their union was blessed in the birth of two children, their son, John M., being reared on a plantation in his native State.   At the age of sixteen years he determined to carve out his own future, and accordingly went to Texas, where he remained seven months, and then took up his abode in Arkansas, locating first in Lafayette County, where he was engaged in tilling the soil and learning the blacksmith's trade, and afterward, in 1860, settled in Franklin County.   In

February, 1863, he joined the Federal army, and served in Company C, First Arkansas Infantry, until 1864, and was then promoted to lieutenant in Company A, same regiment, and served until the close of the war, participating in the following battles: Elk Horn, Poison Spring and Jenkin's Ferry, besides numerous skirmishes. He was married while in Lafayette County, Ark., in 1858, to Miss Mary J. Waldrip, who was born in Alabama in 1840, and by her became the father of four children: Mary E., James Monroe, Sarah A. and Henry D. Mr. Robinson remained in Franklin County, Ark., farming and working at his trade until 1873, when he came to Washington County, locating near Elm Springs, and in 1883 became a member of the blacksmith firm of Smith & Robinson. Mr. Robinson is a stanch supporter of the principles of the Republican party, and is a member of the A. F. & A. M. and G. A. R. All the family belong to the Christian Church.

Dr. Samuel E. Rogers, of Prairie Grove, Ark., was born at Pendleton Court House, S. C., January 28, 1834, and is a son of Hugh Rogers, who was a native of the same State. His father and three brothers were born in Ireland, and were among the very early settlers of South Carolina. Hugh Rogers was married to Miss Martha W. McWhorter, and moved to Hall County, Ga., in 1839, making that State their home until 1851, when they moved to Arkansas, and settled in Washington, where the father is still residing at the extreme old age of ninety-two years. His wife died in 1873. Dr. Samuel E. Rogers received a good education in the common schools and academies of Georgia and Arkansas, and began the study of his profession in the former State, continuing the same after coming to Arkansas under the preceptorship of Dr. Clark and, afterward, Dr. Rogers. He began practicing his profession during the war, and has continued the same until the present time, and now ranks among the first physicians of the county. He has also been largely engaged in farming, and has upward of 900 acres in three farms, with 500 acres under cultivation. He was married January 23, 1834, to Miss Julia Ann West, a native of East Tennessee, and by her is the father of four children: Samuel H., Annie (wife of W. T. Neal), James C. and John E. The Doctor and his wife are members of the Methodist Episcopal Church, South, and he is a Master Mason.

James M. Russell, one of the well-to-do farmers and merchants of Washington County, Ark., and a native of the county in which he resides, was born on the 17th of February, 1837. His parents, J. B. and Ann (Coulter) Russell, were Tennesseeans, and came to Arkansas about 1831, locating on a farm in Washington County. Since the death of his wife, in 1865, the father has resided with his son, James M. The latter received a good practical business education in the common schools and at Cane Hill College, and assisted his father on the farm until the breaking out of the war. In 1862 he enlisted in Col. Brooks' regiment, and at the battle of Prairie Grove lost his right arm, which was shot off by a cannon ball, just below the elbow. He was taken to the hospital, and his arm was amputated above the elbow. After receiving his discharge he returned home, and has since been engaged in tilling the soil. He has 225 acres of land, a portion of which was part of the old homestead; has 100 acres under cultivation and 175 acres fenced. He has an apple orchard of ninety acres, on which are 3,600 trees, of the Ben Davis variety, and the yield from his orchard this year amounts to 25,000 bushels of apples. He has an evaporator, and dries about 100 bushels of green fruit per day. Since 1886 he has been engaged in the mercantile business in Newton, and is doing a fair business. In July, 1861, he was married to Miss Mary Beller, a native of Hempstead County, Ark. She is a teacher of instrumental music, and is exceptionally well educated. Her children are as follows: William C., Ewert, Ola and Nona.

Robert A. Rutherford, one of the leading merchants of Washington County, and president of Elkins Mercantile & Mill Company, was born in McMinn County, Tenn., September 17, 1830. The company was organized August 6, 1888, with Henry Stoklenberry as secretary, and J. F. Hood, treasurer. These are roller process mills, with four double sets of rollers, and one set of corn buhrs. The firm carry a stock of goods valued at $4,000, and do a business of $8,000, but expect to do better. Larkins and Frances (Hester) Rutherford, parents of Robert A. Rutherford, were born in South Carolina in 1799 and 1796, respectively. The father died in McMinn County, Tenn., in 1854, and the mother in the same county in 1856. They were married in their native State, and moved to McMinn County a short time before the birth of Robert A. The father was a miller all his life, and in 1836 assisted in gathering up the Cherokee Indians in order to place them in their Territory. Both parents were members of the Missionary Baptist Church, and the father was a Democrat in politics. To their marriage were born nine children, six now living: Sarah, widow of William Harris; J. M., deceased; A. H.; W. P., deceased; C. H., a fruit grower; Robert A.; Elizabeth, deceased; L. B., and Adaline, wife of H. P. Moss. In 1852 Robert A. Rutherford left home and went to Chattanooga, where he worked at the brick mason's trade. He then returned to McMinn County and began farming, which he continued until he came to Washington County, Ark., in 1857, and here he has remained ever since, engaged in farming and merchandising. Although starting with little or no means, he has been quite successful, and is accounted one of the successful merchants of the county. During the war he served three years in the quartermaster's department, Federal army, stationed at Raleigh, Mo. After the war he held the office of justice of the peace for seventeen years, and is now notary public. He was postmaster at Hood three years, and through his influence the office was established. On the 3d of May, 1885, he married Miss Lough Miller, who was born in Meigs County, Tenn., July 9, 1836. Both he and wife are members of the Methodist Episcopal Church. He is a member of the Masonic fraternity, and of the K. of the H.; he is a Republican in politics, and an excellent citizen.

Dr. S. P. Sample, whose career as a medical practitioner of Washington County, Ark., has met with marked success, was born in Greene County, Tenn., May 9, 1841, being one of two surviving members of a family of four children born to the marriage of Robert Sample and Mary Johnson, both of whom were born and reared in Tennessee. They were married about 1837, and after the father's death, which occurred in 1846, the mother was married to a man by the name of Alexander Rice, and spent the remainder of her days in Illinois, dying in 1880. She became the mother of one child by her last union. Samuel P. Sample grew to maturity in Sullivan and Grundy Counties, Mo., and after receiving a good education in the English branches, began the study of medicine under the instruction of Dr. Mantlow, and afterward was graduated from the Nashville Medical College as an M. D. He immediately located at Modena, Mo. At the breaking out of the Rebellion, in 1861, he enlisted in Company A, Twenty-third Missouri Infantry, and served under Gens. Grant and Sherman until the close of the war. He was wounded at the battle of Shiloh, and was with Sherman on his famous march to the sea, and witnessed the surrender of Gen. Johnston. After the war he located in Mercer County, Mo., and in 1866 was united in marriage to Mary E. Bradley, a daughter of James Bradley, a prominent merchant and stock dealer of that county, and in 1870 took up his abode in Franklin County, Ark., thence to Washington County in 1877. Since 1881 he has resided at West Fork, and has become one of the leading physicians of the county, being one of the examining surgeons of the Springdale Examining Pension Board. He takes an active interest in politics, and is a strong supporter of the principles of the Republican party, and belongs to the G. A. R. He is a Master Mason, and is a member of the I. O. O. F., and represented that fraternity in the Grand Lodge. He is the father of the following children: Emma E., William D., Belle and Eddie. He and family worship in the Methodist Episcopal Church.

John Sanders may be mentioned as one of the prosperous farmers and fruit growers of Washington County, Ark., and was born in Orange County, Ind., in 1834, being a son of Henry and Sarah (Laswell) Sanders. The father was born in Kentucky in 1810, but was reared in Indiana, whither he had been taken with his parents at an early day. He was a farmer and school-teacher by occupation, and is still residing in Lawrence County, Ind. The mother died when her son John was very young, and he was reared to manhood by his father. Through his own exertions he has acquired a good education, and spent several years in teaching school. In 1873 he came to Arkansas, and at the end of five years went to Kansas, but after remaining a short time returned to Washington County, where he has since made his home. He is one of the leading Prohibitionists in the county, and has always taken a deep interest in educational matters and affairs pertaining to the welfare of the county, and has held the office of justice of the peace for two years. While residing in Indiana, in 1852, he was married to Miss Mary Way, by whom he became the father of nine children: T. C., the eldest, a daughter, died in Texas; Eli H.,

Alfred N., G. W. P., died in Indiana; Miss E. L., J. G., John D., Sallie M. and Naomi C. Mr. Sanders is a member of the Argricultural Wheel and the I. O. O. F., and he and family worship in the Missionary Baptist Church. Mr. Sanders' paternal grandfather, Joseph Sanders, was a Virginian, and a son of Henry Sanders, who was a Baptist minister in England, but died in America.

L. A. Sanders, another of Washington County's most wide-awake, thorough-going farmers, was born in that county, and is the son of Anderson Sanders. of Spring Valley. The father was born in Indiana, and came to this State in 1859, locating at or near Spring Valley, where he has followed farming and merchandising ever since. His son, L. A., attended school in Washington County, and secured the best education that the county afforded. He has followed in the footsteps of his father, has tilled the soil all his life and has been very successful. He owns 280 acres of as fine land as there is in the county, 175 being cultivated and well improved. In 1884 he selected his life's companion in the person of Miss Mollie McCarthy, and they are the parents of two children: Paul and Welmet. Mrs. Sanders is the daughter of John and Mary McCarthy, of Fort Smith, Ark. Both Mr. and Mrs. Sanders are members of the church, he of the Baptist denomination and she of the Catholic, and both are respected and esteemed by all their acquaintances.

John W. Scott. In mentioning the prominent farmers of Washington County, Ark., the list would be incomplete without the name of Mr. Scott, who is a native of the State in which he now resides, being born in Crawford County September 2, 1832. It is not known where his parents, Joseph and Mary (Larremore) Scott, were born, but they were very early residents of Crawford County, Ark. Cove Creek Valley was then a solid cane-brake, and the country was in a very wild and unsettled condition. The father was a farmer, and died in 1850 at the age of sixty-five years. His wife died in 1878, aged about sixty years. After Mr. Scott's death she was married to W. C. Maxey, and moved to Franklin County, Ark. Mr. Scott was also twice married, but his first wife's name is not known. To his last marriage were born one daughter (deceased), and three sons (living): James W., William N. and Joseph M. James M., being the eldest of the family, was the main support of the family after his father's death. He managed the farm for his mother until 1854, and then located on his present farm, which consists of 300 acres. May 1, 1851, he married Emily, a daughter of Roland E. Hodge, who was a Tennesseean. Mrs. Scott was born in Tennessee January 10, 1833, and died in Washington County, Ark., March 16, 1871, deeply mourned by her family and friends. The following are her children: William H., Mary A. (wife of Jasper Cole), Charlie C., Martha A. (wife of W. V. Walker), John and Edwin W. In 1871 Mr. Scott married Mary F. Hardesty, who was born in Washington County, Ark., March 2, 1844, and is a daughter of Loving Hardesty. Mr. and Mrs. Scott are church members, and he is a Republican and a member of the K. of H. In August, 1862, he was conscripted into the Confederate army, but about the 12th of October he left the Confederate army and later came home. In April, 1863, he went to Springfield, Mo., and joined the Federal service, and was a forage teamster for three years. In June, 1863, the family moved to Missouri, but in the spring of 1864 returned to Arkansas, and in April went to Fort Smith. In August of the same year Mr. Scott took his family to Fayetteville, but very shortly after took them to Pope County, Mo., where they remained until the close of the war. In 1866 he returned with his family to Arkansas, where he found his house burned to the ground and his property destroyed, but he immediately set to work, and with the assistance of his wife and sons soon replaced what had been destroyed, and is now one of the prosperous farmers of Washington County.

Peter S. Scott was born in Montgomery County, Ky., September 28, 1814, and is the son of James and Elizabeth (Sholtz) Scott. The father was born in North Carolina about 1787, and the mother in the same State in 1791. They both came to Kentucky when young, were married in this State, and after several years they moved to Floyd County, Ind. Both died in this State, the father in 1835 and the mother about 1873. They reared nine children, Peter S. being the seventh child. He remained with his parents on the farm until twenty-five years of age, when he engaged in farming for himself in Indiana, and continued at this ten years. He then went to Decatur County, Iowa, remained there nineteen years, and then moved to the northern part of Washington County, Ark., and after an eighteen months' residence in this county moved to the southeast part of Benton County, of the same State. He had been a farmer previous to this time, but now he began operating a saw and grist-mill, and continued this for eleven years. He then moved to the place where he now lives, in Washington County, two miles east of Goshen, in the mountains. Here he has 130 acres of land, eighty under cultivation, and has been very successful in all his business transactions. In 1839, while in Indiana, he married Miss Sophia Miller, a native of that State, and to them were born twelve children, eight of whom are now living and married and have families: Mary E., widow of T. K. Gardner; Lucinda A., wife of W. B. Still; Rachel, wife of B. Homesley; Houston M.; Peter J.; Sarah J., wife of John Webb; Indiana I., wife of Thomas Dutton, and Nevada T., wife of Moses Dutton, Jr. The mother of these children died November 16, 1886. She was a member of the Church of God, and an excellent lady. Mr. Scott is a member of the same church, is a Democrat in politics, and has filled a number of township offices.

Robert R. Scott, a prominent young farmer of Washington County, Ark., is a native of Pulaski County, Ark., born December 17, 1861. His parents, Robert A. and Eliza (Hix) Scott, were born in Tennessee, and the father was first married to a Miss Patty Haines, by whom he has a family of three children. His last marriage, to Miss Hix, was blessed in the birth of four children: Elizabeth, Mrs. Horner; Robert R. and two children who died in infancy. Mr. Scott came to Pulaski County, Ark., when a young man, and was engaged in farming in that county until 1879, when he brought his family to Washington County, and here resided until his death, which occurred June 11, 1887. He was a devout Christian and an earnest worker in the Methodist Episcopal Church, South, and was also a strong supporter of the principles of the Democratic party. His wife, who was born on the 10th of August, 1819, is still living, and resides in Washington County. Robert R. Scott was reared in Pulaski County, and in 1879 came with his parents to Washington County. Here he was married on the 12th of November, 1882, to Miss Edna E. Barnes, who was born in November, 1863, and a daughter of Wiley Barnes. They have three interesting little children: Gertrude M., Ida B. and Robert B. In starting out in life for himself, Mr. Scott's sole possessions consisted of a span of horses, but by judicious management and indomitable energy he is now the owner of an excellent farm of 169 acres, nearly all of which is under cultivation. Although a young man, he has already taken a prominent place among the representative farmers of the county, and is a good calculator, financier and business man. He is a worthy member of the Knights of the Horse, and has always supported the Democratic party.

Rufus R. Seay, merchant, miller and blacksmith, is the son of Obadiah and Sallie (Rice) Seay. The parents moved from Tennessee to Van Buren, Crawford Co., Ark., in 1829, and here the father left the remainder of the family and went on foot to Washington County, of the same State, in order to find a good location. With an ox team he moved to Cane Hill, of the last named county, and lived for some time in a log house, 16x18 feet, the logs of which he carried on his back. He was a farmer all his life, was a Democrat in politics, and both he and wife were members of the Methodist Episcopal Church. After the death of his wife Mr. Seay married again. To his first marriage were born three children and to the second marriage five children. Rufus R. was the eldest of all the children. He was born October 12, 1830, in Washington County, Ark., was reared to farming, and educated in the old subscription schools. At the age of eighteen he began learning the blacksmith trade, at which he worked until 1880. In the fall of 1861 he enlisted in Capt. Buchanan's company, Arkansas State troops, and served about three months. A year later he hired as blacksmith for Col. Waitey's regiment, but was soon released, returned to Cane Hill, this county, and here followed his trade. In 1868 he married Miss Jane Kimbrough, daughter of Thomas and Elizabeth Kimbrough, and by her became the father of five children: Bettie S., Austell, Thomas Obadiah, Belle and Ellen. In 1880 Mr. Seay moved to Dutch Mills. He is the owner of a store, half of the mill at Dutch Mills, and is also the owner of 240 acres of land; is a Democrat in his political views, and a Master Mason. Mrs. Seay is a member of the Baptist Church at Dutch Mills.

Thomas J. Shannon, a successful and enterprising agriculturist of Vineyard Township, was born in this township April 7, 1842, and is the son of Alexander and Pernarza (Oliver) Shannon, both natives of Kentucky. They were married in Washington County, Ark., where each had moved with their parents when small, and reared a family of seven children, three sons and four daughters. The mother died at the age of thirty, and the father afterward married Mrs. Sarah Crutchfield, who bore him one child. The father is still living, is seventy-six years old, and has followed agricultural pursuits all his life. His son, Thomas J., reached years of manhood on the farm, and received a limited education in the common schools. In 1862 he enlisted in Company A, Second Cherokee Regiment, Confederate States Army, and served until the close of hostilities, being promoted to the rank of third lieutenant the last two years. Since the war he has followed agricultural pursuits. In 1867 he married Miss Cynthia Denton, a native of Tennessee, born February 3, 1846, and the daughter of Greenberry Denton. Eight children, five sons and three daughters, were the fruit of this union. Mrs. Shannon died November 16, 1887. She was a member of the Methodist Episcopal Church, South, and an excellent woman. Mr. Shannon is the owner of 125 acres, of which ninety are tillable. He has made this county his home all his life, and is a man well respected by all who know him. He is a Democrat in his political principles.

Joseph Bryant Shannon, county clerk of Washington County, Ark., was born in Crawford County, of the same State, November 20, 1851, and is the son of Jeremiah and Elizabeth (Bryant) Shannon. The father was a native of Virginia, of the Old Dominion, and a farmer by occupation. He came with his father, John Shannon, to Arkansas when a young man (1827), and settled in Sebastian County, of that State. He was married in Crawford County to Miss Elizabeth Bryant, a native of Crawford County, Ark., and the daughter of Joseph Bryant, who was also a native of Sebastian County, and who settled in Crawford County, Ark., in 1832. Jeremiah Shannon died when his son, Joseph B., was a small boy, and the mother afterward married Rev. Thomas Dodson, who made a home in Madison County, Ark., where Joseph B. grew to manhood. The subject of this sketch was reared on a farm, and when a young man engaged in merchandising as clerk in a store at Wesley, Ark. He afterward embarked in the grocery business at Wesley for himself, but sold out and bought land in Washington County, Ark., in 1879. He then engaged in trading and dealing in live stock for about five years, and in 1884 he was elected clerk of the county, and was re-elected in 1886 with an increased majority. After moving to this county he married Miss Minerva Adaline Garrett, daughter of James and Charity (Kimmins) Garrett, and a native of Tennessee. To them were born six children: Dora Gertrude, Maggie H. (deceased), James Gunter, Martha Hasselteen, Tommie Juanita and an infant named Mary. Mr. Shannon is a member of the K. of H. and K. of P. societies, and a member of the Baptist Church. During the Grange movement in Wesley he took an active part, and was a charter member of Wesley Grange.

John Allen Shepard, farmer and stock raiser, was born in Vermilion County, Ind., in 1828, and is a son of Hiram and Linda (Markham) Shepard, who were born, reared and married in Kentucky, the latter event taking place in 1816. They resided on a farm in their native State until 1826, then moving to Indiana, where the father worked at the blacksmith's trade until 1832. They then returned to Kentucky, and eventually became the owners of a fine farm of 400 acres, but sold out and came to Arkansas in 1859, where he died in 1868. His wife died December 3, 1849. They became the parents of six children, only three of whom lived to maturity: James, Rhoda J. and John A. The latter was reared on a farm, and learned the blacksmith's trade of his father. In 1851 he was married to Miss Frances Wilson, and after farming in his native State until 1857 moved to Randolph County, Ark., and engaged in farming. His wife was born in Virginia, and died in 1861, being a daughter of James Wilson, who was a soldier in the Revolutionary War, and the mother of five children, all of whom are dead. In 1862 Mr. Shepard joined the Confederate army, and was on active duty, under Gen. Price, until the close of the war. He then returned to his farm in Randolph County, and in connection with his agricultural labors worked at his trade. In 1865 he was married to Mary S. Killcrese, of Randolph County, and in 1870 came to Washington County, and has since been a farmer of the county. He has 175 acres of land, with ninety acres under cultivation, on which are good buildings and a nice orchard. Mrs. Shepard was born and reared in Mississippi, and is the mother of nine children: Celert, wife of James Graham; Ben, John, Clyde, Quincy, Hiram, Lambert, Everett and Mary. The family are members of the Missionary Baptist Church.

Berry V. Sherrod, a wide-awake, stirring young farmer of Goshen Township, was born in Madison County, Ark., seven miles south of Hindsville, where Garrett Williams lives, March 29, 1859, and is the son of Sterling B. and Margaret (Lankford) Sherrod. The father was born in Tennessee, and came to this county with his father, William Sherrod, when a young man. Here he grew to maturity, and later in life moved to where G. Williams lived. He was a farmer. He died in 1864, and his wife died just three weeks and two days before his death. They left a family of eight children. Seven of the family died within seven months, leaving only three children, of whom our subject is the only one positively known to be living. He was reared an orphan, began farming when quite young, and this occupation he has since continued. June 24, 1877, Miss Mary K. Wilkerson became his wife, and to them were born five children: Sterling T., Eva M., Arva L., William V. and Mamie. The same year of his marriage Mr. Sherrod settled on the farm where he now resides, which consists of 181 acres, fifty acres being rich bottom land, and ninety acres under cultivation. He has a nice home, and has succeeded well.

Baylis Shumate is a native of Harlan County, Ky., born in 1835, and is a son of William and Sarah (Ball) Shumate, who were born, reared and married in Kentucky, and had a family of two children before coming to Arkansas. They located in Madison County, of the latter State, and there improved a farm and lived for about twelve years, and then came to Washington County, where the father died, January 12, 1877, aged sixty-three years, one month and twenty-one days. His widow is still living, and resides with one of her sons, near Farmington, Ark., being seventy-two years of age. The following are her children who are living: Baylis, Anna, Clarissa, Mark and Nancy. Baylis Shumate was reared to maturity under the home roof, and throughout his life has been engaged in farming. At the age of nineteen years, nine months and twenty-two days he was wedded to Nancy Homesley, who died in 1858, leaving three children: William, Sarah and Viola (deceased). Elizabeth Cole became the second wife of Mr. Shumate, and their union resulted in the birth of eight children: James, John B., Clarissa A., Edie J., Ida B., Bennett and two infants (deceased). Mrs. Shumate was born in Madison County, Ark., her parents being natives of Kentucky, and early residents of Arkansas. Mr. Shumate served in the Confederate army in the late war, and in his political views is a Democrat. He owns a good farm of 420 acres of land, 120 being under cultivation and 300 in timber. He is a member of the Knights of the Horse. His son William is married and resides near Farmington; Sarah is the wife of George Thomas, residing on Richland Creek, and James and John married twin sisters, Cora and Nora Ratliff; Clarissa is the wife of James Benton, and the other children reside with their parents.

William Madison Simmons, a member of the firm of Simmons & Ferguson, liverymen of Fayetteville, Ark., was born in DeSoto County, Miss., December 5, 1848, and is a son of Charles L. and Margaret A. (Roach) Simmons, who were born in South Carolina and Alabama, respectively. They were both reared and married in Alabama, their ancestors being originally from South Carolina. Nathaniel Roach, the maternal grandfather, served in the War of 1812 and the Mexican War. William M. Simmons was reared to manhood in Mississippi, and was married in his native county to Miss Julia M. Boyce, who died there, leaving one daughter, Ellen. After coming to Arkansas he married his present wife, Miss Nora Mayes, a daughter of W. Z. Mayes, by whom he has two daughters: Jeanita and Claudine. Mrs. Simmons is a consistent Christian, and is an honored and valuable member of the Missionary Baptist Church and the Woman's Aid Society. Mr. Simmons belongs to the K. of H. and the Masonic fraternities.

Capt. David Tucker Smith, one of the leading and enterprising citizens of Richland Township, was born in Henderson County, West Tenn., November 7, 1824. His parents, Merideth and Elizabeth (Tucker) Smith, were natives of North Carolina, and when children came to Tennessee, where after growing up they were married. They then lived in West Tennessee for a few years, and then moved to Bedford County, of the same State, where they received their final summons, both in 1853. He died at the age of sixty-three, and there was but a few months difference in their ages. He was a blacksmith all his life, and was a natural mechanic; could make almost anything out of iron or steel. He made money rapidly, but spent it at the same rate. He was a Democrat in politics, and a soldier in the War of 1812. To their marriage were born eight children, Capt. David T. being next to the youngest. He remained at home with his parents, learned his father's trade, and worked at the same until 1850, when he came to Madison County, Ark., locating at Huntsville, where he lived a few years. He then moved to his present location, and worked at his trade for several years after the war. He has since been engaged in tilling the soil. Early in 1861 he enlisted in Capt. S. Inyard's company, afterward Capt. Palmer's company, for two years as Home Guards; first went out as State troops, but were afterward Home Guards. The two last years of the war he was captain of a company that bore his name, and was in Col. Brooks' Regiment. He was in many battles and numerous skirmishes. He was twice wounded by bursting shells, once in the thigh and once below the knee. Two days afterward he was in the service and in another fight. June 5, 1844, many years previous to the war, Capt. Smith married Miss Elizabeth Trollinger, a native of Bedford County, Tenn., born October 5, 1824, and the daughter of John Trollinger. This union has been blessed by the birth of a large family of children: Joseph M. and Andrew J., twins, born February 25, 1845; Rebecca J., born July 13, 1847, wife of W. Duncan; George W., born July 15, 1849; P. F., born July 18, 1853; Daniel F., born March 21, 1855; Julia Ann, born April 2, 1857, wife of John Clark; Birdine T., born April 7, 1859, wife of Charles Gordon; Jefferson D., born April 18, 1863; Nancy J., born May 28, 1866, at home; Susan E., born November 9, 1868. Those deceased were named as follows: Sarah E., born May 17, 1851, and died November 7, 1860, and Laura L., born May. 27, 1865, and died July 11, 1866. Mr. Smith is a stanch Democrat in politics, and is one of the enterprising citizens of the county.

James W. Smith, farmer and stock raiser of Washington County, Ark., is a Virginian, and was born in Botetourt County June 14, 1832. His father, Philip Smith, and grandfather Smith, were also Virginians, and of German descent. The father was married in his native State, to Mary Anderson, and in 1849 moved to Arkansas, purchasing a farm near where James W. now resides, and there spent the remainder of his days, dying in 1855. He was a harness and saddle maker by trade, and was highly esteemed and respected by all who knew him. His widow is still living, and has attained the age of ninety-two years. They were the parents of five sons and four daughters, and seven of their children grew to mature years, and became the heads of families. Two sons died during the war. James W. took the management of affairs into his own hands after the death of his father, and continued to care for the family until 1861, when he enlisted in the Confederate service, being a member of the Second Arkansas Infantry. After serving three months, and participating in the battle of Wilson's Creek, he joined Col. Brooks' regiment, with which he served until the close of the war, then returned home and engaged in farming. He has a fine farm of 210 acres, nearly all of which is bottom-land, with 130 acres under cultivation, and a splendid orchard of 250 trees. June 1, 1880, he was married to Miss Mary Crouches, a daughter of John Crouches. Mrs. Smith was born in Washington County, and is the mother of five children: Thomas E., William L., Nora, Pearl Lee and Alice.

Thomas H. Smith, one of the leading citizens of Richland Township, was born where he now resides, in Washington County, Ark., July 22, 1855, and is the son of Andrew J. and Mary J. (Trammel) Smith, natives of Tennessee and Arkansas, and born in 1825 and 1827, respectively. The father was in T. D. Smith's company, Arkansas cavalry, Confederate service, and was killed at the battle of Fayetteville. He had followed the occupation of a farmer and merchant all his life, and at the time of his death was in a prosperous condition, although the war made sad havoc with most of his property. He was a Democrat in politics, and a member of the Christian Church, of which he was an elder. He was a member of the Masonic fraternity. His widow married H. M. McGuire, who has recently died. The mother is now living with her son, Thomas H. Smith, who was one of eight children, seven now living: Eva, wife of George W. North; Adaline, wife of John H. Merrick; Sallie, wife of G. H. Warrenberry; Thomas H.; Kate, wife of E. G. Sanders; Alice, wife of James Williams; Lee H., and Nannie, deceased. Mr. Smith has been living most of the time on the farm where he now lives. He sold out at one time and moved to Arkansas City, Kas., but only remained a short period, when he returned to Washington County and purchased the old place again. January 24, 1880, he married Miss Lallie Buchanan, who was born February 18, 1864, and who is the daughter of A. P. and Martha E. Buchanan, old settlers of Washington County. Four children blessed the union of Mr. and Mrs. Smith, three of whom are now living: Gussie, Andrew Graham, Kate E. (who died when three years of age) and Thomas Hubert. Mr. Smith is a Prohibitionist in politics, and he and wife are members of the Christian Church.

John P. Stafford, editor of the Springdale *News*, was born in the town in which he now resides in 1868, and is the youngest of three children born to the marriage of John Stafford and Mary Holcomb. He was left fatherless when a child, and at an early day began serving an apprenticeship at the printer's trade in Springdale, Ark.; at the end of three years he began working on the Fayetteville *Democrat*, continuing about two years. Subsequent to this he attended school in Missouri for a short period, and in May, 1887, returned to his home in Springdale and became proprietor of the Springdale *News*, being next to the youngest editor in the State of Arkansas. His paper was at first a small six-column, patent outside paper, but is now a five-column quarto, and is published in the interests of the Democratic party. It is ably edited, and has a rapidly increasing circulation. Mr. Stafford was married Tuesday, November 13, 1888, to Miss Lena Claypool, of Springdale.

James A. Stapp, stock dealer, was born in Fayetteville, Ark., September 19, 1848, the son of Dr. Silas S. and Lucinda (Strickland) Stapp, natives of Tennessee and Illinois, respectively, and grandson of Joshua Stapp, who was a native of North Carolina, and a farmer by occupation, and the great-grandson of Killis Stapp, whose father, Killis Stapp, Sr., with a brother, Duncan Stapp, settled in North Carolina from Scotland about 1773; and from these brothers descended the Stapps of American descent. Lucinda Strickland was the daughter of Rev. Stephen Strickland, who was a pioneer minister in Washington County and Northwest Arkansas. He was a native of North Carolina, and preached from early manhood through Indiana, Tennessee, Illinois and Arkansas. In 1852 he removed to Georgetown, Williamson Co., Tex. His father, Isaac Strickland, was a Scotchman, who served all through the War for Independence, and settled in North Carolina afterward. Dr. Silas Stapp removed from Washington County, Ark., to Williamson County, Tex., in 1852, where he now resides in Coleman County of that State. James A. Stapp was reared in Texas and grew up to ranching life. He afterward went to Washington County, Ark., and in Fayetteville of that county was married to Miss Angie Graham, daughter of U. N. Graham, a native of Tennessee. They have a family of four children, two sons and two daughters: Luta, Ewing, Gay and Mabel. Mrs. Stapp is a member of the Cumberland Presbyterian Church, and an active worker in the same. In 1887 Mr. Stapp returned here for the better school advantages afforded for his children, and here he has since remained engaged in stock dealing, which occupation he has followed all his life.

Stinson S. Stearnes, farmer, was born in New Castle, Me., January 25, 1811, and is the second of seven children, three sons and four daughters, born to Ezekiel and Nancy (Dodge) Stearnes. The parents were natives of Massachusetts and Maine, respectively, and both were of Scotch descent. After marriage they spent the greater part of their lives in Maine, although both died in Boston, Mass. He lived to be seventy-six years of age, and she ninety-eight. He was a cooper by trade, although he made farming his chief occupation through life. Their son, Stinson S., received a very limited education, and when about nine years of age began working in a tannery, grinding bark. Here he remained until about nineteen years of age, when he removed to Boston, and worked in a currying shop for about two years. He then went to Martinsburg, Va., where he superintended a tan-yard for about five years. He then went across the mountains to Ohio, and, after working in that State for a time, rode on westward until he reached Huntsville, Mo., where he located. In 1842 he married Miss Minerva Reed, who was born in Howard County, Mo., February 14, 1822, and soon after they removed to Osceola, Mo., where Mr. Stearnes purchased a tan-yard, and operated the same until the breaking out of the war. In 1866 he and family moved to Washington County, Ark., and here they have since made their home. Mr. and Mrs. Stearnes are the parents of seven children: Martha J., Theodocia, Cyrus P., John W., Charles S., Bettie and Moses. Mr. Stearnes is the owner of over 161 acres, of which 125 are under cultivation, and he and Mrs. Stearnes are members of the Christian Church.

Dr. Marion D. Steele, an enterprising and thorough-going merchant, of Elm Springs, and the son of Price C. and Elizabeth B. (Cooper) Steele, was born in Bedford County, Tenn., in the year 1824. The parents were of Irish and Dutch extraction, respectively. Price C. Steele moved with his parents to Tennessee at a very early day, and, like his father, was a farmer all his life. He was a justice of the peace of Bedford County for many years, and was also associate justice of the county court. He died in 1881, at the hale old age of eighty-one years. His son, Dr. Marion D. Steele, was educated in Bedford County, Tenn., and remained on the farm, engaged in agricultural pursuits with his father, until he was nineteen years of age, when he began the study of medicine. In 1847 he moved to Lawrence County, Ark., and at once began the practice of his profession, which he continued for nine years in that county, meeting with remarkably good success. In 1849 he was united in marriage to Miss Frances S. Poer, of Lawrence County, Ark., and the fruits of this union are two children: William B., and Elizabeth, who married William D. Wasson, of Springtown. Mr. Steele lost his wife in 1860, and one year later he married Mrs. Mary E. Deaver, of Washington County, Ark. They were the parents of nine children, seven now living: Thomas D., who married Miss Mollie Hobbs, of Missouri; James C.; Joseph A., who married Miss Jennie Venable; Mary I., Sarah Frances, H. S. and David A. In 1856 Dr. Steele moved to Benton County, Ark., but remained there only one year, when he moved to Washington County, of the same State, and located at Elm Springs, where he continued to practice until 1874. He then engaged in merchandising at this point, and has remained engaged in this business up to the present. He owns the store building and the stock of goods, which comprises all the articles usually kept in a first-class country store, and amounts to over $5,000. He also owns forty acres of land, besides several lots in the village of Elm Springs. He is a member of the Masonic fraternity. He, his wife and daughters are members of the Methodist Episcopal Church.

W. V. Steele, son of Dr. M. D. Steele, was born in Washington County, Ark., in 1856, and in this county received his education. He remained with his parents until reaching his majority, and in 1880 he engaged in the drug business in the town of Elm Springs, where he has since remained, and where he has a stock of drugs to the amount of $800. He is also postmaster of this little town, which position he has held since 1886. In 1884 he selected Miss Laura E. Railey for his companion in life. She is a native of Benton County, Ark., and was the daughter of Alex. Railey, who was killed during the late civil struggle. To Mr. and Mrs. Steele have been born two children, viz., Fannie E. and Marion R. Mr. Steele owns a nice house and lot in the town of Elm Springs, and is a successful and enterprising citizen. He is a member of the Masonic fraternity, is a Democrat in politics, and Mrs. Steele is a member of the Methodist Episcopal Church, South.

Searing S. Stelle (deceased) was born in Preble County, Ohio, July 20, 1820, and was the son of Alexander and Phoebe (Marsh) Stelle. The father moved to Ohio when young and died in that State in 1826, at the age of sixty. The mother was born May 14, 1787, in New Jersey, and in 1828 removed from Ohio to Illinois. In 1836 she moved to Washington County, Ark., where she died May 11, 1884. She was a member of the Primitive Baptist Church, and the mother of six children, five of whom lived to be grown: John (deceased), Isaac (deceased), Nancy, Searing S. (deceased), Timothy (deceased), and Hannah, widow of Archibald Smith. The mother of these children married Reding Putman, and bore him one son, Reding who is now living in Fayetteville. When Searing S. Stelle was about twenty-three years of age he married Miss Elizabeth Landers, who was born in Washington County, Ark., January 26, 1820. To them were born six children: Sarah E., wife of J. D. Carlisle; John T., who was born June 16, 1850, was married to Miss Martha Baker, daughter of Eli Baker, October 27, 1881, and became the father of two children, Ella, born March 20, 1884, Pearl, born January 12, 1887; an infant (deceased), William A. (deceased), Alexander P., born October 9, 1857, and an infant (deceased). The mother of these children died June 7, 1861, and Mr. Stelle was married April 11, 1869, to Mrs. Catherine Wakfield, widow of Henry Wakfield, the daughter of Robert and Elizabeth Reed, and to them was born, July 30, 1870, a daughter, Elizabeth. Mr. Stelle died May 3, 1888. He was an honored, respected citizen, a member of the Christian Church, and his death was lamented by his many friends and acquaintances. The family are Republicans in their politics, and the widow and her daughter are members of the Christian Church.

L. Granville Stephens, farmer and stock dealer of Washington County, Ark., was born in Monroe County, Tenn., May 1, 1859. His father, Lewis Stephens, was born in Rowan County, N. C., April 26, 1811, and until fifteen years of age resided in his native State. He was then taken by his father, Richard Stephens, who was a soldier in the War of 1812, to Tennessee, and was there married to Miss Elizabeth D. Dyer, a native of that State. They came to Washington County, Ark., in 1869, and in 1874 purchased the farm on which he now resides, and on which his son, L. Granville, was reared to manhood. The latter received a good education in the school at Viney Grove, and after attaining a suitable age took charge of his father's farm, which he has now managed for about eight years. He is largely engaged in buying and shipping stock, shipping nine car loads in 1887, besides selling a large amount of stock at home. The home farm consists of 180 acres of good bottom land, on Moore's Creek, all of which is fenced, and 100 acres under cultivation. He has two other farms of eighty acres each, with nearly all under cultivation, besides forty acres of timber land. His mother, Mrs. Elizabeth Stephens, is a member of the Methodist Episcopal Church.

Rev. John Calvin Stockburger was born in Stokes County, N. C., January 26, 1829, and is a son of Jacob and Nancy (Davis) Stockburger, and grandson of John Stockburger, who was born in Germany, and came to America with his parents about 1871, locating in North Carolina, where he became an extensive planter and large slave owner. He died at the age of about fifty-four years. His wife was also born in Germany, and lived to be about one hundred years old. Jacob Stockburger was born in Stokes County, N. C., in 1804, and in 1824 was married, and located on a farm of his own, eventually becoming the owner of a number of slaves. In 1840 he moved to Georgia with his family, locating on a plantation in Murray County, where he died in 1861. His wife is of English parentage, a native of North Carolina, and is now residing on the old home farm, with two of her children. John C. Stockburger is one of seven surviving members of a family of ten children. In 1849 he was married to Martha A. Reed, who is of German-Irish descent, and by her became the father of twelve children, ten of whom are now living: Marcus A., Nancy E. (wife of J. E. Stockburger), Jacob W., John R., Anna, Joseph, Mary E., Edward E., Emma, Calvin C.; Willie and an infant are deceased. In 1852 Mr. Stockburger came to Washington County, Ark., and moved to where he now lives, having bought 410 acres of land, 200 acres of which are under cultivation, and he is considered one of the successful farmers of the county. Having made the study of medicine a profession, he engaged in practicing after coming to Washington County, and has since been one of the successful practitioners of the county. At the age of eighteen years he embraced Christianity, and a few years after was ordained an elder in the Cumberland Presbyterian Church. He was one of four charter members of the Cumberland Presbyterian Church that was organized in the southern part of the county, and has had practical charge of the same up to the present time, himself, wife and Mrs. Mariah Reed Brown being the only charter members now living.

W. L. Stokes, senior member of the livery firm of Stokes & Son, of Springdale, Ark., was born in the "Palmetto State" in 1822, and at an early day immigrated to Kentucky, thence to Tennessee, and afterward resided in the following States in the order in which they are named: Missouri, Arkansas, Texas and Arkansas. His wife, Lucy Stokes, is the mother of eleven children, and is his second wife. S. L. Stokes, of the above named firm, was born in Missouri in 1855, and after coming to Arkansas erected a large livery stable in Rogers, and was also engaged in merchandising in that place. He is married and has one child, Mary. His brother, H. L. Stokes, also a member of the livery firm, was born in Tennessee in 1846, and was taken by his parents to Missouri when about one year old, and after living in that State for about three years was brought to Arkansas, locating first in Benton County, and then in Crawford County, where they lived until 1861. They then moved South, and H. L. Stokes, at a very early age, joined the Confederate army, and served about three years. After the war he returned to Arkansas, and since 1867 has been a resident of Washington County, and for seven years has been a member of the present livery firm. He was married, in 1869, to Miss A. E. Hinson, who was born in Arkansas in 1856, and by her is the father of five children: F. D., C. N., W. L., J. H. and Ivy D. The family are Democrats.

Alfred D. Strickler. The biographical department of Washington County, Ark., would be incomplete without the sketch of Mr. Strickler, who is a native of the county, and was born January 11, 1838. His parents, Benjamin and Nancy T. (Newman) Strickler, were Tennesseeans, the father being born in Sullivan County, of that State, October 3, 1810. He died in Washington County, Ark., on the 23d of September, 1884, being a son of Jacob and Barbara (Slaughter) Strickler, who were among the early settlers of Washington County, Ark. Mrs. Nancy T. Strickler died on the 17th of February, 1863. She came with her parents to Arkansas at an early day, and was here married to Mr. Strickler on the 14th of February, 1837. They were members of the Primitive Baptist Church, and he was a Mason, a Democrat, and one of the successful farmers of the county, until the breaking out of the war, when he lost heavily during that period. He was the father of five children: Alfred D., M. M. (the widow of William Brewster), A. T., Arthulia P. (deceased) and W. C. Alfred D. Strickler remained with his father until he attained the age of twenty-two years, and on the 10th of November, 1859, was married to Mary S. Morrow, a daughter of John and Maria Morrow, who were from Kentucky, and among the early settlers of Washington County, Ark. Mrs. Strickler was born in Washington County April 25, 1837, and died April 26, 1879. She was a member of the Cumberland Presbyterian Church, and became the mother of three children: Dorcas T., was born September 20, 1860, and is the wife of James Vorhees; Sallie D., born August 11, 1861, is also married, and Walter S., born July 21, 1868. July 18, 1880, Mr. Strickler was united in marriage to his second wife, Martha R. Crawley, a native of the county, born July 21, 1855, and a daughter of William Crawley, who is still living, and is one of the old settlers of the county. Mr. Crawley is the father of two children by his last wife: Sarah, born November 19, 1882, and Mary T., born July 11, 1887. In the spring of 1862 Mr. Strickler enlisted in Company B, of Brook's regiment, and served until the close of the war. He was in a number of important engagements, and was captured while at Saline, and was kept a prisoner at Rock Island, Ill., for ten months. After the cessation of hostilities he returned to his home in Arkansas, and by industry and good management has become one of the well-to-do farmers and stock raisers of the county. He and wife are church members, and he is a Democrat politically.

Silas L. Suttle. Among the many old and prominent citizens of Washington County, who have lived long and honorable lives, and whose early existence was one of privation and trouble, not one is more worthy of mention than Silas L. Suttle, who was born in North Carolina in 1810, and who is the son of George P. and Susan Suttle. The parents were both natives of North Carolina, and in this State they both died about 1816. The father was a tiller of the soil and a hard-working, industrious man. His son, Silas, was left an orphan at the youthful age of six years, and was taken and reared by his uncle. At a very early age he was obliged to start out for himself, and although meeting with many discouragements, had the energy and perseverance to stick to whatever he undertook, and to-day is in very comfortable circumstances. In his twenty-first year he married, in her seventeenth year, Miss Rebecka Elrod, of Tennessee, daughter of Peter and Nancy Elrod, and to this union were born twelve children, six now living: Ewing Greenbery, John L., Adaline F. M., Mary, Caroline and Silas L., Jr. Mr. Suttle commenced life by farming in Tennessee, but left that State in 1840 and moved to Arkansas, and located in Madison County, where he remained fifteen years. He then went to Missouri, and remained in that State for eight months, or until the war broke out. In 1861 he enlisted in Company C, Hunter's regiment, Confederate army, in which he served until the close of the war, and, although he was in three noted battles, he escaped without a scar. After the war he returned to Arkansas, settling in Madison County, but in 1868 moved to Washington County, where he is living at the present time, and where he and F. M. have 163 acres of land, which is well improved and about eighty under cultivation. Mr. Suttle joined the Cumberland Presbyterian Church in 1841; was licensed to preach in 1843, and ordained as minister in that church in 1845. He has been a local preacher ever since. Mrs. Suttle is also a member of the same church. Mr. Suttle is a member of the Masonic fraternity, and is also a member of the Farmers' Alliance.

George Sutton, harness manufacturer, and one of the wide-awake, thorough-going business men of Fayetteville, was born in this city February 5, 1848, and is the son of Seneca and Isabella (Houston) Sutton, natives of Kentucky and Missouri, respectively. The father was born and reared in Lincoln County, and learned the hatter's business, which he followed for many years. In 1834 he married Miss Isabella Houston, and became the father of four children, two sons and two daughters: James T., a merchant and resident of Caston, Ind. T.; Mary and Isabella, who are now residing on the old homestead, and George, subject of this sketch. The father of these children moved to Missouri, and followed his trade in this State until 1840, when he moved to Washington County, Ark., and here received his final summons October 25, 1857. His eldest son, James T., served in the Confederate army from 1862 to 1863, in the Northwestern Fifteenth Arkansas Infantry, McCreas' battalion. He was married in Fayetteville, Ark., to Miss Francena L. Martin, a native of Arkansas, and the daughter of William Martin (deceased). This union resulted in the birth of two sons and a daughter: William Seneca, Henry Stevinson and Mary Bell. William Seneca Sutton is superintendent of the public schools of Houston, Tex., and Mary Bell is a graduate of the Peabody Institute, of Nashville, and is now a teacher in the schools at Morrillton, Ark. George Sutton reached his majority in Washington County, Ark., learned the harness-maker's trade, and has followed the same up to the present, being prominently identified with that industry in the county. He was married to Miss Maggie Cooper, a native of Mississippi, and to them have been born two daughters, Mabel and Bertha. Mr. Sutton is a stockholder in the Fair Association, and he and Mrs. Sutton are members of the Methodist Episcopal Church, she being an active worker in the same.

Dr. D. C. Summers, whose birth occurred in Marion County, Ark., in 1856, is a son of Calvin and Lucinda H. (Porter) Summers. The father was born in Rutherford, Tenn., in 1819, and was by occupation a farmer and tanner, and followed the latter occupation for many years. He enlisted in the Mexican War, but peace was declared before he entered service. He also enlisted in the late war, but was sent home by the Government to tan leather for shoes, etc. He was one of the very early settlers of Northern Arkansas, and is now living at Sylva, Marion County, engaged in merchandising. Dr. D. C. Summers received a rather limited education in Marion County, and later attended the Missouri Medical College at St. Louis one session. At the age of twenty-four he began practicing his profession in Marion County, but at the end of two years he moved to Benton County, and from there to his present property in Washington County. He located at Elm Springs, where he has his share of the practice, and is succeeding very well. In 1877 he married Miss Lida Dingle, daughter of Judge W. B. and Nancy Dingle, of Madison County, Ark., and to them have been born two children, both of whom are deceased. Dr. Summers became a member of the Methodist Episcopal Church, South, in 1872, and after a membership of one year he was ordained a minister of that church and an elder in 1879. He at present occupies the position of local preacher, and for five years he was pastor of the church and in charge of the Mountain View Circuit, also other circuits, and spends a goodly portion of his time in ministering to the spiritual wants of his fellow-men.

Eliphaz Taylor, farmer, of Durham Township, Washington Co., Ark., was born in Fayette County, Ohio, in 1817, the son of Elisha and grandson of William Taylor. The latter served in the Revolutionary War as train-master, and died in Ross County, Ohio, at the age of ninety years. He was the father of fourteen children, all of whom lived to be over sixty years of age, and some attained the age of one hundred years. Elisha Taylor was born in Pennsylvania, and in 1796, when he was about twelve years of age, was taken to Kentucky by his parents, who removed to Ohio four years later. At the age of twenty-seven he was married, and engaged in farming, locating shortly afterward in Kentucky, where he learned the tanner's trade, but never made that occupation a business. He moved to Henry County, Ill., in 1856 or 1857, and there died about 1878, at an advanced age. His wife, whose maiden name was Sarah Adair, was born near Baltimore, Md., and died in Cincinnati, Ohio, where she had gone to have her eyes treated, at the age of sixty-one or sixty-two years. She was the mother of sixteen children, twelve of whom grew to maturity, and four are now living: Eliphaz; Alexander, living in Nebraska; Elisha, residing in Texas, and Jasper, residing in Kansas. Eliphaz Taylor was reared in his native county, and educated in the common schools, and for several years was engaged in teaching school during the winter months, and farming during the summer months.   When he attained his twenty-first year he purchased a farm near the old home place, where he lived until 1854, then sold out and moved to Illinois, and resided on a farm in Henry County until 1868.   Since that time he has resided in Washington County, Ark., and has a farm of about 240 acres, with about 100 under cultivation.   He is a Republican in politics, and is a member of the Cumberland Presbyterian Church.

Z. A. Thomas, cigar manufacturer of Fayetteville, Ark., was born in Hardin County, Ky., December 10, 1854, and is the son of John and Margaret (Jones) Thomas, who were born in Kentucky.   He was reared in his native State, and in 1876, in company with a brother, J. W. Thomas, went to Missouri, and engaged in manufacturing cigars, carrying on a successful business in different parts of that State until 1886, when they came to Arkansas, locating at Eureka Springs, where they were engaged in business until November, 1887, since which time they have resided in Fayetteville, and are doing a thriving and remunerative business.   Since locating in the latter place Z. A. Thomas has been united in marriage to Miss Sarah C., the accomplished daughter of Preston Johnson [see sketch].   J. W. Thomas was married to Miss Anna E. Crutcher, by whom he has two sons and one daughter: Blanche, Roy and Charley.   The brothers are enterprising and public-spirited young men, and during their business career in Fayetteville have established an enviable reputation for business ability, upright dealing and honorable citizenship.

Andrew J. Thompson, one of the prominent farmers of Washington County, Ark., and one of the old and well-known citizens of the same, was born in Campbell County, Tenn., on the 7th of October, 1816, and is the fourth of ten children born to the marriage of Blackburn Thompson and Lucretia Lawson, who were born in Virginia in 1791 and Tennessee in 1792, respectively.   After reaching man's estate Blackburn Thompson was seized with the passion of immigration, and went to Tennessee, where he met and married Miss Lawson, with whom he immigrated to Madison County, Ark., in 1856.   He was a soldier in the War of 1812, under Gen. Jackson, and died in the State of his adoption in 1861, his wife's death occurring in the same county and State in 1880.   Andrew J. Thompson is the only one of his father's family now living, and at the age of twenty-one years left his father's house and came westward, reaching Arkansas in very limited circumstances, his sole possessions being a good constitution, a pair of willing hands and an old flint-lock rifle. He immediately set to work, and by energy, industry and economy has fought the battle of life successfully, and is now the owner of 489 acres of land and has a good and comfortable home.   He is a representative man of the county, and stands high in the estimation of the people.   April 11, 1839, he was married to Phoebe Gray, who was born in Campbell County, Tenn., in 1815, and Henry G., Lucretia, Nancy J., Lewis W. and Mary Ann are the children born to their union.   The parents have been active members of the Baptist Church for many years, and in his political views Mr. Thompson is a Democrat.   His son, Henry G. Thompson, was born in 1840 near where he now lives, and most of his life has been spent in Washington County.   When the late Civil War broke out he joined the Confederate forces, and was promoted to the rank of third lieutenant of Boone's company, Company I, Sixteenth Arkansas Regiment   He afterward left the company, and upon his return to it was given the post of sergeant, and participated in the battles of Elkhorn, Prairie Grove and numerous other minor engagements.   After peace was declared he returned home and resumed work on the old homestead, but was burned out in October, 1872, and soon after removed to a farm on the main fork of the White River, where he lived three years, and then came to his present farm of 280 acres, with about eighty acres under cultivation.   He was married in 1866 to Miss Sarah F. Malloy, who was born in Tennessee and died April 10, 1873, leaving a family of three children: James, Ina, wife of David Griffe, and Mary O., who is residing with her grandfather, Andrew J. Thompson.   August 8, 1876, Mr. Thompson married his present wife, whose maiden name was Sarah Bushart, by whom he has one son, Lewis L.   Mrs. Thompson was born in Tennessee, and is a member of the Cumberland Presbyterian Church.   Mr. Thompson is a member of the Knights of the Horse, and votes the Democratic ticket.

Hon. John N. Tillman, present State senator from the Fifth Senatorial District of the State of Arkansas, although but a young man, ranks among the prominent citizens of Northwestern Arkansas. He was born near Spring-field, Mo., December 13, 1859. His parents, Newton J. and Mary (Mullins) Till-man, were natives of Tennessee and South Carolina, respectively, although the ancestors of both were early settlers of the latter State. The Tillmans are of Scotch-Irish descent. The parents of our subject came to Arkansas from Missouri when John N. was but a child. Here he grew to manhood and received a common-school education. He then entered the Arkansas Industrial University, from which he graduated in 1880. Wishing to become a disciple of Blackstone he taught school two years in order to accumulate the means to enable him to study. He then studied in the office of Judge J. M. Pittman until the latter was elected judge of the circuit court of his district, after which he read with Holsinger and Wall. He was admitted to the bar of Arkansas July 3, 1883, and immediately began the practice of law. In 1882 he was appointed county examiner of the schools of Washington County, which position he filled with so much credit that in 1884, as the Democratic nominee, he was elected circuit clerk. In 1886 he was re-elected to the latter position, and in 1888, at the age of twenty-eight, he was elected State senator from the Fifth Senatorial District. He is a lawyer of marked ability, and is one of the leading members of the Arkansas bar. He is an encampment member of the I. O. O. F., a Royal Arch Mason, and a Knight of the Uniform Division of the Knights of Pythias. On March 4, 1885, Mr. Tillman married Miss Tempy Walker, daughter of M. K. Walker, Esq., and they have one son, John N., Jr.

Rowland C. Tollett, farmer and stock raiser of Washington County, Ark., was born in Hempstead County, Ark., in 1821. His parents, Henry and Eliza (Brown) Tollett, were born and reared in Tennessee and Virginia, respectively. The father was a soldier in the War of 1812, and soon after the close of that war was married, and in 1819 moved to Arkansas. After residing in Hempstead County until 1829 he located in Washington County, near Farmington, where he became the owner of several hundred acres of land. He served as justice of the peace for several years, and was a strong Southern sympathizer during the late war. He died in 1867, and his wife in 1886. Four of their five children are living: Margaret (wife of James Barrington), Harriet (wife of James A. Morton), William J. and Rowland C. The latter was reared and educated in Washington County, and in 1850 was married to Martha J. Johnston, who was born in Washington County a few weeks after her parents, Abel and Mary Johnston, came to the county. She is the mother of five children: William A., C. L., Henry J., Emma and Maggie G. Mr. Tollett owns a good and well-improved farm of 200 acres, and is in comfortable circumstances. He was left almost destitute at the close of the war, but by indomitable energy and perseverance has become one of the well-to-do farmers of the county.

Capt. John C. Toney was born in Powhatan County, Va., February 15, 1833, and is one of four surviving members of a family of six children born to George T. and Sarah (Wattel) Toney, who were natives respectively of Powhatan and Albemarle Counties, Virginia. They were married in their native State, and afterward became residents of Missouri, and still later of Arkansas. The father died in Van Buren County, Ark., in 1867, and the mother in Crawford County in August, 1884. The former followed the occupation of farming and merchandising throughout life, and was a son of John Virgil Toney, who served throughout the Revolutionary War, and was a participant in all the principal battles. He died at the age of sixty-three, and his wife when about seventy-two or seventy-three. She was closely related to John Randolph, the celebrated Virginian. The children born to George T. Toney are as follows: Sarah M., John C., George T. and Cornelia. Those deceased are Victoria, and Virginia P., the wife of J. S. Mattock. At the early age of seventeen years, John C. Toney, who was a lad of energy and pluck, determined to seek his fortune in the far West, and accordingly crossed the plains to California, and spent three years in the mines of that State and Oregon, and afterward dealt in stock for some time. He was very successful for a boy, and returned to his home in Missouri, via the Isthmus of Panama and New York. At the breaking out of the late war he enlisted in the Confederate service, Capt. Dickey's company, and after serving three months organized a company and was chosen its captain. He was with Coffee's regiment, and was a participant in many fiercely contested battles. His company consisted of 125 men when it was organized, and at the close of the war only twenty-seven men were left, only one of whom was never wounded. Capt. Toney was severly wounded several times, and at the last engagement, at Springfield, was taken prisoner, but succeeded in effecting his escape after a short retention. After the cessation of hostilities he went to Crawford County, Ark., but only resided there a short time, when he went to Texas, and remained until 1867, at which time he again located in Crawford County, Ark., and purchased a tract of land. One year later he sold out and came to Washington County, where he has since been engaged in tilling the soil. He owns an excellent farm, well tilled and well located. November 12, 1854, he was married to Elizabeth, a daughter of James Johnson. She was born in Tennessee, and died in Missouri in 1855, leaving one son, J. M. Toney, who is now living in Madison County, Ark. Three years later Mr. Toney married Martha Ayers, who was born in Bedford County, Tenn., in 1839, and died in Washington County, Ark., in 1886. She was a devoted wife and mother, and was a consistent member of the Baptist Church. Nine of her twelve children are living: Joseph S., Robert S. L., Charles R., Jasper N., Sydney J., Alexander S., Virginia P., Tennessee and Effie. Those deceased are Lafayette, Elizabeth J. D. and infant. Capt. Toney is a Democrat.

J. M. Toney, a leading citizen, stock trader and farmer of Richland Township, Washington Co., Ark., is a native of Lawrence County, Mo., born on the 12th of November, 1855, and is a son of Capt. J. C. and Elizabeth (Johnston) Toney, whose sketch appears in this work. Owing to the early death of his mother J. M. Toney was reared by his grandfather, J. W. Johnston, in Lawrence County, Mo. Mr. Johnston was born in Tennessee, and moved to Missouri at an early day, and became a very prominent citizen of Lawrence County. He was a Republican, and died in 1874 at the age of seventy years. At the age of twenty-one J. M. Toney left home and began traveling in the West. He was engaged in no particular business, but the most of his attention was given to stock trading, Texas, Iowa, Kansas, California, Oregon, Colorado and the Territories being the scenes of his operations. At the end of six years he located in Madison County, Ark., but in 1884 located on his present excellent farm in Washington County, where he bears the reputation of being a hard-working and prosperous farmer. February 3, 1884, he was married to Marietta Vail, a daughter of J. T. Vail, who was a leading citizen of Madison County. Mr. Vail was born in North Carolina, and married Elizabeth Robertson. He moved to Dyer County, Tenn., in the spring of 1847, and from there to Arkansas in 1866; he died in 1872. Elizabeth Vail was the mother of nine children, six now living, two sons, G. F. and J. R., now in Madison County, Ark., and four daughters, Mrs. Hattie Warren, Mrs. Toney, Mrs. Mattie Bishop, and Alice, unmarried, who lives with her two brothers. Mrs. Toney was born in Dyer County, Tenn., April 7, 1859, and became the mother of four children, only one of whom is now living, Eula Lou, born August 6, 1885. Mr. Toney is a Republican in his political views.

Josiah W. M. Trent was born in Washington County, Ark., on the 22d of February, 1842, in the house where he now lives. His grandfather, Henry Trent, was one of twelve brothers, nearly all of whom served in the Revolutionary War, and was born and reared in Virginia. For his services during the war he was given a land warrant of ninety-nine acres by the Government, where the city of Milledgeville, Ga., now stands, and afterward became a very extensive land-holder about Grand Gulf, Miss., but neglecting to give proper attention to this very valuable property in each of these States, it passed into other hands without profit to him or his posterity. He located in Louisiana, and after living there for some time moved to the Choctaw Nation, where he died at the ripe old age of about eighty-three years. His son Josiah was born near Milledgeville, Ga., about 1802, and grew to manhood in Mississippi, Louisiana, and the Choctaw Nation. He obtained his education by his own efforts, studying evenings by the light of the fire, and in February, 1829, he came to Washington County, Ark., where he entered a good tract of land, on which he erected a comfortable dwelling-house. February 21, 1833, he was married to Sallie Woolsey, who was born in Illinois on the 22d of February, 1813, and their union resulted in the birth of eleven children, seven of whom are now living. The mother died July 11, 1885, and the father March 26, 1877. He professed religion when quite a young lad, and throughout life was an earnest and consistent Christian. He was ordained a minister of the Methodist Episcopal Church, South, and expounded the doctrines of that church as a local preacher until his death.   Albert L., youngest son and child of Josiah and Sallie Trent, is a man of good education, excellent morals, splendid business qualifications, and is at present cashier of Washington County Bank.   Josiah W. M. Trent was educated in the subscription schools of Washington County, and in 1862 enlisted in Company A, Col. Brooks' Regiment, Confederate States Army, but was captured in 1863, and kept a prisoner at St. Louis until the close of the war.   While in prison he lost the use of his legs, which he has never recovered, and after his return home he attended school and also engaged in teaching.   He engaged in pedagoguing in 1870, and became a successful educator of the county.   In 1878 he was elected county assessor, and has filled the duties of that office, to the entire satisfaction of all, for four successive terms.   He is a member of the Methodist Episcopal Church, South, and the first church of that denomination in the county was organized in his father's house about the year 1831.

Thomas A. Towler, one of the leading farmers and traders of Richland Township, was born in Lunenburgh County, Va., in 1822, April 21, and is the son of James and Elizabeth (Averett) Towler, both natives of Lunenburgh County, Va., and the grandson of Jickanias Towler, who was a soldier in the Revolutionary War, and lost his leg in the cause of independence.   James Towler was, in his younger days, a merchant by occupation, but by unfortunate investments lost his money, and this caused his death.   His son, Thomas A., was but eleven years old at that time.   Mr. and Mrs. Towler were the parents of five children: Thomas A.; Joseph, who was killed at the second battle of Manassas, and was captain of a Confederate company; Elizabeth, Martha F. and Rebecca. The last heard of the mother she was living at Clarksville, Va., and nothing has been heard of the rest of the children since the war.   Thomas A. left his home in Virginia in 1848, traveled to Nashville, Tenn., and from there to Washington County, Ark., where he has since resided, and is now the only man living who was in Richland Township in 1843.   He learned the brick-mason's trade, but that not suiting him, he worked in the tobacco business in Clarksville, Va. When first coming to Washington County, Ark., he began the manufacture of plug tobacco, and continued this until the breaking out of the late war.   Previous to the war, May 8, 1845, he married Miss Rebecca Anderson, a native of Virginia, and the daughter of James Anderson.   Soon after her marriage she was thrown from a horse, and died from the effects March 3, 1846.   May 9, 1847, he married Miss Mary E. Trammel, a native of Georgetown, Mo., born May 19, 1830, and the daughter of John Trammel.   She died in Washington County, Ark., August 29, 1875.   To this marriage were born twelve children, eight now living: Margaret, wife of James Hinds; Nannie, wife of David Dickey; Mary E., wife of William Rough; John, Thomas J., Euen, Ben F.; and those deceased were infants.   Mr. Towler, besides his manufacturing of tobacco, was also engaged in buying, and driving south, mules and horses, and has driven forty-six droves of mules and horses to Louisiana in his time.   Since the war he has followed farming and stock dealing, but has also carried on his tobacco business. During that eventful period he served three years and fifteen days, and was in some important battles.   He was captured at Fayetteville and taken to Springfield, but escaped at the end of seventeen days.   Although a manufacturer of tobacco, Mr. Towler has never used the weed in any shape or form, and has never been intoxicated.   He has been sworn but three times in court, and was instrumental in organizing the Masonic Lodge No. 93.   April 8, 1879, Mr. Towler married Miss Martha Womack, a native of Madison County, Ark., born September 15, 1847, and the daughter of John Womack, who was one of the first settlers of Arkansas.   Mr. Towler is a member of no church, but his wife and all the children are members of the Methodist Episcopal Church.

Junius W. Tucker, a farmer, and a prominent citizen of White River Township, Washington Co., Ark., was born in Tazewell County, Ill., on the 29th of August, 1839.   His parents, John W. and Louisa (Wathen) Tucker, were born, reared and married in Kentucky, and about 1838 became residents of Tazewell County, Ill., moving one year later to Woodford County, where they died in 1874 and 1861, respectively.   The father followed the occupation of distilling while in Kentucky, and on first coming to Illinois, but lost all his property by fire shortly after, and determined to retrieve his fortunes in the gold mines of California.   He made the overland trip by ox teams to that State, in company with some friends, and returned home about two years later with considerable money. In 1858 he made a trip to Pike's Peak, which was not a success financially, and at the end of two years returned to his home in Illinois, where he resided until his death. He and wife had nine children, five of whom are living: Mary E., Junius W., Anna, Frances A. and Henry (city marshal of Eureka, Ill). Junius W. Tucker made his parents' house his home until eighteen years of age, when he, in company with his father, went to Pike's Peak, where he remained four years, then removed to Montana Territory, and was engaged in mining in Virginia City three years, making in his first week's work $7,500, which money he spent in mining property. After making a short trip to British America he returned to the United States, and went to Arizona Territory, in company with 175 men, where he remained during the winter, going the following spring to California, Oregon, Idaho, Wyoming Territory, and back to Illinois, having spent about nine years in the West. After returning home he spent about seven years extensively engaged in stock farming and stock dealing, and then went to Texas in search of health, but a short time after removed to Dakota, and then to Colorado, where he spent two years engaged in freighting. In 1884 he came to Washington County, Ark., locating near Sulphur Springs, where he has a good 120-acre farm, in a good state of cultivation, which, with its substantial and commodious dwelling and convenient out-buildings, make it one of the desirable farms of the county. April 20, 1869, his marriage with Miss Fannie White was celebrated. She was born in the "Emerald Isle," and was brought to America when a child of six years, locating in Massachusetts, where she grew to maturity. When about eighteen years of age she went to Illinois, where she was afterward married to Mr. Tucker. They have four children: Anna Macie, Frances Louisa, May Ellen and John Wesley. Mrs. Tucker is an earnest and consistent Christian, and is an honored member of the Catholic Church. In politics Mr. Tucker is a pronounced Democrat, ready at all times to support his political convictions, and is a true type of the successful, self-made men of Arkansas.

Pleasant B. Tucker, Sr., farmer of Washington County, Ark., was born in Hawkins County, Tenn., July 12, 1817. His mother was born and reared in Greene County, Tenn. Her maiden name was Mary D. Burkhart. She married Davis Howell, and they moved to Hawkins County, Tenn., and by him she reared five children, four of whom are living. He served under Jackson in the Indian War, and returned home and died in a short time. His mother then married Flemon Tucker, and P. B. Tucker, their only child, was born to them. When he was about three or four months old his father and mother separated. She remained at home and reared her child until he was twelve years old. She then removed to Kentucky, and located in Hardin County; then to Indiana in 1836 or 1837, and died at the home of her son, S. D. Howell, in Vermilion County, in 1845. Pleasant B. Tucker made his home with his mother until nineteen years of age, and then started out to fight his way through the world. He worked on a farm and flat-boated out of the Wabash River to New Orleans, and in the spring of 1840 came to Arkansas and located in Washington County. There he followed the occupation of teaming with James E. Howell. In 1845 he enlisted in the Mexican War, but his company was not needed, and he returned to Washington County, and for several years he was engaged in the tanning business in different parts of the State. In 1850 he went overland to California, and after two years spent in mining in that State he returned home, and settled on a farm, which he had purchased before going West. In May, 1852, he was married to Lucinda H. Crawford, a daughter of John Crawford, the pioneer of Washington County, and to them were born ten children, seven of whom are living: James P., Squire D., Pleasant B., Amasa H., Flemmon R., Edward E. and Eldalena. At the beginning of the late war he joined the Southern army as a minute-man. After the battle of Elkhorn he moved with his family to Bell County, Tex., where he worked at his trade until the close of the war. He then returned to Washington County, and began life anew on his farm of 291 acres of fine land. He has 135 acres under cultivation, and has a good, comfortable home. He and his family attend the Methodist Episcopal Church, South.

John G. Tunstill, another prominent and enterprising citizen of Goshen, was born in Wilson County. Tenn., April 21, 1835, and is the son of John S. and Eliza (Baldwin) Tunstill. The father was born in Virginia about 1775, and came to Tennessee soon after marriage. He died in Wilson County, Tenn., in

1842. He was a tailor by occupation, but also carried on farming. The mother was also born in Virginia, at Petersburg, and died in Logan County, Ky., about 1863. John G. Tunstill was the youngest child but one born to his father by his second marriage. He remained in Wilson County, Tenn., until fourteen years of age, and then moved to Logan County, Ky., where he was married in 1859, and afterward moved to Southeastern Arkansas, where he followed farming, and continued this occupation until he moved to Goshen. He had one-half interest in a drug store in Hamburg, Ark., with a brother. During the war he was in Company G, First Trans-Mississippi Regiment, and was second chief commissary of the western department most of the time. He served nearly four years in the Confederate army. In 1876 he removed to Oxford's Bend, in Goshen Township, and farmed here very successfully for six years. He then began the erection of the Goshen Mill, and after selling the farm moved to Goshen, and purchased a farm here. He also purchased a farm of 230 acres in Richland, 140 under cultivation. Mr. Tunstill has given his son one-third interest in the mill. He engaged in merchandising six years ago, and continued the same until July 1, 1888, when he sold out to J. A. Bryant & Co., and is now engaged in running his farms and in dealing in stock. He has been very successful in all his business transactions. He was married in 1856 to Miss Margaret C. Yancey, of Kentucky, and the results of this union were ten children, four deceased: James A. (connected with the mill), John W. (a farmer), Charles S., William M., Mary V. and George G. Those deceased were named Eliza H., Owen, Maggie and Homer G. Mr. Tunstill is a Democrat in politics, is a Master Mason, and is a strictly moral, upright man. He is a member of the Cumberland Presbyterian Church, and Mrs. Tunstill of the Methodist Episcopal Church, South.

James Hayden Van Hoose, mayor of Fayetteville, was born near Paintsville, in Johnson County, Ky., January 8, 1830, the son of John and Lydia (Lewis) Van Hoose, grandson of John Van Hoose, and great-grandson of John Van Hoose, who was a native of Holland. The Van Hoose ancestors, from far back, were large of stature, long lived, were of the Baptist faith, and were honest, God-fearing people. Valentine Van Hoose, brother of John Van Hoose, was a soldier in the Revolutionary War, and rendered honorable service under Gen. Marion. John Van Hoose, father of subject, was a native of Montgomery County, N. C., and his mother, Mrs. Lydia (Lewis) Van Hoose, was also a native of North Carolina. Her father, Zachariah Lewis, was a native of Orange County, N. C., and died when a young man. His widow then married Peter Mankins, who was a native of the District of Columbia, and who, when a lad, saw the American army in its march to attack Cornwallis at Yorktown, and he, with other lads, followed the army some distance out of the city. He was a member of the Baptist Church, and died December 31, 1881, at the great age of one hundred and eleven years, three months and ten or eleven days, and had been a deacon in his church for over seventy years. James Hayden Van Hoose came to Arkansas from Kentucky May, 1839, and grew to manhood in what is now called White River Township. He followed agricultural pursuits until his twenty-first year, when he went to Ozark Institute, and worked for Robert W. Macklin, founder of that institute, for $13 a month, to pay for his education, which had been sadly neglected. March 8, 1852, he came to Fayetteville, and began clerking for James Sutton, with whom he remained until Sutton quit business and sold out to McIlroy in November, 1855. August 9, 1855, he married Melinda Ann, only daughter of William McIlroy (whose sketch appears elsewhere in this work), and after the bank failure of D. D. Stark & Co., in 1875, Mr. Van Hoose, with Mr. McIlroy, took charge of that business, which he continued until 1877, after which he resumed merchandising, and continued this business alone until 1882, when he abandoned it, and has since engaged in the insurance line, severing his connection with the bank of William McIlroy, of which he had been cashier for two years previous to 1876. In September, 1864, Mrs. Van Hoose died, and Mr. Van Hoose afterward married Miss Martha W. Skelton, daughter of William Skelton, Esq. Mr. Van Hoose has reared two orphan girls: Mary Eaton, whom he educated at the university, and who is now the accomplished wife of Samuel Jarman, of Barton, Ark., and Minnie Brooks, who is now at home. In 1880 Mr. Van Hoose was elected mayor and served until 1881. In 1888 he was elected to the same position, and is now filling it. He has always entertained liberal views, and has acted as correspondent for several papers outside of his home town, and never failed to say something good for Fayetteville and for Washing ton County, in fact for all of Arkansas, and contributed largely toward inducing immigration into his State and county. In politics he is a Democrat; in religion a member of the Protestant Episcopal Church. He has written many sketches of early history, and graphically portrayed some of the scenes of pioneer life in Arkansas. He was a friend of education, and, although having no children of his own, he willingly paid his school tax, that the rising generation might be educated. As there were no schools in the early days, when he was a boy growing up in the backwoods of Arkansas, he knew how to appreciate the need of them. He is the oldest notary public in this county, having been appointed by Gov. Conway in 1857, and has held the position ever since. He was made a Mason in 1853, and has since passed all the chairs in the several grand bodies in Arkansas. Mr. Van Hoose is a man noted far and near for his many charitable deeds, and an appeal to him is never in vain. As one example of his many benevolent actions and of his goodness of heart, the following may be mentioned: Some time in January, 1884, he received a letter from a little orphan girl living in one of the Southern counties in the State of Arkansas, of which this letter is a perfect copy, name and address only omitted:

Arkansas
January 13, 1884.

Master of the granD lodg of Arkansas.

Dear Sir, I thought I would write and see if there wasent School funs to edgCate Massons offens that was not able to edgCate theirselves, if so I wousht you would try and help us, there are 3 of us an nun of us has any edgCation. We all hafter work in the fleld to make a livin. I hav a Brother he is 15 years old, and a sister 17 I am 13 years old. If we had a edgCation we could make a livin without any help. I have Sumpthen to Show that my father was in good Standen and if it is nesesery to send it you can write and I will send it to you. I think we oughter be helped for we are young an cannot help ouseelves. We are the orphens of John T——— he was in Good Standen till death

please write Sune
I remain your Young frien
Minnie ———.

Mr. Van Hoose, whose kind heart was not proof against appeals far less touching than this, did "write sune" and gave her all the encouragement he could, but was compelled to tell her that there was "no funs" set apart by the Grand Lodge to educate Masons' orphans. He, however, corresponded with the girl for some time, and soon learned her family history. She was the youngest of three children, was born in Louisiana, and her father died when she was a babe. The widowed mother then moved to Southern Arkansas, where she died in 1881 of pneumonia. The children were thus thrown upon their own resources, and struggled long and hard to pay doctors' bills and funeral expenses. Mr. Van Hoose was anxious to see this little girl, who was ambitious to learn, to receive a good education, and wanted to do something practical in the way of assisting her to gratify her laudable ambition, and wanted it done in the name of Masonry. He therefore appealed to every lodge in Arkansas, to every true Mason, to their wives and daughters, to only give 10 cents each, and succeeded beyond his most sanguine expectations. The little girl was sent to school, and received the much longed for education. When it became certain that Gen. Harrison had been elected President of the United States, Mayor J. H. Van Hoose wrote him a letter of "best wishes," and received by return mail a kind and courteous reply. This congratulatory note of Mayor Van Hoose was spoken of in the dispatches sent out from Indianapolis as one of the most highly prized Gen. Harrison received, and its sincerity is the more appreciable as it comes from a Democrat, the mayor of a Democratic city, in a Democratic State, and from one who (as Mayor Van Hoose himself says) is "not an applicant for office."

George W. Van Hoose, carpenter and builder of White River Township, Washington Co., Ark., was born in Floyd County, Ky., in September, 1832, and is a son of John and Lydia Van Hoose. He was seven years old when brought to Arkansas, and grew to maturity under the home roof, attending the common schools and the Ozark Institute, near Fayetteville, which institution he attended until he acquired a common education. He then taught school for one term, but not liking that work he gave up the idea of a teacher's career, and began learning the carpenter's trade in July, 1853, serving an apprenticeship of three years with George D. Baker. He then worked at his trade in Fayetteville,

Ark., Jackson County, Mo., and other places, until the summer of 1861, and the first house he assisted in erecting was that of James H. Van Hoose, and among the first was the old court-house that was burned during the war. At the breaking out of the Rebellion he made up a company of infantry, was made captain of it (Company D, Seventeenth Arkansas Regiment Infantry, Confederate States Army), but was captured in 1863 in Louisiana, and taken to Johnson's Island, where he was kept a prisoner until the 11th of June, 1865. During his imprisonment he took the names of many of his prison comrades who were members of the Masonic fraternity (he being also a Mason). After the close of the war he traveled around for some time, and then returned home to Fayetteville, Ark., and was married to Miss Nancy Rowton, who was born in Washington County, Ark., April 7, 1851, and daughter of William Rowton, who was a soldier in the Mexican War. Their union resulted in the birth of two sons: Henry B. and Peter P., who both reside with their parents, and one daughter, Lydia Abie (deceased). The family are all members of the Cumberland Presbyterian Church. In his political views Mr. Van Hoose is a Democrat, although formerly an old-line Whig. He has held the office of coroner two terms, and is now filling that position, having been re-elected for the third term. He is a Royal Arch Mason, having been a member of that order for thirty-five years, and is a member of the A. F. & A. M.

Peter Van Winkle (deceased). Among the many noble men and prominent citizens who receive honorable mention in the biographical department of this work may be mentioned the gentleman whose name heads this sketch. He was born in New York City February 25, 1814, and comes of a long line of ancestry who have resided in the "Empire State" and who have arisen to prominence in the history of the country. When in his youth he removed to Illinois with his father, and was reared to manhood in that State. They were among the pioneer settlers, and suffered all the privations and hardships incident to life on the frontier, but by industry and economy became well-to-do citizens. Peter received but meager educational advantages in his early days, and in 1839 came to Washington County, Ark., where he was engaged in farming and mechanical work for eleven years. In 1850 he removed to Benton County, Ark., where he was engaged in milling and lumber dealing, increasing those interests to a marked degree in Northwest Arkansas, and throughout life was ever ready to support those enterprises which tended to advance and benefit the community in which he resided. In 1879 or 1880 he completed a large hotel at Fayetteville, which bears his name, and upon the establishment of the 'Frisco Railroad he lent as much aid and contributed as much money as any other citizen in Northwest Arkansas. He built an extensive sash and door factory, and supplied the majority of the material used in the buildings in Eureka Springs, Fayetteville and other places. Up to 1880 he was supposed to have the most extensive lumber mills in the State. In early life he was married to a lady of more than ordinary ability and strength of character, who proved to be a true helpmate to him in his labors in Washington and Benton Counties. To them were born a family of seven sons and five daughters, all of whom occupy honored places in the citizenship of their respective localities. Calvin, their eldest son, lost his life in the Confederate service, and Washington died at the age of about sixteen years. Norman is a lumber dealer of Eureka Springs; Jefferson B. has a book and stationery store at Fayetteville; Robert E. L. is a lumber dealer of Pittsburg, Kas.; Wallace and Peter are completing their educations, and still reside under the paternal roof. Their eldest daughter, Ann, is the wife of Martin K. Walker, of Benton County, Ark.; Mary is the wife of J. B. Steele, of Rogers, Ark.; Lucy died at the age of fourteen years; Ellen is the deceased wife of J. A. C. Blackburn, and Emily is the wife of J. K. P. Stringfield, a leading merchant and mill owner of Benton County, Ark. Mr. Van Winkle gave all his children excellent educational advantages, and reared them to love honor, truth and their country. On the 10th of February, 1882, he was called to his last rest, and was buried with Masonic honors. He led an exemplary and useful life, and his memory will ever remain green in the minds of the present generation, as one whose enterprise and liberality contributed so much to the business interests of the town and county. He was an earnest and honored member of the Baptist Church.

Jefferson Davis Van Winkle, the founder of the A. I. U. Book and Stationery Store, at Fayetteville, Ark., and son of Peter Van Winkle [see sketch], was reared and educated in Washington County, and in his boyhood days received a fair common-school education, supplemented by a three-years' course in the scientific and classical departments of the Arkansas Industrial University, but left before graduating, owing to the death of his father. He was appointed administrator of the estate, and did not again return to college, but turned his attention to his present business, which has proved to be a decided success, owing to Mr. Van Winkle's energy and business ability. He is very public-spirited, and upon the organization of the Building & Loan Association became one of the stockholders and a charter member of the same. He is also a stockholder in the Fair Association, and is an active and useful member of the Young Men's Christian Association, and belongs to the Masonic fraternity. He built the handsome brick block in which his store is situated, and has taken an active part in the general development of Fayetteville. He was married to Miss Ada D. Pape, a lady of culture and refinement, and their union has been blessed in the birth of two sons and one daughter: Clarence Pape, Charles Arthur and an infant daughter. He and wife are worthy members of the Presbyterian Church.

Joseph Elkanah Vaughan, liveryman, and son of James and Matilda (Rader) Vaughan, was born near Jonesboro, Washington Co., Tenn., February 9, 1836. The father was a native of Eastern Virginia, a mill-wright by occupation, and the son of James Vaughan, Sr., who was also a native of Virginia, but who moved to Hawkins County, Tenn., at a very early period in the history of the State. Peter Rader, the maternal grandfather of Joseph E. Vaughan, was born in Pennsylvania, and was of German ancestry. The subject of this sketch grew to manhood in Washington County, Tenn., and spent some time in the livery business, at Wytheville, Va., where he was engaged in business at the opening of the late Civil War. In the latter part of 1862 he was appointed to the commissary department, Confederate army, of Virginia, and served in that State, Kentucky, North Carolina and Tennessee through the entire war, surrendering at Bristol, Va. After cessation of hostilities he engaged in the livery business at Bristol, Va., and after spending short periods in Kentucky and Tennessee he came to Arkansas in 1871, locating in Fayetteville, of that State, and engaged in his former business, which he has continued up to the present, and at which he has been very successful. Miss Mary E. Haun, daughter of Christopher and Mary A. (Scott) Haun, became his wife. She was born in Tennessee, and by her marriage became the mother of six children, three sons and three daughters: James C. (manufacturer, of Atlanta, Ga.), Robert Lee, Cordie, Rufus A., Mollie M., Daisy Ducker. Mr. Vaughan, his wife and eldest son are members of the Missionary Baptist Church, and she is a member of the Ladies' Missionary Society of the same. Mr. Vaughan has served in the city councils of Fayetteville, and he is a member of the I. O. O. F.

Augustus Volner. Among the prominent industries of Washington County, Ark., worthy of mention, is the foundry and machine shop belonging to Mr. Volner, who was born in Oshkosh, Wis., June 14, 1850, and is a son of Charles and Henrietta Volner. The father was born in Berlin, Prussia, and was married in Albany, N. Y., moving at a later period to Wisconsin, where his son Augustus was born and reared. The latter learned the machinist's trade at La Crosse, Wis., whither the father had moved, and in 1870 went as a journeyman to Springfield, Mo., and worked in the machine department of the iron works of that city during 1875 and 1876. At the latter date he went to Carthage, and was foreman in the Eagle Foundry of that city until 1877, when he returned to Springfield and opened a shop there, which he conducted under the firm name of Volner, Farnsworth & Co. Here he remained until the fall of 1878, and then came to Fayetteville, bringing his machinery with him. This he sold, but afterward leased it, and is now doing a thriving business. He was married in Springfield, Mo., to Miss Florence, a daughter of Capt. H. Davey. She was born in Ohio, and is the mother of three sons and two daughters: Charles, Homer, Lafayette, Edith and Ida. Mr. and Mrs. Volner are members of the Baptist Church, and he belongs to the K. of H., and is a member of the city council for the First Ward.

Thomas Wainwright is a native of Madison County, Ala., and was born near the city of Huntsville, on the 12th day of September, 1828, a son of William and Nancy Wainwright, and grandson of Samuel Wainwright, who came with a brother of his from England to America, prior to the Revolutionary War. His brother located in the State of New York. Samuel located in Dinwiddie County, near Petersburgh, Va., where he became an extensive planter and slave-holder. Here his son William was born in 1785, and after the completion of his education he left his father's and went to Charleston, S. C., where, after spending what money he had, rather than return back to his father's and be dependent upon him, he learned the carpenter's trade, and in 1811 went to Huntsville, Ala. He entered the Seminole War under Gen. Jackson, at the close of which he went to Lincoln County, Tenn., where he married a Miss Nancy Turner, who was a native of Virginia, near Lynchburg. Immediately after his marriage he settled in Florence, Ala., where he lived for three years, at the close of which time he moved back to Madison County and settled near Huntsville. In 1815 his father died, and he received his portion of the estate, consisting of money and slaves. He then purchased a plantation and engaged in cotton raising. In 1835 he became security for some of his friends to the amount of some $13,000. In 1837 he had these security debts to pay, which consumed about all he had. Later in life he retrieved to some extent his fallen fortune. William and Nancy Wainwright were the parents of nine children, seven sons and two daughters. He died in 1855, and she in 1864. They were both members of the Methodist Episcopal Church, South. Their son Thomas was reared on his father's plantation in his native State, and attended the common schools of that county. Was converted to God on the 29th day of August, 1845, and was received in the Methodist Episcopal Church, South, immediately afterward. Was licensed to preach in September, 1846, and admitted into the Tennessee Conference in the following October as an itinerant preacher, filling circuits, stations and districts. In order to extend his knowledge in the sciences and of literature, he entered the best academies in his circuits, and the best colleges in the towns where he was stationed; by so doing he acquired an extensive knowledge of his own language and the different sciences, embracing medicine and law. On September 26, 1854, he was united in marriage with Miss Henrietta A. House, who died in 1859. She gave birth to two children: Cornelius Porter, and Henrietta, now deceased. His second marriage was to Mrs. Fannie Venerable, by whom he has seven children: Thomas (deceased), Lily M. (wife of J. J. Peer), William H., Fannie P., M. Lula, Cornelia J. and John. Politically he has ever been a Democrat. He first voted for Pierce, Buchanan and Douglas, against secession.

Hon. Charles Whiting Walker, a prominent legal practitioner, and son of Chief Justice Walker, was born in Fayetteville, Ark., December 24, 1835, and was reared in that city. He received a thorough scientific and literary course in the College of New Jersey, at Princeton, and afterward read law with his father for about eighteen months, when he entered the Law School of Tennessee, at Lebanon. He here completed the middle course of study, but the war breaking out at this juncture caused him to fling his books aside, shoulder his musket and take his part in the great struggle. He enlisted in the Thirty-fourth Arkansas (Brooks' regiment), Capt. J. W. Walker's company (his brother), and was in active and honorable service until the close of the war. He was tendered the colonelcy of the Third Arkansas Regiment upon the organization of the Arkansas troops, but declined it on the grounds of field service and also being with his brother. After the war he returned to Fayetteville and resumed the practice of law. He was married in this city to Miss Serena Jernigan, September 26, 1867, daughter of C. L. Jernigan, and the fruits of this union were three daughters: Nannie, Louisa and Jennie. Mr. Walker has always taken an active interest in the political spirit of his locality, and represented Washington County, Ark., as a delegate to the constitutional convention of 1868. He also represented that county in the Lower House of the General Assembly in 1877. He was mayor of Fayetteville in 1884, and had previously been on the board of aldermen of this city. He is at present the candidate for election to the circuit clerkship; is a member of the I. O. O. F., and he and family are members of the Missionary Baptist Church.

John A. Walker, farmer of West Fork Township, Washington Co., Ark., was born in Hawkins County, Tenn., July 23, 1853, and is a son of Thomas and Cassandra (Moore) Walker, both of whom were Tennesseeans, the father being a carpenter and farmer by occupation. When our subject was six years old the family moved to Greene County, Tenn. (the father having married a second time), and in 1869 they came to Arkansas, and in 1870 the father purchased about 300 acres of land. His first wife, who died in 1859, became the mother of three children: John A.; William Floyd, born May 31, 1856, and Elizabeth Ann, born October 15, 1858. The father in 1860 married Mrs. Cynthia (Collett) Hartman, by whom he became the father of one child, Margaret Jane, born April 16, 1861. John A. Walker received a good practical education in his native State. He was married in March, 1876, to Miss Serena Strickland, a daughter of Jacob Strickland, who was a prominent Union man during the war, and had three sons in that army, one of whom was killed. Mr. and Mrs. John A. Walker became the parents of five children, three sons, Willie C., born October 17, 1877; George F., born January 7, 1880; an infant boy that died when two days old; and two daughters, Ardia Cliow, born May 20, 1883, and Sidney E., born July 5, 1886. They have a good farm of 120 acres, with 100 acres under cultivation, on which is a comfortable and commodious frame house and substantial out-buildings. Mr. Walker is quite extensively engaged in dealing in horses and cattle, and in his political views is a firm Republican.

William Robert Ward, farmer of Prairie Township, is the son of Squire and Winnie (Duncan) Ward. The father was born in South Carolina, but was reared in Tennessee, and the mother was born in Washington County, Va. Both lived near the Tennessee and Virginia line. After marriage they moved to Hancock County, Ind., and were among the early settlers. In 1853 they moved to Schuyler County, Mo., and four years later to Washington County, Ark. The mother died in Dallas, Tex., at the age of sixty-six. She was a member of the Methodist Episcopal Church, South. The father was a house carpenter and wagon-maker by trade; was a Democrat previous to the war, but after that memorable struggle he affiliated with the Republican party. In their family were thirteen children, nine sons and four daughters, the fifth child being William R. Ward. He was born in Hancock County, Ind., March 16, 1838, was reared to farm life and educated to a limited extent. When about sixteen years of age he began learning the carpenter's trade, at which he worked about three years, and then, not liking the trade, abandoned it. October, 1861, he entered the quartermaster's department, Confederate service, and was most of the time in that department until the close of the war. In 1865 he returned to Washington County, and has since made it his home. In 1866 he married Miss Hannah Stelle, daughter of Timothy and Permelia (Skelton) Stelle, and a native of Washington County, Ark., born on the place where Mr. Ward now lives, February 12, 1845. Four children were born to this union: Timothy S., Hiram D., Miles V. (deceased) and Homer O. Mrs. Ward was a member of the Christian Church, and died March 24, 1888. After marriage Mr. Ward settled on the place where he now lives, which consists of 161 acres, seventy-five under cultivation. Mr. Ward has lived in this county for thirty-one years, and is a good citizen. He is a Democrat in politics, and a member of the Christian Church.

Abner W. Wasson, a successful agriculturist, and the son of Josiah and Artmissia (Bone) Wasson, is a native of Tennessee, born in the year 1820. The father was born in North Carolina, was a farmer by occupation, and also carried on the blacksmith trade. He moved from Tennessee to Alabama in 1834, and here received his final summons. Abner W. was educated in the public schools of Tennessee, and was but fourteen years old when his parents moved to Alabama. In 1842 he concluded to immigrate farther west, and soon after located in Washington County, Ark., where he settled down to farming. In 1843 he married Miss Hannah Trotter, of Missouri, who bore him eleven children, ten now living: Artmissia E., Josiah H., William D., Alfred W., Dick P., James F., Rebecka I., John C., Abner G., Mary and Sarah. In 1863 Mr. Wasson enlisted in the Confederate army, Brown's company, that made the raid through Texas, and was in service until the close of the war, when he returned to his home to gather his scattered fortunes that the war had devastated. In 1872 Mr. Wasson lost his wife, and in 1873 he married Miss Marinda Pearson, of Washington County. In 1855 Mr. Wasson purchased his present home place, which consists of 320 acres of valuable land, with about 120 acres under cultivation. He is a member of the Masonic fraternity, and is Democratic in his political opinions. He held the office of justice of the peace for a great many years previous to the war, and after that memorable struggle he held the same office until 1886, when he retired. He is a member of the Methodist Episcopal Church, South, as are also his wife and children.

Joel Waterman was born in Windsor County, Vt., September 15, 1817, and is the son of Abram and Hannah (Boardman) Waterman, natives of Rhode Island and Vermont, respectively. The father was a farmer by occupation, and died in Vermont in December, 1842. The mother died when Joel Waterman was but a year old. The latter was reared on a farm, and when grown, married, settled to farm life, and in connection also engaged in mechanical work. At the age of twenty-six he moved to McHenry County, Ill., where he remained for about four years engaged in farming. He then moved to Winnebago County, Wis., and after remaining there about ten years removed to Chippewa County, of the same State, where he resided about twenty-one years engaged in farming, lumbering, hotel-keeping and merchandising. He then moved to Fort Worth, Tex., and engaged in hotel-keeping, which he continued from 1877 to 1885. In the last named year he moved to his present property, where he has a farm of 200 acres, 175 under cultivation. In 1843 he married Miss Belinda Joslin, of Waitsfield, Vt., who bore him five children: Eugenia, wife of Ambrose B. Manakan, of California; L. H., now in Nebraska; Leslie E., at Chippewa Falls, Wis.; Lillian, wife of C. E. George, and Jessie, who is unmarried, and is now visiting her sister in California. Mr. Waterman is a firm Republican, and has taken an active interest in public affairs, but has never aspired to office. He has a beautiful place one and a half miles south of the city of Fayetteville; intends making his home here, and is one of the prominent farmers. His father was a Revolutionary soldier, and at the age of sixteen, was at the battle of White Plains, near the city of New York. He was a pensioner at the time of his death. His wife's parents were Hooker and Lucia Joslin, of Vermont.

J. Watkins, one of the prominent jewelers of Fayetteville, and the son of J. and Amanda (Knight) Watkins, natives of Tennessee and Illinois, respectively, was born in Richland County, Ill., November 7, 1851. He reached his majority in his native State, and completed the jeweler's trade at Friendsville. In 1874 he left his home in Illinois and went westward, spending four years in Pineville, Mo., and was then in Rogers, Ark., for some time, but finally, in 1887, located in Washington County, of the same State. He chose for his companion in life Miss Eliza Noel, daughter of B. S. and Irene (Dabney) Noel, who were natives of Kentucky, and the father a farmer by occupation. Mr. and Mrs. Watkins are the parents of three daughters: Stella Belle, Alpha May and Ethel Irene. Mr. Watkins is one of the first-class citizens of the county, and he and wife are members of the Methodist Episcopal Church, South.

James A. Watson, whose name is synonymous with the best farming interests of Washington County, Ark., is a son of John and Martha (Martin) Watson, both natives of Ireland, he born in 1778, and she in 1779. They came to America on the same vessel, when only twelve years of age. He was reared in South Carolina and she in North Carolina, both close to the line. Grandfather Watson was killed in the Revolutionary War, and grandfather Martin also served in the same war, both on the side of the Colonists. The parents of the subject of this sketch were married in 1800, and settled in Roane County, Tenn., where they lie buried. He served in Gen. Carroll's brigade during the War of 1812, and both he and wife were members of the Presbyterian Church. In their family were ten children, four sons and six daughters. He was a Democrat in politics, and died in 1834, and she in 1862. James A. Watson was born October 30, 1820, in Roane County, Tenn.; worked on the farm, and although he received very little schooling learned to read and write by his own exertions. Like a dutiful son he remained with his mother until twenty-four years of age, when he went to Calhoun County, Ala., here worked in a tan-yard, and also clerked in a store. In 1846 he enlisted in Company I, First Alabama Regiment, commanded by Col. John R. Coffey, and served twelve months. In 1848 he returned to Alabama, and entered a tan-yard. In 1851 he married Miss Jane C. Brooks, a native of Bedford County, Tenn., and a school-teacher by occupation. In 1853 they moved to Madison County, Ark., and here engaged in merchandising for six years. In 1859 they moved to Washington County, where he now has a fine farm of 200 acres, 120 under cultivation. To Mr. and Mrs. Watson were born five children: Charles A., principal of a school at Harrison, Ark.; Sarah M., deceased; John J., a miner of Australia; William B., at home, and Kate, wife of Geo. P. Eidson. Mr. Watson is a Democrat in politics, has been a member of the Masonic fraternity for forty-four years, and Mrs. Watson is a member of the Methodist Episcopal Church, South.

Elijah Webb, merchant and postmaster at Wedington, was born in Washington County, Va., September 24, 1838, and is one of a large family of children born to Wesley and Sarah (Dinsmore) Webb, natives of Washington County, Va., where they were married, and soon after the birth of the subject of this sketch moved to Hawkins County, Tenn., where they passed the remainder of their days, the father dying in 1855, at the age of sixty years, and the mother dying in 1885, at the age of seventy-four years. Both were members of the Methodist Episcopal Church. He was a farmer all his life, was in the War of 1812, where he was wounded, and was a life-long Democrat in politics. He was twice married, the first time to Miss Chapman, who bore him one son, James, who died at the age of forty years. Of the large family born to his second marriage, only four are now living: Elizabeth (wife of Henry Malony, a farmer of Hawkins County, Tenn.), Fannie, Sarah, (wife of Jacob Anderson, a stone-mason of Hawkins County, Tenn.), and Elijah, who is the only son now living of seven boys. He left home at the age of twenty-one, engaged in agricultural pursuits, and has continued this occupation ever since until the last two years, when he has been engaged in merchandising. He carries a stock of goods valued at from $1,600 to $2,000, and is doing a good business. August 19, 1860, he married Miss Elizabeth Howe, daughter of Nancy Howe, and a native of Hawkins County, Tenn., born January 6, 1841. To them were born six children: Andrew J., Sarah E., Nancy C., William W., John and James H. In August, 1863, he was in the Federal service, as recruiting officer, and served until the close. In 1870, he moved from Hawkins County to Washington County, Ark., where he has since lived. He has been justice of the peace for the last ten years, and served to the satisfaction of all law-abiding citizens. Mr. Webb is a Republican in politics, and he and wife are members of the Missionary Baptist Church. Mr. Webb is a Royal Arch Mason, and has represented Wedington Lodge four different times, and was H. P. of the Cincinnati Chapter.

Thomas F. Webster, a successful farmer, was born in Fayetteville, Ark., in 1838, the son of John B. and Margaret S. Webster. The father was born in Tennessee, and at a very early date moved to Arkansas, settling in Fayetteville, where he assisted in erecting the first court-house in the county. He was also in charge of the United States arsenal at that place when the Indians were removed from Georgia to the Choctaw Nation, Indian Territory. He was justice of the peace for many years, and was an excellent citizen. He died in 1883. His son, Thomas F., was educated in Fayetteville and Elm Springs, and received the best schooling that the county afforded. In 1862 he married Miss Elizabeth A. Poer, daughter of David and Rachel Poer, and ten children were the result of this union, eight of whom are yet living: Mrs. Maggie Crocksdale, David, John, Ada, Ruth, Orlando, Maude and Cleveland. The same year of his marriage Mr. Webster enlisted in the Confederate army, Company H, Seventh Missouri Infantry, and served with this company until the close of the war. During the latter part of the war he was sent to Texas, in the ordnance department, and during his long term of enlistment was never wounded or captured. He returned to his family and resumed agricultural pursuits, which occupation he has since continued. Later he purchased his present home place, which consists of 270 acres, of his brothers and sisters, who held an undivided interest. This farm is one of the best in Northwest Arkansas, and is well improved and well cultivated. Mr. Webster is a Democrat in politics; is a member of the Masonic and Temperance lodges, and he and wife are members of the Methodist Episcopal Church, South.

Dr. Thomas G. Welch is a member of the medical firm of Welch & Summers, of Elm Springs, Ark., and was born in Madison County, Mo., in 1837, being a son of Henry R. and Eleanor M. (Hooser) Welch, who were born in Tennessee and Kentucky in 1810 and 1818, and died in Missouri in 1847 and 1874, respectively. They were worthy people, farmers by occupation, and were the parents of two sons and five daughters. Dr. Thomas Welch was reared in Cape Girardeau County, Mo., and after attending the common schools entered the Bloomfield Academy, which institution he attended for some time, acquiring a good, practical, business education. After reading and practicing medicine for some time he entered the American Medical College at St. Louis, Mo., and began practicing his profession in Ripley County, Mo., moving to Randolph County, Ark., in 1871. Afterward he removed to Washington County, and since 1885 has been a practicing physician of Elm Springs, and has a large and lucrative practice. In 1869 he was married, in Ripley County, Mo., to Miss Sarah I. Rife, a native of

Tennessee, born in 1847, and by her became the father of eight children, three boys and five girls: H. Aora, W. Aretes, Annie, Gussie, Maud and Claud (twins), Emma and Lelia. Since 1873 Dr. Welch has been a minister of the Methodist Episcopal Church, South, being ordained deacon in 1877, and elder in 1884 and the last year. Each month he preaches once at the following places: Elm Springs, White Oak School-house and Smith's Chapel. He is Deputy Grand Master in the A. F. & A. M., and in his political views is a Democrat. During the late Civil War he was in Jeff. Thompson's State Guards, and after it was disbanded joined Marmaduke's cavalry, and was captured in Kansas and taken to St. Louis. He was afterward sent to Cincinnati, and thence to Johnson's Island, where he was kept until the close of the war.

Alvah G. West was born in Washington County, Ark., near Viney Grove, November 25, 1837, and is one of four surviving members of a family of nine children born to James S. and Mary A. (Crawford) West, who were Tennesseeans by birth. The father came to Arkansas when a young man (about 1834), and located in Washington County, where he reared his family and became a wealthy land owner. He was married three times, and died in 1881. Alvah G. West attended the common schools and the Cane Hill College, receiving an excellent education in the higher English branches and higher mathematics in the latter institution. In 1859 he went to the Rocky Mountains, locating at Pike's Peak, where he was engaged in mining for about three years, then removed to Nevada Territory, where he mined nearly two years. About this time he met with a serious accident, which unfitted him for further hard work, and in the latter part of 1866 he returned home, and in 1867 engaged in agricultural pursuits. On January 22, 1868, he was married to Elizabeth J. Blair, a native of the county, and daughter of Rev. Jesse M. Blair, formerly of Tennsssee, and soon after his marriage took charge of his father-in-law's farm of 220 acres. He has made some valuable improvements, and has 135 acres cleared and under cultivation, with a fine orchard, consisting of fourteen acres. Mr. West has been a member of the school board for a number of years, and takes a great interest in educational matters. He is a member of the Cane Hill Lodge of A. F. & A. M., No. 57, and is a Master Mason, and secretary of his lodge, which position he has held for a number of years. His children are as follows: Jesse Blair, James E., Mary J., George C., Maggie E., William R. and Hattie E. Mrs. West is a member of the Cumberland Presbyterian Church.

James Sanders West (deceased), who was one of the early settlers of Washington County, Ark., was born in Lincoln County, Tenn., April 30, 1814, and died in the first named county February 5, 1881, the son of James and Ann West. At the age of fifteen Mr. West left his home in Tennessee, and went with a company of surveyors to Florida. He afterward returned to Tennessee, and when eighteen years of age came, without means, to Washington County, Ark., where he passed the remainder of his days engaged in farming and stock raising. He was quite an extensive dealer, driving cattle North and horses and mules South, and although a heavy loser by the war, soon regained all he had lost by his extraordinary business ability. Before the war he had been a Democrat in his political views, but after that eventful struggle he became a Republican, and remained true to that party's interests until his death. He was married three times, first to Miss Mary Crawford (a distant relative of the present widow of the deceased), who bore him seven children, four of whom are now living: William P., a farmer and stock raiser, and a soldier of the Confederacy, of the State of Texas; Mrs. Ann Beaty, wife of Capt. Alvin Beaty, a famous Confederate soldier, and farmer of Texas; Alvah G., a farmer of Washington County, and Mrs. Harriet Mason, wife of C. H. Mason, a resident of Indian Territory. Mr. West's second marriage was to Mrs. Pitman, and was blessed by the birth of three children: Mrs. E. E. Sharp, wife of Ed. Sharp, of Cane Hill, Ark.; Nathan T. and Cecil Eugene, who are now residents of California. October 18, 1859, Mr. West married his third wife, Miss R. Jane Crawford, a native of Lincoln County, Tenn., born June 13, 1827, and the daughter of Col. Hay and Susan Crawford, who moved from Lincoln County, Tenn., to Arkansas in 1829, and were early settlers of this State, coming here with a colony which settled at Cane Hill. Her father was colonel of the militia in Tennessee, and was afterward a very prominent man in Arkansas. Her mother was Susan Harris, kin of the Harrises of Tennessee. To Mr. West's last marriage were born four children, two now living: Mary L., wife of J. C. Mitchell, a prominent farmer of Illinois Township, Washington Co., Ark., and Samuel H., named after Sam Harris, a pioneer Cumberland Presbyterian preacher of Arkansas, who is a successful lawyer of Fayetteville. Mrs. West is still living, and is residing with her daughter, Mrs. Mitchell, near Cincinnati, Washington Co., Ark. Mr. West was a liberal member of the Cumberland Presbyterian Church, was a Royal Arch Mason and an excellent citizen.

Thomas M. West was born in Jackson County, Ala., August 19, 1828, and is one of thirteen surviving members of a family of sixteen children born to the marriage of Jonathan R. West and Nancy McIntire, who were also natives of Jackson County, Ala. They came to Arkansas about 1830, and here the father was ordained a minister of the Methodist Episcopal Church, and preached the Gospel throughout Northwest Arkansas and Southwest Missouri for forty years. He was presiding elder of the Arkansas Conference from 1857 to 1861, and was one of the few ministers of his doctrine who adhered to the old church when the Southern members withdrew. He was a strong Union man during the war, and was so persecuted on account of his belief that in 1863 he was compelled to leave home and go to Kansas. He died at the home of his son-in-law, Franklin Johnson, at Carthage, Mo., in 1874. His wife was a daughter of Rev. John McIntire, of Alabama, and was a noble and self-sacrificing mother. She was of a very energetic disposition, and for years spun and wove the clothing for her large family of children. Her death occurred at the home of her son, Thomas M., in Bourbon County, Kas., in 1863. Thomas M. West grew to manhood in Washington County, Ark., and, being the eldest son, took charge of his father's farm, and consequently received but little education. In 1860 he was married to Miss Alpha C. Cook, a native of Sevier County, Tenn., born in 1840, and a daughter of Samuel Cook, and in 1862 removed to Bourbon County, Kas., where he remained until 1866, when he returned to Washington County, and located on the farm where he now lives. He owns a good farm of ninety-three acres on Clear Creek bottom, and has a comfortable and pleasant home. His family consists of the following children: Jonathan C., Samuel C., Lemuel E., Rebecca E., Arthur M. and John T. H. Mr. West is a stanch Republican; is a member of Lodge No. 101, A. F. & A. M., at Cincinnati, Ark., and a member of the Methodist Episcopal Church. His paternal grandfather, Thomas West, was the youngest of six sons, and when a young boy was bound out until he was twenty-one years old. He then married and located in Jackson County, Ala., and in 1830 moved to Washington County, Ark., locating near the Indian Territory, on a farm. He reared six sons and two daughters in Alabama, and died March 31, 1860, at the advanced age of one hundred years.

Joseph White is a native of Knox County, Tenn., born in 1825, and the son of Abraham D. and Elizabeth (Douglas) White. The paternal grandfather, Joseph White, was a North Carolinian, and served in the Revolutionary War under Col. Cleveland. He was a prisoner, and kept in his barn, but got away from Gen. Ferguson, of the English army, the morning of the same day, and informed his comrades before the British attacked them. He was an extensive planter, and owned a large number of slaves. Gen. Ferguson made his headquarters at his house, dying there from wounds received at the battle of King's Mountain. After the war Joseph White located in Knox County, Tenn., where he was killed by the kick of a horse. Benjamin White, the noted hunter and Indian scout, was his brother. Abraham D. White was born in North Carolina in 1790, and went to Tennessee with his father in 1802, where he received a good education in a college in Maryville. He spent a number of years engaged in farming and teaching school, and in 1820 married and settled on a farm, moving to Missouri in 1840, where he followed the same occupations. In 1862 he moved to Texas, where he remained until the close of the late Civil War, and then returned to Missouri, locating in Morgan County. His wife was born and reared in Knox County, Tenn., and was a daughter of Thomas Douglas, who was a farmer, miller and boat-builder, of Knoxville. Her brother, Kelsey H. Douglas, was one of the early settlers of Texas, and was a general in the Texas Rebellion, being the first President elected in the Texas Republic. He was one of the wealthy men of the State, and left a large estate at the time of his death. Mr. and Mrs. White became the parents of the following family: Nancy H., wife of T. I. Murray; Elizabeth, Isabella, Martha and Joseph B. The mother died in 1837, and the father afterward married (in 1846) Jane Austin. He was a consistent member of the Presbyterian Church, and died at the home of his son,

Joseph, in 1868. The latter was educated at the Forest Hill Academy, at Athens, Tenn., and was reared to manhood on his father's farm. In 1848 he was united in the bonds of matrimony to Miss Martha C. Daniels, who was born in Sumner County, Tenn., in 1830, and who was taken to Missouri by her parents in 1839. The following are the children born to her union with Mr. J. B. White: Hugh L., Julius E., Joseph A., Monroe, Elanora (wife of N. P. Williams), Sophronia (wife of George Son), and Lew, his youngest daughter. After his marriage Mr. J. B. White located on the Sioux River, in Greene County, Mo., and was engaged in farming and general merchandising, being also postmaster of Richland for six years. When the war broke out he went to Texas, and traded his slaves for land, and in 1862 entered the Confederate service as a post guard, and was first lieutenant of his company. When the war closed he returned to Missouri, and located on a farm in Morgan County, but removed to Miller County in 1869, where he was engaged in merchandising until 1883. His health began failing him at this time, and he retired to his farm, and two years later came to Washington County, Ark., where he has a fine farm of 205 acres near Farmington. He belongs to the Presbyterian Church, and is a member of the A. F. & A. M. and is a Royal Arch Mason.

Thomas B. Whitehead, farmer, was born in Dade County, Ga., November 12, 1839, and is the son of Lewis and Scarbray (Keenam) Whitehead, both natives of Georgia. The father moved to Marion County, Tenn., when T. B. was a child, and followed agricultural pursuits the principal part of his life. He left Tennessee in the year 1859, moved to Sebastian County, Ark., and died at Fort Smith, of that State, in 1863. The mother died in the same place in 1865. They were the parents of six children, and Thomas B. is the only one of this family now living. He grew to manhood on the farm, and learned the carpenter's trade, which he followed at Little Rock until the beginning of the war. During the latter part of that eventful period he served six months in the Federal army, as first lieutenant of Company H, Second Arkansas Infantry. After that he followed farming in Crawford County, Ark., for two years, and then moved to Washington County, and was three years on Middle Fork. Fours years subsequent to this he was in Madison County, and afterward he moved back to Washington County. In 1883 he settled on his present farm, eight miles east of Fayetteville, and which consists of 200 acres of land, 125 under cultivation. He also raises and deals in stock. December 25, 1867, Mrs. Arissa (Simpson) Little became his wife; she was born in North Carolina, and by her union to Mr. Whitehead became the mother of seven children: Minerva, Mary E., James E., Thomas J., Joseph B., Hugh A. and Nellie. Mr. Whitehead was married previous to the war to Miss Mary Ann Roane, who died in 1866, having borne one son, John W. The present Mrs. Whitehead is a member of the Missionary Baptist Church, as is also her eldest daughter. Mr. Whitehead is a Republican in politics, and is one of the respected and enterprising citizens of the county.

Jay Manuel Whitham, superintendent of mechanic arts and professor of engineering in the A. I. U., was born in Warren, Jo Daviess Co., Ill., August 24, 1858, and is the son of John and Caroline A. (Rowe) Whitham. The father was born in Leeds, England, and when about twelve years of age he immigrated to America with his parents. The mother was born in North Granby, Conn., and their marriage was solemnized in North Colesville, N. Y. After remaining in this State until 1857, they moved to Illinois, and here the father died at the age of sixty-eight. The mother is still living, and is sixty-two years of age. In their family were six children, four sons and two daughters, of whom our subject is the youngest. He received his early literary education in the high-school at Warren, Ill., and when nineteen years of age entered the United States Naval Academy, at Annapolis, Md., where he pursued a course in engineering, graduating with first honors in that course in 1881. Two years following this he cruised on the United States men-of-war Quinnebaug and Galena, visiting ports in the Mediterranean, on the coasts of Africa and South America. After returning he stood an examination at the academy for promotion, and was commissioned assistant engineer in the United States Navy, spending the summer of 1883 on duty in that department at Washington. From 1883 to 1885 he held the position of professor of mechanical engineering in St. John's College, Annapolis, Md. In the last named year he resigned from the United States Navy to accept the chair of applied mathematics and commandant of cadets in the A. I., U., and in June, 1887, he was made superintendent of mechanic arts and professor

****

of engineering.   In 1884 he married Miss Rebekah E., daughter of J. M. Dashiell, D. D.   She was born near Baltimore, Md., and by her marriage became the mother of two children: Jay Dashiell and Lloyd Bankson.   Prof. Whitham is a member of the American Society of Mechanical Engineers, and is corresponding secretary of Arkansas Society of Engineers, Architects and Surveyors. He is also the author of a book, published by John Wiley & Sons, New York, entitled "Steam Engine Design," and a forthcoming text book on "Elements of Analytical Mechanics," besides several professional papers.   Prof. and Mrs. Whitham are members of the Episcopal Church.

W. H. Whitlow, a leading druggist of Fayetteville, member of the Pharmaceutical Association of Arkansas, was born in Hickory County, Mo., July 14, 1851, and is the son of Henry and Ella (Culbertson) Whitlow, natives of Kentucky, who married in Marion County, Mo., at Palmyra.   After marriage they moved to Hickory County, Mo., and from there to Cooper County, Mo., where their son, W. H., grew to manhood, and where he received a good education, but finished the same after moving to Washington County, in 1869, at the Ozark Institute.   In 1870 he engaged as clerk in the drug store of Dr. P. M. Cox, of Fayetteville, and in 1875 he engaged in business for himself, and has since been identified with that industry in Fayetteville.   He was married, at Fort Smith, to Miss Annie Birnie, daughter of Charles Birnie, of Fort Smith, and is now the father of two living children: Annie May and Charles Birnie.   They buried their eldest child, Ethel, at Fort Smith.   Mr. Whitlow is a Royal Arch Mason, and he and family worship at the Presbyterian and Episcopal Churches.   He is a good citizen, and has the respect of all who know him.

Zadok Winn, farmer and stock raiser, of Washington County, Ark., was born in West Fork Township, of that county, February 28, 1836, and is a son of James and Nancy (Bloyd) Winn.   The father was born in Bedford County, Tenn., May 10, 1810, and after reaching manhood located in Illinois; thence to Washington County, Ark., in 1832, locating on the farm now owned by his son, Zadok.   He was married March 17, 1833, to Miss Bloyd, who was born in Kentucky, and became a resident of Washington County, Ark., in 1829, and to their union were born thirteen children, ten of whom grew to manhood and womanhood: Eli; Zadok; Matilda, wife of W. C. Graham; Marinda, wife of Z. C. Winn; Rachel W., wife of John Carris; John; Mary, wife of Samuel Hale; Ednonia, wife of H. Darin; Joel, and Margaret, wife of James Reed.   The mother of these children died in the spring of 1862, and the father afterward married Eliza Hancock, who bore him four children: Martha W., wife of James Carris; Walker, George A., and James.   The mother is now the wife of Daniel Carnes.   Mr. Winn lived a prosperous and useful life until 1869, when he departed this life, deeply regretted by his relatives and friends.   He had been a member of the Christian Church for thirty years, and in his political views was a strong Republican.   The Winn family was first represented in America by three brothers who came from Ireland to North Carolina, a number of years prior to the Revolutionary War, and served the Colonists in their struggle for liberty.   Zadok Winn, whose name heads this sketch, has resided in Washington County all his life, and in his boyhood days received such education as the schools afforded. September 4, 1853, he was united in the bonds of matrimony to Mary Caughman, who was born in Washington County, January 20, 1835, and is a daughter of Nathan and Matilda Caughman, who came to the county in 1829.   She is the mother of ten children: Melvia, wife of John Hutchinson; Nancy, deceased; Matilda, wife of J. M. Bloyd; Lucinda, wife of J. W. Fitts; William; Hettie, wife of J. A. Oxendine; Nettie, Albert L., Almedia and John.   Mrs. Winn is a member of the Christian Church, and Mr. Winn is a member of the following secret organizations: Lodge 336 of the A. F. & A. M., Lodge No. 90 of the I. O. O. F., Post No. 7 of the G. A. R., and the Masons.   In September, 1863, he enlisted in Company D, First Arkansas Cavalry, and did honorable and active duty for the Union until he received his discharge, August 23, 1865.   He is a very active member of the Republican party, serving as deputy marshal under Thomas Boles, and in all enterprises for the public weal he has aided materially with his influence and money.   He is in good circumstances financially, and is the owner of a fine farm as the result of his own industry.

Alfred L. Williams.   The subject of this brief biography belongs to that enterprising class of men who have done so much toward building up the present commercial standing of this thriving city of Fayetteville, and who in their breadth of citizenship have extended material and substantial aid to its social and moral status. He is a native "to the manor born," and comes of a worthy line of pioneer stock in this State from Tennessee. October 2, 1852, he was born here, the son of Thomas W. and Sarah (McGarah) Williams. The former was also a native Arkansan, being born in Washington County November 1, 1832, the son of David and Mary (Smith) Williams, who made a settlement in Washington County about 1828, and, after living worthy and exemplary lives, passed to their last rest, and lie buried under the sod of their adopted State. Thomas W., their son, prosecuted actively the vocations of farmer and dealer in live stock, and was esteemed a very successful operator in that line. The Civil War breaking out, he entered into the spirit of it with all the fervor of a Southern patriot, and did active and honorable duty in Company K, Thirty-fourth Arkansas Infantry, Confederate service, for four years, giving up his arms, only when hope was abandoned for the cause he espoused, at Fort Smith, Ark., June, 1865. Returning from the war, with health and fortune shattered, and for a time with citizenship lost, he put his shoulder to the wheel and bent all his energies to the arts of peace in which he had been engaged previously, farming and trading and dealing in stock, till his death, which occurred July 3, 1886. He died full in the faith of the Cumberland Presbyterian Church, and was buried with the honors of the Masonic body, of which he had been a member for over twenty years. His worthy wife, Sarah McGarah, was the daughter of William McGarah, who is reckoned as the first settler of Fayetteville. The pages of history note the connection of these families with the industrial and social life of this locality, and we forbear further comment. The subject of our sketch was the eldest in a family of six sons and eight daughters, of whom six sons and five daughters survive. He attained his manhood here, and engaged in trading and merchandising, both interests of which he has always pushed vigorously, and to his credit has made for himself a creditable success. Upon the organization of the Washington County Bank, he gave that enterprise material aid, and has held stock in it ever since. He has worked in the sheriff's and collector's office, and rendered effective and valuable service. He is an active member of the lodge of Masons, and a liberal contributor to all worthy objects having for their aim the general advancement of the social and industrial life of his locality. He formed a happy marital union in this county with Miss Josie, second daughter of the Hon. Hosea Maguire [see sketch elsewhere], and two bright little boys have come to bless their domestic circle: Roy Welch, born May 11, 1884, and Hosea L., born October 25, 1886. Walton A., born July 10, 1881, died June 4, 1883. Mrs. Williams is an active member of the Cumberland Presbyterian Church, a lady of estimable attainments, and a co-worker in all Christian work. Her parents, the Hon. Hosea M. Maguire and Louisa (Trammel) Maguire, were pioneers of Washington County, and were reckoned among the most esteemed of this county's citizens. The Maguires came from near Covington, Ky., and settled here in very early times. In their Kentucky home they hold kinship to the Covingtons and many other of the leading families of that section of the country. Hosea M. Maguire was a gentleman of strict integrity and honesty of purpose, and was held in high esteem by Washington County's citizens. He held a seat in the Legislative Assembly of this fair State, and was an acknowledged leader in his party (the Democratic). He was charitable to a fault, the alms-seeker was never turned from his door without material aid and kind words of good cheer, and public interests always received a cordial support from his bountiful hand. He passed to his last rest July 23, 1888, in full communion with the faith of the Cumberland Presbyterian Church, of which he had been a consistent member since his early manhood. He was buried by the Masons, followed by a large concourse of friends. To the posterity of this marital union of Alfred L. and Josie (Maguire) Williams will be found a correct starting point in their Arkansas genealogy for all time to come.

Robert R. Williams, a retired farmer, of White River Township, Washington Co., Ark., was born in Greene County, Tenn., on the 16th of July, 1812. His parents, John and Mary (Rankin) Williams, were Pennsylvanians, and moved to Greene County, Tenn., with their parents when quite young. They were married in this State, and here reared their family and spent the remainder of their lives. The father followed the occupation of boating, and his wife managed the farm. He died in September, 1815, at the age of forty-nine years. The mother died October 27, 1848, at the age of eighty-two years. Robert R.

Williams is the youngest of their seven children, and the only one now living. He remained with his mother until he attained his majority, and assisted her on the farm. His educational advantages were very meager, yet he succeeded in obtaining a fair English education. July 26, 1838, he was married to Catherine Missimer, who was born in Greene County, Tenn., and died in Arkansas July 4, 1870, having borne ten children: John, Mary (deceased), Elvira (deceased), Joseph, Samuel, James, David, Andrew (who is a deaf mute), Narcis (wife of B. F. Harris) and Florence. After the death of his first wife Mr. Williams was married to Mrs. Rachel (Van Hoose) Dickerson, who was the mother of nine children, six living, by her first husband, James Dickerson: Rebecca J. (deceased), Annette (wife of Dr. Wood), Robert M., Hugh H., Lydia A. (deceased), Louisa (wife of R. Ciper), Mary E. (wife of G. McGuire), Albert P. and John G. The father of these children was born in Virginia in 1816, and died in Washington County, Ark., October 31, 1858. His wife was born in Floyd County, Ky., November 9, 1816. Mr. and Mrs. Williams are members of the Methodist Episcopal Church, and he is a Democrat, and has been justice of the peace for six years. He also held the office of associate county judge previous to the war. He is now retired from active life, but still owns his fine farm.

Joseph Williams is a son of Robert R. Williams, and was born in Greene County, Tenn., October 22, 1844. He came west with his parents in 1852, and was reared to manhood in Washington County, Ark. He assisted his parents on the farm until the breaking out of the war, and then enlisted in Company K, Thirty-second Arkansas Infantry, Confederate States Army, and served until April 13, 1865, when he returned home and remained with his parents two years. He was married at this time, and engaged in farming for himself. He shortly after learned the carpenter's trade, at which he has worked the most of the time up to the present date. His wife's maiden name was Selina Lewis. She was born in Madison County, Ark., February 22, 1846, and is a daughter of William Lewis, who died in Washington County, Ark., in February, 1868. Seven of the eight children who were born to Mr. and Mrs. Williams survive: William R., Sarah E., Martha N., Hiram A., George D., Silas and Lizzie P. Mr. Williams is a Democrat.

Andrew J. Wilson, a successful farmer and stock raiser of Washington County, Ark., and native of the same, was born in Pulaski March 25, 1851. His father, William Wilson, was born in Jackson County, Ga., in 1807, and was married in that State to Eliza B. McCulloch, also of Georgia, and of English parentage. They came to Arkansas in 1833, and made their home near Little Rock for eighteen years, coming to Washington County in 1855, where he purchased 600 acres of land, and dealt very extensively in stock. December 6, 1886, the father died at the age of seventy-nine years, leaving a wife and a large family of children to mourn his loss. His sons, John and Anthony, were soldiers in the Confederate army, and died during the war. His sons, Albert and Andrew, are intelligent and enterprising young men, and are residing on and managing the home farm. They have 1,040 acres of prairie land, nearly all in pasture, 1,420 acres of bottom timber land, and are very extensively engaged in raising cattle, horses, mules, hogs and sheep. In 1887 they shipped eight car loads of stock and sold at home 265 head of cattle. On their land is a fine artificial pond, one and a half acres in extent, stocked with German carp, which affords them plenty of fish.

Arkansas Wilson, farmer, was born in Hardin County, Ky., November 1, 1830, and is a son of William and Margaret (Starns) Wilson, both of whom were born in Hawkins County, Tenn. They were married about 1827, and about two years later moved to Hardin County, Ky., and in December of the following year came to Washington County, Ark. The father was a farmer throughout life, and became a large land-holder, owning at one time 1,160 acres of land. He departed this life June 11, 1876, followed by his wife September 15, 1880. They were the parents of three sons: Eldridge H., Arkansas and John T. Arkansas Wilson's boyhood days were spent in following the plow and in attending the common schools. After attaining a suitable age he entered the Arkansas College at Fayetteville, and is one of a class of six who graduated from that institution. After leaving college he taught school in Madison County for two years, and two years more was instructor in the Huntsville Institute, and the following two years was engaged in teaching the young idea at Springhill, Ark. In 1861 he joined the Confederate army, and served as forage master under Gen. McCulloch till the battle of Wilson's Creek, participating in the battles of Oak Hill, Wilson's Creek, Prairie Grove, Jenkin's Ferry and others. He was wounded and captured at Prairie Grove, but after being kept a prisoner for one week was removed to the hospital. After recovering from his wound he rejoined his company as third lieutenant, and after the battle of Prairie Grove was made captain of the company, and remained so until the end of the war. After the cessation of hostilities he went to Texas, where he dealt in horses for some time, and in March, 1866, returned to Washington County, Ark., where he cared for his parents until their respective deaths. April 5, 1883, he was married to Alice Simes, who was born in Monroe County, Ind., April 5, 1858, and by her is the father of one child, Robert Simes, born February 14, 1886. Mrs. Wilson is a daughter of Robert Simes, who died in Monroe County, Ind. Her mother resides in Washington County, Ark. Mr. Wilson owns 280 acres of fine land, the home farm consisting of 120 acres. He is a member of the A. F. & A. M., and is one of the highly cultured gentlemen and well-to-do farmers of Northwestern Arkansas.

William F. Wilson (deceased), who was one of the successful farmers of Prairie Township, was born in Kentucky September 6, 1815, and when quite a small boy came with his parents to this county. They were among the first settlers, and growing up, as Mr. Wilson did, on the frontier, it was not wonderful that his education was rather limited. He followed agricultural pursuits all his life, and when quite a bachelor he married Mrs. Matilda Phelan, nee Barren, May 15, 1827. She was the daughter of James and Jemima (Murray) Barren, both of whom were natives of Tennessee. Her parents remained in Tennessee until 1851, when they moved to this county, and here spent the remainder of their days on the farm. Both were members of the Missionary Baptist Church. In their family there were eleven children, five sons and six daughters, Mrs. Wilson being the fifth child. The father lived to be about seventy years of age, and the mother lived to be about fifty. After coming with her parents to Washington County, Mrs. Wilson married William Phelan, a native of Washington County, Ark., and by him became the mother of five children: James, John, William, Lafayette and Joseph. William is the only one now living. After the death of Mr. Phelan she married Mr. Wilson, and to this union were born three children: Andrew (deceased), George F. and Elizabeth. Mr. Phelan was a member of the Methodist Episcopal Church, but Mr. Wilson was a member of the Christian Church, to which Mrs. Wilson also belonged. Mr. Wilson died in 1882, leaving his widow and children in possession of a large tract of land. He was a self-made man, and was a plain, honest, upright, farmer, and one highly respected. His son, George F., assists his mother in running the farm.

John Proudfit Wood, one of the prominent business men of Fayetteville, Washington County, was born in Brownsville, Tenn., August 14, 1845, and comes of a long line of mercantile ancestors of that State. He is the son of William P. and Ariadne Leonard, the former a pioneer merchant of Brownsville, Tenn., and a native of North Carolina. The Wood family date their ancestry back to an Englishman, who came to America in very early colonial times, and made a settlement either at Boston or Plymouth Rock. The Leonard ancestors were early settlers of Tennessee, and were also more or less engaged in mercantile pursuits. At the youthful age of five years John Proudfit Wood lost his parents, their deaths occurring about two months apart, and a sister and himself were left to the care of his uncle, Spencer R. Wood, a merchant of Brownsville, Tenn., who afterward established himself in business at Memphis, of the same State, where he died during the yellow fever scourge of 1878. Mr. Wood received a thorough collegiate and business training at Brownsville, but afterward removed to Memphis, where for six years he was engaged in business. In 1872 he accepted a position with a wholesale house in St. Louis, Mo., and there remained for fourteen years in active and reputable connection with the wholesale commercial trade, traveling through Tennessee, Kentucky, Mississippi, Alabama, Northwest Arkansas and Indian Territory, as a "knight of the grip-sack." In 1883 he engaged in business for himself, and made investments in Fayetteville, with a small stock of bankrupt goods, increasing with the trade, and four years later had so increased his sale of goods that he felt compelled to abandon his sample trunks, giving his exclusive attention to his already extensive business. From a small stock of goods he had, by dint of persistent industry and economy, coupled with clever business ability, so increased his trade that he was forced to seek larger quarters. He moved into the double store-room of the large Opera House Block, 48x90 feet, his stock of merchandise averaging between $30,000 and $40,000, and aggregating about $60,000 annual sales. Mr. Wood formed a happy union at Helena, Ark., with Miss Fannie Nelson, a lady of refinement, a graduate of the West Tennessee Female College, at Jackson, Tenn., and a daughter of W. L. Nelson, of Helena, Ark. They are the parents of two bright little children: Mattie and John. Mr. Wood is a member of the Western Commercial Travelers' Association, K. of H. and K. of P. societies, and he and wife worship at the Episcopal Church, in which she is an active worker. During the last two years Mr. Wood has made improvements in the Opera House Block, and has fitted it up in first-class style, preparing stage, scenery, folding opera chairs, etc., making it altogether of a character in keeping with his other interests. He has a beautiful home on College Avenue, and being very fond of hunting, his fine Irish setters can be seen at any time playing around his handsome yard.

William T. Woolsey, one of the earliest settlers and the oldest merchant in Washington County, Ark., was born in the State of Illinois in 1811, and is a son of Samuel and Matilda (Thompson) Woolsey. His paternal grandfather was born in Tennessee, and removed from there to Arkansas at a very early day, and settled in what is now Hempstead County. In the War of 1812, before coming to Arkansas, he scouted after Indians, and on one of his expeditions was shot at nine times, the balls passing through his shirt sleeve without injuring his person. He died in Texas at the ripe old age of eighty-two years. Samuel Woolsey was born in Kentucky, and grew to manhood on a farm. Like his father, he was a noted hunter and scout. In 1808 he married and removed to Illinois, where his days were spent in hunting and trapping, and, after serving from his adopted State in the War of 1812, came in 1814 to what is now Hempstead County, then removed to Washington County in 1829 or 1830, and settled near Farmington, where he spent the remainder of his days, dying at the age of sixty-three years. His wife was born in Kentucky, and died at the age of seventy-seven years. They were the parents of thirteen children, six of whom are living at the present time: William T., James, Henry, Lourania W., Louisa, and Elizabeth, wife of James Davis. William T. Woolsey grew to manhood in Hempstead County, Ark., and was educated in the common and subscription schools, his attendance being confined to the winter terms. In 1835 his marriage with Miss Elvira H. F. Davison took place. She was born near Fort Smith, Ark., in 1815, a daughter of John Davison, and seven children were born to her union with Mr. Woolsey: Mary, wife of O. L. Kearns; Matilda, wife of N. Fellows; Sarah, deceased; Lewis; Caroline, wife of Benjamin Little; John and Martha (twins), the latter being the wife of J. Farmer. The mother of these children died in 1849, and Mr. Woolsey took for his second wife Mrs. Charity Robinson, to whom was born one child, Charity, wife of Jacob Stockberger. Mr. Woolsey located on his present place in 1854, and since the late war has been engaged in merchandising. During that conflict he was a Union man, but did not serve as a soldier, his assistance being confined to freighting a portion of the time, the rest of the time being spent in Missouri. After the cessation of hostilities he returned to his home in Arkansas to find his property destroyed, but immediately set to work on his farm, and so continued four years, and then embarked in mercantile business, soon building up a good trade. He was postmaster at West Fork (now Pitkin) for about twelve years; for three years he has been a member of the Cumberland Presbyterian Church; in politics he is a stanch Republican. He was one of the men detailed as a life guard over Barnes and Bailey, the men who were hung at Cane Hill for the murder of William Wright.

John Young, M. D. The subject of this sketch was born in Overton County, Tenn., in 1836, received a common-school education and commenced the study of medicine when about nineteen years of age, under the preceptorship of Dr. D. S. Booth, of Missouri (now of Sparta, Ill.). He went West in the winter of 1862–63, spending about twelve years on the plains and in the mountains freighting, mining, etc. Took his degree in the Missouri Medical College in 1875. Located at Springdale, Ark., in 1879, where he stands at the head of the profession. He has seen the town grow from a few houses to its present proportions. Was married in 1877 to Miss Sophia Franklin, of Dixon, Mo. Their union has been blessed with three children: Franklin Booth, Daisy and John

Benjamin Hill. Mrs. Young was born in London, Canada, in 1848; is a member of the Cumberland Presbyterian Church. The Doctor is a member of the A. F. & A. M., I. O. O. F. and A. O. U. W. The Young family, which is scattered over a number of the Southern States, has a decided predilection for the profession of medicine, and quite a number of the family have become prominent as physicians and surgeons.